Improving International Investment Agreements

This book presents the reflections of a group of researchers interested in assessing whether the law governing the promotion and protection of foreign investment reflects sound public policy. Whether it is the lack of "checks and balances" on investor rights or more broadly the lack of balance between public rights and private interests, the time is ripe for an in-depth discussion of current challenges facing the international investment law regime.

Through a survey of the evolution in International Investment Agreement (IIA) treaty-making and an evaluation from different perspectives, the authors take stock of developments in international investment law and analyze potential solutions to some of the criticisms that plague IIAs. The book takes a multidisciplinary approach to the subject, with expert analysis from legal, political and economic scholars. The first part of the book traces the evolution of IIA treaty-making whilst the other three parts are organized around the concepts of efficiency, legitimacy and sustainability. Each contributor analyzes one or more issues related to substance, treaty negotiation, or dispute resolution, with the ultimate aim of improving IIA treaty-making in these respects.

Improving International Investment Agreements will be of particular interest to students and academics in the fields of International Investment Law, International Trade Law, Business and Economics.

Armand de Mestral is a specialist in international trade and investment law and comparative federalism. Teaching at McGill's Faculty of Law since 1976, Professor de Mestral is also an arbitrator and panellist for the WTO, CUFTA, NAFTA, international commercial arbitration. He is co-author of *International Law* and *The Canadian Law and Practice of International Trade*.

Céline Lévesque is Associate Professor at the Faculty of Law, Civil Law Section, of the University of Ottawa. Her research focuses on international investment law. In 2008–09, she was a Scholar-in-Residence at the Trade Law Bureau of Foreign Affairs and International Trade Canada.

Routledge Research in International Economic Law

Available:

Recognition and Regulation of Safeguard Measures Under GATT/WTO
Sheela Rai

The Interaction between WTO Law and External International Law
The Constrained Openness of WTO Law
Ronnie R.F. Yearwood

Human Rights, Natural Resource and Investment Law in a Globalised World
Shades of Grey in the Shadow of the Law
Lorenzo Cotula

The Domestic Politics of Negotiating International Trade
Intellectual Property Rights in US-Colombia and US-Peru Free Trade Agreements
Johanna von Braun

Foreign Investment and Dispute Resolution Law and Practice in Asia
Vivienne Bath and Luke Nottage (eds)

Improving International Investment Agreements
Armand De Mestral and Céline Lévesque (eds)

Public Health in International Investment Law and Arbitration
Valentina Vadi

Forthcoming:

Trade Remedies
A Development Perspective
Asif Qureshi

Improving International Investment Agreements

Edited by Armand de Mestral
and Céline Lévesque

Routledge
Taylor & Francis Group
LONDON AND NEW YORK

First published 2013
by Routledge
2 Park Square, Milton Park, Abingdon, Oxfordshire OX14 4RN

Simultaneously published in the USA and Canada
by Routledge
711 Third Avenue, New York, NY 10017

Routledge is an imprint of the Taylor & Francis Group, an informa business

First issued in paperback 2014

British Library Cataloguing in Publication Data
A catalogue record for this book is available from the British Library

Library of Congress Cataloguing in Publication Data
Improving international investment agreements / [edited by] Armand De Mestral, Céline Lévesque.
   p. cm.—(Routledge research in international economic law)
   ISBN 978-0-415-67197-2 (hardback)—SBN 978-0-203-10709-6 (e-book)   1. Investments, Foreign—Law and legislation.
   2. Investments, Foreign—Political aspects.
   3. Investments, Foreign—Economic aspects.
   4. Investments, Foreign—Government policy.
   I. De Mestral, Armand L. C.   II. Lévesque, Céline.
K3830.I47 2012
346'.0920261—dc23   2012002347

ISBN 978-0-415-67197-2 (hbk)
ISBN 978-1-138-84338-7 (pbk)
ISBN 978-0-203-10709-6 (ebk)

Typeset in Garamond
by Keystroke, Station Road, Codsall, Wolverhampton

To Rosalind, Philippe and Charles
A. de M.

To Benjamin, Jonas, André and Jeff
À la mémoire de mon père
C.L.

Contents

Editors' preface   xi
List of contributors   xiii
Table of abbreviations   xvii
Editors' notes on references   xix

Introduction   1
CÉLINE LÉVESQUE AND ARMAND DE MESTRAL

PART I
IIA Treaty-making: evolution and evaluation   13

1 Developments in IIA treaty-making   15
ANDREW NEWCOMBE

2 The evolution of IIA practice in Canada and
  the United States   25
CÉLINE LÉVESQUE AND ANDREW NEWCOMBE

3 The evolving role of the European Union in
  IIA treaty-making   42
ARMAND DE MESTRAL

4 The evolution of Chinese approaches to IIAs   59
CHUNBAO LIU

5 A quantitative perspective on trends in IIA rules   76
MARK S. MANGER

6 The costs and benefits of IIAs to developing
countries: an economic perspective 93
AMRITA RAY CHAUDHURI AND HASSAN BENCHEKROUN

PART II
Efficiency 113

7 Investment provisions in regional trade
agreements: a more efficient solution? 115
ARMAND DE MESTRAL AND ALIREZA FALSAFI

8 Increasing the use of alternative dispute
resolution in IIAs 135
CÉLINE LÉVESQUE

9 Is it necessary to avoid substantive and procedural
overlaps with other agreements in IIAs? 158
ANDREAS R. ZIEGLER

PART III
Legitimacy 177

10 Corporate investors' international legal
personality and their accountability for
human rights violations under IIAs 179
PATRICK DUMBERRY

11 Investor misconduct 195
ANDREW NEWCOMBE

12 Balancing IIA arbitration through the
use of counterclaims 212
HELENE BUBROWSKI

13 Issues of corporate nationality in
investment arbitration 230
JEAN-FRANÇOIS HÉBERT

14 Enhancing the legitimacy of international
investment law by establishing an appellate
mechanism   247
DEBRA P. STEGER

PART IV
Sustainability   **265**

15 The use of general exceptions in IIAs:
increasing legitimacy or uncertainty?   267
ANDREW NEWCOMBE

16 Sustainable development and IIAs: from
objective to practice   284
MARKUS W. GEHRING AND AVIDAN KENT

17 Direct taxation, tax treaties and IIAs:
mixed objectives, mixed results   303
MARTHA O'BRIEN AND KIM BROOKS

18 The impact of international law on IIA interpretation   323
AUGUST REINISCH

19 The contribution of international investment
law to public international law   342
ARMAND DE MESTRAL

Table of treaties and international instruments   357
Table of cases   366
Bibliography   376
Index   410

Editors' preface

This book is the result of the common work and individual reflections of a group of scholars and practitioners who collaborated on a research project funded by the Canadian Social Sciences and Humanities Research Council between 2008 and 2011. The research group was composed principally of academics, but we were fortunate to enlist the support and participation of a number of current and former Canadian public servants involved in investor-state arbitrations. Members of the group were primarily Canadian but we were joined by a number of distinguished European colleagues whose contributions have greatly enriched our work. The research team, consisting mostly of legally trained scholars, also benefitted from the participation of colleagues trained in economics and political economy. Several members of the research group were actively engaged in the completion of their doctoral studies. Their commitment and enthusiasm greatly contributed to the work of the group.

The research group began its work in March 2008 at a time when international investment law was undergoing extraordinary development and facing unprecedented challenges. The number of bilateral investment agreements has continued to rise, an increasing number of regional trade agreements include significant provisions or entire chapters on foreign investment, important new regional agreements on investment protection such as the Asean Comprehensive Agreement have emerged and the European Union is in the process of extending its competence in the field. In addition, investor-state arbitration, in various fora such as the ICSID or under the NAFTA, has experienced unprecedented growth and has come to play a significant role in international law. At the same time, not all commentators have viewed these developments in a positive light. Throughout the world, there have been critics ready to decry BITs and investor-state arbitration as reflecting a private multinational corporate agenda, which risks endangering the public interest.

The central question addressed by the research group has been to ask whether the law governing the promotion and protection of foreign investment reflects sound public policy. This is a very ambitious objective since it involves questions of equity and public policy on both the domestic and international planes. It requires judgments as to the balance of interests between foreign and domestic interests, the interests of developing and developed countries and as to the most appropriate procedural remedies to deal with disputes. Contemporary international investment agreements are placed in context with regional trade agreements and international taxation agreements. This book does not purport to be a general overview of the law, but it does attempt to deal with some of the most controversial issues which currently face the international investment law regime and to assist the reader in making a judgment on the underlying policy issues.

The editors wish to thank the Social Sciences and Humanities Research Council of Canada as well as the Law Foundation of Ontario for making this project financially possible. They also wish to thank the numerous research assistants who participated in the project, and in particular, Shawn Kupfert and Krista Zeeman who worked on the preparation of the manuscript. Above all, the editors wish to thank their co-authors with whom it has been such a pleasure to work.

Armand de Mestral C.M., McGill University
Céline Lévesque, University of Ottawa
December 2011

List of contributors

Hassan Benchekroun
Hassan Benchekroun is an Associate Professor in the Department of Economics at McGill University. His research interests include international agreements and cooperation, international trade, environmental economics and applied game theory.

Kim Brooks
Kim Brooks is an Associate Professor and the Dean and Weldon Professor of Law at the Schulich School of Law at Dalhousie University. She formerly held the H. Heward Stikeman Chair in the Law of Taxation at McGill's Faculty of Law. Her primary research interests lie in the areas of corporate and international tax, and tax policy.

Helene Bubrowski
Helene Bubrowski holds a doctoral degree from the University of Cologne, the German State Examination and a Maîtrise/LL.M. from the Université de Paris I. Her dissertation focuses on investment arbitration. She practiced arbitration at an international law firm and acted as the Secretary to the Tribunal in several international arbitration proceedings.

Amrita Ray Chaudhuri
Amrita Ray Chaudhuri is currently an Assistant Professor in the Department of Economics at the University of Winnipeg. She is also an extramural Fellow of the Center for Economic Research and Tilburg Law and Economics Center, Tilburg University. Her primary fields of research are Industrial Organization, Environmental Economics and International Trade.

Patrick Dumberry
Patrick Dumberry is Assistant Professor at the Faculty of Law, Civil Law Section, of the University of Ottawa. He practiced international

arbitration for several years with law firms (in Geneva and Montreal), as well as with the Trade Law Bureau of Foreign Affairs and International Trade Canada. He holds a Ph.D. from the Graduate Institute for International Studies, Geneva.

Armand de Mestral C.M.

Armand de Mestral C.M. is Emeritus Professor, Jean Monnet Professor of Law at McGill University. His principal areas of recent research are regional trade and international investment agreements, the law of international economic integration and comparative federalism. He is also an arbitrator and panellist (WTO, CUFTA, NAFTA, international commercial matters).

Alireza Falsafi

Alireza Falsafi received his PhD from McGill University in 2011. During his doctoral program, Dr. Falsafi also worked on the Social Sciences and Humanities Research Council of Canada (SSHRC) Projects on Regional Trade Agreements and International Investment Agreements. His experience further includes in-house work dealing with international oil contracts.

Markus W. Gehring

Markus Gehring is the *ad personam* Jean Monnet Chair in Sustainable Development Law at the Faculty of Law, Civil Law Section, of the University of Ottawa. He is also affiliated with Cambridge University's Law Faculty and Robinson College. He serves as Lead Counsel for Sustainable International Trade, Investment and Competition Law with the Centre of International Sustainable Development Law (CISDL).

Jean-François Hébert

Jean-François Hébert is a Foreign Service officer and a lawyer at the Trade Law Bureau of Foreign Affairs and International Trade Canada. He currently pursues doctoral studies at McGill University in the area of investor-state arbitration. Prior to joining the Canadian Foreign Service, Jean-François practiced in civil litigation in Montreal.

Avidan Kent

Avidan Kent is a PhD candidate at Cambridge University (POLIS), and an Associate Fellow with the CISDL in the Trade, Investment and Competition Law Research Programme. Avidan Kent's research interests include international trade and investment law and intersections with other legal disciplines such as competition law and climate change law.

Céline Lévesque
Céline Lévesque is Associate Professor at the Faculty of Law, Civil Law Section, of the University of Ottawa. In 2008–2009, she was a Scholar-in-Residence at the Trade Law Bureau of Foreign Affairs and International Trade Canada. Prior to joining the Faculty, she worked at the World Bank (1995–1998).

Chunbao Liu
Chunbao Liu is a doctoral candidate at McGill University Faculty of Law. His dissertation research focuses on Chinese IIAs and trade agreements. He obtained his undergraduate law degree from China.

Mark S. Manger
Mark S. Manger is Assistant Professor at the Munk School of Global Affairs at the University of Toronto, where he teaches courses on political economy. Prior to joining the Munk School in 2012, he was Lecturer in International Political Economy at the London School of Economics, Assistant Professor in the Department of Political Science at McGill University, and a US-Japan Fellow (2007–2008) at the Weatherhead Center for International Affairs at Harvard University.

Andrew Newcombe
Andrew Newcombe is Associate Professor, Faculty of Law, University of Victoria, British Columbia. Professor Newcombe is the co-author of *Law and Practice of Investment Treaties: Standards of Treatment* (Kluwer, 2009) and co-editor of *Sustainable Development in World Investment Law* (Kluwer, 2010). He manages italaw.com, a research website on international investment law.

Martha O'Brien
Martha O'Brien is a Professor of Law at the University of Victoria. Before her academic career, she practised tax law in Vancouver and undertook graduate legal studies in law of the European Union in Brussels. Her research is concentrated on EU taxation and internal market law, and Canadian and international tax law.

August Reinisch
August Reinisch is Professor of International and European Law at the University of Vienna, Austria and Adjunct Professor at the Bologna Center/SAIS of Johns Hopkins University, Italy. His research in international law focuses on investment law and the law of international organizations. Dr Reinisch acts as expert and arbitrator in investment arbitration disputes.

Debra P. Steger

Debra P. Steger is Professor in the Faculty of Law, University of Ottawa and Senior Fellow with the Centre for International Governance Innovation (CIGI). Her research is focused on global economic governance, international trade, investment, and dispute settlement. She was the first Director of the WTO Appellate Body Secretariat from 1995–2001.

Andreas R. Ziegler

Andreas R. Ziegler is a Professor at the University of Lausanne since 2002, where he is also director of the LLM Program in International and European Economic and Commercial law. He practiced for several years before joining the Faculty and studied international economics, international relations and law at the universities of St. Gallen, Paris (Sciences Po) and the European University Institute.

Table of abbreviations

ASEAN	Association of South East Asian Countries
BIT	Bilateral Investment Treaty
CAFTA-DR	Central America-Dominican Republic-United States Free Trade Agreement
CJEU	Court of Justice of the European Union
CUFTA	Canada-United States Free Trade Agreement
DFAIT	Foreign Affairs and International Trade Canada
ECHR	European Convention on Human Rights
ECT	Energy Charter Treaty
EU	European Union
ICC	International Chamber of Commerce
FDI	Foreign Direct Investment
FIPA	Foreign Investment and Protection Agreement
FTA	Free Trade Agreement
GATT	General Agreement on Tariffs and Trade
ICJ	International Court of Justice
ICSID	International Centre for Settlement of Investment Disputes
ICSID Convention	Convention on the Settlement of Investment Disputes between States and Nationals of other States
IIA	International Investment Agreement
ILC	International Law Commission
MAI	Draft OCDE Multilateral Agreement on Investment
MFN	Most Favored Nation
MNE	Multinational Enterprise
NAFTA	North American Free Trade Agreement
NGO	Non-Governmental Organization

OECD	Organisation for Economic Co-operation and Development
PCA	Permanent Court of Arbitration
PCIJ	Permanent Court of International Justice
RTA	Regional Trade Agreement
SADC	Southern African Development Community
TPA	Trade Promotion Agreement
UN	United Nations
UNCITRAL	United Nations Commission on International Trade Law
UNCTAD	United Nations Conference on Trade and Development
United States or US	United States of America
Vienna Convention	Vienna Convention on the Law of Treaties
WTO	World Trade Organization

Editors' notes on references

For ease of reference, BITs have been referred to using their short-form. For example, Canada-Egypt BIT (1996) refers to the following agreement:

Agreement between the Government of Canada and the Government of the Arab Republic of Egypt for the Promotion and Protection of Investments, November 13, 1996, Can TS 1997 No. 31, (entered into force November 3, 1997).

The full text of BITs can be found on a number of internet sites, including those of many individual governments as well as UNCTAD's BIT database at <http://www.unctadxi.org/templates/docsearch____779.aspx>.

Also, individual online references have not been provided for arbitral awards. They are available at the following sites (amongst others):

ICSID: <http://icsid.worldbank.org/ICSID/FrontServlet?requestType=CasesRH&reqFrom=Main&actionVal=ViewAllCases>

Investment Treaty Arbitration (by Andrew Newcombe): <http://italaw.com/>

NAFTA Chapter 11 (Investment) awards can be found on the parties' internet sites:

DFAIT: <http://www.international.gc.ca/trade-agreements-accords-commerciaux/disp-diff/gov.aspx?lang=en&view=d>

US Department of State: <http://www.state.gov/s/l/c3741.htm>

Secretaríat de Economía: <http://www.economia.gob.mx/>

Introduction

Céline Lévesque and *Armand de Mestral***

International Investment Agreements or "IIAs" have become a key feature of international law over the past 60 years. More than 175 states have concluded IIAs. As of 2011 there are over 3,000 IIAs in existence, including more than 2,800 BITs and 300 other economic agreements containing investment provisions.[1] On average, during 2010, one BIT a week was concluded and 20 of those were between developing countries and/or transition economies.[2] While the extent of IIA coverage is wide, room for growth remains. According to UNCTAD, "[t]oday's IIA regime offers protection to more than two-thirds of global FDI stock, but covers only one-fifth of possible bilateral investment relationships."[3] UNCTAD estimates that 14,100 more BITs would be required to cover all bilateral investment relationships![4] Of course, for a number of different reasons, "all" possible relationships will never be covered. However, the subject of this book—Improving IIAs—is still very much one that needs in-depth study. This book aims to inform the conclusion of new IIAs as well as the renegotiation of BITs, in particular those that were signed before the full extent of the impact of investor-state arbitration was felt.

The last ten years have seen an explosion in the number of arbitration claims made by investors against states under IIAs. At the end of 2010, UNCTAD put the total number of known cases filed under IIAs at

---

* Associate Professor, Faculty of Law, Civil Law Section, University of Ottawa. Thanks go to Otabek Ismailov, Shawn Kupfert and Samantha McKenzie for their assistance with this Introduction.
** Emeritus Professor, Jean Monnet Professor of Law, McGill University.

1 See UNCTAD, *World Investment Report 2011: Non-equity Modes of International Production and Development* (New York and Geneva: UNCTAD, 2011) at 100 [UNCTAD, *World Investment*].
2 *Ibid.*
3 *Ibid* at 102.
4 *Ibid* at 102–3.

390.[5] Notably, most of these cases have been filed within the last few years.[6] The number of states that have had to defend investor claims is also impressive: 83 states, including 51 developing countries, 15 economies in transition and 17 developed countries.[7] As of 2011, over 200 cases have been concluded.

With this growing experience came growing dissatisfaction with the regime in general and investor-state arbitration in particular. Among the wide-ranging criticism levelled at the regime is that IIAs do not fulfil their great bargain, the promotion of investment, while they effectively protect powerful economic interests; that IIAs protect investor's rights over the public interest of the host country; that the dispute settlement system put in place by IIAs lacks legitimacy due to the fundamentally *ad hoc* nature of investor-state arbitration; and the complexity and cost of the system are out of control. The literature regarding IIAs has also grown exponentially.[8]

5 *Ibid* at 101.
6 See UNCTAD, 'Latest Developments in Investor-State Dispute Settlement' (2010) IIA Issues Note No. 1, International Investment Agreements, online: UNCTAD <http://www.unctad.org/en/docs/webdiaeia20103_en.pdfIn 2009>, which states: 'the number of known treaty-based investor-state dispute settlement cases filed under international investment agreements (IIAs) grew by at least 32 bringing the total number of known treaty-based cases to 357 by the end of 2009 . . . Of those, 202——or 57 per cent——were initiated during the last five years (starting 2005)' [notes omitted].
7 UNCTAD, *World Investment, supra* note 1 at 101.
8 Recent book-length contributions include: José Enrique Alvarez, *The Public International Law Regime Governing International Investment* (The Hague: The Hague Academy of International Law, 2011); Jose E Alvarez and Karl P. Sauvant, *The Evolving International Investment Regime Expectations, Realities, Options* (Oxford: Oxford University Press, 2011); Christina Binder et al, *International Investment Law for the 21st Century: Essays in Honour of Christoph Schreuer* (Oxford: Oxford University Press, 2009); Chester Brown and Kate Miles (eds), *Evolution in Investment Treaty Law and Arbitration* (Cambridge: Cambridge University Press, 2011); Marie-Claire Cordonier Segger, Markus W. Gehring and Andrew Paul Newcombe (eds), *Sustainable Development in World Investment Law* (The Hague: Kluwer Law International, 2011); Pierre-Marie Dupuy et al (eds), *Human Rights in International Investment Law and Arbitration* (Oxford: Oxford University Press, 2009); Santiago Montt, *State Liability in Investment Treaty Arbitration* (Oxford: Hart Publishing, 2009); Catherine Rogers (ed), *The Future of Investment Arbitration* (Oxford: Oxford University Press, 2009); Jeswald W. Salacuse, *The Law of Investment Treaties* (Oxford: Oxford University Press, 2010); Stephan W. Schill, *International Investment Law and Comparative Public Law* (Oxford: Oxford University Press, 2010); Stephan Schill, *The Multilateralization of International Investment Law* (Cambridge: Cambridge University Press, 2009); Kyla Tienhaara, *The*

This book seeks to contribute to reflections on the ways IIAs could be improved. First, it takes stock of developments in international investment law and then analyzes potential solutions to some of the noted criticisms from the perspective of international public policy. The first part of the book traces the evolution in IIA treaty-making and provides an evaluation from a political economy and economics perspective. The other three parts are organized around the concepts of efficiency, legitimacy and sustainability. Each author, or set of authors, analyzes one or more issues of treaty negotiation, substance or dispute resolution, with the ultimate aim of improving IIA treaty-making.

The three organizing concepts have been used in order to give a thematic guide to the book's discussions. These concepts, as well as the chapter topics that fall under each, are presented below. However, it should be noted that the classification of topics under different organizing concepts is not strict but rather exists to support the analytical framework chosen for the book. In other words, some of the topics could fall under more than one heading.

Part I—IIA Treaty-making: evolution and evaluation

The objective of Part I is to take stock of the evolution of IIA treaty-making and provide an evaluation from different perspectives of law, political economy and economics. After a general description of developments in IIA treaty-making, three specific cases are studied, looking at the evolution in Canada and the United States as well as the EU and China. These countries and the EU have been selected due to their role as major players in the global economy and thus their possible game-changing impact. Finally, a quantitative analysis of trends in IIA rules is presented, followed by an economic analysis of IIAs.

Andrew Newcombe opens with a "table-setting" chapter that presents three trends that have characterized the evolution of IIA treaty-making over the past 60 years. First, Newcombe describes the move towards the "treatification" of international investment law. He also notes the appearance of the defining feature of modern IIAs: investor-state arbitration. Newcombe then surveys the "modelization" trend in IIA treaty-making and discusses the increasing use of model IIAs and its impact. Finally, he focuses on the recent trend towards "renegotiation"

Expropriation of Environmental Governance (Cambridge: Cambridge University Press: 2009); Michael Waibel et al, *The Backlash Against Investment Arbitration: Perceptions and Reality* (The Hague: Kluwer Law International, 2010). Thanks to Andrew Newcombe for his help with this list.

of IIAs and the challenges posed to states that seek to conclude more balanced IIAs.

Céline Lévesque and Andrew Newcombe follow with a chapter focusing on the IIA treaty-making practice of Canada and the United States. Both countries started their BIT programs in the 1980s and draw most of their experience with investor-state arbitration from the workings of Chapter 11 (Investment) of NAFTA. Both countries current BIT models date from 2004. The chapter provides an overview of the evolution of their practice through the lenses of efficiency, legitimacy and sustainability (defined below).

Next, Armand de Mestral's chapter reviews the evolving role of the EU in IIA treaty-making. From a minor role 10 years ago, the EU now has growing but yet unclear responsibilities in this field. De Mestral describes the evolution in the role of the EU, looking at its competence over FDI as well as the positions of different stakeholders. He then analyzes the impact of expanded EU competence with regard to IIA treaty-making, including a possible EU Model BIT. He concludes that the EU's expanded competence will have a dynamic impact both on the law within the EU and on international investment law.

The final chapter under legal evolution is provided by Chunbao Liu who presents a portrait of Chinese IIA treaty-making. While China only launched its program in the early 1980s, today it has concluded 130 BITs, making it a major player. Liu first describes the history of the Chinese BITs program, showing how three generations of treaties correspond to a gradual opening of China's economy to inward and outward FDI. The second part of the chapter highlights key features of current Chinese IIA policy, organized around the concepts of efficiency, legitimacy and sustainability.

The next chapter describes the evolution of IIA treaty-making seen through the eyes of a political economist. Mark Manger notes that political economists have only begun to seriously study IIAs in the last ten years. He explains that their perspective differs considerably from that of legal scholars, "as the primary focus of political economists is on causal explanation and empirical puzzles." As such, this chapter gives an overview of theoretical and empirical research of political economists on the exploration of casual links between the conclusion of IIAs and economic development. The first part discusses two dominant approaches in studying IIAs: rational design and legalization of international relations. The strengths and weaknesses of both schools of thought are analyzed in a comparative way. The second part presents the recent research findings by political economists on the identification of reasons for signing IIAs by states and their possible links to legal scholarship. Then it presents the economic analysis on the role of developed countries in promoting IIAs as major capital exporters. In the last part, the author analyzes trends in the conclusion of IIAs, putting emphasis on three dimensions of international law: "obligation," "precision" and "delegation."

The first part of the book ends with an evaluation of the impact of IIAs on developing countries from a micro-economics perspective. In line with the literature on the subject, Amrita Ray Chaudhuri and Hassan Benchekroun view IIAs as mechanisms that increase the enforceability of contracts negotiated between potential investors (such as a Multinational Enterprise [MNE]) and the government or local agents of the host country (i.e. the country receiving the FDI). The chapter first discusses the main advantage of such a commitment to the host country, which is to attract foreign investment that would otherwise have been directed to some other recipient. It then presents a game theory framework, namely Markusen's knowledge capital model, to analyze the possible disadvantages to the host country from making these commitments. The authors analyze the main disadvantages that IIAs have on the host country: "namely that by signing an IIA, the local agents in the host country collaborating with or being employed by the MNE may end up obtaining a lower share of the MNE's profits deriving from the investment." Thus, although more investment is attracted to the host country in the presence of an IIA, the host country earns a lower share of the profits in comparison to what it would earn in the absence of the agreement. Nonetheless, Ray Chaudhuri and Benchekroun conclude that empirical findings show that the net effect of IIAs is to make the host country better off.

Part II—Efficiency

The second part of the book focuses on ways to increase efficiency in the negotiation of IIAs as well as in matters of dispute settlement. A first way in which to view "efficiency" is the ability of IIAs to achieve one of their main goals: the promotion of FDI. In this perspective, Armand de Mestral and Alireza Falsafi explore one specific question: whether the inclusion of investment provisions in RTAs is a more "efficient" solution than concluding BITs? In order to answer this question, the authors first present some of the background to the inclusion of investment provisions in RTAs (called the "collocation" of trade and investment obligations). They then discuss the impact of collocation on the international investment law regime. Finally, the authors analyze the efficiency of collocation from an economics perspective but also from the perspective of meeting public policy challenges. Their conclusion is that collocation may well be more efficient.

The next chapter considers the high costs of investor-state arbitration and options for increasing the efficiency of the dispute settlement regime existing under IIAs. Céline Lévesque's point of departure is that some investor-state disputes, which took many years and millions of dollars to be resolved, could have been dealt with more efficiently and in line with the public interest, had they avoided international arbitration. As such, Lévesque proposes ways to increase the use of alternative dispute resolution (ADR) in the context of IIAs. The author has recourse to a "merits spectrum" in order to match disputes to the best ADR method, which she describes briefly. In the second part, she explores current IIA practices related to ADR and improvements that could be made in future IIAs in order to resolve disputes more efficiently (i.e. with less transaction costs).

In the last chapter of Part II, Andreas Ziegler asks whether it is necessary to avoid substantive and procedural overlaps *with other agreements* in IIAs? Specifically, he asks whether "the current 'spaghetti bowl' of dispute settlement provisions in RTAs, IIAs and the WTO require 'efficiency' promoting changes in the negotiation of IIAs?" In order to answer these questions, he first analyzes the overlapping provisions on dispute settlement in international economic agreements. Ziegler also provides examples of situations where overlap was at issue. He then provides a survey of international economic law treaty-making. His third part focuses on the substantive and procedural interactions of IIAs with dispute settlement provisions of other treaties. In the end, Ziegler concludes "that the 'spaghetti bowl' effect may not be as detrimental to efficiency as one might first think."

Part III—Legitimacy

A search for improved legitimacy in IIAs would have to start with a search for the meaning of the term (at a minimum) in international law. Even that is not an easy task. For our purposes, it suffices to briefly mention two views, that of Thomas Franck and of Daniel Bodanski, which both frame some of the book's discussions.

In one of his influential works, Thomas Franck defines legitimacy as "a property of a rule or rule-making institution which itself exerts a pull toward compliance on those addressed normatively because those addressed believe that the rule or institution has come into being and operates in accordance with generally accepted principles."[9] In sum,

---

9 Thomas Franck, *The Power of Legitimacy Among Nations* (New York: Oxford University Press, 1990) at 16 [Franck].

actors in a system voluntarily comply with the rules of that system because they perceive those rules emanating from a right and accepted process thus conveying a sense of legitimacy.[10]

In contrast to the normative perspective of legitimacy set forth by Franck, Daniel Bodansky's sociological perspective examines legitimacy as it is perceived by the relevant actors. Bodansky's sociological perspective provides for a practical approach to the concept of legitimacy by focusing on the views of the internal actors in a given system. Bodansky's sociological perspective incorporates an element of social reality by including the views of states, stakeholders and constituencies in gauging why these actors accept or perceive as legitimate an institution's right to rule.[11] Sociological legitimacy serves as a credible method in discerning why international actors voluntarily comply with the institutional rules in a given system.

In this book, legitimacy will be considered from the point of view of acceptability of normative structure to state parties and stakeholders (internal acceptability). When considering how to increase the legitimacy of IIAs, the authors focus most of all on the provision of "checks and balances" on investors' rights. Since IIAs have by design been one-sided (i.e. they provide benefits but no obligations to investors), they have often been criticized as lacking in legitimacy in this way.

Patrick Dumberry discusses the issue of the international legal personality of corporate investors and the possibility of holding them accountable for human rights violations under IIAs. The author first analyzes the legal personality of corporations particularly in the context of IIAs and concludes that corporations have an international legal personality, although it is both "limited" and "derivative." Based on this conclusion, he submits that corporate investors are capable of having obligations under international law. The author then examines the possibilities for holding corporations accountable for human rights violations under current IIAs and possible improvements to future IIAs.

Andrew Newcombe, for his part, asks how IIA tribunals and treaty practice can respond to serious misconduct by foreign investors. First, the author presents different stages of the investment process at which misconduct can occur: establishment, operation and after an investor-state dispute has arisen and draws (potential) consequences on jurisdiction, admissibility and merits in investor-state cases. The author uses the term "misconduct" to refer to conduct that is either illegal under

10 *Ibid.*
11 Daniel Bodansky, "The Concept of Legitimacy in International Law," in *Legitimacy of International law* (Berlin: Springer, 2008) at 313–14.

domestic or international law, or would be considered contrary to international public policy. Thus far, Newcombe believes that tribunals have been able to ensure that investors have not been rewarded for their misconduct even though IIAs do not have express provisions on the matter. He would still suggest that IIAs include an "in accordance with local law" provision in the definition of investment, that they provide preliminary objection mechanisms and also have arbitration provisions which permit the host state to make claims and counterclaims against investors for breaches of international and domestic law.

Picking up on the issue of counterclaims, Helene Bubrowski explores the possibility of states also making claims against investors in the context of investor-state disputes. Bubrowski's chapter provides an analytical overview of various obstacles that defendant states encounter in pleading counterclaims in investment treaty arbitration. The first obstacle is that IIAs typically do not provide rights for host states *vis-à-vis* foreign investors. The chapter then discusses another obstacle, which is the possibility that counterclaims do not fall within the scope of the consent clauses of IIAs. This may serve as a ground for arbitral tribunals to reject jurisdiction over them. Finally, the author addresses the issue of connection or "connexity" between a claim and a counterclaim which is considered a requirement for admissibility in bringing a counterclaim. In conclusion, Bubrowski makes proposals on facilitating the possibility of filing counterclaims in investment treaty arbitration.

Jean-François Hébert follows with a discussion of issues of corporate nationality in investment arbitration. Specifically, he discusses the issue of abuse of corporate structure and "treaty-shopping" in the context of IIAs. The author offers an analytical approach that sheds light on the ways investment tribunals have handled these issues. It focuses on two main approaches used by arbitral tribunals in interpreting the "incorporation test." First, the formalistic approach, which defends the position of strict interpretation of the incorporation test by rejecting any implied additional requirement such as "economic link" in treaty text, is analyzed. This approach is contrasted with the flexible approach, which is based on the abuse of rights theory. The flexible approach has led some tribunals to "deny jurisdiction in cases where claimants have attempted to manufacture the required diversity of nationality through the incorporation of companies of convenience." The chapter also provides a fresh look into the limits of the abuse of rights doctrine and the ways states can limit the potential for such abuse by corporate investors. The chapter covers "denial of benefits" clauses, rarely found in IIAs, which allow states to unilaterally withdraw treaty protection granted to foreign investors.

Debra Steger's chapter concludes Part III with a proposal for the creation of an appellate mechanism for IIAs. This chapter draws specifically on Thomas Franck's writing on legitimacy. In particular, Steger notes that Franck "posits that vague treaty terms can be clarified by being interpreted consistently and coherently by an authority recognized as legitimate."[12] She also notes that other scholars have cited Franck to emphasize "that coherence of rules, including through interpretation, is critical to the legitimacy of any international rules-based system." In the first part of her chapter, Steger provides the reasons for and against the establishment of an appellate mechanism. In the second part, she proposes a model for a comprehensive, standing appeals body that would be applicable to all investment awards.

Part IV—Sustainability

The last part of the book considers ways to increase the sustainability of the IIA regime, focusing on improving the balance between public rights and private interests. Sustainability is considered from the point of view of the stability of the regime, its ability to reconcile different forces and reduce the strains on the system (external perspective as compared to legitimacy). This part notably considers how much flexibility currently exists in IIAs to accommodate different interests.

Andrew Newcombe opens this part with an analysis of whether general exceptions clauses (modeled after article XX GATT) are the proper way of ensuring a balance between public and private interests in IIAs. While an increasing number of countries are adopting this practice (especially in RTAs), the author raises some concerns regarding the adequacy of this practice in the context of international investment law. In particular, it remains unclear how investor-state tribunals will interpret such clauses. The author also questions the necessity of these clauses since tribunals, while interpreting IIA obligations, have already balanced public and private interests at the level of primary obligations. The author concludes that instead of using general exceptions, this balancing should be done by tribunals according to proportionality at the level of primary obligations and also through the clarification of the scope of obligations by states in their IIAs.

Markus W. Gehring and Avidan Kent tackle the issue of incorporating sustainable development principles into IIA practice. The goal of improved sustainability in IIAs is the focus of the Brundtland Report, which almost 25 years ago described "sustainable development" as

---

12 See Franck, *supra* note 9 at 61.

"development that meets the needs of the present without compromising the ability of future generations to meet their own needs."[13] The authors argue that the time is ripe to think further about integrating sustainable development in IIAs, which can be done at three different stages: before the conclusion of IIAs, within the procedural dimensions of IIAs' dispute settlement mechanisms, or within the substantive provisions of IIAs. The authors concentrate on two dimensions: impact assessments (pre-IIA conclusion) and substantive provisions of IIAs.

On impact assessments, the authors argue that such mechanisms allow treaty negotiators to be aware of the (potential) future impacts of their negotiations and allow them to weigh the advantages and dis-advantages of each proposal. When it comes to the substantive dimen-sion, the authors give several solutions but insist on the fact that because of its nature, sustainable development requires different approaches. One of the proposed solutions is to include sustainable development objectives in the preambles of IIAs. Another possibility is the use of exceptions and reservations in the IIAs. The authors encourage negoti-ators to use exceptions with care and not make them overly inclusive. A third tool available is to clarify the language used in IIAs or to improve the definitions that they contain in order to avoid conflicts. A fourth solution suggested by the authors is to refer to corporate social respon-sibility norms in IIAs. While these norms are voluntary and rely on self-governance, the authors believe that by adhering to these external norms, higher standards of behavior can be achieved. The last tool sug-gested in the chapter is to address the possible interactions between IIAs and other sustainable development treaties.

Next, Martha O'Brien and Kim Brooks' chapter provides an "exter-nal perspective" on the interrelations between taxation and investment law. The title of their chapter "Direct Taxation, Tax Treaties and IIAs: Mixed Objectives, Mixed Results" gives a sense of the insufficient atten-tion previously given to these issues, which could have an impact on the sustainability of both regimes going forward. The authors highlight that while tax treaties and IIAs have much in common, "international direct taxation and FDI policy as embodied in IIAs seem to inhabit sep-arate spheres of international law and policy." Their chapter captures the tax treaty provisions most relevant to FDI and their potential inter-action with IIAs. They first provide a general description of tax treaties, using Canada's tax treaty network as an example, and present the rela-

---

13 Gro Harlem Brundtland et al, *Our Common Future: World Commission on Environment and Development* (Oxford: Oxford University Press, 1987).

tionship between tax treaty claims and investor-state claims under IIAs. The authors then examine the consequences of tax treaties for FDI. In order to do so they explore the three primary functions served by tax treaties in relation to FDI: reducing administrative barriers, reducing tax costs to cross-border activity, and ensuring a level playing field for non-nationals. Their parting word is that: "there is much that tax, trade and investment policy makers could learn from working more closely together."

The last two chapters under "sustainability" are mirrors of each other. They both consider the relationship between IIAs and general international law. August Reinisch considers the impact of international law on the interpretation of IIAs while Armand de Mestral considers the impact of IIAs on international law. The study and understanding of these relations is key to ensuring the sustainability of the investment law regime in the future.

August Reinisch first analyzes the use by investment treaty tribunals of the rules of treaty interpretation found at articles 31 and 32 of the Vienna Convention. He discusses under different headings (e.g. ordinary meaning, object and purpose), how tribunals have complied (or not) with those rules. In a second part, he provides examples of the influences of international law (especially customary international law) on IIA interpretation, using the concept of necessity as an illustration. He ends with an appeal: for international law to play a useful role in the clarification of IIA provisions, "[t]his requires, of course, a thorough knowledge of general international law. Only with such knowledge IIAs, as instruments of public international law, will be properly interpreted and applied by tribunals."

In the final chapter, Armand de Mestral asserts that "international investment law is indeed making a significant contribution both to international dispute settlement procedures . . . and to the substance of public international law." In order to demonstrate this contribution, he first discusses the following influences in matters of dispute settlement: (1) the role of private parties as claimants, (2) the participation of non-parties, and (3) the advent of open proceedings. In matters of substance, he discusses the following influences: (1) the capacity of BITs and investor-state arbitrations to serve as sources of international law, (2) BITs and investor-state arbitration as a source on matters of treaty interpretation, (3) the significance of using public international law to resolve private claims, and (4) the strengthening of the direct effect of public international law. His conclusion is that "far from contributing to the 'fragmentation' of international law, international investment law should be seen as a source of enrichment for public international law."

Part I

IIA treaty-making: evolution and evaluation

1 Developments in IIA treaty-making

*Andrew Newcombe**

Introduction

There has been significant legal evolution in IIA treaty-making since the conclusion of the first BIT between Germany and Pakistan in 1959. The number of IIAs has increased exponentially over the past 50 years, creating a complex overlapping network of IIAs with varied procedural and substantive protections for foreign investors. According to UNCTAD, by the end of 2010, there were 2,807 BITs, 309 other international agreements with investment related provisions and 2,976 double taxation treaties.[1] IIAs have not only significantly increased in number, but also in length and complexity. Investment promotion and protection obligations are increasingly being integrated into comprehensive FTAs, creating complex interactions between trade and investment obligations and other international regimes, including international environmental law and international human rights law. Further, IIA treaty-making has begun responding to an array of controversial legal issues that have arisen in investor-state arbitrations. As the contributions in this book demonstrate, IIA treaty-making continues to evolve by adopting procedural innovations in the investor-state arbitration process and clarifying the scope of investment protections.

This chapter provides a brief overview of the legal evolution of IIAs. Part I describes the move towards the "treatification" of international investment law in the 1950s and 1960s and the evolution of IIAs up until the early 1990s. This period is distinguished by the increasing inclusion of investor-state arbitration provisions in treaty texts—the defining feature of the modern IIA. Part II surveys the "modelization"

* Associate Professor, Faculty of Law, University of Victoria.
1 See UNCTAD, *World Investment Report 2011: Non-equity Modes of International Production and Development* (New York and Geneva: UNCTAD, 2011) at 100.

trend in IIA treaty-making—the proliferation of model IIAs—and their use in the treaty–making process. Part III highlights the recent trend towards renegotiation of first generation IIAs and analyzes changes in IIA practice resulting from the fact that an increasing number of countries have both "offensive" and "defensive" interests when negotiating IIAs.

Treatification and investor-state arbitration

The defining trend in international investment law post-WWII has been the process of "treatification."[2] Prior to the development of BITs, treaty-based investment protection was sometimes available under bilateral economic treaties. After WWII, a number of states, including the United States and the United Kingdom, continued this practice, concluding treaties of friendship, commerce and navigation ("FCN") that included provisions on the protection of property rights and the business interests of foreigners.[3] In light of uncertainties regarding investor protection standards in customary international law and the lack of access to effect-ive dispute settlement mechanisms, host states sought to promote and protect foreign investment by concluding treaties that would provide both procedural and substantive protections. Although there were early efforts to create an international framework for foreign investment, dis-agreements between capital exporting and importing states about stan-dards of treatment for foreign investors were an obstacle to the conclusion of a multilateral treaty. As a result, capital exporting states began con-cluding BITs dedicated to foreign investment promotion and protection.

Germany was the first state to develop a BIT program, concluding its first BIT with Pakistan in 1959.[4] The Germany-Pakistan BIT (1959) addressed the scope of protections by defining protected investment and investors and contained many of the substantive provisions that are now common in IIAs.[5] In addition, the BIT provided state-to-state dispute

2 See Jeswald Salacuse, "The Treatification of International Investment Law" (2007) 13 Law and Business Review of the Americas 155; Jeswald W. Salacuse, *The Law of Investment Treaties* (Oxford: Oxford University Press, 2010) at ch 4 [Salacuse]. For the history of the development of BITs and for references to source materials, see Andrew Newcombe and Lluís Paradell, *Law and Practice of Investment Treaties: Standards of Treatment* (The Netherlands: Kluwer Law International, 2009) at ch 1 [Newcombe and Paradell].

3 A number of states had also concluded FCN treaties before WWII.

4 This paragraph and the next is drawn from Newcombe & Paradell, *supra* note 2 at §1.30–§1.31.

5 See J Karl, "The Promotion and Protection of German Foreign Investment Abroad" (1996) 11 ICSID Rev 1.

settlement before the ICJ if the parties agreed, or if they did not agree, to an arbitration tribunal upon the request of either party. This recourse to state-to-state arbitration before a three-person arbitral tribunal, as an alternative to ICJ jurisdiction, represents one of the major differences between early post-WWII FCN treaties, such as the Nicaragua-US FCN treaty, and the BITs that were developed in the early 1960s.

The defining feature of the modern BIT—consent to investor-state arbitration—was, however, still to come. The traditional form of consent to international arbitration between a foreign investor and a state was through an arbitration clause in a contract, such as a natural resource concession or a foreign investment agreement. Until 1968, BITs only provided for state-to-state dispute resolution through the establishment of an arbitral tribunal or submission of the dispute to the ICJ.[6] During the negotiations of the ICSID Convention (1965), negotiators recognized that states could consent to arbitrate future disputes by making an offer to arbitrate in a foreign investment code or law, or by means of a treaty. In 1969, ICSID published a series of model arbitration clauses for use in BITs.[7] The Chad-Italy BIT, concluded in 1969, appears to be the first BIT that provides for investor-state arbitration with unqualified state consent. It was this BIT, not the Germany-Pakistan BIT, that marked the true beginning of modern BIT practice because it combined substantive investment promotion and protection obligations with binding investor-state arbitration.

Although the defining features of the modern BIT existed in practice, states concluded only a small number of BITs through the 1970s. This period was characterized by intense disagreement between capital exporting and importing states over the treatment of foreign investment, as exemplified by the 1974 *Declaration on the Establishment of a New International Economic Order* and the *Charter of Economic Rights and Duties of States*.[8] By 1979, states had concluded only 100 BITs.[9] The majority of these BITs were between capital exporting states in Western Europe[10] and developing states.

6 See *ibid* at §1.31; Jason Webb Yackee, "Bilateral Investment Treaties, Credible Commitment, and the Rule of (International) Law: Do BITs Promote Foreign Direct Investment?" (2008) 42(4) Law and Soc'y Rev 805.

7 *Model Clauses Relating to the Convention on the Settlement of Investment Disputes Designed for Use in Bilateral Investment Agreements*, 1969, 8 ILM 1341.

8 *Declaration on the Establishment of a New International Economic Order*, GA Res 3201 (S-VI), UN, 1974, 13 ILM 715.

9 See Newcombe and Paradell, *supra* note 2 at §1.32–§1.33.

10 Austria, the Belgo-Luxembourg Economic Union, Denmark, France, Germany, Italy, The Netherlands, Norway, Sweden, Switzerland and the United Kingdom.

In contrast to the 1970s, the end of the 1980s and the 1990s witnessed an exponential growth in the conclusion of international investment and trade treaties. An important development in the early 1980s was the development of the United States BIT program.[11] Unlike European BITs, which focused on investment protection, the US model BIT provided for entry and establishment rights—investment liberalization, not just protection.[12] Further, China, which now has 130 BITs, signed its first BIT in 1982.[13]

The number of BITs quintupled during the 1990s. By the end of the 1990s, states had concluded 1857 BITs. By the early 1990s, the vast majority of new IIAs included an investor-state arbitration mechanism. Importantly, BITs were increasingly being concluded between non-industrialized states.[14] Several industrializing states, including Argentina, Chile and India concluded their first BITs, and other OECD states, such as Canada and Australia, followed the United States by initiating BIT programs. The 1990s saw an increasing complexity in treaty provisions and the integration of investment provisions into a variety of international economic treaties, including the NAFTA, the ECT and the WTO *General Agreement on Trade and Services* ("GATS") and *Agreement on Trade-Related Investment Measures* ("TRIMs").[15]

This complexity continues to increase. In 2008, UNCTAD aptly summarized the network of IIAs as universal, atomized, multi-layered and multifaceted:

> The system is *universal*, in that nearly every country has signed at least one BIT and the majority of them are members to several, if not numerous, IIAs. The structure of agreements is *atomized*, that is, it consists of thousands of individual agreements that lack any system-wide coordination and coherence. The IIA universe

---

11 For in-depth commentary, see Kenneth J. Vandevelde, *United States Investment Treaties: Policy and Practice* (Boston: Kluwer Law and Taxation, 1992) [United States Investment Treaties] and Kenneth J. Vandevelde, *United States International Investment Agreements* (Oxford: Oxford University Press, 2009).
12 United States Investment Treaties, *ibid* at 72.
13 See Chunbao Liu at ch 4 on the legal evolution of Chinese BITs.
14 In 2009 an UNCTAD Report noted that IIAs are being concluded amongst a diverse group of states—26% of IIAs are between developing states. See UNCTAD, *Recent Developments in International Investment Agreements (2008–June 2009)*, IIA Monitor 3, UNCTAD/WEB/DIAE/IA/2009/8 at 4.
15 *Agreement on Trade-Related Investment Measures*, April 15, 1994, reproduced in WTO, *The Legal Texts: Results of the Uruguay Round of Multilateral Trade Negotiations* (Cambridge: Cambridge University Press, 1999) at 143.

is *multi-layered*—as IIAs now exist at the bilateral, regional, intraregional, interregional, sectoral, plurilateral and multilateral level—and IIAs at different levels may overlap. The system is also *multifaceted*, meaning that IIAs include not only provisions that are specific to investment, but also rules that address other related matters, such as trade in goods, trade in services, intellectual property, labor issues or environmental protection.[16]

In light of this complexity, and controversial rulings that have resulted from some of the early investor-state arbitration cases, IIA treaty-making practice has continued to evolve.

"Modelization" trend

An important trend in IIA treaty-making is the creation by many states of model or prototype BITs to serve as the basis for the negotiation of new treaties.[17] This trend might contribute to efficiency gains in IIA treaty-making, but also presents difficulties when two countries negotiate on the basis of very different model IIAs.

The beginning of state-based proposals for "modelization" can be traced to the 1962 OECD *Draft Convention on the Protection of Foreign Property*,[18] which was revised and approved by the OECD in 1967 (1967 Draft OECD Convention).[19] Although the 1967 Draft OECD Convention failed to gain sufficient support among OECD countries for adoption as a multilateral convention, its substantive provisions have subsequently served as an important model for BITs.[20] Further, as noted

16 See also UNCTAD, *The Development Dimension of International Investment Agreements*, TD/B/C.II/MEM.3/2, December 2, 2008 [Development Dimension] at para 21.
17 See Mark A. Clodfelter, "The Adaptation of States to the Changing World of Investment Protection through Model BITs" (2009) 24(1) ICSID Rev 165 [Clodfelter].
18 OECD *Draft Convention on the Protection of Foreign Property*, 1963 2 ILM 241. See Newcombe and Paradell, *supra* note 2 at ch 1 for earlier attempts to draft treaties and codify international investment law.
19 OECD *Draft Convention on the Protection of Foreign Property*, October 12, 1967 7 ILM 117.
20 Rudolf Dolzer and Margrete Stevens, *Bilateral Investment Treaties* (The Hague: Martinus Nijhoff Publishers, 1995) at 2; Patrick Juillard, "The Law of International Investment: Can the Imbalance be Redressed?" in Karl P. Sauvant (ed), *Yearbook in International Investment Law and Policy 2008–2009* (New York: Oxford University Press, 2009) 273 at 277; Patrick Juillard, "Bilateral Investment Treaties in the Context of Investment Law" (Paper delivered at the OECD Investment Compact Regional Roundtable on Bilateral Investment Treaties for the Protection and

above, in 1969, ICSID published a series of model BIT arbitration clauses for use in BITs.

Almost all OECD states, and a growing number of industrializing states (including China,[21] India and Mexico), have model BITs.[22] An increasing number of developing states have created model BITs.[23] Regional groups have also put forward models. In the early 1980s, the Asian-African Legal Consultative Organization ("AALCO") published three draft BITs, which provided different models of investment liberalization and protection.[24] In addition to model BITs developed by states, another development in the "modelization" trend has been the creation of a model investment treaty by the International Institute for Sustainable Development (IISD) in 2005—the Model International Agreement on Investment for Sustainable Development (IISD Model).[25]

Promotion of Foreign Investment in South East Europe, Dubrovnik, Croatia, May 28–29, 2001) online: OECD <http://www.oecd.org/dataoecd/44/41/1894794.pdf>.

21 See Chunbao Liu in this book at chapter 4. See also Norah Gallagher and Wenhua Shan, *Chinese Investment Treaties: Policies and Practice* (Oxford: Oxford University Press, 2009).

22 Clodfelter, *supra* note 17 at 167 traces model BITs to at least 32 different states. See also Chester Brown and Devashish Krishan (eds), *Commentaries on Selected Model Investment Treaties* (Oxford University Press, forthcoming), which will analyse the following country models: Australia, Austria, Canada, China, Colombia, France Germany, India, Italy, Japan, Korea, Latvia, China, Netherlands, Russia, Singapore, Switzerland, United Kingdom and the United States, as well as analyse Chapter Eleven of the NAFTA, which has served as a model for IIAs and model BITs.

23 The UNCTAD IIA Compendium includes copies of model treaties for the following developing states: Benin, Burundi, Mauritius, Mongolia, Peru, Thailand and Turkey. See online: UNCTAD <http://www.unctadxi.org/templates/DocSearch____780. aspx.>

24 Model A provides the highest standards of investment protection. Model B provides for more restrictive investment promotion and protection provisions. Model C provides protection similar to Model A but the protections apply to specific types of investments. See *Model Agreement for Promotion and Protection of Investment* (1984) 23 ILM 237, online: <http://www.aalco.int/PROMOTION%20AND%20 PROTECTION%20OF%20INVESTMENTS.pdf >.

25 See International Institute for Sustainable Development's work on Investment and Sustainable Development, online: IISD <http://www.iisd.org/investment/>. The IISD model appears to have had some influence on developing state IIA practice. Since 2007, the IISD has convened an annual forum for developing country investment negotiators, at which the IISD Model has been discussed (see online: IISD <http://www.iisd.org/investment/dci/>). On the IISD Model, see Mahnaz Malik, "The IISD Model International Agreement on Investment for Sustainable Development" in Marie-Claire Cordonier Segger, Markus Gehring and Andrew Newcombe (eds), *Sustainable Development in World Investment Law* (The Hague: Kluwer Law International, 2011) at 565–84. Some of the elements in the IISD model, such as its focus on balancing investor rights and obligations, are reflected in

Model BITs have a number of benefits.[26] First, they enable a state to establish and clarify foreign investment policy and negotiating positions for BIT negotiations. Secondly, since BITs are signed with many treaty partners, a model serves to promote uniformity in state treaty practice. Consistency amongst a state's IIAs may be particularly important in light of arbitral awards holding that investors can use MFN treatment provisions to obtain the advantage of the substantive and procedural protections in the state's other BITs.[27] A broad application of MFN treatment raises concerns that specifically negotiated provisions in a particular BIT (that the state may not want to extend to other treaty partners—for example, if it wants to differentiate between investors from developed and developing states) can be bypassed through the MFN treatment provision. Recent treaty practice suggests that states are increasingly concerned with consistency amongst their various BITs and clarifying limits on the application of MFN treatment.[28] The use of a model BIT has the practical benefit of reducing the risk of potential inconsistencies amongst a state's BITs, particularly where the state is engaged in multiple simultaneous negotiations or concludes a series of BITs over a period of time. Thirdly, from the perspective of a home state's foreign investors, consistency in their home state's BIT practice promotes certainty and predictability with respect to the treatment they can expect when they invest in a host state that has agreed to treat investors in accordance with their home state's model BIT treatment standards. Fourthly, the use of a model BIT provides a strategic negotiating advantage to the proffering state—the model becomes the basis for negotiations and the potential treaty party is put in the position of having to react to an established framework.[29]

the Investment Agreement for the Common Market for Eastern and Southern Africa Common Investment Area (COMESA Investment Agreement). On the COMESA Investment Agreement, see Peter Muchlinski, "The COMESA Common Investment Area: Substantive Standards and Procedural Problems in Dispute Settlement," SOAS School of Law Research Paper No. 11/20102, online: SSRN <http://papers. ssrn.com/sol3/papers.cfm?abstract_id=1698209>, who identifies COMESA as a "significant new model" for investor-state dispute settlement provisions.

26 See Salacuse, *supra* note 2 at 116–17; Clodfelter, *supra* note 17 at 167.

27 See Newcombe and Paradell, *supra* note 2 at ch 5, on the use of MFN treatment standards to obtain the benefit of IIAs with other states.

28 For example, the 2004 Canadian Model FIPA provides that MFN treatment "shall not apply to treatment accorded under all bilateral or multilateral international agreements in force or signed prior to the date of entry into of this Agreement." See DFAIT, online: DFAIT <http://www.international.gc.ca/trade-agreements-accords-commerciaux/assets/pdfs/2004-FIPA-model-en.pdf> at Annex III(1).

29 Salacuse, *supra* note 2 at 116.

Although model BITs have common elements and many similar provisions, modelization is not synonymous with harmonization and standardization. Model agreements display important differences. The current United States or Canadian model agreements, which reflect these countries' experience with the NAFTA, differ significantly from the models of their European counterparts, such as the Dutch, German or Swiss models. Further, model BITs develop over time—for example, there are significant differences between the 1987 and 2004 US Model BITs.[30]

As model BITs proliferate, however, negotiators will increasingly be faced with situations of competing model BITs, with potentially conflicting policies, approaches and provisions. For example, Canada and China began BIT negotiations in 1994. Those negotiations were suspended pending China's accession to the WTO and were resumed in 2004, but have not yet resulted in a signed agreement. Part of the difficulty in reaching an agreement has been attributed to divergences in each state's respective BIT programs.[31]

Renegotiations and the search for balance

The legal evolution of IIA treaty-making is also reflected in the fact that early BITs are now being renegotiated. By the end of 2008, 132 BITs had been renegotiated.[32] For example, in 2009, Germany and Pakistan replaced their 1959 BIT, with a new treaty providing for investor-state arbitration and a broader range of investment protections than the earlier treaty. To date, most BIT renegotiations have followed the trend reflected by the new German-Pakistan BIT (2009)—the replacement of an earlier, "weaker" BIT with a BIT with stronger investment protection standards and more expansive investor-state arbitration provisions.[33] A smaller number of renegotiations have been motivated by the need for

---

30 José E Alvarez, "The Return of the State" (2011) 20(2) Minnesota Journal of International Law 223.

31 Justin Carter, "The Protracted Bargain: Negotiating the Canada-China Foreign Investment Promotion and Protection Agreement" (2009) 47 Can YB Int'l L 197.

32 UNCTAD, Recent Developments International Investment Agreements (2008– June 2009), IIA Monitor No. 3 (2009), (New York and Geneva: United Nations, 2009), online: UNCTAD <http://www.unctad.org/en/docs/webdiaeia20098_en. pdf>. See Development Dimension, *supra* note 16 at 3, noting that as of June 2008 Germany had renegotiated the most BITs (16), followed by China (15), Morocco (12) and Egypt (11).

33 For example, many communist era BITs restrict investor-state arbitration to determining the amount of compensation for expropriation. See Chunbao Liu at ch 4 on the development of Chinese IIA practice.

new EU members—the Czech Republic, Hungary, Latvia, Poland, Romania, and the Slovak Republic—to renegotiate their existing BITs to bring them into compliance with EU law.[34]

As states become more concerned about the need to balance defensive interests as potential respondents with offensive interests in terms of protecting their investors abroad, there may well be increased attention dedicated to revising BITs in an effort to limit investor rights and to clarify the right of host states to regulate on environmental and other social issues.[35] In reaction to their experiences as respondents in NAFTA investor-state claims, Canada and the United States have revised their model investment treaties to address concerns with the scope of investor's procedural and substantive rights.[36] Further, as Armand de Mestral's chapter highlights, with the EU taking competence over FDI, the re-negotiation of 100s of European BITs becomes a possibility. There continues to be an intense debate within the EU about the shape of a model EU BIT.[37]

Conclusion

The treatification of international investment law over the past 50 years has been driven by uncertainty regarding the international minimum standard of treatment of foreign investment and the need for effective dispute settlement mechanisms. Modelization—the creation of model BITs and programs to promote the conclusion of BITs—has contributed to the proliferation of the global network of BITs by reducing transactions cost associated with the conclusion of a bilateral treaty. And although the overall trend in the renegotiation of BITs has been a transition to more investment-protective BITs, there is no inevitability to this trend. As Alvarez has argued in "The Return of the State", compared to the 1987 US Model BIT, the 2004 US Model BIT has "dramatically" shrunk "virtually every right originally accorded to foreign investors."[38] For

---

34 See DFAIT, "Background on the Canada-'EU6' Foreign Investment Promotion and Protection Agreement (FIPA) Negotiations," online: DFAIT <http://www.international. gc.ca/trade-agreements-accords-commerciaux/agr-acc/fipa-apie/eu6-ue6.aspx?menu_ id=30&menu=R>. With the EU gaining competence for FDI under the Lisbon Treaty the consistency between IIAs and EU law has become the subject of much debate. See Armand de Mestral at ch 3 in this book.
35 See Development Dimension, *supra* note 16 at 3; Alvarez, *supra* note 30.
36 See ch 2 by Céline Lévesque and Andrew Newcombe on the Canadian and American Model IIAs.
37 See Armand de Mestral at ch 3 in this book.
38 Alvarez, *supra* note 30 at 235.

Clodfelter, the innovations of recent Model BITs "reflect the efforts of an increasing number of States to find a new balance between two competing objectives: the promotion and protection of investments, and the right to properly regulate for public welfare purposes."[39] Whether the right "balance" has been achieved remains to be seen and treaty-making in this dynamic area will undoubtedly continue to evolve.

39 See Clodfelter, *supra* note 17 at 174.

2 The evolution of IIA practice in Canada and the United States

Céline Lévesque and Andrew Newcombe**

Introduction

American and Canadian IIA practices have evolved significantly since each state began their formal BIT programs and concluded their first BITs—the US-Egypt BIT (1986) and the Canada-USSR BIT (1989). A significant development for both states was the inclusion of an investment chapter in the NAFTA in 1992.[1] The IIA practice of both the United States and Canada has been significantly influenced by their experience of acting as respondents in investor-state arbitrations under NAFTA. The current model IIAs of both states, respectively the 2004 US Model BIT ("US Model")[2] and the 2004 Canadian Model Foreign Investment Promotion and Protection Agreement ("Canadian Model"),[3]

* Associate Professor, Faculty of Law, Civil Law Section, University of Ottawa.
** Associate Professor, Faculty of Law, University of Victoria.

1 North American Free Trade Agreement Between the Government of Canada, the Government of Mexico and the Government of the United States, 17 December 1992, Can TS 1994 No. 2 (entered into force January 1, 1994) [NAFTA].

2 Treaty between the Government of the United States of America and Government of [Country] Concerning the Encouragement and Reciprocal Protection of Investment (2004 Model BIT), online: US State Department <http://www.state.gov/documents/organization/117601.pdf> [US Model]. For commentary on the current US Model BIT and the evolution of US BIT practice, see Lee Caplan and Jeremy Sharpe, "The 2004 U.S. Model Bilateral Investment Treaty", in Chester Brown and Devashish Krishan (eds), *Commentaries on Selected Model International Investment Agreements* (Oxford: Oxford University Press, forthcoming) [*Commentaries on Selected Model IIAs*].

3 Agreement between Canada and _____ for the Promotion and Protection of Investment, online: DFAIT <http://www.international.gc.ca/trade-agreements-accords-commerciaux/assets/pdfs/2004-FIPA-model-en.pdf> [Canadian Model]. For commentary on the current Canadian Model BIT and the evolution of Canadian BIT practice, see Céline Lévesque and Andrew Newcombe, "Commentary on the

include procedural and substantive provisions that reflect Canadian and American concerns with various aspects of investor-state arbitration under NAFTA Chapter Eleven.

It is beyond the scope of this chapter to discuss in detail the evolution of Canadian and American BIT practice and the various model BITs each state has used over time. Canadian practice since 1989 can be divided into three generations of BITs,[4] while the United States developed six model BITs between 1983 and 2004.[5] In addition to the different models used by each state over time, the texts of individual BITs often diverge from the model texts used in negotiations. Each state's IIA practice now also encompasses a series of FTAs with investment chapters. These investment chapters are typically based on the state's model BIT, with modifications to reflect the legal architecture and particular features of the FTA.[6]

This chapter focuses on the current Canadian and US Models, both of which are products of the relatively unique position that Canada and the United States have faced as serial respondents in NAFTA investor-state arbitrations, even though their IIAs policies have been primarily focused on "offensive" interests—protecting their investors abroad. This NAFTA "laboratory" has significantly affected Canadian and American BIT practices in a number of areas. Many of these specific developments are explored in chapters of this book. The purpose of this chapter is to provide an overview of these developments through the lenses of efficiency, legitimacy and sustainability.

Efficiency

As described in the Introduction to this book, improved efficiency has many facets and can be attained by different means. The IIA practice of the United States and Canada has demonstrated a trend toward increased efficiency over time, both related to the coverage of IIAs as well as the settlement of investment disputes.

Canadian Model Foreign Investment Promotion and Protection Agreement", in *Commentaries on Selected Model IIAs, ibid.*

4 See Lévesque and Newcombe, *ibid.*

5 The six models (1983, 1984, 1992, 1994, 1998 and 2004) are reprinted as annexes in Kenneth J. Vandevelde, *United States International Investment Agreements* (Oxford: Oxford University Press, 2009).

6 For Canadian FTAs, see online: DFAIT <http://www.international.gc.ca/trade-agreements-accords-commerciaux/agr-acc/index.aspx?view=d>. For US FTAs, see online: Office of the United States Trade Representative <http://www.ustr.gov/trade-agreements/free-trade-agreements>.

Scope and coverage of IIAs

For about 20 years, the IIA practice of the United States and Canada has been characterized by its use of the "pre-establishment" model. In other words, American and Canadian IIAs impose obligations on states not to discriminate against foreign investors, at the time of admission, on the basis of their nationality. Thus, both national treatment and MFN treatment obligations apply at the time of "establishment" or "acquisition" of an investment.[7] This approach can be contrasted with that in European BITs, where obligations only apply "post-establishment."

American and Canadian IIAs pair this "pre-establishment" protection with a system of exclusions for existing non-conforming measures as well as some future measures. Different variations exist on this theme, but the general idea is for states not to *adopt* measures that are more restrictive than those in existence at the time of conclusion of the IIA and not to *modify* existing measures in a way that would make them more restrictive than at the time of conclusion. This is sometimes referred to as the "standstill principle."[8] US and Canadian IIAs often include long lists of sectors and specific measures that are excluded from investment obligations (a system of "negative lists" or "carve-outs").

From this perspective, American and Canadian IIAs are not liberalization instruments.[9] Rather, they attempt to create a minimum standard of liberalization by preventing additional restrictions on the admission of foreign investment. This may, in turn, have a promotional effect on FDI. At least one econometric study on the promotional effect of US BITs has found that: "1. A U.S. BIT is more likely than not to exert a strong and positive role in promoting U.S. investment. 2. A U.S. BIT is more likely

7 The performance requirement provisions of both models also apply in the context of establishment. See US Model, *supra* note 2 at art 8, and Canadian Model, *supra* note 3 at art 7.
8 OECD, Drafting Group No. 2 on Selected Topics Concerning Treatment of Investors and Investment (Pre/Post Establishment), Note by the Chairman, *Mechanisms for Standstill, Rollback and Listing of Country Specific Reservations*, February 15, 1996, DAFFE/MAI/DG2(95)3/REV1, online: OECD <http://www.oecd.org/daf/mai/pdf/dg2/dg2953r1e.pdf>.
9 See online: DFAIT <http://www.international.gc.ca/trade-agreements-accords-commerciaux/agr-acc/fipa-apie/fipa-purpose.aspx?lang=en&menu_id=43&view=d>. "Does the FIPA eliminate restrictions to invest in the foreign country? No. The FIPA is not an instrument of liberalization. It can, however, support the goals of liberalization. For example, most FIPAs, but not all, contain provisions that commit Parties not to adopt measures that are more restrictive with respect to investment; and not to reverse any new liberalization measures that they may adopt."

than not to exert a strong and positive role in promoting overall investment. 3. A U.S. BIT is likely to exert more of an impact than other
OECD BITs in promoting overall investment."[10] Although the debate
over the promotional effect of BITs is notoriously controversial,[11] there
are good reasons to think that the pre-establishment model followed by
the United States and Canada has the *potential* for more investment
promotion effect than a post-establishment model.

A second dimension to the "efficiency" of the American and
Canadian IIA practice in terms of promotion effect is the increased
number of FTAs with investment chapters.[12] As will be discussed further in Chapter 7 of this book, UNCTAD has found that FTAs (and
other regional integration and cooperation agreements) that include
investment chapters have a stronger impact in terms of increased FDI
flows than BITs.[13] Looking at the FTA negotiations currently taking
place between Canada, the United States and their respective partners,
this trend is likely to continue.[14]

Settlement of investment disputes

American and Canadian IIA practice has incorporated a number of procedural mechanisms to promote early resolution of claims, to make the
investor-state arbitration process more efficient and to handle overlapping dispute settlement mechanisms.[15] Several of these procedural
innovations first appeared in NAFTA Chapter Eleven, and have subsequently found their way into the US and Canadian Models.

---

10 See Jeswald W. Salacuse and Nicholas P. Sullivan, "Do BITs Really Work?: An
    Evaluation of Bilateral Investment Treaties and Their Grand Bargain" (2005) 46
    Harv Int'l LJ 67 at 111.
11 See Karl P. Sauvant and Lisa E. Sachs, *The Effect of Treaties on Foreign Direct Investment*
    (Oxford: Oxford University Press, 2009). See also Mark Manger at ch 5 in this book
    and for a micro-economics perspective see Amrita Ray Chaudhuri and Hassan
    Benchekroun at ch 6.
12 For Canadian and US FTAs, see *supra* note 6.
13 UNCTAD, The Role of International Investment Agreements in Attracting Foreign
    Direct Investment to Developing Countries, UNCTAD/DIAE/IA/2009/5, at 110,
    online: UNCTAD <http://www.unctad.org/Templates/webflyer.asp?docid=12543&
    intItemID=2068&lang=1>. See Armand de Mestral and Alireza Falsafi at ch 7 in
    this book.
14 See listing of current Canadian and US FTA negotiations, online: DFAIT<http://
    www.international.gc.ca/trade-agreements-accords-commerciaux/agr-acc/index.
    aspx?view=d> and Office of the United States Trade Representative <http://www.
    ustr.gov/trade-agreements/free-trade-agreements>.
15 On overlaps, see Andreas Ziegler at ch 9 in this book.

In common with other IIAs, the US and Canadian Model BITs promote the settlement of claims through consultations and negotiations.[16] The US Model refers to the use of non-binding, third party procedures.[17] The Canadian Model requires the parties to hold consultations within 30 days of the submission of a notice of claim.[18] The US and Canadian Models have both adopted the requirement in NAFTA Chapter Eleven[19] that a disputing investor must deliver a notice of intent to submit a claim to arbitration at least 90 days before a claim is submitted to arbitration.[20] This notice requirement provides the respondent state essential information about the claim, which can be used in the context of consultations and, potentially, settlement discussions. Under both Models, there is a waiting period of six months from the occurence of the events in question before a claim may be made.[21] This provides a "cooling-off" period, during which consultations can occur before the formal institution of arbitral proceedings.

The US and Canadian Models have also adopted a number of other procedural requirements that appear in NAFTA Chapter Eleven and that promote efficiency in dispute settlement. The Models address concurrent dispute settlement procedures regarding the same measure by requiring that the notice of arbitration be accompanied by a waiver of the right to initiate or continue other dispute resolution procedures.[22] The Models promote timely claims by imposing a requirement to bring a claim within three years.[23] And both Models include a provision, almost identical to the one in the NAFTA,[24] for consolidating multiple claims that have a question of law or fact in common.[25]

Another important efficiency-related development in IIA practice is the use of expedited procedures for addressing preliminary objections by host states that a claim is frivolous or without legal merit.[26] Both Models provide that claims may be submitted to arbitration under the ICSID Rules,[27] which were amended in 2006 to provide for an expedited

---

16 See Céline Lévesque at ch 8 on the use of ADR in the resolution of IIA claims.
17 US Model, *supra* note 2 at art 23.
18 Canadian Model, *supra* note 3 at art 25(2).
19 NAFTA, *supra* note 1 at art 1119.
20 See US Model, *supra* note 2 at art 24(2), and Canadian Model, *supra* note 3 at art 24.
21 US Model, *ibid* at art 24(3), and Canadian Model, *ibid* at art 26(1)(b) and 26(2)(b).
22 US Model, *ibid* at art 26(2)(b), and Canadian Model, *ibid* at art 26(1)(e) and 26(2)(e).
23 US Model, *ibid* at art 26(1), and Canadian Model, *ibid* at art 26(1)(c) and 26(2)(c).
24 NAFTA, *supra* note 1 at art 1126.
25 US Model, *supra* note 2 at art 33, and Canadian Model, *supra* note 3 at art 32.
26 See also Céline Lévesque at ch 8 in this book.
27 As of 1 December 2011, Canada had signed, but not yet ratified the ICSID Convention.

preliminary objection procedure.[28] The US Model expressly provides a preliminary objection process, allowing the state to object to claims for which, as a matter of law, an award could not be made.[29] If a preliminary objection is made, proceedings on the merits are suspended. There is an additional expedited procedure for bringing a preliminary objection within 45 days after the tribunal is constituted.[30] This provision specifically refers to objections that a claim is not within the tribunal's competence.[31] The Canadian Model states that where there is a preliminary objection as to jurisdiction or admissibility, the tribunal shall "wherever possible" decide the matter before proceedings on the merits.[32] In contrast to the US Model, which mandates the tribunal to suspend proceedings on the merits and render a decision, the Canadian Model leaves the tribunal discretion in how to address preliminary objections.

Legitimacy

The IIA practice of Canada and the United States has not been immune from the criticism by stakeholders and different constituencies that the regime lacks legitimacy.[33] Some of the claims related to the absence of obligations for investors under IIAs—instruments pathologically unbalanced.[34] Regarding dispute settlement procedures, critics complained of the secret and closed nature of the investor-state arbitration process.[35]

---

28 ICSID Arbitration Rule 41(5), online: ICSID <http://icsid.worldbank.org/ICSID/ICSID/RulesMain.jsp>.
29 US Model, *supra* note 2 at art 28(4).
30 *Ibid* at art 28(5).
31 *Ibid* at art 28(4) and (5). A similar procedure is available under the CAFTA and has been used in a number of cases. See *Pac Rim Cayman LLC v Republic of El Salvador*, Decision on the Respondent's Preliminary Objections under CAFTA arts 10.20.4 and 10.20.5, ICSID Case No. ARB/09/12 (August 2, 2010) and *Commerce Group Corp. and San Sebastian Gold Mines, Inc v Republic of El Salvador*, Award, ICSID Case No. ARB/09/17 (March 14, 2011).
32 Canadian Model, *supra* note 3 at art 37.
33 For book-length treatments, see Gus Van Harten, *Investment Treaty Arbitration and Public Law* (Oxford: Oxford University Press, 2007); Michael Waibel et al, *The Backlash Against Investment Arbitration* (The Netherlands: Kluwer, 2010); and José Enrique Alvarez, *The Public International Law Regime Governing International Investment* (The Hague: The Hague Academy of International Law, 2011), especially Chapter V, "The Once and Future Investment Regime".
34 See ch 11 in this book by Andrew Newcombe on investor misconduct and ch 10 by Patrick Dumberry on corporate investors' international legal personality.
35 See the discussion of "secret" NAFTA tribunals, in the transcript of Bill Moyers's story "Trading Democracy", online: Public Broadcasting System, <http://www.pbs.org/now/transcript/transcript_tdfull.html>.

In the last decade, both countries reacted to these criticisms and others, at times in different ways.

Scope and coverage of IIAs

The regulation of the behavior of multinational corporations ("MNCs") through IIAs is a controversial issue.[36] In its recent FTAs, however, Canada has taken a (small) step to address issues of corporate social responsibility ("CSR"). The United States does not appear to have moved on this front.

The first FTA to include a CSR clause is the Canada-Peru FTA signed in 2008. It states:

> Each Party should encourage enterprises operating within its territory or subject to its jurisdiction to voluntarily incorporate internationally recognized standards of corporate social responsibility in their internal policies, such as statements of principle that have been endorsed or are supported by the Parties. These principles address issues such as labour, the environment, human rights, community relations and anti-corruption. The Parties remind those enterprises of the importance of incorporating such corporate social responsibility standards in their internal policies.[37]

The wording of this clause demonstrates the difficulty in addressing CSR in an IIA. First, it is a "best efforts" clause. Secondly, the CSR norms it refers to are voluntary. Thirdly, the norms are not specific as the two countries are not necessarily signatories to the same codes and other instruments dealing with CSR. Thus, its main purpose appears to be a signalling device for commitment to CSR. These difficulties may explain why the United States has not followed suit.

Another "legitimacy" issue that the United States and Canada have addressed in their IIAs is the potential for "forum shopping" by foreign

---

36 See Patrick Dumberry at ch 10 in this book.
37 *Free Trade Agreement between Canada and the Republic of Peru*, May 29, 2008 (entered into force August 1, 2009), at art 810 (Corporate Social Responsibility), online: DFAIT <http://www.international.gc.ca/trade-agreements-accords-commerciaux/agr-acc/peru-perou/peru-toc-perou-tdm.aspx?lang=eng&view=d>. See also *Free Trade Agreement between Canada and the Republic of Colombia*, 21 November 2008 (entered into force August 15, 2011) at art 816 (Corporate Social Responsibility), online: DFAIT<http://www.international.gc.ca/trade-agreements-accords-commerciaux/agr-acc/colombia-colombie/can-colombia-toc-tdm-can-colombie.aspx?view=d> [Canada-Colombia FTA].

investors. Both countries include so-called "denial of benefits" clauses in their model BITs and their recent IIAs.[38] One situation that such a clause aims to prevent is for corporate investors, without "substantial business activity" in the territory where they are constituted (i.e. home state of convenience), to take advantage of the BIT to sue the host state.[39] Denial of benefits clauses ensure that investors cannot use shell-companies to obtain the benefit of home state IIA protections.

Settlement of investment disputes

Legitimacy-related innovations in American and Canadian treaty practice have focused on the transparency of investor-state arbitration. Transparency became a controversial issue as a result of a number of early NAFTA investment claims in which investors challenged government measures related to the environment.[40] In response, the NAFTA parties (Canada, Mexico and the United States), through the NAFTA Free Trade Commission, issued a Note of Interpretation in 2001 stating that NAFTA does not impose a general duty of confidentiality on the disputing parties to a Chapter Eleven arbitration.[41] Then, in 2003, the NAFTA parties, through the NAFTA Free Trade Commission, issued a statement on the operation of Chapter Eleven, outlining provisions for non-party participation.[42] At the same time, Canada and the United States stated individually that they would consent to open hearings of investor-state cases, subject to the protection of confidential information.[43]

---

38 US Model, *supra* note 2 at art 17, and Canadian Model, *supra* note 3 at art 18.
39 On denial of benefits, see Jean-François Hébert at ch 13 in this book.
40 See *Ethyl Corpn v Government of Canada*, Award on Jurisdiction, UNCITRAL (June 24, 1998); *Metalclad Corpn v The United Mexican States*, ICSID, Case No. ARB (AF)/97/1 (August 30, 2000); *Methanex Corpn v United States of America*, Final Award of the Tribunal on Jurisdiction and Merits, UNCITRAL (August 3, 2005) [*Methanex*].
41 See NAFTA Free Trade Commission, Notes of Interpretation of Certain Chapter 11 Provisions, July 31, 2001, online: DFAIT <http://www.international.gc.ca/trade-agreements-accords-commerciaux/disp-diff/NAFTA-Interpr.aspx?lang=en& view=d> [FTC Notes].
42 See NAFTA Free Trade Commission, Statement on non-disputing parties, online: DFAIT   <http://www.international.gc.ca/trade-agreements-accords-commerciaux/ assets/pdfs/Nondisputing-en.pdf>.
43 See Statement of Canada on Open Hearings in NAFTA Chapter Eleven Arbitrations, October 2003, which affirms that Canada will make all efforts to ensure "that hearings in Chapter Eleven disputes be open to the public, except to ensure the protection of confidential information, including business confidential information." Online: DFAIT   <http://www.international.gc.ca/trade-agreements-accords-commerciaux/agr-acc/nafta-alena/open-hearing.aspx?lang=eng>. For the United

The US and Canadian Models reflect and incorporate these changes. With respect to hearings, both Models provide that hearings shall be open to the public, subject to appropriate protections for confidential information.[44] The open hearing requirements in both Models can be contrasted with the position under the ICSID Arbitration Rules, the ICSID Additional Facility Rules and the UNCITRAL Arbitration Rules under which a party may object to open the hearings to the public.[45]

Both Models provide that documents submitted to and issued by a tribunal shall be publicly available, subject to protection for the disclosure of confidential or protected information.[46]

Further, both Models establish procedures for submissions by non-disputing parties.[47] The Canadian Model establishes a series of criteria for the tribunal to consider whether to grant leave to a "non-disputing party,"[48] which are substantially based on the criteria listed in the NAFTA Free Trade Commission statement issued in October 2003.[49] In contrast, the US Model simply confirms that tribunals have the authority to accept and consider *amicus curiae* submissions.[50] These transparency-related developments are also reflected in the 2006 amendments to the ICSID Arbitration Rules, which now expressly provide that an ICSID tribunal may accept submissions from non-disputing parties.[51]

The US Model reflects two other legitimacy-related provisions that address the interpretation of BIT provisions. First, the US Model includes a mechanism under which, at the request of a disputing party,

States, see Press Release, online: Office of the United States Trade Representative <http://www.ustr.gov/about-us/press-office/press-releases/archives/2003/october/nafta-commission-announces-new-transparen>.

44 US Model, *supra* note 2 at art 29(2), and Canadian Model, *supra* note 3 at art 38(1).

45 ICSID Arbitration Rule 32(2) and ICSID Additional Facility Rule 39(2), online: ICSID <http://icsid.worldbank.org/ICSID/ICSID/RulesMain.jsp>; UNCITRAL Arbitration Rules (1976) at art 25(4), and UNCITRAL Arbitration Rules (2010) at art 28(3), online: UNCITRAL <http://www.cnudmi.org/uncitral/en/uncitral_texts/arbitration/1976Arbitration_rules.html>.

46 US Model, *supra* note 2 at art 29(2)–(4) and Canadian Model, *supra* note 3 at art 38(2)–(8). The Canadian model refers to "documents", in contrast, the US Model lists specific documents that must be made available. The US Model, for example, does not specifically refer to documentary evidence.

47 US Model, *supra* note 2 art 28(3), and Canadian Model, *supra* note 3 at art 39.

48 Canadian Model, *ibid* at art 39.

49 See Statement of the Free Trade Commission on non-disputing party participation, online: DFAIT <http://www.international.gc.ca/trade-agreements-accords-commerciaux/assets/pdfs/Nondisputing-en.pdf)>.

50 US Model, *supra* note 2 at art 28(3).

51 ICSID Arbitration Rules, *supra* note 45 at rule 37(2).

the tribunal must transmit its proposed decision or award to the disputing parties and the other non-disputing state party. The disputing parties are then given 60 days to comment on "any aspect" of the proposed decision or award. The tribunal "shall consider" comments and then must issue its decision or award within 45 days.[52] Secondly, the US Model contemplates the addition of a "bilateral appellate body or similar mechanism to review awards."[53] Debra Steger discusses the review of awards and proposals for appellate review in Chapter 14 of this book.

Sustainability

As described in the Introduction to this book, the concept of sustainability refers to the ability of the international investment law regime to reconcile different forces, to accommodate different interests in a way that ensures its stability and its long-term viability. Improving the balance between public rights and private interests is a key component of sustainability.[54] Both the United States and Canada have made changes to their IIA practice that support sustainability in substantive as well as dispute settlement matters.

Substance

States have different options when they aim to address the balance between investor and state rights in their IIAs. One way is to clarify the interpretation of substantive provisions. Another way is to provide for exceptions. More generally, parties can imbed "sustainable development" values in different parts of the agreement. The United States and Canada have both espoused this trend, but in different ways.

Clarification of substantive provisions

The interpretation of the "fair and equitable treatment" ("FET") provision has been the object of many controversies. Under NAFTA, the question arose early as to whether the minimum standard of treatment ("MST") provision was "autonomous" or referred to the customary international minimum standard of treatment. Apparently dissatisfied with the answer provided by some tribunals, the NAFTA parties agreed in

---

52 US Model, *supra* note 2 at art 28(9)(a).
53 US Model, *ibid* at Annex D.
54 See Introduction to this book.

2001 on an interpretation of article 1105.[55] The interpretation stated that:

1. Article 1105(1) prescribes the customary international law minimum standard of treatment of aliens as the minimum standard of treatment to be afforded to investments of investors of another Party.
2. The concepts of "fair and equitable treatment" and "full protection and security" do not require treatment in addition to or beyond that which is required by the customary international law minimum standard of treatment of aliens [. . .].[56]

This clarification is reflected in both the US and Canadian Models.[57] The US Model goes further than the Canadian Model in that it provides a definition of customary international law[58] and "for greater certainty" provides examples at article 5 of what "fair and equitable treatment" and "full protection and security" cover.[59] Similar elaborations have since been found in Canadian practice.[60]

Arguably the threshold for violation of an MST clause referring to customary international law is higher than for violation of an "autonomous" FET clause. In principle, then, such an MST clause would provide more balance between public and private interests as it reflects the practice and *opinio juris* of states related to the treatment of foreign investors. In practice, however, much depends on the interpretation given by arbitral tribunals and their view on the evolution of customary international law. As NAFTA practice post-2001 has demonstrated, tribunals can diverge widely on the interpretation of customary MST.[61]

Another subject of controversy has been the interpretation of the expropriation provision of IIAs, in particular in matters of indirect expropriation. The US and Canadian Models both include an Annex, worded in very similar fashion, that aims to provide more direction to

---

55 See FTC Notes, *supra* note 41.
56 *Ibid*.
57 US Model, *supra* note 2 at art 5 and Annex A, and Canadian Model, *supra* note 3 at art 5.
58 US Model, *ibid* at Annex A.
59 US Model, *ibid* at art 5(2)(a) and (b).
60 See Canada-Colombia FTA, *supra* note 37 at art 805, ft 2.
61 Compare *Glamis Gold, Ltd v The United States of America*, Award, UNCITRAL (June 8, 2009) at paras 598–627 and *Merrill & Ring Forestry L.P. v Canada*, Award, UNCITRAL (March 31, 2010) at paras 182–213.

tribunals, namely by offering factors to be weighed in making a determination of indirect expropriation.[62] The US Annex states:

(a) The determination of whether an action or series of actions by a Party, in a specific fact situation, constitutes an indirect expropriation, requires a case-by-case, fact-based inquiry that considers, among other factors:

   (i) the economic impact of the government action, although the fact that an action or series of actions by a Party has an adverse effect on the economic value of an investment, standing alone, does not establish that an indirect expropriation has occurred;

   (ii) the extent to which the government action interferes with distinct, reasonable investment-backed expectations; and

   (iii) the character of the government action.

(b) Except in rare circumstances, non-discriminatory regulatory actions by a Party that are designed and applied to protect legitimate public welfare objectives, such as public health, safety, and the environment, do not constitute indirect expropriations.[63]

The Canadian Model differs in this last regard as it defines what are "rare circumstances" in the following manner:

Except in rare circumstances, such as when a measure or series of measures are so severe in the light of their purpose that they cannot be reasonably viewed as having been adopted and applied in good faith, non-discriminatory measures of a Party that are designed and applied to protect legitimate public welfare objectives, such as health, safety and the environment, do not constitute indirect expropriation.[64]

In both instances, such wording appears to reflect elements of the police power doctrine of international law.[65] This doctrine, which aims to

---

62 US Model, *supra* note 2 at Annex B, and Canadian Model, *supra* note 3 at Annex B. 13(1).
63 US Model, *ibid.*
64 Canadian Model, *supra* note 3 at Annex B. 13(1).
65 For example in *Saluka Investments B. V. v the Czech Republic*, Partial Award, UNCITRAL (March 17, 2006), the tribunal noted that "the principle that a State does not commit an expropriation and is thus not liable to pay compensation to a dispossessed

balance public rights and private interests, fits squarely within the theme of sustainability.[66]

The provision of exceptions

Exceptions in IIAs often seek to balance the investment protection obligations of states with the broader public interest. Both the US and Canadian Models include security exceptions in their IIAs, while only Canada provides for general exceptions of the GATT article XX variety.[67]

Canada is unique in its early adoption and continuous use of general exceptions in its IIAs.[68] All of its IIAs since 1994 include such a provision. In contrast, NAFTA's general exception provision does not apply to Chapter Eleven (Investment). The explanation likely lies in the view that exceptions cannot "excuse" discrimination on the basis of nationality. As described in Chapter 15, despite their broad appeal, it is questionable whether GATT article XX type exceptions are an efficient means of achieving sustainability in IIAs.[69] That being said, Canada also provides exceptions applicable, amongst others, to cultural industries, prudential measures and access to information.[70]

Security exceptions exist in both American and Canadian IIAs. While the formulations are different, both provisions are worded in a way that makes clear that they are "self-judging."[71] In the case of the United States, this evolution occurred in the light of considerable debate on the interpretation of article XI of the 1991 US-Argentina BIT, which refers to "measures necessary for . . . the Protection [sic] of its own essential security interests."[72]

alien investor when it adopts general regulations that are 'commonly accepted as within the police power of States' forms part of customary law today" (para 262).

66 The impact of the factors proposed to identify an indirect expropriation, notably the interference "with distinct, investment-backed expectations" is less clear. As described elsewhere, these factors have their source in US Supreme Court decisions. See Céline Lévesque, "Influences on the Canadian FIPA Model and the US Model BIT: NAFTA Chapter 11 and Beyond" (2006) Can YB Int'l Law 249 at 286–90.

67 See *General Agreement on Tariffs and Trade* [GATT] at art XX reproduced in World Trade Organization, *The Legal Texts: The Results of the Uruguay Round of Multilateral Trade Negotiations* (Cambridge: Cambridge University Press, 1999) [WTO Agreements].

68 See Andrew Newcombe at ch 15.

69 See *ibid.*

70 See Canadian Model, *supra* note 3 at art 10.

71 Article 10(4) of the Canadian Model is almost identical to art 2102 (National Security) of NAFTA and very similar to GATT art XXI (Security Exceptions).

72 US-Argentina BIT, art XI: "[t]his Treaty shall not preclude the application by either Party of measures necessary for the maintenance of public order, the fulfillment of

Sustainable development

Both the United States and Canada include provisions in their IIAs that refer to the protection of health, safety and the environment, and in the case of the United States, labor rights. The preamble to the Canadian Model refers specifically to the "promotion of sustainable development."[73] The preamble in the US Model rather refers to the desire "to achieve these objectives in a manner consistent with the protection of health, safety, and the environment, and the promotion of internationally recognized labor rights."[74] Both states also aim to prevent a "race to the bottom" by encouraging parties not to relax their environmental standards in order to attract investment. In the case of Canada, health and safety are also covered in the substantive provision[75] while the US Model covers the environment and labor in separate provisions.[76] Considering the interpretative value of preambular language, as well as the soft language of the other provisions, one can question how effective these provisions will be in promoting sustainable development.

Settlement of investment disputes

The long-term sustainability of the IIA regime will be put at risk if tribunals interpret IIA provisions in a way that is fundamentally inconsistent with the common intention of the state parties and their understanding of the meaning and scope of the provision. At the same time, the sustainability of the regime will be affected if states re-interpret investment obligations in unforeseen ways. Tribunal interpretations that are methodologically flawed or not firmly based on accepted principles of treaty interpretation are a serious concern in a regime where arbitral awards are final and not subject to appellate review.

The US and Canadian Models include procedural provisions that focus on treaty interpretation. First, both Models incorporate provisions

---

its obligations with respect to the maintenance or restoration of international peace or security, or the Protection of its own essential security interests." See José Enrique Alvarez, *The Public International Law Regime Governing International Investment* (The Hague: The Hague Academy of International Law, 2011), especially Chapter IV, "Lessons from the Argentina Crises Cases".

73 See Markus Gehring and Avidan Kent at ch 16 in this book on sustainable development.

74 US Model, *supra* note 2 Preamble.

75 Canadian Model, *supra* note 3 at art 11.

76 US Model, *supra* note 2 at art 12 (Investment and Environment) and art 13 (Investment and Labor).

similar to NAFTA articles 1127 to 1129 providing for notification to, and participation by, the non-disputing state party in any investor-state arbitration. NAFTA state parties have made extensive use of the right provided to them individually by article 1128 to make submissions to tribunals on questions of interpretation of NAFTA.[77] Articles 33 to 35 of the Canadian Model ensure that a "non-disputing Party" is to be informed of all claims submitted to arbitration under the Agreement, can obtain all of the documents relating to an arbitration from the disputing Party, can make submissions to the tribunal "on a question of interpretation of this Agreement"[78] and has the right to attend any hearings. Article 28(2) of the US Model provides that a non-disputing Party may make oral and written submissions to the tribunal regarding the interpretation of the treaty. Article 29(1) requires transmission of arbitration related documents to the non-disputing Party.

Secondly, both Models provide that the state parties' joint decision on the interpretation of a treaty provision is binding on a tribunal and that any tribunal award[79] must be consistent with the joint decision.[80] The requirement that tribunal awards must be consistent with joint interpretations addresses issues that have arisen in the NAFTA context about interpretative statements made by the Free Trade Commission.[81]

Thirdly, both Models provide a mechanism for the state parties to jointly make binding interpretations of exceptions and reservations to obligations in treaty annexes, including reservations for existing measures and liberalization commitments, reservations for future measures and exceptions from MFN treatment.[82]

Conclusion

Current Canadian and American IIA practices, as reflected in these states' Model BITs and recent IIAs, reflect concerns relating to the

---

77 See listings of cases filed against Canada, Mexico and the United States and links to the legal pleadings, online: DFAIT <http://www.international.gc.ca/trade-agreements-accords-commerciaux/disp-diff/nafta.aspx?lang=en&view=d>.

78 Canadian Model, *supra* note 3 at art 35.

79 The provision in the US model refers to "any decision or award." The Canadian Model only refers to an "award."

80 US Model, *supra* note 2 at art 30(3), and Canadian Model, *supra* note 3 at art 40(2).

81 See *Pope & Talbot Inc v The Government of Canada*, Award in Respect of Damages, UNCITRAL (31 May 2002) at paras 8–66 and *Methanex, supra* note 40 at Part IV, Chapter C.

82 US Model, *supra* note 2 at art 31, and Canadian Model, *supra* note 3 at art 41.

themes of efficiency, legitimacy and sustainability addressed in this book. The Canadian and US Model BITs represent clear attempts to engage in a rebalancing of rights between investors and states.[83] The extent of this rebalancing, particularly in the context of the US BIT, is hotly contested—for some representatives of business it goes too far— for some representatives of labor and environmental interests it does not go far enough.[84] Judge Stephen Schwebel, the former president of the International Court of Justice, has referred to the 2004 US Model as a "regressive development" in international law.[85] Another commentator, José Alvarez, has argued that, compared to the investor-protective 1984 US Model BIT, the 2004 Model "has now shrunk, sometimes dramatic-ally, virtually every right originally accorded to foreign investors while at the same time increasing, sometimes vastly, the discretion accorded host states."[86]

It is beyond the scope of this overview to assess the extent to which the new Models, with their detailed provisions now running over 40 pages each, simply "clarify" the scope of investment obligations existing under previous treaties rather than reduce their scope. However, as to substantive changes, even if some are characterized as clarifications, they are uniformly focused on providing the host state more "policy space" in its treatment of investors and investment.

On the procedural side, it is clear that American and Canadian IIA practices have evolved to impose more conditions on the institution of investor-state arbitration, to make it easier to have frivolous claims dismissed earlier and to provide for more transparency in the process. From this perspective, the Canadian and US Model BITs make the process for invoking and proceeding with investor-state arbitration more onerous than it was under earlier Models.

---

83 Kenneth Vandevelde, "A Comparison of the 2004 and 1994 US Model BITs: Rebalancing Investor and Host Country Interests" (2008–2009) Yearbook of International Investment Law and Policy 283.

84 See the different views of the business and labor representatives in: Report of the Advisory Committee on International Economic Policy Regarding the Model Bilateral Investment Treaty, presented to the Department of State, 30 September 2009, online: Department of State, Press Release <http://www.state.gov/r/pa/prs/ps/2009/sept/130097.htm>.

85 Stephen M. Schwebel, "The United States 2004 Model Bilateral Investment Treaty: An Exercise in the Regressive Development of International Law" in Gerald Aksen et al (eds), *Global Reflections on International Law, Commerce and Dispute Resolution: Liber Amicorum in Honour of Robert Briner* (Paris: ICC Publishing, 2005) at 815.

86 José Enrique Alvarez "The Return of the State" (2011) 20(2) Minn J Int'l L 223 at 235.

In sum, current Canadian and American IIA practice demonstrates that both countries have made significant modifications to address efficiency, legitimacy and sustainability concerns. And as the chapters in this book highlight, evolutions in this area continue.

3 The evolving role of the European Union in IIA treaty-making

*Armand de Mestral**

Introduction

The EU played a minor role in the IIA treaty-making process up until the turn of the new century. In the first place, it had no specific treaty mandate to act independently of its Member States. Secondly, its Member States have been among the most active negotiators of BITs and as a result did not look to the EU to further their objectives in this area. The result was that, leading up to the new millennium, the law governing the EU and the law governing the international protection of FDI were considered to be two distinct spheres. The only area where the EU had been involved in international investment protection was in the negotiation of regional and bilateral trade agreements. A number of EU trade agreements concluded before 2000 as mixed agreements contain articles or chapters on the protection of FDI.[1] Since 2000, the EU has continued to negotiate trade treaties, often including provisions on investment protection.[2] The EU has also been a party to the ECT since 1994,[3] an agreement that contains

---

* Emeritus Professor, Jean Monnet Professor of Law, McGill University. The author would like to thank Ramona Schmitt, doctoral candidate at the University of St. Gallen, Switzerland, for her research and editorial assistance.

1 Some agreements contain an obligation on the free transfer of capital related to FDI, see e.g. *Euro-Mediterranean Agreement establishing an association between the European Communities and their Member States, of the one part, and the Republic of Tunisia, of the other part* [1998] OJ, L 97 at arts 33–4; other agreements grant MFN and national treatment for companies established according to the law of the host state, see e.g. *Partnership and Cooperation Agreement between the European Communities and their Member States, and Ukraine,* [1998] OJ, L 49 at art 30.

2 *Agreement establishing an association between the European Community and its Member States, of the one part, and the Republic of Chile, of the other part* [2002] OJ, L 352 at 3.

3 EC, *Council and Commission Decision 98/181/EC, ECSC, Euratom of 23 September 1997 on the conclusion, by the European Communities, of the Energy Charter Treaty and the Energy Charter Protocol on energy efficiency and related environmental aspects* [1998] OJ L 69 at 1.

extensive provisions on the protection of investments in the energy sector as well as an investor-state arbitral procedure.[4] Thus, although the EU has not been entirely absent from this field, it has not played a major role in developing the international law governing the protection of investments.

Since 2000, the situation has been changing rapidly. As a matter of policy, the EU Commission has become increasingly concerned over the possibility that Member States' BITs might distort the internal market, with each state seeking its own advantage rather than being subject to common rules. In proving that at least some typical BIT-provisions contravene EU law, the Commission successfully argued before the CJEU that the provisions governing the free transfer of capital in certain Swedish, Austrian and Finnish BITs[5] were in violation of the EU treaties. Proposals granting EU competence over FDI were included in the ill-fated Constitution for Europe,[6] and when that was not adopted, the negotiators of the Treaty of Lisbon[7] carried forward the proposal to expand the Common Commercial Policy (CCP) by amending articles 206 and 207 of the Treaty on the Functioning of the European Union (TFEU).[8]

This chapter reviews the treaty changes that have occurred and assesses the impact that expanded EU powers may have on the development of the law governing the protection of FDI in the future. Part I describes the evolution in the EU's role, looking at its competence over FDI as well as the positions of the Commission and EU Member States. Part II analyzes the impact of expanded EU competence with regard to treaty-making, including the possibility of an EU Model BIT as well as potential changes to current practices. The chapter focuses on the external policy of the EU and sets aside discussions regarding the internal market impact (which is nonetheless important).[9] In conclusion,

---

4 *Energy Charter Treaty*, December 17, 1994, 2080 UNTS 36116, 34 ILM 360 at art 26 [ECT].

5 *Commission v Austria*, C-205/06, [2009] ECR I-1301; *Commission v Sweden*, C-249/06, [2009] ECR I-1335; *Commission v Finland*, C-118/07, [2009] ECR I-10889.

6 *Treaty Establishing a Constitution for Europe* [2004] OJ C 310 at 1 [not in force].

7 *Treaty of Lisbon amending the Treaty on European Union and the Treaty establishing the European Community* [2007] OJ C 306, at 1.

8 *Consolidated versions of the Treaty on European Union and the Treaty on the Functioning of the European Union* [2008] OJ C 115 at 1 [TFEU].

9 For a discussion on the impact of expanded EU competence on the Internal Market, see Armand de Mestral, "The Lisbon Treaty and the Expansion of EU Competence Over Foreign Direct Investment and the Implications for Investor-State-Arbitration" in Karl P. Sauvant (ed), *Yearbook on International Investment Law and*

it is submitted that the expanded competence of the EU will have a dynamic impact both on the law within the EU and on the international law governing the protection of foreign investment.

The evolution of the role of the EU

The primary focus of this chapter is the potential influence of the EU on IIA treaty-making and on the development of international investment law. In this regard, much depends on the extent of EU competence. Further, the potential for the Commission and Member States to agree on the future of the EU's IIA policies will be determinant.

EU competence over FDI

Many of the questions regarding EU competence concern not only the future of EU policy but also the capacity of the EU to implement a complete and coherent policy. It may take many years before the CJEU has an opportunity to rule on the extent of EU competence in this area and it will certainly take many more years before any such decision can be fully implemented by the Commission and EU Member States.

The EU Commission, often described as the "conscience" of the EU, has become increasingly concerned that the authority of Member States to negotiate the terms of BITs both with each other and with third states could distort or frustrate the realization of the "internal market." If Member States can conclude or maintain BITs between themselves, and each state is free to seek its own advantage with third states to the detriment of other EU members, then the principles of free movement of goods, services, persons and capital might be frustrated. Foreign investors might be induced to invest and to remain in one Member State only. The conditions under which foreign investment occurs may involve the granting of special advantages by one state to the detriment of competition in the broader internal market. The EU has been developing policies designed to ensure the mobility of capital,[10] corporations[11] and business persons[12] throughout

---

Policy 2009–2010 (New York: Oxford University Press, 2010) 365 at 389 [de Mestral].

10 TFEU, *supra* note 8 at arts 63 ff.
11 *Ibid* at art 49 in connection with *ibid* at art 54.
12 *Ibid* at arts 45 ff

the internal market. Given the importance of foreign investment in the promotion of economic development,[13] it was inevitable that the Commission would wish to ensure that foreign investment occur in a manner compatible with the fundamental principles of the treaties. Furthermore, the EU has its own policies on the promotion of investment,[14] especially in its less developed regions, which could be compromised by beggar-thy-neighbor investment policies of Member States.

The expansion of EU competence to include FDIs was accomplished with the passage of articles 206 and 207 TFEU. These articles define the Common Commercial Policy (CCP) as one of the EU's five exclusive competences.[15] As will be explained below, these changes have been interpreted by the Commission as implying that the EU now enjoys complete and exclusive competence to regulate the entry of FDI into the EU and to set the terms governing the treatment of direct investments and investors once they have entered.[16] The Commission has also asserted that existing *intra*-EU BITs be rescinded and that it has the competence and capacity to negotiate BITs on behalf of the EU. The Commission's position follows a similar path as it has in the past with respect to other spheres of competence such as authority

---

13 Carolynn Hjälmroth and Stefan Westerberg, "A Common Investment Policy for the EU" in *The contribution of trade to a new growth strategy*, online: Kommers <http://www.kommers.se/upload/Analysarkiv/In%20English/Analyses/LS%20 Investments.pdf>; for a different view see Mary Hallward-Driemeier, "Do Bilateral Investment Treaties Attract FDI? Only a bit . . . and they could bite," World Bank Policy Research Working Paper Series No. 3121, online: SSRN <http://papers.ssrn. com/sol3/cf_dev/AbsByAuth.cfm?per_id=327728>.
14 See the EU website on EU policies on development of poorer region, online: EUROPA <http://europa.eu/pol/reg/index_en.htm>.
15 TFEU, *supra* note 8 at arts 206, 207.
16 EU Commission, Communication from the Commission to the Council, the European Parliament, the European Economic and Social Committee and the Committee of the Regions. Towards a comprehensive European international investment policy, 7 July 2010, COM (2010)343 final, online: EUROPA <http:// trade.ec.europa.eu/doclib/docs/2011/may/tradoc_147884.pdf>; EU Commission, Proposal for a Regulation of the European Parliament and the Council establishing transitional arrangements for bilateral investment agreements between Member States and third countries, July 7, 2010, COM(2010)344 final, online: EUROPA<http://trade.ec.europa.eu/doclib/docs/2011/may/tradoc_147884. pdf>.

over telecommunications,[17] energy monopolies[18] and air transport services.[19]

The fact that the Commission is staking a maximum position does not mean that Member States are in complete agreement and that they will not challenge the Commission's claims. In all probability, we will witness in the years to come both claims and counterclaims of a legal and political nature. These claims may be resolved by political cooperation, legislation and compromise between the EU and its Member States, but at this point, compromise does not appear to be the likely outcome. Most probably, there will be a complex mix of negotiation within the EU Council in response to the Draft Regulation[20] proposed by the Commission, accompanied by litigation before the CJEU if the Commission is not satisfied with the role that Member States wish it to play. The central issue that is likely to arise in litigation before the CJEU will be the extent of exclusive competence over FDI now enshrined in the CCP. This is not a simple matter, as the CJEU has, in a number of decisions since 1994,[21] held that the CCP accords exclusive competence over external trade relations, but that it does not necessarily bestow total correlative authority to regulate the internal market. Reasonable people can differ as to whether exclusive competence over FDI involves a correlative exclusive authority to set the standards of treatment of foreign investment within the *internal* market. Thus, even if a cooperative *modus vivendi* is rapidly concluded between the Commission and Member States, the working out of the new system as it affects existing *intra* and

---

17 In the field of telecommunication, the Commission published a document in which it held for a full-scale Community telecommunications policy, see European Commission, Towards a Dynamic European Economy. Green Paper on the Development of the Common Market for Telecommunications Services and Equipment. Appendices, June 30, 1987, COM (87) 290 final/appendices.

18 The European Commission opened the debate on a European energy policy with the publication of a Green Paper in March 2006, see European Commission, A European Strategy for Sustainable, Competitive and Secure Energy, 8 March 2006, COM (2006) 105 final, online: EUROPA <http://europa.eu/legislation_summaries/energy/european_energy_policy/l27062_en.htm>. An overview of the secondary EU legislation in the field of energy currently in force can be found online: EUROPA <http://ec.europa.eu/energy/doc/energy_legislation_by_policy_areas.pdf>.

19 See European Commission, Communication from the Commission on relations between the Community and third countries in the field of air transport. Proposal for a European Parliament and Council Regulation on the negotiation and implementation of air service agreements between Member States and third countries, February 26, 2003, COM(2003) 94 final.

20 EU Commission Proposal, *supra* note 16.

21 *Opinion 1/94*, [1994]ECR I-5267; *Opinion 2/00* [2001] ECR I-09713.

extra-EU BITs and the negotiation of new BITs by the Commission or member states will almost certainly take many years.

Positions of the Commission and of Member States

Prior to the entry into force of the TFEU articles 206 and 207, the Commission had already begun to define a position concerning BITs concluded by EU Member States. In the first place, officials of the Commission took a position in the *Eastern Sugar*[22] arbitration suggesting that existing EU BITs between Member States had been overtaken by EU law when these states joined the Union. Similar arguments appear to have been made in several other investor-state arbitrations.[23] Secondly, the Commission has successfully taken legal action against Austria, Sweden and Finland,[24] arguing that the provisions in their BITs with several third countries[25] dealing with the free movement of capital interfered with the competence of the EU to restrict capital movements in the event of an economic emergency.[26] As a result, the Commission succeeded in demonstrating that *extra*-EU BITs can be in conflict with EU law, and in which case they must be brought into conformity with the treaties.[27] Thus the Commission had already begun to take positions with respect to both *intra* and *extra*-EU BITs before the entry into force of the TFEU articles 206 and 207.

The Commission has also played a part in adjusting the BITs of new Member States prior to their joining the Union prior to 2004 and 2007. The Commission warned future members that their BITs might not be compatible with the EU *acquis*,[28] and in anticipation of their joining,

---

22 *Eastern Sugar B.V. (The Netherlands) v The Czech Republic*, Partial Award, UNCITRAL (27 March 2007) [*Eastern Sugar*]; See also James Chalker, "Case Note: Eastern Sugar B.V. v. The Czech Republic" (2009) *Transnational Dispute Management* 1.

23 *Saluka Investments BV (The Netherlands) v The Czech Republic*, Partial Award, UNCITRAL (17 March 2006); *Vattenfall AB, Vattenfall Europe AG, Vattenfall Europe Generation AG v Federal Republic of Germany*, Award, ICSID Case No. ARB/09/6 (March 11, 2011); *Eureko B.V. v The Slovak Republic*, Award on Jurisdiction, Arbitrability and Suspension, UNCITRAL (October 26, 2010)

24 *Commission v Austria*, C-205/06, [2009] ECR I-1301; *Commission v Sweden*, C-249/06, [2009] ECR I-1335; *Commission v Finland*, C-118/07, [2009] ECR I-10889.

25 See e.g. *Agreement Between the Republic of Korea and the Republic of Austria for the Encouragement and Protection of Investments*, March 14, 1991, online: UNCTAD <http://www.unctadxi.org/templates/docsearch.aspx?id=779>.

26 ECT *supra* note 4 at arts 57.2, 59, 60.1; now TFEU *supra* note 8 at arts 64.2, 66, 75.1.

27 ECT *supra* note 4 at art 307.2; now TFEU *supra* note 9 at art 351.2.

28 No official document was published, but the demand was subject to congressional review, see "U.S.-Bulgaria Investment Treaty Additional Protocol Sent to Senate,"

the Commission offered to assist in negotiations with third states. To this end, it led negotiations with the United States on behalf of eight future members[29] that had BITs with the United States. These negotiations concluded with the adoption of a Memorandum of Understanding[30] with the United States by which certain actions by the EU would not be deemed to be in conflict with the BITs in question. The Commission also offered to assist six future members in renegotiating their BITs with Canada.[31] However, in this case the six, after initially working with the Commission, decided to act on their own to renegotiate their BITs with Canada directly, and proceeded to negotiate and conclude entirely new agreements, without the assistance of the Commission.[32] Thus the record of action by the Commission is rather equivocal.

Since the entry into force of the TFEU and the extension of the CCP, the Commission has taken a more comprehensive position with respect to EU competence over FDI. In July 2010, the EU Commission issued two documents: first, a *Draft Regulation proposing a Transitional Regime for Bilateral Investment Agreements between Member States and Third Countries* (the Draft Regulation) to govern existing agreements while a European investment policy was being elaborated. Secondly, a communication entitled *Towards a Comprehensive European International Investment Policy* (the Communication),[33] containing the Commission's view related to the core features of a European international investment policy. These documents, submitted to the European Council and the European Parliament in July 2010, set out a strategy for dealing with the over 1,200 BITs in force with third states, pending the adoption of

22   January 2004, online: America <http://www.america.gov/st/washfile-english/2004/January/200401221522291CJsamohT0.7042353.html>; see Chris Brummer, "The Ties That Bind? Regionalism, Commercial Treaties, and the Future of Global Economic Integration" (2007) 60(5) V and L Rev 1349 at 1372 [Brummer].

29   The Czech Republic, Estonia, Latvia, Lithuania, Poland and the Slovak Republic, which joined the EU in 2004, as well as Bulgaria and Romania, which joined in 2007.

30   *Understanding Concerning Certain U.S. Bilateral Investment Treaties, signed by the U.S., the European Commission, and acceding and candidate countries for accession to the European Union*, 22 September 2003, online: USDS: http://www.state.gov/s/l/2003/44366.htm>; see on this Anca Radu, "Foreign Investors in the EU. Which 'Best Treatment'? Interactions Between Bilateral Investment Treaties and EU Law" (2008) 14 Eur LJ 237; Brummer, *supra* note 28.

31   See Luke Eric Peterson, "Canada releases new BITs with several EU member-states reflect EU requirements and Canadian reform agenda" (2009) 2(8) *IA Reporter* 7.

32   de Mestral, *supra* note 9.

33   EU Commission Proposal, *supra* note 16.

a broader strategy concerning the authority of the Commission to negotiate new BITs or to renegotiate BITs in the future on behalf of the EU as a whole. The Draft Regulation and the Communication call for the abrogation of all BITs between EU Member States, on the assumption that these BITs may constitute a denial of national treatment and other principles of EU law. With respect to BITs with third states, the Draft Regulation and the Communication are predicated on the assumption that the BITs will remain in force, but they call on Member States to renegotiate any provisions that conflict with EU law. This is done pending the adoption of a comprehensive mandate for the Commission to renegotiate these BITs sometime in the future. A review of the policy within five years is envisaged. During the interim period, Member States are also given the right to negotiate new BITs, subject to the scrutiny of the Commission. Given the sheer number of BITs in force with third states and the complexity and the delicacy of the issues that would be raised, any demand that the Commission might begin their renegotiation immediately is out of the question.[34]

The Draft Regulation and the Communication say nothing about the 190 BITs in force between EU members. One is left to infer that the Commission's position remains that these BITs should already have been denounced as several Commission officials have stated.[35]

Interestingly, the Draft Regulation[36] would require that Member States inform the Commission immediately upon receiving a notice of arbitration under a BIT, and would reserve the right for the Commission to be involved in formulating a response to the claim. It thus seems clear that the Commission sees itself in the long term as being not only involved in negotiating BITs for the EU, but also as acting in the defense of EU interests in investor-state arbitral claims. One can assume from this that the Commission is concerned that Member States should take positions in their own defense that are coherent with the general legal position and interests of the EU. One should recall that the Commission

---

34 In September 2011, it was reliably reported that the Commission had obtained negotiating authority, including the authority to negotiate investor-state arbitration with Canada, Singapore and India. See online: Bilaterals <www.bilaterals.org> [Bilaterals].

35 See letter quoted in *Eastern Sugar*, *supra* note 22; Ulrich Wölker, "The EU as a Player in the BIT Arena: Current and Future Legal Challenges" (Paper delivered at the 50 Years of Bilateral Investment Treaties Conference, Frankfurt) reproduced in (2009) 24(2) ICSID Rev 434.

36 EU Commission proposal, *supra* note 16 art 13.

defends all claims against Member States under the WTO Dispute Settlement Understanding (DSU); whether the Commission sees itself as following this model is not yet clear.

The Draft Regulation has been debated by both the European Parliament and the European Council in 2011.[37] Positions taken in the European Parliament have been generally favorable to the position of the Commission, but Member States have shown a considerable reluctance to endorse the policy proposed by the Commission. In the first place, with respect to intra-EU BITs, which are not covered by the Draft Regulation, only the Czech Republic, Italy, Slovenia and Malta have indicated their willingness to rescind their BITs with other EU members.[38] There appears to be little interest on the part of many others to follow suit.[39] With respect to BITs with third states, as far as one can judge, EU members appear very reluctant to endorse a broad mandate for the Commission to renegotiate their BITs. They also appear to be unwilling to concede that the CCP must be interpreted as giving the Union exclusive powers to regulate the treatment of FDI within the internal market. It is certainly possible to settle this matter by political negotiation and compromise, but if this does not happen, litigation seems to be a likely outcome.

37   Council of the European Union, Conclusions on a comprehensive European international investment policy, 3041st Foreign Affairs Council Meeting, October 25, 2010; Committee on International Trade, Draft Report for a regulation of the European Parliament and of the Council establishing transitional arrangements for bilateral investment agreements between Member States and third countries, 18 November 2010. The International Trade Committee recently adopted a report on the draft regulation that limits the power of the European Commission to review and withdraw authorisation from Member States' BITs, see Bilateral investment: less Commission authority, easier EU-level agreements, Press release, online: European Parliament <http://www.europarl.europa.eu/en/pressroom/content/2011 0411IPR17422/html/Bilateral-investment-less-Commission-authority-easier-EU-level-agreements>. However, since the report was adopted by a slim majority, the commitee decided to put the report to a plenary vote.
38   Luke Eric Peterson, "Italy, Slovenia and Malta concur with Czech Republic on lack of necessity for intra-EU BITs; Italy-Czech treaty has been terminated" (2009) 2(13) *IA Reporter*.
39   Council of the European Union, 2007 EFC Report to the Commission and the Council on the Movement of Capital and Freedom of Payments, Doc.-Nr. 5123/08, No. 15: "Most Member States do not share the Commission's concern about arbitration risks and discriminatory treatment of investors. A clear majority of Member States prefers to maintain the existing agreements, in particular with view to the provisions on expropriation, compensation, protection of investments and investor-to-state dispute settlement."

The impact of expanded EU competence on the external market

The emergence of an EU Model BIT

It appears that the Commission envisions a day when it will negotiate BITs on behalf of the EU as a whole in order to replace the many BITs that currently exist. Since this is a likely hypothesis, it is necessary to consider which policies the Commission is likely to adopt. Will it seek to promote an "EU Model BIT" very much as individual states have done?[40] It seems reasonable to expect this, although a Commission official has already warned that a "no size fits all" approach would be advisable.[41] Indeed, in the context of negotiating trade agreements containing investment provisions, the Commission already appears to have a modest model: the *Minimum Platform for Investment for the EU FTAs.* This is a curious document first prepared by the Directorate General (DG) for Trade in 2006[42] that focuses primarily on establishment and trade in financial services related to investment. As the title suggests, it is designed to provide guidance to negotiators of EU trade agreements who may have a mandate to include a chapter on, or at least some general provisions related to, investment. It does not read like a standard BIT and it would have to be considerably amended and expanded to serve as a genuine model BIT capable of providing the standard protections to investors in respect of both EU action and the actions of all Member States. Another issue relates to pre-investment guarantees: unlike Canadian and American BITs,[43] the BITs of EU

---

40 For example the United States, Canada, Germany or France. For Model BITs of these states, see online: Italaw <http://ita.law.uvic.ca/investmenttreaties.htm>.

41 "Towards a comprehensive European international investment policy: An interview with Tomas Baert, European Commission, Directorate General for Trade, Services and Investment," *Investment Treaty News* (23 September 2010), online: IISD <http://www.iisd.org/itn/2010/09/23/towards-a-comprehensive-european-international-investment-policy-an-interview-with-tomas-baert-european-commission-directorate-general-for-trade-services-and-investment/>

42 Council of the EU, Brussels, March 6, 2009, 7242/09, Limited; first issued as *Minimum platform on investment for EU FTAs—Provision on establishment in template for a Title on "Establishment, trade in services and e-commerce,"* Note to The 133 Committee, European Commission DG Trade, Brussels, July 28, 2006, D (2006) 9219. It must be noted that this document, although available on several NGO websites, has never been officially issued. Requests under freedom of information have been denied.

43 Canadian Model BIT (2004), online: DFAIT <http://www.international.gc.ca/trade-agreements-accords-commerciaux/assets/pdfs/2004-FIPA-model-en.pdf> ("Each Party shall accord to investors of the other Party treatment no less favorable than that it accords, in like circumstances, to its own investors with respect to the

Member States have usually avoided such commitments, referring only to "existing law."[44]

Perhaps a better idea of the possible future intentions of the Commission can be found in the text of various trade agreements already concluded or under negotiation. The most recent text under negotiation in 2010 and 2011 is the investment chapter of the Comprehensive Economic and Trade Agreement (CETA)[45] currently under negotiation with Canada. Negotiations are not expected to conclude until early 2012, but several unofficial versions have been made available and all contain a chapter on investment. This text, which has yet to be accepted by both parties,[46] provides for both pre- and post-investment guarantees. Thus, unlike many EU Member States' BITs, it would guarantee market access, MFN and National Treatment in respect of establishment. It also provides for the Minimum Standard of Treatment in accordance with customary international law, meaning that it would restrict the application of performance requirements and it would require full compensation in the case of direct or indirect expropriation.[47] The text also guarantees the right to freely transfer capital between the two jurisdictions. Further, it contains provisions for the protection of health, safety and environmental measures in force in both jurisdictions, encourages respect for the principles of corporate social responsibility,[48] and provides for a range of public policy exceptions. To enjoy the protection of the chapter, investors will be required to have "substantial business

establishment, acquisition, expansion, management, conduct, operation and sale or other disposition of investments in its territory," at art 3.2); US Model BIT (2004), online: USTR <http://www.state.gov/documents/organization/117601.pdf> at art 3.1.

44 German Model BIT (2008), online: Italaw <http://italaw.com/investmenttreaties.htm> ("Each Contracting State shall in its territory promote as far as possible investments by investors of the other Contracting State and admit such investments in accordance with its legislation," at), ; France Model BIT (2006), online: Italaw <http://italaw.com/documents/ModelTreatyFrance2006.pdf> ("Each Contracting Party shall promote and admit on its territory and in its maritime area, in accordance with its legislation and with the provisions of this Agreement, investments made by nationals or companies of the other Contracting Party," at art 2).

45 See Foreign Affairs and International Trade Canada, "Canada-European Union—Trade and Investment Enhancement Agreement", online: DFAIT <http://www.international.gc.ca/trade-agreements-accords-commerciaux/agr-acc/eu-ue/index.aspx>; European Commission, "EU and Canada take stock of historic Free Trade Agreement negotiations", online: Europa <http://trade.ec.europa.eu/doclib/press/index.cfm?id=664&serie=389&langId=en>.

46 CETA negotiating text, as of February 2011 [CETA].

47 *Ibid* at arts X:2–X:9.

48 *Ibid* at arts X:12,13.

activities" in either jurisdiction.[49] Interestingly, the final article of the draft states that it is subject to "other investment agreements" in force between the EU or its Member States and third states.[50]

The draft text dated October 1, 2010 also provides for arbitration in an annex. However, the text as it stands is ambiguous as to whether a private investor can seek arbitration against the EU or Canada, since the annex is drafted in function of the expression "Parties" and does not indicate clearly that this includes a private investor.[51] The annex does not deal with the issue of the applicable law and the applicable rules of arbitration and leaves unresolved the thorny issues posed by the standing of the EU, an international institution and not a state, before certain arbitral rules such as those of the ICSID Convention.[52] As of late 2011, there are no bilateral agreements negotiated by the EU that contain provisions on investment protections that include investor-state arbitration.[53]

In recent years, investment issues appear to have been a constant preoccupation of the EU in its trade negotiations. According to the EU Commission, the reopened talks on a trade agreement with the MERCOSUR will cover investment issues as well as trade.[54] Similarly, discussions with the ASEAN group and individual ASEAN countries such as Singapore, begun in 2009, are reported to cover both trade and investment questions,[55] and both trade and investment are mentioned in the notice of the start of EU-Vietnam trade talks.[56] The

---

49 *Ibid* at art X:16.

50 *Ibid* at art X:15.

51 It appears to follow the model of the EU-Korea FTA which provides only for interstate arbitration, see art 14, not yet in the Official Journal, but the text is available at: <http://trade.ec.europa.eu/doclib/press/index.cfm?id=443&serie=273 &langId=en>.

52 *Convention on the Settlement of Investment Disputes between States and Nationals of Other States*, 18 March 1965, 575 UNTS 159.

53 However, it is now reported that the Commission has the authority to negotiate investor-state arbitration with Canada, see Bilaterals, *supra* note 34.

54 "European Commission proposes relaunch of trade negotiations with Mercosur countries", May 4, 2010, online: EUROPA <http://trade.ec.europa.eu/doclib/press/ index.cfm?id=566&serie=339&langId=en>.

55 For information on the EU and the ASEAN, see online: EUROPA <http://ec.europa. eu/trade/creating-opportunities/bilateral-relations/regions/asean/>; see also "EU to start bilateral trade negotiations with Singapore", March 3, 2010, online: EUROPA <http://trade.ec.europa.eu/doclib/press/index.cfm?id=519&serie=320&langId =en>.

56 "EU and Vietnam To Launch Free Trade Negotiations", March 2, 2010, online: EUROPA <http://trade.ec.europa.eu/doclib/press/index.cfm?id=518&serie=319& langId=en>.

EU-CARIFORUM Economic Partnership Agreement[57] concluded in 2008 contains a chapter on the promotion and protection of investment, although it does not provide for investor-state arbitration. A similar pattern can be seen in the negotiations of the Economic Partnership Agreements with other Africa, Caribbean, Pacific (ACP) countries.[58] The EU-China Comprehensive Competition and Economic Partnership talks begun in 2007 also cover investments as well as trade issues,[59] and in 2011, the EU and China announced the commencement of negotiations for a BIT.[60] The EU-Korea Free Trade Agreement, signed in October 2010,[61] contains provisions on establishment, financial services, payments and capital movements and the settlement of disputes through interstate arbitration (but not investor-state arbitration).

The general pattern of EU trade agreements appears to reveal increased concern by the EU with investment issues in negotiations and trade agreements since 2000.[62] Investor-state arbitration has not been a feature of agreements concluded to date, although some incorporate general interstate arbitration as a procedure for dispute settlement and it appears that investor-state arbitration is contemplated in the Canada-EU CETA negotiations. Should the EU adopt a model BIT, and should it seek to negotiate on the basis of this model, as the largest economy in the world, it is likely to exercise considerable influence on the drafting of BITs over time. The EU has already shown its capacity to impose a pattern by requiring the inclusion of provisions on issues such as respect for democratic values, consumer and environmental protection, and sustainable development in its trade agreements. This pattern was already mandatory as a result of the specific provisions dealing with respect for EU values in its trade agreements and has been strengthened in the TFEU.[63] This capacity of the EU to set a pattern is also displayed in the provisions

57 Online: EUROPA   <http://trade.ec.europa.eu/doclib/docs/2008/october/tradoc_140979.pdf>.

58 See generally online: <http://ec.europa.eu/trade/creating-opportunities/bilateral-relations/regions/africa-caribbean-pacific/>.

59 Online: EUROPA   <http://ec.europa.eu/trade/creating-opportunhttp://trade.ec.europa.eu/doclib/press/index.cfm?id=443&serie=273&langId=enities/bilateral-relations/countries/china/>.

60 See "China, EU could begin investment pact negotiations next month: official", September 22, 2011, online: China Post <http://www.chinapost.com.tw/business/asia-china/2011/09/22/317383/China-EU.htm>.

61 Online: EUROPA <http://trade.ec.europa.eu/doclib/press/index.cfm?id=443&serie=273&langId=en>.

62 See generally on bilateral relations, online: EUROPA <http://ec.europa.eu/trade/creating-opportunities/bilateral-relations/> .

63 TFEU, *supra* note 8 at art 207.1.

found in recent EU trade agreements to allow for public policy exceptions to investment protections and to require the criterion of central ownership and control of investors to replace the criterion of mere incorporation found in many older BITs of EU Member States. Thus, while it is not yet certain whether the EU will seek to impose its model, its capacity to set new standards should not be underestimated.

The potential impact of the EU on the BIT system

Could the EU actually exercise the kind of influence described above upon the international system of investment protection currently in existence? The answer is: Yes. Indeed, there is a precedent in the field of air transport services. In 1999 there were some 500 *intra*-EU bilateral air transport agreements and at least 1,500 bilaterals with third states. As a result of the political decision to exercise EU competence over air transport to develop a more unified EU regulatory regime,[64] and as a result of decisions of the CJEU, which declared provisions of all existing bilateral air transport agreements within the EU and with third states in violation of the freedom of establishment of air transport companies,[65] all *intra*-EU bilateral agreements had to be abrogated and all bilaterals with third states had to be renegotiated. Furthermore, as a result of these developments, the EU has become the principal regulator of air transport services, safety and security, and the Commission has become the principal negotiator of bilateral air transport agreements with third states. New "horizontal" agreements with countries such as the United States and Canada[66] have begun to replace the myriad of agreements of Member States, and the Commission is in the process of gradually replacing Member State bilaterals with single "horizontal" agreements binding the whole of the EU. In the interim, given the impossibility for

64 EC, *Commission Regulation (EC) 847/2004 of the European Parliament and of the Council of 29 April 2004, on the negotiation and implementation of air service agreements between Member States and third countries* [2004] OJ L 157.
65 CJEU, *Commission v Denmark*, C-467/98, [2002] ECR I-9519; *Commission v Sweden*, C-468/98, [2002] ECR I-9575; *Commission v Belgium*, C-471/98, [2002] ECR I-9681; *Commission v Finland*, C-469/98, [2002] ECR I-9627; *Commission v Luxemburg*, C-472/98, [2002] ECR I-9855; *Commission v Austria*, C-475/98, [2002] ECR I-9797; *Commission v Germany*, C-476/98, [2002] ECR I-9855.
66 See EC, *Commission Decision 2007/339/EC on the signature and provisional application of the Air Transport Agreement between the European Community and its Member States, on the one hand, and the United States of America, on the other hand* [2007] OJ, L 134 at 1, 4; *Agreement on Air Transport between Canada and the European Community and its Member States* [2010] OJ, L 207 at 32.

the Commission to replace over 1,500 bilaterals in short order, member Member States have been required to bring existing agreements into conformity with EU law. The whole process will thus be spread over some 20 years. But there can be no doubt that the changes within the EU have led to dramatic demands for change within the larger structure of international air law; given the commitment of the EU to completely open skies within the Union, it has been pressing other states for the adoption of similar policies worldwide.[67] The similarity of what has happened to air transport bilateral agreements and what might happen to BITs is striking. It is estimated by UNCTAD that some 2,800 BITs currently exist.[68] This includes some 190 *intra*-EU BITs and 1,200 EU Member States' BITs with third states. International change has been driven by the EU, but this change has been a long and complex process.

The potential for change is evident. At first blush, there appears to be a strong argument to be made that the same scenario as the one driving change in the law governing bilateral international air transport agreements may be followed. It would appear that the Commission is seeking to promote this outcome and considers that EU law now requires such a result. But more mature consideration suggests that this is unlikely to transpire in the same fashion. In the first case, the law governing the two areas is not the same and, in particular, the CJEU has yet to render a major decision concerning BITs. The other major difference to be found is in the calculus of the interests of the EU and of its Member States in general. It can be argued that the EU will gain by the transfer of competence from Member States to the centre and by rewriting all existing BITs, but this is by no means certain. The existing BITs with third states have been carefully negotiated, some as recently as 2009,[69] and it has yet to be proven that it would be wise to abandon the guarantees that they contain, or that new, stronger and more comprehensive BITs can be successfully negotiated with the EU's trading partners around the world. It takes two partners to conclude a treaty and apparently some partners would like nothing better than to abandon their BITs with EU Member States.[70]

67 See generally Paul Stephen Dempsey, "Competition in the Air: European Union Regulation of Commercial Aviation" (2001) 66(3) J Air L & Com 979.
68 See UNCTAD, *World Investment Report 2011: Non-equity Modes of International Production and Development* (New York and Geneva: UNCTAD, 2011) at 100.
69 Germany-Pakistan BIT (2009).
70 Ecuador, for example, has denounced a number of BITs to which it was party and Venezuela has denounced its BIT with the Netherlands, see UNCTAD, Recent Developments in International Investment Agreements (2008–June 2009) 3 IIA Monitor 1 at 6. Furthermore, Bolivia and Ecuador withdraw from the ICSID Convention, see on this Ignacio A. Vincentelli, "The Uncertain Future of ICSID in Latin America" (2010) 16 Law and Business Review of the Americas 409 at 410.

The Commission has yet to prove that it can negotiate new and better BITs than those currently in force. Member States, and even more the investment community, are understandably skeptical that the Commission can exchange new lamps for old. On top of this are the many questions concerning the capacity of the Commission to commit the EU to investor-state arbitration, particularly under the ICSID Convention, and to manage such arbitrations.

What would be the point of renegotiating the hard-won commitments of existing BITs for a new model filled with public policy exceptions, human rights, labor rights, environmental protections and protection of consumer interests? From a human rights perspective, perhaps every-thing, but it may take time to build strong support within the EU for this approach. Currently it appears that Member States do not even want to abandon their BITs among themselves and the Commission may have to go to the CJEU to force them.

From the perspective of Member States and of investors, there may be many negative implications regarding a complete shift of BIT negotiation to the Commission and the gradual abandonment of existing BITs. Article 64.1 of the TFEU currently protects non-conforming measures governing the treatment of capital that existed in 1993, and the new TFEU does not appear to do away with this provision. The hands of the Commission may be partially tied. Nor is it certain that the Commission could negotiate the same advantages as those found in existing agree-ments. Furthermore, it is not clear that the Commission would be cons-titutionally permitted to adopt the same hard-nosed approach as shown by Member States in the past. The treaty language governing EU treaty-making requires that new agreements reflect the broad values of the EU, covering a wide spectrum of democracy and human rights.[71] This is very much to the EU's credit, but it may make for weaker investment pro-visions. The image of the Commission as a careful steward of the economic interests of its Member States may suffer.

On the other hand, there are a number of arguments that can be made by the Commission in support of a new approach. An argument already being put forward by the Commission[72] is that it would in fact be able to negotiate more favorable terms on behalf of its 27 members than each

71 See *Treaty on European Union*, February 7, 1992, 31 ILM 247 at art 21.1; see also TFEU, *supra* note 8 at art 207.1.
72 EU Commission, Communication from the Commission to the Council, the European Parliament, the European Economic and Social Committee and the Committee of the Regions. Towards a comprehensive European international investment policy, July 7, 2010, COM (2010)343 final, at 5.

member could individually negotiate with third states. As the largest market in the world, the EU can offer considerable advantages in a BIT and gain considerable advantages in return. This is a serious argument and one that the Commission is in the process of proving with the terms of the many regional trade agreements containing investment provisions that it has negotiated in recent years. There is little evidence that the Commission has proceeded to abandon the economic interests of its members as it negotiates trade agreements.[73] Indeed, the Commission is known as a very hard negotiator.

Conclusion

At this point many hypotheses as to the role of the EU in international investment law can be envisaged. However, it is clear that, in the long term, the Commission will be able to influence the course of development of all BITs. An EU model BIT, something that has yet to be proposed outside the context of trade agreements, could have considerable influence on the development of international investment law. Given the fact that the EU has to negotiate with over 100 ACP states at the very minimum, and is in process of doing so, and that, if it sought to renegotiate existing BITs, it would have to renegotiate BITs with even more states, an EU model BIT could not fail to have very considerable influence on the future development of the law. In particular, the greater concern that would have to be shown for democracy, human rights and environmental values, as well as general public policy concerns, could well constitute a breath of fresh air in what has become a politically contested body of law. One has only to consider such an approach applied to the many current cases against Argentina to think that the law might well be changed forever. Investors may shudder at the prospect. Many others will cheer.

---

73 See e.g. the Comprehensive Economic and Trade Agreement currently under negotiation with Canada or the Free Trade Agreements currently under negotiation with India or Singapore, online: EUROPA <http://ec.europa.eu/enterprise/policies/international/facilitating-trade/free-trade/index_en.htm>.

4 The evolution of Chinese approaches to IIAs

*Chunbao Liu**

Introduction

Following three decades of spectacular growth, China became the world's second largest economy in 2010, second only to the United States.[1] It is now the largest exporter and second largest importer of goods in the world. China has long been the largest recipient of FDI among developing countries and is now one of the largest recipients of FDI in the world. Recently, it has also emerged as a significant capital exporter.[2] Corresponding with China's rapid growth in economic muscle has been its increasing activism in the international arena. As a result, China's role and influence within a variety of international regimes is in the midst of an important evolution.[3] In particular, once a harsh critic of IIAs, China has become one of its most active players. To date, China has concluded 130 BITs[4] and has included investment chapters in an increasing number of RTAs.[5]

* Doctoral Candidate, McGill University, Faculty of Law.

1 IMF, World Economic Outlook April 2011, online: IMF <http://www.imf.org/external/pubs/ft/weo/2011/01/pdf/text.pdf> at 72–5.
2 UNCTAD, World Investment Report 2011, online: UNCTAD <http://www.imf.org/external/pubs/ft/weo/2011/01/pdf/text.pdf> at 45–51.
3 Stephen Olson and Clyde Prestowitz, "The Evolving Role of China in International Institutions," (Research report prepared for the US-China Economic and Security Review Commission, January 2011), online: US-China Economic and Security Review Commission <http://www.uscc.gov/researchpapers/2011/TheEvolvingRole ofChinainInternationalInstitutions.pdf>.
4 This data was reported by the Chinese Ministry of Commerce (MOFCOM) on November 1, 2010. "Signed BITs with 130 countries" *Xinhua* (November 1, 2010), online: Xinhua <http://news.xinhuanet.com/fortune/2010-11/01/c_12724364.htm>. The texts of Chinese BITs are available online: UNCTAD <http://www.unctadxi.org/templates/DocSearch.aspx?id=779>; online: MOFCOM <http://tfs.mofcom.gov.cn/aarticle/Nocategory/201111/20111107819474.html>.
5 Texts of Chinese FTAs are available online: MOFCOM <http://fta.mofcom.gov.cn/english/index.shtml>.

This chapter aims to take stock of China's evolving IIA practice. Part I describes the evolution of IIA treaty-making in China. Part II presents the key features of current IIA policy, emphasizing the values of "efficiency," "legitimacy" and "sustainability."

A brief history of China's IIA program

China joined the IIA trend late, but caught up fast. Launched in 1982, China's IIA program evolved over three stages in the process of liberalizing its IIA regime. The 1980s witnessed the first-generation IIAs; the second-generation IIAs account for most of the 1990s; and the third-generation IIA emerged in the late 1990s. Each generation of IIAs was represented by a China Model BIT that highlighted the crucial changes in the Chinese approaches to international investment law.

China's decision to participate in IIAs was a result of its "Reform and Opening-up" policy adopted in 1978. China has a bitter history with Western colonialism and "unequal treaties."[6] After the Communist Party came to power in 1949, foreign investment was gradually excluded from China. Correspondingly, the government denied the legitimacy of the investment protection system under international law. However, three decades of self-reliance failed to bring stability or prosperity to China. To the contrary, by the late 1970s the Chinese national economy was on the edge of collapse. Against this backdrop, China embarked on a policy of "Reform and Opening-up" in 1978. A primary objective of this policy was to open China's doors to foreign investments. As such, in the following years, a number of laws and regulations were adopted to address investment-related issues. In particular, China amended its constitution in 1982, adding a new article specifying the protection of foreign investment. However, the Chinese government realized that a mere change in domestic law was insufficient and that international legal commitments were needed to "strengthen domestic promises and reduce mistrust."[7]

First-generation IIAs

China signed its first BIT with Sweden in 1982. In the subsequent three years, it concluded BITs with capital exporting countries, such as

---

6 See generally William L. Tung, *China and the Foreign Powers: The Impact of and Reaction to Unequal Treaties* (NY: Oceana Publications, 1970); Dong Wang, *China's Unequal Treaties: Narrating National History* (Maryland: Lexington Books, 2005).

7 Shishi Li, "Bilateral Investment Promotion and Protection Agreements: Practice of the People's Republic of China" in Paul de Waart, Paul Peters and Erik Denters (eds), *International Law and Development* (Netherlands: Martinus Nijhoff Publishers, 1988) at 165 [Li].

Germany, France, Belgium-Luxembourg, Finland and Norway. This is not surprising since the main purpose of the Chinese BITs was to promote and protect FDI in China. In 1985 China started to sign BITs with developing countries while continuing to enter into BITs with other developed countries. Thailand was the first developing country to sign a BIT with China. This was followed by Singapore, Kuwait, Sri Lanka, Malaysia, Pakistan and Ghana. Between 1985 and 1989, China signed BITs with developed countries including Denmark, the Netherlands, Austria, the United Kingdom, Switzerland, Australia, Japan and New Zealand. In addition, China also concluded BITs with transition economies such as Poland, Bulgaria and Romania.[8]

With a few years of BIT negotiations under its belt, China formulated its first Model BIT around 1984.[9] In it, China incorporated basic provisions such as definitions, fair and equitable treatment, MFN treatment, expropriation and compensation, compensation for damages and losses, transfer rights and subrogation. It also stipulated that investor-state disputes concerning the amount of compensation for expropriation could be submitted to an *ad hoc* tribunal at the request of either party.[10] This prototype was replaced by the second Model BIT in the late 1980s. It generally retained the same framework of the first Model BIT, but added a qualified national treatment standard and an umbrella clause. In addition, the standard of compensation for expropriation was modified, with the concept of "market value" included in the provision.[11]

Overall, the first-generation BITs were, for the most part, similar and relatively conservative. Nevertheless, as noted by Shishi Li, Chinese BITs with developing countries displayed certain distinct features compared to those with developed countries.[12] The former tended to focus on investment promotion and encouragement, emphasize state sovereignty and national jurisdiction, and allow more flexibility for the needs of BIT partners.

---

8 For a review of Chinese practice of BITs in the 1980s, see Norah Gallagher and Wenhua Shan, *Chinese Investment Treaties: Policies and Practice* (Oxford: Oxford University Press, 2009) at 35–8 [Galllagher and Shan].

9 This Model BIT can be found in UNCTAD: *International Investment Instruments: A Compendium, Vol III* (New York: UN, 1996), online: UNCTAD <http://www.unctad.org/sections/dite/iia/docs/Compendium//en/65%20volume%203.pdf> at 151–7.

10 *Ibid* at art 9.

11 See second Model BIT at art 4. An English translation of the second Model BIT by Wenhua Shan can be found in Gallagher and Shan, *supra* note 8 at 427–31.

12 Li, *supra* note 7 at 177–80.

Second-generation IIAs

The 1990s experienced a worldwide BIT boom and China was no exception. In less than a decade, China entered into BITs with more than 60 countries. The second-generation BITs were characterized by the inclusion of clauses for the submission of disputes concerning the amount of compensation for expropriation to ICSID arbitration.[13] Like many other developing countries, China was initially very skeptical of the ICSID Convention. It perceived the ICSID Convention as a threat to state sovereignty and national jurisdiction. However, after a decade of reforms, China formally signed the ICSID Convention in February 1990 and subsequently ratified it in January 1993.[14] The final decision to ratify the ICSID Convention was largely attributed to Deng Xiaoping's famous "Southern Tour Talks" in 1992. During the tour, Deng campaigned for further economic reform and "opening up" of the country. More importantly, he advocated the establishment of a socialist market economy in the communist country.[15] According to Chinese leaders, the ratification of the ICSID Convention signaled to the international community that China was committed to further liberalizing its economy.[16] Nevertheless, China proceeded with caution. In accordance with article 25(4) of the Convention, China notified the Center that it would only consider submitting disputes over compensation for expropriation under ICSID jurisdiction.[17]

Once China became a signatory to the ICSID Convention, it started making reference to ICSID in its BITs. The Lithuania BIT signed in November 1993 was said to be the first BIT with such a reference. Nevertheless, it is worth noting that not all BITs signed by China after 1993 followed this model. Rather, many of them avoid any reference to ICSID jurisdiction, even when the counterparty is a member of the Convention.[18] This highlighted the persistent reluctance on the part of the Chinese to accept ICSID arbitration.

13 See e.g. China-Chile BIT (1994) at art 9(3); China-Israel BIT (1995) at art 8(1); China-Morocco BIT (1995) at art 10(2).
14 Gallagher and Shan, *supra* note 8 at 38.
15 See Yingyi Qian, "The Process of China's Market Transition (1978–1998): The Evolutionary, Historical, and Comparative Perspectives" (2000) 156 Journal of Institutional and Theoretical Economics 151.
16 Gallagher and Shan, *supra* note 8 at 38–9.
17 ICSID, Notifications Concerning Classes of Disputes Considered Suitable or Unsuitable for Submission to the Centre, online: ICSID <http://icsid.worldbank.org/ICSID/FrontServlet?requestType=ICSIDDocRH&actionVal=ShowDocument&Measures=True&language=English> ICSID/8-D at 1.
18 See e.g. China-Ecuador BIT (1994) at art 9.

Third-generation IIAs

The third-generation BITs were launched in the late 1990s with China's inclusion of a comprehensive arbitration provision as well as further liberalized substantive provisions. A new Model BIT reflecting these policy changes was formulated in 1997.[19] The first BIT that gave consent to international arbitration for all disputes was signed with Barbados on July 20, 1998.[20] In fact, the breakthrough was achieved in 1997 during the course of BIT negotiations with Canada. It was then that China's State Council approved certain key changes in their negotiation policies, including investor-state dispute settlement.[21]

There are a number of reasons behind China's turn toward the new IIA regime. First, China's domestic legal framework relating to foreign investment had experienced dramatic changes since the early 1990s, particularly on the eve of its entry into the WTO. Ongoing domestic reforms enhanced China's ability to accept more liberal investment treaties.[22] Secondly, competition for foreign investment had significantly intensified by the 1990s as more countries shifted to a more neoliberal investment policy. The Chinese authorities felt an urge to improve their investment regime in order to maintain China as an attractive FDI destination.[23] Most importantly, China founded its "Go Global" strategy in the late 1990s primarily by promoting outward FDI. China is no longer only a passive recipient of foreign investment but is a significant capital exporter as well. As such, the Chinese government perceived the need to enter into new treaties in an effort to protect its increasing outgoing investments.[24]

Closely following its new prototype, China has entered into approximately 40 new BITs. Most of them were signed with African and South American countries. The most recent BIT was concluded with Libya on August 4, 2010, bringing the total number of BITs involving China to 130.[25] China also revised a dozen of its existing BITs in the form of either a new BIT or an amendment protocol in the 2000s. Most of the renegotiated BITs were concluded with European states. They

---

19 China Model BIT (1997) in Gallagher and Shan, *supra* note 8 at 433–7.
20 See China-Barbados BIT (1998) at art 9.
21 See Gallagher and Shan, *supra* note 8 at 40.
22 See Nicholas R. Lardy, *Integrating China into the Global Economy* (Washington, DC: Brookings Institution Press, 2002) at 29–62.
23 Gallagher and Shan, *supra* note 7 at 41.
24 Axel Berger, "The Politics of China's Investment Treaty-Making Program" in Tomer Broude, Marc L. Busch and Amelia Porges (eds), *The Politics of International Economic Law* (Cambridge: Cambridge University Press, 2011) at 162–85.
25 See *supra* note 4.

often went slightly beyond the China Model BIT in favor of investors.[26] Immediately after entering the WTO in 2001, China began negotiating FTAs. By the end of June 2010, China had concluded ten FTAs.[27] Four of them, namely the ASEAN FTA, Pakistan FTA, New Zealand FTA and Peru FTA include a BIT-like investment chapter. The investment chapters in FTAs provide similar protection to investors as the new generation BITs. One exception can be found in the Pakistan FTA. It introduces a framework for the establishment of "China-Pakistan Investment Zones," where investors are entitled to a package of incentives guaranteed by the Pakistan government.[28]

So far, the network of Chinese IIAs has spread to cover most of Asia, Europe, Africa, Latin America and Oceania. However, some important investment partners remain absent. In fact, five of the top ten FDI sources in China, namely Hong Kong, Taiwan, the United States, Macao and Canada, have not yet been covered.[29] In the Economic Cooperation Framework Agreement entered into force in 2010 between the mainland and Taiwan, the parties agreed to negotiate a BIT and the cross-strait BIT is expected to be signed soon. Negotiations with the United States on a BIT started as early as 1983 but failed because of wide divergence between the two parties over a range of issues.[30] After lengthy discussions, China and the United States announced the reopening of BIT negotiations on June 18, 2008. Similarly, negotiations between China and Canada started in 1994, later stopped, and resumed in September 2004.[31]

---

26 For more details, see Part II.
27 There are ASEAN countries (2002), Hong Kong (2003), Macao (2003), Chile (2005), Pakistan (2006), New Zealand (2008), Singapore (2008), Peru (2009), Costa Rica (2010) and Taiwan (2010). For a general picture of Chinese FTA program, see Francis Snyder, "China, Regional Trade Agreements and WTO Law" (2009) 43 *Journal of World Trade* 1; Guiguo Wang, "China's FTAs: Legal Characteristics and Implications" (2011) 105(3) AJIL 493.
28 *Amending Protocol to the Free Trade Agreement Between the Government of the People's Republic of China and the Government of the Islamic Republic of Pakistan*, October 16, 2008, online: MOFCOM <http://fta.mofcom.gov.cn/inforimages/200810/20081023143246189.pdf>.
29 Top ten origins of non-financial FDI in China are Hong Kong, Taiwan, Japan, Singapore, United States, South Korea, United Kingdom, Germany, Macao and Canada. See MOFCOM statistics, online: MOFCOM <http://www.fdi.gov.cn/pub/FDI/wztj/wstztj/lywzkx/t20100115_117047.htm>.
30 Congyan Cai, "China-US BIT Negotiations and the Future of Investment Treaty Regime: A Grand Bilateral Bargain with Multilateral Implications" (2009) 12 J Int'l Econ L 457 at 458.
31 Justin Carter, "The Protracted Bargain: Negotiating the Canada-China Foreign Investment Promotion and Protection Agreement" (2009) 47 Can YB Int'l Law 197 at 198.

Key features of current IIA policy

Some of the key features of China's current IIA policy will be examined within the context of the organizational themes of efficiency, legitimacy and sustainability.[32]

Efficiency

Corresponding to the liberalization of China's IIA policy is the increased efficiency in investment protection. Arguably, China's IIA policy has been characterized by increasing efficiency over time, as it relates to coverage, substantive obligations and dispute settlement procedures.

FTAs containing BIT-like investment chapters

A trend has emerged over the last decade that has featured China signing FTAs with investment chapters that provide similar protections as those afforded to investors under BITs. According to UNCTAD, FTAs (and other regional integration and cooperation agreements) that include investment chapters have a stronger impact in terms of increased FDI flows than BITs.[33] For more discussion on the efficiency of investment chapters in FTAs, see de Mestral and Falsafi's treatment of this topic in chapter 7.

National treatment

The evolution of national treatment provisions in China's IIAs parallels the overall liberalization process relating to international investment in the country. In general, China's first generation BITs do not contain a national treatment provision, with a few exceptions where the provision is only a "best effort" obligation.[34] China's initial reluctance to include national treatment protection was due to several reasons. First and foremost, China wanted to protect its domestic industry which was too weak to withstand international competition. Thus, as China's domestic industries gradually developed over the past three decades, China became more inclined to accept national treatment subject to

---

32 See the Introduction to this book.

33 UNCTAD, *The Role of International Investment Agreements in Attracting Foreign Direct Investment to Developing Countries* (New York and Geneva: United Nations, 2009) at 110. See further de Mestral and Falsafi in ch 7 .

34 See China-UK BIT (1985) at art 3(3); China-Japan BIT (1988) at art 3(2).

certain exceptions.[35] Secondly, the regulatory structure of the Chinese economy evolved from a centrally-planned economy. As a result, there was no "uniform national standard."[36] Enterprises were divided into several categories, including state-owned enterprises, collectively owned enterprises, privately owned enterprises and foreign-invested enterprises. As such, the treatment granted to an enterprise depended on the nature of its ownership.[37]

Starting in the late 1990s, China has increasingly accepted a post-establishment national treatment clause. This change was the result of China's decision to abandon the planned economy and move towards a market economy in the 1990s. However, as a "full market economy" has not yet been established, the third-generation IIAs still contain substantial restrictions in its national treatment provision, as evidenced by article 3.2 of the China Model BIT:

> *Without prejudice to its laws and regulations*, each Contracting Party shall accord to investments and activities associated with such investments by the investors of other Party treatment not less favorable than that accorded to the investments and associated activities by its own investors [emphasis added].[38]

This type of clause makes the national treatment obligation contingent on the domestic legislation of the host country and allows the host country to discriminate against foreign investors by changing old or enacting new laws in favor of domestic investors. However, it would prevent discriminatory measures that are not imposed by formal laws or regulations. In some renegotiated European BITs and some FTAs, the reservation "without prejudice to its laws and regulations" has been replaced by a grandfather clause. A typical example of such a clause can be found in article 141 of the China-New Zealand FTA:

1. Article 138 (National Treatment) does not apply to:

    (a) any existing non-conforming measures maintained within its territory;
    (b) the continuation of any non-conforming measure referred to in subparagraph (a);

---

35 Stephan Schill, "Tearing Down the Great Wall: the New Generation Investment Treaties of the People's Republic of China" (2007) 15 Cardozo J Int'l & Comp L 73 at 95.
36 *Ibid* at 96; See also Gallagher and Shan, *supra* note 8 at 166.
37 *Ibid*.
38 China Model BIT (1998) at art 3(2).

(c)   an amendment to any non-conforming measure referred to in subparagraph (a) to the extent that the amendment does not increase the non-conformity of the measure, as it existed immediately before the amendment with those obligations.

2.   The Parties will endeavour to progressively remove the non-conforming measures.[39]

The scope of the exceptions granted by the grandfather clause is clearly narrower than the one established by "without prejudice to its laws and regulations." The grandfather clause allows the preservation of non-conforming measures but prohibits the introduction of new discriminations. This development reflects the ongoing "national treatment movement" of China's domestic regulatory reform.

MFN

Like many other countries, China has participated in IIAs with the hopes of attracting increased foreign capital. Nevertheless, it has perceived a need to retain control over the admission of investments in accordance with its domestic policy. Chinese IIAs admit investments of other contracting parties only if they comply with the host state's legislation. Article 2.1 of the China Model BIT provides that "Each Contracting Party shall encourage investors of the other Contracting Party to make investments in its territory and *admit such investment in accordance with its laws and regulations*" (emphasis added). This approach has been followed in most of its third-generation IIAs.[40]

Virtually all Chinese IIAs contain an MFN clause. In principle, on the basis of an MFN clause a foreign investor is able to invoke preferential treatment that the host country grants to investors of a third country. Therefore, the ever-evolving Chinese IIA practice will have repercussions on its existing and more restrictive old-generation BITs.[41]

---

39 *Free Trade Agreement between the Government of New Zealand and the Government of the People's Republic of China*, online: New Zealand-China FTA <http://www.chinafta. govt.nz/1-The-agreement/2-Text-of-the-agreement/0-downloads/NZ-ChinaFTA-Agreement-text.pdf> [China-New-Zealand FTA].
40 See e.g. China-Netherlands BIT (2001) at art 2; China-Russia BIT (2006) at art 2(1); China-Mexico BIT (2008) at art 2.
41 For a discussion of the potential impact of MFN regarding Chinese IIAs, see Aaron M. Chandler, "BITs, MFN Treatment and the PRC: The Impact of China's Ever-Evolving Bilateral Investment Treaty Practice" (2009) 43 The International Lawyer 1301 at 1308–10; Wei Shen, "The Good, the Bad or the Ugly? A Critique of the

The MFN clause in most Chinese BITs applies only to the post-establishment stage. However, some new IIAs extend the scope of MFN to cover admission of investments. For example, article 139(1) of the China–New Zealand FTA provides that investors, investments and associated activities from the other contracting party shall receive MFN treatment with respect to *"admission,* expansion, management, conduct, operation, maintenance, use, enjoyment and disposal."[42] The right to establishment is conditional in that it exists only if investors of third parties have been treated in a more favorable way.

Transfer rights

Most IIAs permit the transfer of investment-related funds without delay, in a convertible currency and at the prevailing market exchange rate.[43] China, on the other hand, has traditionally maintained a strict foreign exchange and currency control policy. The China Model BIT subjects the transfer guarantee to the "domestic laws and regulations" of the host country. This restriction could substantially reduce the level of protection as the host country can modify its domestic legislation at any time. Further, the China–Trinidad and Tobago BIT fails to stipulate the speed at which a transfer must take place.

Transfer rules have nevertheless been liberalized in some recent IIAs. For one, China has replaced the local law requirement in the 2009 China–Switzerland BIT by merely subjecting the transfer of funds to "relevant formalities stipulated by the applicable Chinese laws and regulations relating to exchange control."[44] Further, to ensure that these formalities are not used as a means by the host country to avoid its obligations on transfer rights, these relevant formalities are required to be completed within two months. Moreover, if such formalities cease to exist under Chinese law, transfers shall occur without restriction. This

Decision on Jurisdiction and Competence in *Tza Yap Shum v. The Republic of Peru"* (2011) 10 Chinese Journal of International Law 55, at 85–8.

42 China–New Zealand FTA *supra* note 40 at art 139. See also Agreement on Investment of the Framework Agreement on Comprehensive Economic Cooperation Between The People's Republic of China and the Association of Southeast Asian Nations, August 15, 2009 (ASEAN-China IIA (2009)) online: MOFCOM <http://fta.mofcom.gov.cn/inforimages/200908/20090817113007764.pdf> at art 5(1).

43 Andrew Newcombe and Lluís Paradell, *Law and Practice of Investment Treaties: Standards of Treatment* (The Netherlands: Kluwer Law International, 2009) at 405.

44 Protocol to the China–Switzerland BIT (2009) at ad art 5.

liberalized approach to transfer rights can also be found in some renegotiated European BITs and FTAs.[45]

Investor-state arbitration

Generally, investor-state arbitration provides a more effective and efficient remedy for investors than its alternatives—the domestic legal system of the host state or diplomatic protection. Nevertheless, China was initially hesitant to include investor-state arbitration provisions in its IIAs. For instance, its first BIT signed with Sweden in 1982 did not include any provision related to investor-state arbitration. Further, most of its IIAs concluded in the 1980s and 1990s limit the jurisdiction of an arbitral tribunal to "disputes concerning the amount of compensation for expropriation."[46] By 1998, China began accepting comprehensive investor-state dispute settlement clauses. According to the China Model BIT, the host state consents to the arbitration of "any legal dispute between an investor of one Contracting party and the other Contracting party in connection with an investment in the territory of the other Contracting Party."[47]

While China has made strides towards a more effective and efficient dispute settlement policy, there remains room for improvement. Despite its consent to investor-state arbitration, China continues to discourage resort to this mechanism by setting relatively high pre-requisites to arbitration in some recent IIAs. For one, many IIAs only permit a dispute to be submitted to arbitration after a lapse of time, usually six months, designated towards negotiations.[48] Additionally, the investor is required to notify the state party prior to submitting to arbitration. Upon receipt of the notice, the state party is allowed to "require the investor concerned to go through any applicable domestic administrative review procedures specified by the laws and regulations of the state party."[49] Finally, some Chinese IIAs impose a limit on the

45 Protocol to the China-Germany BIT (2003) at ad art 4; China-New-Zealand FTA *supra* note 40 at art 142(3).
46 See e.g. China-UK BIT (1986) at art 7(1); China-Korea BIT (1992) at art 9 (3); China-Morocco BIT (1995) at art 10(2).
47 China Model BIT (1998) at art 9(1).
48 See China-Germany BIT (2003) at art 9 (2); China-New Zealand FTA (2008) at art 153(1). In itself, more time for negotiations is not necessarily inefficient. See Céline Lévesque on improving the use of ADR in IIAs at ch 8.
49 China Model BIT (1998) at 9(2). See also Protocol to the China-Germany BIT (2003) at ad art 9.

time frame within which a claim may be submitted, typically three years.[50]

Although there has traditionally been reluctance on the part of the Chinese to accept investor-state arbitration as a means of resolving disputes, there are indications that China is becoming more at ease with this mechanism. For instance, to ensure that the host state does not abuse the administrative review procedure, some renegotiated European BITs and FTAs set a three-month limit for this procedure.[51] Moreover, the China Model BIT contains a "fork in the road" clause, whereby an investor's choice of one remedy between domestic courts and ICSID arbitration precludes the invocation of another.[52] Some IIAs allow the investor to withdraw a dispute from a domestic court before a final judgment has been reached in the case and submit it instead to international arbitration.[53]

Legitimacy

Whether it is investor misconduct, abuse of corporate nationality or even a lack of transparency, the international investment regime has long suffered from a perceived legitimacy crisis. In fact, prior to embarking on economic reform, China was suspicious of the international investment regime, and often questioned its legitimacy.

Investor misconduct

As detailed in Andrew Newcombe's chapter 11 on investor misconduct, international investment law was developed as a protection mechanism for foreign investors. As a result, IIAs usually provide asymmetrical rights and obligations in favor of foreign investors. This imbalance between investor rights and state obligations threatens the legitimacy of contemporary IIAs, especially as issues relating to investor misconduct become increasingly prevalent.

In line with Newcombe's recommendations to curb investor misconduct, the China Model BIT employs an asset-based definition of

---

50 See e.g. China-New Zealand FTA, *supra* note 40 at art 154(1); China-Mexico BIT (2008) at art 13(7).
51 See e.g. Protocol to the China-Germany BIT (2003) at ad art 9; China-New Zealand FTA, *supra* note 40 at art 153(2).
52 See China Model BIT (1998) at art 9(2).
53 Protocol to the China-Germany BIT (2003) at ad art 9; China-New Zealand FTA *supra* note 40 at art 153(3).

"investment" that defines "investment" as "every kind of asset invested by investors of one Contracting Party *in accordance with the laws and regulations* of the other Contracting Party in the territory of the latter, and in particular, though not exclusively, include . . . [emphasis added]."[54] Under this definition, an investment will enjoy treaty protection only if a claimant establishes that its investment has been owned and controlled in accordance with the host state's legislation. Conversely, a host government may deny treaty protection to an investment found to be illegal. Notably this qualification does not appear in the definition of investment in some recent Chinese IIAs, such as the 2003 China-Germany BIT and the 2004 China-Uganda BIT. Both, nevertheless, emphasize in another provision that each contracting party shall "admit such investments in accordance with its laws and regulations."[55]

Abuse of corporate nationality

As described in Jean-François Hébert's chapter 13, the extension of treaty rights to legal persons with only minimal connections to their alleged home state can lead to an abuse of the treaty's protections and in some cases, treaty shopping. These abusive practices raise further doubts regarding the legitimacy of the international investment regime as a whole.

In many cases, the main problem lies with the definition of investors in IIAs. Defining which investors can benefit from a treaty is essentially one of determining what link needs to exist between an investor and a contracting party to the treaty. In the case of natural persons, Chinese IIAs generally specify the link on the bases of nationality, which is determined by the domestic law of the home country. For investors that are companies or other legal entities, determining an appreciable link with a contracting party is more complex. The China Model BIT requires that the treaty partner be the country of the company's incorporation and the country of the company's seat.[56] In some recent IIAs, the "seat" criterion has been replaced by "substantive business operations" to allow for more flexibility in an attempt to reduce the possibility of abuse.[57] On the other hand, many recent IIAs extend to include the country whose nationals own or control the company making the

---

54 China Model BIT (1998) at art 1(1).
55 See e.g. China-Germany BIT (2003) at art 2(1); China-Uganda BIT (2004) at art 2.
56 China Model BIT (1998) at art 1(2).
57 See e.g. China-Mexico BIT (2008) at art 1.

investment.[58] This development has the effect of extending benefits to considerable investors based in Hong Kong who are owned or controlled by nationals of a partner.

Transparency

Finally, a long lasting criticism of the international investment regime is the lack of transparency with respect to investment arbitration. Although there remains much work to be done, it is notable that some Chinese IIAs have responded to these concerns regarding a lack of transparency. For example, the China-New Zealand FTA includes a provision addressing the issue of transparency in investment arbitration. According to article 48(5) of the ICSID Convention, the Center shall not publish the arbitral award without the consent of the disputing parties. However, this can be problematic as an award that is closed to the public can affect the interests of a variety of groups beyond merely the parties.[59] Consequently, article 157 of the China-New Zealand FTA authorizes the state party, at its discretion, to make all tribunal documents public without the consent of the disputing investor.[60] It nevertheless does not go as far as the article 29 of the US Model BIT, which creates an obligation on the disputing state to make the document public.[61]

Sustainability

A main issue in the development of IIA policy is the long-term sustainability of the IIA regime. In order to promote sustainability, China's IIA policy has evolved and now incorporates measures that will help its IIAs sustain the test of time.

Preamble

A common strategy employed by the Chinese government is the inclusion of provisions, in the preamble of its IIAs, highlighting its

---

58 Protocol to the China-Netherlands BIT (2001) at ad art 1; China-New Zealand FTA, *supra* note 40 at art 135.
59 *Convention on the Settlement of Investment Disputes Between States and Nationals of Other States*, March 18, 1965 575 UNTS 159 (entered into force October 14, 1966) at art 48(5).
60 China-New Zealand *FTA, supra* note 39 at art 157.
61 See Céline Lévesque and Andrew Newcombe on the evolution of IIA practices in Canada and the United States at ch 2.

sustainability objectives. The preambles of some recent Chinese IIAs articulate that investment promotion and protection must respect other key public policy objectives. For example, the preamble in the China-Trinidad and Tobago BIT states that "these objectives can be achieved without relaxing health, safety and environmental measures of general applications."[62] Additionally, the preamble of the ASEAN Agreement explicitly identifies sustainability as a core objective of the treaty. It refers to "allowing flexibility to the Parties to address their sensitive areas . . . in the realization of the sustainable economic growth and development goals . . ."[63] The inclusion of sustainability-like provisions in the preamble of recent IIAs points towards an increasing cognizance on the part of the Chinese regarding the significance of establishing an IIA policy that can co-exist and adapt to future policy objectives.[64]

General exceptions

Foreign investment protection is not the only objective of investment treaties and such protection should not be granted at any cost. A state seeking the benefits of foreign investment is often confronted with the tension between the state's perceived national interests and its required treaty obligations. One device employed to mediate this tension is the inclusion of treaty-exceptions to assure the host state maintains sufficient regulatory power. While Chinese IIAs are increasingly being liberalized, the types and number of exceptions finding their way into newly negotiated treaties is increasing too.

At least four categories of exceptions can be identified in recent Chinese IIAs, ranging from wide exceptions applying to all IIA obligations to narrowly defined reservations for specific measures. The Model BIT does not contain express exceptions to protect security interests. Many newer Chinese IIAs, however, include an essential security provision.[65] A small number of IIAs have general exceptions from IIA obligations for measures necessary to meet specific objectives, including public order and protection of human, animal and plant life or health.[66] These exceptions are typically very closely patterned after the general exception provisions in GATT

---

62 See China-Trinidad and Tobago BIT (2002).
63 See ASEAN-China BIT (2009), *supra* note 42.
64 On sustainable development, see Markus Gehring at ch 16.
65 See e.g. China-India BIT (2006) at art 14; ASEAN–China BIT (2009), *supra* note 42 at art 17.
66 ASEAN-China BIT (2009), *supra* note 42 at art 16.

article XX or GATS article XXIV.[67] Also, some IIAs exclude specific industrial sectors or types of measures from IIA obligations. In addition, as mentioned above, there are "grandfather" provisions that allows for the continuation, renewal and amendment of an existing non-conforming measure.

The exceptions represent an explicit compromise between competing policy objectives—the first to promote and protect investment, and the second to enable regulatory authority in support of legitimate national interests. In the terms of John Ruggie, this phenomenon can be described by a political commitment to "embedded liberalism."[68] The desire to increase the efficiency of international investment was "embedded" within a larger vision: a shared commitment to legitimacy and sustainability.

Expropriation and police powers

Given China's history of expropriation of foreign property following the communist takeover, Chinese leaders publicly promised that China would refrain from nationalizing or expropriating foreign investment unless such expropriation became necessary. This expropriation policy was then translated into IIAs.

Most contemporary arbitral tribunals have struggled to distinguish legitimate regulation from indirect expropriation. In response to concerns over the possibility of an over-expansive interpretation of "indirect expropriation," some newer Chinese IIAs add explicit criteria on how to determine whether a particular measure amounts to expropriation. Among other things, Annex 13 of the China-New Zealand FTA makes clear that (1) in order to constitute indirect expropriation, the state's deprivation of the investor's property must be either severe or for an indefinite period, and disproportionate to the public purposes; and (2) "measures taken in the exercise of a state's regulatory powers as may be reasonably justified in the protection of the public welfare, including public health, safety and the environment, shall not constitute an indirect expropriation," unless in rare circumstances such as the measure is discriminatory in its effect.[69]

---

67 On general exceptions, see Andrew Newcombe at ch 15.
68 John Ruggie, "International Regimes, Transactions, and Change: Embedded Liberalism and the Post-war Economic Order" (1982) 36 International Organization 379.
69 See China-New Zealand FTA, *supra* note 39 at annex 13.

Conclusion

The preceding overview suggests that China's IIAs have slowly evolved over the past three decades. The main evolutionary trend has been the increase of efficiency in investment protection. Legitimacy concerns such as transparency of dispute settlement have also been reflected in recent Chinese IIAs. Furthermore, efforts are being made to ensure that IIAs are sustainable instruments for investment policy. Nevertheless, it is very difficult to predict the future direction of China's IIA program. On the one hand, given the dramatic increase of outward investment from China to the rest of the world and the negotiations with the United States and Canada, it would seem realistic to expect that China will continue to liberalize the regime. On the other hand, with the entry into force of the new generation IIAs and a growing public understanding of the instruments, it is believed that the government of China and its investors will be increasingly engaged in investor-state arbitration cases.[70] When such changes take place, China may be expected to seek more balance in its IIAs.

---

70 Despite of signing such a large number of IIAs, so far the government and its investors have very limited involvement in investment arbitration. *Tza Yap Shum v The Republic of Peru* is the single reported case initiated by a Chinese investor. *Tza Yap Shum v Republic of Peru*, Decision on Jurisdiction and Competence, ICSID Case No. ABR/07/6 (June 19, 2009). There is another recent case administered by the PCA: see *China Heilonjiang International Economic & Technical Cooperative Corp. et al. v Mongolia*, PCA online <http://www.pca-cpa.org/showpage.asp?pag_id=1378>. Recently a Malaysian company filed a case against Chinese government before the ICSID. *Ekran Berhad v People's Republic of China*, ICSID Case No. ABR/11/15 (suspended as of July 22, 2011).

5 A quantitative perspective on trends in IIA rules

*Mark S. Manger**

As evident from the contributions to this volume, the governance of international investment is one of the most active areas in the development of international economic law. Surprisingly, despite decades of research by legal scholars, political economists[1] have only begun to seriously study investment agreements in the last ten years. Less surprising is the fact that their perspective differs considerably from that of legal scholars, as the primary focus of political economists is on causal explanation and empirical puzzles. In this instance, how can we characterize the evolution of the international regime for foreign investment, and what explains its development? To help answer these questions, this chapter introduces key findings in the political economy literature and presents some insights obtained from a quantitative view on the international investment regime to complement the legal perspective and to stimulate further interdisciplinary research.

Initially, most research in political economy treated IIAs the same way as other international institutions.[2] Hence all that mattered was whether two countries had an agreement, irrespective of the substance of that

---

* Lecturer in International Political Economy, Department of International Relations, London School of Economics.
1 By "political economists" I mean economists and political scientists (currently in the majority) working in the tradition of positive economic analysis, usually applying formal and empirical methods to explain policy outcomes.
2 Peter Egger and Michelle Pfaffermayr, "The Impact of Bilateral Investment Treaties on Foreign Direct Investment" (2004) 32(4) Journal of Comparative Economics 788 [Egger and Pfaffermayr]; Rodolphe Desbordes and Vincent Vicard, "Foreign Direct Investment and Bilateral Investment Treaties: An International Political Perspective" (2009) 37(3) Journal of Comparative Economics 372 [Desbordes and Vicard]; Eric Neumayer and Laura Spess, "Do Bilateral Investment Treaties Increase Foreign Direct Investment to Developing Countries?" (2005) 33(10) World Development 1567 [Neumayer and Spess].

agreement. This perspective slighted international legal scholarship. To move beyond such a reductionist view, political economists have started to take the content of IIAs seriously. At the same time, an empirical approach offers some interesting new insights for legal scholars.

In political economy two approaches dominate, implicitly or explicitly, the study of IIAs: the "rational design" and "legalization of international relations" schools of thought. The first assumes that the creation of international law is the result of actions by rational agents who may be faced with uncertainty and incomplete information about the actions and intentions of other agents.[3] Nonetheless, these agents are quite certain about the consequences of the institutional arrangements they choose, including the effects of specific legal clauses. The strength of this approach is that it can be formalized using the mathematical apparatus of game theory. At its best, it provides parsimonious yet powerful explanations of generic problems of cooperation and interaction in international affairs. For example, it has shown that the higher the stakes for states, the shorter is the period that states are willing to be contractually bound through international law. International treaties dealing with issues related to state security tend to have a shorter lifespan, while commercial agreements on the other hand tend to have much longer timeframes.[4] This is in line with rationalist predictions, as countries will adapt contracts to reflect uncertainty about the future and the stakes involved. The view of international law as consisting of specific contracts is prevalent in this approach. If agreements are similar, then they probably represent a rational solution to a generic cooperation problem, but international law has no "life of its own" beyond the sum of individual contracts.[5]

Despite such straightforward and compelling explanations, the "rational design" approach does not fare as well as when dealing with the legal details of treaties. Consider specifically IIAs. Without any provisions for dispute settlement, IIAs are not likely to be enforceable unless we consider such vague notions like "diplomatic pressure." Accordingly, whether or not an IIA contains a dispute settlement procedure in the form of arbitration should have an effect on how much protection it offers to investors and investments. More protection for investors should make a country more attractive for FDI, if the aim of

3 Barbara Koremenos et al, *The Rational Design of International Institutions* (Cambridge: Cambridge University Press, 2004).
4 Barbara Koremenos, "Contracting around International Uncertainty" (2005) 99(4) American Political Science Review 549.
5 *Ibid.*

IIAs is really to promote foreign investment. And yet, as some authors note,[6] it makes no difference for bilateral investment flows whether or not an agreement contains an arbitration clause.

In contrast, the "legalization" approach focuses squarely on international law itself. It remains within the rational choice tradition in that states are goal-directed actors, but it pays much greater attention to the content of IIAs.[7] The intellectual authors of this approach propose three dimensions of international law that are to be analyzed as the outcome of a political process: *Obligation*, *Precision* and *Delegation*. A definition of the terms follows.

Obligation reflects the extent to which a state is bound by a specific legal agreement notwithstanding the general doctrine of *rebus sic stantibus*. International instruments range from non-binding and voluntary (e.g. the OECD Guidelines for Multinational Enterprises)[8] to fully binding international treaties without even an explicit withdrawal option, as is the case with the European Union prior to the Treaty of Lisbon.[9] Signatories deliberately vary the degree of obligation through individual reservations, exclusions and general exceptions. Other international agreements have a built-in "sunset clause" that lets them expire unless renewed. Most, however, simply allow for withdrawal after a specific period of time—usually ten years in the case of IIAs.[10]

Precision narrows the scope for the interpretation of rules. It is not identical with clarity, as the attempt to limit the range of possible understandings often leads to particularly dense language. At other times, general language covers situations not foreseeable by the parties, while highly specific text deals with known issues over which often intense bargaining unfolds. Finally, imprecise text may reflect the political inability to agree on language, or deliberate vagueness to preserve future freedom of action.

---

6   Todd Allee and Clint Peinhardt, "Contingent Credibility: The Impact of Investment Treaty Violations on Foreign Direct Investment" (2011) 65(3) International Organization 401 [Allee and Peinhardt, "Contingent Credibility"].

7   Judith Goldstein et al, "Introduction: Legalization and World Politics" (2000) 54(3) International Organization 385; Frederick Abbott, "NAFTA and the Legalization of World Politics: A Case Study" (2000) 54(3) International Organization 519.

8   OECD Guidelines are available at <http://www.oecd.org/dataoecd/56/36/1922428.pdf>.

9   *Treaty of Lisbon amending the Treaty on European Union and the Treaty establishing the European Community* (December 13, 2007), online: EUROPA <http://europa.eu/lisbon_treaty/full_text/index_en.htm> at art 50.

10   For example, the US-Uruguay BIT (2005) states that "A Party may terminate this Treaty at the end of the initial ten-year period or at any time thereafter by giving one year's written notice to the other Party" at art 22(2).

The third and final dimension is *Delegation*, or the extent to which the interpretation of rules in the case of a dispute is left to neutral third parties, whether they are courts or arbitration tribunals. Delegation ranges from effectively zero, i.e. when all disagreements are subject to direct negotiations between the parties, to pre-commitment to have disputes arbitrated by a neutral third party and to accept the outcome of its ruling.

For political economists, delegation is the easiest dimension to observe and understand. Treaties clearly state when and how states (and in the case of IIAs, investors) will have access to a dispute settlement body. Obligation and precision are more challenging concepts, to the point where many legal scholars doubt that they can be quantified at all. Against this objection it should be kept in mind that without common principles, there could be no law beyond individual bargains, and it would certainly be impossible to teach these principles.

The first part of this chapter introduces recent research in political economy, identifies possible links to legal scholarship, and indicates some gaps in our knowledge. The second part examines the role of developed countries in the promotion of IIAs. The third part presents an analysis of trends in IIAs. In conclusion, suggestions are offered for future interdisciplinary research.

The emergent literature on IIAs in political economy

Empirically, the central question for political economists is this: why do countries sign international legal agreements in the first place? By definition, a legal agreement constrains the freedom of action of a government (i.e. the state incurs a "sovereignty cost"), so an agreement must have specific benefits that outweigh the cost. An argument from contract theory called "credible commitment" is often used as the basis of theoretical explanations.[11]

Many developing countries have a history of expropriating foreign investors, especially in the natural resources sector. Often, the regulatory environment in such a country is unstable, so that unexpected changes in government policy can make an investment suddenly unprofitable. However, before an investment is made, countries generally have to appear as

11 Jason Webb Yackee, "Bilateral Investment Treaties, Credible Commitment, and the Rule of (International) Law: Do BITs Promote Foreign Direct Investment?" (2008) 42(4) Law & Soc'y Rev 805 [Yackee]. For the concept of "credible commitment," see Oliver E. Williamson, "Credible Commitments: Using Hostages to Support Exchange" (1983) 73(4) The American Economic Review 519.

investor-friendly as possible. Once the investment has been made, with capital transferred, and construction of the new facilities completed, the balance of power shifts toward the host government. Since the investment cannot be pulled out without losses, the host government can now alter the terms of the agreement, e.g. demand a greater share of resource revenues, or impose other restrictions that burden the foreign company. Knowing this, investors are wary of "political risk" in developing countries, so that potentially profitable investments are not made—an inefficiency since economic returns are not realized. International agreements solve this "time-inconsistency" problem by substituting international for domestic institutions. By means of an IIA, a developing country can make a credible commitment to respect the property rights of foreign investors. Credible, because if it violates these rights, it has previously conceded that the foreign investor can seek binding arbitration at ICSID, under UNCITRAL arbitration rules, etc. In the worst case, if a country simply rejects the ruling of a tribunal, it (presumably) will suffer considerable damage to its reputation.

The "credible commitment" argument rests on three further assumptions of varying degrees of realism. First, investors must know and care about the effects of IIAs, or at least be indirectly influenced by them in their decision-making. This would be the case if the absence of a BIT resulted in increased insurance cost. Second, the legal standards in IIAs must be so clear and unambiguous that they are easily understood by investors or their counsels and applied consistently by arbitration tribunals. The probability of being wrong about the implications of an IIA should be lower than the likelihood of misreading the political risk in a potential host country. Finally, there should be no other formal (legal) or informal means that make IIAs unnecessary.[12] Clearly, these assumptions are not to be taken as absolutes, but they need to be approximately correct for the commitment device to work, and consequently for the IIA to help attract FDI.

Despite these challenging requirements, some studies find that IIAs have a positive effect on investment inflows. Neumayer and Spess submit that the more BITs a country has signed, the greater its share of global FDI in a given year. Their findings are echoed by other studies.[13] There is little evidence, however, that BITs increase bilateral flows from the more developed country to the less developed partner.[14] But this may be

12 *Ibid* at 810.
13 Egger and Pfaffermayer, *supra* note 2; Desbordes and Vicard, *supra* note 2; Neumayer and Spess, *supra* note 2.
14 Mary Hallward-Driemeier, "Do Bilateral Investment Treaties Attract FDI? Only a

due to the statistical approach taken. For example, a country that already attracts FDI for reasons not captured in the statistical model has little incentive to sign and ratify a BIT (consider the example of Brazil, where all signed BITs to date have floundered in Congress and have not been ratified).[15] The statistical result could be an underreporting of the positive effects of BITs.

More problematic is that these early studies in political economy ignore the substantive content of IIAs and the substantial differences between them. BITs are either treated as identical on-off variables, or simply counted. This means that 20 BITs without any reference to arbitration are 20 times better than one recent BIT with the United States—a finding that legal scholars would surely consider odd.

A clear step forward is therefore found in the work by Yackee, who investigates whether or not BITs with arbitration clauses, i.e. those that actually represent a credible commitment, have an effect on bilateral FDI flows.[16] The surprising answer is that regardless what outcome is measured (bilateral flows, the share of the FDI outflows of the capital-exporting partner in a BIT pair, or the share of global FDI outflows that a country captures), it does not seem to matter whether or not a BIT contains arbitration clauses.[17] Even in the rare instances where the effect is statistically significant, it is very modest in substantive terms, and smaller than many of the awards rendered in recent years. Other studies corroborate this result.[18] Signing on to IIAs therefore does not seem to make much sense for developing countries. A remaining possibility is that IIAs are not meant to attract new investment, but to entice firms to reinvest capital. In other words, *existing* rather than future investment is at the heart of government efforts to negotiate IIAs. While

Bit . . . and They Could Bite" (2003) World Bank Policy Research Working Paper 3121; Susan Rose-Ackerman and Jennifer Tobin, "Foreign Direct Investment and the Business Environment in Developing Countries: The Impact of Bilateral Investment Treaties" (2005) Yale Law & Economics Research Paper No. 293.

15 Luke E. Peterson and Ana C. Simões e Silva (2008) "Brazilian Government Mandated to Pursue Limited Range of Investment Protection Standards; Prospects for Ratification of 1990s-era BITs With Various Developed Countries Remain Highly Unlikely" (2008) 1(9) IA Reporter 7.

16 Yackee, *supra* note 11.

17 *Ibid* at 826.

18 Allee and Peinhardt, "Contingent Credibility", *supra* note 6; Todd Allee and Clint Peinhardt, "The Least BIT Rational: An Empirical Test of the 'Rational Design' of Investment Treaties" (Presentation delivered at the Political Economy Organization Conference in Monte Carlo Verità, Switzerland February 3–8, 2008) online: <http://www.cis.ethz.ch/events/past_events/PEIO2008/Allee.Peinhardt_BITs.Rational.Design> [Allee and Peinhardt, "The Least BIT Rational"].

the evidence is still limited, initial findings suggest that this may be the case.[19]

All of these studies at least implicitly assume that developing countries compete to attract foreign capital.[20] But they lead to the conclusion that developing countries should sign as many BITs as possible while holding the line and keeping obligations and commitments in these agreements to the absolute minimum.

The "rational design" argument therefore runs into difficulties. If the legal content of IIAs does not matter for investment decisions, what then explains the differences between treaties? Why would developed countries expend money employing legal experts to (re-) design model treaties? Negotiating BITs might at the margin improve the governance of capital flows, but providing this for free makes little sense for governments.

What's more, the vague language of many IIAs makes them a poor commitment device compared to common investment contracts. For decades, investors have negotiated contracts to reduce investment risk. These individual contracts are, as pointed out by Kolo and Wälde, enforceable through arbitration.[21] In fact, they often include pre-consent to arbitration by the same body as IIAs. They may still be commitment devices, but given that investment contracts are usually confidential, it is nearly impossible to identify which IIAs actually govern investments that are not covered by separate contracts as well.

Developed countries as promoters of IIAs

If we shift the focus of our analysis to the legal content of IIAs, then we must necessarily direct our attention to the providers of the legal language—in the majority capital-exporting developed countries. Three observations guide the analysis.

First, while competition between developing countries may promote the negotiation of BITs and RTAs with investment chapters, the

19 Deborah L. Swenson, "Why Do Developing Countries Sign BITs?" (2005) 12(1) UC Davis J Int'l L & Pol'y 131.

20 Zachary Elkins et al, "Competing for Capital: The Diffusion of Bilateral Investment Treaties, 1960–2000" (2006) 60(4) International Organization 811 [Elkins et al, "Competing for Capital"]; Andrew T. Guzman, "Why LDCs Sign Treaties That Hurt Them: Explaining the Popularity of Bilateral Investment Treaties" (1998) 38(4) Va. J Int'l L 639.

21 Abba Kolo and Thomas W. Wälde, "Renegotiation and Contract Adaptation in International Investment Projects—Applicable Legal Principles and Industry Practices" (2000) 1(1) The Journal of World Investment and Trade 5.

"templates" or "models" are provided by the capital-exporting country, i.e. usually but not always the developed country. Developing countries may bargain over some more marginal issues or exceptions and reservations, but by and large, to what extent a specific IIA deviates from a template agreement is strongly determined by the power asymmetries between the partners.[22]

Secondly, existing research on the effects of IIAs on investment flows has not given any consideration to the evolution of international investment law over time. The typical approach of empirical researchers has been to seek to identify how the effects of changes in one variable (e.g. whether or not an arbitration clause is included in a treaty) affect the outcome variable (e.g. investment flows to a specific country), while holding all other variables constant—including possibly an underlying time trend towards the inclusion of such clauses in IIAs. Yet as Newcombe makes clear, international public law on foreign investment has evolved rapidly.[23]

Finally, all classical econometric analysis necessarily rests on the "conditional independence" assumption—after controlling for what affects the outcome, the remaining term is simply a random variable unrelated to the others. This cannot be true in a system like the current network of IIAs. Practically all BITs concluded in the last three decades incorporate an MFN clause. In other words, the effective legal protection provided by a BIT depends not only on the specific treaty, but also on the legal clauses in other IIAs with third parties in force with the same host country. Most problematically, we do not even know for certain to what extent such an MFN clause applies until tested, although recent work argues that the MFN clause has led to the creation of a de-facto multilateral regime for international investment.[24]

Theoretical framework

Most political economy research focuses on "cross-sectional" variation, e.g. differences between countries during the same time period. IIAs, rather than varying across country-pairs, differ primarily because of the model treaties of the principal capital-exporting countries and because of the evolution of international investment law over time. Developing countries are often faced with a take-it-or-leave-it option for the treaty

---

22 Allee and Peinhardt, "The Least BIT Rational", *supra* note 18.
23 See Andrew Newcombe, ch 1.
24 Stephan W. Schill, *The Multilateralization of International Investment Law* (Cambridge: Cambridge University Press, 2009).

text, and can only bargain over a limited set of more marginal issues, exceptions or reservations. In other words, variation in the legal content of IIAs appears at least as much over time as cross-sectionally. Our analytical focus here is on the evolution of IIA provisions over time.

From a social science perspective, three theoretical approaches appear suited to the problem. First, legal scholars are close to the ideal type of an "epistemic community" as defined by Haas.[25] Epistemic communities are made up of experts with specialized knowledge, similar professional interests, shared principled beliefs, and common professional or scientific norms for how to validate claims. For governmental decision-making, they matter most when there is considerable uncertainty regarding the consequences of a policy, or when societal and political interests are not articulated or organized, so that governments do not simply respond to lobbying. Scholars of international law fit this description well, especially given their transnational connections, interaction in professional conferences, workshops and panels. For example, the 1948 *Draft Statutes of the Arbitral Tribunal for Foreign Investment and the Foreign Investment Court* proposed by the International Law Association clearly influenced the policies of individual countries.[26]

Unfortunately, the concept of epistemic communities offers a description of a causal pathway for how international legal rules emerge, but very little insight into what drives the specific content of the rules. By definition, a focus on the commonalities of an epistemic community does not provide any leverage to explain variation between the model treaties of individual countries, and only a partial explanation of change over time.

Policy learning is a candidate explanation as well insofar as it can take place at a different pace among governments, but clearly predicts a process over time. Moreover, even if governments update their policies based on the experience of their effects, they may learn selectively depending on available "templates" and because of their own ideological leanings.[27]

Policy learning describes well how legal templates such as proposed conventions and model treaties spread across different countries.[28] The

25 Peter M. Haas, "Introduction: Epistemic Communities and International Policy Coordination" (1992) 46(1) International Organization 1.
26 Andrew Newcombe and Lluís Paradell, *Law and Practice of Investment Treaties* (The Netherlands: Kluwer Law International, 2009) at 21.
27 Frank Dobbin et al, "The Global Diffusion of Public Policies: Social Construction, Coercion, Competition, or Learning?" (2007) 33(1) Annual Review of Sociology 449.
28 Fabrizio Gilardi, "Who Learns from What in Policy Diffusion Processes?" (2010) 54(3) American Journal of Political Science 650.

negotiation of BITs and investment chapters in RTAs provides frequent opportunities for different experiences, negotiations with other parties, and preexisting ideology, leading to the adoption of different IIA models. As long as international law evolves, new templates become available and can be adopted by governments. Clearly, the policy learning and epistemic community frameworks are not mutually incompatible.

The main alternative to the two frameworks above is an explanation based on competition. Research indicates that developing countries likely see IIAs as a policy to attract foreign direct investment by offering stronger commitments than their competitors.[29] Existing work has not extended this to the legal content of IIAs, which presumably could be endogenized in the model in some form.

We therefore need to move toward a theory that explains the evolution and (selective) adaptation of international legal rules. The logical starting point for such a theory is with developed countries and their model treaty templates, since most developing countries have little influence over the content of the treaties.[30] The spread of BITs and other IIAs is best seen as a process of "legal exports" from developed countries to their developing country partners. Major capital-exporting developed countries in particular shape the character of public international law as it applies to foreign direct investment.

If bargaining between the partners explains little variation, as suggested by the highly similar character of IIAs signed by the same developed country, then we should focus on the different preferences of their governments. Using the concepts outlined above, we can observe that capital-exporting governments vary in their preferred degrees of precision, obligation and delegation.

Operationalization and measurement

The three concepts as originally developed are generally applicable to international law, but the framework does not give precise guidance of how to operationalize them in a given issue-area of international relations. Partly because of this problem, the "legalization" framework has not generated as much empirical research as anticipated. A further challenge is that the assessment of specific legal clauses is not easily turned into a quantitative measure because of the high degree of uncertainty surrounding specific meanings and intentions—otherwise

---

29 Elkins et al, *supra* note 20.
30 A partial exception is the "legal export" by major developing countries such as China (see Liu, ch 4 *supra*) and India.

disputes would hardly ever arise because the consequences of violation of an agreement would be easily foreseeable.

Nonetheless, when limiting our operationalization to investment rules we can draw on the burgeoning legal literature that tries to interpret rules prior to the adjudication by a tribunal. At the same time, by restricting our analysis to one issue-area we avoid the challenge of assessing the equivalence of similar clauses or wordings in different domains. This does not suggest that we perceive investment law as static, since much of the interpretation of rules takes place in tribunal proceedings. However, it tends to feed back into scholarship only after some delay. When designing our operationalization, we therefore have to take this delay into account. More concretely, the legal scholarship on which we can draw rests on the analysis of cases decided and agreements written several years ago. In practice, the endpoint of our dataset will therefore lie in the past because our measurement of the most recent developments becomes less and less adequate.

To operationalize the three concepts and turn them into a quantifiable index measure of the language in IIAs, we proceeded as follows.[31] First, we collected all texts of BITs and trade agreements with investment chapters that were publicly available in electronic format in English and French. We then assembled a corpus of "typical wordings" without prejudice to their weight or legal implication based on frequency, an endeavor that is greatly simplified by the similarity of actual treaties and templates.

Secondly, we aggregated these wordings in various categories, based on a reading of individual BITs and the recording of specific clauses when they appeared in the text. An example follows for the category "definition of investment" that lists one or more of several keywords:

a.   Every kind of asset.
b.   Any kind of asset.
c.   Movable and immovable property.
d.   Property rights.
e.   Mortgages.
f.   Liens.
g.   Pledges.
h.   Shares.
     (. . .)

---

31 "We" refers to the author and his research assistants. We do not implicate the legal scholars who have advised us in any way in our specific choices, but we take some consolation that many of our observations resonate with the legal literature that we did *not* consult during the design of our index.

We recorded the appearance of each keyword, and asked several scholars of international economic law[32] to provide a ranking of the clauses according to the three dimensions of legalization. This provided us with an ordinal ranking. We then gave the clauses in this ordinal ranking a weight. This step obviously introduces measurement error. However, given that we compare individual clauses, we find that it is often less problematic than we assumed. For example, a tautological definition of investment is considered less precise than an asset-based definition.

What this means is that precision logically precedes obligation and delegation. An obligation will only be binding (or will not be disputed) if it is stated with some precision in the legal text, irrespective of the specific wording. We then calculated scores for the obligation and delegation embedded in the clauses based on our ordinal ranking. Finally, we assigned weights to individual clauses to reflect their relative importance. For example, we value the preamble less than the substantive text, even though the preamble quite often precisely states intentions. Our raw data is fully transparent, so that our data collection process is in principle replicable and open to challenge.

An analysis of trends in IIAs

We analyze data of BIT texts between 1965 and 2007.[33] Figure 1 shows a smoothed plot of legal precision over time. It is immediately obvious that there is considerable variation across BITs and across time. Remarkably, the heyday of precision in BITs in the late 1990s appears to have passed, and we now observe a slight downward trend. Ranking BITs according to their precision, we find that the top five are UK-Swaziland (1995), Canada-Ecuador (1996), Canada-Costa Rica (1998), Germany-Lebanon (1997) and United States-Kazakhstan (1994). These are both cases that directly reflect asymmetrical investment flows from important sources as well as countries that appear to set standards in international law more broadly. BITs at the lower end of the spectrum of precision tend to be South-South BITs and those in earlier time periods. The bottom three are Libya-Malta (1973), W. Germany-Singapore (1975), and surprisingly, Japan-Russia (1998).

---

32 Among them are several contributors to this volume. The author does not implicate them in the judgments made here; all errors and misjudgments are his own.

33 While we coded BITs since 1959, our earliest data points are omitted in this analysis because with few model BITs, we have only a weak basis for comparison and have less faith in our ordinal ranking.

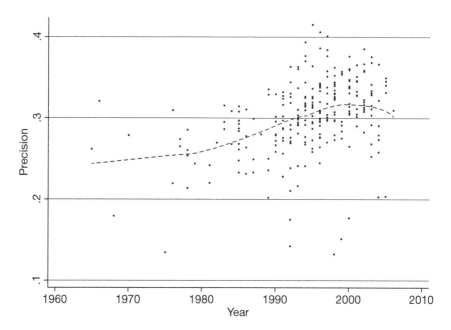

Figure 1 Precision in BITs

Figure 2 shows our index of obligation over time. Again, we observe considerable variation, but much less change over time and no further change since the mid-1990s. This suggests that the standards for BITs are less disputed than often thought. Overall, there is much more convergence towards similar levels in obligation than in precision. Nonetheless, there is enough variation to identify categories. Among the top 20 treaties by obligation, 17 are US BITs, including four data points that jump out: the US BITs with Azerbaijan, Bolivia, Jamaica and Nicaragua. At the low end of the range, we find BITs concluded by Belgium and Germany with various developing country partners from the 1960s through the 1980s.

Note that this measure considers obligation in BITs in isolation, but ignores the effect of the MFN clause. This is clearly problematic, as there is at least one example of the MFN clause providing access to better dispute settlement procedures via a second BIT.[34] There is no obvious solution to this short of calculating the theoretical retroactive effect of the MFN clause. We leave this for future research, but we note that even though our measure does not immediately tell us

---

34 *Emilio Agustin Maffezini v Kingdom of Spain*, Decision of the Tribunal on Objections to Jurisdiction, ICSID Case No. ARB/97/7 (January 25, 2000).

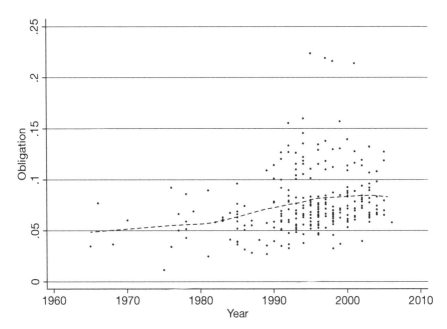

Figure 2 Obligation in BITs

what level of obligation applies for a given investor-host state combination, it gives us a good indication of the relative *increase* in obligation.

Lastly, consider the trend and variation in the degree of delegation shown in figure 3. Early treaties offered virtually no delegation. Even in recent years, some IIAs limit the parties' access to arbitration, making them effectively unenforceable. If either side refuses to agree to arbitration, the only means to settle disputes is in the domestic courts or bilateral state-to-state negotiations.[35] Compared to the two other dimensions, it is evident that there is less convergence. The cross-sectional variation in each year does not change much, suggesting that the menu of delegation options is relatively fixed. Measured by delegation, the top five BITs are Austria-FRY Macedonia (2002), Canada-Costa Rica (1998), Croatia-Kuwait (1997), the interesting case of Lebanon-Belarus (2002) and Switzerland-Mexico (1996).

An econometric analysis of the determinants of these trends is challenging because of the obvious interdependence of observations,

35 Consider the Iran-Sri Lanka BIT (2000) that does not bind a contracting party to arbitration requested by an investor from the other party, and instead relies on the consent of both parties.

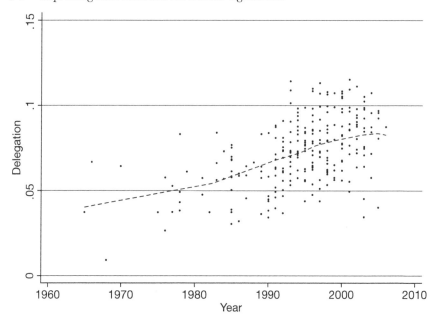

Figure 3 Delegation in BITs

both because of the countries involved and the MFN clause, and is therefore beyond the scope of this chapter. Yet even without further statistical analysis, we can discern trends.

The first observation is a slight convergence toward a common model of bilateral investment treaty in the degrees of precision and obligation. Second and more importantly, we observe a leveling off toward a steady state in all three measures and even a slight downward trend in precision.

What does this tell us about our candidate explanations? A competition model would suggest that developing countries observe that the more BITs an FDI host has, the greater the share of global FDI available in a given year it will receive. In consequence, they should try to maximize the number of BITs they can obtain, but probably refuse to sign BITs that contain obligations beyond their individual threshold at which the cost in loss of "policy freedom" becomes unbearable. Developed countries, on the other hand, still tend to benefit from more precise and obliging treaties (at least as long as they are not regularly the target of investor claims under IIAs).

A learning model, on the other hand, would suggest that developed countries update their treaty models and use them as templates in negotiations until they reach an (individually) optimal level. Developing countries might still pursue the "competitive" policy, but we would observe convergence toward a common level of standards among all IIAs driven by developed countries.

A further possibility is that once developed countries are targeted by claims, they stop signing BITs or include general exceptions.[36] This might simultaneously increase precision and reduce the level of obligation in the treaty.

Conclusion

The international investment regime, consisting of thousands of individual BITs and other IIAs, has only recently attracted the attention of researchers in political economy. In the early stages, the emerging research program has overlooked differences in BITs and, in particular, the evolution of international investment law over time. We may attribute this to an excessive emphasis in consideration of the "rational design" of international institutions. The "legalization" approach described here has been brought to bear less frequently on investment law. This chapter has presented an introduction to this research program and its first findings in a quantitative survey of BITs.

Based on the three concepts of precision, obligation and delegation, we have found that there is a clear trend toward higher legal standards evident during the past decades. What's more, there appears to be a leveling off, suggesting that we may not see the same rapid evolution of investment law in the future, and that a consolidation of existing standards can set in. While investors would in principle benefit from ever-increasing protection, it is possible that host countries have now reached the threshold level at which the commitments enshrined in international investment law bring no further benefits that outweigh the loss of policy freedom.

Nonetheless, several questions remain. We do not know if developed countries keep promoting higher standards and fail to find partners to implement them, or if they are content with the steady state the system is approaching. We also do not know why some countries are willing to aim for higher standards, while others are content to follow and obtain benefits only indirectly via the MFN clause. Perhaps most importantly, we do not have a good theoretical explanation for how decision-makers

---

36 Lauge S. Poulsen, "Sacrificing Sovereignty by Chance: Investment Treaties, Developing Countries and Bounded Rationality" (2011) [unpublished, archived at Department of International Relations, London School of Economics].

in governments deal with the high level of uncertainty regarding the implications of the treaties they conclude. Answering these questions will help guide legal scholars and practitioners in dealing with some of the challenges laid out in this volume.

6 The costs and benefits of IIAs to developing countries: an economic perspective

*Amrita Ray Chaudhuri**
and Hassan Benchekroun**

Introduction

By any measurement, the number of IIAs in existence is significant: over 2,800 BITs existed as of the end of 2010, not counting "other IIAs" which number over 300. The number of countries party to them—over 175—is also telling.[1] Some countries, such as China and India, have respectively signed over 80 agreements each.[2] One would tend to assume that if countries have generally continued to sign and ratify IIAs it is because they promote FDI. Empirical studies, however, have revealed a less obvious picture.[3] This chapter does not seek to present an econometric analysis of the link between IIAs and increased FDI between member countries—an issue that has been the subject of a series of recent papers.[4] Rather, this chapter weighs the theoretical benefits and costs to developing countries from committing to IIAs using a game-theory framework, specifically Markusen's knowledge capital model.[5]

* Assistant Professor, Department of Economics, University of Winnipeg and Extramural Fellow, CentER, TILEC, Tilburg University.
** Associate Professor, Department of Economics, McGill University.
1 See UNCTAD, *World Investment Report 2011: Non-equity Modes of International Production and Development* (New York and Geneva: UNCTAD, 2011) at 100. See also "International Investment Agreements", online: WLU <http://investmentadr.wlu.edu/resources/page.asp?pageid=592>; For a history, see also Andrew Newcombe and Luis Paradelle, *Law and Practice of Investment Treaties: Standards of Treatment* (New York: Kluwer Law International, 2009) at ch 1.
2 See UNCTAD, Country-specific Lists of BITs, online UNCTAD: <http://www.unctad.org/Templates/Page.asp?intItemID=2344&lang=1>.
3 See e.g. Karl P. Sauvant and Lisa E. Sachs (eds), *The Effect of Treaties on Foreign Direct Investment Bilateral Investment Treaties, Double Taxation Treaties, and Investment Flows* (Oxford: Oxford University Press, 2009).
4 *Ibid.*
5 James R. Markusen, "Commitment to Rules on Investment: The Developing Countries' Stake" (2001) 9(2) Review of International Economics 287 [Markusen, "Commitment to rules"].

The starting point of our analysis is that IIAs increase the ability of host states to commit. As such, this chapter views IIAs as a mechanism that increases the enforceability of contracts negotiated between potential investors (such as an MNE) and the government or local agents of the host country (i.e. the country receiving the FDI). Under the knowledge capital model, key aspects are the enforcement of intellectual property rights "IPR" protections and of contracts (either between MNE-state or MNE-local manager). Under an IIA, a systematic lack of enforcement of IPR protections could be considered a violation of fair and equitable treatment protection or, if discriminatory, the lack of enforcement could be a violation of national treatment protection.[6] Further, the "taking" by the government of IPR could constitute an expropriation.[7] With respect to contracts between an MNE and the state (or a State-Owned Enterprice (SOE)), an umbrella clause in an IIA (whereby a state promises to respect its commitments) provides further assurances to the foreign investor.[8] As relates to contracts between an MNE and a (private) local manager or agent, one can imagine scenarios where a lack of enforcement amounts to a denial of justice and a breach of fair and equitable treatment by the state. The possibility for investors (here, MNEs) to have recourse to investor-state arbitration provides a credible commitment device to uphold IIA obligations.

In sum, while we may observe (empirically) more FDI after a BIT enters into force this does not mean that the receiving country is enjoying a higher degree of welfare. Markusen's model provides a rationale as to why not all receiving countries are enthusiastic about signing BITs. We conclude, however, that the main benefit to developing countries in committing to IIAs is to attract otherwise unattainable FDI and that this effect more than compensates for the various disadvantages.

By signing an IIA, a host country effectively directs foreign investment away from other recipients towards itself. We begin by discussing this advantage of the host country committing to an IIA (Part I). We then present Markusen's knowledge capital model (Part II). Using this model, we analyze the main disadvantages that IIAs have on the host

---

6 This analysis assumes that IPR is covered under the definition of investment in the IIA. See UNCTAD Series on Issues in International Investment Agreements II, *Scope and Definition* (New York and Geneva: United Nations, 2011) at 24, 47–8.

7 Markusen, "Commitment to rules", *supra* note 5 at 294.

8 On umbrella clauses, see amongst others Rudolf Dolzer and Christoph Schreuer, *Principles of International Investment Law* (Oxford: Oxford University Press, 2008) at 153–62; OECD, Working Papers on International Investment, Number 2006–3, *Interpretation of the Umbrella Clause in Investment Agreements* (October 2006), online: OECD <http://www.oecd.org/dataoecd/3/20/37579220.pdf>.

country—namely that by signing an IIA, the local agents in the host country collaborating with or being employed by the MNE may end up obtaining a lower share of the MNE's profits deriving from the investment. From an economic perspective, the loss in the share of profits occurs directly (when a contract exists between the state and the foreign investor) or indirectly (when the foreign investor has a contract with a local agent). In both instances, the host country is disadvantaged (Part III). When incentives to renege on a contract are taken into account, it is argued that the increase in the volume of investment attracted to the host country under an IIA may come at the expense of the host country earning a lower share of the profits generated by these investments.[9] Thus, the net impact of the increase in investments on the host country's welfare is, in theory, ambiguous. We review the empirical findings on this issue and conclude that the net effect of IIAs is to make the host country better off (Part IV).

The advantages of commitment

According to UNCTAD (2009), "Overall, developing countries stand to benefit from engaging in IIAs in terms of increasing their attractiveness for FDI, and therefore the likelihood that they receive more FDI."[10] How does this work?

Avoiding the "holdup" problem

Consider the following example: A MNE must decide the mode of entry into a new market, hereby referred to as the host country. The MNE can either export its product to the host country or invest in setting up a production facility (subsidiary) within the host country. The host country prefers that the MNE invest rather than export. This is mainly because the subsidiary that is set up within the host country will employ local agents who will enjoy a share of the MNE's profits. However, the investment involves sunk costs to be paid by the MNE, that is, costs that are irredeemable once the investment is made. An

9 Other studies to analyze this economic tradeoff of signing an IIA include B. Hoekman and K. Saggi, "Multilateral Disciplines for Investment-Related Policies" in Paolo Guerrieri and Hans-EckartScharrer (eds), *Global Governance, Regionalism and the International Economy* (Baden-Baden: NomosVerlagsgesellschaft, 2000).
10 See UNCTAD, "The Role of International Investment Agreements in Attracting Foreign Direct Investment to Developing Countries" (2009) UNCTAD Series on International Investment Policies for Development, Executive Summary at xv [UNCTAD, "The Role of IIAs"].

example of this is investment in industry specific physical capital that is immobile geographically. The host country realizes that once the investment has been undertaken, the MNE is not likely to leave since the MNE cannot redeem the sunk cost. Therefore, the host country has an incentive to take a greater share of the profits (in economic terms "expropriate" the profits) of the MNE post-investment through a variety of measures, such as increasing the taxes charged to the MNE. This problem is exacerbated if future political leaders refuse to honor the commitments made to the MNE by the previous administration in power at the time of the investment. This could make the MNE worse off than if it chose to export. The MNE, anticipating such behavior from the host country, chooses to export instead of invest thus decreasing the welfare of the host country. This is known as the "holdup" problem.[11]

This problem can be avoided if the host country can commit to refrain from taking a greater share of the MNE's profits after it has invested. A credible way for the host country to make such a commitment is by signing an IIA whereby the host country would be punished for reneging on its commitment under the investor-state arbitration process. As long as the MNE realizes that the punishment exceeds the gains to the host country from reneging, the MNE will invest and the holdup problem will be overcome.[12]

Reputation effects

Consider a scenario where there are several MNEs, each of which, instead of dealing with the host country's government, deals with different local agents within the host country. For instance, consider different local managers of the subsidiaries who may take a greater share of the MNE's profits once the investment has been made. The larger the number of agents the lower is the number of MNEs that each agent deals with. In this case, each local agent does not internalize the negative impact on the country's reputation whilst reneging on his own contract with the subset of MNEs that he deals with. Thus, the respective gain that each individual agent receives from reneging is greater than the loss that would be incurred from a damaged reputation to the country as a whole in terms of lower future foreign investment.[13] One way of solving this problem is for the host country's government to commit to laws and

11 Markusen, "Commitment to rules", *supra* note 5 at 289.
12 *Ibid* at 289.
13 *Ibid* at 291–2.

IIAs that prevent individual agents within the host country from defecting from contracts signed with foreign investors.[14]

Our discussion thus far points to some of the potential advantages for a host country in committing to IIAs. These would seem to explain the high number of IIAs concluded as well as the fact that most countries in the world have seen it fit to enter into these agreements. At the same time, however, in the 1990s developing countries vociferously protested against the MAI. The MAI was proposed by the OECD in 1995 and was directed at both OECD and non-OECD member countries. It was aimed at fostering FDI liberalization and protecting investment on a multilateral basis by relying on both investor-state and state-state dispute settlement procedures. Developing countries that protested against the MAI at a range of international political forums during the late 1990s included India, Indonesia, Malaysia and Zimbabwe.[15] In light of these objections to the MAI, it seems there are some disadvantages associated with such commitments.

In order to gain further insights into these disadvantages, it is useful to follow an analytical approach. We begin by explaining the factors that induce firms to become MNEs by presenting the "knowledge capital model."[16]

The knowledge capital model

This model is based upon the observation that MNEs are frequently involved in using production processes that depend on the existence of knowledge-based assets and activities such as research and development "R&D," management, finance and marketing. More specifically, the

---

14 *Ibid* at 292.

15 See e.g. 1996 WTO Ministerial meeting in Singapore; See also Zdenek Drabek, "A Multilateral Agreement on Investment: Convincing the Sceptics" (1998) WTO ERAD Staff Working Paper 98–05; "Trade By Any Other Name", *The Economist*, November 3, 1998; see Alessandro Turrin and Dieter M. Urban, "A Theoretical Perspective on Multilateral Agreements on Investment" (2008) 16(5) Rev Int Econ 1023 for further details.

16 David L. Carr, James R. Markusen and Keith E. Maskus, "Estimating the Knowledge Capital Model of the Multinational Enterprise" (2001) 91(3) The American Economic Review 693 [Carr, Markusen and Maskus]. James R. Markusen, "Contracts, Intellectual Property Rights, and Multinational Investment in Developing Countries" (2001) 53 Journal of International Economics 189.; James R. Markusen and Keith E Maskus, "Discriminating Among Alternative Theories of the Multinational Enterprise" (2002) 10 Review of International Economics 694.

model assumes that the production process used by MNEs possesses the following features:

1. Fragmentation: the services of the knowledge-based asset can be applied to production facilities in geographically distant locations.
2. Factor intensity: the knowledge-based activity requires the use of skilled labor.
3. Jointness: the services of the knowledge-based activity can be applied to multiple production facilities without reducing its utility at each facility.[17]

Consider McDonalds for example. The knowledge-based assets it possesses include kitchen equipment and management skills. Judging from the standardized facilities used, and the services provided by McDonalds outlets worldwide, this knowledge is cheap to transport and apply to geographically distant outlets thus fulfilling the fragmentation and jointness criteria. The development of more efficient management techniques requires the use of skilled labor and occurs at the headquarters, rather than at individual outlets, thus fulfilling the factor intensity criterion. The first two criteria induce McDonalds to have a vertically integrated structure by locating its headquarters in a developed country with plenty of skilled labor whilst locating its subsidiaries or outlets in others. The jointness criterion enables McDonalds to open many outlets in different countries globally.

Like McDonalds, any firm whose production process satisfies the three above assumptions has a natural tendency to evolve into an MNE. As long as the fragmentation and factor intensity criteria are satisfied, it becomes a vertical multinational, fragmenting its production process to produce the skill intensive part in developed countries and the rest in developing countries. Indeed, this theory is empirically validated, as follows. Let inward FDI for country A denote investment in A by a firm headquartered outside A. Let outward FDI for country A denote investment outside A by a firm headquartered within A. As shown by UNCTAD's World Investment Report, the inward FDI flow to the developing world has steadily increased to reach approximately $500 billion in 2007.[18] According to Foreign Affairs and International Trade Canada's report on Trade Policy Research (2010), the developed world

17 Markusen, "Commitment to rules", *supra* note 5 at 288.
18 See UNCTAD, *World Investment Report 2008: Transnational Corporations, and the Infrastructure Challenge* (New York and Geneva: UNCTAD, 2008) in Overview and at 8.

accounted for 88 per cent of the world's outward FDI during 1980–2008 and the inward FDI received by developing countries rose sharply in 2008–09.[19] More than two-thirds of the inward FDI received by developing countries, during 1987–2007, was in the form of greenfield investments, that is, MNEs setting up subsidiaries in the host countries and re-investment of retained earnings.[20]

Having identified some of the features common to most MNEs, we are now in a position to understand how they can be used by the host country to bargain for a share of the MNE's profits once the MNE has invested.

The disadvantages of commitment

The "knowledge capital model" allows us to consider a specific channel through which the host country's agents can expropriate the profits of the MNE *ex post*, that is, by "stealing" the services of the MNE's knowledge-based asset. As noted by Glass and Saggi, several technology-intensive goods are costly to imitate.[21] Host countries pay up to 65 per cent of the cost of innovation to uncover production techniques through backward engineering, a cost they can avoid by setting low standards of intellectual property protection which allows local agents to first learn the techniques from the MNE and then to re-use it to generate private profits.[22] As Maskus points out, intellectual property rights play an even more important role in those industries where the cost of imitation has been decreasing over the decades such as pharmaceuticals, chemicals, food additives and software.[23] The fact that MNEs are concerned with IPR enforcement when deciding whether to set up a local production unit in a foreign country is well documented by numerous authors that show a clear positive relationship between the degree of IPR enforcement in developing countries and investment by US firms.[24]

19 Someshwar Rao, Malick Souare and Weimin Wang, "Canadian Inward and Outward Direct Investment: Assessing the Impacts" Foreign Affairs and International Trade, Trade Policy Research 2010: Exporter dynamics and productivity 315 at 317.
20 *Ibid* at 317–18.
21 Amy Glass and Kamal Sassi, "Intellectual Property Rights and Foreign Direct Investment" (2002) 56(2) Journal of International Economics 387 at 388 [Glass and Sassi].
22 *Ibid* at 388.
23 Keith Maskus, *Intellectual Property Rights in the Global Economy* (Washington: Institute for International Economics, 2000) at 35–6.
24 Walter Park, "Intellectual Property Rights and International Innovation" in Keith Maskus, *Frontiers of Economics and Globalization: Intellectual Property Rights and*

Bargaining over the distribution of profits

The host country's objective is to attract the investment of the MNE whilst still extracting as much of its profits as possible. By committing *ex ante* to a set of rules regarding foreign investment by signing an IIA, the host country effectively diminishes the bargaining power of its local agents to later renegotiate with the MNE for a greater share of its profits.

Let us consider again the knowledge capital model. Consider a scenario where the MNE develops a new technology, which yields returns for two periods, after which a new technology is developed by the MNE. When the MNE establishes a subsidiary in the host country, it uses the new technology in the production process. The local managers employed in the subsidiary sign a contract to stay with the MNE forever. However, after learning the new technology in the first period, they can leave and start a rival firm in the second period. This reduces the MNE's profits since it must hire a new local manager for the second period and compete against the rival firm in the second period. If this is, indeed, a credible threat to the MNE, then this can be used by the local managers to negotiate a higher salary. As a result of this bargaining process, a self-enforcing agreement will arise between the MNE and the local managers that ensures that in future periods (i) the MNE finds it profitable to invest instead of exporting, and (ii) the local managers do not wish to leave the MNE.

If, however, the host country's government commits to the enforcement of contracts and of IPR protection through an IIA (in this case, this would be functionally equivalent to committing to restrict the local managers' ability to leave the MNE in the second period) then the local managers cannot extract the higher share of profits from the MNE. This illustrates one of the main reasons why the host country may choose to retain some flexibility in its dealings with the MNE by not signing an IIA.

Globalization (Amsterdam: Elsevier Science Ltd, 2008); Jeong-Yeon Lee and Edwin Mansfield, "Intellectual Property Protection and US Foreign Direct Investment" (1996) 78(2) Review of Economic and Statistics 181; Edwin Mansfield, Mark Schwartz and Samuel Wagner, "Imitation Costs and Patents: An Empirical Study" (1981) 91(364) The Economic Journal 907. Peter Nunnenkamp and Julius Spatz, "Intellectual Property Rights and Foreign Direct Investment: A Disaggregated Analysis" (2004) 140(3) Review of World Economics 393; Lee G. Branstetter, Raymond Fisman and C Fritz-Foley, "Do Stronger Intellectual Property Rights Increase International Technology Transfer? Empirical Evidence from US Firm-Level Data" (2006) 121(1) Quarterly Journal of Economics 321; Lee Branstetter et al, "Intellectual Property Rights, Imitation, and Foreign Direct Investment Theory and Evidence" (2007) NBER Working Paper 13033.

Inability to discriminate amongst investment projects

If the returns on investment from the various MNEs differ, the host country would like to sign different contracts with each MNE where each contract matches the self-enforcing agreement between that particular MNE and the local managers.

In practice, there are many reasons why different investment projects may offer different levels of benefit to the host country. For example, some investment projects might cause a negative externality such as environmental damage. Other projects may generate positive externalities such as technological spillovers. Different projects might involve different types of knowledge transfer, some more valuable to the host country (such as knowledge of more efficient production techniques) than others (such as brand identification and advertising). The host country would benefit from retaining the flexibility to offer different financial incentives to these investors in accordance with the magnitude of the damages or benefits that each causes.[25] Indeed, nondiscrimination has emerged as one of the most sensitive issues and has dominated the arguments against MAI put forth by developing countries.[26]

Bilateral moral hazard

It is not only the host country that has an incentive to renege, the MNE may have similar incentives as well.[27] An IIA does not directly address the MNE's failure to comply with its contractual obligations. However, the contract with the state (if present) does. Also, an improvement in the "rule of law" (resulting from the conclusion of an IIA), as per the standard assumption in the related economic literature, increases the potential for enforcement of contractual obligations, for example by requiring states to provide access to impartial courts and due process.[28] Then, who gains and who loses from the MNE's commitments? By using the knowledge capital model, we illustrate using a fictitious numerical example that, under certain conditions, the MNE gains at the expense of the host country from the enforcement of IIAs.

---

25 Markusen, "Commitment to rules", *supra* note 5 at 296.
26 *Ibid* at 296.
27 *Ibid* at 297–8.
28 See also C. Schreuer, "Why Still ICSID?" (2011) *Transnational Dispute Management* at 2 who states: "Development is not just a matter of investment flows and GDP. It is also reflected in good governance and the rule of law. Investment arbitration has made a contribution to this form of development that was perhaps not intended by the drafters of the ICSID Convention and of BITs."

Consider the following scenario, similar to the one used by Markusen.[29] Time is decomposed into multiple discrete periods. The MNE produces a new product every second period. Examples of industries where new products are launched frequently include clothing lines and electronic gadgets such as cell phones and portable music devices. After two periods the product becomes obsolete and cannot be sold any longer. In other words, the "product cycle" consists of two periods. The MNE can choose whether to export the product to the host country (and earn a profit of 800 per period) or to invest in setting up a subsidiary in the host country (and earn licensing fees L_1 in period 1 and L_2 in period 2 minus the fixed cost of setting up a subsidiary F). Due to costs related to exporting (such as tariffs and transport costs), once the subsidiary has been set up, it is more profitable to produce the products within the host country rather than to export.

The MNE hires a local agent to run the subsidiary in the host country. Throughout the analysis below we follow Markusen's framework and consider the relationship between a private agent and a foreign investor, however the analysis carries through when the local agent is a state-owned firm or a joint venture owned by both the foreign investor and the local government; e.g. when the host country has several regions, provinces or states that can compete to attract the foreign investment and the MNE collaborates with provincial or regional governments in order to operate its subsidiary or the joint venture. For example, consider the leading producer of passenger cars in India: Maruti Suzuki India Ltd, a subsidiary of SMC, Japan. This company was set up in 1981 as a joint venture between the Government of India and SMC.[30]

---

29 Markusen, "Commitment to rules", *supra* note 5 at 297.
30 The energy industry also provides cases of joint ventures between governments of developing countries and MNEs. For example, Enron, between 1993–2001, had a contract with a state-owned enterprise in India, the Maharashtra State Electricity Board, whereby the latter had to pay plant maintenance fees and purchase the electricity produced by Enron at a pre-determined price. In December 1993, Enron signed a 20-year power-purchase contract with the Maharashtra State Electricity Board. The contract allowed Enron to construct a 2,015 megawatt power plant. In 1996 when India's Congress Party was no longer in power, the Indian government assessed the project as being excessively expensive and refused to pay for the plant and stopped construction. The Maharashtra State Electricity Board (MSEB), the local state run utility, was required by contract to continue to pay Enron plant maintenance charges, even if no power was purchased from the plant. The MSEB determined that it could not afford to purchase the power at Rs 8 per unit kWh charged by Enron. The plant operator was unable to find alternative customers due to the absence of an open free market in the regulated structure of utilities in India. From 1996 until Enron's bankruptcy in 2001 Enron tried to revive the project without success. See

In the following model, for simplicity, any contractual payment made by the local agent (private or state-owned) to the MNE is labeled as "licence fees." Also, it is assumed that in order to set up the subsidiary, the MNE incurs a fixed cost of F, which includes the cost of transferring the required technology, transporting or buying physical capital and training the local agent. Per period, the total profit generated by the subsidiary is 1,000 out of which the local agent must pay a licensing fee of L_i in period i to the MNE. Therefore, assuming, for simplicity, a zero discount rate between the two periods that constitute a product cycle, the agent earns $V = 2000 - L_1 - L_2$ per product cycle. Similarly, the local agent would continue to earn V per product cycle if she continued to work with the MNE forever. If the discount rate,[31] r, between product cycles is given by 0.05, then it is straightforward to show that the present value to the local agent of maintaining this relationship with the MNE forever is $V/0.05$.

A long-term contract is signed between the MNE and a local agent, but it is not "binding" in the sense that either party can defect. More specifically, a local agent who learns how to produce the new product in the first period can quit and start a rival firm in the second period. The local agent incurs a fixed cost of G to set up the new rival firm, which includes, for example, the cost of buying physical capital.

Thus far, the scenario is similar to that presented in the previous section. However, now we introduce the possibility that the MNE can also defect by firing the local agent after the first period and hiring a new one in the second. The training cost of the new agent to the MNE is 100. It is reasonable to assume that this training cost is less than the fixed cost of setting up a new subsidiary, F. In the event the local agent is a state-owned entity and the subsidiary is run by a regional government, the MNE can defect by relocating after the first period in another region (province or state) of the host country.

In the following analysis, we assume that when the MNE (or local agent) defects, it must pay a penalty of $P_M(P_A)$. The penalty is contract

Sylvie Choukroun, *Enron in Maharashtra: Power Sector Development and National Identity in Modern India* (MA Thesis, University of Pennsylvania, 2002) online: <http://lauder.wharton.upenn.edu/pages/pdf/SylvieChoukroun_Thesis.pdf>.

31 Instead of being the discount rate, the term r has an alternative interpretation. Assume that there is uncertainty over whether or not the firm will successfully develop the next generation of product. Let the probability of successfully developing a new product in the next cycle be $1/(1 + r)$ if there is a product in the current cycle, zero otherwise (i.e. once the firm fails to develop a new product, it is out of the game). The probability of having a product in the third cycle is $1/(1 + r)^2$, etc. The algebra in the model (as detailed in the appendix) is valid under either interpretation of r.

specific: that is, there exists a clause in the contract that specifies the amount of the penalty and to whom it must be paid if either the MNE or the local agent defects. To simplify the analysis, we assume that the penalty is payable to a third party (e.g. the government of the host country). However, the results hold even in the scenario where the penalty is payable by the defecting party to the other party in the contract and the economic intuition driving the results remains unchanged (this is discussed in more detail below). The levels of P_M and P_A are taken to be measures of contract enforcement. In order for the two parties to continue in this relationship, the contract must be designed in a way such that neither party has any incentive to defect, that is, the contract must be self-enforcing.

Self-enforcing contract versus exporting

In this subsection, we focus on the case where the only possibilities are that the MNE offers a self-enforcing contract and that it exports.

Let $P = P_M + P_A$. Figure 1 shows the combinations of F and G under which different outcomes occur, for a given P. More specifically, there can arise three possible outcomes depending on the values of F and G. First, the MNE may offer a contract (which specifies L_1 and L_2) to the local agent such that the MNE captures all the profits from the investment project (i.e. $V = 0$). This is known as the Rent Capture contract, denoted by RC in Figure 1. Secondly, the MNE may offer a contract to the local agent such that the local agent gets a positive share of the profits from the investment project (i.e. $V > 0$). This is known as the Rent Sharing contract, denoted by RS in Figure 1. Thirdly, the

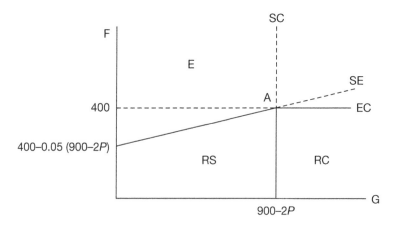

Figure 1

MNE can export to the host country, without investing in a subsidiary, denoted by E in Figure 1. For the algebraic details of the exact conditions under which each outcome occurs, please refer to the Appendix at the end of the chapter.

In Figure 1, the line SE represents the locus of points such that the MNE is indifferent between exporting and offering the Rent Sharing contract: that is, the MNE's payoff from exporting, 1,600, is equal to the payoff from the Rent Sharing contract, $L_1 + L_2 - F$.[32] SE is upward sloping because, the lower is G, the easier it is for the agent to defect and, therefore, the lower the incentive of the MNE to invest in setting up a subsidiary. The line EC represents the locus of points such that the MNE is indifferent between exporting and offering the RC contract: that is, the MNE's payoff from exporting, 1,600, is equal to the payoff from the RC contract, $2,000 - F$. The line SC represents the locus of points such that the MNE is indifferent between offering the Rent Sharing and the Rent Capture contract: that is, the MNE's payoff from the Rent Sharing contract, $L_1 + L_2 - F$, is equal to the payoff from the Rent Capture contract, $2,000 - F$.

The area to the right of SC and below EC represents those combinations of F and G such that the rent capture contract is offered. G is sufficiently large such that the local agent does not defect. The MNE takes advantage of this and captures all the profit.

The area to the right of SC and above EC represents those combinations of F and G such that the MNE exports rather than invests, since the fixed cost of setting up a subsidiary, F, is too high.

The area to the left of SC and below SE represents those combinations of F and G such that the MNE offers a rent sharing contract, RS. The area to the left of SC and above SE represents those combinations of F and G such that the MNE exports rather than invests.

Now consider an increase in contract enforcement, denoted in our model by an increase in P, as would presumably occur upon the entry into force of an IIA. Given F and G, if the optimal contract offered by the MNE is a Rent Capture contract both before and after P is increased, then both parties' earnings remain unaffected by the change in P.[33] On the other hand, if the optimal contract offered by the MNE is a Rent Sharing contract both before and after P is increased, then the MNE gains and the local agent loses. Under these conditions, therefore, the MNE gains at the expense of the host country as a result of the entry

---

32 L_1 and L_2 are given by (8) and (7) respectively in the Appendix.
33 This is shown by (5) and (6) in the Appendix.

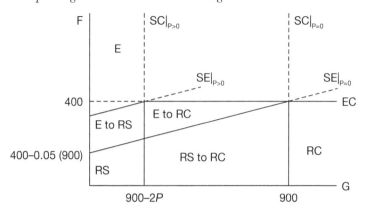

Figure 2 Note: In Figure 2, RC denotes the Rent Capture contract, RS denotes the Rent Sharing contract and E denotes Exports.

into force of an IIA that increases P. This is because when P_A increases it becomes costlier for the agent to defect. The MNE can thus charge higher license fees and still induce the agent to comply with the contract.[34]

The question that naturally arises is the following: Is it possible for a change in P to cause a switch from RS to RC or from either RS or RC to exporting. Figure 2 addresses these issues by comparing the scenario for a given $P > 0$ to that of $P = 0$.

It is assumed that, in the absence of an IIA, the penalty payable by either party if defection occurs is not enforceable. This is equivalent to setting P_A and P_M to zero in the model. Signing an IIA is assumed to provide a guarantee regarding the enforcement of an agreed upon penalty. This is equivalent to setting P_A and P_M strictly positive in the model. This is in line with UNCTAD (2009), which states that "IIAs . . . improve investment protection and add to the security, transparency, stability and predictability of the investment framework."[35] Thus both P_A and P_M would increase due to an IIA.

For a given G, as P increases, it is more likely that the contract offered will be Rent Capture rather than Rent Sharing. This is shown in Figure 2 by a shift to the left of the SC line from $SC|_{P=0}$ to $SC|_{P>0}$. In addition, SE shifts up from $SE|_{P=0}$ to $SE|_{P>0}$. This is because the increase in P_A allows the local agent to defect for a lower range of F, given any G. This decreases the holdup problem and the MNE prefers to invest rather than export, for a greater range of F, given any G.

---

34 This is shown by (9) and (10) in the Appendix.
35 See UNCTAD, "The Role of IIAs" at xii.

For those combinations of F and G such that RS switches to RC, the local agent is worse off and the MNE better off as a result of the increase in P. For those combinations of F and G such that there is a switch from exporting to RC, the local agent is indifferent and the MNE better off as a result of the increase in P. For those combinations of F and G such that there is a switch from exporting to RS, both parties are better off as a result of the increase in P.

Thus, Figure 2 illustrates that the economic intuition driving the above analysis reduces the host country's incentive to sign an IIA. In the above example, this incentive depended on the magnitudes of the set up costs of the MNE and the local agent, although in reality there may be additional factors involved that determine whether the IIA benefits the host country.

Trade costs

Thus far, we assumed that there was no cost involved in exporting. If we now allow for such a cost (e.g. a tariff or transport cost) then the host country is not indifferent between RC and exporting. This is because more is sold within the host country if the subsidiary is set up within its borders than if the MNE exports its product, due to the export cost. Hence, price is lower and consumers are better off under RC than exporting. In this case, the host country prefers the rent sharing contract over the rent capture contract *and* the rent capture contract over the exporting outcome.

Optimal policy

Suppose the host country does not commit to any international agreement and is free to set P to maximize its own welfare. Our previous discussion shows that, ideally, the host country would like to end up with a Rent Sharing contract, which is more likely to occur the lower P is. Also, from (10) it follows that the share of profits of the local agent, V, is decreasing in P. Therefore, the host country would like to set the minimum possible P such that the MNE still invests in the host country instead of exporting. The host country would also like to constrain P to be non-negative so as not to subsidize defection.

In Figure 2, if (G, F) lies above EC or to the right of $SC|_{P=0}$, then the choice of P is irrelevant. Either the MNE exports or, if it does invest, it captures all the profits, even if P is set to zero. If (G, F) lies under the line $SE|_{P=0}$ then $P = 0$ is optimal. If (G, F) lies above $SE|_{P=0}$ and below EC, then the host country sets $P > 0$ such that (G, F) lies on $SE|_{P>0}$. This makes the MNE indifferent between exporting and investing. In other words, the host country captures all profits from the investment by choosing P optimally.

This clearly demonstrates that under specific conditions, it is indeed beneficial for the host country to retain the flexibility to set P in order to maximize its own welfare, rather than having to set a high value of P due to an international agreement.

Second-period duopoly between the MNE and the first-period agent

The previous discussion has assumed that the MNE offers a self-enforcing contract to the local agent in the form of the Rent Sharing contract. However, in reality, it is often observed that local agents do defect. For example, in Latin America and East Asia, locally owned firms often employ agents who have been trained by an MNE. An example is the American Insurance Group (AIG), which spent up to 18 months training each local agent in Nigeria and the Philippines only to lose some of the trainees to other local companies in these countries during the period 1970–80.[36] The local firms are, generally, either rivals of or suppliers to the MNE. In the following discussion, we present the case where the MNE offers a contract that the MNE and the local agent know will not be self-enforcing in the second period, with the MNE and the local agent knowing that they will compete as a duopoly in the second period.

In Figure 3, DD represents the region where defection occurs and the MNE and the local agent compete in quantities in the second period. This only occurs for sufficiently low values of both F and G. The local agent defects because the cost of doing so is low, and the MNE invests anyway since the cost of setting up the subsidiary is also low. If the cost of training local agents is too high, then this region does not exist. Within DD, relative to RS, the consumer surplus is higher since the price is lower due to increased competition. However, the MNE captures all the profits generated by the subsidiary. As a result, it is not clear what the net effect on the welfare of the host country is.

The effect of raising P, for example due to the signing of an international agreement, is to shift out SE as before. This might lead to DD disappearing, as shown in Figure 4. Since a rise in P allows the MNE to pay a lower share of profits to the local agent and still satisfy the local agent's incentive compatibility constraint, as P increases it

36 Ronald Shelp et al, *Service Industries and Economic Development: Case Studies in Technology Transfer* (New York: Praeger Publishing, 1984).

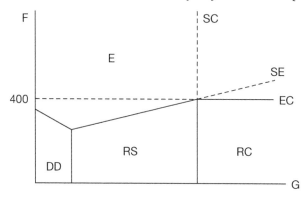

Figure 3 Note: In Figure 3, RC denotes the Rent Capture contract, RS denotes the Rent Sharing contract, and E denotes Exports.

becomes more likely that the MNE chooses the Rent Sharing contract rather than the DD outcome.

Alternative specification of penalties

Consider the following punishment scheme. Instead of paying a penalty to a third party, the defector must pay the penalty to the other party to the contract. Further, assume that the only possibilities are that the MNE offers a self-enforcing contract to the local agent or exports to the host country. In this case, it is clear that the conditions required for the MNE and the local agent to comply with the contract in the second period are the same as those when the penalty is paid to a third party, that is inequalities (1)–(3) in the Appendix. Thus, the previous analysis can be extended to this alternative specification of the penalty mechanism.

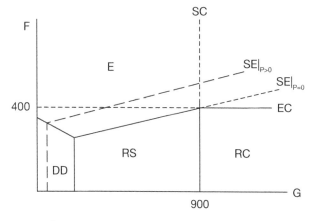

Figure 4

Empirical evidence

We submit that the main benefit to developing countries from signing an IIA is to attract otherwise unattainable FDI. The main cost is the loss of bargaining power *vis-à-vis* MNEs regarding the share of profits generated by this investment that the developing country can retain. The natural question that arises is which of these two effects dominates in reality?

Since the latter effect is mainly illustrated through the knowledge capital model in the economics literature, a first step to answering the above question is to empirically validate the main predictions of this model. This is done by a number of authors including Brainard, Ekholm, Carr, Markusen and Maskus, Chellaraj et al and Markusen and Maskus.[37] The second step is to measure the welfare effect of increased foreign investment by calibrating this model. Markusen and Strand focus on industries providing business services and find evidence that the host countries' welfare increases with inward investment. More generally, Markusen and UNCTAD, in a special report on "The Role of International Investment Agreements in attracting Foreign Direct Investment to Developing Countries"[38] summarize the empirical findings in the literature as inward direct investment generally being beneficial to developing countries.

37 Lael Brainard, "An Empirical Assessment of the Factor Proportions of Multinational Sales" (1993) NBER Working Paper 4580; Lael Brainard, "An Empirical Assessment of the Proximity-Concentration Tradeoff between Multinational Sales and Trade" (1997) 87 American Economic Review 520; Karolina Ekholm, "Mulinational Production and Trade in Technological Knowledge" PhD dissertation, Lund Economic Studies (1995); Karolina Ekholm, "Factor Endowments and the Pattern of Affiliate Production by Multinational Enterprises" (1997) CREDIT Working Paper 97/19, University of Nottingham; Karolina Ekholm, "Headquarter Services and Revealed Factor Abundance" (1998) 6 Review of International Economics 545; Karolina Ekholm, "Proximity Advantages, Scale Economies, and the Location of Production", in Pontus Braunerhjeim and Karolina Ekholm (eds), *The Geography of Multinational Firms* (Boston: Kluwer Academic, 1998); Carr, Markusen and Maskus, *supra* note 17; Ganaraj Chellaraj, Keith E Maskus and Aaditya Mattoo, "Labor Skills and Foreign Direct Investment in a Dynamic Economy: Estimating the Knowledge Capital Model for Singapore" (2009) East West Centre Working Paper, Economic Series 100; James R. Markusen and Keith E. Maskus, "Multinational Firms: Reconciling Theory and Evidence" in Magnus Blomstrom and Linda Goldberg (eds), *Topics in Empirical International Economics: A Festschrift in Honour of Robert E. Lipsey* (Chicago: University of Chicago Press, 2001).
38 James R. Markusen and Bridget Strand, "Adapting the Knowledge Capital Model of the Multinational Enterprise to Trade and Investment in Business Services" (2009) 32(1) World Economics 6; UNCTAD, "The Role of IIAs" *supra* note 11.

Appendix

In the section entitled "Bilateral Moral Hazard," we have the following.

The agent's conditions for entering and continuing the relationship

In our example, the agent earns non-negative profits as long as $V \geq 0$. In order for the agent not to want to defect it must be that its second period earnings, $1,000 - L_2$, plus the present value of continuing the relationship with the firm, $V/0.05$, exceeds the returns from defecting, $(1,000 - G - P_A)$. That is,

$$L_2 \leq G + P_A + V/0.05 \tag{1}$$

The MNE's conditions for entering and continuing the relationship

The MNE must earn more per product cycle by setting up the subsidiary, $L_1 + L_2 - F$, than from exporting, $1,600$. That is,

$$L_1 + L_2 - F \geq 1,600 \tag{2}$$

Also, for the MNE not to want to defect, it must be that the second period license fee, L_2, is greater than or equal to the returns from firing the first agent and hiring a second one, $1,000 - 100 - P_M$. That is,

$$L_2 \geq 900 - P_M \tag{3}$$

Together, (1) and (3) imply that if the following holds, then one may find values of L_1 and L_2 such that neither party defects:

$$G + P_A + V/0.05 \geq 900 - P_M \tag{4}$$

Given these constraints on the contract (that ensure that it is self-enforcing), we can have two possible outcomes depending on the magnitude of the costs associated with defection for both parties (G, P_A and P_M). Let Case 1 (2) denote the scenario where these costs are sufficiently large (small) relative to the profits per period.

Case 1: $G + P_A + P_M \geq 900$

If $G + P_A + P_M \geq 900$, then (4) is satisfied for $V = 0$. That is, as long as the costs of defection for both the MNE and the local agent are sufficiently large, the MNE captures all profits from running the subsidiary.

This is because the MNE can ensure that the contract offered to the local agent is self-enforcing without sharing any profits with the local agent, given the large cost of defection. The contract is indeed self-enforcing as long as the following conditions are met.

$$L_2 = G + P_A \tag{5}$$

satisfying (1) and

$$L_1 = 2000 - G - P_A, \tag{6}$$

satisfying $V = 0$, that is, the agent's earnings are not negative. This contract is referred to henceforth as the Rent Capture (RC) contract.

Case 2: $G + P_A + P_M < 900$

If $G + P_A + P_M < 900$, then (4) is only satisfied if $V > 0$. That is, as long as the costs of defection for both the MNE and the local agent are sufficiently small, the MNE can only ensure that the contract offered to the local agent is self-enforcing if it shares some of the profits with the local agent. This contract is referred to henceforth as the Rent Sharing (RS) contract. This contract consists of

$$L_2 = 900 - P_M, \tag{7}$$

which satisfies the MNE's condition for not defecting, as given by (3). The MNE would like to offer the minimum possible V to the local agent which still guarantees that the agent will not defect. This would be the case if (4) held with equality. Thus, we have $G + P_A + V/0.05 = 900 - P_M$ where $V = 2000 - L_1 - L_2$ and $L_2 = 900 - P_M$. This yields

$$L_1 = 1100 - 0.05\,(900 - G - P_M - P_A) + P_M \tag{8}$$

As a result, in Case 2, when the rent sharing contract is offered, the MNE earns

$$L_1 + L_2 - F = 2{,}000 - F - 0.05\,(900 - G - P_M - P_A) \tag{9}$$

and the local agent earns

$$V = 2{,}000 - L_1 - L_2 = 0.05\,(900 - G - P_M - P_A) \tag{10}$$

Part II

Efficiency

7 Investment provisions in regional trade agreements: a more efficient solution?

Armand de Mestral* and Alireza Falsafi**

Introduction

This chapter discusses the growing trend in international investment law of including investment chapters or provisions in international trade agreements. This chapter will examine the origin and development of this trend and evaluate its impact on the international investment law regime. The discussions will also touch on some of the advantages and disadvantages of including investment chapters in RTAs as opposed to BITs. The convergence or "collocation" of trade and investment provisions, whether in RTAs or BITs, is contributing to the substantive and procedural development of international investment law. There are new issues of interpretation and an overlap of standards and dispute resolution processes. The possible decline of the self-standing BIT also raises new questions concerning the efficiency of an investment chapter or provisions in an RTA, as opposed to a self-standing BIT, to promote and protect investment while at the same time maintaining the protection of public interests.

Part I surveys the background to the collocation of trade and investment treaty obligations. Part II examines the impact of collocation on the international investment law regime. Part III analyzes the efficiency of collocation from an economics perspective but also from the perspective of meeting public policy challenges.

The collocation of trade and investment obligations

This part describes the recent trend to collocate trade and investment obligations and explores the reasons explaining this trend.

* Emeritus Professor, Jean Monnet Professor of Law, McGill University.
** PhD McGill University, 2011.

What has been happening?

RTAs are a significant feature of contemporary international trade law. Since 1994, we have witnessed the adoption of some 300 RTAs alongside the 2,800 existing BITs, most of which have been negotiated and entered into force during the same period. In 2011, some 267 RTAs had been notified to the WTO Committee on Regional Trade Agreements.[1] Traditionally, RTAs and BITs have existed in separate legal universes. But in recent years, a number of RTAs have addressed investment issues, either in the form of complete chapters or general provisions. This phenomenon ushers in a distinct pattern of investment "agreement" as part of trade and investment treaties and constitutes a new category of treaty: the trade and investment agreement "TIA."

TIA is used to refer to trade agreements that include investment chapters or provisions but do not include agreements that refer solely to future negotiations or cooperation as to investment. This emerging trend finds some of its origins in earlier Friendship, Commerce and Navigation Treaties "FCN" that covered both trade and investment liberalization.[2] So far, close to 40 TIAs exist at the bilateral, regional and interregional levels.[3] It is certainly too early to suggest that the age of the BIT is

1 Committee on Regional Trade Agreements (CRTA), online: WTO <http://www.wto. org/english/tratop_e/region_e/regcom_e.htm> [CRTA].
2 See Alireza Falsafi, "Regional Trade and Investment Agreements: Liberalizing Investment in a Preferential Climate" (2008) 36(1) Syracuse J Int'l L & Com 43 at 85. (This ranges from economic communities to free trade agreements and economic partnership agreements with varying objectives, scopes, and contents at regional or interregional levels and between two states, several states or groups of states in the body of the economic agreement or in a separate instrument.)
3 Some recently concluded agreements include: *Free Trade Agreement between Canada and the Republic of Panama*, May 14, 2010, online: DFAIT< http://www.international. gc.ca/trade-agreements-accords-commerciaux/agr-acc/panama/panama-toc-panama-tdm.aspx?lang=eng&view=d > [*Canada–Panama FTA*]; *Agreement between the Government of the United States of America and the Government of the Sultanate of Oman on the Establishment of a Free Trade Area*, January 1, 2009, online: USTR <http://www. ustr.gov/sites/default/files/uploads/agreements/fta/oman/asset_upload_file345_8820. pdf>; *India-Korea Comprehensive Economic Partnership Agreement*, August 7, 2009, online: India Department of Commerce <http://commerce.nic.in/trade/india%20 korea%20cepa%202009.pdf> [*India-Korea Partnership*]; *Free Trade Agreement between the People's Republic of China and the Government of the Republic of Peru*, April 28, 2009, online: MOFCOM <http://fta.mofcom.gov.cn/topic/enperu.shtml>; *Agreement Establishing the ASEAN-Australia-New Zealand Free Trade Area*, February 27, 2009, online: ASEAN <http://www.asean.org/22260.pdf>; *Free Trade Agreement Between The Government of New Zealand And the People's Republic of China*, October 1, 2008, online: MFAT <http://www.chinafta.govt.nz/1-The-agreement/2-Text-of-the-agreement/ index.php> [*New Zealand–China FTA*]; *Agreement on Free Trade and Economic Partnership between Japan and Swiss Confederation*, 1 September 2009, online: MOFA <http://www.

over—many are currently under negotiation.[4] But there is reason to conclude that because an increasing number of trade agreements, including trade agreements under negotiation,[5] do include investment provisions, that we may well be seeing the end of RTAs that do not deal with investment issues at all.

The majority of contemporary RTAs include whole chapters, or at least significant provisions, on trade in services such as financial services. This trend began with the adoption of the Canada-United States Free Trade Agreement in 1988.[6] The pattern was further set with the adoption of NAFTA in 1994, when the US Model BIT was used as the basis for drafting Chapter 11.[7] It is most apparent in the context of regional trade arrangements involving a number of countries such as the MERCOSUR,[8] ASEAN,[9] which adopted a major self-standing investment agreement in

---

mofa.go.jp/region/europe/switzerland/epa0902/agreement.pdf>; *Australia-Chile Free Trade Agreement*, July 30, 2008, online: DFATA <http://dfat.gov.au/fta/aclfta/ Australia-Chile-FTA.html>; *Peru-Singapore Free Trade Agreement*, May 29, 2008, online: OAS <http://www.sice.oas.org/TPD/PER_SGP/Final_Texts_PER_SGP_e/ index_e.asp> [*Peru-Singapore FTA*]; *Agreement between Japan and Brunei Darussalam for an Economic Partnership*, June 18, 2007, online: MOFA <http://www.mofa.go.jp/ region/asia-paci/brunei/epa0706/agreement.pdf>; *The EU-South Korea Free Trade Agreement (FTA)*, October 6, 2010, online: EC <http://ec.europa.eu/trade/creating-opportunities/bilateral-relations/countries/korea/> [*EU South Korea FTA*]; and some Agreements signed by Singapore, see online: Singapore government website <http:// www.fta.gov.sg/>. See also Falsafi, *supra* note 2 at notes 16–17.

4 See UNCTAD, *World Investment Report 2011*, UNCTAD/WIR/2011 at 100 [UNCTAD, *World Investment*]. 23 new BITs were concluded in the first five months of 2010 and many are currently being negotiated; see also "Canada's Foreign Investment Promotion and Protection Agreements" for a list of Canada's FIPAs currently being negotiated and those recently concluded, online: DFAIT <http://www.international. gc.ca/trade-agreements-accords-commerciaux/agr-acc/fipa-apie/index.aspx?view=d>.

5 See e.g. Canada-EU negotiating text for a Comprehensive International Trade Agreement. *Canada-European Union: Comprehensive Economic and Trade Agreement (CETA) Negotiations*, online: DFAIT <http://www.international.gc.ca/trade-agreements-accords-commerciaux/ agr-acc/eu-ue/can-eu.aspx?view=d>.

6 *Free Trade Agreement Between Canada and the United States of America*, January 2, 1988 (entered into force January 1, 1989), online: DFAIT <http://www.international.gc.ca/ trade-agreements-accords-commerciaux/agr-acc/us-eu.aspx?lang=eng&view=d>.

7 *North American Free Trade Agreement Between the Government of Canada, the Government of Mexcio and the Government of the United States*, December 17, 1992, Can TS 1994 No. 2 (entered into force January 1, 1994) [NAFTA].

8 See *Treaty of Asuncion*, Argentina, Brazil, Paraguay and Uruguay, March 26, 1991, online: Mercosur—(common market of the south) <http://www.worldtradelaw.net/ fta/agreements/mercosurfta.pdf>.

9 See *ASEAN Declaration (Bangkok Declaration)*, Indonesia, Malaysia, Philippines, Singapore and Thailand, 8 August 1967, online: Association of Southeast Asian Nations <http://www.asean.org>.

2009, COMESA,[10] the Andean Community,[11] the CARICOM,[12] and the EEA.[13] The most complete regional agreement, the EU, has always involved extensive commitments on the free movement of services and the right of establishment of service providers. EU treaties deal extensively with investment issues, although frequently under the rubric of freedom of establishment or the regulation of financial services.[14] One major multilateral treaty, the ECT,[15] contains significant provisions on investment protection.

Why has it been happening?

The context for this trend is one of enduring tension between free trade and social concerns.[16] In this chapter, "social concerns" or the "social dimension" are expressions used broadly to encompass consumer protection, intellectual property rights, labor rights, human rights, environmental protection, climate change and other social concerns that have traditionally been disconnected from trade. Some of these social concerns, such as intellectual property rights, have already been included in the multilateral trading system, but most have not.[17]

---

10 The Common Market for Eastern and Southern Africa (COMESA) was formed in December 1994 to replace the former Preferential Trade Area (PTA) as an organization of free independent sovereign states that agreed to cooperate in developing their natural and human resources for the good of all of their people. See online: COMESA <http://about.comesa.int/>.

11 The Andean Community is made up of four countries (Bolivia, Colombia, Ecuador and Peru) that decided voluntarily to join together for the purpose of achieving more rapid, better-balanced and more autonomous development through Andean, South American and Latin American integration. See online: Comunidad Andina <http://www.comunidadandina.org/>.

12 See *Treaty Establishing the Caribbean Community*, July 4, 1973, online: Caribbean Community <http://www.caricom.org/>.

13 *Agreement on the European Economic Area—Final Act—Joint Declarations—Declarations by the Governments of the Member States of the Community and the EFTA States—Arrangements—Agreed Minutes—Declarations by one or several of the Contracting Parties of the Agreement on the European Economic Area*, May 2, 1992, online: EU Treaties Office Database <http://ec.europa.eu/world/agreements/prepareCreateTreatiesWorkspace/treatiesGeneralData.do?step=0&redirect=true&treatyId=1>.

14 As of 2009, *Treaty on the Functioning of the European Union*, March 30, 2010, online: Europa <http://eur-lex.europa.eu/LexUriServ/LexUriServ.do?uri=OJ:C:2010:083:0047:0200:en:PDF> at arts 206, 207: explicit reference to "direct foreign investment."

15 *Energy Charter Treaty* 17 December 17, 1994, 2080 UNTS 36116, 34 ILM 360.

16 Sungjoon Cho, "Linkage of Free Trade and Social Regulation: Moving Beyond the Entropic Dilemma" (2005) 5 Chicago J Int'l L 625 at 626 [Cho].

17 *Agreement on Trade-Related Aspects of Intellectual Property Rights*, reproduced in WTO, *The Legal Texts: Results of the Uruguay Round of Multilateral Trade Negotiations* (Cambridge: Cambridge University Press, 1999) [WTO Agreements].

In reality, it is very difficult, for example, to separate trade in services and the regulation of foreign investment. On the one hand, governments value trade liberalization and the accompanying liberalization of financial services, because it is economically beneficial and ultimately welfare-enhancing. Indeed, since the mid-1990s, contemporary international trade negotiations, whether multilateral, regional or bilateral, have been marked by an ever-increasing realization that trade liberalization must include the liberalization of services if it is to capture the reality of contemporary international commerce.[18] On the other hand, governments want to maintain a certain measure of regulatory sovereignty over domestic social issues to guarantee a better quality of life in the face of global unfamiliarity and unpredictability. As a compromise, an effective domestic regulatory framework was given autonomy within the multilateral trading system in order to address social concerns. However, it is by no means clear that an effective domestic regulatory framework exists in many countries or indeed that it is envisaged by most BITs. There is an increasing realization that a social dimension should be included in the current global trading system to build an "integrated, more viable and durable multilateral trading system."[19]

Many reasons can be advanced to explain the increasing practice in recent years of collocating trade and investment provisions in trade agreements. The most obvious reason is that investment issues, which formed part of the "Singapore Issues" included in the Doha Round of Multilateral Trade Negotiations, were subsequently taken out of the negotiations.[20] This limited the negotiating options of those WTO members that wished to expand foreign investment protection and moderate investment controls by other states at the multilateral level. The removal of investment issues from the WTO trade agenda has made it necessary for states to pursue other options in regional and bilateral trade agreements. This phenomenon predated the Doha Round,

---

18 Mona Haddad and Constantinos Stephanos (eds), *Financial Services and Preferential Trade Agreements: Lessons from Latin America* (Washington, DC: The World Bank, 2010) at 4; see also "The Benefits of Services Trade Liberalization," International Chamber of Commerce Policy Statement, 7 September 1999, ICC Doc 103/210, online: ICC <http://www.iccwbo.org/policy/trade/id413/index.html>.

19 Cho, *supra* note 16 at 646.

20 "Doha Round" refers to the trade negotiations that were launched by the Ministerial Conference, the WTO's highest decision-making body, in Doha, Qatar in November 2001. The Doha Round was followed by Fifth Session of the Ministerial Conference in Cancún, Mexico, of September 10–14, 2003 where investment issues were taken out of the negotiations. See WTO, online: The Fifth WTO Ministerial Conference <http://www.wto.org/english/thewto_e/minist_e/min03_e/min03_e.htm>.

but it appears to have been accelerated by the declining pace of the Round.

Another reason for the inclusion of investment provisions in trade agreements, also linked to the pace of negotiations within the WTO, is the entry into force of the General Agreement on Trade in Services "GATS"[21] in 1994 as part of the new WTO package of agreements (that includes a Protocol on Financial Services[22]). Despite the initial reservations of many developing countries, the Uruguay Round of Multilateral Trade Negotiations was expanded to include services and succeeded in adopting the GATS as an integral part of the WTO package of legally binding agreements. The GATS has set off a pattern of negotiating the liberalization of services, such as financial services, and this has had a direct impact on the treatment of foreign investment. Thus the liberalization of certain forms of investment controls has been launched under the guise of service liberalization. The pace of the negotiation of concessions by WTO members liberalizing trade in financial services under the aegis of the GATS has been relatively slow. While the GATS opens up this field to negotiations, it has not compelled all states to seek to liberalize their trade in financial services, and those states wishing to make progress have again had to look to their regional and bilateral trade agreement options. Generally, the commitments made in the context of an FTA are more extensive than those required under the GATS.[23]

Another equally significant reason for the trend to include investment provisions in trade agreements is the fact that, until the adoption of the *Treaty of Lisbon* in 2009,[24] the EU, one of the principal negotiators of RTAs, could only negotiate investment issues in the context of trade agreements.[25] Although the Common Commercial Policy of the EU has

21 *General Agreement on Trade in Services* (GATS), in WTO Agreements, *supra* note 17.
22 *WTO: Financial Services: Protocols*, online: WTO <http://www.wto.org/english/tratop_e/serv_e/5prote_e.htm>.
23 See Jean-Pierre Chauffour and Jean-Christophe Maur (eds), *Preferential Trade Agreement Policies for Development: A Handbook* (Washington, DC: The World Bank, 2011) at 257; Jane Kelsey, "Embedding the Neoliberal Transformation of Government Services Through Trade in Service Agreements" in Shawkat Alam, Natalie Klein and Juliette Overland (eds), *Globalisation and the Quest for Social and Environmental Justice: The Relevance of International Law in an Evolving World Order* (New York: Routledge, 2011) at 119.
24 *Treaty of Lisbon amending the Treaty on European Union and the Treaty establishing the European Community*, December 13, 2007, online: Europa <http://eur-lex.europa.eu/JOHtml.do?uri=OJ:C:2007:306:SOM:en:HTML> at 1.
25 The *Treaty of Lisbon* expanded the Common Commercial Policy by amending arts 206 and 207 of the *Treaty on the Functioning of the European Union (TFEU)*. See also De Mestral, "The Lisbon Treaty and the Expansion of EU Competence Over Foreign

now been expanded to include "foreign direct investment," the EU Commission has not sought to, nor has it been given a mandate to, negotiate a self-standing BIT and it continues, as it is doing with Canada,[26] to negotiate investment issues in the context of FTAs.

As the experience of the EU demonstrates, it is very difficult to separate trade in services and the regulation of foreign investment. Indeed, in many respects, freedom of establishment accomplishes many of the things that are achieved under trade agreements by commitments as to entry of services and service providers. The two are inseparable in many respects. The chapters on services in the Canada-United States FTA and NAFTA were thus quite naturally complemented by chapters on the protection of foreign investment. This pattern has continued in a number of more recent agreements such as the China-New Zealand FTA of April 2008.[27] This close link between services and investment protections is surely one of the principal reasons that it has been deemed appropriate to incorporate investment provisions into trade agreements.

Finally, it would appear that we are witnessing the broadening of the trade agenda, which now embraces a variety of issues that only a few years ago would have been deemed to be "non-trade" matters. The "non-trade" matters have been inevitably extended to matters touching upon investment protection and promotion. This broadening of the trade agenda has been necessitated by the realization that international trade must include a social dimension to ensure scope for domestic social policy choices, which run the risk of being rendered ineffective by external pressures in an increasingly globalized world.

Impact on the international investment law regime

The broadening of the international trade agenda is also contributing to the substantive and procedural development of the international investment law regime. In particular, the increasing inclusion of investment provisions in trade agreements poses new questions regarding the proper interpretation of such provisions. Should they be interpreted in exactly the same manner as similar provisions in a self-standing BIT or does the

---

Direct Investment and the Implications for Investor-State-Arbitration" in Karl P. Sauvant (ed), *Yearbook on International Investment Law and Policy* (Oxford: Oxford University Press, 2010) at 365–89.

26 See e.g. *the Comprehensive Economic and Trade Agreement currently under negotiation with Canada or the Free Trade Agreements currently under negotiation with India or Singapore*, Online: Europa <http://ec.europa.eu/enterprise/policies/international/facilitating-trade/free-trade/index_en.htm>.

27 *New Zealand-China FTA, supra* note 3.

fact that they are collocated with trade liberalization provisions in a trade agreement require that they be interpreted in the broader context provided by the TIA? In other words, does the inclusion of investment provisions in a broader context not have an impact upon their meaning and purpose? Besides the interpretation issues, the convergence of trade and investment may also have led to a blurring of the lines between trade and investment law, an overlap of their standards and dispute resolution processes, a decline in the number of self-standing BITs and structural changes within the WTO.

Interpretation of investment provisions in trade agreements

The first question in response to the new trend is whether investment provisions inserted into a trade agreement should be interpreted in the broader context provided by the TIA. The interpretation issue concerns the qualification of a trade activity as a foreign investment and, where the activity is a covered investment, the scope of the protection provided for under the investment provisions. These issues have been raised in a number of NAFTA cases.

Qualification as investment

On the jurisdictional issue, the *Pope and Talbot* tribunal held that a trade in goods might qualify as investment under NAFTA Chapter 11.[28] Similarly, adopting the approach of the WTO Panel in the *Korean Dairy Products* case,[29] the *S.D. Myers* tribunal considered that different provisions of a trade agreement should be regarded as complementary and cumulative unless a conflict arises where adherence to one leads to the violation of another.[30] On that basis, the tribunal concluded that a measure that concerns goods under Chapter 3 of NAFTA could also relate to an investor or investment under Chapter 11 and that disputes regarding investments concerning those goods are covered under Chapter 11 unless excluded.[31] In the damages phase, the *S.D. Myers* tribunal also referred to the cumulative concept to hold that the trade

28 *Pope & Talbot Inc v Government of Canada*, Award, UNCITRAL (January 26, 2000) at para 26.
29 *Korea—Definitive Safeguard Measure on Imports of Certain Dairy Products* (1999), WTO Doc WT/DS98/R (Panel Report).
30 *S.D. Myers, Inc. v Government of Canada*, Partial Award, UNCITRAL (November 13, 2000) at paras 292–5.
31 *Ibid* at paras 294–6.

activity of a service provider under Chapter 12 of NAFTA that also qualifies the service provider as an investor under Chapter 11 opens the recourse to investor-state arbitration under Chapter 11.[32] The tribunal ruled that the existence of one right under one chapter of the trade agreement did not take away the other unless they were mutually exclusive or expressly excluded.[33] The tribunal further suggested that once the investment chapter is engaged, its application is not limited to investment activities but applies to cross-border services of the investor involved in its investment.[34] Apparently, the tribunal considered the overall investment activity of the service provider without separating the cross-border services involved for the purposes of the losses incurred by the investor. This line of reasoning was upheld in the recent Chapter 11 sweeteners cases against Mexico.[35] In *Cargill*, the tribunal notably held that there is "no express or implied presumption that measures dealing with goods cannot *ipso facto* be alleged to be measures 'relating to' investors or investments per Article 1101."[36]

A different issue arose in the *Canadian Cattlemen* case.[37] In this case, the claimants argued that the existence of an investment chapter in the context of NAFTA carried the implication that those who invested in one of the three integrated markets for the purpose of exporting to the two others should be considered as investors in all three,[38] or put in other words, that NAFTA carried no territorial limitation as to where they should invest to enjoy the protections of Chapter 11. The claimants contended that the NAFTA tribunal had jurisdiction for the dispute arising from the US ban on the importation of the Canadian cattle into the United States in 2003 that allegedly gave rise to a breach of the national treatment obligation under NAFTA article 1102 and caused

32 *S.D. Myers, Inc. v Government of Canada*, Second Partial Award, UNCITRAL (October 21, 2002) at paras 131–9.
33 *Ibid* at paras 131–2.
34 *Ibid* at para 139: "[t]he fact that some of the totality of SDMI's losses due to interference with its investment involved cross-border services does not prevent SDMI from recovering them."
35 *Cargill, Incorporated v United Mexican States*, Award, ICSID Case No. ARB (AF)/05/2 (September 18, 2009); *Corn Products International, Inc. v United Mexican States*, Decision on Responsibility, ICSID Case No. ARB (AF)/04/1 (January 15, 2008); *Archer Daniels Midland and Tate & Lyle Ingredients America, Inc. v United Mexican States*, Award, ICSID Case No. ARB (AF)/04/5 (November 21, 2007).
36 *Cargill, supra* note 35 at para 153.
37 *The Canadian Cattlemen for Fair Trade v The United States of America*, Award on Jurisdiction, UNCITRAL (January 28, 2008) [*Cattlemen*].
38 *Ibid* at paras 39, 99.

damages to their investment located in Canada.[39] They argued that, by raising cattle in Canada for trade to the United States, they were in fact investors in the United States. The United States objected to the jurisdiction of the tribunal, arguing that NAFTA Chapter 11 did not cover investment located solely in the home state and that the claimants were not in fact investors in the United States.[40] The United States argued that NAFTA Chapter 11 did not have a broader scope than BITs.[41] The tribunal agreed with the United States' position, holding that only investors whose investments were located in the territory of another NAFTA party could benefit from NAFTA Chapter 11.[42] But the tribunal did state, contrary to US claims, that Chapter 11 "cannot be reduced simply to an ordinary bilateral investment treaty," in part because "it functions as part of a larger agreement that requires analysis of how the different parts of the treaty interrelate in a range of circumstances."[43] Ultimately, the tribunal declined jurisdiction under Chapter 11 because the object of NAFTA Chapter 11 is to protect *foreign* investors.[44]

Scope of investment protection

The interaction between the trade and investment chapters of TIAs is also evident with respect to the substantive protection of investment. This aspect of the question primarily relates to the extent of the obligations of state parties under the investment chapter in relation to other provisions of the TIA. More broadly, the issue concerns the question of the extent of investment protection in view of the overall framework of TIAs in contrast to BITs.

39 *Ibid* at paras 39, 78–105.
40 See *ibid* at paras 3, 38, 52–77. The United States argued that the claimants' disputes were trade disputes that were subject to a state-to-state settlement mechanism under NAFTA ch 20 or elsewhere, and that allowing claimants to invoke the NAFTA ch 11 dispute settlement mechanism for such cross-border trade disputes "constitutes a radical departure from the obligations that NAFTA Parties, or any State Party to an international investment agreement, have ever undertaken with respect to foreign investors" (para 38).
41 See *ibid* at para 53.
42 See *ibid* at para 111. The decision of the tribunal in rejecting the claimants' assertion was also based on the broader context of NAFTA: see *ibid* at paras 113–14, 130.
43 *Ibid* at para 164.
44 *Ibid* at paras 169, 193, 233. The tribunal held that the remedy for the dispute, being a cross-border trade, fell under ch 20 of NAFTA (state-to-state arbitration) (para 193).

In the *Metalclad* case, the tribunal found that the transparency provisions set out in Chapter 18 of NAFTA and drawn from the principles of article 102(1) that set out the objectives of NAFTA provide a clear legal framework to investors.[45] This aspect of the award was set aside by the Supreme Court of British Columbia (BC).[46] The BC Supreme Court held that, by relying on transparency as one of the objectives of NAFTA, the *Metalclad* tribunal exceeded the scope of the submission to arbitration because there was no transparency obligation in Chapter 11.[47]

The *Pope and Talbot* tribunal also took an expansive approach to interpreting the objectives of NAFTA. That tribunal relied on the objectives of NAFTA to decide that, by placing an investment chapter in a trade agreement, the state parties had intended to set a higher standard of fairness than might be required by a mere BIT. The tribunal suggested that this was its preferred approach despite Canada's insistence that, whatever the meaning of fair and equitable treatment in BITs, the NAFTA parties had not intended to go beyond customary international law.[48] The tribunal reasoned that Canada and the United States had, in their BITs with other countries, adopted the additive fairness elements of fair and equitable treatment and, by reference to the NAFTA objective under article 102(1) to "increase substantially investment opportunities," found itself unable to accept that NAFTA parties intended to limit investment protection between themselves.[49] The three NAFTA parties vigorously objected to the expansive interpretation given by the tribunals in *S.D. Myers, Metalclad* and *Pope and Talbot* including regarding the consequences of placing an investment chapter in a trade agreement. In order to prevent such interpretations by other tribunals under Chapter 11, the parties issued a Statement of Interpretation in July 2001, explaining that article 1105 prescribed the minimum standard of treatment of aliens at customary international law.[50] Several Chapter 11 tribunals held that it was their duty to abide by the

---

45 *Metalclad Corpn v The United Mexican States*, ICSID, Case No. ARB (AF)/97/1 (August 30, 2000) at paras 88 and 99.
46 *The United Mexican States v Metalclad Corpn*, 2001 BCSC 664 at para 72.
47 *Ibid* at paras 71–2.
48 *Pope & Talbot Inc. v Government of Canada*, Award on the Merits of Phase 2, UNCITRAL (April 10, 2001) at paras 114–15.
49 *Ibid* at para 115.
50 Notes of Interpretation of Certain Chapter 11 Provisions. This interpretation was adopted pursuant to NAFTA art 1131 (NAFTA Free Trade Commission, July 31, 2001), online: DFAIT http://www.international.gc.ca/trade-agreements-accords-commerciaux/disp-diff/NAFTA-Interpr.aspx?lang=en>.

Statement of Interpretation.[51] In 2009, the *Glamis* tribunal again followed this approach.[52]

The *Cattlemen* case also involved a substantive dimension in terms of the objectives of the NAFTA as a TIA rather than as a BIT. Despite rejecting jurisdiction because of the lack of investment as defined under NAFTA, the tribunal in that case stated that NAFTA Chapter 11 "cannot be reduced simply to an ordinary bilateral investment treaty."[53] According to the tribunal, that chapter "functions as part of a larger agreement that requires analysis of how the different parts of the treaty interrelate in a range of circumstances."[54]

While the *Metalclad* and *Cattlemen* tribunals tended to expand the substantive investment protection in comparison to BITs, the *Pope and Talbot* tribunal attempted to place NAFTA above BITs and asserted an even broader standard of protection based on the general objectives of NAFTA. The *Glamis* tribunal and others ruling after the July 2001 Statement of Interpretation stand in contrast. These cases reflect the NAFTA standard but may not demonstrate a definitive conclusion as to the special position of TIAs for either broadening or narrowing the extent of investment protection in substantive terms. State practice, as witnessed by the Statement of Interpretation, sheds light as to what the NAFTA states intended, but not necessarily what other states using similar language in BITs intended.

In conclusion, it is still too early to assert that the inclusion of investment provisions in trade agreements changes the scope of both the trade and investment provisions. However, the collocation of two broad fields of law, which have long remained separate, can hardly be without legal consequences. As with all trade and investment treaties, the text in context must be the first consideration when it is interpreted. Interestingly, while the words do not always change, the context may well be changing. The words of treaties must always be given meaning and it is a truism to suggest that the same words in different contexts can have different meanings. Exactly where this is leading is not yet clear, but it would be wrong to suggest that nothing has changed.

---

51 See e.g. *ADF Group Inc. v United States of America*, Award, ICSID Case No. ARB(AF)/00/1 (January 9, 2003); *Mondev International Ltd v United States of America*, Award, ICSID Case No. ARB(AF)/99/2 (October 11, 2002).
52 *Glamis Gold Ltd v the United States of America*, Award, UNCITRAL (June 8, 2009) at para 606.
53 *Cattlemen, supra* note 37 at para 164.
54 *Ibid.*

The possible coalescing of trade and investment law

As demonstrated by the NAFTA cases, the line between trade and investment is no longer as bright under the new regime as it was in the age of the self-standing BIT. Arguably, we are witnessing the beginning of the end of the rigid distinction between trade and investment law. The most fully integrated of all regional trade agreements, the EU, clearly demonstrates that the free movement of goods and services cannot be separated from the movement of capital within a customs union. Even the WTO, the multilateral arrangement that constitutes the lowest level of economic integration binding on its 153 members, is moving in this direction through the TRIPS Agreement and financial service commitments under the GATS. The walls are still high between the worlds of international trade and finance, but they do appear to be coming down. This is certainly the direction suggested by the more than 40 TIAs now in existence and those currently under negotiation.

Overlap in trade and investment standards

With the blurring of the line between trade and investment, comes the convergence of the standards used in both. We are witnessing an increasing use in international investment law of a number of standards originally developed in the context of trade law. That the two should fit relatively well should be no surprise as the basic standards such as MFN and National Treatment emerged from the practice surrounding FCN Treaties, which embraced matters of trade in goods and services, establishment and investment, as well as standards of treatment of aliens. The MFN Treatment, National Treatment, and Fair and Equitable Treatment standards have been grafted into BITs, as well as into TIAs, with little need for adaptation, except for the obvious need to distinguish no less favorable treatment of "similarly situated" investments for the application of MFN and National Treatment obligations.[55] If there is a process of coalescing of trade and investment law occurring in TIAs, the process is being assisted by recourse to common legal standards used in international trade.

Confusion of dispute resolution processes

A further consequence of the convergence of trade and investment relates to dispute settlement. The practice under many BITs has been to

---

55 See *India-Korea Partnership, supra* note 3; *Peru-Singapore FTA, supra* note 3; *Canada-Panama FTA, supra* note 3.

provide for investor-state arbitration, frequently having recourse to the services of ICSID. Some investment chapters in trade agreements, such as Chapter 11 of NAFTA or Chapter 11 of the China-New Zealand FTA of April 2008,[56] incorporate exactly the same process. Other recent agreements, such as the EU-Korea FTA of October 6, 2010,[57] have adopted a form of investor-state claim that is submitted to an interstate arbitration procedure rather than allowing a direct claim by an investor against a state party. Given the reservations expressed by EU parliamentarians in the 2011 debates concerning the extension of EU competence over foreign direct investment,[58] it is possible that the EU Commission may not wish to commit to true investor-state procedures in the future. Australia has recently announced its intention to avoid commitment to investor-state arbitration in future RTAs and TIAs.[59] There is thus the possibility of divergent dispute settlement practice between BITs and TIAs. This may be compounded by the fact that many trade agreements incorporate a WTO-style panel process, which is almost always on an interstate basis and not necessarily adapted to the particularities of investment disputes.[60]

From the investor's standpoint, the inclusion of an investor-state procedure in a TIA is the optimal outcome of such negotiations. So far, the majority of the TIAs reviewed appear to adopt this approach. But some do not and there is the possibility that investment disputes under TIAs in the future will come to be subject to more general dispute settlement processes. There is a distinct possibility that investor-state

---

56 See *New Zealand-China FTA, supra* note 3.

57 *EU-South Korea FTA, supra* note 3.

58 See "EU investment policy needs to balance investor protection and public regulation, says International Trade Committee", Press release, online: European Parliament <http://www.europarl.europa.eu/en/pressroom/content/20110314IPR 15476/html/EU-investment-policy-needs-to-balance-investor-protection-and-public-regulation>.

59 Australian Government, Department of Foreign Affairs and Trade, "Gillard Government Trade Policy Statement: Trading our way to more jobs and prosperity", April 2011, online: Australian Government <http://www.dfat.gov.au/publications/ trade/trading-our-way-to-more-jobs-and-prosperity.html>.

60 See e.g. *Free Trade Agreement Between the Government of Canada and the State of Israel*, July 31, 1996 (entered into force January 1, 1997), online: DFAIT <http://www. international.gc.ca/trade-agreements-accords-commerciaux/agr-acc/israel/toc-tdm. aspx?lang=eng&view=d> *Economic Partnership Agreement between the CARIFORUM States, of the one part, and the European Community and its Member States, of the other part*, October 15, 2008, OJ Ref L/289, 30.10.08 (WTO Consideration ongoing), online: EU <http://ec.europa.eu/world/agreements/prepareCreateTreatiesWorkspace/ treatiesGeneralData.do?step=0&redirect=true&treatyId=7407>.

arbitration will disappear between Member States of the EU[61] and, for a variety of reasons, this may also happen under other trade agreements negotiated by the EU.

Possible desuetude of the self-standing BIT?

Another possible impact of the inclusion of investment provisions in trade agreements may ultimately be a decline in the number of self-standing BITs. It is certainly too early to assert that there is a definite trend in this direction. There are some 2,800 BITs in existence,[62] while only some 40 TIAs and one major energy agreement, which include investment provisions, have been counted. All that can be asserted with certainty is that this number appears to be increasing, and that it represents a much more important proportion of the 300 existing RTAs than of the total number of BITs. BITs continue to be negotiated, often by governments that are also negotiating comprehensive TIAs with other states. The BIT is often seen as the precursor to the development of deeper economic ties.[63] What does seem to have happened is that it has become much less common to negotiate a comprehensive economic relationship at the regional or bilateral level without including investment considerations in the trade treaty.

Convenience

Another possible cause of the current trend is that governments are realizing the convenience of including investment issues in a total trade package. Given the close links between trade and investment issues in the modern global economy, this development is very understandable and seems likely to continue.

WTO review of investment provisions

The increasing convergence of trade and investment may also affect the structure of the current multilateral trading system, embodied by

---

61 See de Mestral, "The Evolving Role of the European Union in International Investment Agreement Treaty-Making", at ch 3 of this book.

62 See UNCTAD, *World Investment, supra* note 4 at 100, which refers to 2,807 BITs (proper). It must be noted, however, that the UNCTAD database that justifies this number includes a variety of agreements apart from pure self-standing BITs.

63 See e.g. "Middle East Free Trade Area Initiative," online, Office of the United States Trade Representative: <http://www.ustr.gov/trade-agreements/other-initiatives/middle-east-free-trade-area-initiative-mefta>; Cliff Sosnow, "Canada-China Investment Protection Agreement—A Significant Stepping Stone to Deeper Economic Co-Operation," online: Blakes <http://www.blakes.com/english/view_disc.asp?ID=43>.

the WTO. In 1996, the WTO established a major standing committee, the Committee on Regional Trade Agreements (CRTA), with a view to strengthening the degree of scrutiny of these agreements under the GATT article XXIV.[64] Ten years later, in order to further strengthen the process, the WTO adopted the "Transparency Mechanism."[65] The purpose of the CRTA, acting pursuant to the Transparency Mechanism, is to review the operation of new RTAs and to report to the WTO membership. The CRTA takes no decision on the conformity of the RTAs with the GATT. These issues are formally left to dispute settlement, although, in the process of review, WTO members are able to question the parties to new RTAs as to their conformity with the letter and the spirit of WTO law. The CRTA must review the complete agreement, including the investment provisions; in this way, the WTO, whose general mandate in respect of investment issues is relatively limited, is gradually being drawn into debate on these questions.

Overall, the full legal impact of including investment provisions in trade agreements is far from clear at this point. The most obvious implication drawn by a few arbitrators, namely that such inclusion is a sign that the states party to the TIAs in question intended to raise the level of protection, has been repudiated by the three NAFTA governments, and EU parliamentarians appear to be following suit. But it remains a serious argument in the context of other treaties. Other possible impacts have been examined above and it is likely that these matters will be the object of pleadings and decisions in arbitral proceedings in the future.

Increasing efficiency as a matter of economics as well as public policy

This Part briefly surveys some of the evidence relating to the economic efficiency of including an investment chapter in a trade agreement as opposed to a BIT. It also discusses whether the new TIA trend is better suited to addressing public policy interests than the self-standing BIT.

Regarding economic efficiency, several economic studies have shown that investment provisions in various types of treaties have positive effects on the inflow of FDI to the implementing countries. One such study, conducted by Lesher and Miroudot, concludes that: "substantive investment provisions matter for both trade and investment, and that

64 See CRTA, *supra* note 1.
65 See Regional Trade Agreements: Transparency Mechanism for RTAs, online: WTO <http://www.wto.org/english/tratop_e/region_e/trans_mecha_e.htm>.

trade complements, more than it substitutes for, investment in the context of RTAs that contain substantive investment provisions."[66] Given this "dual positive effect," the authors conclude that investment, when stimulated by such TIAs, may be more "efficiency-seeking" than "market-seeking."[67] Understanding the effects that investment agreements have on foreign investment can help policy-makers build better policies for economic development by, for example, incorporating investment provisions into a broader strategy of attracting FDI for the purposes of sustainable growth, a strategy that is also likely to include trade agreements.

Indeed, the 2009 Report issued by UNCTAD on the role of international investment agreements in attracting FDI to developing countries identifies three groups of determinants that affect the attractiveness of a given host country for foreign investment: policy determinants, economic determinants and business facilitation.[68] While policy determinants include legislation and the overall economic, political and social stability of a location, economic determinants include market size, and the cost or availability of resources; business facilitation covers investment protection measures. The Report suggests that the inclusion of investment provisions in trade agreements is more efficient than simply concluding BITs because, while BITs address the policy determinants of a country's attractiveness to foreign investment, TIAs, with their broader scope, improve both the policy and the economic determinants of attractiveness to foreign investment. Such improvements can, more significantly than can an independent investment agreement, impact a company's decision on where to invest.

The pursuit of a broader strategy for sustainable economic development has seen not only the inclusion of investment provisions in trade agreements, but also of public policy terms in investment treaties. Although the incorporation of public policy issues in investment treaties has been driven by the North American and EU practice, the practice has largely developed under RTAs.[69] A recent study finds that in a sample study of 26 TIAs and 269 BITs, the majority of TIAs, in

---

66 UNCTAD, *The Role of International Investment Agreements in Attracting Foreign Direct Investment to Developing Countries* (New York and Geneva: United Nations, 2009) at 90.
67 *Ibid.*
68 *Ibid* at 110.
69 The North American practice is less surprising as Canada, Mexico, and the United States have followed the same program for investment provisions under their BITs and RTAs.

comparison to only a few of the 269 BITs, embody provisions on social issues such as environment or labor.[70] Recent TIAs appear to be following this trend,[71] thus suggesting that this format is particularly suited to promoting broader policy objectives over and above a pure trade or investment agenda.

The current trend, therefore, adds an interesting dimension to the efficiency discourse of investment treaties. The efficiency of concluding an investment agreement to promote and protect investment while at the same time maintaining the protection of public interests falls at the core of this development. A few arbitral tribunals have tended to afford a different level of protection to investments because of the inclusion of the investment chapter in a trade agreement. In parallel, the treaty practice developed by TIAs appears to clarify the position that investment promotion and protection is not designed to undermine public interests usually falling within the sustainable development discourse.[72] Arguably this latter development imparts a broader textual context to TIAs, in contrast to RTAs and to BITs.

Besides being more efficient in promoting investment at the same time as public policy interests, TIAs are also more explicit in advancing general public policy objectives. The inclusion of provisions regarding public policy objectives in TIAs associates the advancement of general public policy objectives with investment provisions in a more explicit manner than is the case in most BITs. The practice has widened in terms of the countries employing a policy to address such objectives in their investment treaties. Countries like Belgium, Finland, Luxembourg, Netherlands, Sweden, Chile and Latvia are joining their North American counterparts by incorporating this policy into their investment treaty practice.[73] The EU has also been placing greater emphasis on public policy objectives in relation to investment provisions. The EU has adopted a model in relation to trade agreement negotiations, *the Minimum Platform for Investment for the EU FTAs*.[74] This document

---

70 OECD, International Investment Law: Understanding Concepts and Tracking Innovations (2008) at 135 et seq [OECD, International Investment Law].

71 See *India-Korea Partnership*, *supra* note 3; *Peru-Singapore FTA*, *supra* note 3; *Canada-Panama FTA*, *supra* note 3.

72 See Markus Gehring and Avidan Kent, on sustainable development at ch 16 of this book.

73 See OECD, International Investment Law, *supra* note 71 at 144.

74 Council of the EU, Brussels, March 6, 2009, 7242/09, Limited (first issued as *Minimum platform on investment for EU FTAs—Provision on establishment in template for a Title on "Establishment, trade in services and e-commerce,"* Note to the 133 Committee, European Commission DG Trade, Brussels, July 28, 2006, D (2006) 9219)

primarily addresses investment establishment and, in line with the general practice of the EU, avoids substantive investment protection provisions or investment arbitration. The document incorporates a clause ensuring that environment, health, safety, or labor standards are not sacrificed at the expense of encouraging investment.[75]

Despite their variation in scope and language on social issues, recent TIAs have been promoting this dimension of investment treaties. It appears that, while developed countries have included such provisions in their model investment treaties, the level of success in actual negotiations and concluded treaties is currently higher in TIAs than in BITs, as TIAs often include provisions on other issues such as trade in goods, trade in services, and competition policies.[76] In their coverage of a range of issues other than investment, TIAs have a larger textual capacity than BITs to emphasize the public policy considerations required to achieve social and economic goals. The broader textual capacity of TIAs to address these issues may be in part because RTAs have a broader negotiating platform addressing different issues, leaving more room for negotiators to highlight certain social issues. In contrast, the narrow negotiating platform of BITs does not provide the opportunity for a textual emphasis on social aspects of the treaties. Instead, the inclusion of social provisions is achieved mainly through contextual objectives. The narrow platform of BITs notwithstanding, in the long-run, future BITs may well be led to follow the practice developed in highlighting certain social aspects, particularly if the approach proposed by the EU Parliament is followed.[77]

Conclusion

It is far from clear where the trend to include investment provisions in trade agreements is leading. However, the trend demonstrates the close link between services and investment protections and underscores the importance of creating a social dimension within the multilateral

---

[*Minimum platform on investment for EU-FTAs*]. It must be noted that this document, although available on several NGO websites, has never been officially issued. Requests under freedom of information have been denied.

75 *Ibid.*

76 See UNCTAD, "International Investment Arrangements: Trends and Emerging Issues" UNCTAD/ITE/IIT/2005/11 at 10. The so-called "new regionalism" reflects the widening of regional trade agreements in surpassing trade tariffs to a whole range of other issues. See UNCTAD, "Trade and Development Report" (2007) UNCTAD/TDR/2007 at 54.

77 See e.g. *Minimum platform on investment for EU-FTAs*, *supra* note 75.

trading system. Without such a social dimension within the WTO, members that wish to expand foreign investment protections are turning to regional and bilateral agreements. This convergence of investment and trade is also contributing to the substantive and procedural development of the international investment law regime. It is still too early to assert that the inclusion of investment provisions in trade agreements changes the scope of both the trade and investment provisions, but the trend is tearing down the walls between the worlds of international trade, investment and finance. These developments are likely to lead to structural changes within the WTO. It is far from clear whether the trend will be more effective at addressing public policy concerns than was achieved under the self-standing BIT. However, what is clear is that the trend is likely to continue.

8 Increasing the use of alternative dispute resolution in IIAs

*Céline Lévesque**

Introduction

Recent years have confirmed that the international arbitration of investor-state disputes under IIAs is generally a lengthy and expensive affair.[1] This fact, combined with the rapid multiplication of investor claims under IIAs, has led to calls in search of alternatives or complements to international arbitration.[2] This chapter aims to contribute to this

* Associate Professor, Faculty of Law, Civil Law Section, University of Ottawa. The author would like to thank many of the participants in the Washington and Lee University and UNCTAD Joint Symposium on International Investment and Alternative Dispute Resolution held in Lexington, Virginia, in March 2010, for their helpful discussions and pointers. Special thanks go to Susan Franck for her continued support. Thanks also go to Filip Balcerzak, my research assistant on this chapter.

1 See United Nations Conference on Trade and Development (UNCTAD), *Investor-State Disputes: Prevention and Alternatives to Arbitration* (New York and Geneva: United Nations, 2010) at 16–19 [UNCTAD, *ADR I*].
2 See *ibid*; UNCTAD, *Investor-State Disputes: Prevention and Alternative to Arbitration II:Proceedings of the Washington and Lee University and UNCTAD Joint Symposium on International Investment and Alternative Dispute Resolution, held on 29 March 2010 in Lexington, Virginia, United States of America* (New York and Geneva: United Nations, 2011) [UNCTAD, *ADR II*]. In the literature, see e.g. Jack J. Coe Jr, "Towards a Complementary Use of Conciliation in Investor-State Disputes—A Preliminary Sketch," (2005) 12(7) UC Davis J Int'l L & Pol'y 7 [Coe, "Preliminary Sketch"]; Jack Coe, "Settlement of Investor-State Disputes Through Mediation—Preliminary Remarks on Processes, Problems and Prospects" in R. Doak Bishop (ed), *Enforcement of Arbitral Awards Against Sovereigns* (New York: Huntington, JurisNet LLC, 2009) at 92 [Coe, "Mediation"]; Susan Franck, "Integrating Investment Treaty Conflict and Dispute Systems Design" (2007) 92(1) Minn L Rev161 [Franck, "Dispute System Designs"]; Susan Franck, "Challenges Facing Investment Disputes: Reconsidering Dispute Resolution in International Investment Agreements" in Karl P. Sauvant and Michael Chiswick-Patterson (eds), *Appeals Mechanisms In International Investment Disputes* (New York: Oxford University Press, 2008) at 144 [Franck, "Reconsidering Dispute Resolution"]; Bart Legum, "The Difficulties of Conciliation in Investment

discussion, with an emphasis on the promotion of efficiency (including the reduction of transaction costs) but also of the public interest. The analysis focuses on the perspective of states—the perennial respondents in investor treaty-based claims—and on a specific point in time—when a state receives from a foreign investor a notice of intent to submit a claim to arbitration or a notice of arbitration.[3] This chapter demonstrates that, even at this juncture, many options could be considered by states to improve dispute resolution under IIAs. Further, it suggests ways in which future IIAs can better integrate alternatives and complements to international arbitration.

The analysis relies at its core on a rights-based framework for assessment of conflicts, called here the "merits spectrum." However, some of the options considered draw on interest-based methods of conflict resolution and include hybrids of rights-based and interest-based methods.[4] The idea to use a "merits spectrum" to channel investor-state disputes to more appropriate dispute resolution mechanisms came from the realization that some disputes, which took many years and millions of dollars to be resolved, could have been dealt with more efficiently and in line with the public interest had they avoided international arbitration. This seemed to be most obvious at the extremes of the spectrum: for claims that were meritorious and for claims that lacked legal merit. Even in the middle of the spectrum, where lay claims of uncertain merit (either as a matter of law, fact or mixed questions of law and fact), room seemed to exist for improvement over the single international arbitration model.

The chapter uses the merits spectrum to explore different alternative dispute resolution (ADR) options available to states. Faced with a

Treaty Cases: A Comment on Professor Jack C. Coe's 'Toward a complementary use of conciliation in investor-state disputes—A preliminary sketch'" (2006) 21(4) Mealey's International Arbitration Report 1 [Legum]; Noah Rubins, "Comments to Jack C. Coe Jr's Article on Conciliation" (2006) 21(4) Mealey's International Arbitration Report 1 [Rubins]; Jeswald W. Salacuse, "Is There a Better Way? Alternative Methods of Treaty-Based, Investor-State Dispute Resolution" (2007) 31 Fordham Int'l LJ 138 [Salacuse]; Margrete Stevens and Ben Love, "Investor-State Mediation: Observations on the Role of Institutions" in Arthur W. Rovine (ed), *Contemporary Issues in International Arbitration and Mediation: Fordham Papers 2009* (The Netherlands: Martinus Nijhoff, 2009) at 389 [Stevens and Love].

3 Also called the "formalized dispute phase", see Brandon Hasbrouk and Jason Ratigan, "The Way forward" in UNCTAD, *ADR II, supra* note 2 at 128.

4 For a brief presentation, see UNCTAD, *ADR I supra* note 1 at xv–xvi and Mariana Hernandez Crespo, "From Paper to People: Building Conflict Resolution Capacity and Frameworks for Sustainable Implementation of IIAs to Increase Investor-State Satisfaction" in UNCTAD, *ADR II, supra* note 2 at 65.

possible or actual claim, states will evaluate as best they can the merit of the investor's case. This early assessment may often be difficult due to limited access to the facts and by uncertainty in the law but it is nonetheless necessary. In addition to providing an early assessment of potential state liability, it could be used to explore alternatives or complements to international arbitration under the IIA.[5] There are many options including direct negotiations, early neutral evaluation, mediation, conciliation, expedited review of claims, and arbitration with a mediation window.[6]

In an ideal world, conflicts between foreign investors and states would be managed efficiently and resolved early on before they escalate into disputes. Many governments in recent years have turned their attention to conflict management with investors and put in place services, including ombudsman services, which aim to further this goal.[7] As a matter of fact, most investor-state "disagreements" or "conflicts" get resolved outside of the formal arbitration process provided by IIAs or contracts between investors and states. A comparison between the amounts of FDI worldwide and the number of known investor-state arbitration cases and awards leads to no other conclusion.[8]

Still, recent years have witnessed an explosion of investor claims under IIAs as well as the very real possibility that a government only first hears about a complaint when investors deliver a notice of intent to submit a claim to arbitration under an IIA.[9] It may be that the conflict developed at the sub-national government level—far away from the central government's ears. It may be that the investor has no relationship with the government other than through its regulation (now alleged to be discriminatory or expropriatory) and that early discussions with the sectoral department involved did not lead to a resolution of the conflict.

5 Céline Lévesque, "Preliminary Legal Assessments of Investor Claims as a Tool to 'Fitting the Forum to the Fuss'" in UNCTAD, *ADR II*, *supra* note 2 at 77 [Lévesque].
6 On the idea of "fitting the forum to the fuss" see Frank E.A. Sander and Stephen B. Goldberg, "Fitting the Forum to the Fuss: A User-Friendly Guide to Selecting ADR Procedure" (1994) 10(1) Negotiation Journal 49 [Sander and Goldberg].
7 See UNCTAD *ADR I*, *supra* note 1 at 87–93; Franck, "Dispute System Designs", *supra* note 2 at 212–14.
8 See W. Michael Reisman, "International Investment Arbitration and ADR: Married but Best Living Apart" in UNCTAD *ADR II*, *supra* note 2 at 22–3; see also Salacuse, *supra* note 2 at 165 who estimates that: "Because of the confidentiality usually surrounding such settlements, accurate, comprehensive statistics on negotiated settlements of investor-state conflicts are not available. Still, one would suppose that over the last eighteen years, such settlements vastly outnumber the estimated 229 investor-state arbitrations that have been lodged."
9 Franck, "Dispute System Designs", *supra* note 2 at 200.

Or, it may be a case of an unscrupulous investor trying to (ab)use the IIA dispute settlement regime.[10]

Thus, while the improvement of conflict resolution between foreign investors and states is a wide ranging topic, this chapter only looks at one point in time (i.e. when an IIA claim or notice of intent is submitted) and considers options available to governments. Part I introduces the "merits spectrum" and considers different ADR options. Part II explores current practices and improvements that could be made in future IIAs in order to resolve disputes more efficiently by encouraging recourse to ADR.

The merits spectrum and ADR options

This part attempts to "match" the most appropriate ADR options to the type of claims being made. Organised according to the merits spectrum they are: meritorious claims, unmeritorious claims and claims of uncertain merit.

Meritorious claims

Some cases come along where the breach of an IIA obligation is fairly clear. For example, a sub-national government may have proceeded to expropriate the investment of a foreign investor without compensation or may have blatantly discriminated against a foreigner. The early assessment of the merit of the claim performed by the (central) government would reveal a high risk of liability. In such a case, direct negotiation or facilitated negotiation, with the assistance of a neutral third-party (such as a conciliator or mediator), could be considered as options.

While there are likely to be many differences between any two conciliators or mediators,[11] it is useful to briefly define the main characteristics and the pros and cons of some of the different ADR options available. It should also be noted that these options are not necessarily mutually exclusive.

Direct negotiations: In this process, parties are in direct contact to attempt to resolve their dispute and there are normally no third parties involved.[12] Salacuse describes the process as one "whereby the parties themselves through direct discussion of their conflict agree to settle their dispute."[13] This process has the advantage of leaving the parties in

---

10 Lévesque, *supra* note 5 at 77.
11 UNCTAD, *ADR I*, *supra* note 1 at 28.
12 *Ibid* at xiv.
13 Salacuse, *supra* note 2 at 154.

control but presents the corresponding disadvantage—the parties may not be able to come up with a solution on their own. IIAs often include "amicable settlement" provisions that encourage the parties to settle a claim through "consultation and negotiation."[14] However, as discussed further below, many tribunals have interpreted such clauses as "procedural" rather than "jurisdictional" requirements and have not rejected claims even though the "waiting period" for the consultations had not elapsed at the time investors made their claims.[15]

Conciliation: One of the means of facilitated negotiations, conciliation has also been called "non-binding arbitration."[16] This connection to arbitration is due to the relatively formal and structured nature of conciliation (as opposed to mediation).[17] Also, conciliation usually ends with a written agreement or at least written recommendations by the conciliator or a panel of conciliators.[18] As such, the process is geared towards finding a concrete solution to a problem rather than improving the relationship between the parties.[19] According to some commentators, one of the reasons why the ICSID conciliation rules have rarely been used relates to its high degree of formality.[20]

Mediation: An informal process of assisted negotiation, mediation involves a third-party (the mediator) who aims to facilitate a settlement.[21] An important part of this process is usually the maintenance of a constructive relationship between the parties. As such, mediators often consider issues that are broader than the specific point of disagreement between the parties.[22] As with all ADR, the success of mediation depends on the cooperation of both parties.

While it would appear highly beneficial and efficient for a government to try to resolve a "losing" case early through direct or assisted

---

14 See e.g. *North American Free Trade Agreement Between the Government of Canada, the Government of Mexico and the Government of the United States*, December 17,1992, Can TS 1994 No. 2 (entered into force January 1, 1994) [NAFTA] at art 1118; see also Salacuse *supra* note 2 at 161.

15 See Claudia Ludwig, "Negotiation Clauses in BITs—Empty Words?" May 24, 2011, online: Kluwer Arbitration Blog <http://kluwerarbitrationblog.com/blog/2011/05/24/negotiation-clauses-in-bits-%E2%80%93-empty-words/>.

16 Salacuse, *supra* note 2 at 173; UNCTAD, *ADR I, supra* note 1 at xiii–xiv.

17 UNCTAD, ADR I *supra* note 1 at xiii, 26.

18 *Ibid* at xiii, 27.

19 *Ibid* at xiii–xiv, 27.

20 See e.g. Stevens and Love, *supra* note 2 at 410–11.

21 The terms "mediation" and "conciliation" do not have shared meanings across borders. Some authors use one term to refer to both. e.g. Coe, "Preliminary sketch", *supra* note 2 at 14; see also Salacuse *supra* note 2 at 173.

22 UNCTAD, *ADR I, supra* note 1 at xix, 27.

negotiations, states face a number of obstacles or barriers in settling claims even though they have merit. The obstacles—both real and perceived—to the use of ADR by governments include: (a) the lack of political cover provided by a negotiated solution as opposed to a third-party binding decision; (b) the risk of appearing to cave in to foreign investors, especially where the claim is of public interest; (c) intergovernmental issues such as when the claim relates to sub-national measures adopted by municipalities or provinces/states that are not signatory to the IIA; (d) intra-governmental issues such as when multiple ministries and agencies are involved and not a single decision-maker can make the decision to settle; (e) the risk of upsetting public expectations when ADR is confidential and arbitration would be more transparent; (f) the fact that ADR may unnecessarily lengthen the dispute settlement process if the parties ultimately have recourse to arbitration in any case.[23] Such potential obstacles have to be explored with the aim of reducing their impact.

Despite these obstacles, settlements do happen rather frequently. According to UNCTAD, "by the end of 2009, 164 [treaty-based investor-state dispute settlement] cases had been brought to conclusion. Out of these, 38 per cent were decided in favor of the State (62) and 29 per cent in favor of the investor (47), while 34 per cent (55) cases were settled."[24] Recent statistics released by ICSID are in line with this finding since, as of June 30, 2011, 39 per cent of arbitration proceedings under the ICSID Convention and Additional Facility Rules had been settled or otherwise discontinued.[25] This number, however, includes cases other than treaty-based cases. As such, the percentage would be lower once disputes based on contracts and domestic investment law are excluded.[26] Still, upwards of 34 per cent is substantial.[27]

Unfortunately, little is publicly known about these cases and why or how they were settled. Many factors could influence such an outcome.

23 This is an excerpt from Lévesque, *supra* note 5 at 78. For more on obstacles to the use of ADR, see Salacuse, *supra* note 2 at 149–50, 166–8, 172, 177–9; Coe, "Preliminary Sketch", *supra* note 2 at 29–32, 36; Legum, *supra* note 2 at 1–3; Rubins, *supra* note 2 at 2; Stevens and Love, *supra* note 2 at 403–4, 413.
24 UNCTAD, "Latest Developments in Investor-State Dispute Settlement" (2010) IIA ISSUES NOTE No. 1 International Investment Agreements, online: UNCTAD <http://www.unctad.org/en/docs/webdiaeia20103_en.pdf> at 3.
25 See ICSID, "The ICSID Caseload—Statistics", online: ICSID <http://icsid.worldbank.org/ICSID/FrontServlet?requestType=ICSIDDocRH&actionVal=ShowDocument&CaseLoadStatistics=True&language=English21> at 13.
26 *Ibid* at 10.
27 For a comparison with other rates of settlements see Coe, "Preliminary Sketch", *supra* note 2 at 35.

It may be that the parties were bound by a long-term contract and ultimately showed a willingness to maintain their relationship in the future (interest-based assessment); it may be that the respondent government did not have the expertise or resources to sustain a prolonged battle in arbitration against a deep-pocketed investor (power-based assessment); or it may be that the government knew it was going to lose on the merits (rights-based assessment).

Two examples taken from Canada's experience under NAFTA's investment chapter[28] serve to illustrate that investor claims can and do get settled but not without some controversy and difficulties. In 1998, Canada settled the first claim submitted to it by American investors under NAFTA Chapter 11. Twelve years later, in 2010, it settled another high profile claim.[29]

In 1997, Ethyl Corporation submitted its notice of arbitration in a case related to the gasoline additive "MMT."[30] The investor complained that an Act of Parliament banned the interprovincial trade and import of MMT (while the production and sale of MMT was still allowed in Canada).[31] The investor challenged the reasons provided by Canada for adopting the ban, including those related to the protection of health and the environment. In 1998, after a decision had been rendered on the jurisdiction of the tribunal, the government decided to settle the claim for a reported CAN$19 million.[32] Although the settlement was not made public, on the government website one finds the following statement: "In response to a similar challenge launched by three Canadian

---

28 See NAFTA, *supra* note 14 at ch 11.

29 Another case was settled in 2011 in the *Dow AgroSciences LLC v Canada*. For the settlement agreement in this case, see online: DFAIT <http://www.international. gc.ca/trade-agreements-accords-commerciaux/assets/pdfs/DowAgroSciences_ Settlement-eng.pdf>. Other cases that appear in the "withdrawn or inactive" category on the DFAIT website may have also been settled, but information is not readily available from the government about them.

30 *Ethyl Corporation v Government of Canada*, Notice of Arbitration, April 14, 1997, online: DFAIT <http://www.international.gc.ca/trade-agreements-accords-commer ciaux/assets/pdfs/ethyl2.pdf>.

31 *Ethyl Corpn v Government of Canada*, Award on Jurisdiction, UNCITRAL (June 24, 1998) at paras 5–6 [*Ethyl*].

32 See Shawn McCarthy, "Failed ban becomes selling point for MMT. Not enough scientific evidence to prove additive a risk, minister says, promising to give manufacturers $19-million," *The Globe and Mail* (July 21, 1998) A3 [McCarthy]; Sylvia Ostry and Julie Soloway, "The MMT case ended too soon. Taking it to arbitration would have helped settle some crucial questions," *The Globe and Mail* (July 24, 1998) A15; Julie A. Soloway, "NAFTA's Chapter 11—The Challenge of Private Party Participation" (1999) 16(2) Journal of International Arbitration 1 at 5.

provinces, a Canadian federal-provincial dispute settlement panel, established under the Agreement on Internal Trade, subsequently found against the federal measure. Accordingly, Canada and Ethyl settled all outstanding matters, including the Chapter Eleven claim."[33]

Since the measure was found to be discriminatory under Canada's own *Agreement on Internal Trade*,[34] the government probably decided to cut its losses by not defending the case further under NAFTA—as it was likely to have a similar outcome. Some NGOs, however, did not see it this way.

For some NGOs, the *Ethyl* case became a "test" as to whether investor claims under IIAs could force governments to overturn environmental regulations. While some groups were concerned with the merits of the case (arguing that the ban was necessary for the protection of health and the environment), others were concerned with the restriction investor claims imposed on the governments' abilities to pass environmental and health legislation.[35] Further, some NGOs saw the *Ethyl* case as a "warning for things to come" notably under the OECD's MAI that was being negotiated at the time.[36]

Meanwhile, it took over ten years before Canada would settle another high profile case, concerning Abitibi Bowater's Chapter 11 claim.[37] The settlement in this case was also criticized by NGOs.[38] But the case also provides a perfect example of the difficulties facing federal states (such as Canada) when a sub-national measure is the object of an investor claim.

33 Online, DFAIT <http://www.international.gc.ca/trade-agreements-accords-commerciaux/disp-diff/ethyl.aspx?lang=en&view=d>.

34 See Julie A. Soloway, "Environmental Trade Barriers Under NAFTA: The MMT Fuel Additives Controversy" (1999) 8(1) Minn J Global Trade at 77–8, 83 [Soloway, "Environmental Trade Barrier"].

35 See McCarthy, *supra* note 32; See also online, Suns Online <http://www.sunsonline.org/trade/areas/environm/06030297.htm>.

36 Stephen J. Kobrin, "The MAI and the Clash of Globalizations", *Foreign Policy* (September 1998) 97 at 102–4; See also Soloway, "Environmental Trade Barrier", *supra* note 34 at 88.

37 It is hard to tell whether the response to the *Ethyl* case settlement acted as a deterrent to other settlements or if later cases were considered not to be "meritorious" enough to engage in settlement discussions. Nevertheless, one thing appears certain. A settlement in response to a challenge to another environmental measure (such as was the case in *S.D. Myers v Canada*) could probably not be fathomed by the Canadian government—even though the case was later lost on the merits.

38 See e.g. The Council of Canadians, "Blame NAFTA, not Williams, for costly AbitibiBowater settlement", online< http://www.canadians.org/media/trade/2010/27-Aug-10.html>.

This case centered on the adoption by the provincial government of Newfoundland and Labrador of an Act which effectively expropriated assets, lands and various other rights belonging to AbitibiBowater and its subsidiaries in the province.[39] The Act was passed, in a single day in 2008, less than two weeks after AbitibiBowater announced its planned closure of a pulp and paper mill in the province (due to financial difficulties). Abitibi chiefly complained that the Act did not provide for appropriate compensation of the expropriated property and denied the company judicial avenues for legal redress.[40] The NAFTA Chapter 11 claim was for an estimated CAN$500 million in damages.[41]

Following the notice of arbitration in February 2010, a tribunal was constituted. In August, the parties informed the tribunal that they had reached a settlement of the dispute. This settlement, once different conditions were met, was later recorded by the tribunal as a consent award. This award, dated December 15, 2010, contained the obligation for Canada to pay CAN$130 million to a new company that was to continue operations in Canada.[42] To understand the circumstances better, consideration has to be given to the fact that AbitibiBowater had filed for bankruptcy protection (or equivalent) both in the United States and Canada in 2009 and that it had operations in five other Canadian provinces.[43]

One would assume that the decision by the Canadian federal government to settle the claim and pay CAN$130 million on account of a provincial measure that breached NAFTA, was difficult to take. In response to questions regarding the settlement, Prime Minister Stephen Harper provided the following response:

> I do not intend to get back the monies expended in this case from the government of Newfoundland and Labrador. But I have indicated that in future, should provincial actions cause significant legal obligations for the government of Canada, the government of Canada will create a mechanism so that it can reclaim monies lost through international trade processes.[44]

39 See *AbitibiBowater Inc v Government of Canada*, Notice of Arbitration and Statement of Claim, February 25, 2010, at paras 13 ff [AbitibiBowater NOA].
40 *Ibid* at para 13.
41 *Ibid* at para 100.
42 See *AbitibiBowater Inc. v Government of Canada*, Consent Award, ICSID (December 15, 2010).
43 AbitibiBowater NOA, *supra* note 39 at paras 80–5.
44 Bertrand Marotte and John Ibbitson, "Provinces on hook in future trade disputes: Harper" *The Globe and Mail* (August 26, 2010).

Thus far no such mechanism has been implemented.

In conclusion, the settlement of meritorious claims, through direct or assisted negotiations, may be the most efficient solution to a dispute. However, as the two examples above demonstrate, there are many obstacles to governments settling cases. More should be done to explore these obstacles in order to reduce their impact.

Unmeritorious claims

Some claims lack legal merit because they are either frivolous, brought in bad faith or represent an abuse of process.[45] The assessment of the merit performed by the government would point to a low risk of liability. This does not mean, however, that the government should proceed with a fully-fledged arbitration. Even if the government prevails in the end, the cost and energy involved in defending such claims are substantial. For obvious reasons, some of those claims cannot be settled (e.g. where there is some evidence of corruption).[46]

There are still some options that could be considered, two of which will be presented here: recourse to "Early Neutral Evaluation" (ENE) and to the ICSID expedited review of claims process.

ENE, a sort of "advisory ADR," occurs early in a case.[47] UNCTAD defines ENE as follows:

> Early neutral evaluation involves an evaluator, usually an attorney or other expert with specific knowledge of the subject matter of a case, who hosts an informal meeting with investors and their counsel. At such a meeting, both sides of the dispute (i.e. representatives of the investor and the State) will present their evidence and arguments, based on which the evaluator identifies areas of agreement and issues to focus on. The evaluator then writes a confidential

---

45 See Salacuse, *supra* note 2 at para 65 ("it must be acknowledged that any system of litigation entails the risk of frivolous lawsuits, and investor-state arbitrations are no exception. Investors may bring baseless arbitrations either because they honestly have misevaluated the strength of their claims, because they view the arbitration as a means to pressure a negotiated settlement from the host state, or because they believe they have relatively little to lose and the potential to gain a great deal.")

46 Lévesque, *supra* note 5 at 78.

47 Nancy A. Welsh and Andrea K. Schneider, "Of Fireworks and Flames: The Thoughtful Integration of Mediation into International Investor State Dispute Resolution" [manuscript—on file with author]. See also Sander and Goldberg, *supra* note 6 at 51.

evaluation of the prospects of a case and offers to present it to the disputants [. . .].[48]

Arguably, the ENE result of a claim that is "unmeritorious" could discourage the investor from proceeding any further. In other words, a neutral evaluation to the effect that the claim is likely to fail on jurisdiction or merits may be enough for an investor to re-evaluate its risks and chances of prevailing in arbitration. For ENE to be successful, both parties would have to trust in the judgment and evaluation of the evaluator.[49] One of the potential difficulties with this process, however, is that it requires early access to evidence, which may be difficult for a state to muster especially if the challenged measure has been taken by a sub-national government.

A government facing a claim under the ICSID Convention Arbitration Rules or ICSID Additional Facility Rules can also have recourse to the process of expedited review of claims (also called "summary dismissal of claims" or "expeditious dismissal of claims"). Under ICSID Arbitration Rule 41(5) a party can submit an objection on the grounds that a claim is "manifestly without legal merit."[50] If the tribunal finds that it is the case, it renders an award to that effect.[51] This process was adopted in 2006 and as such is relatively new. Thus far, four cases have been through this process.

Rule 41(5) provides:

Unless the parties have agreed to another expedited procedure for making preliminary objections, a party may, *no later than 30 days after the constitution of the Tribunal*, and *in any event before the first session of the Tribunal*, file an objection that a claim is manifestly without legal merit. The party shall specify as precisely as possible the basis for the objection. The Tribunal, after giving the parties the opportunity to present their observations on the objection, shall, *at*

48 UNCTAD, *ADR I, supra* note 1 at xvii referring to Stephanie Smith and Janet Martinez, "An Analytical Framework for Dispute Systems Design" (2009) 14 Harvard Negot L Rev.
49 See Salacuse, *supra* note 2 at 169.
50 "Rules of Procedure for Arbitration Proceedings," in *ICSID Convention, Regulations and Rules* (effective April 2006), online: ICSID <http://icsid.worldbank.org/ICSID/StaticFiles/basicdoc/basic-en.htm> at Rule 41(5) [ICSID Arbitration Rules]. The same process exists under the ICSID, *ICSID Additional Facility Rules* (effective April 2006), online: ICSID <http://icsid.worldbank.org/ICSID/ICSID/AdditionalFacilityRules.jsp> at art 45(6) [ICSID Additional Facility Rules].
51 ICSID Arbitration Rules, *supra* note 50 at Rule 41(6).

its first session or promptly thereafter, notify the parties of its decision on the objection [. . .] (emphasis added).[52]

As appears from the wording of Rule 41, the process occurs early in the arbitral procedure and could be a useful tool for governments to object to clearly "unmeritorious" claims.

The first decision regarding a request for early dismissal was rendered in 2008 in *Trans-Global Petroleum Inc v Jordan*.[53] In this case, the tribunal decided to proceed to the merits regarding two claims concerning a petroleum exploration venture, while the third claim was decided to be manifestly without legal merit (as it happens, it was also withdrawn by the Claimant).[54] The tribunal found that no duty of consultation was owed to the investor (under article VIII of the BIT) and as a result the third claim was missing an essential legal basis.[55] The case was subsequently settled and the settlement was adopted in the form of a consent award.[56] It is certainly possible that the early venting of issues contributed to the settlement of the case.

The second decision was rendered in 2009 in *Brandes Investment Partners LP v Venezuela*.[57] In this case, the tribunal, after weighing both parties' arguments, decided that none of the claims were manifestly without merit.

Finally, in 2010, two cases were dismissed for manifestly lacking merit: *Global Trading Resource Corpn and Globex International, Inc. v Ukraine*[58] and *RSM Production Corpn v Grenada*.[59] In the case of *Global Trading*, the alleged investment boiled down to a contract for the supply of poultry. The tribunal held that it was a pure commercial transaction and not an investment for the purpose of ICSID (and under one element of the definition of investment of the applicable BIT).[60] As such, the

---

52 *Ibid* at Rule 41(5).
53 *Trans-Global Petroleum Inc v Jordan*, Decision on Rule 41(5) Objection, ICSID Case No. ARB/07/25 (May 12, 2008) [*Trans-Global Petroleum*, Decision].
54 *Ibid* at para 120.
55 *Ibid* at paras 118–19.
56 *Trans-Global Petroleum Inc v Jordan*, Consent Award, ICSID Case No. ARB/07/25 (April 8, 2009).
57 *Brandes Investment Partners LP v Venezuela*, Decision on Rule 41(5) Objection, ICSID Case No. ARB/08/3 (February 2, 2009) [*Brandes Investment*].
58 *Global Trading Resource Corpn and Globex International, Inc. v Ukraine*, Award, ICSID Case No. ARB/09/11 (December 1, 2010).
59 *RSM Production Corpn v Grenada*, Award, ICSID Case No. ARB/10/6 (December 10, 2010) [*RSM Production*].
60 *Global Trading supra* note 58 at para 56.

claim "manifestly lacked legal merit."[61] In the case of *RSM Production*, the dispute concerned a petroleum exploration agreement that had already been the object of a contract claim at ICSID and had been dismissed. The tribunal held that the case was "manifestly without legal merit" because "as pleaded and argued, the present case is no more than an attempt to re-litigate and overturn the findings of another ICSID tribunal . . .".[62]

Although they had different outcomes, the four decisions share many holdings that will be useful to guide future tribunals in this new process.[63] First, the tribunals agreed that objections can be made as to both jurisdiction and merit.[64] Secondly, objections have to concern legal arguments and not facts—unless the facts are manifestly incredible.[65] Thirdly, the term "manifestly" means that a claim must be clearly and obviously without merit. In other words, it is a high standard.[66] While there is no special procedure provided under Rule 41(5), at least one tribunal has specifically held that the claimant should have an opportunity to be heard, both in writing and orally—since the result may be the dismissal of the claim.[67]

Regarding the cost of proceedings and who should bear them, the tribunals have reached different conclusions. There is a marked contrast between the two 2010 decisions. Whereas the tribunal in *Global Trading* took into account the newness of the procedure and the concise nature of the parties' arguments to let the costs of the procedure "lie where they fall" and make no order as to cost,[68] the tribunal in *RSM Production* ordered the claimant to fully indemnify the respondent for all its costs.[69]

---

61 *Ibid* at para 58.

62 *RSM Production, supra* note 59 at para 7.3.6.

63 See John R. Crook, "Four Tribunals Apply ICSID Rule for Early Ouster of Unmeritorious Claims", 15(10) ASIL Insights (2011), online <http://www.asil.org/insights110426.cfm> who comments that: "The four unanimous decisions are in harmony on key points and set out standards and procedures that are likely to influence future tribunals."

64 See e.g. *Brandes Investment, supra* note 57 at para 50; *Global Trading, supra* note 58 at para 30.

65 See e.g. *Trans-Global Petroleum*, Decision, *supra* note 53 at para 97 and 105; *Brandes Investment, supra* note 57 at para 61.

66 See e.g. *Trans-Global Petroleum*, Decision, *supra* note 53 at para 88; *Global Trading, supra* note 58 at para 35; *Brandes Investment, supra* note 57 at para 64; *RSM Production, supra* note 59 at paras 6.1.1–6.1.2.

67 See *Global* Trading, *supra* note 58 at para 33.

68 *Ibid* at para 59

69 See *RSM Production, supra* note 59 at paras 8.3.4, 8.3.6.

Since an award of costs may act as a deterrent to "unmeritorious" claims, the approach of the tribunal in *RSM Production* may be more appropriate in many cases.[70] As the procedure loses its "newness" over time, the loser-pays-principle might come to prevail. In general, as one author has concluded "[The cases] show that the new rule can be an effective device to limit states' burden and expenses in the face of legally dubious claims."[71]

Finally, it should at least be mentioned that there are also claims that do not "lack legal merit" but, for other reasons—such as the amount of damages claimed is relatively minor—do not belong in international arbitration. Because of the high cost of arbitration, alternatives should be explored to resolve such claims as well.

Claims of uncertain merit

Most investor claims will probably lie in the middle of the spectrum. However, claims of uncertain merit (either as matter of law or fact) might still be more efficiently handled, for example, through mixed ADR/arbitration models. The uncertainty regarding the interpretation of many obligations in IIAs makes it difficult for governments to perform the type of risk assessments required to make decisions regarding settlements. For example, a preliminary legal assessment may present the holdings of divergent awards on a certain legal issue and be unable to conclude either way on the risks of liability. Nonetheless, the legal assessment can be useful in weighing the strengths and weaknesses of different claims and arguments. This analysis can in turn be used to tailor a more efficient dispute settlement process.[72]

Often there will be room for improvement from the single international arbitration model. In many cases, investors have a tendency to make numerous claims in the hope that some claims will "stick." This strategy involves costs and delays. Mediation prior to arbitration or concurrent with arbitration could help narrow and refine claims for the arbitration (if not lead to a settlement).[73] Arbitration with a "mediation window," as discussed recently at the Centre for Effective Dispute Settlement (CEDR), could be useful in this context.

---

70 See Salacuse, *supra* note 2 at 165 who states: "[o]ne way for arbitrators to dissuade such frivolous cases is to allocate all or a substantial portion of the arbitration costs to such claimants if they lose their case."

71 Crook, *supra* note 63.

72 Lévesque, *supra* note 5 at 79.

73 See Coe, "Preliminary Sketch", *supra* note 2 at 19–20.

In 2007, the CEDR formed a Commission on Settlement in International Arbitration in order to review the practice of arbitral tribunals in promoting settlements and to make recommendations to improve this aspect of the process.[74] After consultations, the Commission, chaired by Lord Woolf and Professor Gabrielle Kaufmann-Kohler, produced a final report in November 2009. In Appendix 1 of the Report, one finds the CEDR Rules for the Facilitation of Settlement in International Arbitration.

The Rules lay out principles and guidelines to be followed by arbitrators in promoting settlements while avoiding the possibility that an award (ultimately required) be open to challenge. The Commission warns in particular of the risks related to "med-arb" processes that involve arbitrators meeting privately with each party as part of the mediation part of the process.[75] Arbitration with a "mediation window", however, is included in the Rules. In the definitions, "mediation window means a period of time during an arbitration that is set aside so that mediation can take place and during which there is no other procedural activity."[76] Further, the Rules provide that: "The Arbitral Tribunal shall: 3.1. insert a Mediation Window in the arbitral proceedings when requested to do so by all Parties in order to enable settlement discussions, through mediation or otherwise, to take place."[77] In order to induce compliance, the Rules also provide that "any unreasonable refusal by a party to make use of a Mediation Window" could be considered when the time comes to award costs at the end of the arbitration.[78] According to some authors, "some of the CEDR recommendations might well lead to processes that could bring about more efficient and cost-effective outcomes in investment arbitration, but others should probably be approached with caution in the investor-state context."[79]

---

74 Centre for Effective Dispute Resolution, CEDR Commission on Settlement in International Arbitration, Final Report, November 2009, online: CEDR <http://www.cedr.com/about_us/arbitration_commission/Arbitration_Commission_Doc_Final.pdf> at 2.

75 *Ibid* at 3.

76 *Ibid* at Appendix, art 1.5.

77 *Ibid* at Appendix 1, art 5.3.1.

78 *Ibid* at art 6.1.

79 Stevens and Love, *supra* note 2 at 400. The authors also suggest that ICSID Arbitration Rule 21 could be used as a "mediation window" (at 414). See ICSID Arbitration Rules, *supra* note 50, ("Rule 21, Pre-Hearing Conference (1) At the request of the Secretary-General or at the discretion of the President of the Tribunal, a pre-hearing conference between the Tribunal and the parties may be held to arrange for an exchange of information and the stipulation of uncontested facts in order to expedite the proceeding. (2) At the request of the parties, a pre-hearing

Other authors have promoted the concept of "concurrent med-arb" or "shadow conciliation."[80] In this scenario, both a mediator(s) and an arbitrator(s) are appointed. The mediator(s) sit on the arbitration proceedings, which go on concurrently, and can meet the parties at different junctures to help them come to a settlement.[81] This process has the advantage of not delaying the arbitration and preserving the authority and integrity of the tribunal in case settlement discussions fail and an award is rendered.[82]

Extensive literature exists on different ADR options and their advantages and disadvantages. The important point here is to suggest that options other than single-model arbitration should be considered in order to increase the efficiency of investor-state dispute resolution.

Improvements in future IIAs

While some IIAs provide for ADR in a limited fashion, more could be done to facilitate and encourage recourse to it.

Current IIA practice

The majority of IIAs contain "amicable settlement clauses," i.e. provisions which state that parties should try to settle their dispute amicably.[83] Usually, amicable settlement clauses do not mention any ADR option in particular. As a result, "amicable settlement" does not have a clear meaning and may allow any kind of ADR (direct negotiations, facilitated negotiations, etc.). This openness can be a source of flexibility but it can also cause problems. One author notes that it can create "confusion for legal cultures with different dispute resolution traditions or working definitions of mediation and other forms of nonbinding dispute resolution."[84]

conference between the Tribunal and the parties, duly represented by their authorized representatives, may be held to consider the issues in dispute with a view to reaching an amicable settlement.")

80 See UNCTAD, *ADR II*, *supra* note 2; see also Coe, "Preliminary Sketch", *supra* note 2 at 32–4, 42–3.

81 See Coe, "Preliminary Sketch", *supra* note 2 at 33, 39; see also Robert N. Dobbins, "The Layered Dispute Resolution Clause: From Boilerplate to Business Opportunity" (2005) 1 Hasting Business Law Journal 176.

82 Coe, "Preliminary Sketch", *supra* note 2 at 37.

83 See e.g. Salacuse, *supra* note 2 at 169; Stevens and Love, *supra* note 2 at 392.

84 Franck, "Dispute System Designs", *supra* note 2 at 196–7 [notes omitted]; Rubins, *supra* note 2 at 3.

Also, as recent awards have demonstrated, the mandatory nature of the process can be doubted.[85] In the recent *Alps Finance Trade AG v Slovak Republic*, the tribunal noted that what the relevant BIT clause required was that "consultations be at least attempted and that the six months lapse without any resulting solution."[86] The tribunal reviewed the relevant case-law which, but for one exception, did not consider "deficiencies" in complying with the clause a jurisdictional matter. In this instance, the tribunal held that some exchange of correspondence amply fulfilled the requirement.[87] In particular, the tribunal noted the relevant articles "do not impose specified formalities for the consultations."[88] In another case, *Salini v Morocco*, the tribunal also noted that the clause "does not set out any procedure to be followed in relation to reaching an amicable settlement of the dispute between the two Parties."[89]

The 2004 US Model BIT (and a few examples from earlier US IIAs)[90] goes a step further in specifically providing for the possibility of recourse to "non-binding, third-party procedures." Article 23 (Consultation and Negotiation) of the Model BIT states: "In the event of an investment dispute, the claimant and the respondent should initially seek to resolve the dispute through consultation and negotiation, which may include the use of non-binding, third-party procedures."[91] This wording, while it does not clarify the extent of the obligation to engage in such processes, at least has the virtue of bringing the possibility to the attention of the parties.[92] For an author, "[t]his language appears to represent an attempt by states to underscore the importance of alternative dispute resolution techniques and to introduce them into the investor-state dispute resolution process."[93] Importantly, it can eliminate the possible feeling that the party who proposes to use ADR considers its position "weaker" and that is why it wants to settle.[94]

85 Franck, "Dispute System Designs", *supra* note 2 at 198.
86 *Alps Finance Trade AG v The Slovak Republic*, Award, UNCITRAL (March 5, 2011).
87 *Ibid* at 200–9.
88 *Ibid* at 209.
89 *Salini Costruttori S.P.A. and Italstrade S.P.A. v Kingdom of Morroco*, Decision on Jurisdiction, ICSID Case No. ARB/00/4 (July 23, 2001) at 19. See also Ludwig *supra* note 15.
90 See e.g. US-Turkey BIT (1985) at art VI(2); US-Poland BIT (1990) at art IX.2. See also Salacuse, *supra* note 2 at 170–1.
91 See US Model BIT, online: US State Department <http://www.state.gov/documents/organization/117601.pdf> at art 18.
92 See Stevens and Love *supra* 2 at 392.
93 Salacuse *supra* 2 at 171; See also Coe, "Preliminary Sketch", *supra* note 2 at 37, 129.
94 *Ibid* at 172.

In contrast, the 2004 Canadian Model FIPA does not clarify what the word "consultation" might entail process wise, but clearly makes the process mandatory. Article 25 (Settlement of a Claim through Consultation) of the Model states:

1. Before a disputing investor may submit a claim to arbitration, the disputing parties shall first hold consultations in an attempt to settle a claim amicably.
2. Consultations shall be held within 30 days of the submission of the notice of intent to submit a claim to arbitration, unless the disputing parties otherwise agree.
3. The place of consultation shall be the capital of the disputing Party, unless the disputing parties otherwise agree.[95]

The process details (time, location) as well as the fact that the consultation has to occur before a notice of arbitration has been submitted (unless otherwise agreed) will likely contribute to a more efficient process.

A limited number of IIAs specifically provide for conciliation, in addition to negotiations and before arbitration. For example, article 12 of the Australia-India BIT (1999) provides the following process:

1. Any dispute between an investor of one Contracting Party and the other Contracting Party in relation to an investment of the former under this Agreement shall, as far as possible, be settled amicably through negotiations between the Parties to the dispute.
2. Any such dispute which has not been amicably settled may, *if both Parties agree*, be submitted:
   (a) for resolution, in accordance with the law of the Contracting Party which has admitted the investment to that Contracting Party's competent judicial or administrative bodies; or
   (b) to international conciliation under the Conciliation Rules of the United Nations Commission on International Trade Law.
3. Should the Parties fail to agree on a dispute settlement procedure provided under paragraph 2 of this article or where a dispute is referred to conciliation but conciliation proceedings are terminated other than by signing of a settlement agreement, the

---

95 2004 Canadian Model FIPA, online: DFAIT <http://www.international.gc.ca/trade-agreements-accords-commerciaux/assets/pdfs/2004-FIPA-model-en.pdf> at art 25.

dispute may be referred to Arbitration [. . .][96] (emphasis added). However, access to conciliation is only available "if both Parties agree," which in practice would likely limit its use.[97]

In terms of early case dismissal, Article 28 of the 2004 US Model BIT provides:

4. Without prejudice to a tribunal's authority to address other objections as a preliminary question, a tribunal shall address and decide as a preliminary question any objection by the respondent that, as a matter of law, a claim submitted is not a claim for which an award in favor of the claimant may be made under Article 34.

    (a) Such objection shall be submitted to the tribunal as soon as possible after the tribunal is constituted, [. . .]
    (b) On receipt of an objection under this paragraph, the tribunal shall suspend any proceedings on the merits, [. . .]
    (c) In deciding an objection under this paragraph, the tribunal shall assume to be true claimant's factual allegations [. . .]
    (d) [. . .]

5. In the event that the respondent so requests *within 45 days* after the tribunal is constituted, the tribunal shall decide on *an expedited basis* an objection under paragraph 4 and any objection that the dispute is not within the tribunal's competence. The tribunal shall suspend any proceedings on the merits and issue a decision or award on the objection(s), stating the grounds therefor, no later than 150 days after the date of the request. However, if a disputing party requests a hearing, the tribunal may take an additional 30 days to issue the decision or award. Regardless of whether a hearing is requested, a tribunal may, on a showing of extraordinary cause, delay issuing its decision or award by an additional brief period, which may not exceed 30 days.

6. When it decides a respondent's objection under paragraph 4 or 5, the tribunal may, if warranted, award to the prevailing disputing party reasonable costs and attorney's fees incurred in submitting or opposing the objection. In determining whether such an

96 Cited in Stevens and Love, *supra* note 2 at 393–4.
97 See Rubins, *supra* note 2 at 3 who cites the Sweden-India BIT (2000) as a nearly unique example of a BIT providing for "mandatory conciliation."

award is warranted, the tribunal shall consider whether either the claimant's claim or the respondent's objection *was frivolous*, and shall provide the disputing parties a reasonable opportunity to comment[98] (emphasis added).

This process is similar to the one discussed above in the context of ICSID. Notably, in case the tribunal finds that the claim was "frivolous," it is directed to consider this fact when awarding costs.

Potential options

As a general matter, parties to an investor-state dispute who are willing to engage in ADR can do so without running afoul of IIA dispute settlement provisions.[99] The question addressed here is what could be *included in IIAs* that would make this process more accessible and efficient.[100] The approach is "minimalist" in the sense that the provisions suggested would force parties to a dispute to at least consider engaging in an ADR process without adding much delay or cost to the arbitration process— in the eventuality that it takes place anyway.[101] States who wish to take "bolder" initiatives could consider mandatory mediation prior to or concurrent with arbitration.[102] "Half-compulsory mediation" could also be considered. An IIA provision could state that if an investor requests it, the respondent state is obliged to accept the request for mediation. In this way, mediation would only take place when an investor really wants to engage with the state.[103]

Also, the opportunity of including an early-dismissal clause in an IIA will not be discussed further. This process currently applies under ICSID, and ICSID Additional Facility Arbitration Rules, but not under UNCITRAL Arbitration Rules. As the United States has done, it may be wise to include such a process in IIAs.[104]

The first suggested addition to IIAs would be a "convening clause."[105] In general, a convening clause:

98 2004 US Model BIT, *supra* note 91 at art 28.
99 See Salacuse, *supra* note 2 at 169; Rubins, *supra* note 2 at 3.
100 For other suggestions, see Salacuse, *supra* note 2 at 184.
101 Concerns regarding delay and cost are often voiced by practicing lawyers who are not favorable to ADR. See e.g. Salacuse *supra* note 2 at 177–8.
102 See Coe, "Preliminary Sketch", *supra* note 2 at 37; see also Nancy A. Welsh, "Mandatory Mediation and its Variations" in UNCTAD, *ADR II*, *supra* note 2 at 108–13.
103 On "half-compulsory mediation" see Welsh and Schneider, *supra* note 48.
104 See 2004 US Model BIT, *supra* note 99 and corresponding text.
105 Thanks to Laurence Boulle for bringing this possibility to my attention.

provides that an independent third person or organisation is to convene a meeting between the parties (usually after direct negotiations have broken down) to assist them to evaluate and choose an appropriate dispute resolution process, and if necessary, to select a service provider. The clause may provide that, in the absence of an agreement between the parties, the third party is to choose an appropriate process.[106]

In the context of IIAs, the convening clause could be added to the "amicable settlement" provision. It could state:

(2) If after [90] days a dispute has not been settled amicably through negotiations according to paragraph one, the parties shall meet under the direction of a convenor for the purpose of conflict analysis and to consider appropriate alternative dispute resolution.

(3) The convenor, a neutral person, will be selected by agreement of the parties to the dispute. If after 30 days a convenor has not been selected, the nomination shall be made by the [appointing authority].

(4) The convenor will meet [at least twice] with the parties within a [60] days period and provide the parties with recommendations as to possible alternative dispute resolution mechanisms.

Such a process would add limited time to the schedule (around three months), while it could provide substantial benefit in the long run, if appropriate ADR can be identified and eventually succeed. Also, it would avoid the issues described above where tribunals have not given full effect to the negotiation clauses because they did not provide "specific formalities" or "procedures."[107]

A second proposal would be the inclusion in IIAs of a provision on "early neutral evaluation" (ENE). As discussed above, ENE involves an evaluator who hosts informal meetings between the state, investors and their counsel.[108] The provision could also be an add on to the amicable negotiation clause. It could state:

---

106 Bobette Wolski, "Recent Developments in International Commercial Dispute Resolution: Expanding the Options" (2001) 13(2) Bond Law Review, online <http://epublications.bond.edu.au/blr/vol13/iss2/2>.

107 See *supra* notes 87–91 and corresponding text.

108 See ENE *supra* note 48 and corresponding text.

(2) If after [90] days a dispute has not been settled amicably through negotiations according to paragraph one, the parties shall meet with an evaluator.

(3) The evaluator, a neutral person, will be selected by agreement of the parties to the dispute. If after 30 days the evaluator has not been selected, the nomination will be made by the [appointing authority].

(4) Within [30] days, the evaluator will convene a first meeting to set out a schedule to hear the parties. This meeting should take place within [X] days.

(5) During a second meeting, the evaluator will hear the parties. Based on this, the evaluator will attempt to identify areas of agreement and issues to focus on.

(6) A third meeting will take place during which the evaluator will present his views to the parties and get their comments.

(7) The evaluator then writes a confidential evaluation of the prospects of a case and offers to present it to the parties.

(8) The discussions that took place during the ENE process and the evaluator's report shall not be disclosed in the event of an arbitration.[109]

Admittedly, this proposal is more involved than the first one. In terms of process, it poses the key challenge of timing. The ENE should take place early enough in the dispute settlement process (to be most efficient) but will only be useful and successful once the state has the necessary knowledge of the claim to engage with the evaluator. As a benefit, the ENE can help parties settle or move the case ahead more efficiently through the arbitration.

Conclusion

In view of the evidence regarding the substantial time and cost involved in the arbitration of investor-state disputes, the moment has come to consider increasing the use of ADR in the context of IIAs. The chapter addresses a specific point in time—when a notice of intent or a notice of arbitration has been submitted to a government by an investor. Even at this "late" point (when nothing was done successfully to resolve the conflict before it escalated into a full-fledge dispute), the chapter demonstrates that different ADR options are still available. From the perspective of the respondent state, a useful prism is to consider the options

---

109 Some of the language is taken from the definition of ENE provided above. See *ibid.*

that best match the different cases, categorized along a "merits spectrum." Direct or assisted negotiations may be most useful when the state is faced with a "meritorious" claim, while ENE and the expedited review of claims may be better suited to "unmeritorious" claims. Claims of "uncertain merit" may call for recourse to arbitration with a mediation window, concurrent med-arb, or other options which could be more appropriate than the single-model arbitration. As one author has noted: "Effective use of [Dispute Systems Design] to manage investment treaty conflict is likely to reduce the transaction costs of dispute resolution. This could decrease investment risks, lower the cost of investing, and produce economic incentives that make host governments more attractive investment opportunities."[110]

In order to facilitate and encourage the use of ADR, states should consider including specific provisions in their IIAs. While current IIAs arguably provide the room for ADR to occur (by not limiting it), more could be done in order to increase the efficiency of investor-state dispute resolution. At a minimum, two provisions could be considered: a convening clause and ENE. The expedited review of claims (provided in the context of ICSID) could also be extended through its inclusion in IIAs.

---

110 Franck, "Dispute System Designs", *supra* note 2 at 183 [notes omitted]; see also Andrea Kupfer Schneider, "Using Dispute System Design to Add More Process Choices to Investment Treaty Disputes" in UNCTAD, *ADR II*, *supra* note 2 at 95; Salacuse, *supra* note 2 at 153.

9 Is it necessary to avoid substantive and procedural overlaps with other agreements in IIAs?

Andreas R. Ziegler[*]

Introduction

Does the current "spaghetti bowl" of dispute settlement provisions in RTAs, IIAs and the WTO require "efficiency" promoting changes in the negotiation of IIAs? Most of the investment-related literature in recent years has focused on parallel or incoherent dispute settlement procedures within the area of investor-state proceedings. It has generally neglected the fact that dispute settlement provisions in IIAs (including investment chapters in RTAs) may interfere with the functioning of the multilateral trading system and its dispute settlement system—as well as the fast-growing parallel structure of RTAs. The key concepts normally associated with this development may be summarized as including, amongst others: forum shopping, conflicting requirements, parallel proceedings, institutional overlap and divergent interpretation.[1]

Many modern IIAs and RTAs contain investor-state dispute settlement provisions that are open to private parties (foreign investors). These procedures have been increasingly used over the last ten years and investors have been very innovative in using them to extend their protection from government action in a broad area of policies. This

---

* Professor of Law and Director of the LLM Programme in International and European Economic and Commercial Law at the Law Faculty of the University of Lausanne (Switzerland); Conjoint Professor at the Faculty of Law of the University of New South Wales (Australia); Visiting Professor at the Swiss Federal Institute of Technology Zurich and the University of St Gallen (Switzerland).
1 See e.g. Ernst-Ulrich Petersmann, "Justice as Conflict Resolution: Proliferation, Fragmentation and Decentralization of Dispute Settlement in International Trade" (2004) EUI Working Paper Law No. 2004/10, online: SSRN <http://ssrn.com/abstract=836324>; Anne van Aaken, "Fragmentation of International Law: The Case of International Investment Protection" (2008) 17 Finnish Yearbook of International Law 93.

new trend has most prominently come to the fore under NAFTA,[2] as investors have pursued investment claims that challenge states' trade policy measures. A number of claims under NAFTA's Chapter 11 have indeed been related to trade issues (including public procurement[3], countervailing duties[4] etc.) and this can also arise in the context of IIAs and other RTAs involving investor-state dispute settlement.[5] It has been argued that this may be a way to allow private parties to challenge trade measures before arbitral tribunals without having to rely on their home-state's willingness to take a case to the WTO or state-to-state dispute settlement in various RTAs (such as Chapter 20 under NAFTA).[6]

Part I of this chapter analyzes the overlapping provisions on dispute settlement in international economic agreements and provides examples of (problematic) situations that may arise as a result of the overlap. Part II surveys international treaty-making in international economic law. Part III focuses on the interactions (both substantive and procedural) of IIAs with dispute settlement provisions of other treaties. The chapter concludes that the "spaghetti bowl" effect may not be as detrimental to efficiency as one might first think.

---

2 *North American Free Trade Agreement Between the Government of Canada, the Government of Mexico and the Government of the United States*, December 17, 1992, Can TS 1994 No. 2, 32 ILM 289 (entered into force January 1, 1994) [NAFTA].

3 *ADF Group Inc v United States of America*, Award, ICSID Case No. ARB(AF)/00/1 (January 9, 2003); see also CJ Michael Flavell, QC, Martin G. Masse and Cyndee Todgham Cherniak, "Buy American or What?" (2009) International Trade Brief, online: McMillan <http://www.mcmillan.ca/Buy-American-or-What>.

4 Besides the famous softwood lumber cases—*infra* note 13 and corresponding text— see also Tania Voon, "NAFTA Chapter 19 Panel Follows WTO Appellate Body in Striking Down Zeroing" (2010) 14(29) American Society of International Law, 14(29) ASIL Insights, online: ASIL <http://www.asil.org/files/insight100923pdf. pdf>. With regard to the cases: *Re Stainless Steel Sheet and Strip In Coils from Mexico (Mexico v United States)* (2010), USA-MEX-2007-1904-01 (ch 19 Panel), online: NAFTA <http://registry.nafta-sec-alena.org/cmdocuments/edce701c-9720-424b-b232-1fd714d318ba.pdf>; *United States—Final Anti-Dumping Measures on Stainless Steel from Mexico (Complaint by the United States)* (2008), WTO Doc WT/DS50/AB/R (Appellate Body Report), online: WTO <http://docsonline.wto.org>.

5 An example involving SPS issues is a recent dispute involving the cigarettes producer Philip Morris International (PMI) challenging labelling requirements in Uruguay under an IIA (Switzerland-Uruguay), see "News in Brief: Uruguay prepares defense against Philip Morris" *Investment Treaty News* (December 16, 2010), online: IISD <http://www.iisd.org/itn/2010/12/16/news-in-brief-2/>.

6 Armand de Mestral, "NAFTA Dispute Settlement: Creative Experiment or Confusion" in Lorand Bartels and Federico Ortino (eds), *Regional Trade Agreements and the WTO Legal System* (Oxford: Oxford University Press, 2006) at 359 ff.

Overlapping dispute settlement provisions in international economic agreements

WTO, RTAs and IIAs

The co-existence of the WTO, RTAs and IIAs can lead to legal problems when it comes to the use and outcomes of their respective dispute settlement provisions.[7] Especially in the late 1990s the WTO Dispute Settlement Understanding (DSU) was welcomed as a major achievement for the resolution of trade disputes. The number of notifications of disputes and the number of panel and Appellate Body reports is certainly impressive in comparison to the general numbers of cases adjudicated by international courts and tribunals.[8]

At the same time, the WTO is silent with regard to the existence of specific dispute settlement procedures in other agreements and one must rely on the language of the DSU and possibly the exceptions for RTAs found in the GATT and the General Agreement on Trade in Services (GATS) to address the issue.[9] While the number of cases relating to dispute settlement procedures in RTAs seems rather small[10] to date, there is an increasing number of arbitral awards under IIAs and investment chapters of RTAs.[11] Often, they do not call for any comparative or

---

7 See also Jennifer Hillman, "Conflicts Between Dispute Settlement Mechanisms in Regional Trade Agreements and the WTO" (2009) 42(2) Cornell Int'l LJ 193; Joost Pauwelyn and Luiz Eduardo Salles, "Forum Shopping Before International Tribunals" (2009) 42(1) Cornell Int'l LJ 77.

8 According to the WTO, as of April 1, 2011 424 disputes have been registered under the WTO system. 102 cases have led to an Appellate Report by June 1, 2011; see the lists online: WTO <http://www.wto.org/english/tratop_e/dispu_e/dispu_e.htm#disputes>. For more statistics see Kara Leitner and Simon Lester, "WTO Dispute Settlement 1995–2010—A Statistical Analysis" (2011) 14(1) J Int'l Econ L 191. See *Understanding on Rules and Procedures Governing the Settlement of Disputes* [DSU] in World Trade Organization, *The Legal Texts: The Results of the Uruguay Round of Multilateral Trade Negotiations* (Cambridge: Cambridge University Press, 1999) [WTO Agreements].

9 See DSU, GATT and *General Agreement on Trade in Services* (GATS) in WTO Agreements *ibid.* The leading decision is *Turkey—Restrictions on Imports of Textile and Clothing Products* (1999), WT/DS34/AB/R, (Appellate Body Report), online: WTO <http://www.wto.org/english/tratop_e/dispu_e/34abr_e.pdf>; a more recent significant decision is *Brazil—Measures affecting Imports of Retreaded Tires* (2007), WT/DS332/AB/R (Appellate Body report) online: WTO <http://www.wto.org/english/tratop_e/dispu_e/cases_e/ds332_e.htm>.

10 Maybe with the exceptions of NAFTA and Mercosur. See for the latter and other agreements in Latin America: online: UN IDATD <http://idatd.eclac.cl/controversias/index_en.jsp>.

11 UNCTAD reported 390 known investor-state cases at the end of 2010. See UNCTAD, "Latest Developments in Investor-State Dispute Settlement" (2011) IIA

comprehensive analysis with regard to trade rules contained in RTAs or the WTO, but increasingly there are overlaps with regard to the interpretation of certain terms or the use of specific venues and procedures (forum shopping).[12]

Typical situations

The Softwood Lumber Dispute (or disputes—depending on the view of the various contentious measures and the timing) between the United States and Canada has not only led to NAFTA claims of all types[13] but has also been dealt with by the WTO and most recently even by traditional bilateral arbitration proceedings outside of the NAFTA and WTO setting. It is a typical example of the overlap that can arise in complex economic situations where obligations under several treaties in various areas of international economic law—in particular trade and investment—arise. The complexity of the dispute led to several phases and a plethora of proceedings. As an example, we can cite the so-called Lumber III dispute (1991–96) that led to proceedings under Chapter 19 of the United States-Canada Free Trade Agreement (UCFT—the predecessor to NAFTA) and the Agreement on Subsidies and Countervailing Measures of the old GATT of 1947 (before the coming into force of the WTO Agreement). It was finally settled in a 13-page US-Canada *ad hoc* agreement—a negotiated settlement between the two states. In a later phase of the dispute, often referred to as "Lumber IV" (2001–06), 11 NAFTA Chapter 19 panels (Antidumping/Countervailing duty determination) were constituted in addition to four NAFTA Chapter 11 (Investment) tribunals and six WTO dispute settlement panels. Apart from this plethora of international cases, due to the construction of the NAFTA provisions, five US Court of International Trade cases, two District Court cases and three Court of Appeals petitions were filed. In its most recent iteration, this dispute has been the object of two arbitral awards

Issues Note 1, online: UNCTAD <http://www.unctad.org/en/docs/webdiaeia20113_en.pdf> at 1.

12 See Gabrielle Marceau and Julian Wyatt, "Dispute Settlement Regimes Intermingled: Regional Trade Agreements and the WTO" (2010) 1(1) Journal of International Dispute Settlement 67.

13 See e.g. on the various procedures available Taylor G. Stout, "NAFTA Dispute Settlement Procedures" (2011) International Judicial Monitor, online: International Judicial Monitor <http://www.judicialmonitor.org/archive_winter2011/spotlight.html>.

by the London Court of International Arbitration (LCIA) in 2009[14] and 2011.[15]

A second leading case exemplifying the use of various dispute settlement procedures in the investment and trade fields is the so-called Sweetener or Soft Drink Dispute in which typical trade questions were addressed under both the WTO and NAFTA (Chapter 19) while other aspects were brought by private investors before investor-state arbitral tribunals.[16] This case involved a series of trade or investment-related measures taken by Mexico to protect its sugar producers against the import from the United States, and local production, of cheaper High Fructose Corn Syrup (HFCS) to be used in the production of soft drinks. This led to the United States challenging certain Mexican anti-dumping duties at the WTO[17] while Mexico, for its part, sought to bring the United States to state-to-state arbitration under Chapter 20 of the NAFTA, in an effort to force the United States to permit a greater level of duty-free Mexican sugar imports.[18] However, Mexico accused the United States of blocking the appointment of a tribunal to hear this claim under NAFTA and asked the panel under the WTO Dispute Settlement to take this into account and to dismiss the WTO claim in favor of the NAFTA proceedings—which was rejected by the Panel and the Appellate Body of the WTO as they lacked the power to do this.[19]

14 See *United States of America v Canada*, Decision, LCIA Case No. 91312 (September 27, 2009).

15 *United States of America v Canada*, Award, London Court of International Arbitration Case No. 81010 (January, 20 and 28 2011).

16 See William J. Davey and André Sapir, "The Soft Drinks Case: The WTO and Regional Agreements" (2009) 8(1) World Trade Review 5; Sandy Hamelmann, "Internationale Jurisdiktionskonflikte und Vernetzungen transnationaler Rechtsregime: Die Entscheidungen des Panels und des Appellate Body der WTO in Sachen 'Mexico—Tax Measures on Soft Drinks and Other Beverages'" (2006) 58 Beiträge zum transnationalen Wirtschaftsrecht 1.

17 *Mexico—Anti-Dumping Investigation of High-Fructose Corn Syrup (HFCS) from the United States (Complaint by the United States)* (2001), WTO Doc WT/DS132/AB/RW (Appellate Body Report), online: WTO <http://wto.org/english/tratop_e/dispu_e/cases_e/ds132_e.htm>.

18 See *Mexico—Measures on Soft Drinks and Other Beverages (Complaint by the United States)* (2005),WTO Doc WT/DS308/R (Panel Report), online: WTO <http://www.wto.org/english/tratop_e/dispu_e/cases_e/ds308_e.htm> at para 4.92 [*Mexico Soft Drinks*].

19 See *Mexico Soft Drinks, ibid*; *Mexico—Taxes Measures on Soft Drinks and Other Beverages (Complaint by the United States)* (2006), WTO Doc WT/DS308/AB/R (Appellate Body Report), online: WTO <http://www.wto.org/english/tratop_e/dispu_e/cases_e/ds308_e.htm> [*Mexico—Soft Drinks Appellate Body*] See Joost Pauwelyn, "Adding Sweeteners to Softwood Lumber: the WTO–NAFTA 'Spaghetti Bowl' is Cooking" (2006) 9(1) J Int'l Econ L 197 [Pauwelyn, "Adding Sweetners"].

Moreover, on December 31, 2001 the Mexican Congress approved a new tax of 20 per cent on soft drinks and syrups sweetened with sweeteners other than sugar. It was this tax that gave rise to three separate claims by US investors under NAFTA Chapter 11. As well, the tax led to WTO[20] and NAFTA proceedings initiated against Mexico by the US government. Ultimately, the tax was repealed by Mexico at the outset of 2001 in order to comply with a WTO ruling. However, the private claimants persisted with their NAFTA Chapter 11 claim, seeking damages for losses during the period when the tax was in effect.[21]

Plethora of treaties relating to international economic law

Treaties regulating, or at least including, aspects of bilateral economic relations have a very long tradition. In particular during the late 18th and the 19th centuries they were usually concluded in the form of integrated instruments comprising trade between the contracting parties and the establishment and treatment of nationals of another contracting party. The most common form used was the Treaty on Friendship, Commerce and Navigation (FCN) among two or more states. For land-locked countries—like Switzerland—the title was often changed to Treaty on Friendship, Commerce and Establishment thereby making this comprehensive approach even more evident.

After World War II, an attempt to create a comprehensive multilateral treaty in the context of the United Nations Conference on Trade and Employment failed. Not only was it impossible to establish the International Trade Organization (ITO) with a broad mandate, but the attempts to codify investment rules had, even prior to the signature of the Final Act, led to rather meagre outcomes. This was due in large part to the absence of a clear consensus on the scope and role of such rules.[22]

While the creation of the WTO in 1994 has led to a truly multilateral framework for trade and the resolution of trade disputes, the area of investment and investment disputes remains outside of this framework. This has led to a classical dichotomy in the teaching and negotiations of

---

20 *Mexico Soft Drinks, supra* note 18 and *Mexico Soft Drinks Appellate Body, supra* note 19.
21 See *Archer Daniels Midland Co and Tate & Lyle Ingredients Americas, Inc v United Mexican States*, Award, ICSID Case No. ARB (AF)/04/5 (November 21, 2007); *Corn Products International, Inc v United Mexican States*, Decision on Responsibility, ICSID Case No. ARB (AF)/04/1 (January 15, 2008); *Cargill, Inc v United Mexican States*, Award, ICSID Case No. ARB (AF)/05/2 (September 18, 2009).
22 See for details Andreas R. Ziegler, "Multilateraler Investitionsschutz im Wirtschaftsrecht" in Dirk Ehlers and Hans-Michael Wolffgang (eds), *Rechtsfragen internationaler Investitionen* (Frankfurt: Verlag Recht und Wirtschaft 2009).

the two fields as "international trade law" and "international investment law."[23] Although the inclusion of investment rules into the WTO has been discussed, the major direct overlap of the two regimes relates to the Agreement on Trade Related Investment Measures (TRIMS) and the market access and treatment of foreign services suppliers (GATS Mode 3).[24]

The situation has become even more confusing as more IIAs[25] have been negotiated that include ambitious investor-state dispute settlement procedures that allow investors to challenge host state measures in a rather comprehensive way that potentially leads to overlaps between investment measures under an IIA and trade measures governed by the WTO. This tendency has been exacerbated by the fact that an increasing number of comprehensive RTAs have been negotiated since the early 1990s that include trade and investment rules[26], normally accompanied by various types of dispute settlement procedures.[27] In some cases, even older RTAs have been completed by dispute settlement mechanisms where they had not been included in the original agreements.[28]

The fact that the existence and increased focus on RTAs can affect the efficiency and legitimacy of the WTO (and divert members' interests

---

23 See Asif Qureshi and Andreas R. Ziegler, *International Economic Law*, 3rd edn (London: Thomson Sweet & Maxwell, 2011).

24 See TRIMS and GATS in WTO Agreements, *supra* note 8. See e.g. Rudolf Adlung and Martín Molinuevo, "Bilateralism in Services Trade: Is There Fire Behind the (BIT-) Smoke" (2008) 11(2) J Int'l Econ L 365, online: JIEL <http://jiel. oxfordjournals.org/content/11/2/365.abstract>.

25 According to UNCTAD, by the end of 2010 there were 2,807 BITs, 309 other international agreements with investment related provisions, see UNCTAD, *World Investment Report 2011: Non-equity Modes of International Production and Development* (New York and Geneva: UNCTAD, 2011) at 100.

26 See WTO RTA Gateway, online: WTO <http://www.wto.org/english/tratop_e/ region_e/region_e.htm>. (As of May 15, 2011, some 489 RTAs, counting goods and services notifications separately, have been notified to the GATT/WTO. Of these, 358 RTAs were notified under art XXIV of the GATT 1947 or GATT 1994; 36 under the Enabling Clause; and 95 under art V of the GATS. At that same date, 297 agreements were in force.)

27 See Pauwelyn, "Adding Sweetners", *supra* note 19.

28 See e.g. the agreement recently concluded between Tunisia and the European Community (now the European Union): EC, *Council Decision 2010/91/EC of 10 November 2009 on the conclusion of an Agreement in the form of a Protocol between the European Community and the Republic of Tunisia establishing a dispute settlement mechanism applicable to disputes under the trade provisions of the Euro-Mediterranean Agreement establishing an Association between the European Communities and their Member States, of the one part, and the Republic of Tunisia, of the other part* [2010] OJ L 40/75 [*EC-Tunisia Protocol Agreement*]; see on this Andreas R. Ziegler, *Droit international économique de la Suisse— Une introduction* (Berne, Stämpfli: 2010) at para 162.

from the WTO) has been discussed elsewhere. From a legal perspective, article XXIV GATT[29] and article V GATS[30]—which allow WTO members to enter such agreements—have been subject to long-running negotiations and tensions within the WTO. Although most states claim to enter only into agreements that fully comply with their WTO obligations,[31] this has often been questioned. In addition, for several years the co-existence between the WTO and RTAs has been described as a "spaghetti bowl" where WTO disciplines and commitments are only applicable between an ever smaller group of members while more and more of them rely on preferential rules—a fact that leads to little transparency and increasingly distorts international trade flows.[32]

IIAs and dispute-settlement mechanisms in other treaties

Substantive overlap

One reason why the dispute settlement mechanisms of various agreements may apply to the same situation stems from the very fact that, in certain RTAs, the contracting parties simply affirm existing rights and obligations with respect to each other under the WTO Agreement or another treaty. For example, article 1.2 of the 2006 US-Peru TPA confirms the parties' obligations under another agreement and in particular the WTO ("The Parties affirm their existing rights and obligations with respect to each other under the WTO Agreement and other agreements to which such Parties are party"). This is repeated throughout the agreement, for instance with regard to the Agreement on Technical Barriers to Trade (TBT).[33] The same is true for other recent

29 See GATT in WTO Agreements, *supra* note 8.
30 *Ibid.*
31 This even figures as a prominent statement in the text (often the preamble) of most RTAs. Provisions confirming the Parties' WTO obligations are very common in RTAs with regard to various areas covered.
32 The WTO Committee on Trade and Development, on October 4, 2010, approved a proposal by Brazil, China, India and the United States to establish a transparency mechanism for preferential trade arrangements adopted by the General Council at its meeting of December 14, 2010. See WTO General Council, *Minutes of Meeting* (held on December 14, 2010) WTO Doc WT/COMTD/71, online: WTO <http://www.wto.org/english/thewto_e/gcounc_e/meet_dec10_e.htm>; WTO General Council, *Minutes of Meeting* (held on December 14, 2010) WTO Doc WT/L/806, online: WTO <http://www.wto.org/english/news_e/news10_e/summary_gc_dec10_e.htm>.
33 *The United States-Peru Trade Promotion Agreement*, April 12, 2006, online: USTR <http://www.ustr.gov/trade-agreements/free-trade-agreements/peru-tpa/final-text> [US-Peru TPA].

agreements like the ones concluded by European Free Trade Association (EFTA).[34]

In certain cases, parties to RTAs explicitly repeat existing (WTO) obligations or refer to them. This often leads to a so-called incorporation of those rules and normally makes their violation also a violation of the agreement in which they are confirmed. This is a well-known practice, as evidenced (already with regard to the GATT 1947) under NAFTA and in the EU- and EFTA-Agreements with third states. To take a recent example from US practice, article 7.3.2 of the US-Peru TPA explicitly incorporated the existing work undertaken within the WTO with regard to the rules of the TBT Agreement.

If this happens in an IIA or in the investment chapter of an RTA, it may have the additional effect of not only incorporating WTO disciplines or disciplines from other agreements into the bilateral or regional agreement, but also making them subject to the investor-state arbitration that is typical of both investment agreements and investment chapters. A good example is article 10.7.5 of the US-Peru TPA. In the context of the definition of an expropriation in the investment chapter of the agreement (Chapter 10), the agreement incorporates WTO law. In order to assess the legality of a compulsory license, the parties refer to the rules of the Agreement on Trade-related Aspects of International Property Rights (TRIPS) Agreement. This practice exists also in other IIAs and RTAs.[35] Certain IIAs even explicitly exclude the possibility to

---

34　In the recently concluded Free Trade Agreement between the EFTA States and Peru of July 14, 2010 the Preamble includes the following statements: "Building on their respective rights and obligations under the Marrakesh Agreement Establishing the World Trade Organization (hereinafter referred to as 'the WTO Agreement') and the other agreements negotiated thereunder and other multilateral and bilateral instruments of co-operation . . ."; and in art 1.4 (Relation to Other International Agreements) one can read: "The provisions of this Agreement shall be applied without prejudice to the rights and obligations of the Parties under the WTO Agreement and the other agreements negotiated thereunder to which they are a party and any other international agreement to which they are a party." See *Free Trade Agreement Between The Republic of Peru and the EFTA States*, July 14, 2010, online: EFTA <http://www.efta.int/~/media/Documents/legal-texts/free-trade-relations/peru/EFTA-Peru%20Free%20Trade%20Agreement%20EN.pdf> at III, art 1.4 [*Peru-EFTA FTA*].

35　See *Agreement on Trade-related Aspects of International Property Rights* (TRIPS) in WTO Agreements *supra* note 8. The same can be found in the *Agreement Between the Swiss Federation and the Republic of Columbia on the Promotion and Reciprocal Protection of Investments*, May 17, 2006, online: seco <http://www.seco.admin.ch/themen/00513/00594/04638/index.html?lang=en> at 15: "(1) It is understood that the said Article is without prejudice to the issuance of compulsory licenses granted in relation to intellectual property rights or other measures taken in accordance with

challenge the WTO compatibility of compulsory licenses under their investor-state dispute settlement provisions.[36]

Similarly the incorporation of the WTO's TRIMs into IIAs or investment chapters of RTAs is very common. The following example stems from the 2009 Switzerland-Japan FTA:

> Article 96 Prohibition of Performance Requirements
> For the purposes of this Chapter, the Annex to the Agreement on Trade-Related Investment Measures in Annex 1A to the WTO Agreement is hereby incorporated into and made part of this Agreement, *mutatis mutandis.*[37]

A similar idea can be found in the trilateral FTA between ASEAN, Australia and New Zealand.[38] In article 5 of Chapter 11 (Investment), the agreement incorporates the existing WTO obligation under the TRIMS. This article, however, is excluded from the dispute settlement procedure of the investment chapter—possibly in order to avoid the interpretation of WTO law by investor-state arbitration tribunals.[39] However, such an exclusion from dispute settlement does not exist in other agreements, such as the Japan-Switzerland RTA quoted above that also incorporates the TRIMS. The latter case could therefore easily lead to an investor-state dispute settlement procedure in which the arbitral tribunal might have to interpret the TRIMS.

the WTO Agreement on Trade-Related Aspects of Intellectual Property Rights." See on this issue in detail Christopher Gibson, "A Look at the Compulsory License in Investment Arbitration: The Case of Indirect Expropriation" (2010) 25 Am U Int'l L Rev 357.

36 See e.g. Columbia Model Bit (2007), online: Italaw <http://italaw.com/documents/inv_model_bit_colombia.pdf> at art 6.7. ("The Contracting Parties confirm that issuance of compulsory licenses granted in accordance with the TRIPS Agreement of the WTO, may not be challenged under the provisions set out in this Article").

37 *Agreement on Free Trade and Economic Partnership between Switzerland and Japan*, February 19, 2009, online: Seco <http://www.seco.admin.ch/themen/00513/02655/02731/02970/index.html?lang=en> at art 96 [*Switzerland-Japan FTA*].

38 *ASEAN-Australia-New Zealand Free Trade Agreement*, February 27, 2009, online: ASEAN <http://www.asean.fta.govt.nz/chapter-11-investment/>.

39 *Ibid.* ("Claim by an Investor of a Party: If an investment dispute has not been resolved within 180 days of the receipt by a disputing Party of a request for consultations, the disputing investor may, subject to this Article, submit to conciliation or arbitration a claim: that the disputing Party has breached an obligation arising under Article 4 (National Treatment), Article 6 (Treatment of Investment), Article 7 (Compensation for Losses), Article 8 (Transfers), and Article 9 (Expropriation and Compensation) . . ." at art 20.)

Of particular importance is the apparent widespread trend of incorporating WTO exceptions into investment chapters of RTAs.[40] A typical example (though relating to trade in services) is article 5.8 of the EFTA-Peru FTA that reads: "The exception in subparagraph (d) of article XIV of the GATS is hereby incorporated into and made part of this Chapter [investment Chapter], *mutatis mutandis*."[41] Another example of a WTO-based exception clause in an investment chapter of an RTA can be found in the 2009 Switzerland- Japan FTA:

> Article 95 General and Security Exceptions
>
> 1. In respect of the making of investments, Articles XIV and XIV*bis* of the GATS, which are hereby incorporated into and made part of this Agreement, mutatis mutandis, shall apply.
> 2. Paragraph 1 of Article XIV*bis* of the GATS shall also apply, mutatis mutandis, to investments made.
> 3. This Article shall not apply to paragraph 1 of Article 86 [General Treatment], and Articles 91 [Expropriation] and 92 [Treatment in Case of Strife]. [. . .][42]

Apart from the reference to, or incorporation of, existing obligations in other agreements in IIAs, there may result a substantive overlap from the scope of some of the rather vague notions with regard to treatment and protection usually used in IIAs. A number of authors have analyzed the question whether typical treatment standards found in IIAs can be used by investors to challenge potential violations of the WTO (or other agreements) by the host state.[43] Certain tribunals have also dealt with this question.[44] Here the substantive overlap in the protection is used to bring a breach of another treaty obligation into the reach of the dispute settlement mechanism of the IIA[45]:

---

40 See Andrew Newcombe in this book at ch 15.
41 *Peru-EFTA FTA, supra* note 34.
42 *Switzerland-Japan FTA, supra* note 37.
43 See Gaetan Verhoosel "The Use of Investor-State Arbitration under Bilateral Investment Treaties to Seek Relief for Breaches of WTO Law" (2003) 6(2) J Int'l Econ *L* 493.
44 See e.g. *Grand River Enterprises et al v United States of America*, Award, UNCITRAL (January 12, 2011) [*Grand River*].
45 The contrary is also possible; in a recent decision by the European Court of Human Rights the non-enforcement of an arbitral award was considered a violation of the Additional Protocol to the European Convention on Human Rights. See *Kin-Stib and Majkíc v Serbia*, No 12312/05 (April 20, 2010).

- Of particular importance in past cases was the question of whether the "fair and equitable treatment" obligation could be interpreted as requiring a host state to comply with all its obligations under international law, including treaty obligations outside the IIA. Arbitral tribunals so far have tried to avoid clearly answering this question and relied on a self-contained interpretation of the investment treaty standards.[46]
- Also "umbrella clauses," which potentially make any other legal obligation that a state has entered into a breach of the IIA, have been identified by some legal writers as potentially allowing investors to make an IIA claim on the basis of the breach of another treaty.[47]
- A discriminatory treatment of imports can easily be considered a violation of the national treatment and/or most-favored-nation standards contained in most IIAs if it can be shown that this discriminatory treatment affects the foreign investment or the foreign investor.[48]
- Any violation of intellectual property rights according to the TRIPs can easily be construed as treatment that is not fair and equitable as requested under most IIAs or even to constitute an expropriation where intellectual property rights are covered by the IIA (as it is very often the case). For example, there are discussions in several fora on new labeling requirements for cigarettes. In particular, the requirement to sell cigarettes in plain-packaging is highly controversial and has led to a (test) case launched in 2010 by Tobacco giant Philip Morris International (PMI) against Uruguay under an IIA on the one hand,[49]

---

46 See Charles Owen Verrill Jr, "Are WTO Violations Also Contrary to the Fair and Equitable Treatment Obligations in Investor Protection Agreements" (2005) 11(2) ILSA Journal of International and Comparative Law 287.

47 See Gaetan Verhoosel, *supra* note 43.

48 See also Jürgen Kurtz, "National Treatment, Foreign Investment and Regulatory Autonomy: The Search for Protectionism or Something More?" in P. Kahn and T. Wälde (eds), *New Aspects of International Investment Law* (Leiden: Martinus Nijhoff, 2007) at 311. In addition, the different concepts of discrimination underlying the WTO and IIAs may be of relevance; see on this issue Nicholas DiMascio and Joost Pauwelyn, "Nondiscrimination in Trade and Investment Treaties: Worlds Apart or Two Sides of the Same Coin?" (2008) 102(1) AJIL 48.

49 In an investor-state dispute settlement proceeding initiated in 2010, tobacco giant Philip Morris International (PMI) has initiated an ICSID arbitration against Uruguay over new rules requiring that 80% of cigarette pack surfaces be devoted to graphic warnings of the dangers associated with smoking. See *FTR Holding SA, Philip Morris Products S.A. and Abal Hermanos S.A. v Oriental Republic of Uruguay*, ICSID Case No. ARB/10/7 (March 26, 2010), online: Italaw <http://italaw.com/chronological_list_if_content.htm>.

and discussions at the WTO with regard to the TRIPs on the other.[50]

- Many IIAs refer to (general) international law with regard to the treatment of foreign investors and investment, without limiting it to specific areas or sources of law. Often treaties require treatment no less than "that required by international law," as is the case in most IIAs negotiated by the United States.[51] This could, of course, be used to argue that the violation of any obligation under international law shall be considered a violation of the IIA governed by the dispute settlement available only for such violations of the IIA. This issue was explicitly addressed by the NAFTA parties in an Interpretation by the NAFTA Free Trade Commission (FTC) of July 31, 2001: "A determination that there has been a breach of another provision of the NAFTA, or of a separate international agreement, does not establish that there has been a breach of Article 1105(1)" and article 1105 "do[es] not require treatment in addition to or beyond that which is required by the customary international law minimum standard of treatment of aliens."[52]

- Finally, there is great potential for overlaps in those areas of the WTO system where we have proper investment-rules, in particular—as mentioned above—under mode 3 supply of services in the GATS.[53]

So far, arbitrators in investor-state proceedings have shied away from allowing the import of other treaty obligations into IIAs. They seem to avoid, as far as possible, a situation where they have to interpret other treaties (like human rights treaties, RTAs or the WTO). A possible argument in favor of this approach is that importing other treaties tends to expand the available protection and can overload the IIAs as well as the balance that was agreed upon when negotiating the IIA. A recent example

---

50 A new Australian draft law that would require cigarettes—and eventually other tobacco products—to be sold in plain packages, came under scrutiny in the June 7, 2011 WTO intellectual property (TRIPS) council meeting. Some members said it could violate trademark rights while others defended it as a legitimate step to protect public health. See WTO, "Members debate cigarette plain-packaging's impact on trademark rights", June 7, 2011, online: WTO <http://www.wto.org/english/news_e/news11_e/trip_07jun11_e.htm>.

51 See e.g. US-Egypt BIT (1982) at art II(4); US-Argentina BIT (1991) at art II(2).

52 NAFTA Free Trade Commission, *Notes of Interpretation of Certain Chapter 11 Provisions* (July 31, 2001), online: DFAIT <http://www.international.gc.ca/trade-agreements-accords-commerciaux/disp-diff/NAFTA-Interpr.aspx?lang=en&view=d>.

53 This question is beyond the scope of this chapter.

is the award in *Grand River v United States*, a dispute brought by a Canadian investor under NAFTA Chapter 11.[54] The arbitrators declined to consider the possibility that a breach of non-NAFTA obligations may give rise to a breach of the treatment obligations guaranteed under NAFTA. In reaching this decision, the arbitrators expressly deferred to the 2001 interpretive note. The tribunal stated that it would not "import" other rules of international law into the NAFTA, nor would the tribunal permit "alteration of an interpretation established through the normal interpretive processes of the Vienna Convention."[55] Some authors have raised the issue that the arbitrators should be more open to such arguments in view of article 31(3)(c) of the Vienna Convention, which provides that interpretations shall take account of "any relevant rules of international law applicable in the relations between the parties."[56] For example, one commentator argued that "[w]hile Article 31(3)(c) does not operate as a springboard for 'importing' external norms into a given treaty, such as the NAFTA—and providing claimants with the ability to claim for the breach of such external obligations—it might be the case that other relevant rules of international law might shape an arbitral tribunal's interpretation of a given investment treaty or trade agreement obligation."[57]

Procedural overlap

Traditionally, RTAs did not address the possible overlap with the GATT 1947. Furthermore, even after the coming into force of the WTO as the successor framework, they are often silent or ambiguous with respect to the relationship. Also, with regard to other dispute settlement mechanisms, the RTAs normally do not contain specific rules. However, a comprehensive approach can be found in some recent trade agreements.[58] The new agreement between Tunisia and the European Union[59] foresees:

54 *Grand River, supra* note 44.
55 *Ibid* at para 71.
56 See *Vienna Convention on the Law of Treaties*, May 23, 1969, 1155 UNTS 331, 8 ILM.679 (entered into force January 27, 1980).
57 See Luke Eric Peterson, "Analysis: Tribunal in Grand River v. U.S.A. arbitration declines to import non-investment law obligations into NAFTA; role of other 'relevant' legal obligations in treaty interpretation under Vienna Convention is not discussed" *IA Reporter*, March 6, 2011, online: IA Reporter <http://www.iareporter.com/articles/20110306_3>.
58 See also for Mercosur: Guilherme Morales de Paula, "A cláusula de eleição de foro do Protocolo de Olivos e seus efeitos contraproducentes para o Mercosul" (2005) 6(1) Revista Escuela Direito Pelotas 167.
59 See *EC-Tunisia Protocol Agreement, supra* note 28; an alternative example can be found in the US-Peru TPA *supra* note 33 at art 21.3.

Article 20 Relation with WTO obligations

1. Recourse to the dispute settlement provisions of this Protocol shall be without prejudice to any action in the WTO framework, including dispute settlement action.

2. However, where a Party has, with regard to a particular measure, instituted a dispute settlement proceeding, either under this Protocol or under the WTO Agreement, it may not institute a dispute settlement proceeding regarding the same measure in the other forum until the first proceeding has ended. In addition, a Party shall not seek redress for the breach of an obligation which is identical under the Association Agreement and under the WTO Agreement in the two forums. In such case, once a dispute settlement proceeding has been initiated, the Party shall not bring a claim seeking redress for the breach of the identical obligation under the other agreement to the other forum, unless the forum selected fails for procedural or jurisdictional reasons to make findings on that claim.

3. For the purposes of paragraph 2:

   • dispute settlement proceedings under the WTO Agreement are deemed to be initiated by a Party's request for the establishment of a panel under Article 6 of the Understanding on Rules and Procedures Governing the Settlement of Disputes of the WTO (DSU) and are deemed to be ended when the Dispute Settlement Body adopts the panel's report, and the Appellate Body's report as the case may be, under Articles 16 and 17(14) of the DSU,

   • dispute settlement proceedings under this Protocol are deemed to be initiated by a Party's request for the establishment of an arbitration panel under Article 5(1) and are deemed to be ended when the arbitration panel notifies its ruling to the Parties and to the subcommittee on industry, trade and services under Article 8.

4. Nothing in this Protocol shall preclude a Party from implementing the suspension of obligations authorised by the Dispute Settlement Body of the WTO. The WTO Agreement shall not be invoked to preclude a Party from suspending its obligations under this Protocol.

It is mostly with regard to trade disputes and the states involved therein that a number of potential frictions have been identified (in particular with regard to the WTO). First, a respondent may try to dismiss a

WTO claim by invoking an existing claim based on an obligation under another treaty.[60] This argument cannot be made with regard to related investor-state proceedings as the home state of the investor is not directly involved in the arbitral proceedings under the IIA. Secondly, a respondent state may seek to justify its conduct inconsistent with a treaty by referring to the claimant's conduct inconsistent with another treaty, as was the case in Mexico—Taxes on Soft Drinks (DS308) where Mexico sought to justify its (discriminatory) tax by arguing that it was necessary to secure the US compliance with its obligation to establish a NAFTA panel in order to resolve the sugar dispute.[61]

When it comes to investment chapters in RTAs or IIAs, certain treaties contain an obligation to choose a forum, but traditionally this clause is concerned with the choice between international investment arbitration procedures and domestic courts (choice of forum, fork in the road).[62] The problem regarding such a choice of forum lies in the very fact that under trade agreements (including the WTO) there is no possibility for private investors to use them and hence they normally only have investor-state dispute-settlement procedures at their disposal. To exclude recourse to such proceedings in the case where the home state has taken up the issue in trade-related proceedings seems exaggerated and would appear to be incompatible with the spirit of investor-state dispute settlement. It is often the intention of contracting states to allow investors to defend their rights without relying on diplomatic protection.

60 See e.g. *Argentina—Definitive Anti Dumping Duties on Poultry* (2003), WTO Doc WT/DS241/R (Panel Report), online: WTO <http://www.wto.org/english/traptop_e/dispu_e/cases_e/ds241_e.htm> (Argentina asked the WTO panel to dismiss the case filed by Brazil in light of prior Mercosur panel ruling or, alternatively, to treat the latter as binding; the panel declined to do so as it could not take the Mercosur proceedings into account); see also Caroline Henckels, "Overcoming Jurisdictional Isolationism at the WTO-FTA Nexus: A Potential Approach for the WTO" (2008)19(3) EJIL 571. Henckels argues that in the interest of the effective administration of justice, the WTO's judicial organ should use its inherent power of comity to decline to exercise jurisdiction so that the dispute can be resolved by an FTA tribunal where a dispute is inextricably connected with a dispute under an FTA and that exercising jurisdiction would not be reasonable in the circumstances. Another case involved the European Union arguing that the United States were estopped from bringing claims under WTO SCM Agreement in view of bilateral 1979 and 1992 agreements between the EU and the US (*EC—Measures Affecting Trade in Large Civil Aircraft* (2011), WTO Doc WT/DS316/AB/R)). See also *Mexico—Taxes on Soft Drinks (DS308)*, *supra* note 18 (Mexico asked the WTO panel to dismiss in favor of dispute under NAFTA ch 20 over US restrictions on sugar imports: both the established Panel and the Appellate Body found no power in the applicable law to decline jurisdiction).

61 See *Mexico Soft Drink*, *supra* note 18 and corresponding text.

62 See e.g. Qureshi and Ziegler, *supra* note 23 at 523.

Conclusion

While in trade chapters of RTAs we increasingly find certain rules that try to avoid parallel proceedings among the same state parties, this approach is not applicable to overlaps between IIAs and their investor-state dispute settlement provisions as well as the substantive and procedural overlap with trade law. The parties are not the same and investors have only this venue to obtain an arbitral award.[63] Therefore, we cannot speak of a typical case of forum shopping, as it may be the case for a state that chooses between various procedures among different RTAs or the WTO. Investors can often choose between various venues (*fora*) under the same IIA or use various IIAs. This can lead to "forum shopping" and parallel proceedings, but there is no overlap issue with other treaty regimes.[64]

However, the fact that various arbitral tribunals under IIAs, RTAs and the WTO can interpret similar language and concepts differently cannot be tackled with the existing mechanisms. Within the WTO, one of the Appellate Body's functions is to create legal certainty and avoid "incoherent" outcomes.[65] Within ICSID, the Annulment Proceedings could in principle serve a similar function, although to a lesser extent.[66] The annulment process creates an option to re-examine the original award. However, as the scope of review is highly limited and there is no permanent annulment body, the current situation is a far cry from creating a proper appellate body leading to greater coherence.[67] These factors have contributed to the criticisms leveled against ICSID for a lack of coherence in its annulment jurisprudence.[68]

What does this mean regarding the promotion of efficiency in the negotiation of IIAs? As long as we do not have a fully integrated system

---

63 The issue of parallel investor-state proceedings shall not be treated here.

64 See Jean-François Hébert's ch 13 in this book on measures to prevent the abuse of corporate structure. See also Robin F. Hansen "Parallel Proceedings in Investor-State Treaty Arbitration: Responses for Treaty-Drafters, Arbitrators and Parties" (2010) 73(4) The Modern Law Review 523, online: SSRN <http://ssrn.com/abstract= 1638173 or doi:10.1111/j.1468-2230.2010.00807>.

65 Although even in the WTO system panels do sometimes dare to differ—which has been corrected and criticized by the Appellate Body. See Qureshi and Ziegler, *supra* note 23 at ch 14.

66 See Karl P. Sauvant (ed), *Appeals Mechanism in International Investment Disputes*, (New York: Oxford University Press, 2008).

67 See Debra Steger's ch 14 in this book on an appellate mechanism for investment.

68 See the recent cases involving Argentina Dohyun Kim, "The Annulment Committee's Role in Multiplying Inconsistency in ICSID Arbitration: The Need to Move Away from an Annulment-based System" (2011) 86 NYU Law Review 242.

where one institution (possibly) with an Appellate Body—as in the case of the WTO—adjudicates all economic disputes (trade and investment), we will not be able to prevent this development. Even in an integrated international economic law system, possible divergences with other areas of international law (like human rights, environment etc.) will prevail. This has been described as the fragmentation and risk of incoherence resulting from the existence of various unrelated dispute settlement mechanisms in international law. Obviously, an integrated system where a single permanent body deals with trade and investment-related disputes can possibly solve this problem. However, no such developments are on the horizon.

For the time being, however, it may be useful to encourage arbitrators and the members of judicial bodies of multilateral organizations like the WTO and ICSID to refer to each other's case law and engage in a judicial debate. This could avoid the scenario where each system operates in clinical isolation and would certainly be beneficial for the development of an inter-institutional debate on specific issues affecting global trade and investment flows. At the same time, creating a fully-fledged permanent appellate mechanism for IIAs that can be used to challenge outcomes of arbitral proceedings under IIAs might be an interesting option to test whether such a body can operate in a similar way as the WTO Appellate Body despite the absence of a multilateral agreement, and purely based on a myriad of IIAs. [69] In my view this could be done by creating an additional body under ICSID while leaving the existing annulment proceedings in place in order to let states choose which mechanism they consider appropriate for their own IIAs.

At the same time, perhaps the current situation where various bodies (WTO Panels, the WTO Appellate Body, dispute settlement tribunals under various RTAs, arbitral tribunals constituted according to various procedural rules based on different IIAs, ICSID annulment committees, domestic judges[70] etc.) shape international economic law is not as bad as it seems. First, it seems that increasingly these bodies try to learn from each other (judicial dialogue). Secondly, they all contribute to the case law on certain legal concepts and notions—not always completely consistently but generally so. Thirdly, the existence of diverging outcomes stimulates debate and may make negotiators aware of shortcomings in

---

69 See Debra Steger in this book at ch 14.
70 See on the role of domestic judges, Andreas R. Ziegler and Bertram Boie, "The Relationship Between International Trade Law and International Human Rights Law" in Erika de Wet and Yure Vidmar (eds), *Hierarchy in International Law* (Oxford: Oxford University Press, forthcoming).

their treaty models or in existing frameworks.[71] Fourthly, this system is very ambitious and requires academia, panellists/arbitrators and negotiators to pay attention to developments in various fields—which is not always easy to track and find (a situation generally criticized with regard to investment disputes)—but this may be the price for a judicialization of the international economic law based on the rule of law.

I would thus agree with Andrea Bjorklund and Sophie Nappert: "The international investment arena, with its myriad *ad hoc* tribunals and legal doctrines enshrined in treaties that either codify or build on customary international law, offers an excellent laboratory in which to theorize about communication between the nuclei and when such communication is appropriate."[72] This may also be true with regard to the overlap between the WTO, RTAs and IIAs, as the doctrinal developments in each should not be too isolated and occasions for informed dissent may lead to a more sophisticated system. Even the interpretation of WTO or RTA provisions by arbitral tribunals established under IIAs may ultimately not threaten the coherence of the existing system as long as the arbitrators involved enter into a judicial dialogue with panels and the Appellate Body and do not ignore or completely neglect the reasoning of previous tribunals. From this point of view, I do not see any need to change current negotiations of investment Chapters in RTAs or IIAs regarding the operation of investor-state dispute settlement.

---

71 A highly interesting example is the case law regarding the MFN clause in BITs and the resulting new treaty language used by many states; see Andreas R. Ziegler, "The Nascent International Law on Most-Favoured-Nation (MFN) Clauses in Bilateral Investment Treaties (BITs)" in Christoph Herrmann and Jörg Philipp Terhechte (eds), *European Yearbook of International Economic Law* (Heidelberg, Germany: Springer, 2010).

72 See Andrea K. Bjorklund and Sophie Nappert, "Beyond Fragmentation" (2011) UC Davis Legal Studies Research Paper No. 243, online: SSRN <http://ssrn.com/abstract=1739997>.

Part III
Legitimacy

10 Corporate investors' international legal personality and their accountability for human rights violations under IIAs

*Patrick Dumberry**

Introduction

This chapter examines the controversial question of the international legal personality of juridical persons (i.e. corporations or partnerships). It is generally recognized that an entity qualifies as a subject of international law to the extent that it holds rights and is given the possibility to commence a direct claim against a state before an international tribunal. These conditions are clearly met by corporate investors in the context of modern IIAs. These treaties are, however, asymmetrical insofar as investors are being accorded substantive *rights* without being subject to any specific *obligations*. Investors under IIAs are therefore a very unique and peculiar type of subject of international law: they have rights, but no obligations.

The lack of obligations for investors under IIAs is part of a broader debate about how to best address human rights violations committed by corporations doing business abroad. At present, such allegations can be addressed under domestic law: the host state can initiate litigation in its own courts against a corporation accused of human rights violations.[1] This approach, however, is generally considered ineffective particularly whenever the host state itself is complicit in the commission of the breach. In any event, not all host states are keen on enforcing human rights compliance against powerful foreign investors.[2] Human rights

* Assistant Professor, Faculty of Law, Civil Law Section, University of Ottawa. The author would like to thank Ms Gabrielle Dumas-Aubin for her research assistance.

1 The *home* state of the investor could also initiate litigation in its own courts against the accused corporation. There is, however, no obligation under international law for home states to sanction investors breaching international law. See Penelope Simons, "Corporate Voluntarism and Human Rights: The Adequacy and Effectiveness of Voluntary Self-Regulation Regimes" (2004) 59(1) Industrial Relations 101 at 104.
2 Jorge Daniel Taillant and Jonathan Bonnitcha, "International Investment Law and Human Rights" in Marie-Claire Cordonier Segger, Markus W. Gehring and Andrew

violations may therefore remain unaddressed. The question then arises whether international law can be of any help. The issue of whether or not corporations can be accountable for upholding rights contained in international human rights instruments is controversial in doctrine.[3] This is because, in general,[4] international law does not impose any direct legal obligations on corporations.[5]

In this context, one question that has been increasingly debated in academia is whether there is need for a greater degree of balance in IIAs between the legitimate interests of investors and host states. One option put forward is for IIAs to impose some obligations on corporations when they invest in the host state. This chapter examines how new IIAs could be drafted (and existing ones be amended) to take into account human rights, labor, and environmental obligations. Arguably, these suggested changes are likely to increase the legitimacy of IIAs in the future.[6] Part I of the chapter analyzes the legal personality of corporations particularly in the context of IIAs. Part II examines the possibilities of making corporations accountable for human rights violations under IIAs.

Corporations as subjects of international law

The debate in international law

Corporations are, of course, subjects of law and have a legal personality within the internal legal order of the country where they

Newcombe (eds), *Sustainable Development in World Investment Law* (Netherlands: Kluwer Law International, 2011) at 79.

3 See e.g. the discussion in United Nations Sub-Commission on the Promotion and Protection of Human Rights, *Draft Norms on the Responsibility of Transnational Corporations and other Business Enterprises with Respect to Human Rights (Draft Norms)*, UN Doc E/CN.4/Sub.2/2003/12/Rev.2 (August 26, 2003). Steven R. Ratner, "Corporations and Human Rights: A Theory of Legal Responsibility" (2001) 111 Yale LJ 443; David Kinley and Rachel Chambers "The UN Human Rights Norms for Corporations: The Private Implications of Public International Law" (2006) 3 Human Rights Law Review; N. Jägers, Corporate Human Rights Obligations: In Search of Accountability (Antwerpen: Intersentia, 2002); David Kinley and Junko Tadaki, "From Talk to Walk: The Emergence of Human Rights Responsibilities for Corporations at International Law" (2004) Va JL Int'l L 931 at 931–1023.

4 One exception is *jus cogens* obligations. See Lahra Liberti, "Investissements et droits de l'homme" in Phillipe Kahn and Thomas W. Walde (eds), *New Aspects of International Investment Law* (Hague Academy of International Law, 2007) at 836 [Liberti].

5 *Report of the Special Representative of the Secretary-General of the United Nations on the issue of human rights and transnational corporations and other business enterprises*, HRC, UNGAOR, 4th Sess., UN Doc A/HRC/4/74 (2007) at paras 60–1.

6 See Introduction to this book.

are registered. But, can they also have an international legal personality?[7]

As mentioned in the introduction, the proposition that corporations should be granted (or recognized as having) international legal personality is not a novel one. By the early 1950s, some writers had already begun exploring the role of corporations as international legal actors.[8] This question generated a great amount of controversy in the 1960s and 1970s when the prominence of such entities began to increase significantly. The period was marked by decolonization and the willingness of developing states to create a "New International Economic Order," as illustrated *inter alia* by the adoption in 1974 of the *Charter of Economic Rights and Duties of States* by the UN General Assembly.[9] At that time, the question of what treatment should be accorded to foreign investors under international law was at the heart of a heated debate that existed between developing and developed states. Especially controversial was the question of the existence of a "minimum standard" of protection under international law and the scope of compensation required when a state expropriated foreign property.[10] The rise of multinational corporations was considered by many states as a serious threat to their national sovereignty, especially with respect to their control over natural resources. In this context, scholars began debating the best ways to control the activities of these corporations in order to prevent what was then perceived as their negative impact on the host state's economy. One method envisaged was the elaboration of different "codes of conduct" imposing non-binding obligations on corporations investing abroad.[11]

---

7 See Patrick Dumberry, "L'entreprise, sujet de droit international? Retour sur la question à la lumière des développements récents du droit international des investissements" (2004) 108(1) RGDIP at 103–22 [Dumberry]; Patrick Dumberry and Érik-Labelle-Eastaugh, "Non-State Actors in International Investment Law: The Legal Personality of Corporations and NGOs in Investor State Arbitration" in Jean d'Aspremont (ed), *Participants in the International Legal System: Multiples Perspectives on Non-State Actors in International Law* (New York: Routledge-Cavendish, 2011).

8 Myres S. McDougal, "International Law, Power and Policy: A Contemporary Conception" (1953) Rec des Cours 82 at 160–2, 249–53; Philip C. Jessup, *A Modern Law of Nations, an Introduction* (New York: Macmillan Co, 1948) at 20–1, 33–4.

9 United Nations, Charter of Economic Rights and Duties of States, GA Res. 3281 (XXIX) (December 12, 1974).

10 Stephen M. Schwebel, "The United States 2004 Model Bilateral Investment Treaty: An Exercise in the Regressive Development of International Law" in Gerald Aksen et al (eds), *Global Reflections on International Law, Commerce and Dispute Resolution: Liber Amicorum in Honour of Robert Briner* (Paris: ICC Publishing, 2005).

11 Patrizio Merciai, *Les entreprises multinationales en droit international* (Brussels: Bruylant, 1993); Norbert Horn (ed), *Legal Problems of Codes of Conduct for Multinational*

Not surprisingly, the majority of scholars strongly rejected the possibility of recognizing corporations as subjects of international law for various different reasons. Some authors, adhering to an orthodox view of the international legal order as exclusively governed by states, were necessarily opposed to the idea of according any international legal personality to non-state actors.[12] Others were opposed to granting natural persons (i.e. individuals) such personality and logically came to the same conclusion regarding corporations.[13] Yet more opposed granting international legal personality to corporations in an effort to minimize their power and influence.[14] Still others pointed to the need to preserve stability in international relations as a reason not to grant them any legal personality.[15] Finally, some academics raised what might be characterized as formalist objections, pointing to the fact that corporations cannot conclude treaties[16] or create new norms of international law,[17] and that they cannot hold rights or obligations under international law.[18] In a similar vein, some argued the fact that corporations are creatures of municipal law bars them from obtaining legal personality under international law.[19]

Enterprises (Boston: Kluwer, 1980). See also the debate at the Institut de droit international, "Les entreprises multinationales" (1978) II: 57, Ann inst dr int at paras 195, 221–4.

12 Louis Henkin, "International Law: Politics, Values and Functions" (1989) IV: 216 Rec des Cours at 199.

13 Christian Dominicé, "La personnalité juridique dans le système du droit des gens" in Jerzy Makarczyk (ed), *Theory of International Law at the Threshold of the 21st Century: Essays in Honour of Krzysztof Skubiszewski* (The Hague: Kluwer, 1996) at 154, 163–4; Prosper Weil, "Le droit international en quête de son identité" (1992) VI: 237 Rec des Cours at 101, 112, 121.

14 Fleur Johns, "The Invisibility of the Transnational Corporation: An Analysis of International Law and Legal Theory" (1994) 19 Melbourne UL Rev 893 at 913; Georges Abi Saab, "The International Law of Multinational Corporations: A Critique of American Legal Doctrines" (1971) 2 Annales d'études internationals 97 121; François Rigaux, "Transnational Corporations" in M Bedjaoui (ed), *International Law: Achievement and Prospects* (Paris: Unesco, 1991) at 129.

15 Jonathan I. Charney, "Transnational Corporations and Developing Public International Law" (1983) Duke LJ 773.

16 Chris N. Okeke, *Controversial Subjects of Contemporary International Law*, 3rd edn (Rotterdam: Rotterdam University Press, 1974) at 214–15, 218–20.

17 Hans W. Baade, "The Legal Effect of Code of Conduct for Multinational Enterprises" in N. Horn, *supra* note 11 at 7–8.

18 Louis Henkin et al, *International Law, Cases and Materials*, 3rd edn (St-Paul: West Publ. Co, 1993) at 369.

19 K.P. Sauvant and V. Aranda, "The International Legal Framework for Transnational Corporations" in A.A. Fatouros (ed), *Transnational Corporations—The International Legal Framework* (New York: Routledge, 1994) at 84.

These different arguments are not entirely convincing and not especially helpful in answering the question of whether or not corporations are subjects of international law within the context of IIAs. Some of the controversy may stem from a certain amount of confusion regarding what is meant by "international legal personality." To say that corporations possess international legal personality is not to say that they are co-equal to states. As was famously stated by the ICJ in the *Reparations* case, "subjects of law in any legal system are not necessarily identical in their nature or in the extent of their rights, and their nature depends upon the needs of the community."[20] This personality will, of course, be circumscribed by the will of the constituent states. In the *Reparations* case, the ICJ recognized that an international organization like the UN can possess a form of international legal personality, but that this personality will be more limited than that of states.[21] At issue in that case was whether or not the UN could bring a claim against a state for injuries suffered by a UN official. The court reasoned that whether or not an entity has the competence to bring an international claim is, first and foremost, a question of whether or not that entity possesses international legal personality. For the Court, the international personality of the UN means that it is "a subject of international law" which is "capable of possessing international rights and duties" and has "the capacity to maintain its rights by bringing international claims."[22] In other words, possession of legal personality gives an entity the right to bring a claim against a state before an international tribunal.

The analytical framework developed by the ICJ in the *Reparations* case has since been endorsed in doctrine.[23] It has also been applied in other contexts in reverse order: the fact that an entity has been granted substantive rights in a treaty as well as a direct right of action has been used as evidence that it possesses international legal personality. For example, private individuals are subjects of international human rights law where, as in the case of the ECHR, they are given a direct right of action.[24]

---

20 *Reparations for Injuries Suffered in the Service of the United Nations*, Advisory Opinion [1947] ICJ Reports 174 at 179.
21 *Ibid.*
22 *Ibid.*
23 C. Berezowski, "Les problèmes de la subjectivité internationale" in V. Ibler (ed), *Mélanges offerts à Juraj Andrassy* (The Hague: Martinus Nijhoff Publ., 1968) at 33–5; Julio A. Barberis, "Nouvelles questions concernant la personnalité juridique internationale" (1983) I: 179 Rec des Cours 168–9 [Barberis].
24 *Protocol No. 11 to the Convention for the Protection of Human Rights and Fundamental Freedoms*, November 1, 1998, 155 Eur TS, art 34, online: Council of Europe—Treaty

The undeniable international legal personality of corporations under IIAs

There are two circumstances in which corporations possess both sub-stantive rights and the ability to bring a claim on the basis of those rights before an international tribunal. First, state contracts are often governed by international law and typically contain an arbitration clause. According to the *Texaco-Calasiatic* arbitral tribunal[25] as well as numerous authors,[26] the combination of substantive and procedural rights found in such contracts, which are the product of a direct nego-tiation between an investor and the host state for the purpose of under-taking a specific project, is an indication that corporations possess international legal personality. Investors also benefit from this combina-tion of substantive and procedural rights under most modern IIAs. Under such treaties, a state typically gives its consent to arbitration in advance to all investors from the other contracting states that meet the applicable standing requirements.[27] This amounts to granting these investors international legal personality for the purpose of the treaty.[28] It does not follow from this conclusion, however, that corporations also have a legal personality in *general* public international law. The present analysis is limited to international investment law.

Office <http://conventions.coe.int/treaty/en/treaties/html/009.htm>. For an over-view of doctrine, see Christian Dominicé, "L'émergence de l'individu en droit inter-national public" (1987–88) 16 Annales d'études internationales 8.

25 *Texaco Overseas Petroleum Co & California Asiatic Oil Co v Libyan Arab Republic*, Award (January 19, 1977) ILR, 53, 1977 at 459.

26 David Adedayo Ijalaye, *The Extension of Corporate Personality in International Law* (New York: Oceana Publications, 1978) 5 at 226, 243; Barberis, *supra* note 23 at 206; Gérard Cohen-Jonathan, "L'arbitrage Texaco-Calasiatic contre Gouvernement Libyen" (1977) 23(1) AFDI 452 at 457–9; W. Friedmann, "General Course in Public International Law" (1969) II 127 Rec des Cours 121; I Seidl-Hohenveldern "The Theory of Quasi-International and Partly International Agreements" (1975) 11 Rev BDI 570.

27 See e.g. *North American Free Trade Agreement Between the Government of Canada, the Government of Mexico and the Government of the United States*, December 17, 1992, Can TS 1994 No. 2, 32 ILM 289 (entered into force January 1, 1994) at art 1116 and 1117 [NAFTA].

28 See also F. Poirat, "L'article 26 du Traité relatif à la Charte de l'énergie : procédures de règlement des différends et statut des personnes privées" (1998) 102 RGDIP at 73–4, 79–81; C. Leben, "Quelques réflexions théoriques à propos des contrats d'Etat" in *Souveraineté étatique et marchés internationaux à la fin du 20ᵉ siècle: Mélange en l'honneur de Philippe Kahn* (Paris: Litec, 2000) at 128–31, 142; Robin F. Hansen, "The International Legal Personality of Multinational Enterprises: Treaty, Custom and the Governance Gap" (2010) 10(1) Global Jurist at 15–16 [Hansen].

The nature of rights held by investors under IIAs was recently the subject of debate in the context of NAFTA.[29] In three separate claims, US producers and suppliers of high fructose corn syrup (HFCS) complained of the imposition by Mexico of a 20 per cent excise tax on soft drinks that used sweeteners other than cane sugar (including HFCS). Between 2007 and 2009, the three arbitral tribunals reached divergent conclusions on the nature of rights held by investors. In each case, Mexico argued in defense that the tax measure it adopted was a legitimate "countermeasure" under customary international law. This countermeasure was allegedly in response to a breach by the US government of its own obligations notably under Chapter 20 of NAFTA. In *ADM*, the tribunal took the view that NAFTA's *substantive* investment protections were not individual rights possessed by investors, but rather rights possessed by the investor's home state. The only right directly possessed by investors was the *procedural* right to submit a claim to arbitration.[30] However, in the *CPI* arbitration, the tribunal concluded that "the NAFTA confers upon investors substantive rights separate and distinct from those of the State of which they are nationals"[31] and that "an investor which brings a claim is seeking to enforce what it asserts are its own rights under the treaty and not exercising a power to enforce rights which are actually those of the State."[32] The *Cargill* tribunal, while rejecting this dichotomy (between substantive and procedural rights), in fact adopted a reasoning consistent with that of the *CPI* tribunal.[33] Most writers have observed that the "direct" rights theory is more persuasive than the "derivative" one adopted by the *ADM* tribunal.[34] The conclusion is in line with investors having an international legal personality in the context of IIAs.

29 NAFTA, *supra* note 27.

30 *Archer Daniels Midland Company and Tate & Lyle Ingredients Americas, Inc v United Mexican States*, Award, ICSID Case No. ARB (AF)/04/5 (November 21, 2007) at paras 161–80 (see the different conclusion reached on this point by arbitrator Rovine in his Concurring Opinion).

31 *Corn Products International, Inc v United Mexican States*, Decision on Responsibility, ICSID Case No. ARB (AF)/04/1 (January 15, 2008) at para. 167.

32 *Ibid* at para. 174.

33 *Cargill, Inc v United Mexican States*, Award, ICSID Case No. ARB (AF)/05/2 (September 18, 2009) at paras 420–8.

34 Zachary Douglas, *The International Law of Investment Claims* (New York: Cambridge University Press, 2009) at 10–39; Campbell MacLachlan QC, Laurence Shore and Matthew Weiniger, *International Investment Arbitration: Substantive Principles* (Oxford: Oxford University Press, 2007) at 60 ff; J. Robbins, "The Emergence of Positive Obligations in Bilateral Investment Treaties" (2006) 13 U Miami Int'l & Comp L Rev, 403 at 403 ff.

Against such a backdrop, two conclusions can be drawn as to the nature of a corporation's international legal personality.[35] First, that it is a *limited* personality, in the sense that corporations, like international organizations, do not possess the full range of capacities recognized to states under international law. A corporation may only exercise those limited powers and claim those rights that its "constituting instrument" has granted it. In practice, the extent of an investor's legal personality is determined by the arbitration clause, which will indicate the substantive rights contained in the treaty that can form the basis of a claim.

Secondly, the legal personality is *derivative* in the sense that a corporation is a "secondary" subject of international law. Its personality is not inherent, but rather emanates from the express will of (at least) one state, either in an IIA or a state contract.[36] In the context of IIAs, corporations are also *passive* subjects in the sense that they are not direct participants in the negotiation and generation of the legal norms on which their personality rests. Indeed, this personality can be modified or withdrawn without their consent as treaties may always be modified by the contracting states.[37] However, the situation is somewhat different in the context of state contracts, where a corporation is a direct participant in the *creation* of legal norms (the contractual terms) which must be complied with by the contracting state. In these circumstances, a corporation is not a mere bystander, but rather a direct participant in the *creation* of legal norms (the contractual terms) which must be complied with by the contracting state.

Subjects of international law have not only rights, but also obligations under international law. For instance, in contemporary international law there is no doubt that individuals have rights that are typically contained in human rights treaties. They also have obligations which are directly imposed upon them by rules of international law,

---

35 This is discussed in Dumberry, *supra* note 7 at 114. See also Quoc Dinh Nguyen, Patrick Daillier and Alain Pellet, *Droit international public*, 6th edn (Paris: L.G.D.J., 1999) at 690; Peter Malanczuk, "Multinational Enterprises and Treaty-Making: A Contribution to the Discussion on Non-State Actors and the Subjects of International Law" in V. Gowlland-Debbas (ed), *Multilateral Treaty-Making: The Current Status of Challenges to and Reforms Needed in the International Legislative Process* (The Hague: Martinus Nijhoff Publishers, 2000) 55 at 72.

36 *Contra* Hansen, *supra* note 28 at 15–16, 19–21 (suggesting that corporations' capacity for international legal personality has developed into a customary international norm operational against *all states*).

37 Dumberry, *supra* note 7 at 116.

such as in the area of international criminal law.[38] Because a corporation possesses an international legal personality in the context of IIAs, it is submitted that it is also capable of having obligations under international law. There are no theoretical objections to impose obligations on corporations under international law. One example where obligations are imposed on corporations is in the context of state contracts. Nothing prevents IIAs from also imposing such obligation upon investors. This question is further examined in this next section.

Corporations' accountability for human rights violations under IIAs

As mentioned above, several academics[39] and organizations[40] have argued in recent years that IIAs are asymmetrical and imbalanced insofar as investors are being accorded substantive rights without being subject to any specific obligations. This section examines (1) the prevailing situation under IIAs, and (2) how these treaties could be drafted in the future (and existing ones amended) to take into account these developments. It should be noted that this section is solely aimed at mapping some of the most salient issues and not to provide an exhaustive analysis of the question.

---

38 The now famous *dictum* of the Nuremberg International Military Tribunal who had to judge the Nazi war criminals after World War II: "Crimes against international law are committed by men, not by abstract entities, and only by punishing individuals who commit such crime can the provision of international law be enforced", in Judicial Decisions: International Military Tribunal (Nuremberg) , Judgment and Sentences (1947) 41(1) AJIL 172 at 221.

39 Marc Jacob, *International Investment Agreements and Human Rights* (2010) INEF Research Paper Series, at 21 [Jacob]; Jose E. Alvarez, "Critical Theory and the North American Free Trade Agreement's Chapter Eleven" (1997) 28 U Miami Inter-Am L Rev at 303–12 [Alvarez]; Glen Kelley, "Multilateral Investment Treaties: A Balanced Approach to Multinational Corporations" (2001) 39(2) Colum J Transnat'l L 483 [Kelley]; A.V. Lowe, "Corporations as International Actors and International Law Makers" in Benetto Conforti et al (eds), *The Italian Yearbook of International Law* (Leiden: Martinus Nijhoff Publishers, 2004) 23 at 31 [Lowe]; Dr Efraim Chalamish, "The Future of Bilateral Investment Treaties: A De Facto Multilateral Agreement?" (2009) 34(2) Brook J Int'l L 304 at 346 [Chalamish]; Rémie Bachand and Stéphanie Rousseau, "International Investment and Human Rights: Political and Legal Issues" (2003) International Centre for Human Rights and Democratic Development 16; Joseph E. Stiglitz, "Regulating Multinational Corporations: Towards Principles of Cross-border Legal Frameworks in a Globalized World" (2008) 23 Am U Int'l L Rev at 468, 536 [Stiglitz].

40 ILA, "Final Report of the International Law on Foreign Investment Committee" (2008) at 15 [ILA].

The current situation prevailing under IIAs

Under most IIAs, arbitral tribunals only have jurisdiction to adjudicate claims brought *by investors* (and not those submitted by the host state or any other actors) as well as disputes originating from alleged breaches of a treaty provision.[41] Typically, IIAs do not contain any provisions dealing with substantive human rights or labor law obligations.[42] There are a limited number of exceptions where BITs contain references to human rights in their preamble,[43] or in a treaty provision. For instance, in the US 2004 Model BIT, the parties acknowledge that it is "inappropriate" to encourage investment by weakening or reducing the protections afforded in domestic environmental or labor laws.[44] Importantly, however, these standards do *not* impose any *direct* obligations and responsibilities upon foreign investors.

The same can be said of the recent Canadian practice to include a corporate social responsibility clause in its FTAs. While innovative, one can question the effectiveness of a clause which states as follows:

> Each Party should encourage enterprises operating within its territory or subject to its jurisdiction to voluntarily incorporate

41 This issue is further discussed in ch 12 of this book.
42 Howard Mann, "International Investment Agreements, Business and Human Rights: Key Issues and Opportunities" (2008) IISD 9 [Mann]; OECD, "International Investment Agreements: A Survey of Environmental, Labour and Anti Corruption Issues" (2008).
43 See the draft version of the Norway Model BIT (2007) online: Investment Treaty Arbitration <http://italaw.com/investmenttreaties.htm>. Apparently, the Model BIT was later abandoned by the government: Damon Vis-Dunbar, "Norway Shelves its Draft Model Bilateral Investment Treaty", June 8, 2009, online: Investment Treaty News   <http://www.iisd.org/itn/2009/06/08/norway-shelves-its-proposed-model-bilateral-investment-treaty/>. Other agreements refer in their preambles to human rights protection instruments: European Free Trade Area–Singapore Free Trade Agreement, 2002; *Free Trade Agreement* between *Canada and the Republic of Colombia*, November 21, 2008 (entered into force August 15, 2011), online: DFAIT <http://www.international.gc.ca/trade-agreements-accords-commerciaux/agr-acc/colombia-colombie/can-colombia-toc-tdm-can-colombie.aspx> [Canada-Colombia FTA].
44 The US 2004 Model BIT indicates that the parties "shall strive to ensure that it does not waive or otherwise derogate from, or offer to waive or otherwise derogate from, such laws in a manner that weakens or reduces the protections afforded in those laws as an encouragement for the establishment, acquisition, expansion, or retention of an investment in its territory" at arts 12, 13, online, State Department <http://www.state.gov/documents/organization/117601.pdf>. See also Canada's FIPA Model (2004) where the parties "recognize that it is inappropriate to encourage investment by relaxing domestic health, safety or environmental measures" (at art 11) online: DFAIT <http://www.international.gc.ca/trade-agreements-accords-commerciaux/assets/pdfs/2004-FIPA-model-en.pdf>.

internationally recognized standards of corporate social responsibility in their internal policies, such as statements of principle
that have been endorsed or are supported by the Parties. These
principles address issues such as labor, the environment, human
rights, community relations and anti-corruption. The Parties
remind those enterprises of the importance of incorporating
such corporate social responsibility standards in their internal
policies.[45]

This conclusion does not mean human rights and labor concerns are
altogether irrelevant to investor-state arbitration. Despite the lack of
any explicit references in the treaty, allegations of human rights and
labor law violations committed by the investor can nevertheless be
raised in several different ways under IIAs (in their current form).

For one, human rights concerns can be raised *by the host state* in defense
during the arbitration proceedings.[46] A tribunal would thus have jurisdiction over such allegations to the extent that they are *related or connected* to the investor's investment about which it filed a claim.[47] Whether
or not the same logic applies to allegations of human rights violations
that are *not* directly related to the investor's investment examined by the
tribunal but connected to, for instance, *another* investment project is
controversial. Some authors have suggested that a tribunal should take
into account such allegations when the IIA refers to "international law"
as the applicable law to the dispute.[48] Others have argued that a tribunal

---

45 See e.g. Canada-Colombia FTA, *supra* note 43 art 816 (Corporate Social Responsibility); *Free Trade Agreement between Canada and the Republic of Peru*, May 29, 2008
(entered into force August 1, 2009), online: DFAIT <http://www.international.gc.
ca/trade-agreements-accords-commerciaux/assets/pdfs/Canada-PeruFTA_
chapter8-en.pdf> at art 810 (Corporate Social Responsibility).

46 The other issue of human rights arguments raised by governments in defense in
order to justify their actions taken against investors are discussed in: UNCTAD,
"Selected Recent Developments in IIA Arbitration and Human Rights" (2009) 2
IIA MONITOR 8 [UNCTAD]; Luke E. Peterson and Kevin Gray, "International
Human Rights in Bilateral Investment Treaties and Investment Treaty Arbitration"
(2003) Working Paper for the Swiss Ministry for Foreign Affairs at 22 [Peterson and
Gray]. For a critical analysis, see James D. Fry, "International Human Rights in
Investment Arbitration: Evidence of International Law's Unity" (2007) 18 Duke
J Comp & Int'l L 77.

47 Jacob, *supra* note 39 at 26.

48 Jacob, *supra* note 39 at 27; A. Van Aaken, "Fragmentation of International Law: the
Case of International Investment Protection" (2008) 1 Univ St Gallen Law and
Economics Research Paper Series 2–3, 10 [Van Aaken]; Clara Reiner and Christoph
Schreuer, "Human Rights and International Investment Arbitration" in Pierre-
Marie Dupuy, Francesco Francioni and Ernst-Ulrich Petersmann (eds), *Human*

should always take into account allegations that an investor breached *jus cogens* obligations,[49] or customary human rights obligations.[50] In fact, several authors believe that under presently-drafted IIAs a tribunal should find inadmissible a claim submitted by an investor having committed *jus cogens* violations. Support for this proposition is found in the *Phoenix Action* case where the tribunal held that protection "should not be granted to investments made in violation of the most fundamental rules of protection of human rights, like investments made in pursuance of torture or genocide or in support of slavery or trafficking of human organs."[51] Secondly, human rights concerns could be raised before an arbitral tribunal by *third parties* to the IIA, for instance, if the tribunal allows *amicus curiae* participation.[52] Some authors have also referred to the much less likely scenario of human rights concerns being raised before an arbitral tribunal by the *home* state of the investor starting arbitration proceedings.[53]

In sum, tribunals have jurisdiction over allegations of human rights violations committed by an investor in only a limited number of circumstances under IIAs.

How could IIAs be drafted (or amended) to include corporate responsibility?

According to some authors, the issue of corporate responsibility should be addressed in a multilateral investment agreement.[54] This solution, however, is unlikely to be achieved in the near future given the failure of past attempts (for instance, the "MAI") and persisting disagreement between developed and developing states on the specific content of such

---

Rights in International Investment Law (Oxford: Oxford University Press, 2009) at 84 [Reiner and Schreuer].

49 UNCTAD (2009), *supra* note 46 at 14; Peterson and Gray, *supra* note 46 at 18–19; A. Van Aaken, *supra* note 48 at 11.

50 Hansen, *supra* note 28 at 6, 42 ff (identifying nine such customary obligations under international law that must be observed by corporations).

51 *Phoenix Action Ltd v Czech Republic*, Award, ICSID Case No. ARB (AF)/06/5 (April 15, 2009) at para. 78.

52 Mann, *supra* note 42 at 27 ff; Reiner and Schreuer, *supra* note 48 at 90.

53 Peterson and Gray, *supra* note 46 at 20. More generally, several authors argue for home states to have a more prominent role in sanctioning their national investors. See M. Sornarajah, *The International Law on Foreign Investment*, 2nd edn (New York: Cambridge University Press, 2004) at 169, 182; Stiglitz, *supra* note 39 at 536–9; ILA, *supra* note 35 at 15.

54 Kelley, *supra* note 39 at 483; Chalamish, *supra* note 39 at 348.

a global agreement.[55] Another, rather illusionary, solution that has been mentioned is amending the ICSID Convention to include a provision allowing tribunals to consider environmental, public health, and labor concerns.[56] A more realistic perspective favored in recent years by several authors[57] and international organizations, such as UNCTAD,[58] would be to include specific language on corporate obligations in IIAs.

IIAs should be drafted to include corporate responsibility in a *separate provision*. Otherwise, a mere reference in the IIA's *preamble* would only have a limited impact insofar as it would not create any substantive obligations for investors. Such a reference would only be relevant with respect to the interpretation of the treaty's provisions. The clause should make reference to a limited number of clear and precise mandatory obligations and responsibilities that must be respected by corporations.[59] However, a clause where states simply agree to "encourage" investors to conduct their investment activities in compliance with a non-binding code of conduct, such as the OECD Guidelines for Multinational Enterprises, is unsatisfactory because it does not create any mandatory obligations for investors.[60] The scope of the clause should be confined to obligations arising in only a limited number of areas such as, for instance, human rights, labor law and the environment. Also, the clause should expressly refer to obligations contained in international instruments widely-recognized by states, such as the 1948 *Universal Declaration of Human Rights*, the 1966 UN *International Covenant on Civil and Political Rights*, the 1998 ILO *Declaration on Fundamental Principles and Rights at Work,* etc. Another, more cumbersome, option would be to include a comprehensive list of specific obligations to be respected by corporations. The obvious difficulty with this "pick and choose" approach is that both parties would have to negotiate and specifically agree on what these obligations are.

The IIA's investor-state dispute resolution clause should also contain an express reference as to how investor's obligations can be enforced.[61]

---

55 OECD, *Negotiating Group on the Multilateral Agreement on Investment*, Draft Consolidated Text of February 11, 1998, online: OECD <http://www.oecd.org/daf/mai/pdf/ng/ng987e.pdf> at 58–64.

56 Kate M. Supnik, "Making Amends: Amending the ICSID Convention to Reconcile Competing Interests in International Investment Law" (2009–10) 59 Duke LJ 343.

57 Jacob, *supra* note 39; Chalamish, *supra* note 39 at 346 ff: Liberti, *supra* note 4 at 842, 846; Peterson and Gray, *supra* note 46.

58 UNCTAD, "Development Implications of International Investment Agreements" (2007) 2 IIA Monitor 6.

59 *Ibid* at 6; Lowe, *supra* note 39 at 31.

60 See e.g. (now abandoned) Norway Model BIT (2007) *supra* note 43 at art 32.

61 Jacob, *supra* note 39 at 36, 45; Peterson & Gray, *supra* note 46 at 36.

At least three different enforcement possibilities can be envisaged under IIAs.

First, an investor's substantive rights under an IIA could be *conditioned* to its respect of human rights and labor obligations ("the clean-hands option"). This option should be expressly mentioned in the IIA's arbitration clause.[62] As discussed in Chapter 11 of this book, recent tribunals have held that they either lack the necessary jurisdiction or that a claim is inadmissible when faced with the illegal conduct of an investor, such as misrepresentations made by the claimant[63] or bribery/corruption.[64] Tribunals have also held that substantive protections offered under BITs cannot apply to investments made contrary to the host state's domestic law.[65] Tribunals should be allowed (under new or amended IIAs) to decide on the admissibility of a claim based on human rights violations committed by an investor.[66]

Secondly, another option would be to permit an investor's claim, even in the face of human rights violations, but to allow the host state to raise any such allegations during the arbitral proceedings (the "mitigation option").[67] A tribunal would thus take into account such allegations when making its determination on the merits of the dispute, the assessment of compensation for damage, the allocation of costs, fees, etc. One variant of this option would be to allow human rights allegations to be raised by the host state in a counterclaim.[68] As discussed in Chapter 12, one notable difficulty with this approach is that most IIAs do not expressly mention the right of host states to submit counterclaims. This is why the possibility for counterclaims by host states should be expressly mentioned in the IIA's arbitration clause.[69]

---

62 Peterson & Gray, *supra* note 46 at 36. See e,g, *IISD Model International Agreement on Investment for Sustainable Development,* online: Investment Treaty Arbitration < http://italaw.com/investmenttreaties.htm> at art 18(A) [IISD Model]
63 *Plama Consortium Limited v. Bulgaria,* Award, ICSID Case No. ARB (AF)/03/24 (27 Aug. 2008).
64 *World Duty Free Company Limited v. Kenya,* Award, ICSID Case No. ARB (AF)/00/7 (4 Oct. 2006).
65 *Plama, supra* note 63 paras 138–139; *Phoenix Action supra* note 1 at para 101.
66 Peterson & Gray, *supra* note 46 at 33, 36.
67 Jacob, *supra* note 39 at 36, 45. The investor-state dispute resolution clause should expressly mention that tribunals have the authority to take into account human rights obligations in the context of the proceedings.
68 Chalamish *supra* note 39 at 348; Liberti, *supra* note 4 at 840.
69 See e.g. IISD Model, *supra* note 56 at art 18(E).

Under a third option, supported by some writers,[70] the host state (or even one of its nationals) would be allowed to file an arbitration claim directly against an investor based on a breach of human rights or labour obligations. Of course, most current IIA dispute resolution clauses restrict the right to claim solely to investors.[71] Should these treaties allow host states to bring human rights claims against investors? This option should be discarded because of the absence of any consent to arbitration by the investor.[72] Consent, by both the investor and host state, is a basic requirement to arbitration. In any event, arbitral tribunals constituted under IIAs are probably not the best forum to address such issues.[73]

Conclusion

One of the undeniable effects of globalization has been the relative decline of states in the sphere of international economic relations, as non-state actors such as corporations and NGOs, have emerged as important players therein. As the unparalleled growth in trans-border commercial exchanges continues, states are under constant pressure to further open their markets in order to attract foreign investment, which is deemed by many to be essential to economic development. In this context, states are willing to grant foreign investors maximum protections in IIAs against discriminatory, unfair, arbitrary or expropriatory measures taken by the host state in order to allay concerns they might have about investing there. Modern IIAs include arbitration clauses granting investors a direct right of action against the host state before an international tribunal. The current state of international economic relations is such that, in the context of international investment law, states have granted in certain circumstances and to a limited extent, international legal personality to corporate investors. Naturally, with rights come obligations.

In recent years, there has been mounting concerns regarding the unbalanced nature of IIAs. There is, indeed, a notable backlash against some of the most fundamental aspects at the core of the investor-state

---

70 See Todd Weiler, "Balancing Human Rights and Investor Protection: a New Approach for a Different Legal Order" (2004) 27 BC Int'l & Comp L Rev ICLR at 449; Chalamish *supra* note 39 at 351, 354.

71 The issue is discussed in details in Chapter 13 of this book.

72 See also Peterson & Gray, *supra* note 46 at 33, Mann, *supra* note 42 at 14.

73 The host state can initiate proceedings in its own courts against the investor. See James D. Fry, "International Human Rights in Investment Arbitration: Evidence of International Law's Unity" (2007) 18 Duke J Comp & Int'l L 77.

arbitration system.[74] In this context, it is timely to assess whether the very nature of IIAs should be modified in order to impose some *obligations* on corporations (such as human rights or labor standards) in addition to granting them rights. At present, the prospect of a new generation of IIAs balancing the rights and obligations of corporations is uncertain. There does not seem to be any clear political will amongst states for such changes. Ultimately, continuous concerns about the legitimacy of these treaties may eventually push states toward including corporate responsibilities in IIAs. An appropriate balance between corporate rights and obligations under IIAs would certainly increase the legitimacy of these vital instruments for global economical growth. Ultimately, all states, both developed and developing, would have a great interest in pursuing this goal and should, accordingly, envisage taking into account these changes in future treaties.

74 See e.g. M Waibel et al, *The Backlash against Investment Arbitration* (Alphen aan den Rijn, The Netherlands: Kluwer Law International, 2010).

11 Investor misconduct

*Andrew Newcombe**

Introduction

The possibility that host states might misuse sovereign powers and harm foreign investment is one of the primary purposes of international investment law. Modern investment treaties allow foreign investors to hold a host state accountable for breaching its commitments to them and, more generally, for misuse of sovereign powers. International investment law serves as a commitment mechanism to address the problem of the "obsolescing bargain"[1]—that once a foreign investor invests in the host state (particularly in the case of large-scale infrastructure and other "bricks and mortar" investments), its bargaining power can rapidly diminish. An investor with a "sunk" investment of $250 million in a natural resources project cannot simply exit the host state with its investment if the host state reneges on its commitments. IIAs serve to reduce the risk of a host state acting opportunistically by providing foreign investors *ex ante* unilateral commitments about the treatment they can expect if they invest in the state and the ability to subject state conduct to independent scrutiny *ex post* through irrevocable pre-consent to investor-state arbitration.

Although this legal framework does much to protect the interests of foreign investors, it reflects asymmetrical international legal obligations. As discussed in Chapter 1, IIAs have traditionally focused on imposing enforceable obligations on host states and have not addressed the issue of the obligations of foreign investors within the host state (or the obligations of home states with respect to the conduct of their nationals abroad).[2] The asymmetry in the structure of IIAs arises from

* Associate Professor, Faculty of Law, University of Victoria.
1 See Raymond Vernon, *Sovereignty at Bay: The Multinational Spread of U.S. Enterprises* (New York: Basic Books, 1971) at 46.
2 See Sara L. Seck, "Unilateral Home State Regulation: Imperialism or Tool for Subaltern Resistance?" (2008) 46(3) Osgoode Hall LJ 565; Sara L. Seck, "Conceptualizing the

the traditional position that foreign investors are not subjects of inter-national law with international law obligations.[3] It also arises from the fact that since the foreign investment is located within the territorial jurisdiction of the host state, the domestic law (the panoply of the host state's executive, legislative and judicial powers) governs and regulates the conduct of the foreign investor and investment.[4] From this perspective, the asymmetry in IIAs reflects the reality that the host state can unilaterally exercise state sovereign powers in ways that seriously harm foreign investors.

The legitimacy of the IIA framework of unilateral commitments made by states is brought into question, however, if foreign investors seek the benefit of host state IIA commitments when they have also engaged or are engaging in serious misconduct. What about the investor that has engaged in fraud, corruption or illegality? Is this investor entitled to the benefits of investment treaty protection or does it, as a result of its misconduct, forfeit the protection afforded by the treaty?

Although foreign investors and investments are theoretically subject to the full force of domestic law and its enforcement by the host state, the reality is that many developing states have weak governance, regulatory and enforcement regimes.[5] Further, investor misconduct might involve fraud, corruption or other activities designed to evade or pervert the application of domestic law (including lobbying to ensure that regulation contrary to foreign investor interests is not adopted). Media and NGO reports are rife with allegations of various types of abuses by foreign investors—violations of human rights, labor standards, environmental degradation, fraud and corruption. Whatever the merits of indi-

---

Home State Duty to Protect Human Rights" in Karin Buhmann et al (eds), *Corporate Social and Human Rights Responsibilities: Global Legal and Management Perspectives* (New York: Palgrave Macmillan, 2010); Robin Hansen, "The Systemic Challenge of Corporate Investor Nationality in an Era of Multinational Business" (2010) 1(1) Journal of Arbitration and Mediation 81.

3 See ch 10 in this book on foreign investors as subjects of international law.

4 Where serious misconduct is present, there will likely be a breach of the domestic laws of the host and home states. For example, Siemens AG, which has been the subject of corruption and bribery investigations by numerous domestic authorities, pleaded guilty to a series of offences and agreed to pay massive fines. See report on "Legal Proceedings" (December 3, 2009), online: Siemens AG <http://w1.siemens.com/press/pool/de/events/corporate/2009-q4/2009-q4-legal-proceedings-e.pdf>.

5 See e.g. the work of the Extractive Industries Transparency Initiative online: <http://eiti.org> and the Oil, Gas and Mining Unit of the World Bank. Also see the OECD's work on weak governance zones, online: <http://www.oecd.org/document/5/0,3746,en_2649_33765_36899994_1_1_1_1,00.html>.

vidual allegations may be, it is evident that international economic actors (just like host states) are sometimes responsible for serious misconduct. This gives rise to the question—how can and should IIA tribunals and treaty practice respond to serious misconduct by foreign investors?

This chapter analyzes the various ways in which IIA tribunals can treat investor misconduct, and questions whether treaty practice should change to address this issue explicitly.[6] The chapter proceeds in two parts. Part I identifies and maps investor misconduct by stage of investment and stage of arbitration and analyzes the various mechanisms currently available to IIA tribunals to address such misconduct. In light of the variety of issues that fall under the rubric of "misconduct," as well as the differing levels of severity of misconduct (i.e. from inadvertent and minor technical breaches and oversights of a regulation to wide-scale fraud, corruption and serious harm to humans and the environment), this chapter suggests there is no single answer to how IIA tribunals should address misconduct issues and that a series of procedural and substantive rules and mechanisms are available to IIA tribunals. For example, on the one hand, serious misconduct at the stage of making the investment may prompt an IIA tribunal to find that it either lacks jurisdiction or that claims are substantively inadmissible. On the other hand, misconduct during the operation of the investment, particularly failure to comply with legal requirements, may provide a host state with a justification for its challenged conduct (such as where the host state revokes an investor's license or concession because of misconduct).

Part II turns to a brief analysis of current treaty practice aimed at investor misconduct. Since serious misconduct is invariably illegal under host state law, this part recommends that IIAs specify that, in order for investments to qualify for protection under the IIA, the investment must be made in accordance with domestic law.

The chapter concludes by highlighting the risk of treating investor misconduct solely as an issue of jurisdiction. In cases where there is misconduct by both the foreign investor and the host state, IIA tribunals should be wary of denying jurisdiction due to an investor's misconduct if a host state has also engaged in misconduct.

---

6 Parts of this chapter draw on the author's analysis and work in Andrew Newcombe, "Investor Misconduct: Jurisdiction, Admissibility or Merits" in Chester Brown and Kate Miles (eds), *Evolution in Investment Treaty Law and Arbitration* (Cambridge: Cambridge University Press, 2011) and a series of blogs on the topic of investor misconduct, online: Kluwer Arbitration Blog <http://kluwerarbitrationblog.com>.

Mapping investor misconduct by phase of investment and arbitration proceedings

In analyzing investor misconduct it is useful to distinguish between misconduct at three different phases of the investment process: establishment, operation and after an investor-state dispute has arisen. Further, in assessing the consequences of misconduct, it is useful to consider the various phases of the arbitration: jurisdiction of tribunal, admissibility of claims, arbitral procedures (such as fact-finding, inferences and the burden of proof), the assessment of the merits (which may involve defenses and counterclaims), quantum of damages and the award of costs. The fundamental point is that an IIA tribunal has a variety of mechanisms to address investor misconduct and can take such misconduct into account at various stages of the arbitral process.

The issue of investor misconduct arises in IIA cases in myriad ways and circumstances. Accordingly, general statements about the effect of investor misconduct on investment treaty protection should be made with care. Although I use "misconduct" as a generic label, I am referring to conduct that is either illegal under domestic or international law, or would be considered contrary to international public policy, rather than simply undesirable conduct that may not comport with normative conceptions of corporate social responsibility.[7] The term "misconduct" is used in this chapter to refer in general to investor conduct that might have a bearing on whether the investor is entitled to obtain treaty protection or that might have consequences for the merits of a claim or reparation. Further, I only address cases in which the investor misconduct is proven and the issue is the legal significance of the misconduct. Each form of misconduct—be it corruption of public officials,[8] non-compliance with regulatory requirements (illegality), criminal activity,[9]

---

7 See Benjamin Richardson, *Socially Responsible Investment: Regulating the Unseen Pollutors* (Oxford: Oxford University Press, 2008); Michael Kerr et al, *Corporate Social Responsibility: A Legal Analysis* (Markham, Ont: LexisNexis, 2009).

8 On the treatment of corruption in international arbitration, see M. Scherer, "International Arbitration and Corruption—Synopsis of Selected Arbitral Awards" (2001) 19(4) ASA Bulletin 710; Kristine Karsten and Andrew Berkely (eds), *Arbitration—Money Laundering, Corruption and Fraud* (Paris: ICC, 2003); Alexandre Court de Fontmichel, *L'arbitre, le juge et les pratiques illicites du commerce international* (Paris: Editions Panthéon Assas, 2004); Abdulhay Sayed, *Corruption in International Trade and Commercial Arbitration* (The Hague: Kluwer Law International, 2004); Alexis Mourre, "Arbitration and Criminal Law: Reflections on the Duties of the Arbitrator" (2006) 22(1) Arb Int'l 95.

9 See M.S. Kurkela, "Criminal Laws in International Arbitration—the May, the Must, the Should and the Should Not" (2008) 26(2) ASA Bulletin 280; Dragor Hiber and

contractual illegality,[10] fraud, lack of due diligence or human rights violations—raises different issues and may well require a different response based on the type and severity of the misconduct in question.

Misconduct by phase of investment

The first phase of the investment process that can give rise to misconduct is the establishment or acquisition of the investment. Where an investment has been acquired through illegal means—such as through fraud, corruption or contravention of regulatory requirements—investment tribunals have generally found that either they have no jurisdiction (*Inceysa v El Salvador*,[11] *Fraport v Philippines*[12] and *Anderson v Costa Rica*[13]) or that the claim cannot proceed because of the misconduct at issue (*World Duty Free v Kenya* and *Plama v Bulgaria*).[14]

Inceysa, *Fraport* and *Anderson* stand for the general principle that investments acquired in contravention of host state law are not protected

Vladimir Pavić, "Arbitration and Crime" (2008) 25(4) J Int'l Arb 461. On the treatment of corruption in the context of IIAs, see Bernardo Cremades, "Corruption and Investment Arbitration" in Gerald Aksen et al (eds), *Global Reflections on International Law, Commerce and Dispute Resolution, Liber Amicorum in honour of Robert Briner* (Paris: International Chamber of Commerce, 2005) at 203; Hilmar Raeschke-Kesslar, "Corruption" in Peter Muchlinski et al (eds), *The Oxford Handbook of International Investment Law* (Oxford: Oxford University Press, 2008); Florian Haugeneder, "Corruption in Investor-State Arbitration" (2009) 10(3) J World Investment and Trade 319.

10 See Richard H. Kreindler, "Aspects of Illegality in the Formation and Performance of Contracts" in Albert Jan van den Berg (ed), *ICCA Congress Series No. 11* (The Hague: Kluwer Law International, 2003) at 209; Karen Mills, "Corruption and Other Illegality in the Formation and Performance of Contracts and in the Conduct of Arbitration relating Thereto" in Albert Jan van den Berg (ed), *ICCA Congress Series No. 11* (The Hague: Kluwer Law International, 2003) at 295; and H. Raeschke-Kesslar, "Corrupt Practice in the Foreign Investment Context: Contractual and Procedural Aspects" in Norbert Horn (ed), *Arbitrating Foreign Investment Disputes: Procedural and Substantive Aspects* (The Hague: Kluwer Law International, 2004); Zdenek Novy, "The Illegality of a Contract Contrary to Fundamental Principles of International Law" (2010) online: SSRN <http://ssrn.com/abstract=1685293>.

11 *Inceysa Vallisoletana, S.L. v El Salvador*, Award, ICSID Case No. ARB/03/26 (August 2, 2006) [*Inceysa*].

12 *Fraport AG Frankfurt Airport Services Worldwide v Philippines*, Award, ICSID Case No. ARB/03/25 (August 16, 2007) at paras 396–404 [*Fraport*].

13 *Alasdair Ross Anderson and others v Republic of Costa Rica*, Award, ICSID Case No. ARB(AF)/07/3 (May 19, 2010) [*Anderson*].

14 *World Duty Free Company Limited v Kenya*, Award, ICSID Case No. ARB/00/7 (October 4, 2006) [*World Duty Free*]; *Plama Consortium Ltd v Bulgaria*, Award, ICSID Case No. ARB/03/24 (August 27, 2008) [*Plama*].

investments under IIAs.[15] In *Inceysa*, the tribunal found that the foreign investor had made false statements when it bid on an investment contract. The tribunal held that it did not have jurisdiction because the El Salvador-Spain BIT only protected investments made in accordance with El Salvadoran law and "any investment made against the laws of El Salvador is outside the protection of the Agreement, and therefore, from the competence of this Arbitral Tribunal."[16] In *Fraport*, the majority of the tribunal found that the investor had knowingly and intentionally circumvented host state law by acquiring more than 40 per cent control of a public utility (a concession for the construction and operation of an airport). The majority of the tribunal found that the Germany-Philippines BIT required that, in order to qualify for BIT protection, the investment had to be in accordance with host state law. The failure to comply with national law meant the tribunal had no jurisdiction *ratione materiae* with respect to the investment.[17] Finally, in *Anderson*, even though the investors were unwitting victims of a fraudulent and illegal ponzi scheme,[18] the tribunal found that it had no jurisdiction under the Canada-Costa Rica BIT because investment was defined to mean assets owned "in accordance with" Costa Rican law.[19] The tribunal noted that:

> The fact that the Contracting Parties to the Canada-Costa Rica BIT specifically included such a provision is a clear indication of the importance that they attached to the legality of investments made

15 On illegality and IIAs, see Christina Knahr, "Investments 'in accordance with host state law'" (2007) 4(5) *Transnational Dispute Management* [Knahr]; Ursula Kriebaum, "Illegal Investments" in Klausegger et al (eds), *Austrian Yearbook on International Arbitration* (Austria: Manz, 2010) at 307 [Kriebaum].

16 *Inceysa, supra* note 11 at para 203.

17 The *Fraport* Award, *supra* note 12, was annulled on the basis that there was a serious departure from the fundamental rule of procedure entitling the parties to be heard. See *Fraport AG Frankfurt Airport Services Worldwide v Philippines*, Decision on the Application for Annulment, ICSID Case No. ARB/03/25 (Annulment Proceedings) (December 23, 2010).

18 In *Anderson* the investors did not engage in active misconduct—it was their lack of due diligence that was fatal: ". . . prudent investment practice requires that any investor exercise due diligence before committing funds to any particular investment proposal. An important element of such due diligence is for investors to assure themselves that their investments comply with the law. Such due diligence obligation is neither overly onerous nor unreasonable. Based on the evidence presented to the tribunal, it is clear that the Claimants did not exercise the kind of due diligence that reasonable investors would have undertaken to assure themselves that their deposits with the Villalobos scheme were in accordance with the laws of Costa Rica." *Anderson, supra* note 13 at para 58. See para 25 regarding the Ponzi scheme.

19 *Ibid* at para 55.

by investors of the other Party and their intention that their laws with respect to investments be strictly followed. The assurance of legality with respect to investment has important, indeed crucial, consequences for the public welfare and economic well-being of any country.[20]

Since most forms of serious misconduct, including fraud, corruption and criminal conduct, are likely to be illegal under host state law, an express requirement in an IIA that the investment comply with host state law as a condition of the application of the IIA serves as a very strong mechanism to weed out IIA claims involving investor misconduct.[21] However, as exemplified by the IIAs considered in *Inceysa*, *Fraport* and *Anderson*, there is significant variation in IIA provisions dealing with local law.[22] Although some treaties include the requirement that the investment be made in accordance with domestic law in the definition of "investment,"[23] the reference to domestic law sometimes occurs in the context of the substantive protections (such as admission of the investment).[24] Even in the absence of an express provision requiring that an investment comply with domestic law, at least one IIA tribunal has found that the substantive protections of the IIA in question does not apply to an investment made contrary to law. In *Plama*, a case under the ECT, the tribunal concluded that there had been deliberate concealment of the true identity of the investor amounting to fraud[25] and that the investor's conduct was illegal under Bulgarian law.[26] The tribunal concluded that "the substantive protections of the ECT cannot apply to investments that are made contrary to law"[27] and that the "Claimant is not entitled to any of the substantive protections afforded by the ECT."[28]

---

20 *Ibid* at para 53.
21 As noted in *Salini Costruttori S.P.A. and Italstrade S.P.A. v Kingdom of Morocco*, Decision on Jurisdiction, ICSID Case No. ARB/00/4 (July 23, 2001), this type of provision "seeks to prevent the Bilateral Treaty from protecting investments that should not be protected, particularly because they would be illegal" (at para 46).
22 See Knahr, *supra* note 15; Kriebaum, *supra* note 15.
23 See Canada-Costa Rica FIPA at art I, discussed in *Anderson, supra* note 13.
24 See El Salvador-Spain BIT (1995) at arts II & III, discussed in *Inceysa, supra* note 11.
25 In *Plama, supra* note 14, the tribunal concluded that Vautrin (the indirect controlling shareholder) deliberately misrepresented the true identity of the investor to Bulgarian authorities (see para 129) and that the investment was the result of deliberate concealment amounting to fraud (see para 135).
26 *Ibid* at para 137.
27 *Ibid* at para 139.
28 *Ibid* at para 325.

Although the consequence of a finding of illegality can be severe (as discussed below, it can result in a denial of jurisdiction or the inadmissibility of the claim), not all forms of illegality are (or should be) treated the same. IIA jurisprudence has distinguished a number of different types of illegality. First, IIA tribunals have suggested that technical or minor illegalities should not result in a loss of jurisdiction.[29] This is a sound position. It would be anomalous if a large infrastructure development was deprived of IIA protection because the foreign investor inadvertently failed to submit a form to a regulatory agency on time. Trivial or minor illegalities should not provide the host state a license for its own misconduct. Secondly, tribunals have distinguished between illegality at the time of establishment and illegality during the operation of the investment. In this regard, the *Fraport* tribunal stated that:

> Moreover the effective operation of the BIT regime would appear to require that jurisdictional compliance be limited to the initiation of the investment. If, at the time of the initiation of the investment, there has been compliance with the law of the host state, allegations by the host state of violations of its law in the course of the investment, as a justification for state action with respect to the investment, might be a defense to claimed *substantive* violations of the BIT, but could not deprive a tribunal acting under the authority of the BIT of its jurisdiction.[30]

Similarly, in *Gustav FW Hamester GmbH & Co KG v Republic of Ghana*, the tribunal noted "that a distinction has to be drawn between (1) legality as at the initiation of the investment ("made") and (2) legality during the performance of the investment."[31] The *Hamester* tribunal found

---

29 See *Rumeli Telekom A.S. and Telsim Mobil Telekomunikasyon Hizmetleri A.S. v Republic of Kazakhstan*, Award, ICSID Case No. ARB/05/16 (July 29, 2008) ("Indeed, in order to receive the protection of a bilateral investment treaty, the disputed investments have to be in conformity with the host State laws and regulations. On the other hand, as was determined by the arbitral tribunal in the *Lesi* case, investments in the host State will only be excluded from the protection of the treaty if they have been made in breach of fundamental legal principles of the host country" at para 319). Also see *Tokios Tokeles v Ukraine*, Decision on Jurisdiction, ICSID Case No. ARB/02/18 (April 29, 2004): "to exclude an investment on the basis of such minor errors would be inconsistent with the object and purpose of the Treaty" at para 64; *Accord Alpha Projektholding GmbH v Ukraine*, Award, ICSID Case No. ARB/07/16 (November 8, 2010) at para 297.

30 *Fraport, supra* note 12 at para 343.

31 *Gustav FW Hamester GmbH & Co KG v Republic of Ghana*, Award, ICSID Case No. ARB/07/24 (June 18, 2010) at para 127 [*Hamester*].

that, based on the BIT at issue, legality at the initiation of the investment is a jurisdictional issue, while the legality during performance is a
merits issue.[32] Finally, where the host state knew of or participated in
the illegality, the state might be estopped from raising a violation of its
own law as a jurisdictional defense.[33]

In addition to illegality under host state law, in assessing the conduct
of an investor in making an investment, tribunals have also referred to
general principles of international law as the basis for denying jurisdiction. In *Inceysa*, the tribunal referred to: (i) the principle of good faith,[34]
noting that El Salvador's consent to arbitrate "presupposed good faith
behavior on the part of future investors;"[35] (ii) the principle of *nemo audi-
tur propriam turpitudinem allegans*,[36] noting that a "foreign investor cannot seek to benefit from an investment effectuated by means of one or
several illegal acts;"[37] (iii) violation of international public policy;[38] and
(iv) violation of the principle that prohibits unlawful enrichment.[39]

As highlighted by the citations quoted above in *Fraport* and *Hamester*,
misconduct can also arise during the operation of the investment. As
noted by these tribunals, this form of misconduct is more likely to give
rise to a ruling on the merits, rather than jurisdictional issues. Further,
investor misconduct may well provide a justification for the state conduct
at issue, such as where the state revokes a license, permit or concession as
a result of non-compliance with its terms or with domestic law. For
example, in *Genin v Estonia*, the investor's misconduct provided the host
state the basis upon which it could revoke the investor's banking license.[40]

---

32 *Ibid* at para 127.
33 In *Fraport, supra* note 12 the tribunal noted that "There is, however, the question of
    estoppel. Principles of fairness should require a tribunal to hold a government
    estopped from raising violations of its own law as a jurisdictional defense when it
    knowingly overlooked them and endorsed an investment which was not in
    compliance with its law" (at para 346).
34 *Inceysa, supra* note 11 at paras 230–9.
35 *Ibid* at para 238.
36 *Ibid* at paras 240–4.
37 *Ibid* at para 242.
38 *Ibid* at paras 245–52.
39 *Ibid* at paras 253–7.
40 In *Genin et al v Estonia*, Award, ICSID Case No. ARB/99/2 (June 25, 2001), the
    tribunal considered the investor's unreasonable reluctance to divulge information
    relevant in assessing whether the state breached treaty obligations in revoking a
    banking license (see paras 348–73). Likewise in *Joseph Charles Lemire v Ukraine*,
    Decision on Jurisdiction and Liability, ICSID Case No. ARB/06/18 (January 14,
    2010) [*Joseph Charles Lemire*], the tribunal noted that the investor's duty to perform
    an investigation before effecting the investment is relevant in assessing a breach of
    fair and equitable treatment (see para 285).

Finally, investor misconduct can also arise in the dispute resolution process, such as where the investor engages in sham transactions in order to obtain the benefit of investment treaty protection—a form of abusive forum shopping[41]—after a dispute has arisen. Tribunals have found that this type of investor conduct is an abuse of process.[42] Another form of forum shopping—albeit not involving a fraudulent transaction or a false assertion of ownership—arises where an investment is purchased solely for the purpose of commencing litigation.[43] This occurred in *Phoenix Action Ltd v Czech Republic*, where the tribunal found that share transactions through which an Israeli company obtained shares in Czech companies were an illegitimate device to transform a claim by a Czech national (who owned the Czech companies) into an international claim under the Czech Republic-Israel BIT. Even though the tribunal found that the claim met all the general jurisdiction requirements of the treaty and that there was no illegality, the tribunal held that it had no jurisdiction if the investment was not made in good faith:

41 Forum shopping—in the sense of restructuring an investment after a dispute has arisen in order to obtain the benefit of IIA protection—is here distinguished from more general forms of treaty-shopping, where an investor, at the time of establishment, structures an investment in order to obtain investment treaty protection. See *Mobil Corporation and others v Bolivarian Republic of Venezuela*, Decision on Jurisdiction, ICSID Case No. ARB/07/27 (June 10, 2010) (noting that restructuring of investments in order to gain access to ICSID arbitration is "a perfectly legitimate goal as far as it concerned future disputes" but that with "respect to pre-existing disputes, the situation is different and the Tribunal considers that to restructure investments only in order to gain jurisdiction under a BIT for such disputes would constitute, to take the words of the Phoenix Tribunal, an abusive manipulation of the system of international investment protection under the ICSID Convention and the BITs" at paras 204 and 205).

42 See *Cementownia "Nowa Huta" S.A. v Turkey*, Award, ICSID Case No. ARB(AF)/06/2 (September 17, 2009) [*Cementownia*] ("The Arbitral Tribunal is of the opinion that the Claimant has intentionally and in bad faith abused the arbitration; it purported to be an investor when it knew that this was not the case. This constitutes indeed an abuse of process. In addition, the Claimant is guilty of procedural misconduct: once the arbitration proceeding was commenced, it has caused excessive delays and thereby increased the costs of the arbitration" at para 159); *Europe Cement Investment & Trade S.A. v Republic of Turkey*, Award, ICSID Case No. ARB(AF)/07/2 (August 13, 2009) ("If, as in *Phoenix*, a claim that is based on the purchase of an investment solely for the purpose of commencing litigation is an abuse of process, then surely a claim based on the false assertion of ownership of an investment is equally an abuse of process" at para 175) [*Europe Cement*].

43 *Europe Cement*, *ibid* ("In the above cases, the lack of good faith was present in the acquisition of the investment. In the present case, there was in fact no investment at all, at least at the relevant time, and the lack of good faith is in the assertion of an investment on the basis of documents that according to the evidence presented were not authentic" at para 175).

The purpose of the international mechanism of protection of investment through ICSID arbitration cannot be to protect investments made in violation of the laws of the host State or investments not made in good faith, obtained for example through misrepresentations, concealments or corruption, or amounting to an abuse of the international ICSID arbitration system. In other words, the purpose of international protection is to protect legal and *bona fide* investments.[44]

Although *Phoenix* involved forum shopping after the dispute between the Czech companies and Czech authorities arose, since there was a subsequent share transfer to a foreign investor, it is a case that involves both the establishment of an investment and investor conduct after a dispute has arisen. Subsequent tribunals have applied the principle that only investments made legally and in good faith fall within an ICSID tribunal's jurisdiction.[45]

Misconduct by phase of arbitration

As the above references to various awards and decisions indicate, investor conduct can have legally relevant consequences at various stages in the arbitration proceedings. The cases involving illegality have generally been dismissed at the jurisdictional stage on the basis that the tribunal's jurisdiction is limited to investments made in accordance with host state law. *Phoenix* suggests that, at least with respect to arbitrations under the ICSID, good faith and legality are jurisdictional conditions. Although IIA tribunals have cited *Phoenix* with approval,[46] the reasoning has also been criticized for implying jurisdictional criteria not present in the ICSID Convention.[47]

Rather than treating issues of illegality and other forms of misconduct as jurisdictional issues, another approach is for a tribunal to find that it has jurisdiction, but nevertheless rule that the investor's claim (or part

---

44 *Phoenix Action Ltd v Czech Republic*, Award, ICSID Case No. ARB/06/5 (15 April 2009) [*Phoenix*] at para 100. *Accord: Hamester, supra* note 31 at para 123; *Contra: Saba Fakes v Turkey*, Award, ICSID Case No. ARB/07/20 (July 14, 2010) at paras 112–14 [*Fakes*]. (In *Fakes*, the tribunal rejected the *Phoenix* approach of reading the principles of good faith and legality into the definition of investment in ICSID Convention.)

45 *Hamester, supra* note 31 at para 123 and *Cementownia, supra* note 42 at paras 153–7.

46 *Ibid.*

47 In *Fakes, supra* note 44 at paras 112–14, the tribunal rejected the *Phoenix* approach of reading the principles of good faith and legality into the definition of investment in the ICSID Convention.

of it) is inadmissible. In a companion paper to this chapter,[48] I have argued that tribunals have the power to find that claims are substantively inadmissible where the investor has acted contrary to international law. For example, in *Plama*, the tribunal concluded that "the substantive protections of the ECT cannot apply to investments that are made contrary to law."[49] Unlike in *Inceysa*, *Fraport* or *Phoenix*, the investor misconduct was not viewed as a jurisdictional issue, but rather an issue that affects the substantive inadmissibility of the claim.[50] An arguably similar approach was taken in *World Duty Free*, a non-investment treaty case in which the investor bribed the President of Kenya in order to obtain a concession contract. In that case, the tribunal stated that:

> In light of domestic laws and international conventions relating to corruption, and in light of the decisions taken in this matter by courts and arbitral tribunals, this Tribunal is convinced that bribery is contrary to the international public policy of most, if not all, States or, to use another formula, to transnational public policy. Thus, claims based on contracts of corruption or on contracts obtained by corruption cannot be upheld by this Arbitral Tribunal.[51]

More generally, where the misconduct arises during the course of the arbitration proceedings, the tribunal might use various procedural mechanisms to censure investor misconduct, such as granting interim measures, refusing to admit evidence or drawing adverse inferences.[52]

As noted above, investor conduct is often a key consideration in merits issues, in particular when assessing fair and equitable treatment.[53]

---

48 Newcombe, *supra* note 6.
49 *Plama, supra* note 14 at para 139.
50 *Plama, ibid*, might also be read as suggesting that the substantive protections of the ECT are applicable only if the investment is legal, which is a question of the merits of the claim.
51 *World Duty Free, supra* note 14 at para 157. In the investment treaty context, see *Waguih Elie George Siag and Clorinda Vecci v the Arab Republic of Egypt*, Dissenting Opinion of Professor Francisco Orrego Vicuña, ICSID Case No. ARB/05/15 (June 1, 2009) ("Whether the principle of *ex turpi causa non oritur actio*, the doctrine of unclean hands or the policy of eliminating corruption domestically and internationally are relied upon, the result is that an arbitration tribunal cannot find for a claim that is tainted by such practices" at 4–5).
52 See Abba Kolo, "Witness Intimidation, Tampering and Other Related Abuses of Process in Investment Arbitration: Possible Remedies Available to the Arbitral Tribunal" (2010) 26(1) Arb Int'l 43.
53 In interpreting fair and equitable treatment some tribunals have engaged in a form of proportionality analysis. An investor's conduct could be considered in this analysis.

Investor conduct may also be relevant in assessing damages. In *MTD v Chile*, the tribunal found the investor responsible for 50 per cent of damages because its lack of due diligence increased business risks.[54] Investor conduct may be relevant to apportionment of the costs of the arbitration and the parties' legal fees. In *Cementownia*, the tribunal, due to the investor's abuse of process, ordered the investor to bear all the costs of the arbitration, as well as the state's legal fees and expenses.[55]

Is there a need for changes to treaty practice to address investor misconduct?

The above overview of the responses of IIA tribunals to investor misconduct suggests that, when faced with the issue of serious investor misconduct, tribunals have been able to use existing mechanisms to ensure that an investor does not profit from its own misconduct. The question arises whether there is a need for an evolution in treaty practice to address investor misconduct or whether existing IIA mechanisms are adequate. In light of the various mechanisms that IIA tribunals have at their disposal to address serious forms of misconduct, particularly illegality and corruption, can the legitimacy of IIAs overall be increased by including express provisions on investor misconduct?

In my view, existing mechanisms are generally adequate to ensure that an investor is not able to profit from its misconduct. Even though IIAs do not have express provisions on investor misconduct, IIA tribunals have been able to apply general principles of law and rules of treaty interpretation to protect the legitimate interests of host states and ensure that investors are not rewarded for their misconduct.

As a starting point, this chapter recommends that IIAs should define "investment" to include a condition of compliance with local law. Since all forms of serious misconduct are likely to be illegal under host state law, serious illegality will bar the investment from the IIA's protections, either as a matter of jurisdiction, admissibility or the merits of the claim.[56] In

---

See e.g. *EDF (Services) Ltd v Romania*, Award, ICSID Case No. ARB/05/13 (October 8, 2009) at paras 286, 301 and *Joseph Charles Lemire, supra* note 40 at para 285.

54 *MTD Equity Sdn Bhd & MTD Chile S.A. v Chile*, Award, ICSID Case No. ARB/01/7 (May 25, 2004) at paras 242–3 [*MTD*].

55 *Cementownia, supra* note 42 at para 177. For a discussion of abuse of process in investment treaty arbitration, see John Gaffney, "'Abuse of Process' in Investment Treaty Arbitration" (2010) 11(4) Journal of World Investment and Trade 515.

56 See Newcombe, *supra* note 6, in which the author argues that IIA tribunals have the power to dismiss claims as inadmissible and that this approach may be preferable to finding that the tribunal has no jurisdiction.

addition, it is important for there to be procedural mechanisms in place so that host states can apply to strike-out unmeritorious claims (such as those involving serious misconduct) at an early stage. The ICSID Arbitration Rules[57] have such procedures, as do IIAs based on the 2004 US Model BIT.[58]

In addition to restricting investment to assets acquired in accordance with local laws, states could also go one step further and impose a positive obligation on foreign investors to comply with domestic law during the establishing and operation of the investment. This is the approach in article 13 of the Investment Agreement for the COMESA Common Investment Area (COMESA Investment Agreement):[59] "COMESA investors and their investments shall comply with all applicable domestic measures of the Member State in which their investment is made."[60]

This provision raises conceptual difficulties because COMESA investors are not parties to the COMESA Investment Agreement. Rather, they are in the position of third party beneficiaries of investment protections.[61] However, in the COMESA Investment Agreement, the investor-state arbitration provision raises the interesting possibility of a host state making a counterclaim for breach of local law. Article 28(9) provides that:

> A Member State against whom a claim is brought by a COMESA investor under this Article may assert as a defence, counterclaim, right of set off or other similar claim, that the COMESA investor bringing the claim has not fulfilled its obligations under this Agreement, including the obligations to comply with all applicable

---

57 See ICSID, *Rules of Procedure for Arbitration Proceedings*, online: ICSID <http://icsid.worldbank.org/ICSID/ICSID/RulesMain.jsp> at art 41(5).
58 See US Model BIT (2004) at art 28(4) with respect to preliminary objections. See C. Lévesque in this book at ch 8.
59 COMESA is the Common Market for Eastern and Southern Africa.
60 *Investment Agreement for the COMESA Common Investment Area* (2007) at art 13, online: <http://vi.unctad.org/files/wksp/iiawksp08/docs/wednesday/Exercise%20Materials/invagreecomesa.pdf> [COMESA Investment Agreement].
61 The situation is not quite so clear because art 28(4) provides, in part, that "Each investor, by virtue of establishing or continuing to operate or own an investment subject to this Agreement, consents to the terms of the submission of a claim to dispute resolution under this Agreement if he exercises the right to bring a claim against a Member State under this Agreement." It might be argued that by virtue of investing in a Member State territory, the investor has agreed to the terms under which claims will be assessed and that this would include counterclaims for breach of domestic or international law. See *infra*.

domestic measures or that it has not taken all reasonable steps to mitigate possible damages.[62]

As a result of this provision, it can be argued that if a foreign investor accepts the host state's offer to arbitrate, it binds itself to have the dispute governed under the COMESA Investment Agreement, including its obligation to comply with host state law.[63] The COMESA Investment Agreement highlights the need for states to consider both the source of the positive obligation on the foreign investor (based on national and/or international law) and to provide the procedural means to adjudicate breaches of those obligations. It would appear desirable for states to have the ability to raise breaches of both national and international law both in defending against an investor's claims and in making its own claims and counterclaims.

It is beyond the scope of this paper to discuss whether, and the extent to which, foreign investors have international legal obligations. This issue is addressed in Patrick Dumberry's chapter in this book.[64] There is the further procedural issue of the extent to which host states, under the asymmetrical framework of modern IIAs, can bring claims and counterclaims against foreign investors.[65] Helene Bubrowski addresses the issue of host state counterclaims in Chapter 12 of this book.

With respect to specific forms of misconduct, a small number of IIAs (mostly in the form of FTAs with investment chapters) are beginning to address issues such as corruption[66] and corporate social responsibility.[67] Anti-corruption provisions are rare in BITs, but appear in recent American, European and Japanese FTAs and economic cooperation agree-

---

62 COMESA Investment Agreement, *supra* note 60 at art 28(9).

63 *Ibid* at art 31 (Governing Law in Disputes) which provides that: "When a claim is submitted to an arbitral tribunal, it shall be decided in accordance with this Agreement, the COMESA Treaty, national law of the host state, and the general principles of international law."

64 See ch 10.

65 Since investors are not party to IIAs, a state could not under an IIA bring a claim against the investor on the basis of the investor-state arbitration provision, unless consent to arbitrate could be found in some conduct of the foreign investor.

66 See "International Investment Agreements: A Survey of Environmental, Labour and Anti-corruption Issues", in OECD, International Invest Law, Understanding Concepts and Tracking Innovations (Paris: OECD, 2008), online: <http://www.oecd.org/dataoecd/3/5/40471550.pdf>.

67 See Jarrod Hepburn and Vuyelwa Kuuya, "Corporate Social Responsibility and Investment Treaties" in Marie-Claire Cordonier Segger, Markus W. Gehring and Andrew Newcombe (eds), *Sustainable Development in World Investment Law* (The Hague: Kluwer Law International, 2011) at 585 [Hepburn and Kuuyn].

ments and in the CAFTA.[68] For example, article 21.5 (Anti-Corruption), US-Singapore FTA provides:

1. Each Party reaffirms its firm existing commitment to the adoption, maintenance, and enforcement of effective measures, including deterrent penalties, against bribery and corruption in international business transactions. The Parties further commit to undertake best efforts to associate themselves with appropriate international anticorruption instruments and to encourage and support appropriate anticorruption initiatives and activities in relevant international fora.
2. The Parties shall cooperate to strive to eliminate bribery and corruption and to promote transparency in international trade. They will look for avenues in relevant international fora to address these issues and build upon the potential anti-corruption efforts in these fora.[69]

With respect to corporate social responsibility (CSR), the practice is limited to a small number of treaties.[70] For example, the Canada-Peru FTA provides:

Each Party should encourage enterprises operating within its territory or subject to its jurisdiction to voluntarily incorporate internationally recognized standards of corporate social responsibility in their internal policies, such as statements of principle that have been endorsed or are supported by the Parties. These principles address issues such as labour, the environment, human rights, community relations and anti-corruption. The Parties remind those enterprises of the importance of incorporating such corporate social responsibility standards in their internal policies.[71]

---

68 See CAFTA's ch 18.
69 *United States-Singapore Free Trade Agreement*, May 6, 2003, online: USTR <http://www.ustr.gov/sites/default/files/uploads/agreements/fta/singapore/asset_upload_file708_4036.pdf> at art 21.5.
70 Hepburn and Kuuya, *supra* note 67.
71 See *Free Trade Agreement Between Canada and the Republic of Colombia*, November 21, 2008 (entered into force August 15, 2011), online: DFAIT <http://www.international.gc.ca/trade-agreements-accords-commerciaux/agr-acc/colombia-colombie/preamble-preambule.aspx?lang=eng&view=d> at art 816; *Free Trade Agreement Between Canada and the Republic of Peru*, May 29, 2008 (entered into force August 1, 2009), online: DFAIT <http://www.international.gc.ca/trade-agreements-accords-commerciaux/agr-acc/peru-perou/preamble-preambule.aspx?lang=eng&view=d> at art 810.

Conclusion

I have argued elsewhere that serious misconduct on the part of foreign investors should not be condoned. Yet serious misconduct is not necessarily always a jurisdictional issue.[72] Jurisdiction is binary—there is or there is not jurisdiction. Jurisdictional decisions are a very imperfect tool where there is misconduct of various shades on both sides. As noted by Dr Bernardo Cremades' dissent in *Fraport*:

> If the legality of the Claimant's conduct is a jurisdictional issue, and the legality of the Respondent's conduct a merits issue, then the Respondent Host State is placed in a powerful position. In the Biblical phrase, the Tribunal must first examine the speck in the eye of the investor and defer, and maybe never address, a beam in the eye of the Host State.[73]

As outlined in Part I of this chapter, investor misconduct can be addressed at various stages of the arbitration process and there are a range of procedural responses available to a tribunal. Although recent decisions have focused on jurisdiction as the 'control mechanism' for addressing investor misconduct, given its binary function, jurisdiction is a blunt tool for dealing with the complexity and variety of issues that arise in investor misconduct cases.

In light of this complexity, I am skeptical of the ability of states to design new IIA provisions that establish clear rules for addressing various forms of investor misconduct and would recommend a minimalist approach involving three elements. First, requirements that investments be in accordance with host state law are certainly desirable. The best practice would be to include an "in accordance with local law" provision in the definition of investment. Secondly, IIAs should provide preliminary objection mechanisms to allow host states to strike out claims at an early stage. Thirdly, states should consider clarifying arbitration provisions to expressly permit the host state to make claims and counterclaims against investors for breaches of national and international law.

---

72 Newcombe, *supra* note 6.
73 *Fraport*, *supra* note 12 at para 37.

12 Balancing IIA arbitration through the use of counterclaims

*Helene Bubrowski**

Introduction

The emergence of investment treaty arbitration provoked a shift in the parties' respective rights in arbitration proceedings. In 1995, Jan Paulsson delivered the following analysis:

> This new world of arbitration is one where the claimant need not have a contractual relationship with the defendant and where the table could not be turned: the defendant could not have initiated the arbitration, nor is it certain of being able even to bring a counterclaim.[1]

The possibility of bringing a claim against the host state based on a unilateral offer in an IIA considerably strengthens the position of foreign investors. They are no longer charged with the burden of negotiating a separate arbitration agreement with the host state. Conversely, it impairs the host state's means of defense because its ability to plead counterclaims against foreign investors is faced with various obstacles. This chapter explores the viability of counterclaims before treaty-based arbitration tribunals and the difficulties involved therein.

A large number of national legal systems provide the right for the respondent to present a counterclaim against the claimant.[2] The

* Ph.D. (University of Cologne, 2011); currently Law Clerk at the Berlin Superior Court of Justice. The author would like to thank Hinda Rabkin for comments on earlier versions of this article.

1 Jan Paulsson, "Arbitration Without Privity" (1995) 10(2) ICSID Rev 232.
2 Arwed Blomeyer, "Types of Relief Available (Judicial Remedies)" in Mauro Cappelletti (ed), VXI *International Encyclopedia of Comparative Law* (Tübingen: Mohr, The Hague: Nijhoff, 1982) ("In principle, all legal systems admit a cross-action where there exists an inter-relation of claim and counterclaim" at 60). See e.g. art 70

procedural rules of the PCIJ and of its successor, the ICJ, also permit the presentation of counterclaims.[3] With respect to the recognition of counterclaims in international arbitration, some skepticism among scholars existed in the beginning of the last century.[4] However, today, the right of the respondent to file a claim in opposition to the primary claim in the same proceeding is commonly admitted by arbitral tribunals and explicitly included in the legal instruments governing international arbitration proceedings.[5]

Indeed, the possibility to raise counterclaims is beneficial in many respects. Providing an avenue for relief in opposition to the primary

---

NC proc civ; Rule 13 Federal Rules of Civil Procedure (USA); § 33 Code of Civil Procedure (Germany); art 14 Code of Civil Procedure (Switzerland). For other examples of national legal provisions, see Christian Koller, *Aufrechnung und Widerklage im Schiedsverfahren* (Vienna: Manzsche Verlags und Universitätsbuchhandlung, 2009) at 52–68.

3 *Rules of the Court* (1922), PCIJ (Ser. D) No. 1 and *Rules of the International Court of Justice,* [1978] ICJ Acts and Doc 6; for the interpretation of art 63 of the PCIJ rules (4th edition of the rules of April 1940), see the *Asylum Case (Columbia v Peru)*, [1950], ICJ Rep 266 at 280–8. A detailed analysis of the practice of the PCIJ and the ICJ with respect to these rules, see Bradley Larschan and Guive Mirfendereski, "The Status of Counterclaims in International Law, With Particular Reference to International Arbitration Involving a Private Party and a Foreign State" (1986–87) 15 Denv J Int'l L and Policy 11 at 13–17.

4 See e.g. Dionisio Anzilotti, "La Demande Reconventionnelle en Procédure Internationale" (1930) 57 Journal du Droit International 857 ("Il ne pouvait, évidemment, pas être question de demande reconventionnelle dans la procédure internationale, tant que la seule forme judiciaire de solution des litiges entre États a été l'arbitrage, au sens étroit du mot" at *ibid*).

5 *Convention on the Settlement of Investment Disputes between States and Nationals of other States*, March 18, 1965, 575 UNTS 188, 4 ILM 532 (entered into force October 14, 1966) [ICSID Convention] (". . . the Tribunal shall, if requested by a party, determine any incidental or additional claims or counterclaims arising directly out of the subject-matter of the dispute provided that they are within the scope of the consent of the parties and are otherwise within the jurisdiction of the Centre" at art 46), rephrased by ICSID Arbitration Rule 40; art 47 ICSID Additional Facility Rules (". . . a party may present an incidental or additional claim or counter-claim, provided that such ancillary claim is within the scope of the arbitration agreement of the parties"); *Arbitration Rules of the United Nations Commission on International Trade Law*, GA Res. 31/98, UNCITRAL, 31st sess., Supp No. 17, UN Doc A/31/17 (1976) [UNCITRAL Arbitration Rules] ("In his statement of defence, or at a later stage in the arbitral proceedings if the arbitral tribunal decides that the delay was justified under the circumstances, the respondent may make a counter-claim arising out of the same contract or rely on a claim arising out of the same contract for the purpose of a set-off" at art 19(3)); *Rules of Arbitration of the International Chamber of Commerce*, online: International Chamber of Commerce <http://www.iccwbo.org/uploadedFiles/Court/Arbitration/other/rules_arb_english.pdf> ("Any counterclaim(s) made by the Respondent shall be filed with its Answer" at art 5(5)).

claim, this legal instrument assures equality of arms by placing the respondent and claimant on an equal footing in the proceedings. Furthermore, the consolidation of claims brought by the respective parties serves the goals of judicial economy and efficiency because one proceeding is generally less costly in terms of time and money than two parallel or consecutive adjudications.[6] In view of the desire to avoid the risk of inconsistent outcomes, it is also in line with the principle of legal certainty.[7]

While the advantages of allowing counterclaims are relevant to all kinds of national and international legal proceedings, there is a specific beneficial role for counterclaims in international investment law. With the enormous growth of investment disputes, the traditional paradigm of investment arbitration as a mechanism for the sole protection of investors' rights is being shattered.[8] International investment law is increasingly faced with the challenge of improving its legitimacy. The critique asserts that arbitration primarily benefits the investor to the detriment of the state and establishes a disproportionate balance of arms; arbitral tribunals are "private fora for public issues," where social and public interests are ignored.[9] The bias against arbitration is evidenced by the recent

6 Hege Elisabeth Veenstra-Kjos, "Counterclaims by Host States in Investment Treaty Arbitration" (2007) 4(4) *Transnational Dispute Management* 1 at 5 [Veenstra-Kjos]; Yaraslau Kryvoi, "Counterclaims in Investor-State Arbitration", LSE Society and Economy Working Papers 8/2011 at 4 [Kryvoi]. See also the Czech Republic's argument *Saluka Investments B.V. v The Czech Republic*, Decision on Jurisdiction over the Czech Republic's Counterclaim, UNCITRAL (May 7, 2004) ("Moreover, the exercise of jurisdiction by the Tribunal over the Respondent's counterclaim would advance the goals of economy and efficiency in international dispute resolution, since otherwise the Respondent would have to pursue its claim elsewhere" at para 24) [*Saluka*].
7 Christoph Schreuer, *The ICSID Convention: A Commentary* (New York: Cambridge University Press, 2009) at 732.
8 Gustavo Laborde, "The Case for Host State Claims in Investment Arbitration" (2010) 1(1) Journal of International Dispute Settlement 97 at 97–99, presenting the idea of the so-called "reverse paradigm of investment arbitration disputes." *Contra*, Charles Brower and Stephan Schill, "Is Arbitration a Threat or a Boon to the Legitimacy of International Investment Law?" (2009) 9 Chi. J. Int'l L. 471 ("Hence, the criticism that investment treaties afford unilateral benefits to investors presents a very limited and in fact contorted picture of investor-state relations. It disregards the fact that the host state already possesses a power that the foreign investor lacks" at 482).
9 See e.g. Jeffery Atik, "Legitimacy, Transparency and NGO Participation in the NAFTA Chapter 11 Process" in Todd Weiler (ed), *NAFTA Investment Law and Arbitration: Past Issues, Current Practice, Future Prospects* (New York: Transnational Publishers, 2004) 135 at 140; Mehmet Toral and Thomas Schultz, "The State, a Perpetual Respondent in Investment Arbitration?" in Michael Waibel et al (eds),

denunciations of the ICSID Convention by Bolivia and Ecuador and the denunciation of several BITs by Ecuador and Venezuela.[10] Thus, the crucial task is to introduce a balance between protecting foreign investors while simultaneously preserving the host states' margin of maneuver regarding regulatory activity.[11] Giving host states an effective means to defend their own interests is apt to enhance the general acceptance of international investment arbitration and increase the legitimacy of the international investment law regime.[12]

Up until now, however, counterclaims remain a rarity in investor-state disputes.[13] In the "traditional world of arbitration" where the tribunal's jurisdiction is based on contractual arbitration clauses, host states have asserted counterclaims in some instances. In treaty-based arbitration proceedings, thus far very few tribunals have been given the chance to rule on a counterclaim filed by a host state.[14] The awards, in dismissing these counterclaims, provide good examples of the different obstacles that host states face in pleading counterclaims in investment treaty arbitration. This chapter analyzes such obstacles before suggesting, in conclusion, some possible cures. Amongst the obstacles is that IIAs do not provide rights for host states *vis-à-vis* foreign investors (Part I); that the counterclaim might not fall within the scope of the parties' agreement to arbitrate investment disputes (Part II); and that the lack

---

The Backlash Against Investment Arbitration: Perceptions and Reality (The Hague: Wolters Kluwer, 2010) 577 at 577–8 [Toral and Schultz].

10 UNCTAD, Recent Developments in International Investment Agreements (2007–June 2008), IIA Monitor No. 3 (2009) (New York, Geneva, 2009) at 6.

11 For an analysis of the conflict between the interests of foreign investors and the regulatory interests of host states, see Charles Brower II, "Obstacles and Pathways to Consideration of the Public Interest in Investment Treaty Disputes" in Karl P. Sauvant (ed), *Yearbook of International Investment Law & Policy* (2008–09) 347 at 361; Lars Markert, "The Crucial Question of Future Investment Treaties: Balancing Investors' Rights and Regulatory Interests of Host States" in Marc Bungenberg, Jörn Griebel and Steffen Hindelang (eds), *European Yearbook of International Economic Law, Special Issue: International Investment Law and EU Law* (Berlin/Heidelberg/New York: Springer, 2011) at 145–71 .

12 See Introduction to this book.

13 Anne K. Hoffmann, "Counterclaims by Respondent State in Investment Arbitrations" (2006) German Arbitration Journal 317.

14 *Alex Genin, Eastern Credit Limited, Inc and A.S. Baltoil v The Republic of Estonia*, Award, ICSID Case No. ARB/99/2 (June 25, 2001) [*Alex Genin*]; *Saluka, supra* note 6; *Limited Liability Co Amto v Ukraine*, Final Award, SCC Case No. 080/2005 (March 26, 2008) [*Amto*]; *Gustav FW Hamester GmbH & Co KG v Republic of Ghana*, Award, ICSID Case No. ARB/07/24 (June 18, 2010) [*Gustav Hamester*]; *Sergei Paushok, CJSC Golden East Co, CJSC Vostokneftegaz Co v The Government of Mongolia*, Award on Jurisdiction and Liability, UNCITRAL (April 28, 2011) [*Sergei Paushok*].

of so called "connexity" might prevent a tribunal from consolidating the claim and the counterclaim in one set of proceedings (Part III).

The host state's rights *vis-à-vis* foreign investors

In order to bring a claim, the respondent state has to argue a violation of a right *vis-à-vis* a foreign investor. Already for the purpose of determining jurisdiction, tribunals have considered whether the facts alleged in the claim constitute a *prima facie* breach of the provision invoked.[15]

With respect to substantive provisions, IIAs are asymmetrical.[16] Their objective, as reflected in titles and preambles, is the promotion and protection of foreign investments. IIAs produce obligations for host states and corresponding rights for investors. Foreign investors are to IIAs what third-party beneficiaries are to contracts.[17] Reciprocity in IIAs is limited to the promise between the contracting states to accord the same level of protection to their respective investors. However, a debate is ongoing whether investors' duties can be imported into IIAs.[18] Arbitral practice seems to be increasingly sensitive to issues concerning human rights and sustainable development; tribunals have at times taken into account the corresponding rules and provisions of international law when interpreting the applicable IIA.[19] But as of today, IIA fail to impose clear obligations on investors. It remains unresolved whether, in general, private parties can be subject to obligations under international law.[20]

---

15 *Azurix Corpn v Argentine Republic*, Decision on Jurisdiction, ICSID Case No. ARB/01/12 (December 8, 2003) at para 76; *SGS Société Générale de Surveillance S.A. v Republic of the Philippines*, Decision on Jurisdiction, ICSID Case No. ARB/02/6 (January 29, 2004) at para 26 [*SGS v Philippines, Decision on Jurisdiction*]; *SGS Société Générale de Surveillance S.A. v Islamic Republic of Pakistan*, Decision on Jurisdiction, ICSID Case No. ARB/01/13 (August 6, 2004) at para 145 [*SGS v Pakistan*, Decision on Jurisdiction]; *Impregilo S.p.A. v Islamic Republic of Pakistan*, Decision on Jurisdiction, ICSID Case No. ARB/03/3 (April 22, 2005) at para 254.

16 Hoffmann, *supra* note 13 at 320.

17 Laborde, *supra* note 8 at 112.

18 For a detailed analysis see Toral and Schultz, *supra* note 9 at 580–8.

19 See e.g. *Southern Pacific Properties (Middle East) Ltd v Arab Republic of Egypt*, Award on the Merits, ICSID Case No. ARB/84/3 (May 20, 1992) at paras 150–4 where the tribunal examined whether the UNESCO Convention was relevant for deciding the case.

20 According to the classical doctrine of international law, only states are bearers of obligations under international law; see Kryvoi, *supra* note 6 at 17–27. The author explores possible sources of international law creating obligations for investors, among them international conventions, international custom, and general principles of law. See also Patrick Dumberry at ch 10 in this book.

While host states cannot bring claims based on IIAs, they are not devoid of all rights in the matter. Contracts between a foreign investor and a host state generally contain rights and obligations for both parties. Yet, many contracts are not concluded with the host state's central government, but with a separate legal entity having its own legal personality, such as a territorial subdivision, a state-owned enterprise or a national fund.[21] In these cases, the host state is neither a contracting party, nor can contractual rights be attributed to it.[22] Therefore, the host state is not entitled to bring a claim based on these types of contracts.

Rights of host states may also stem from their own national laws. For example, an action against the investor can be based upon violations of the host state's public policy laws, such as tax, safety, employment, and environmental laws. Additionally, a host state's claim against the investor can arise from private law, for instance tort law or the law of unjust enrichment. A breach of the obligations expressed in these laws can render an investor liable to pay compensation to the host state. If the investor has raised a claim against the host state, it may be possible for the state to file a counterclaim based on these grounds in order to avoid or reduce its compensation duty.[23]

With regard to the cost of arbitration proceedings, a tribunal can order an investor to cover the costs incurred by the host state. However, a host state cannot make a counterclaim for arbitration costs. Rather, costs are considered by arbitral tribunals on the basis of the applicable arbitration rules.[24]

Jurisdiction over counterclaims

A central issue regarding the viability of counterclaims in investment treaty arbitration is the tribunals' jurisdiction over claims raised by host

21 See *Saluka, supra* note 6. In its counterclaim, the Czech Republic alleges *inter alia* a breach of the Share Purchase Agreement. However, the contracting party was not the Czech Republic but Czech National Property Fund. The tribunal dismissed the claim for other reasons and did not explicitly address this issue.

22 See "Draft articles on responsibility of States for internationally wrongful acts", Report of the International Law Commission on the Work of Its Fifty-third Session (UN Doc A/56/10) in *Yearbook of the International Law Commission 2001*, vol 2, part 2 (New York: UN, 2007) at 26 ff at arts 4–11 (UNDOC.A/CN.4/SER.A/2001/Add.1) which only allow attribution of internationally wrongful acts to a state.

23 Thomas W. Wälde and Borzu Sabahi, "Compensation, Damages and Valuation" in Peter T. Muchlinski, Federico Ortino and Christoph Schreuer (eds), *Handbook of International Investment Law* (Oxford/New York: Oxford University Press, 2008) 1049 at 1097–8.

24 *Amto, supra* note 14 at para 116.

states. The arbitration agreement defines the extent of jurisdiction with respect to the subject-matter of the dispute (jurisdiction *ratione materiae*) and to the parties (jurisdiction *ratione personae*).

The parties' consent to arbitration

The consent of the disputing parties is the jurisdictional basis of all international arbitration tribunals.[25] In the first three decades of the ICSID Convention, the jurisdiction of ICSID tribunals was primarily based on *clauses compromissoires* in investor-state contracts.[26] In recent years, most investment claims have been brought before treaty-based arbitration tribunals.[27] In this scenario—which is often referred to as "arbitration without privity"[28]—the arbitration agreement is concluded by the host state's offer of arbitration through a dispute settlement clause in an IIA and the investor's acceptance of it which is generally accomplished by the investor instituting arbitration.[29]

The tribunal's jurisdiction over a claim brought by an investor does not imply jurisdiction over a counterclaim brought by the respondent state.[30] Article 46 of the ICSID Convention says that "the Tribunal shall . . . determine any incidental or additional claims or counterclaims . . . provided that they are within the *scope of the consent of the parties* and are otherwise within the jurisdiction of the Centre."[31]

Therefore, the parties have to agree for a counterclaim to be submitted to international arbitration. They can do so by concluding a separate arbitration agreement with regard to the counterclaim. However, if the investor does not give express consent to the jurisdiction over the counterclaim, the question arises whether the parties' respective consents regarding the primary claim are broad enough to encompass a host state's counterclaim.

25 Chittharanjan F. Amerasinghe, *Jurisdiction of International Tribunals* (The Hague: Kluwer Law International, 2003) at 70.
26 See e.g. *Holiday Inns S.A. v Morocco*, Decision on Jurisdiction, ICSID Case No. ARB/72/1 (May 12, 1974); *Klöckner Industrie-Anlagen GmbH and others v United Republic of Cameroon and Société Camerounaise des Engrais*, Award, ICSID Case No. ARB/81/2 (October 21, 1983) [*Klöckner*].
27 The first time an investor raised a claim by virtue of a BIT is in *Asian Agricultural Products Ltd v Republic of Sri Lanka*, Award, ICSID Case No. ARB/87/3 (June 27, 1990). However, in this case, the tribunal's jurisdiction had not been challenged by the respondent state.
28 Paulsson, *supra* note 1 at 232.
29 Schreuer, *supra* note 7 at 212; Christopher F. Dugan et al, *Investor-State Arbitration* (New York: Oxford University Press, 2008) at 221.
30 Veenstra-Kjos, *supra* note 6 at 9–10.
31 ICSID Convention *supra* note 5 at art 46.

The host state's offer through an IIA

Pursuant to a traditional understanding, dispute resolution clauses in IIAs are offers to conclude an arbitration agreement with foreign investors regarding claims alleging wrongful conduct committed by a host state. However, a more liberal interpretation of these clauses reveals that they are potentially capable of grounding the right of host states to plead claims against investors.

The scope of dispute resolution clauses in IIAs

As discussed above, a host state generally cannot base a claim against an investor on an IIA provision. The viability of counterclaims before IIA-based arbitration tribunals depends mainly on the question of whether jurisdiction established through IIAs extends to claims based on other legal grounds, especially those based on contracts between investors and host states.

The starting point for the analysis is the varying wording used in dispute settlement clauses. Several treaties limit the state's consent to claims based on IIA provisions.[32] In these cases, it is clear that a tribunal has jurisdiction only over IIA claims brought by an investor.

Many treaties, in contrast, contain broadly worded dispute resolution clauses, either explicitly including contract claims[33] or generally

---

32 See e.g. *North American Free Trade Agreement Between the Government of Canada, the Government of Mexico and the Government of the United States*, December 17, 1992, Can Ts 1994 No. 2, 32 ILM 289 [NAFTA] ("An investor of a Party may submit to arbitration under this Section a claim that another Party has breached an obligation under [NAFTA]" at art 1116(1)(a)); *Energy Charter Treaty*, December 17, 1994, 2080 UNTS 100, 34 ILM 360 [ECT] ("Disputes . . . which concern an alleged breach of an obligation . . . under Part III" at art 26(1)); Netherlands-Venezuela BIT (1993) at art 9(1); Canada-Venezuela BIT (1998) at art XII(1). Some BITs even limit their consent to particular provision of the IIA, especially those concluded by the former Soviet Union to which the Russian Federation has become a party, e.g. Germany-Soviet Union BIT (1989) ("a dispute relating to the amount of compensation" at art 10(2)); Austria-Soviet Union BIT (1990) at art 7(1); Netherlands-Soviet Union BIT (1989) at art 9(2).

33 See e.g. US Model BIT (2004), online: USTR <http://www.state.gov/documents/organization/117601.pdf> [US Model BIT] ("the claimant, on its own behalf, may submit to arbitration under this Section a claim (i) that the respondent has breached (a) an obligation under Articles 3 through 10, (b) an investment authorization, or (c) an investment agreement" at art 24(1)(a)); Honduras-USA BIT (1995) at art IX(1); Bangladesh-USA BIT (1989) at art VII(1); El Salvador-USA BIT (1999) at art IX(1); *Declarations of the Government of the Democratic and Popular Republic of Algeria Concerning the Settlement of Claims by the Government of the United States of America and the Government of the Islamic Republic of Iran* (January 19, 1981), online:

referring to "disputes with respect to investments,"[34] "all disputes"[35] or "any disputes."[36] The arbitral jurisprudence diverges on the question of what effect should be given to these clauses. The two SGS decisions[37] are famous examples of the conflicting interpretations that can be applied to such clauses.

The ongoing debate between those in favor of, and those against, extending jurisdiction based on broad dispute resolution clauses to contract claims will not be repeated here.[38] After all, there is no uniform interpretation of dispute resolution clauses in IIAs. Each clause must be interpreted individually in accordance with article 31 and following of the Vienna Convention.[39] If the wording and the context of an IIA dispute settlement clause so indicate, the host state offers to arbitrate not only IIA claims, but also those claims arising under a contract or under national legislation.

A *caveat* relates to the applicable law to an arbitration proceeding. Some IIAs explicitly stipulate that arbitral tribunals shall decide the dispute in accordance with the IIA provisions and applicable rules of

Iran-US Claims Tribunal <http://www.iusct.org/claims-settlement.pdf> at art II(1) [Iran-US Claims Settlement Declaration].

34 See e.g. Pakistan-Switzerland BIT (1995) at art 9(1); Philippines-Switzerland BIT (1997) at art VIII(1); China-Germany BIT (2003) at art 9.

35 See e.g. French Model BIT (2006), online: Italaw <http://italaw.com/documents/ModelTreatyFrance2006.pdf> at art 8(1) [French Model BIT]; Italy-Morocco BIT (1990) at art 8(1).

36 *Agreement among the Government of Brunei Darussalam, the Republic of Indonesia, Malaysia, the Republic of the Philippines, the Republic of Singapore and the Kingdom of Thailand for the Promotion and Protection of Investments*, December 15, 1987, online: ASEAN <http://www.asean.org/12812.htm> at art X(1) [ASEAN Agreement]; France-Argentina BIT (1991) at art 8(1).

37 *SGS v Pakistan, supra* note 15 at para 161; *SGS v Philippines, supra* note 15 at paras 130–5.

38 For a detailed analysis see e.g. Christoph Schreuer, "Investment Treaty Arbitration over Contract Claims—the Vivendi I Case Considered" in Todd Weiler (ed), *International Investment Law and Arbitration* (Huntington: JurisNet, LLC, 2008) 281 at 295–9; Emmanuel Gaillard, "Treaty-Based Jurisdiction: Broad Dispute Resolution Clauses", 234 NYLJ 68, 1 at 3; Jörn Griebel, "Die Einbeziehung von 'contract claims' in internationale Investitionsstreitigkeiten über Streitbeilegungsklauseln in Investitionsschutzabkommen" (2006) German Arbitration Journal 306 at 306–11; Lars Markert, *Streitschlichtungsklauseln in Investitionsschutzabkommen* (Baden-Baden: Nomos, 2010) at 142–56.

39 *Vienna Convention on the Law of Treaties*, May 23, 1969, 1155 UNTS 331, (1969) 8 ILM 679 ("A treaty shall be interpreted in good faith in accordance with the ordinary meaning to be given to the terms of the treaty in their context and in the light of its object and purpose" at art 31(1)). See August Reinisch at ch 18 in this book.

international law.[40] In the *Amto* case, the tribunal has held that a claim governed by national law could not be heard because the ECT provides that the applicable law to an ECT dispute is international law.[41] However, in this case, the question of the applicable law is intrinsically linked to the dispute resolution clause of the ECT which only allows for the submission of claims alleging a violation of the treaty.

The standing of the host state

With regard to the counterclaim, a host state takes the position of a proper claimant. Therefore, IIA dispute resolution clauses can only be assessed as offers to arbitrate counterclaims if they accord to host states the right to bring an action against an investor. The fact that claims arising from a multiplicity of legal sources can be heard by IIA-based arbitration tribunals does not necessarily imply that a host state has actual standing to raise these claims.

Article 25 of the ICSID Convention is silent on this question.[42] But it follows from the Report by the World Bank Executive Directors appended to the Convention that host states and foreign investors should have equal access to ICISD arbitration. The Report spells out that "the Convention permits the institution of proceedings by host States as well as by investors and the Executive Directors have constantly had in mind that the provisions of the Convention should be equally adapted to the requirements of both cases."[43] This view on the ICSID Convention erodes the traditional understanding of investment arbitration as a mechanism for the sole protection of foreign investors.[44]

In fact, several IIAs equally offer investors and host states the possibility to bring a claim. The Switzerland-Pakistan BIT at issue in *SGS v Pakistan* provides in article 9(3) that "each party may start the procedure."[45] Similar provisions are contained in the Model BITs of

---

40 See e.g. NAFTA, *supra* note 32 at art 31(1); ECT, *supra* note 32 at art 26(6). Most IIAs, however, either do not contain any provision with respect to the applicable law or provide for several alternatives, among them the national law of the host state, see US Model BIT *supra* note 33 at art 30(2).

41 *Amto, supra* note 14 at para 118. A similar reasoning can be found in *Gustav Hamester*, *supra* note 14 at 355.

42 ICSID Convention, *supra* note 5 at art 25.

43 ICSID Convention, Regulations and Rules, *Report of the Executive Directors on the ICSID Convention*, online: ICSID <http://icsid.worldbank.org/ICSID/StaticFiles/basicdoc/partB.htm> at para 13.

44 Laborde, *supra* note 8 at 100.

45 *SGS v Pakistan, supra* note 15 at para 109.

France[46], Germany[47], in many BITs of the United Kingdom[48] and in the ASEAN Agreement.[49] In these IIAs, the host state's right to initiate arbitration proceedings coexists with a broadly worded dispute resolution clause. It would be pointless if a host state could procedurally initiate a claim against an investor even though the tribunal was only competent to decide over IIAs claims which can only be brought by investors.

Other IIAs do not provide explicitly for the host state's *locus standi*.[50] If such dispute settlement clauses are broadly worded referring "any legal dispute" to international arbitration, they can be construed as conferring standing to the host state.[51] In fact, the wording "any legal dispute" seems to include disputes concerning alleged breaches of the host state's rights.

The same is true if the IIA stipulates that the possibility of counterclaims is excluded for certain subject-matters.[52] *E contrario*, one can conclude that the host state can bring a claim for other matters. Such an interpretation can also be maintained if the IIA restricts the right to initiate arbitration to investors, as it is the case in NAFTA and the ECT.[53] In fact, the express exclusion of claims of a certain nature would be superfluous if the host state could never file a counterclaim. It seems rather that the contracting parties only wanted to exclude the host state's right to initiate arbitration proceedings while preserving its right to respond to the investor's claim by filing a counterclaim.

46 See e.g. French Model BIT, *supra* note 35 ("If this dispute has not been settled . . . it shall be submitted at the request of either party to the arbitration of the International Centre for the Settlement of Investment Disputes" at art 7(2)).

47 See e.g. German Model BIT (2008), online: Italaw <http://italaw.com/investment treaties.htm> ("If the dispute cannot be settled . . ., it shall, at the request of the investor of the other Contracting State, be submitted to arbitration" at art 10(2)).

48 See e.g. UK-El Salvador (1999) at art 9(2); UK-Bulgaria BIT (1995) at art 9(1); UK-Bolivia BIT (1988) at art 8(1); UK-Jamaica BIT (1987) at art 9(1).

49 ASEAN Agreement, *supra* note 36 at art X(2).

50 See e.g. UK-Albania BIT (1994) ("Each Contracting Party hereby consents to submit to [ICSID] any legal dispute arising between the Contracting party and a national . . . of the other Contracting party concerning an investment" at art 8).

51 Laborde, *supra* note 8 at 108; Veenstra-Kjos, *supra* note 6 at 21.

52 See e.g. US Model BIT *supra* note 33 ("A respondent may not assert as a defense, counterclaim, right of set off, or for any other reason that the claimant has received or will receive indemnification or other compensation for all or part of the alleged damages pursuant to an insurance or guarantee contract" at art 28(7)); US-Morocco BIT (1991) at art VI(5); US-Argentina BIT (1991) at art VII(7).

53 NAFTA, *supra* note 32 at art 1137(3); ECT, *supra* note 32 at art 15(3); Canadian Model BIT (2004), online: DFAIT <http://www.international.gc.ca/trade-agreements-accords-commerciaux/assets/pdfs/2004-FIPA-model-en.pdf> at art 46(3).

The investor's acceptance

Characterizing arbitration as consensual does not only mean that an investor has to accept the state's offer to arbitrate, it also implies that a tribunal's jurisdiction is only established to the extent that the parties' respective consents coincide. Therefore, attention must be drawn to the investor's acceptance since it may be narrower than the offer given by the state.[54]

To defeat the possibility of a counterclaim, an investor may be tempted to deny the tribunal's jurisdiction by arguing that his consent was limited to the primary claim. Such a contention is difficult to rebut in the case of tacit consent expressed by the investor instituting arbitration proceedings. Bringing a claim against a host state does not generally imply consent to a counterclaim brought by the respondent.

However, the investor might be advised to consent to the tribunal's jurisdiction over counterclaims for several reasons. The consolidation of reciprocal claims in one forum is not only efficient but also saves the investor from being sued in the host state's domestic courts.[55] Furthermore, a treaty-based arbitration tribunal might be more willing to accept jurisdiction over a contract claim brought by an investor if the parties agree that their consent also encompasses a counterclaim based on the contract. This seemed to be the underlying rationale of SGS's arguments in the case against Pakistan where the claimant promptly acknowledged that the "consent also covers any eventual counter-claims that might be presented by Pakistan."[56] Finally, the investor's consent to a counterclaim may provide an incentive for the respondent state to cooperate during arbitration proceedings.

---

54 Christoph Schreuer, "Consent to Arbitration" in Peter T. Muchlinski, Federico Ortino and Christoph Schreuer (eds), *Handbook of International Investment Law* (Oxford/New York: Oxford University Press, 2008) 830 at 834; Laborde, *supra* note 8 at 109. The "mirror image rule", a principle of common law according to which an offer must be accepted without modifications, does not pose a problem with respect to the parties' consent in international investment arbitration. An IIA dispute settlement clause referring to treaty claims and contract claims is to be construed as two offers to arbitrate which can be independently accepted by the investor. *Contra* Pierre Lalive and Laura Halonen, "On the Availability of Counterclaims in Investment Treaty Arbitration" in Alexander J. Bělohlávek and Naděžda Rozehnalová, *Czech Yearbook of International Law*, vol II (New York: Juris Publishing 2011) 141 at 150 who argue that "[a] BIT is not an à la carte selection of provisions among which the investor can choose."

55 Veenstra-Kjos, *supra* note 6 at 24; Kryvoi, *supra* note 6 at 5.

56 *SGS v Pakistan*, *supra* note 15 at para 108.

The question of the investor's acceptance is linked to the issue of whether the respective consents of both the host state and the investor can ground a tribunal's jurisdiction *rationae personae* over a counterclaim brought against a person other than the investor who has given its consent. In the *Saluka* case, the tribunal was confronted with a situation where the Czech Republic's counterclaim was directed against the English company Nomura and not against the Dutch investor Saluka who filed the primary claim. Without definitively deciding on this matter, the tribunal advanced the proposition that the two companies were so close that they could be seen as interchangeable as parties in the proceedings.[57] However, doubts remain as to the general possibility of piercing the corporate veil of two separate legal entities having different nationalities.[58]

Exclusive jurisdiction of national courts

If there is agreement between the parties to arbitrate a claim brought forth by the host state, an arbitral tribunal might still be prevented from hearing the claim due to the exclusive jurisdiction of national courts.

Investor-state contracts often contain clauses referring contractual disputes to the national courts of the host state.[59] The question arises whether an arbitral tribunal can exercise its jurisdiction over a counterclaim based on such a contract. In fact, in the *Saluka* case, a mandatory forum selection clause in the contract was one of the reasons why the tribunal dismissed the counterclaim brought by the Czech Republic.[60]

The principle of *pacta sunt servanda*, which constitutes a general principle of law,[61] demands that a tribunal faced with a contract claim

---

57 *Saluka, supra* note 6 at paras 41–4. A similar problem with regard to Estonia's counterclaim occurred in *Alex Genin, supra* note 14 at footnote 101. The tribunal noted in an *obiter dictum* that the proper claimant of the sum requested in the counterclaim was not the Republic of Estonia but the Liquidation Committee of the Estonian Innovation Bank that had a separate legal personality.

58 For an analysis of the conditions for piercing the corporate veil in international investment law, see Markus Perkams, "Piercing the Coporate Veil in International Investment Agreements—The Issue of Indirect Shareholder Claims Reloaded" in August Reinisch and Christina Knahr (eds), *International Investment Law in Context* (Utrecht: Eleven International Publishing, 2007) at 93.

59 See Jörn Griebel, *Internationales Investitionsrecht* (Munich: Beck Verlag, 2008) at 32.

60 *Saluka, supra* note 6 at paras 51–8.

61 Bin Cheng, *General Principles of Law as Applied by International Courts and Tribunals* (New York: Cambridge University Press, 2006) at 112–13.

respects all of the provisions of that contract and therefore enforces an agreement representing a choice of jurisdiction.[62] This principle is spelled out in the *Vivendi* decision on annulment: "[i]n a case where the essential basis of a claim brought before an international tribunal is a breach of contract, the tribunal will give effect to any valid choice of forum clause in the contract." [63] Hence, contractual forum selection clauses are a significant obstacle to the viability of counterclaims.

However, they do not always prevent an arbitral tribunal from deciding over a counterclaim based on a contract. There is only a clash of jurisdictional competence if the contract provides for *exclusive* jurisdiction of another forum than the IIA. Furthermore, the parties are generally free to replace the contractual forum selection clause by a subsequent agreement declaring an international arbitration tribunal to be the competent forum for contract claims.[64]

The problem of exclusive jurisdiction of national courts can also occur in the context of counterclaims based on the host state's public laws. In *Paushok v Mongolia*, the tribunal dismissed Mongolia's counterclaim on the basis that it raised issues of non-compliance with the host state's tax law and therefore fell within the scope of the exclusive jurisdiction of Mongolian courts.[65] According to the tribunal, the principle of non-extraterritorial enforceability of national public laws, and especially of tax laws, bars the tribunal from deciding over the counterclaim. The tribunal infers from the possibility to seek recognition and enforcement through the New York Convention on the Recognition and Enforcement of Foreign Arbitral Awards[66] in its member countries that Mongolian tax law could be enforced by non-Mongolian courts in respect to non-Mongolian nationals.

National tax regimes are indeed of a highly sovereign nature. The same is true for other public policy rules such as laws on domestic safety, employment and environment. However, enforcement of an award on damages in another country must be distinguished from extra-territorial

---

62 Yuval Shany, *Regulating Jurisdictional Relations between National and International Courts* (New York: Oxford University Press, 2007) at 146; *contra*, Laborde, *supra* note 8 at 117–20 who argues that contract jurisdiction could not undo treaty jurisdiction but that both jurisdictions coexist.

63 *Compania de Aguas del Aconquija, S.A. and Vivendi Universal (formerly Compagnie Générale des Eaux) v. Republic of Argentina*, Decision on Annulment, ICSID Case No. ARB/97/3 (Annulment Proceeding) (July 3, 2002) at para 98.

64 Veenstra-Kjos, *supra* note 6 at 29.

65 *Sergei Paushok, supra* note 14 at para 694.

66 *Convention on the Recognition and Enforcement of Foreign Arbitral Awards*, June 10, 1958, 330 UNTS 38, 21 UST 2517.

application and enforcement of these laws. An award in favor of the host state imposes pecuniary obligations on an investor due to the fact that his or her actions in the host state infringe national public laws. Enforcing the obligation to pay damages by another country's national courts cannot be equated with requiring compliance with the host state's national laws in another country. Therefore, host states are not precluded from alleging violations of public national laws before arbitral tribunals.

Connexity between claim and counterclaim

If a claim brought by the respondent state falls within the scope of the parties' arbitration agreement and is not subject to the exclusive jurisdiction of national courts, there is still another obstacle to overcome: the requirement of connection or "connexity" between the primary claim and the counterclaim.

Article 46 of the ICSID Convention provides that a tribunal "shall determine any incidental claims or counterclaims arising directly out of the subject-matter of the dispute."[67] In similar terms, this requirement is spelled out in article II(1) of the Iran-US Claims Settlement Declaration stating that the counterclaim must arise "out of the same contract, transaction or occurrence that constitutes the subject matter of [the inital] claims."[68] Article 19(3) of the UNCITRAL Arbitration Rules is even more restrictive requiring that the counterclaim arises out of the "same contract" as the primary claim.[69]

These provisions indicate that connexity constitutes a general legal principle which requires that a connection between a claim and a counter-claim be established in order to justify a tribunal consolidating both claims in one proceeding.[70] *Stricto sensu*, it is not a matter of jurisdiction, but of admissibility.[71] A claim brought by the respondent might be

---

67 ICSID Convention, *supra* note 5 at art 46.
68 Iran-US Claims Settlement Declaration, *supra* note 33 at art II(1).
69 UNCITRAL Arbitration Rules, *supra* note 5 at art 19(3).
70 Hoffmann, *supra* note 13 at 319; Hugh Thirlway, "Counterclaims Before the International Court of Justice: The *Genocide Convention* and the *Oil Platforms* Decisions" (1999) 12 Leiden J. Int'l Law 197 at 203.
71 Schreuer, *supra* note 7 at 751; Veenstra-Kjos, *supra* note 6 at 30. For a detailed analysis of the distinction between admissibility and jurisdiction, see Markert, *supra* note 38 at 82–117; Ian Laird, "A Distinction without a Difference?" in Todd Weiler (ed), *International Investment Law: Leading Cases from the ICSID, NAFTA, Bilateral Investment Treaties and Customary International Law* (London: Cameron May, 2005) 201 at 222; Jan Paulsson, "Jurisdiction and Admissibility" in Gerald Aksen et al,

within the tribunal's jurisdiction without being closely connected to the claim brought by the investor, and *vice versa*. However, in arbitral practice, the distinction between jurisdiction and admissibility with regard to counterclaims often becomes blurred.

A universal definition of the conditions grounding connexity does not exist. The crucial issue in this respect concerns the nature of the link between the claim and counterclaim: is connexity a factual concept which is satisfied if the claim and counterclaim arise out of the same investment? Or does connexity require an interrelation in law, meaning that both claims must be assessed by applying norms emanating from the same legal order or even the same legal source?[72]

The requirement of connexity was at issue in several cases where the primary claim was not based on an IIA, but on a contract. In the case *Klöckner v Cameroon*,[73] the parties relied on different contracts and the dispute resolution clauses contained in them. The tribunal held that the contracts constituted an "indivisible whole" and therefore affirmed that the claim and counterclaim were connected.[74] In other cases, tribunals followed the same reasoning but decided that the linkage between the different contracts was not sufficiently strong in the cases before them.[75] If, however, the respondent's claim was based on provisions of national law, tribunals consistently dismissed jurisdiction over the counterclaim.[76] Altogether, the decisions rendered in the context of non-IIA arbitration provide that connexity does not require that the claim and counterclaim be based on the same legal source, as long as the claimant and respondent both rely on investor-state contracts which are factually interdependent.

In investment treaty arbitration, the setting is fundamentally different. It is unlikely for the investor's claim and the host state's

Global Refections on International Law, Commerce and Dispute Resolution—Liber Amicorum in honor of Rober Briner (Paris: ICC Publishing, 2005) 601 at 601–8.

72 For a detailed discussion on the nature of connexity, *cf*. Veenstra-Kjos, *supra* note 6 at 29–46.

73 *Klöckner, supra* note 26 at 17.

74 The same reasoning was applied in *American Bell International, Inc v The Government of the Islamic Republic of Iran, et al* (June 11, 1984), 6 Iran-US CTR, 74 at 83–4 and *Westinghouse Electric Corpn v The Islamic Republic of Iran et al* (February 12, 1987), 14 Iran-US CTR, 104.

75 *Owens-Corning Fiberglass Corpn. v The Government of Iran et al* (May 13, 1983), 2 Iran-US CTR, 322 at 324; *Morrison-Knudsen Pacific Ltd v The Ministry of Roads and Transportation et al Harris International* (July 3, 1984), 4 Iran-US CTR, 54 at 82–4.

76 *Amco Asia Corpn. and others v Republic of Indonesia*, Resubmitted Case, Decision on Jurisdiction, ICSID Case No. ARB/81/1 (May 10, 1988) at paras 122–7; *Telecommunications, Inc v Islamic Republic of Iran*, Partial Award (November 2, 1987), 17 Iran-US CTR, 31.

counterclaim to allege violations of the same set of rules: While the investor bases his or her claim on IIA provisions, the host state can so far only invoke contractual rights or provisions of national laws. These grounds belong to different legal orders. Only if an investor uses a broadly worded dispute resolution clause in an IIA to raise a claim for breach of an investor-state contract, there could possibly be identity of legal sources. Therefore, if legal connexity is required, there is almost no room for counterclaims before IIA-based arbitration tribunals.

However, this conclusion did not prevent the tribunal in the *Saluka* case from adopting the understanding of connexity as a legal interrelation.[77] Because the legal basis on which the respondent had itself relied on was to be found in the application of Czech law, the tribunal concluded that it had no jurisdiction because the counterclaim was not sufficiently connected to the subject-matter of the primary claim which was based on the Czech-Netherlands BIT.[78] This conclusion was explicitly approved in *Sergei Paushok v Mongolia*.[79]

Conclusion

The "new world of arbitration" brings up considerable obstacles with respect to the host states' ability to file a counterclaim before an arbitral tribunal. However, no general barrier exists which would exclude counterclaims in investment treaty arbitration. This chapter has shown that there are situations where arbitral tribunals can accept jurisdiction over counterclaims and find them admissible.

The central issue in this respect appears to be the fact that IIAs contain very few or no reference to counterclaims. Thus, individual tribunals are given very little guidance as to the question of counterclaims. If arbitrators follow a liberal view on broadly worded dispute resolution clauses, deny the impact of a contractual forum selection clause, and apply very generously the requirement of connexity, a host state has a chance to succeed with its counterclaim. However, if arbitrators share a different opinion on one of these questions, the host state's claim will not pass to the merits stage.

In order to facilitate the possibility of counterclaims in investment treaty arbitration and thereby increase legal certainty in this field, states should include a specific provision on counterclaims in future IIAs. It is

---

77 For an analysis of this award with respect to the requirement of connexity see *Lalive and Halonen*, *supra* note 54 at 154.
78 *Saluka*, *supra* note 6 at paras 79–80.
79 *Sergei Paushok*, *supra* note 14 at paras 688–93.

worth considering whether IIAs could impose obligations on investors, making them subject to both rights and obligations under international law. With respect to forum selection clauses in investor-state contracts, it is advisable for the contracting parties to provide for alternative jurisdiction of either national courts or international arbitral tribunals. Giving host states and investors access to international arbitration for contractual disputes allows both of them more flexibility as to the avenues of relief and solves the problem of competing jurisdictions with respect to treaty claims. Concerning the precondition of connexity, under most arbitration rules, the parties can opt for a less restrictive test limiting connexity to a purely factual relation between claim and counterclaim or even completely waive this requirement.[80]

Altogether, host states, investors and arbitration tribunals should work towards an expansive admission of counterclaims in investment treaty arbitration. Overcoming the current obstacles to bringing counterclaims is not only beneficial for the investor and the host state in individual cases, it also serves the overall integrity and legitimacy of international investment law by infusing balance into the dispute settlement mechanism. Perhaps the future world of investment arbitration will allow for more calibrated and robust proceedings by assuring the equality of arms between investors and host states when a dispute occurs.

---

80 See *Saluka, supra* note 6 at para 62. In this case, the parties have not agreed on derogating the requirement of connexity but the tribunal points out they could have done so.

13 Issues of corporate nationality in investment arbitration

*Jean-François Hébert**

Introduction

The desire to accord broad protection to foreign investments has led many states to extend treaty protection to legal persons that have only minimal connections with their putative home state. This is the case with IIAs that have adopted formalistic criteria, such as the place of incorporation, to circumscribe the class of legal persons that may benefit from treaty protection (also referred to as the "incorporation test").[1]

The application of the incorporation test has proven particularly contentious in many disputes in which respondent states have objected to its rigid application on the grounds that it would lead to abuses of a treaty's protection and encourage treaty shopping. Such would be the case if, for example, an investor from a third state (or the host state) attempted to bring a pre-existing dispute with the host state under the scope and coverage of a treaty through the incorporation of a company in a foreign state whose investors benefit from treaty protection in the host state. Left unchecked, such abuses risk undermining the legitimacy of investor-state treaty arbitration by dramatically altering the careful balance between the protection a state seeks to negotiate for its nationals

---

* DCL candidate McGill University; Lawyer, Trade Law Bureau, Foreign Affairs and International Trade Canada. The views expressed in this article are those of the author and do not necessarily represent the views of, and should not be attributed to, the government of Canada.

1 See e.g. *Energy Charter Treaty*, December 17, 1994, 2080 UNTS 36116, 34 ILM 360 at art 1(7) [ECT], which defines the term "investor" using the place of incorporation: "'investor' means: (a) with respect to a Contracting Party [. . .] (ii) a company or other organization organized in accordance with the law applicable in that Contracting Party;" see also *North American Free Trade Agreement Between the Government of Canada, the Government of Mexico and the Government of the United States*, December 17, 1992, Can Ts 1994 No. 2, 32 ILM 289 at arts 1139, 201 [NAFTA].

investing abroad and the obligations it undertakes *vis-à-vis* foreign investors in its own territory.

The objective of this chapter is to highlight ways in which states can address these concerns. The first part shows that tribunals generally favour a strict formalistic application of the incorporation test. This formalistic interpretation will be contrasted with some recent arbitral awards where tribunals have adopted a more flexible approach and applied the abuse of right doctrine to deny jurisdiction in cases where claimants have attempted to manufacture the required diversity of nationality through the incorporation of companies of convenience. It will also highlight some limits to the abuse of rights doctrine. The second part presents ways in which some states have limited the potential for abuse by requiring that corporate investors have genuine links with their home state in order to benefit from treaty protection. This part also discusses the use of "denial of benefits" clauses in IIAs to counter cases of forum shopping. These clauses, which appear in relatively few IIAs, allow states to unilaterally withdraw the protection granted by a treaty to investors that would otherwise be entitled to it. In light of recent arbitral awards that have raised questions with respect to the application of such clauses, this part will also explore ways to ensure their effectiveness as tools to combat forum shopping.

The interpretation by tribunals of the incorporation test

Respondent states that have had to defend against claims brought by legal persons incorporated in a treaty state but ultimately controlled by investors of a third state (or even by their own nationals) have at times objected to the jurisdiction of arbitral tribunals even though the claimants appeared to satisfy the formal incorporation test provided by the applicable treaties. In objecting to the jurisdiction of arbitral tribunals, respondent states have essentially sought to convince the arbitrators to look beyond the formal legal structures set up by the claimants and consider the economic reality behind the corporate veil. With few exceptions, these challenges have failed.

The dominant approach: a formalistic interpretation

The jurisdictional objections have commonly been based on two sets of arguments. First, respondent states have sought to avoid a strict application of the incorporation test stipulated by the applicable treaty by arguing that, in order to benefit from treaty protection, a corporate claimant must also possess a genuine connection with its state of incorporation. In other words, respondent states have sought to import an implied additional requirement in the treaty text. This requirement has at times been referred to as a "genuine link," "control test" or "social or economic factual links" requirement. Whatever label is used, the implied requirement seeks to disqualify from treaty protection corporations that have only tenuous links with their state of incorporation and, often, whose sole and only link to a jurisdiction is the fact that they have been incorporated under its laws.[2]

These attempts to relax the strict application of the incorporation test have been roundly rejected by arbitrators who have favoured a strict literal interpretation and resisted any interpretation of the treaty text which would effectively incorporate an implied requirement for claimants to establish a genuine connection with their purported home state. Thus, the *Rompetrol* tribunal, for example, observed that in the absence of a general rule of "real and effective nationality" for the purpose of determining the nationality of corporations in customary international law, "there is simply no room for an argument that a supposed rule of 'real and effective nationality' should override [. . .] the prescriptive definitions incorporated in the BIT."[3] Accordingly, the tribunal applied a strict interpretation of the incorporation test to the Netherlands-Romania BIT, which the tribunal found to be "clear and unambiguous,"[4] and consequently dismissed the challenge to its jurisdiction.

The second set of arguments commonly made in support of a jurisdictional objection does not so much challenge the incorporation test *per se*, but rather seeks to bypass it altogether by arguing that the corporate veil of the investor should be pierced for equitable considerations. In the *ADC* arbitration, Hungary argued that the Cypriot investors were in reality the *alter ego* of Canadian investors and pointed to the structure of the airport construction project, the operation of the project as well as the involvement of the Canadian government when the dispute first

---

2 See e.g. *Tokios Tokelés v Ukraine*, Decision on Jurisdiction, ICSID Case No. ARB/02/18 (April 29, 2004) [*Tokios*]; *Saluka Investments v Czech Republic*, Partial Award, UNCITRAL (March 17, 2006) at paras 183, 197 [*Saluka*]; *ADC Affiliate Ltd and ADC & ADMC Management Ltd v The Republic of Hungary*, Award, ICSID Case No. ARB/03/16 (October 2, 2006) at para 336 [*ADC*]; *Rompetrol v Romania*, Decision on Respondent's Preliminary Objections on Jurisdiction and Admissibility, ICSID Case No. ARB/06/03 (April 18, 2008) at para 84 [*Rompetrol*]; *Yukos Universal Ltd (Isle of Man) v The Russian Federation*, Interim Award on Jurisdiction and Liability, UNCITRAL (November 30, 2009) at para 406 [*Yukos*].

3 *Rompetrol, supra* note 2 at para 93. See also *Tokios, supra* note 2 at para 52; *Yukos, supra* note 2 at para 415; *Saluka, supra* note 2 at para 230 and *ADC, supra* note 2 at para 357.

4 *Rompetrol, supra* note 2 at para 108.

arose, as proof that the dispute concerned a Canadian investment rather than a Cypriot one. Similarly, in the *Saluka* arbitration, the Czech Republic argued that the relationship between the claimant and its parent company, a legal person incorporated in England, "was so close that they were in effect interchangeable as parties in these proceedings" and that "the real party in interest" in the arbitration was its parent, which could not benefit from the protection of the BIT between the Netherlands and the Czech Republic.[5]

Although both tribunals dismissed the respondent states' challenge to their jurisdiction, it is noteworthy that the tribunals agreed with the respondents on the principle that the corporate veil can be pierced, and the separate corporate personality of a claimant ignored, on equitable grounds.[6] However, perhaps weary of the discretionary power this principle grants tribunals, the arbitrators in the *Saluka* arbitration echoed the words of the ICJ in the *Barcelona Traction* case and expressly limited its application to exceptional circumstances where the claimant's separate corporate personality has been misused "to perpetrate fraud or other malfeasance."[7] Finding no such evidence of fraud or malfeasance, the arbitrators dismissed the respondent states' jurisdictional challenge.

As evident from this brief review of arbitral awards, the formalistic interpretation of the incorporation test appears to enjoy broad support amongst arbitration tribunals. Indeed, arbitrators have expressed little objection to the strategic routing of investments through foreign companies in order to benefit from the protection afforded by IIAs. Further, arbitrators have recognized their standing as protected investors even when these companies have little connection with their putative home state and could be described as companies of convenience.

The exception: a flexible approach based on the abuse of rights theory

A pair of recent jurisdictional awards appears to have departed somewhat from the trend of applying a literal interpretation of the treaty text. In *Phoenix Action Ltd v Czech Republic*, an Israeli corporation invoked the dispute settlement provisions of the Israel-Czech Republic BIT and began international arbitration proceedings against the Czech Republic to settle a dispute involving two Czech companies it had acquired in the

---

5 *Saluka, supra* note 2 at para 180.
6 *Ibid* at para 230; *ADC, supra* note 2 at para 358.
7 *Saluka, supra* note 2 at para 227.

commodity trading business.[8] Both Czech companies were then mired in domestic legal proceedings concerning tax and custom duty evasion charges as well as a private commercial dispute. The Czech Republic challenged the jurisdiction of the tribunal on the ground that the corporate claimant was nothing more than a "sham Israeli entity created by a Czech fugitive from justice."[9] The respondent relied on the fact that the owner of the Israeli claimant was a Czech national who had been the executive officer of one of the two Czech companies prior to being charged with tax fraud and his subsequent escape to Israel where he incorporated the claimant. It also placed great emphasis on the fact that the two Czech companies were owned, prior to their acquisition by the Israeli corporation, by the wife and daughter of the Czech national in question. In essence, the respondent sought to portray the purported investment by an Israeli corporation as a corporate re-organization within the same family for the sole purpose of gaining access to international arbitration.[10]

Had the tribunal limited itself to a strictly textual interpretation of the jurisdiction conferring provisions of the ICSID Convention and the applicable BIT, it would have had to recognize the separate legal personality of the Israeli claimant and its standing to bring an investment claim even if it clearly was a corporation of convenience. However, the tribunal dismissed Phoenix Action's claim. Rather than addressing the challenge from the perspective of the definition of the term "investor," which included an incorporation and permanent seat test, it dealt with it from the perspective of the definition of "investment." The tribunal relied on the well-known *Salini* test to determine whether the claimant had made an investment in the Czech Republic.[11] In addition to the traditional requirements of contribution, duration, risk, and contribution to the economic development of the host state, the tribunal read into article 25 of the ICSID Convention an obligation that the investment be realized in "good faith."[12] The tribunal relied on a purposive interpretation of the ICSID Convention and the relevant BIT to hold that an economic transaction performed "with the sole purpose of taking advantage of the rights contained in such instruments, without any

---

8 *Phoenix Action Ltd v Czech Republic,* Award, ICSID Case No. ARB/06/5 (April 15, 2009) at para 34 [*Phoenix Action*].

9 *Ibid* at para 34.

10 *Ibid* at para 41.

11 *Ibid* at para 83, referring to *Salini Costruttori S.p.A. and Italstrade S.p.A. v Kingdom of Morocco,* Decision on Jurisdiction, ICSID Case No. ARB/00/4 (July 23, 2001).

12 *Ibid* at para 114.

significant economic activity" could not benefit from the protection of the international investment law system.[13] It stated that such transactions "must be considered as an abuse of the system."[14] Considering the timing of the claimant's alleged investment, which was made after the alleged damages to the two Czech companies materialized, the timing of the claim, which was initially notified to the Czech Republic a mere two months after the alleged investment, as well as the evidence that the claimant never intended to perform any business activity in the market place, the tribunal concluded that the investment was made, not for the purpose of engaging in economic activity in the Czech Republic, but rather to bring international litigation against the respondent. The claim thus constituted an abuse of right: "The abuse here could be called a *'détournement de procédure'*, consisting in the Claimant's creation of a legal fiction in order to gain access to an international arbitration procedure to which it was not entitled."[15]

The award in the *Phoenix Action* arbitration was followed a year later by another jurisdictional award which dismissed part of a claim against Venezuela also on the basis of the abuse of rights theory.[16]

These recent jurisdictional awards demonstrate that, despite favouring a literal application of the incorporation test, arbitration tribunals have at times adopted a more flexible approach and applied exogenous principles, such as the abuse of rights theory, to sanction the most egregious forms of protection shopping. The tribunals have justified recourse to this theory on the basis that it is merely an application of the good faith principle to the exercise of rights.[17]

In effect, the abuse of rights theory has been used by tribunals as a sort of safety valve, to avoid the undesirable consequences of an overly inflexible application of jurisdictional provisions in investment treaties. This use of the abuse of rights theory is by no means novel. Jennings and Watts observe in one of the leading textbooks in public international

---

13 *Ibid* at para 93.
14 *Ibid.*
15 *Ibid* at para 143.
16 *Mobil Corporation and others v Bolivarian Republic of Venezuela*, Decision on Jurisdiction, ICSID Case No. ARB/07/27 (June 10, 2010) [*Mobil*].
17 *Ibid* at para 170; *Phoenix Action, supra* note 8 at para 143; *Abaclat and ors v Argentina*, Decision on Jurisdiction, ICSID Case No. ARB07/05 (August 4, 2011) at para 646. See generally Michael Byers, "Abuse of Rights: An Old Principle, A New Age" (2002) 47(2) McGill LJ 389 at 397 [Byers]; R. Jennings and A. Watts (eds), *Oppenheim's International Law*, 9th edn, vol. 1 (London: Longman, 1992) at 408 [Jennings and Watts]; Bin Cheng, *General Principles of Law as Applied by International Courts and Tribunals* (Cambridge: Cambridge University Press, 2006) at 121.

law that the abuse of rights theory serves as a "useful safeguard in relatively undeveloped or over-inflexible parts of a legal system pending the development of precise and detailed rules."[18]

Despite being founded upon a universally recognized legal principle, the application of the abuse of rights theory is somewhat contentious.[19] In some jurisdictions, particularly those of the *common law* tradition, the theory is viewed as an oxymoron. In fact, even in those jurisdictions that do recognize the theory's existence, its content varies.[20] It is not surprising, therefore, that the invocation of the theory in international investment law has received a lukewarm reception by some arbitrators, particularly those who favour a positivist conception of international law. Thus, in the *Rompetrol* dispute, the arbitral tribunal cautioned that a jurisdictional objection based on this theory "is evidently a proposition of a very far reaching character" as it would require a tribunal to refuse to exercise the jurisdiction expressly conferred upon it by the disputing parties.[21] The arbitrators then questioned whether "so far-reaching a proposition needs to be backed by some positive authority in the Convention itself, in its negotiating history, or in the case-law under it."[22] The arbitrators ultimately expressed no view on the merit of the theory and left their rhetorical question unanswered.

Regardless of their merit, the criticisms of the abuse of rights theory as a normative framework to address treaty shopping practices add to the considerable uncertainty inherent in its application as it requires some subjective determination on the part of individual arbitrators, at least until such time as objective criteria are more fully fleshed out in future arbitral practice. For the moment, the theory arguably vests considerable discretionary power in the hands of arbitrators in drawing the line between circumstances of "legitimate corporate planning" and "abuse of rights"[23] and the question may be put whether the time has come for

---

18 Jennings and Watts, *supra* note 17 at 407.
19 John P Gaffney, "'Abuse of Process' in Investment Treaty Arbitration" (2010) 11(4) Journal of World Investment and Trade 515 at 538. (Gaffney suggests that "the abuse of rights doctrine appears to be less suited as a normative basis for the application of the abuse of process doctrine in investment treaty arbitration.") See also Chester Brown, "The Relevance of the Doctrine of Abuse of Process in International Adjudication" (2011) 2 *Transnational Dispute Management*.
20 Byers, *supra* note 17 at 392–7. (Byers cites for example Lord Halsbury: "If it was a lawful act, however ill the motive, he had a right to do it."); *Mayor of Bradford v Pickles* [1895] AC 587 at 594 (HL).
21 *Rompetrol*, *supra* note 2 at para 115.
22 *Ibid.*
23 *Mobil*, *supra* note 16 at para 191.

international investment law to develop more precise and detailed rules to combat treaty shopping practices, as argued by some authors.[24]

IIA provisions limiting the potential for abuse

It is particularly instructive to note that some states have long limited the potential for abusive treaty shopping by negotiating specific provisions either qualifying the incorporation test and requiring in addition to incorporation some other link with the home state, or reserving for themselves the power to deny the benefits of the treaty to investors in certain circumstances. These two limits to the incorporation test will be examined in turn below.

Treaty clauses requiring additional links with the home state

It may be a truism that states seeking to avoid the abuse of the investor-state dispute settlement system to which a mere incorporation test can sometimes lead may choose not to use the test in favour of some other criteria to delimit the scope of protection afforded to corporate investors. Yet, the prevalence of the incorporation test in IIAs at times obscures other options. As such, a brief overview of some other criteria in use in investment treaties is warranted.

Some IIAs use the *siège social* test to identify protected corporate investors. Under this test, a corporation is deemed a national of the country in which its central administration or effective management is located. An example may be found in the Germany-China BIT which defines the term "investor," with respect to Germany, as "any juridical person as well as any commercial or other company or association with or without legal personality having its seat in the territory of the Federal Republic of Germany, irrespective of whether or not its activities are directed at profit."[25] Another example may be found in the Mexico-Italy BIT which provides that the term "investor" includes "a State enterprise, a company, a firm, an association or any other entity having a seat in the territory of a Contracting Party and recognised in accordance with its legislation as legal person, regardless or whether its liability is limited or otherwise."[26]

---

24 Engela C. Schlemmer, "Investment, Investor, Nationality, and Shareholders" in Peter Muchlinski, et al. (eds), *The Oxford Handbook of International Investment Law* (Oxford: Oxford University Press, 2008) at 87.
25 Germany-China BIT (2003).
26 Mexico-Italy BIT (1999).

Other IIAs adopt what can be described as an economic interest test which usually requires that a corporation carry out business activities in its home state in order to benefit from treaty protection. The wording of the requirement may vary. Some treaties require that the corporation perform "real economic activities"[27] or "actually [do] business"[28] in the home state. This test is rarely used by itself and is usually employed cumulatively with the incorporation test so that corporate investors will only benefit from treaty protection if they satisfy both tests. The objective of such an approach is clear: mailbox corporations are excluded from treaty protection.

Recently, an arbitral tribunal constituted under the Swiss-Czech Republic BIT dismissed a claim brought by a Swiss corporation because it found that the corporation was nothing more than a mailbox corporation that did not satisfy the conditions imposed by the treaty requiring that a claimant have its seat and "actually do business" in Switzerland.[29] The dispute concerned receivables that the claimant had acquired from a bankrupt Slovak company and involved measures by the Slovak judiciary which allegedly prevented the claimant from enforcing the contractual rights it had purchased. The respondent raised a jurisdictional challenge against the claim on the basis that the claimant did not satisfy the definition of "investor" contained in the applicable BIT which provides for three cumulative tests in order to benefit from the protection of the treaty. To satisfy the definition, a legal person must be incorporated under the laws of Switzerland, it must have its seat in Switzerland and it must perform real economic activities in that country.[30] This definition is one of the most restrictive definitions of "investor" found in IIAs. Most definitions only contain an incorporation test. Some treaties reference two tests but rarely require the satisfaction of three tests. The claimant easily cleared the first hurdle by providing an excerpt from a commercial registry but stumbled on the remaining two.

To satisfy the seat requirement, which the tribunal equated with "an effective center of administration of the business operations,"[31] the tribunal required proof that the claimant's board of directors regularly met in Switzerland or that the shareholders' meetings were held in that

---

27 Czech Slovakia-Switzerland BIT (1990).
28 Netherlands-Philippines BIT (1985).
29 *Alps Finance and Trade AG v Slovak Republic*, Award, UNCITRAL (March 5, 2011) [*Alps Finance*].
30 Czech Slovakia-Switzerland BIT (1990) at art 1(1).
31 *Alps Finance, supra* note 29 at para 217.

country. It also required proof that "there is a management at the top of the company sitting in Switzerland;"[32] that the company employed workers at the seat; that the company had means to communicate with third parties at the seat and that the company had a physical location in Switzerland. According to the tribunal, the claimant's assertions that it was incorporated in Switzerland, that the company books were kept in Switzerland and the production of the claimant's Swiss tax declaration was insufficient proof that it had its seat in that country, especially in light of the fact that the claimant had no phone number in Switzerland and could produce no formal written lease for office space.[33]

The tribunal also found that the claimant failed to prove that it per-formed "real economic activities" in Switzerland.[34] It noted that the tax return that had been adduced as evidence demonstrated "a quite modest turnover."[35] Moreover, the claimant was "unable to establish number and type of its clients, type of its operations, kind of contracts it enters into, quantity and type of personnel, nature and composition of its managing bodies" (sic).[36] In the end, the tribunal declined juris-diction over the dispute citing that the claimant failed to demonstrate its standing as an "investor" in order to bring a claim under the applic-able BIT.

This recent award demonstrates the usefulness of the *siège social* or economic interest test in preventing abuses of treaty protection performed through certain companies of convenience. However, the adoption of a *siège social* test or an economic interest test, with or with-out an additional incorporation test, is still an incomplete bulwark against forum shopping investors as investors may decide to locate their head office and/or perform *pro forma* economic activities in the home state for the sole purpose of benefitting from treaty pro-tection. It is obvious, however, that such cases would be exceptional. Another concern with the inclusion of a *siège social* or economic interest test in the definition of "investor" is that while it may constitute a useful tool to combat forum shopping practices, it could also be per-ceived as providing too narrow a scope of protection for corporate investors and as unduly restricting their legitimate corporate planning options.

32 *Ibid.*
33 *Ibid* at paras 217–18.
34 *Ibid* at para 219.
35 *Ibid.*
36 *Ibid.*

Treaty clauses allowing states to deny the benefit of the treaty to corporations of convenience

Another approach to limit the potential for abusive treaty shopping is the so-called "denial of benefits" clause whereby states reserve for themselves the right to deny the benefits of the treaty, in certain circumstances, to companies that may otherwise strictly comply with its formal jurisdictional requirements and would therefore *a priori* fall within the ambit of protection of the treaty. These clauses are often used in tandem with treaty provisions adopting the incorporation test to determine the nationality of corporations. They serve to limit the broad scope of protection accorded by a strict application of the incorporation test by allowing the treaty parties to effectively override the broad jurisdiction-conferring provisions of a treaty when there is evidence that a corporate investor does not have a sufficiently close connection with its putative home state.[37]

A typical example of such a clause may be found in the Austria-Lebanon BIT (2001) which provides that:

> A Contracting Party may deny the benefits of this Agreement to an investor of the other Contracting Party and to its investments, if investors of a Non-Contracting Party own or control the first mentioned investment and the first mentioned investor has no substantial business activity in the territory of the Contracting Party under whose law it is constituted or organized.[38]

Both the 2004 US Model BIT and Canada's model FIPA contain a similar denial of benefits provision modeled on article 1113 of the NAFTA,[39] as does the ECT.[40]

As is apparent from the wording of this clause, and all similarly worded provisions, the right of a state to deny the benefits of a treaty is conditioned upon the fulfillment of two cumulative requirements. First,

---

37 Meg N. Kinnear et al, *Investment Disputes under NAFTA: An Annotated Guide to NAFTA Chapter 11* (The Hague: Kluwer Law International, 2006) at 113–15; Panayotis M. Protopsaltis, "The Challenge of the Barcelona Traction Hypothesis: Barcelona Traction Clauses and Denial of Benefits Clauses in BITs and IIAs" (2010) 11 Journal of World Investment and Trade 561 at 584: "[denial of benefits clauses] use, amongst others, the control test in order to deny the application of the treaty to mail-box companies controlled by nationals of the host State or of a third State."

38 Lebanon-Austria BIT (2001) at art 10.

39 NAFTA, *supra* note 1.

40 ECT, *supra* note 1 at art 17.

the corporation must be owned or controlled by investors of a third party state. Secondly, the corporation must not have substantial business activities in its state of incorporation.[41] Thus, the typical denial of benefits clause allows a state to maintain a broad scope of protection for corporate investors through the adoption of a mere incorporation test, while simultaneously allowing the treaty parties to ensure that the broad scope of protection is not extended to corporate investors that are owned or controlled by third party nationals and that have no substantial business activities in their state of incorporation.

Mistelis and Baltag trace the origins of these clauses to FCN treaties concluded by the United States after 1945.[42] According to Herman Walker, a former official of the State Department, the inclusion of such clauses in post-WWII FCN treaties served to placate fears that extending treaty commitments to foreign corporations could "become a cloak under cover of which rights would be gained by interests of third countries."[43] By guarding against "free-rides" by third-country investors, Walker surmised that such clauses "facilitated the post-1945 advance in the bilateral assumption of undertakings regarding corporations."[44]

Yet, despite their long history, denial of benefits clauses are not (yet) widely included in IIAs. In a survey of 550 BITs, Jagusch could only find 31 that contained such a provision, which perhaps explains why they have been discussed in relatively few arbitral awards.[45]

A denial of benefits clause provides more flexibility to the contracting states than a narrow definition of "investor" in that the right it grants is entirely discretionary. Even where the conditions for its application are met, a foreign investor may still benefit from the protection of the treaty until such time as a state exercises the power granted by the denial of benefits clause. The clause allows states to evaluate, on a case-by-case

---

41 A tribunal, commenting on the similarly worded denial of benefits clause contained in art 17 of the ECT held that "It is clear that the conjunction 'and' makes the test a cumulative one. Both of these conditions must be present for Article 17(1) to apply." *Petrobart Ltd v The Kyrgyz Republic*, Award, Arbitration Institute of the Stockholm Chamber of Commerce, ARB. No. 126/2003 (March 29, 2005) at 59 [*Petrobart*].

42 Loukas A. Mistelis and Crina Mihaela Baltag, "Denial of Benefits and Article 17 of the Energy Charter Treaty" (2009) 113(4) Penn St L Rev 1301 at 1304.

43 Herman Walker Jr, "Provisions on Companies in United States Commercial Treaties" (1956) 50 Am J Int'l L 373 at 388.

44 *Ibid.*

45 Stephen Jagusch, "Denial of Advantages under Article 17(1)" (Presentation delivered to the Investment Protection and the Energy Charter Treaty Conference Washington DC, May 18, 2007) [unpublished] [on file with author].

basis, whether the particular circumstances of a given investment warrant the denial of treaty benefits.

However, the effectiveness of denial of benefits clauses is not without its own limitations. First, most clauses only permit a state to deny the benefits of the treaty when a corporation is owned or controlled by nationals of a third state and thus fail to address the situation where a corporation is owned or controlled by nationals of the denying state. This is the case with NAFTA article 1113, for example, which provides that a NAFTA party may deny the benefits of the treaty to investors and their investments if "investors of a non-Party own or control the enterprise." Article 17 of the ECT contains a similar limit. Conceptually, it is difficult to understand why the policy rationale for denying the benefits of the treaty to corporations owned or controlled by third party nationals should not apply equally, if not more forcefully, to corporations owned or controlled by nationals of the host state. Indeed, just as third party nationals can seek to benefit from a treaty to which their home state is not a party by incorporating a company in the territory of a treaty state, nationals of one state could attempt to bring an international claim against their own home state by incorporating a company in the territory of a state with which their home state has concluded an IIA. To address this issue, some treaties specify that a party may deny the benefits of the treaty if "nationals of any third country, *or nationals of such party* [emphasis added]" own or control the corporation.[46]

A second limitation stems from the uncertainty surrounding the legal effect of a state's right to deny the benefits of a treaty to a foreign-owned corporation. At least three relatively recent arbitral decisions under the ECT have held that the denial of treaty protection can only have a prospective effect and therefore have allowed claims to proceed in circumstances where the respondent state purported to exercise its right to deny the benefits of a treaty *after* a claim was made. In *Plama Consortium Ltd*, Bulgaria challenged the jurisdiction of a tribunal constituted under the ECT on the ground that it had denied the benefits of the treaty to the claimant, a company incorporated in Cyprus, pursuant to article 17 of the ECT.[47] Noting that Bulgaria only exercised its right under article 17 after the claimant had filed its request for arbitration with the ICSID, the tribunal rejected the challenge. According to the tribunal, holding

---

46 US-Argentina BIT (1991); The 2004 US Model BIT departs from the NAFTA model and extends the right of a party to deny the benefits of the treaty to cases where persons of the denying party own or control the enterprise.

47 *Plama Consortium Ltd v Republic of Bulgaria*, Decision on Jurisdiction, ICSID Case No. ARB/03/24 (February 8, 2005) [*Plama*].

that a denial of benefits clause could operate retrospectively to deny a claim already filed would run counter to the object and purpose of the ECT, which is to promote "long-term co-operation in the energy field," as well as investors' legitimate expectations.[48] The tribunal stressed the importance of ensuring legal certainty for investors who can too easily become "hostage" of a state after an investment is made and therefore need to know, before making any investment, whether they will be able to rely on the protection of the ECT.[49] The tribunal therefore held that Bulgaria's denial only deprived the claimant from the benefits of the ECT prospectively, from the date of the denial onwards.[50]

More recently, the tribunals in the *Yukos* and *Liman* arbitrations closely followed the reasoning of the *Plama* tribunal and similarly held that article 17 of the ECT cannot operate to deny the benefits of the treaty to an investor that has already brought a claim.[51]

Arguably, the interpretation adopted by these three arbitration tribunals conflicts with the findings of other arbitral tribunals that appear to have been willing to consider the possibility that a denial of benefits clause could operate retrospectively, although they did not address the issue expressly. In *Generation Ukraine v Ukraine*, an arbitral tribunal constituted pursuant to the US-Ukraine BIT rejected an objection based on the denial of treaty protection raised after the claim had been registered by the ICSID on the grounds that the respondent had failed to discharge its burden of proving that the claimant was owned or controlled by third-party nationals.[52] Similarly, the tribunal set up to decide a dispute between a UK claimant and the Kyrgyz Republic under the ECT rejected an objection by the respondent state raised well after the claim was filed because the weight of the evidence before it tended to demonstrate that the claimant was not owned or controlled by nationals of a third state and had substantial business activities in the UK. As such, the tribunal found that "the conditions for application of article 17(1) of the Treaty are not present in this case."[53] These decisions appear to

---

48 *Ibid* at para 161.
49 *Ibid* at paras 159–65.
50 *Ibid* at para 165.
51 *Yukos, supra* note 2 at para 458; *Liman Caspian Oil BV & NCL Dutch Investment BV v The Republic of Kazakhstan*, Award, ICSID Case No. ARB/07/14 (22 June 2010) at para 225.
52 *Generation Ukraine v Ukraine*, Final Award, ICSID Case No. ARB/00/9 (September 16, 2003) at para 15.
53 *Petrobart, supra* note 41 at 63. To the same effect, see the joined cases *Pan American Energy LLC & BP Argentina Exploration Co v Argentine Republic*, ICSID Case No. ARB/03/13 and *BP America Production Co et al v Argentine Republic*, ICSID Case No. ARB/04/8, Decision on Preliminary Objections (July 27, 2006).

contemplate the possibility that a denial of benefits clause could operate retrospectively and bar a claim brought prior to the exercise of a state's right to deny. Indeed, there otherwise would have been no reason for the arbitrators to delve into the evidence and consider whether the substantive conditions for application of the clause were satisfied since, as in all of the other cases, the respondent state sought to deny the benefits of the applicable treaty after the claims had been filed.

As some commentators have aptly observed, limiting the effects of a state's exercise of a denial of benefits clause to the date of the exercise onwards dramatically limits the usefulness of this tool against treaty shopping.[54] In many states with open economies and liberal investment regimes, foreign investors are not required to register or otherwise seek any formal governmental approval prior to investing in their jurisdiction. Therefore, in many instances, the respondent state will only become aware of the existence of a foreign investment at the time it receives notice of an arbitration claim. In the worst cases, particularly where an investment has been channelled through a complex web of related foreign companies, the respondent state may not even be able to identify the ultimate owner or controller of an investment with any degree of certainty until well into the arbitration proceedings. In this context, the interpretation adopted by the *Plama*, *Yukos* and *Liman* tribunals appears to run counter to the *effet utile* of such clauses. Unless, of course, arbitrators require states to actively seek out and investigate the corporate ownership of all investments within their territory in the event that a dispute arises, which is a monumental task by any measure.[55]

In light of these criticisms and the remaining uncertainty surrounding the effects of denial of benefits clauses, it is interesting to note that certain treaties contain clauses that are drafted slightly differently and would appear not to attract the same controversy concerning the legal effects of a denial of benefits. For example, the denial of benefits clause of the *ASEAN Framework Agreement on Services* provides that:

> The benefits of this Framework Agreement *shall be denied* to a service supplier who is a natural person of a non-Member State or a juridical person owned or controlled by persons of a non-Member State

---

54   Anthony C. Sinclair, "The Substance of Nationality Requirements in Investment Treaty Arbitration" (2005) 20 ICSID Rev-FILJ 357 at 385–7; Zachary Douglas, *The International Law of Investment Claims* (Cambridge: Cambridge University Press, 2009) at 470–2; see also Laurence Shore, "The Jurisdiction Problem in Energy Charter Treaty Claims" (2007) 10 Int'l Arb L Rev 58; James Chalker, "Making the Energy Charter Treaty Too Investor Friendly: Plama Consortium Limited v. Republic of Bulgaria" (2006) 5 *Transnational Dispute Management*.

55   See also Kinnear, *supra* note 37 at 1113–17.

constituted under the laws of a Member State, but not engaged in substantive business operations in the territory of Member State(s) [emphasis added].[56]

The *Plama* tribunal contrasted the use of the words "shall be denied" with the permissive language used in article 17 of the ECT to hold that the denial of treaty benefits under the ECT is not automatic and requires some affirmative action on the part of the denying state.[57] The use of the command "shall" also resolves the temporal effect of a denial of treaty protection as the clause would operate automatically as soon as an investment is made. Investors would therefore not acquire any legitimate expectation of treaty protection as the denial of benefits clause would make clear that, provided its conditions of application are met, investors never acquire treaty protection.

However, such mandatory language also removes any discretion on the part of states not to deny treaty benefits despite the fact that the conditions of application of the clause are otherwise met. This discretionary power undoubtedly forms part of the appeal of denial of benefits clauses and helps explain why they are negotiated instead of merely inserting narrower scope provisions or narrower definitions of "investors" and "investments."

For greater certainty, states that are reluctant to abandon this discretionary power may instead consider adopting language expressly providing for the retroactive application of a denial of treaty protection. Such language could, for example, specify that a denial of treaty protection is retroactive and nullifies a claim already made or language to that effect. Such language would clarify, if necessary, that a claim already brought prior to the denial of treaty benefits would fail for lack of jurisdiction *ratione personae*. In deciding whether to adopt such a clarification, states will need to assess the likelihood that future arbitral tribunals will follow the interpretation favoured by the *Plama, Yukos and Liman* tribunals in light of the relative importance of the policy objective of guarding against treaty shopping.

Conclusion

The liberal extension of treaty protection to legal persons that satisfy a mere incorporation test exposes states to treaty shopping both by third-party nationals and even by their own nationals. Until recently,

---

56 *ASEAN Framework Agreement on Services*, December 15, 1995, 35 ILM 1072, III Compendium IV 43.
57 *Plama*, supra note 47 at para 156.

arbitration tribunals overwhelmingly favoured a strict literal interpretation of the jurisdiction-conferring provisions of IIAs and refused to read into them any implied requirement of a genuine link between a legal person and its state of incorporation, thereby compounding the risk of forum shopping. Two recent arbitral awards have bucked the trend in favour of a more flexible approach through recourse to the abuse of rights theory in an effort to temper the rigors of overly rigid jurisdiction-conferring provisions. It remains to be seen whether these recent awards signal greater sensitivity in the arbitration community with respect to the practice of forum shopping and a new trend toward a more flexible application of the jurisdiction-conferring provisions of IIAs.

Despite its advantages, the abuse of rights theory, by its very nature, is at best a stopgap measure to sanction the most egregious forms of protection shopping. States willing to guard against the very real risk of treaty shopping through corporations of convenience could consider additional jurisdictional requirements in their treaties such as a *siège social* test or an economic interest test. Alternatively, they could consider systematically including denial of benefits clauses in their IIAs. Properly drafted, these clauses constitute powerful tools to combat treaty shopping by granting states the discretion to deny treaty protection if certain conditions, usually related to third-party ownership and lack of substantial business activity in the state of incorporation, are met. By specifying that treaty protection may also be denied to legal persons owned or controlled by nationals of the denying state and, for greater certainty, that such a denial operates retrospectively to bar a claim filed prior to the denial, states could avoid some of the most important limitations to the effectiveness of denial of benefits clauses.

14 Enhancing the legitimacy of international investment law by establishing an appellate mechanism

*Debra P. Steger**

Introduction

There has been considerable debate in the past few years about the idea of an appellate mechanism for international investment arbitration. A number of reasons have been posited for establishing such a mechanism, including ensuring the consistency and accuracy of awards as well as the legitimacy of the system as a whole.

The United States stated in the *Bipartisan Trade Promotion Authority Act of 2002* that one of its key goals in foreign direct investment was the negotiation of ". . . an appellate body or similar mechanism to provide coherence to the interpretations of trade agreements . . ."[1] and similar clauses have appeared in IIAs negotiated by the United States since that time. The ICSID Secretariat estimated that by mid-2005 there would be as many as 20 countries that had signed treaties with clauses contemplating an appellate mechanism for investor-state arbitration and other treaties with similar provisions under negotiation.[2] Concerned both about the consistency of arbitral awards in the future and the possibility of fragmentation if several appellate mechanisms were established under various agreements, the ICSID Secretariat proposed in a 2004 Discussion Paper that an Appeals Facility be established under the ICSID Additional Facility Rules that would have the authority to hear appeals from all ICSID Convention, ICSID Additional Facility and UNCITRAL Rules awards where the parties in their

* Professor of Law, University of Ottawa. I am grateful to David Coker for his able research assistance. Any errors or omissions are mine.
1 *Bipartisan Trade Promotion Authority Act of 2002*, 19 USC § 3802(b)(3)(G)(iv) (2002).
2 ICSID Secretariat, "Possible Improvements of the Framework for ICSID Arbitration" (Discussion Paper), (October 22, 2004) at para 20, online: ICSID <http://icsid. worldbank.org> (ICSID Secretariat Proposal) [ICSID Secretariat Discussion Paper].

international investment treaties had agreed to submit the awards to the Appeals Facility for review.[3]

However, establishing an appellate mechanism in the investment field would be a complicated and challenging endeavor involving major hurdles that several experts have concluded are too high to overcome. Unlike the International Tribunal for the Law of the Sea, the International Criminal Court, the World Trade Organization Appellate Body and other similar tribunals or dispute settlement systems established under a single statute or treaty,[4] there are over 3,000 bilateral investment treaties and investment chapters in trade agreements.[5] Investment arbitration can be brought on the basis of treaty obligations between states or a contract between a state and a private investor. Depending upon the applicable treaty or contract, a claimant may avail itself of several different arbitration rules and facilities.[6]

By design, international investment awards are not subject to appeal, in the traditional sense, before international tribunals. Also, the rules and procedures of the ICSID Convention, on the one hand, and of the ICSID Additional Facility and UNCITRAL, on the other hand, differ

3 *Ibid* Annex. See also *Convention on the Settlement of Investment Disputes Between States and Nationals of Other States*, March 18, 1965 575 UNTS 159 (entered into force October 14, 1966) [ICSID Convention]; ICSID, *ICSID Additional Facility Rules*, ICSID/11 (April 2006) [Additional Facility Rules]; *Arbitration Rules of the United Nations Commission on International Trade Law*, GA Res 31/98, UNCITRAL, 31st sess, Supp No. 17, UN Doc A/31/17 (1976) at art 19(3) [UNCITRAL Arbitration Rules].

4 See the International Tribunal for the Law of the Sea, established under the *United Nations Convention on the Law of the Sea*, December 10, 1982, 1833 UNTS 397 (entered into force November 16, 1994); the International Criminal Court, established under the *Rome Statute of the International Criminal Court*, July 17, 1998, UN Doc 2817 UNTS 90, 37 ILM 999 (entered into force July 1, 2002); WTO Appellate Body established pursuant to the *Understanding on Rules and Procedures Governing the Settlement of Disputes* [DSU], art17. See World Trade Organization, *The Legal Texts: The Results of the Uruguay Round of Multilateral Trade Negotiations* (Cambridge: Cambridge University Press, 1999) [WTO Agreements].

5 See UNCTAD, *World Investment Report 2011: Non-equity Modes of International Production and Development* (New York and Geneva: UNCTAD, 2011) at 100.

6 These include, most commonly, the ICSID Arbitration Rules, the ICSID Additional Facility Arbitration Rules, and the UNCITRAL Arbitration Rules, *supra* note 3, as well as the *Rules of Arbitration of the International Chamber of Commerce*, online: International Chamber of Commerce <http://www.iccwbo.org/uploadedFiles/Court/Arbitration/other/rules_arb_english.pdf> and the Arbitration Institute of the Stockholm Chamber of Commerce, online: <http://www.jurisint.org/en/ctr/17.html>. See also August Reinisch, "Selecting the Appropriate Forum" in UNCTAD (ed), *Dispute Settlement: International Center for the Settlement of Investment Disputes* (New York and Geneva: United Nations, 2003) at module 2.2.

with respect to finality, enforcement and the review of awards. Under the ICSID Convention, article 53 provides that awards are final and may not be appealed. However, there is an annulment committee procedure provided in article 52 which includes limited grounds for annulment (and a high standard of review).[7] For cases brought under the ICSID Additional Facility Rules or the UNCITRAL Rules, applications can be made in national courts to set aside awards based on limited grounds of review.[8] The annulment procedures in the ICSID Convention and the set aside procedures in the UNCITRAL Model Law and the New York Convention contain such limited grounds for review that they cannot be characterized as "appeal" procedures. They are concerned with the legitimacy of the process by which the awards are rendered, rather than with the correctness or accuracy of the decisions.[9]

In the first part of the chapter, I will briefly review the reasons for and against an appellate mechanism. Ultimately, the goals of consistency, coherence and legitimacy of the system of international investment law are too important to subjugate to the goal of finality especially when cost and timing issues can be easily remedied. In the second part, I will propose a model for a comprehensive, standing appeals body applicable to all investment awards that could be adapted for implementation by different legal means.

Reasons for and against an appellate mechanism

In the wide-ranging debate that has ensued on whether or not an appellate mechanism should or could be established in international investment arbitration, five main themes have emerged:

1. whether there has been serious inconsistency or incoherence in arbitration awards so as to threaten the legitimacy of the system, or whether this would be a possible threat in the future;

---

7 The ICSID annulment committee procedures have their shortcomings, which will not be discussed in this chapter.
8 UNCITRAL Model Law on International Commercial Arbitration, 1985, online: <http://www.uncitral.org/uncitral/en/uncitral_texts/arbitration/1985Model_arbitration. html> at art 34 [UNCITRAL Model Law]. *United Nations Convention on the Recognition and Enforcement of Foreign Arbitral Awards*, une 10, 1958, 330 UNTS 38 (entered into force June 7, 1959) at art V [New York Convention].
9 David D. Caron, "Reputation and Reality in the ICSID Annulment Process: Under-standing the Distinction between Annulment and Appeal" (1992) 7(1) ICSID Rev 21 at 24. See also Aristidis Tsatsos, "ICSID Jurisprudence: Between Homogeneity and Heterogeneity. A Call for Appeal?" (2009) 6 *Transnational Dispute Management* 1 at 4 [Tsatos].

2. the impact of the increasing number of IIAs and the different provisions under them on consistency and coherence of decision making
   in the future;
3. the relative costs and timeliness of the current systems of arbitration
   with the possibilities of requests for annulment or set aside in the
   courts as compared with an appeals process;
4. the long-term sustainability of the investment arbitration system,
   in responding to concerns about confidence, credibility and legitimacy of the system;
5. challenges with respect to legal implementation and political
   feasibility.

The (in)consistency debate

One of the key reasons advanced in favor of an appellate mechanism is
the consistency and coherence of awards. In the wake of the significant
increase in investment arbitration since the late 1990s, several commentators have concluded that the different results and apparent inconsistencies in some important awards have threatened the very legitimacy of
the relatively new investment arbitration system.[10] Susan Franck in her
influential study in 2005 warned that "conflicting awards based upon
identical facts and/or identically worded investment treaty provisions
will be a threat to the international legal order and the continued existence of investment treaties."[11]

Some practitioners, however, disagree with the assertion that a problem with the consistency of awards exists, apart from a few notable
exceptions, or that the experience in investment arbitration is any

---

10 See Susan D. Franck, "The Legitimacy Crisis in International Treaty Arbitration:
   Privatizing Public International Law Through Inconsistent Decisions" (2005) 73(4)
   Fordham L Rev 1521 [Susan Franck]; David A. Gantz, "An Appellate Mechanism
   for Review of Arbitral Decisions in Investor-State Dispute: Prospects and
   Challenges" (2006) 39 V and J Transnat'l L 39 [Gantz]; Johanna Kalb, "Creating an
   ICSID Appellate Body" (2005) 10 UCLA J Int'l & Foreign Aff 179; Andrea Kupfer
   Schneider "Getting Along: the Evolution of Dispute Resolution Regimes in
   International Trade Organizations" (1999) 20 Mich J Int'l L 697; Charles H. Brower
   II, "The Functions and Limits of Arbitration and Judicial Settlement under Private
   and Public International Law" (2008) 18 Duke J Comp & Int'l L 259; James
   Crawford, "Is There a Need for an Appellate System?" (2005) 2 *Transnational Dispute
   Management* 8 [Crawford]; Thomas Wälde, "Alternatives for Obtaining Greater
   Consistency in Investment Arbitration: An Appellate Institution after the WTO,
   Authoritative Treaty Arbitration or Mandatory Consolidation?" (2005) 2 *Trans-
   national Dispute Management* 71 at 72 [Wälde].
11 Susan Franck, *supra* note 10 at 1583.

different from national courts in which there will always be some inconsistent decisions.[12] They argue that this is a new field of international law, and therefore, it is not surprising that there is some level of inconsistency which reflects "normal growing pains" for a new area of law.[13] Stephan Schill suggests that, despite international investment arbitration's "embryonic institutional design," investment tribunals have actually achieved a remarkable level of consistency in their decisions and have contributed to a multilateralization of investment law despite the multiplicity of bilateral investment agreements.[14]

Some commentators point to articles 52 and 53 of the ICSID Convention as evidence that finality of awards, not accuracy, was the key objective of the drafters of that Convention. They argue that establishing an appellate mechanism would upset the delicate balance negotiated by the drafters of that Convention and tip the scale too far towards the goals of consistency and accuracy at the cost of finality.[15]

A seasoned arbitrator has maintained that an appeals mechanism is unlikely to improve consistency for three reasons: (1) since this is a relatively new field there is no consensus on what terms mean; (2) the treaties and contracts are imperfect texts; and (3) fundamental norms are open-textured.[16] He also argues that, for the most part, awards are fact-based, not law-based, and therefore appeals would not be appropriate.[17]

Yet, international investment arbitration is a part of international law, part private and part public, and it does not exist in isolation from international law. To the extent that a claim is based on a treaty,

---

12 Judith Gill, "Inconsistent Decisions: An Issue to be Addressed or a Fact of Life?" (2005) 2 *Transnational Dispute Management* 12 at 15.

13 See e.g. Jan Paulsson, "Avoiding Unintended Consequences" in Karl P. Sauvant and Michael Chiswick-Patterson (eds), *Appeals Mechanism in International Investment Disputes* (New York: Oxford University Press, 2008) 241 at 253 [Paulsson]; Doak Bishop, "The Case for an Appellate Panel and its Scope of Review" (2005) 2 *Transnational Dispute Management* 8 at 9 [Bishop].

14 Stephan W. Schill, *The Multilateralization of International Investment Law* (Cambridge: Cambridge University Press, 2009) at 287, 321–39 [Schill].

15 See e.g. Christian J. Tams, "Is There a Need for an ICSID Appellate Structure?" in R. Hoffman and Christian J. Tams (eds), *The International Convention for the Settlement of Investment Disputes: Taking Stock After 40 Years* (Nomos: Baden Baden, 2007) 223 at 226 [Tams]; Gabrielle Kaufmann-Kohler, "In Search of Transparency and Consistency: ICSID Reform Proposal" (2005) 2 *Transnational Dispute Management* 1 at 6 [Kaufmann-Kohler "In search of transparency"]; William H. Knull III and Noah D. Rubins, "Betting the Farm on International Arbitration: Is it Time to Offer an Appeal Option?" (2000) 11 Am J Int'l Arb 531 at 570–1 [Knull and Rubins].

16 Paulsson, *supra* note 13, 241 at 258–9.

17 *Ibid* at 247.

customary international law rules relating to the interpretation of treaties may come into play and there may be other principles of general international law that become relevant.[18] The challenges that treaty terms may be unclear and customary international law principles may be difficult to discern are not unique to international investment law. These are common problems in other fields, such as international human rights law. Thomas Franck in his influential treatise, *The Power of Legitimacy among Nations*, posits that vague treaty terms can be clarified by being interpreted consistently and coherently by an authority recognized as legitimate.[19] Also, although the relevant facts pertaining to each award are typically unique, most awards involve interpretations by tribunals of treaty terms which often include public international law concepts such as expropriation or minimum standard of treatment. The potential risk for undermining the legitimacy of the international investment law with inconsistent legal rulings is particularly acute when it relates to determining questions of public international law, rather than simply interpreting the same or similar treaty terms or deciding similar cases on the facts. Recognizing the importance of international investment arbitration in the development of international law is critical to building respect and legitimacy for the field of international investment law in general.[20]

The multiplicity of IIAs challenge

There are debates among experts about whether or not an appellate mechanism would increase consistency because of the number of international investment treaties. Some argue that there are so many different treaties and contracts with such different provisions that it would be impossible for an appellate mechanism to interpret such provisions with any degree of consistency or coherence.[21] Others point out that there are really not that many different types of provisions, that they are based on common concepts and principles, that the key states that have

18 See August Reinisch in ch 18 of this book.
19 Thomas M. Franck, *The Power of Legitimacy Among Nations* (New York: Oxford University Press, 1990) at 61.
20 See Schill, *supra* note 14 at 359. See also José E. Alvarez, "Implications for the Future of International Investment Law" in Sauvant and Chiswick-Patterson, *supra* note 13, 16 at 32 [Alvarez, Implications for the Future].
21 See Paulsson, *supra* note 13, 241 at 259; Tsatsos, *supra* note 9 at 33–4. See also Gabrielle Kaufmann-Kohler, "Annulment of ICSID Awards in Contract and Treaty Arbitrations: Are There Differences?" in E. Gaillard and Y. Banifatemi (eds), *Annulment of ICSID Awards* (New York: Juris Publishing, 2004) 189 at 211.

negotiated them have used model agreements,[22] and thus, the dissimilarities may not be that stark.

Some observers have noted a related structural challenge: most international tribunals have been created by the consensus of the parties to a single, underlying multilateral agreement or a statute and have been charged with resolving disputes under that agreement, rather than under a multiplicity of different treaties and contracts among different parties.[23] On the contrary, however, the ICJ, although created by a single statute, hears cases relating to numerous different treaties and other matters of international law that Member States and UN agencies bring to it. The various legal issues and cases it hears are not even remotely similar when compared to the legal issues in investment arbitration cases. By contrast, investment arbitration cases are often based on IIAs that have been negotiated from model treaties containing similar clauses. Wording may be different, and nuances are important, but the basic principles in investment law are few and there are high degrees of similarity among agreements. Also, the application of the MFN clause may extend the benefits of the provisions of one agreement to the parties of another agreement even though the precise wording of the similar provision in the other agreement may differ in some respects. The United Nations Appeals Tribunal, also established under a single statute by the Member States of the UN, has broad authority to hear different matters either on appeal from the UN Dispute Tribunal or on reference from specific UN agencies.[24]

Citing the legendary Thomas Franck, scholars have emphasized that coherence of rules, including through interpretation, is critical to the legitimacy of any international rules-based system.[25] International investment arbitration, after all, is often based on treaties between sovereign states and involves issues of treaty interpretation as well as general international law. The problem with "inaccuracies" or inconsistencies in

22 See Patrick Juillard, "Variation in the Substantive Provisions and Interpretation of International Investment Agreements" in Sauvant and Chiswick-Patterson, *supra* note 13, 81 at 90–1; Schill, *supra* note 14 at 293; Gantz, *supra* note 10 at 77.

23 See Barton Legum, "Options to Establish an Appellate Mechanism for Investment Disputes" in Sauvant and Chiswick-Patterson, *supra* note 13, 231 at 235; Paulsson, *supra* note 13, 241 at 259; Donald McRae, "The WTO Appellate Body: A Model for an ICSID Appeals Facility?" (2010) 1 Journal of International Dispute Settlement 371 at 383–4 [McRae].

24 *Resolution adopted by the General Assembly: Administration of Justice at the United Nations*, UN GAOR, 63d Sess, Annex II, Agenda Item 129, UN Doc A/RES/63/253 (2009) 14 [Statute of the UN Appeals Tribunal] at art 2.

25 See Alvarez, Implications for the Future, *supra* note 20 at 32; Susan Franck, *supra* note 10 at 1584.

awards is not simply that the results in some cases could have been different, or that a damages award paid by the taxpayers could have been less or non-existent, the real problem is when there is an accretion of different interpretations of the same or very similar treaty provisions over time or worse, inconsistent statements by different tribunals relating to principles of customary international law.[26]

The issues of costs and delays

A major criticism of the idea of establishing an appeals mechanism is that it would add costs and delays to the investment arbitration process.[27] As will be discussed below, a response to these concerns would be to impose time limits for filing appeals[28] and for the proceedings as a whole.[29] Fees for filing appeals as well as procedures for preliminary awards and costs awards could also help deter frivolous appeals.[30]

Depending upon the powers of the appellate mechanism, if it has the authority to reverse and modify the decision of the arbitral tribunal, the appeal should be final. More generally, however, it is worth noting that annulment committee decisions made under the ICSID Convention are not necessarily the final word in a dispute. If the decision annuls the tribunal's award in full or in part, a new tribunal can be established, leading to ping pongs back and forth between tribunals and annulment committees.[31] Arguably, the current ICSID Convention process can lead

---

26 See e.g. *Archer Daniels Midland Co and Tate & Lyle Ingredients Americas, Inc v United Mexican States*, Award, ICSID Case No. ARB (AF)/04/5 (November 21, 2007); *Corn Products International, Inc v United Mexican States*, Decision on Responsibility, ICSID Case No. ARB (AF)/04/1 (January 15, 2008); *Cargill, Inc v United Mexican States*, Award, ICSID Case No. ARB (AF)/05/2 (September 18, 2009).

27 Rainer Geiger, "The Multifaceted Nature of International Investment Law" in Sauvant and Chiswick-Patterson, *supra* note 13 at 26 [Geiger]; Paulsson, *supra* note 13, 241 at 257, 260; Kaufmann-Kohler, "In search of transparency" *supra* note 15 at 6; Tams, *supra* note 15 at 228.

28 Statute of the UN Appeals Tribunal, *supra* note 24 at art 7.1(c) provides that appeals must be filed from decisions of the UN Dispute Tribunal within 45 days; WTO DSU, *supra* note 4 at art 16.4 provides that panel reports must be adopted by the Dispute Settlement Body or appealed within 60 days after their circulation to WTO members.

29 WTO DSU, *supra* note 4 at art 17.5, the Appellate Body is required to hear and decide an appeal and issue its decision within 60–90 days.

30 Knull and Rubins propose a monetary limit threshold on appeals, security for costs, costs awards, sanctions, and waivers of judicial remedies. Knull and Rubins, *supra* note 15 at 571–4.

31 See e.g. *Compania De Aguas Del Aconquija S.A. and Compagnie Générale des Eaux v Argentine Republic*, Award, ICSID Case No. ARB/97/3 (November 21, 2000); and Decision on annulment (July 3, 2002) resubmitted case: *Compania De Aguas Del*

to greater delays and costs than would an appellate mechanism. Similarly, review by national courts if they set aside all or parts of tribunal awards can also lead to remands or appeals and greater delays and costs than a one-stop shopping resort to an appellate mechanism.

Some have expressed the concern that if appeals are readily available, there will be an increase in applications for review, as compared with annulments.[32] It is interesting to note that from 1966 to September 19, 2011, there were 320 ICSID Convention arbitration cases registered, 139 Convention awards rendered and 47 annulment proceedings registered, and from 2001–11, there were 108 Convention awards and 32 annulment proceedings registered.[33] Therefore, under the ICSID Convention, annulment applications have been registered relating to approximately one-third of all awards despite the fact that only six awards have been annulled in full and five in part (8 per cent of all awards and 3 per cent of all cases registered) in the history of ICSID.

The role of an appellate mechanism in enhancing confidence in an international rules-based system

While of the view that the system is not broken, some experienced arbitrators nevertheless believe that an appeals mechanism is necessary because there is a perceived lack of confidence in the sustainability of the system itself. Doak Bishop, for example, emphasizes that an appellate body "should not be viewed as a reaction to cure problems of the present system, but simply as a phase in the evolution of a new and more sophisticated international law of investment disputes."[34] Another noted expert points to the unquestionable success of the WTO Appellate Body in enhancing confidence in the WTO dispute settlement system and in the organization as a whole.[35] Bishop maintains that a well-functioning appeals mechanism would improve and enhance the consistency of decisions, predictability of the law, objectivity in making decisions as to the meaning of investment provisions, and sensitivity to legitimate values in the international system.[36] Establishing an appellate mechanism as the ultimate legal authority in the field of international investment law

---

Aconquija S.A. & Vivendi Universal S.A. v Argentine Republic, Award, ICSID Case No. ARB/97/3 (August 20, 2007) and Decision on annulment (August 10, 2010).

32 Kaufmann-Kohler "In search of transparency", *supra* note 15 at 6; Paulsson, *supra* note 13, 241 at 257, 260.

33 Statistics on file with ICSID, cited with the permission of the ICSID Secretariat.

34 Bishop, *supra* note 13 at 9.

35 Crawford, *supra* note 10 at 8.

36 Bishop, *supra* note 13 at 10.

could herald a new era in which this field is recognized as a legitimate part of international law, and enable it to contribute effectively and authoritatively to the future development of international law.

Several experienced arbitrators have raised the concern that creating an appellate mechanism would undermine the authority of the arbitrators and devalue the trust placed in them by the parties, particularly if they are regularly appealed.[37] If a roster-type of appeals facility is created, as envisaged in the ICSID Secretariat proposal, some have queried what is the point of having another level of arbitrators and how will these experts be selected?[38] However, the same criticism was also leveled against the WTO Appellate Body; the comment was often made that it would make panels redundant even though it had authority to hear only appeals on questions of law and legal interpretation from panel reports. The response to these questions will depend upon the institutional design of the appeals mechanism and the standard of review. Not all issues will be appealed and the standard of review should be somewhat deferential to the first instance tribunal. There is value in having a second set of eyes and minds consider difficult issues. Legal issues become more precise and fine-tuned upon appeal; parties do not necessarily make exactly the same arguments on appeal that they made at the first instance level. As the legal issues become fewer and more precise on appeal, parties' arguments also tend to become more detailed and in depth. A standing appeals body is preferable to a roster-type system to guarantee consistency and coherence in decision making precisely because a small group of judges or members are more likely to develop a sense of collegiality and an institutional perspective of their common role and responsibility.

While some believe an appeals mechanism would improve the quality of decision making and help to guarantee procedural fairness at the arbitral level,[39] others take the view that a strong, cohesive, institutional, first instance, dispute settlement process is needed before an appeals mechanism, following the WTO model, can be successful.[40] On the contrary, however, in the WTO, there was not a strong, cohesive, institutional, first instance dispute settlement process before the Appellate Body was established. But the existence of the Appellate Body has significantly improved the functioning of the panels, both in terms of improving their procedures and the quality of their decisions.

---

37 Paulsson, *supra* note 13, 241 at 260; Kaufmann-Kohler "In search of transparency", *supra* note 15 at 6.
38 Kaufmann-Kohler, *supra* note 15 at 5–6; McRae, *supra* note 23 at 386.
39 Geiger, *supra* note 27 in Sauvant and Chiswick-Patterson, *supra* note 13, 17 at 25.
40 McRae, *supra* note 23 at 384–5.

Logistics, political feasibility and implementation

Ultimately, the major obstacles to establishing an appellate mechanism are logistics and political feasibility: how to deal with the multiplicity of agreements and arbitration forums, how to obtain state consent, and how to legally implement any proposal? These are major hurdles indeed that have led many esteemed observers to conclude that it is not worth the effort and to look for other means of enhancing consistency and coherence.[41]

Some maintain that it would require an amendment of the ICSID Convention, but there are alternative legal means by which an appellate mechanism could be established.[42] For investment arbitration conducted outside of the ICSID Convention, the logistical hurdles to establish an appellate mechanism would also be complicated because of the availability of review of awards by national courts.

It is not the purpose of this chapter to propose specific legal means of establishing an appellate mechanism for investment arbitration. Rather, I will focus on outlining a possible model for such a mechanism.

A model for consideration

International investment law has come of age and it is precisely in order to overcome the design "challenges" of the multiplicity of treaties, the choice of arbitration fora, and the web of *ad hoc* tribunals, annulment committees and national courts, that it is important to establish, at this point in history, a comprehensive, judicial, appeals mechanism with the authority to interpret treaty provisions, clarify international law and

41 Christoph Schreuer and Gabrielle Kaufmann-Kohler have suggested that use of consolidation procedures and reference of legal questions to an adjudicative or political body may help to improve consistency. Christoph Schreuer, "Preliminary Rulings in Investment Arbitration" in Sauvant and Chiswick-Patterson, *supra* note 13, 207 at 209; Kaufmann-Kohler "In search of transparency", *supra* note 15 at 7–8. Similarly, Christian J. Tams has observed that although there is a serious institutional problem with consistency, creating an appellate mechanism would be a drastic reform that could paralyze the system and has proposed the alternatives of consolidation of cases and possible references to the ICJ. Tams, *supra* note 15 at 247.

42 For example, the ICSID Secretariat proposed that an Appeals Facility could be established by a set of ICSID Appeals Facility Rules adopted by the Administrative Council without amending the Convention. ICSID members, however, would have to provide in their investment treaties for submission of awards to the Appeals Facility. See ICSID Secretariat Proposal, *supra* note 2 at para 2. See also W. Michael Reisman, "The Breakdown of the Control Mechanism in ICSID Arbitration" (1990) 4 Duke LJ 739 at 806, who has suggested that an amendment does not need to be accepted by all members of the Convention.

guarantee fair procedures. In designing an appropriate model for the international investment regime, the specific goals and unique features of the system must be taken into account in order for the model to be successful. Borrowing from another, different system may not work without careful adaptation, but it is equally important to be innovative and bold when creating a new judicial institution.[43] As with any judicial body, certain fundamental principles must be taken into account in designing an appeals mechanism: independence and impartiality of the judges, fair procedures, as well as consistency and coherence in its decisions. Other goals such as timeliness, efficiency and finality are also important.

With these principles and goals in mind, the basic features of a proposed model will be outlined and discussed.

A comprehensive, standing appeals body

To ensure maximum consistency, coherence and legitimacy of the system, a standing appeals body—a comprehensive mechanism for all investment awards—should be considered. The purpose of the ICSID Secretariat proposal was to establish a single Appeals Facility designed for use under both forms of ICSID arbitration as well as under UNCITRAL rules in order to prevent inconsistencies in tribunal awards and the risk of fragmentation if separate appellate mechanisms were to be established in future IIAs.[44]

Obviously, a comprehensive appellate mechanism applicable to all international investment awards would be highly preferable in terms of achieving the goals of maximum coherence, consistency and legitimacy in the development of international investment law. This may be a "rather utopian view" at this point in time.[45] However, starting with an appellate mechanism in a bilateral investment treaty would not be a major step on the road to greater consistency, coherence and legitimacy.

---

43 It can and has been done several times in other fields in recent years: the International Tribunal for the Law of the Sea, the International Criminal Court, and the WTO Appellate Body, *supra* at note 4; the United Nations Appeals Tribunal, established under the Statute of the United Nations Appeals Tribunal, *supra* note 24; the World Bank Administrative Tribunal, established under the *Statute of the Administrative Tribunal of the International Bank for Reconstruction and Development*, International Development Association and International Finance Corporation, online: <http://lnweb90.worldbank.org/crn/wbt/wbtwebsite.nsf/(resultsweb)/42053A8AD4A530 0585256AD8004ABA13>.
44 ICSID Secretariat Discussion Paper, *supra* note 2 at paras 21–3.
45 Wälde, *supra* note 10 at 72.

An appellate mechanism in a plurilateral free trade agreement (PTA) may be an incremental step worth considering, but there are very few PTAs, and it may not be worth the effort especially if the investment disputes under those agreements are brought under the ICSID or the UNCITRAL rules in any case. Therefore, it is worth considering the comprehensive, multilateral option.

A standing appeals body would be preferable to a roster-type system in that it would have the character and personality of a tribunal, with the ongoing jurisdiction and authority not only to hear appeals, but also to establish its own rules of procedure and deal with internal administration such as the selection of divisions or chambers to hear cases as well as conflict of interest matters. The ICSID Secretariat proposed the establishment of an Appeals Panel composed of 15 persons elected by the Administrative Council of ICSID on the nomination of the Secretary-General.[46] In the ICSID proposal, challenges of awards would be referred to an appeal tribunal appointed by the Secretary-General from the Appeals Panel.[47] The Secretary-General was also to act as a gate-keeper in allowing access to the Appeals Facility.[48]

By creating a standing body and giving it the authority to establish its own rules of procedure and govern its internal administration, the ICSID Secretariat would have less influence over the system. Additionally, there would be more of a distinction between the first-instance level and appellate-level decision-making processes, and most importantly, the appeals body would develop as an institution with a long-term view of itself and responsibility for its decisions. A standing body would thus ensure the consistency and coherence of decisions, make its contribution to international law, and add to the legitimacy of the international investment system.

Appointment to the appeals body and composition of divisions or tribunals

The selection and appointment of standing body members and the composition of divisions or tribunals are among the most difficult issues to consider. For reasons of consistency and efficiency, the number of members should be small and appointments could be part-time until the caseload warrants full-time judges. The nomination and appointment of members will depend on what legal means are chosen

46 ICSID Secretariat Discussion Paper, *supra* note 2 at para 5 of Annex.
47 *Ibid* at para 6 of Annex.
48 *Ibid* at para 11 of Annex.

to establish the appeals mechanism. The ICSID Secretariat proposed that an Appeals Facility could be established under a set of ICSID Appeals Facility Rules adopted by the Administrative Council of ICSID. However, the submission of an award to the Appeals Facility would have to be either based on the provisions of a treaty (in the case of ICSID Convention awards) or on the consent of the parties (in the case of other awards).[49] The ICSID Secretariat proposed that the Secretary-General could nominate persons from different countries "of recognized authority, with demonstrated expertise in law, international investment and investment treaties," and the Administrative Council of ICSID would elect 15 persons to serve as members on an Appeals Panel.[50] When an award was challenged, the Secretary-General would appoint a three-member "tribunal" from the Appeals Panel to hear the appeal, after consultation with the parties "as far as possible."[51] Other proposals have included a comprehensive multilateral treaty establishing a single court, housed in the Permanent Court of Arbitration, with 11 judges serving a fixed 10-year term.[52]

The challenge with appointments to a standing body, appeals panel or court is that they will be made by states parties to the convention or legal instrument establishing it, without any apparent input from investors who are stakeholders and bring claims. Perhaps an advisory body could be established to take their views into account.

The issue of composition or selection of a division or tribunal to hear an appeal once it has been filed should be considered an internal matter for the standing body, appeals panel or court. In the case of a standing body or a court, delegation of such responsibility to a chair or chief justice or some other procedure is often established in its rules of procedure. Adopting a similar approach would ensure independence and impartiality, which are fundamental to any judicial body, as well as help to develop an institutional sense of purpose.

The standard of review

Defining the appropriate standard of review is a critical, and perhaps the most difficult part of the design of any appeals or judicial review body. It is important to define the standard clearly,[53] and to get it right. The

---

49 *Ibid* at paras 1–3 of Annex.
50 *Ibid* at para 5 of Annex.
51 *Ibid* at para 6 of Annex.
52 Susan Franck, *supra* note 10 at 1619, 1623–4.
53 Knull and Rubins, *supra* note 15 at 564, 572.

ICSID Secretariat proposed combining the current grounds for annulment set out in article 52 of the ICSID Convention which essentially relate to manifest or serious errors of jurisdiction and procedure[54] with "clear errors of law" and "serious errors of fact."[55] This combination of annulment and added appeal grounds is confusing, and a fresh approach should be considered. First, with respect to jurisdictional or legal errors, any error should be reversible. What is the difference between a "clear" error of law, and an "unclear" error of law? Surely, an error of law is an error of law. Deference should, however, be shown to the arbitral tribunal with respect to matters of procedure and questions of fact. Ensuring that tribunals apply principles of fair procedures is fundamental to the right of the parties to a fair hearing, therefore, a standard providing that "there has been a serious departure from a fundamental rule of procedure"[56] or that the tribunal "committed an error in procedure, such as to affect the decision of the case"[57] would be appropriate. If the key objectives in establishing an appeals mechanism are: (1) to ensure the consistency and coherence of awards, (2) provide greater credibility, authority and sustainability of the system, and (3) maintain the long-term legitimacy of international investment law, then the appeals mechanism does not need the authority to review factual findings of arbitral tribunals. It would have greater authority, and its mission would be more focused as guardian of the law, if its competence was limited to questions of law, jurisdiction and procedure. Alternatively, if it was felt that it was essential for the appeals mechanism to review tribunal awards for issues of fact, the standard of review should be highly deferential to the arbitral tribunal. In the latter case, an appropriate standard might be: "Erred on a question of fact, resulting in a manifestly unreasonable decision."[58]

If the appeals body only has the authority to review tribunal awards for excess of jurisdiction, serious procedural errors and errors of law, then it should have the power to render orders to uphold, reverse or modify the awards of the arbitral tribunals. If it is not engaged in reviewing factual findings of tribunals, it will be less likely to need the authority to remand cases to the arbitral tribunals. To the greatest extent possible, the

---

54 ICSID Convention, *supra* note 3, art 52, the grounds for annulment are: that the arbitral tribunal was not properly constituted; that it manifestly exceeded its powers; that one of its members was corrupt; that there was a serious departure from a fundamental rule of procedure; and that the award failed to state the reasons on which it was based.
55 ICSID Secretariat Discussion Paper, *supra* note 2 at para 7 of Annex.
56 ICSID Convention, *supra* note 3 at art 52.
57 Statute of the UN Appeals Tribunal, *supra* note 24 at art 2.1.
58 *Ibid.*

appeals body should modify the decisions of the arbitral tribunals that it has overturned, rather than remanding them to the tribunals.

Orders and proceedings: finality, timeliness, efficiency and cost concerns

It is critical for finality, cost and efficiency reasons that the orders of the appeals body be final, binding and timely. Also, in order to ensure timeliness and to save costs, time limits should be established both for the filing of appeals and for the length of appellate proceedings.[59] With respect to finality, some commentators believe that it is fundamental to provide for a waiver of any judicial review.[60] Surprisingly, Susan Franck, who was one of the first to promote the idea of a court for review of all investment awards for errors of law and legal interpretation, would maintain in place the annulment and review mechanisms in the ICSID, New York and Panama Conventions.[61] Yet, arguably, adding another review mechanism to the thicket of international and national mechanisms already available would only cause opportunities for delays, added costs and reduced finality of awards. Therefore, annulment under the ICSID Convention should be replaced by the new appeals mechanism. A waiver on judicial remedies is also essential to ensuring finality as well as the authority and legitimacy of the appeals body.

Concerns have been expressed about the costs of the mechanism and how to prevent every case from being appealed. The short answer is that there will probably be more appeals filed in the early days by prospective appellants trying to test the mechanism. There could be some procedural and substantive hurdles: short time limits for filing appeals, fees for filing appeals, and the standard of review. Some commentators have also suggested monetary limits—a threshold amount, cost shifting, security for costs, and penalties[62] as procedural ways to deter frivolous appeals. However, rules of procedure should not deter appeals from being brought by

---

59 Appeals from a WTO panel must be brought within 60 days after the issuance of the panel report and appeals from the UN Disputes Tribunal to the UN Appeals Tribunal must be brought within 45 days; WTO Appellate Body proceedings must, in no case, take longer than 90 days from the filing of the appeal until the issuance of the Appellate Body report. *Supra* notes 4 and 24.

60 Knull and Rubins, *supra* note 15 at 573; Daniel M. Price, "US Trade Promotion Legislation" (2005) 2 *Transnational Dispute Management* 47 at 49; Wälde, *supra* note 10 at 76.

61 Susan Franck, *supra* note 10 at 1621.

62 Knull and Rubins, *supra* note 15 at 572–3. But see Wälde, *supra* note 10 at 76, who disagrees that parties should have to pay the costs of the tribunal for an appeal.

developing country members in cases that may have important public policy implications. It would be more appropriate for the appeals mechanism to develop its own preliminary procedures for rejecting frivolous appeals than to set the monetary threshold or the penalties for bringing appeals too high. In the first few years of the WTO, 100 per cent of panel reports were appealed, but the overall percentage of panel reports that have been appealed from 1995–2010 has dropped to 67 per cent.[63] Under the ICSID Convention, until September 2011, there were 47 annulment proceedings registered which represented approximately one-third of all Convention awards.[64] In the future, the number of appeals will no doubt increase if an appeals body is established. Over time, however, the number of appeals would decrease as experience with the appeals body grows and the case law develops.

Conclusion

Creating an appellate mechanism for international investment arbitration is the next logical step in building the necessary infrastructure for the development of a consistent and coherent international investment law. A comprehensive, standing appeals body for all investment arbitration awards should be established with the necessary authority to guarantee consistency and coherence in the law, but even more important, to build legitimacy and credibility for a new field of law that is not well known and even less well understood. The issue is not simply whether an appellate mechanism is needed because arbitral awards have been inconsistent or inaccurate to date. As noted by commentators, although the significance of inconsistent decisions on the system may be debatable, what is not is the potential for inconsistency, incoherence and fragmentation in the future with the increasing number of international investment agreements and arbitration awards. The warning bells were sounded in 2003–05; it would be wise to take action before they turn into a cacophony.

A strong, internationally-respected judicial institution is required to speak with authority on key issues of law in order to establish and maintain the credibility and legitimacy of this important and vital field of law. It is especially critical that there be an authoritative, unifying legal voice

---

63 World Trade Organization, Appellate Body, *Annual Report for 2010*, WT/AB/15, June 2011 at 5.

64 ICSID Statistics, *supra* note 33. According to the ICSID Secretariat, between 1966–September 19, 2011, there were 320 Convention arbitration cases registered and 139 Convention awards rendered.

in the international investment field precisely because of the multiplicity of international investment treaties and the potential risks of fragmentation and inconsistencies in the interpretations and statements of the law. What is often not recognized is that there is a reciprocal, two-way influence between norms as they develop in a specific field of international law and general international law. Thus, establishing an authoritative tribunal in the international investment field will have a positive impact not only on the development of norms in international investment law, but also a reciprocal benefit on general international law.[65]

It is essential, however, that the appeals mechanism be carefully designed, paying close attention to the fundamental principles governing any international judicial body and the specific goals unique to international investment arbitration. Obviously, there will be advantages and drawbacks associated with each proposal, and the formidable challenge of implementation given the complex existing treaty structure is without a doubt the most significant hurdle of all. However, if there is a will among sovereign governments to take this major step on the path to creating order, enhancing legitimacy, and building credibility for the vitally important system of international investment law, a way can be found.

---

65 José Alvarez suggests that within the WTO context, the normative impact may flow in both directions. Not only has the WTO been changed by resort to general international law, but the WTO Appellate Body has clearly had an influence on general international law. José Alvarez "The Factors Driving and Constraining the Incorporation of International Law in WTO Adjudication", in Merit E. Janow, Victoria Donaldson and Alan Yanovich (eds), *The WTO: Governance, Dispute Settlement and Developing Countries* (New York: Juris Publishing, 2008) at 632. See also Armand de Mestral in ch 19 of this book.

Part IV

Sustainability

15 The use of general exceptions in IIAs: increasing legitimacy or uncertainty?

*Andrew Newcombe**

Introduction

This chapter focuses on the potential that general exceptions clauses offer to create a "sustainable" IIA regime—sustainable in the sense of being able to reconcile competing public and private interests while simultaneously ensuring that IIAs do not hamper host state policies that promote sustainable development.[1]

As recent scholarship attests, there has been a great deal of commentary and a divergence of views on whether IIAs are a threat to public welfare and what, if anything, needs to be done.[2] Although the concerns with IIAs are multifaceted, one recurring concern is that obligations imposed by IIAs with respect to the treatment of foreign investors and investment may limit a state from taking action to protect the public welfare, and, in particular, that regulatory changes designed to protect the environment and living things from harms associated with economic activities may result in IIA breaches. This concern, amongst others, is reflected in the *Public Statement on the International Investment Regime* published in 2010 by a group of more than 35 academics.[3] The preamble to the three-page Statement states:

> We have a shared concern for the harm done to the public welfare by the international investment regime, as currently structured, especially its hampering of the ability of governments to act for

* Associate Professor, Faculty of Law, University of Victoria.
1 See ch 16 of this book on sustainable development and IIAs.
2 The literature in this area has been growing at an exponential rate. See the list of recent book-length contributions in the Introduction to this book.
3 Various, "Public Statement on the International Investment Regime" (August 31, 2010), online: Osgoode Hall Law School <http://www.osgoode.yorku.ca/public_statement>.

their people in response to the concerns of human development and environmental sustainability.

As described in Chapter 1, treaty practice with respect to foreign investors' substantive and procedural rights has continued to evolve, spurred, at least in part, by the type of concerns expressed in the Statement.[4] This chapter focuses on one particular treaty clause, what I refer to as a "general exception," and whether general exceptions clauses modeled on article XX GATT are the preferred method to address the legitimacy and sustainability concerns that have been raised regarding the scope of IIA standards of protection. In other words, should general exception clauses become as ubiquitous as clauses requiring fair and equitable treatment and compensation for expropriation in the next generation of IIAs?

A very small, but growing, number of IIAs include general exceptions. The appeal of general exceptions is understandable—they provide an express and general exemption for regulatory measures that might be found to breach obligations under IIAs. The inclusion of general exceptions clauses in future IIAs is one potential response to the general concern that IIA obligations are too broad. The allure of a general exception clause is that it creates a protected regulatory space for the state to implement a broad range of measures to address unknown future harms to the public welfare as well as to justify existing regulatory measures.

Although on their face general exceptions may appear to offer a holistic and innovative solution to legitimacy and sustainability concerns regarding the scope of foreign investors' rights under IIAs, this chapter questions the advisability of using general exceptions as the preferred treaty mechanism to balance public and private rights. First, there is significant uncertainty about how general exceptions clauses, drawn from international trade treaties, will be applied in the very different context of international investment law. Secondly, in light of that interpretative uncertainty, the inclusion of general exceptions in IIAs does not provide particularly helpful guidance to treaty interpreters (including arbitrators) in determining how to balance the public right to regulate and the protection of investor rights. Uncertainty about the scope of fair and equitable treatment and other generally worded IIA obligations is not resolved by using general exceptions—indeed interpretative outcomes may become even more uncertain. Thirdly, general exceptions arguably simply displace where in the legal analysis the balancing

4 For the author's critical comment on the Statement, see Andrew Newcombe, "A Brief Comment on the 'Public Statement on the International Investment Regime'" (September 3, 2010) online: Kluwer Arbitration Blog <http://kluwerarbitrationblog.com>.

between public and private rights is to occur (i.e. at the stage of analyzing the primary obligation or at the stage of defense by way of exception to the primary obligation) in a way that is potentially quite disruptive to the overall stability of international investment law. Fourthly, international trade and investment law have vastly different legal and institutional structures. Although general exceptions are well integrated into the international trade system, they have a very uneasy relationship with customary international law standards of investment protection, and their transplantation from international trade to investment treaties may have unintended consequences. The chapter concludes that instead of looking for a solution in general exceptions, the better way forward is for any balancing of public and private rights to occur at the level of primary obligations and through states clarifying the scope of investment obligations in their investment treaty practice.[5]

Part 1 provides a very brief introduction to general exceptions in international trade law, in particular article XX GATT, as this provision has served as a model for general exceptions in IIAs. Part 2 provides an overview of IIA treaty practice relating to general exceptions. Part 3 discusses different approaches to the interpretation of general exceptions and the interaction between general exceptions and investment obligations. The chapter concludes with the recommendation that article XX GATT-like general exceptions not be adopted in future investment treaty practice and the suggestion that if states are concerned about the scope of IIA obligations, the focus should be on clarifying the scope of primary obligations and using more focused exceptions.[6]

Article XX GATT, general exceptions

The general exceptions discussed in this chapter are those modeled on the general exceptions in article XX GATT.[7] Article XIV of the General

---

5 On state clarification of existing IIA obligations, see Anthea Roberts, "Power and Persuasion in Investment Treaty Arbitration: The Dual Role of States" (2010) 104 AJIL 178.

6 This chapter draws and builds on the discussion of general exceptions in "Exceptions and Defences" in Andrew Newcombe and Lluís Paradell, *Law and Practice of Investment Treaties: Standards of Treatment* (The Hague: Kluwer Law International, 2009) at ch 10 [Newcombe and Paradell]; Andrew Newcombe, "General Exceptions in International Investment Agreements" in Marie-Claire Cordonier Segger, Markus Gehring and Andrew Newcombe (eds), *Sustainable Development in World Investment Law* (The Hague: Kluwer Law International, 2011) at 351–70.

7 See *General Agreement on Tariffs and Trade* [GATT] at art XX reproduced in World Trade Organization, *The Legal Texts: The Results of the Uruguay Round of Multilateral*

Agreement on Trade in Services (GATS) has a similar form of general exceptions clause, also based on article XX GATT.[8] Article XX, called "General Exceptions" provides exceptions to GATT obligations including MFN treatment (article I), national treatment (article III) and the prohibition of quantitative restrictions (article XI). Article XX consists of 10 enumerated exceptions and an introductory provision, known as the *chapeau*, which focuses on the *application* of the measure in question. Article XX, provides, in part as follows:

> Subject to the requirement that such measures are not applied in a manner which would constitute a means of arbitrary or unjustifiable discrimination between countries where the same conditions prevail, or a disguised restriction on international trade, nothing in this Agreement shall be construed to prevent the adoption or enforcement by any contracting party of measures:
>
> (a) necessary to protect public morals;
> (b) necessary to protect human, animal or plant life or health; . . .
> (c) relating to the conservation of exhaustible natural resources if such measures are made effective in conjunction with restrictions on domestic production or consumption; . . .[9]

The WTO Appellate Body has established a number of principles to be applied in interpreting article XX. With respect to the general purpose of general exceptions, the Appellate Body has stated that general exceptions "affirm the right of Members to pursue objectives identified in the paragraphs of these provisions even if, in doing so, Members act inconsistently with obligations set out in other provisions of the respective agreements, provided that all of the conditions set out therein are satisfied."[10] The

Trade Negotiations (Cambridge: Cambridge University Press, 1999) [WTO Agreements]. For general overviews of art XX jurisprudence, see Michael Trebilcock and Robert Howse, *The Regulation of International Trade*, 3rd edn (London: Routledge, 2005); Mitsuo Matsushita et al, *The World Trade Organization: Law, Practice and Policy* 2nd edn (Oxford: Oxford University Press, 2006); Peter van den Bossche, *The Law and Policy of the World Trade Organization*, 2nd edn (Cambridge: Cambridge University Press 2008).

8 See *General Agreement on Trade in Services* [GATS] in WTO Agreements, *supra* note 7 at art XIV.

9 See GATT, *supra* note 7 at art XX.

10 *United States—Measures Affecting the Cross-Border Supply of Gambling and Betting Services*, WT/DS285/AB/R (adopted April 20, 2005) at para 291 (with respect to the general exception in art XIV, GATS).

analysis of general exceptions is two-tiered: first, justification under one of the enumerated exceptions; and, secondly, a determination of conformity with the *chapeau*. The first tier of the analysis can be broken into two further steps: does the measure fall within the range of objectives permitted by the exception; and does the measure satisfy the nexus requirement of it being "necessary" or "relating to" the objective in question?

With respect to enumerated exceptions requiring that the measure in question be "necessary," the Appellate Body jurisprudence indicates that the meaning of "necessary" can be situated on a continuum stretching from "indispensable to a contribution" to "achieving the objective."[11] Assessing whether a measure that is not indispensable may nevertheless be "necessary" involves, in each case, a process of weighing and balancing a series of factors including: (i) the relative importance of the common interests or values that the measure is intended to protect; (ii) the contribution made by the measure to the achievement of the objective; and (iii) the restrictiveness and impact of the measure.[12]

With respect to the *chapeau*, the Appellate Body has held that it is a manifestation of the principle of good faith and the prohibition of an abuse of rights. The *chapeau* serves to balance the right of a state to invoke the general exception and the duty of that same state to respect the treaty rights of the other members.[13] It is worth noting that in WTO practice, many state attempts to justify measures under general exceptions have foundered at the *chapeau* stage of the analysis because, even though a measure may be justifiably necessary to meet a particular public welfare objective (such as conserving natural resources), the measure might be applied in a way that is discriminatory.[14] The *chapeau* provides a second level of screening to ensure that measures that might, in principle, be aimed at a legitimate objective are not applied in ways that are discriminatory or a disguised restriction on international trade.

Rather than adopting a formalistic approach of either restrictive or wide interpretation to the meaning of "necessary," the WTO Appellate Body has adopted a weighing and balancing analysis. This approach is in keeping with the need to balance the right of a host state to invoke

---

11 *Korea—Measures Affecting Imports of Fresh, Chilled and Frozen Beef*, WT/DS161/AB/R and WT/DS169/AB/R (adopted January 10, 2001) at para 161.

12 *Ibid* at para 164. The Appellate Body affirmed this weighing and balancing approach more recently in *Brazil—Measures Affecting Imports of Retreaded Tyres*, WT/DS322/AB/R (adopted December 17, 2007) at para 210.

13 *United States—Import Prohibition of Certain Shrimp and Shrimp Products*, WT/DS58/AB/R (adopted November 6, 1998) at para 159.

14 See e.g. *United States—Import Prohibition of Certain Shrimp and Shrimp Products, ibid.*

an express exception against ensuring that the host state respects its treaty obligations. Some commentators have characterized this weighing and balancing approach as a form of proportionality analysis reflected in constitutional and human rights jurisprudence.[15] Therein lies the appeal of including general exceptions in IIAs: an article XX-like general exceptions clause provides a boilerplate treaty mechanism for calibrating or recalibrating the balance between public and private rights in IIAs.

IIA treaty practice relating to general exceptions

General exceptions are only one treaty mechanism that IIA parties can use to address concerns that an IIA provides an appropriate balance between public and private rights. Before turning to treaty practice on general exceptions, it is worth highlighting that the majority of IIAs do not contain general exceptions. Indeed, the majority of IIAs do not have express provisions carving out space for host states to regulate in areas such as public health, safety or the protection of the environment.[16]

A 2011 OECD study entitled *Environmental Concerns in International Investment Agreements*[17] is a good barometer of the extent to which state treaty practice has specifically addressed the balance between private and public rights. The first finding of interest is that only 8 per cent of

15 See Alec Stone Sweet and Jud Mathews, "Balancing and Global Constitutionalism" (2008) 47 Colum J Transnat'l L 68, online: <http://ssrn.com/abstract=1569344> at 75, arguing that proportionality analysis "has also migrated to the three treaty-based regimes that have serious claims to be considered 'constitutional' in some meaningful sense: the European Union (EU), the European Convention on Human Rights (ECHR), and the World Trade Organization (WTO). In our view, proportionality-based rights adjudication now constitutes one of the defining features of global constitutionalism, if global constitutionalism can be said to exist at all." On proportionality in WTO Law, see Mads Andenas and Stefan Zleptnig, "Proportionality: WTO Law in Comparative Perspective" (2007) 42(3) Tex Int'l LJ 370; Andrew Mitchell, *Legal Principles in WTO Disputes* (Cambridge: Cambridge University Press, 2008). But see Jürgen Kurtz, "Adjudging the Exceptional at International Investment Law: Security, Public Order and Financial Crisis" (2010) 59 ICLQ 325, questioning whether proportionality analysis in the sense of whether the "costs imposed by the measure are excessive or disproportionate to the benefits of the policy objective" (at 366) should be used in the context of international investment law.

16 On the various types of exceptions and reservations to substantive obligations that appear in IIAs, see Newcombe and Paradell, *supra* note 6 at ch 10.

17 Kathryn Gordon and Joachim Pohl, "Environmental Concerns in International Investment Agreements: A Survey" (2011) *OECD Working Papers on International Investment, No. 2011/1*, OECD Investment Division, online: <http://www.oecd.org/daf/investment> [2011 OECD Study].

the sample of 1,623 IIAs include specific references to environmental concerns. Further, it appears that the vast majority of these references occur in more recent treaties (those signed after 1995). The references occur in a variety of treaty provisions, with great variation in content, including: (i) preambular references addressing environmental concerns; (ii) those reserving policy space for environmental regulation for the entire treaty (sometimes in the form of general exceptions); (iii) those reserving policy space for environmental regulation for specific subject matters (such as performance requirements or national treatment); (iv) those clarifying that non-discriminatory environmental regulation cannot be the basis for claiming an indirect expropriation; (v) those forbidding lowering of environmental standards to attract investment; (vi) those relating to investor-state dispute settlement (such as provisions for expert reports on technical matters); and (vii) those providing for general promotion of progress in environmental protection and cooperation.[18]

Although a 2008 study notes that exception provisions appear in at least 200 IIAs, the majority of these exceptions (what the authors of the study refer to as "non-precluded measures") relate to specific obligations, such as national treatment, or to specific exceptions for essential security interests, public order, prudential measures or taxation.[19] They are not general exceptions modeled on article XX GATT-like language that address more general forms of public welfare regulation. The 2011 OECD Study found 82 examples of clauses reserving policy space for environmental regulation out of a sample of 1,623 IIAs, but only about 30 of those are expressly modeled on Article XX GATT-like language.[20]

A small but increasing number of IIAs (both BITs and FTAs with investment chapters) include general exceptions modeled on article XX GATT and/or article XIV GATS.[21] The majority of these IIAs are Canadian Foreign Investment Promotion and Protection Agreements (FIPAs). Indeed, Canada is unique among OECD states in including article XX GATT-like general exceptions in most of its FIPAs.[22] The

18 *Ibid.*
19 William W. Burke-White and Andreas von Standen, "Investment Protection in Extraordinary Times: The Interpretation of Non-precluded Measure Provisions in Bilateral Investment Treaties" (2007) 48(2) Va J Int'l L 307.
20 See 2011 OECD Study, *supra* note 17.
21 See GATT, *supra* note 7 at art XX and GATS, *supra* note 8 at art XIV.
22 Some recent Japanese agreements contain general exceptions to investment obligations. See *Agreement between Japan and the Republic of Singapore for a New-Age Economic Partnership,* online: Japan Ministry of Foreign Affairs <http://www.mofa.go.jp/region/asia-paci/singapore/jsepa-1.pdf> at art 83; *Agreement between the Government of*

Canadian treaty practice of including general exceptions dates from 1994 and general exceptions now appear in over 20 Canadian FIPAs.[23] A general exception modeled on article XX GATT, appears in article X of Canada's current model FIPA (2004), which provides as follows:

General Exceptions

1. Subject to the requirement that such measures are not applied in a manner that would constitute arbitrary or unjustifiable discrimination between investments or between investors, or a disguised restriction on international trade or investment, nothing in this Agreement shall be construed to prevent a Party from adopting or enforcing measures necessary:

    (a) to protect human, animal or plant life or health;
    (b) to ensure compliance with laws and regulations that are not inconsistent with the provisions of this Agreement; or
    (c) for the conservation of living or non-living exhaustible natural resources.

Although general exceptions in BITs other than Canadian FIPAs are extremely rare,[24] they have begun to appear more frequently in comprehensive bilateral FTAs, particularly those between Asian states.[25]

Japan and the Government of Malaysia for an Economic Partnership, December 13, 2005, online: Japan Ministry of Foreign Affairs <http://www.mofa.go.jp/region/asia-paci/malaysia/epa/index.html> at art 10 [Japan-Malaysia FTA].

23 The Canadian treaty practice is not consistent. Earlier FIPAs do not refer to discrimination in the chapeau (see art XVII(3) in Ukraine FIPA) and about half of Canadian FIPAs use "relating to" rather than "necessary" with respect to the conservation of natural resources. For commentary on art X of the Model FIPA, see Céline Lévesque and Andrew Newcombe, "Commentary on the Canadian Model Foreign Investment Promotion and Protection Agreement" in Chester Brown and Devashish Krishan (eds), *Commentaries on Selected Model International Investment Agreements* (Oxford: Oxford University Press, forthcoming).

24 Another example of a BIT with a general exceptions provision is Jordan-Singapore BIT (2004). Latvia's current model BIT also contains a general exceptions clause. See OECD, "International Investment Agreements: A Survey of Environmental, Labour and Anti-corruption Issues" in *International Investment Law: Understanding Concepts and Tracking Innovations* (Paris: OECD, 2008) at 181.

25 See e.g. Japan-Singapore FTA, *supra* note 22 at art 83; *Comprehensive Economic Cooperation Agreement between the Republic of India and the Republic of Singapore*, online: Export Inspection Council <http://www.eicindia.org/eic/certificates/FTA_CECA_Agreement.pdf> at art 6.11; Japan-Malaysia FTA, *supra* note 22 at art 10.

Another approach has been to incorporate article XIV GATS in relation to investments, as was done in the Panama-Taiwan and Korea-Singapore FTAs.[26] The 2008 China-New Zealand FTA incorporates article XX GATT and article XIV GATS.[27] Furthermore, article 17 of the 2009 ASEAN Comprehensive Investment Agreement contains a general exceptions provision modeled on article XX GATT. Another regional agreement, the Investment Agreement for the COMESA Common Investment Area, also provides for GATT-like general exceptions.[28]

Although the inclusion of general exceptions in IIAs remains fairly limited, three general points can be made about the treaty practice to date. First, although there are differences between the drafting of the various exceptions, the basic structure of general exceptions clauses is based on article XX GATT. In common with article XX GATT, there is an enumeration of a series of legitimate objectives for which the measure in question must be "necessary" or to which it must be "relat[ed]." There are further requirements in the introductory clause or *chapeau* requiring the measure not be applied arbitrarily, discriminatorily or as a disguised restriction on investment. In light of the strong textual affinities between this type of general exception and article XX GATT, there is a strong argument that IIA tribunals should seek guidance from WTO general exceptions jurisprudence in interpreting IIA general exceptions.[29]

---

26 *Free Trade Agreement between the Republic of China and the Republic of Panama*, online: SICE <http://www.sice.oas.org/trade/panrc/panrc_e.asp> at art 20.02(02); *Free Trade Agreement between the Government of the Republic of Korea and the Government of the Republic of Singapore*, online: CommonLii <http://www.commonlii.org/sg/other/treaties/2005/2/KSFTA_Agreement.html> at art 21.2; see also *Malaysia-New Zealand Free Trade Agreement*, online: MFAT New Zealand <http://mfat.govt.nz/downloads/trade-agreement/malaysia/mnzfta-text-of-agreement.pdf> at art 17.1.

27 *Free Trade Agreement Between the Government of New Zealand and the Government of the People's Republic of China*, online: Chinafta <http://www.chinafta.govt.nz/1-The-agreement/2-Text-of-the-agreement/0-downloads/NZ-ChinaFTA-Agreement-text.pdf> at art 200(1) ("1. For the purposes of this Agreement, Article XX of GATT 1994 and its interpretative notes and Article XIV of GATS (including its footnotes) are incorporated into and made part of this Agreement, mutatis mutandis.")

28 See Common Market for Eastern and Southern Africa (COMESA) at art 22.

29 IIA tribunals have been reluctant to rely on WTO jurisprudence in interpreting specific investment obligations, such as national treatment. See *Methanex Corporation v United States of America*, Final Award of the Tribunal on Jurisdiction and Merits, UNCITRAL (August 3, 2005) at Part IV, ch B. But see *Continental Casualty Co v Argentina*, Award, ICSID Case No. ARB/03/9 (September 5, 2008). On the use of WTO jurisprudence to interpret national treatment obligations in IIAs, see Jürgen Kurtz, "The Use and Abuse of WTO Law in Investor-State Arbitration: Competition and its Discontents" (2009) 20 EJIL 749.

Secondly, a number of states that have included general exceptions clauses in their IIAs, including Australia, Canada, China, India, Korea, Japan and Singapore, have inconsistent IIA treaty practice.[30] Some of their IIAs contain general exceptions and others do not. This leads to significant interpretative uncertainty—did these states intend to undertake significantly different obligations in their contemporaneously signed IIAs?[31]

Thirdly, some general exceptions clauses incorporate GATS article XIV, *mutatis mutandis*. Notably, unlike GATT (article XX(g)), GATS does not include an express exception for conservation of natural resources. The absence of an exception for the conservation of natural resources in GATS might be explained by the fact that GATS obligations focus on market access (liberalization) and non-discrimination (national and MFN treatment) for foreign service providers.[32] In principle, it would appear unlikely that a state would need to discriminate between service providers on the basis of nationality to allow for the conservation of natural resources and, accordingly, unlike GATT article XX, GATS article XIV does not include this express exception. However, given the scope of investment protections and the fact that investment physically located within the host state is likely to have a greater environmental impact (and a significant amount of FDI occurs in the natural resource sector), article XX-like exceptions may be better suited for the investment context. The absence of a conservation exception in GATS might explain why in the Thailand-Australia FTA, for the purposes of the investment chapter, article XIV GATS, and article XX (e)–(g) GATT, are incorporated *mutatis mutandis*.[33]

The uncertain consequences of including general exceptions

States that have included general exceptions in IIAs appear to have done so to ensure that they can achieve specific policy objectives without

30 Notably, although the majority of Canada's FIPAs have general exceptions, the NAFTA general exception provision (art 2101) does not apply to the investment chapter (Chapter Eleven).
31 Where a state has inconsistent IIA treaty practice, it would seem unlikely that it intended to undertake radically different investment protection in two contemporaneous treaties. On the other hand, this might be the case if the state adopts a binary investment protection policy: entering highly protective treaties with host states in which its nationals have significant investment (the offensive interest) and less-protective treaties where it is a host state itself (the defensive interest).
32 On GATS obligations and GATS as an instrument of investment liberalization, see Newcombe and Paradell, *supra* note 6 at §3.14.
33 See *Thailand-Australia Free Trade Agreement*, online: DFAIT <http://www.dfat.gov.au/fta/tafta/tafta_toc.html> at art 1601.

breaching IIA obligations.[34] It is unclear, however, whether the inclusion of general exceptions is premised on the assumption that, absent the general exception, state responsibility would arise for breach of IIA obligations because the scope of investment obligations is otherwise too broad, or whether general exceptions are an example of an abundance of caution—a "belt and suspenders" approach to treaty drafting in light of uncertainty over the scope of investment protection standards.

Whatever the reasons may be for the inclusion of general exceptions, there remains significant uncertainty as to how IIA investor-state tribunals will interpret them. This uncertainty arises in part because the vast majority of IIAs do not contain general exceptions and IIA jurisprudence on core investment treatment obligations, including national treatment, fair and equitable treatment and expropriation, has already recognized that many forms of state regulation aimed at the type of public policy objectives identified in general exceptions do not breach IIA obligations. Indeed, in the absence of express general exceptions to IIA obligations, tribunals have arguably implied them by setting limits on the scope of IIA obligations (see below). In other words, tribunals in interpreting IIA obligations have already engaged in balancing at the level of the primary obligation.

The interpretation of GATT- and GATS-like general exceptions in IIAs raises many interpretative issues that to date have not been addressed in IIA jurisprudence. Although the interpretation of any specific treaty must be guided by the specific treaty text, it is possible to identify three different ways that IIA tribunals may in the future approach the interpretation of general exceptions.

The first approach would be that general exceptions are intended to provide greater regulatory flexibility to host states in pursuing the specific legitimate objectives established in the exceptions. Since the inclusion of GATT- and GATS-like general exceptions in IIAs is quite exceptional compared to the standard treaty practice, an *effet utile*

---

34 For example, the description of the 2004 Canadian Model FIPA states that: "General exceptions to the disciplines of the Agreement are included in order to meet several important policy goals: the protection of human, animal or plant life or health, as well as the conservation of living or non-living exhaustible resources; to ensure that Parties may adopt or maintain reasonable measures for prudential purposes; to guarantee a Party's ability to protect information related to, or to take measures necessary to protect, its essential security interests; and to exclude cultural industries from the provisions of the Agreement." DFAIT, Canada's Foreign Investment Promotion and Protection Agreements (FIPAs) Negotiating Programme, online: < http://www.international.gc.ca/trade-agreements-accords-commerciaux/agr-acc/ fipa-apie/what_fipa.aspx?lang=en&menu_id-45&menu=R#structure>.

interpretation might suggest that the parties intended to provide the host greater regulatory flexibility and a corresponding lower level of investment protection than that provided by other IIAs without general exceptions.

The second approach would be to interpret general exceptions clauses as an express reflection of the balancing of public and private interest inherent in existing IIA jurisprudence. For example, IIA national treatment jurisprudence recognizes that states can differentiate between investments on the basis of rational (and non-protectionist) policy objectives.[35] On this view, general exceptions provide an IIA tribunal explicit guidance on how to balance investment protection obligations with legitimate objectives. Further, general exceptions might be seen as an insurance policy or control mechanism to address the risk of a "runaway" tribunal making overreaching and unwarranted interpretations of IIA obligations. Since investor-state arbitration awards can only be reviewed on very limited grounds (not including a mere error of law), the inclusion of general exceptions might be viewed as serving as an important check against a tribunal interpreting an investment obligation in an unexpected and expansive manner. Although a tribunal might be able to distinguish or otherwise ignore jurisprudence that implies limits or exceptions to IIA obligations, a tribunal faced with an express general exception must interpret it in accordance with the rules of treaty interpretation. Hence, general exceptions may reflect a cautionary approach, mitigating the risk of overly broad interpretations of IIA obligations in awards that are not subject to appellate review.

Thirdly, general exceptions might be interpreted restrictively, i.e. as providing even less regulatory flexibility to host states.[36] In interpreting IIA obligations, tribunals have generally highlighted the investment promotion and protection purposes of IIAs, as reflected in IIA titles and preambles.[37] Most tribunals have construed IIA exceptions quite narrowly.[38] One of the reasons that the International Institute for

---

35 See discussion below of national treatment.

36 See Céline Lévesque, "Influences on the Canadian FIPA Model and US Model BIT: NAFTA Chapter 11 and Beyond" (2006) 44 Can YB of Int'l Law 249 at 271–7.

37 *Siemens A.G. v The Argentine Republic*, Decision of Jurisdiction, ICSID Case No. ARB/02/8 (August 3, 2004) at para 81. See also *Compañiá de Aguas del Aconquija S.A. and Vivendi Universal S.A. v The Argentine Republic*, Award, ICSID Case No. ARB/97/3 (August 20, 2007) at para 7.4.4; *SGS Société Générale de Surveillance S.A. v Republic of the Philippines*, Decision of the Tribunal on Objections to Jurisdiction, ICSID Case No. ARB/02/6 (January 29, 2004) at para 116.

38 See *Canfor Corporation v United States of America* and *Terminal Forest Products Ltd v United States of America*, Decision on Preliminary Question, UNCITRAL (June 6,

Sustainable Development did not include an article XX-like general exception in its *Model International Investment Agreement for Sustainable Development* appears to have been the concern that, based on GATT article XX jurisprudence, general exceptions in IIAs may be interpreted too narrowly, resulting in a limitation, rather than a widening, of policy space.[39] One risk with the use of general exceptions is that, since they provide a closed list of legitimate policy objectives, their inclusion might have the unintended consequence of limiting the range of legitimate objectives available to the state (*expressio unius est exclusio alterius*). In other words, IIA tribunals might interpret general exceptions as providing states less regulatory flexibility, rather than more. For example, article X of the Canadian Model FIPA only refers to measures necessary "to protect human, animal or plant life or health." The exception does not include a range of other legitimate objectives such as "safety," "public morals," and "consumer protection." This might suggest that there is less regulatory space for these types of measures (which do not benefit from an express exception) compared to measures where the objective is specifically identified in the general exception.

Further interpretative questions arise with respect to the interaction between general exceptions and specific investment obligations. A brief consideration of the national treatment, minimum standard of treatment and expropriation obligations in IIAs highlights these difficulties.

In the case of national treatment, a number of tribunals have essentially read-in GATT article XX-like general exceptions to the national treatment obligation. They have done so, however, without being constrained by a GATT article XX-like closed list of exceptions. This is the case in particular under the NAFTA, where the general exceptions clause does not apply to Chapter 11 (Investment).[40]

In determining whether investments are in like circumstances, NAFTA tribunals have found that investments are not in "like circumstances" when there is a legitimate policy rationale, not motivated by protectionism, for differentiating between investments.[41] However,

2006) at para 187 and *Enron Corpn and Ponderosa Assets, L.P. v Argentine Republic*, Award, ICSID Case No. ARB/01/3 (May 22, 2007) at para 331.

39 See Aaron Cosbey, "The Road to Hell? Investor Protections in NAFTA's Chapter 11" in Lyuba Zarsky (ed), *International Investment for Sustainable Development: Balancing Rights and Rewards* (London: Sterling, VA: Earthscan, 2005).

40 See *North American Free Trade Agreement Between the Government of Canada, the Government of Mexico and the Government of the United States*, December 17, 1992, Can TS 1994 No. 2, 32 ILM 289 (entered into force January 1, 1994) at art 2101.

41 See *Pope & Talbot Inc v The Government of Canada*, Award on the Merits of Phase 2, UNCITRAL (April 10, 2001) [*Pope and Talbot*] at paras 78–9; *GAMI Investments, Inc*

NAFTA jurisprudence does not provide clear guidance on what amounts to a legitimate policy rationale and the standards by which legitimate policy rationales will be assessed. In *Pope & Talbot v Canada*, the tribunal referred to the requirement that there be a:

> reasonable nexus to rational government policies that (1) do not distinguish, on their face or *de facto*, between foreign-owned and domestic companies, and (2) do not otherwise unduly undermine the investment liberalizing objectives of NAFTA.[42]

In *GAMI v Mexico*, the tribunal took a similar view and stated that the differential treatment must be "plausibly connected with a legitimate goal of policy . . .. and . . . applied neither in a discriminatory manner nor as a disguised barrier to equal opportunity."[43] In *S.D. Myers v Canada*, the tribunal found that even if the NAFTA investment chapter had article XX-like general exceptions, the ban on polychlorinated biphenyl (PCB) exports could not be justified under the *chapeau* of article XX, given the tribunal's finding that the ban was motivated by protectionism of the domestic PCB industry.[44] The concurring opinion expressly noted that "like circumstances" requires the same kind of analysis as article XX GATT.[45]

DiMascio and Pauwelyn note in their article on non-discrimination obligations in trade and investment treaties that,[46] unlike GATT, IIAs do not have closed lists of exceptions and do not impose a strict necessity test:

> Generally, tribunals were open to any legitimate policy objective, in contrast to the closed list of policy exceptions in GATT Article XX. Finally, tribunals have begun to address the appropriate standard of

v The Government of the United Mexican States, Final Award, UNCITRAL (November 15, 2004) [*GAMI*] at para 114.

42 *Pope and Talbot, supra* note 41 at para 78. The *Pope and Talbot* tribunal found that the exclusion of some provinces and different quota provisions for new entrants had a reasonable nexus with a rational policy and were not discriminatory. See paras 88 and 93.

43 *GAMI, supra* note 41, at para 114 (ensuring that the sugar industry was in the hands of solvent enterprises).

44 *S.D. Myers, Inc v Government of Canada*, Partial Award, UNCITRAL (November 13, 2000) at para 298.

45 *S.D. Myers, Inc v Government of Canada*, Separate Concurring Opinion, UNCITRAL (November 13, 2000) at para 129.

46 Nicholas DiMascio and Joost Pauwelyn, "Nondiscrimination in Trade and Investment Treaties: Worlds Apart or Two Sides of the Same Coin" (2008) 102 AJIL 48.

review for these policies. The majority of tribunals have once again taken a considerably softer approach than the "necessity test" under many GATT Article XX exceptions, looking only for a "reasonable" or "rational" nexus between the measure and the policy pursued.[47]

In their view, the absence of express exceptions allows tribunals to consider an unlimited list of legitimate government concerns:

> In the investment context, the broad reference to investors "in like circumstances" has consistently enabled tribunals to balance investor interests with an unlimited list of legitimate government concerns— a list far *broader* than the exceptions in GATT Article XX.[48]

This line of argument suggests that inclusion of general exceptions might result in a stricter review of host state measures—a more restrictive approach than is present in the current national treatment jurisprudence.[49]

The interpretation of general exceptions raises particularly difficult issues in relation to minimum standards of treatment provisions. With respect to breaches of minimum standards of treatment, including fair and equitable treatment, it is unclear in what circumstances general exceptions would or *could* apply. On its face, if state conduct breaches the minimum standard of treatment, then it is unlikely that the state would be able to meet the threshold for justifying the conduct under the general exception. The conduct in question would have to (i) be necessary to meet one of the enumerated exceptions (there was no other alternative that would reasonably meet the policy objective); (ii) not have been applied in a manner that would constitute arbitrary or unjustifiable discrimination; and (iii) not constitute a disguised restriction on international investment. If a measure could be justified under the stringent requirements of a general exception provision, it is difficult to envisage a situation in which it would have violated minimum standards of treatment in the first place. At a conceptual level, it is difficult to see the utility of having a general exception to a minimum standard of treatment, which is intended to be an absolute baseline standard of protection.

Finally, with respect to expropriation, even if a measure (such as the creation of a park) meets the requirements of the general exception, if an

---

47 *Ibid* at 77.
48 *Ibid* at 82–3.
49 It is important to note that it is not clear that all IIA tribunals will take the same approach as NAFTA tribunals and that there are differences in the drafting of national treatment provisions.

investment has been expropriated, why should compensation not be payable? It would be surprising if, by effect of general exceptions, parties to IIAs intended to provide less protection to foreign investors than that accorded under customary international law. The negotiations on the draft Multilateral Agreement on Investment provide support for the view that a general exception is not intended to exclude the obligation to pay compensation: article VI, General Exceptions of the MAI negotiating text, provides that it does not apply to article IV, 2 and 3 (Expropriation and compensation and protection from strife). The commentary on the text notes that the "majority view was that the MAI should provide an absolute guarantee that an investor will be compensated for an expropriated investment."[50] It should also be noted that the general exceptions in the ECT do not apply to expropriation and compensation for losses.[51]

Conclusion

The problem of applying general exceptions to minimum standards of treatment (including the requirement to pay compensation in the event of expropriation) is symptomatic of the difficulty of transplanting a clause from a trade treaty into an investment protection treaty with a very different purpose and legal structure.[52] The foreign investor who has invested in an energy infrastructure project on the basis of promised returns over a 30-year period is in a very different situation from a trader whose goods cannot access a foreign market because of the implementation of protectionist policies. The trade-in-goods regime seeks to discipline protectionist measures and ensures that states do not cheat on their tariff bargains. It uses state-to-state dispute settlement, the aim of which

---

50 Commentary to the MAI Negotiating Text, online: OECD <www1.oecd.org/daf/mai/pdf/ng/ng988r1e.pdf>.
51 See *Energy Charter Treaty*, December 17, 1994, 2080 UNTS 36116, 34 ILM 360 at art 24(2).
52 See José Enrique Alvarez and Tegan Brink, "Revisiting the Necessity Defense" (2011–12) *Yearbook of International Investment Law and Policy* (forthcoming), online <http://www.iilj.org/publications/documents/2010–3.Alvarez-Brink.pdf>. As noted in Alvarez and Brink's critique of the use of art XX jurisprudence by the *Continental Casualty* tribunal, GATT's primary purposes are the reduction of tariffs and other barriers to trade and the elimination of discriminatory (protectionist) treatment. In contrast, foreign investment law provides minimum standards of protection to foreign investors, who are vulnerable to opportunistic and arbitrary state conduct once they have made an investment. International trade and investment law deal with very different types of commitment problems.

is for the state to bring its measures into compliance with its trade obligations. It does not provide compensation to the trader who has lost sales as a result of the inconsistent trade measures. In contrast, the very fact that foreign investors and investments are located within the jurisdiction of a foreign state and, accordingly, are subject to the full panoply of state jurisdiction and conduct gives rise to unique vulnerabilities. Minimum standards of treatment in customary international law and, now, the minimum standards of treatment provided by IIAs, provide investors minimum guarantees of treatment in light of these vulnerabilities.[53]

Rather than addressing concerns about the scope of IIA protections by importing a treaty clause developed and used in a very different institutional context, it is preferable to address concerns about balancing of private and public rights directly by clarifying the scope of the primary obligations (i.e. fair and equitable treatment or expropriation). Some tribunals have engaged in forms of proportionality balancing in their interpretation of primary obligations.[54] This approach should be encouraged. States, for their part, are also introducing forms of proportionality balancing at the level of the primary obligations. This approach is evident in how the Canadian and American models address the meaning and scope of expropriation. The interpretative annexes on expropriation included in both model treaties provide for a form of proportionality analysis.[55] Obligation-specific clarification of exceptions provides more useful guidance to tribunals and more predictability in the law in the long term compared to broad general exceptions.

---

53 See Newcombe and Paradell, *supra* note 6 at ch 6.

54 See e.g. *EDF (Services) Ltd v Romania*, Award, ICSID Case No. ARB/05/13 (8 October 2009) at paras 286, 301; *Joseph Charles Lemire v Ukraine*, Decision on Jurisdiction and Liability, ICSID Case No. ARB/06/18 (January 14, 2010) at para 285. On proportionality analysis under IIAs, see Alec Stone Sweet and Jud Mathews, *supra* note 15; Benedict Kingsbury and Stephen W. Schill, "Investor-State Arbitration as Governance: Fair and Equitable Treatment, Proportionality and the Emerging Global Administrative Law" (September 2, 2009), NYU School of Law, Public Law Research Paper No. 09–46. Available at SSRN: <http://ssrn.com/abstract=1466980>; J Krommendijk and Dr John Morij, "'Proportional' by What Measure(s)? Balancing Investor Interests and Human Rights by Way of Applying the Proportionality Principle in Investor-State Arbitration" in Pierre-Marie Dupuy et al (eds), *Human Rights in International Investment Law and Arbitration* (Oxford: Oxford University Press, 2009); Roland Kläger, *'Fair and Equitable Treatment' in International Investment Law* (Cambridge: Cambridge University Press, 2011) at 236–45.

55 See 2004 Canadian Model FIPA (online: <http://www.international.gc.ca/trade-agreements-accords-commerciaux/assets/pdfs/2004-FIPA-model-en.pdf>) at Annex B.13(1); US Model BIT (2004) (online: <http://www.state.gov/documents/organization/117601.pdf>) at Annex B.

16 Sustainable development and IIAs: from objective to practice

Markus W. Gehring and *Avidan Kent***

Introduction

The concept of "sustainable development" has been recognized by the world's nations in a line of international documents and global events.[1] While many have attempted to define this term,[2] perhaps the most commonly accepted definition of "sustainable development" is the one proposed almost 25 years ago by the Brundlant Report, in which it was described as "[D]evelopment that meets the needs of the present without compromising the ability of future generations to meet their own needs."[3] In essence, the ultimate objective of sustainable development is the integration of economic development with environmental protection and social well-being.[4] Sir Elihu Lauterpacht has recently explained in this respect: "Sustainable development, therefore, represents a commitment to a different kind of economic development, one that focuses on achieving important improvements in the opportunities and quality of life without jeopardizing the interests of future generations."[5]

* Associate Professor, Faculty of Law, Civil Law Section, University of Ottawa. With special thanks to Erika Arban and Misha Benjamin for invaluable research assistance.
** PhD Candidate, Cambridge University.
 1 See amongst others, *The Rio Declaration on Environment and Development*, June 3–14, 1992, online: UNEP <http://www.unep.org/Documents.Multilingual/Default.asp?documentid=78&articleid=1163>; *Johannesburg Declaration on Sustainable Development*, UN Doc A/CONF/199/20 (2002); *Doha Ministerial Declaration*, Ministerial Conference, Fourth Session, November 14, 2001, WTO Doc WT/MIN(01)/DEC/W/1. For a more detailed review, see Marie-Claire Cordonier Segger and Ashfaq Khalfan, *Sustainable Development Law: Principles, Practices & Prospects* (Oxford: Oxford University Press, 2004) [Cordonier Segger and Khalfan].
 2 *Ibid* at 3–4.
 3 Gro Harlem Brundtland et al, *Our Common Future: World Commission on Environment and Development* (Oxford: Oxford University Press, 1987).
 4 Cordonier Segger and Khalfan, *supra* note 1 at 103.
 5 Sir Elihu Lauterpacht, "Foreword" in Marie-Claire Cordonier Segger, Markus W. Gehring and Andrew Newcombe (eds), *Sustainable Development in World Investment*

On the other hand, FDI, as defined by the OECD, "reflects the object-ive of establishing a lasting interest by a resident enterprise in one econ-omy (direct investor) in an enterprise (direct investment enterprise) that is resident in an economy other than that of the direct investor."[6] In economic terms, it is often assumed that these investments include common features such as the transfer of funds, long-termed activity, participation, at least to some extent, of the investor in the management of the project, and business risk.[7] IIAs are one of the means used for the promotion of FDI. These treaties are designed to provide security and certainty for foreign investors, in order to promote FDI, with the ultim-ate goal of development.

The relationship between FDI and sustainable development is two-sided. While FDI can support sustainable development, sustainable development can also support the interests of Transnational Corpora-tions. The great economic potential embedded in the prospect of a "green economy" is indeed noticeable.[8] For example, in the context of climate change, according to some estimation the demand for emis-sion credits may reach US$100 billion by 2050.[9] An increase in the demand for low-carbon technologies is therefore expected, resulting in substantial economic gains for the owners of these technologies. Moreover, ignoring sustainable development issues can be bad for businesses. For example, as identified by the Stern Report, the effects of climate change are expected to damage economic growth and disrupt the economy "on a scale similar to those associated with the great wars and the economic depression of the first half of the 20th century."[10]

Law (Netherlands: Kluwer Law International, 2010) [Cordonier Segger, Gehring and Newcombe].

6 Secretary-General of the OECD, *OECD Benchmark Definition of Foreign Direct Investment*, 4th edn (Paris: OECD, 2008), online: OECD <http://www.oecd.org/dataoecd/26/50/40193734.pdf> at para 117 [OECD Benchmark Definition of Foreign Direct Invest-ment].

7 Rudolf Dolzer and Christoph Schreuer, *Principles of International Investment Law* (Oxford: Oxford University Press, 2008) at 60 [Dolzer and Schreuer].

8 See e.g. Céline Kauffmann and Cristina Tébar Less, *Transition to a Low-carbon Economy: Public Goals and Corporate Practices* (Paris: OECD, 2010) online: OECD <http://www.oecd.org/dataoecd/40/52/45513642.pdf>"] at paras 105–9 [OECD, "Transition to a low-carbon economy"].

9 UNFCCC, *Investment and Financial Flows to Address Climate Change* (2007), online: UNFCCC <http://unfccc.int/cooperation_and_support/financial_mechanism/items/4053.php> at para 637 [UNFCCC 2007].

10 Nicholas Stern, "The Stern Review on the Economics of Climate Change", online: National Archive <http://webarchive.nationalarchives.gov.uk/+/http://www.hm-treasury.gov.uk/stern_review_report.htm> at ii [The Stern Review].

As explained in this chapter, the integration of sustainable development in IIAs can take place in several ways. First, sustainable development objectives can be integrated in the process of negotiations before the conclusion of IIAs. For example, impact assessment mechanisms can assist decision-makers in understanding the impact that an investment treaty may have on sustainable development objectives. Secondly, sustainable development can be integrated within the procedural dimensions of IIAs' dispute settlement mechanisms. For example, the principle of public participation, as phrased by the International Law Association's *New Delhi Declaration of Principles of International Law Relating to Sustainable Development*,[11] can be integrated through the inclusion of the public's right to submit *amicus curiae* briefs in investment disputes, or by allowing free access to documents.[12] Lastly, sustainable development can be integrated within the substantive provisions of IIAs. For example, the substantive rules of IIAs can be phrased in a manner that does not restrict states from enacting environmental or social laws. Moreover, IIAs can also be designed so as to actively promote sustainable investment. This can be achieved *inter alia* by creating a secured business environment for these investments.

This chapter explains how sustainable development objectives can be integrated into international investment law. Part I considers the procedural dimension, with a focus on impact assessments of IIAs. Part II analyzes the substantive dimension including the various tools available to states in order to integrate sustainable development goals into their IIAs. Challenges faced by policy-makers when making policy choices in this field are highlighted throughout.

Impact assessments as a new procedural dimension of IIAs[13]

FDI can bring social, economic and environmental benefits to countries. Indeed, FDIs have a positive impact on a variety of issues such as income growth, modernization, employment and productivity.[14] Yet without

---

11 International Law Association, *New Delhi Declaration of Principles of International Law Relating to Sustainable Development* (2002) 49(2) Netherlands International Law Review 299 [*New Delhi Declaration*].

12 See Céline Lévesque and Andrew Newcombe in ch 2 of this book on the progress the United States and Canada have made in terms of transparency and openness.

13 See Markus W. Gehring, "Impact Assessments of Investment Treaties" in Cordonier Segger, Gehring and Newcombe, *supra* note 5 at 149 [Gehring].

14 OECD, Committee on International Investment and Multinational Enterprises, *Foreign Direct Investment for Development: Maximising Benefits, Minimising Costs* (Paris: OECD, 2002) online: <http://www.oecd.org/dataoecd/47/51/1959815.pdf> [OECD, "FDI for development"].

careful crafting, IIAs can frustrate sustainable development objectives and create potential conflicts between the commercial, social and environmental goals.[15] Conversely, well-drafted agreements can achieve more than their inherent goals. For example, trade and investment agreements can support and promote climate change, or poverty eradication objectives. One way to avoid potential conflicts on the one hand, and promote possible synergies on the other, is the use of impact assessment mechanisms.[16]

Impact assessments are comprehensive studies in which the future impact of negotiated agreements is assessed. In the past, the focus of these mechanisms was limited to the environmental effects of trade agreements. These assessments are known as Environmental Impact Assessments ("EIAs"). Nowadays, however, the scope of impact assessments is increasingly expanding. For example, some impact assessments are specifically designed to review the impact of international trade or foreign investments on human rights.[17]

More widely, and in accordance with the "holistic" concept of sustainable development,[18] some impact assessment mechanisms attempt to provide a fuller picture, by assessing the economic, environmental and social implications of investment and trade agreements. For example, the EU Commission "Handbook" on this topic proposes the examination of energy use, poverty, gender equality, external debt, public health, living conditions, access to education, labor standards, unemployment and more.[19] These wider assessments are known as Sustainability Impact Assessments ("SIAs").

15 For a review of the potential conflicts, see Cordonier Segger, Gehring and Newcombe, *supra* note 5.

16 For a more detailed review of this topic, see Gehring, *supra* note 13.

17 For a detailed review, see James Harrison and Alessa Goller, "Trade and Human Rights: What Does 'Impact Assessment' Have to Offer?" (2008) 8(4) *Human Rights Law Review* 587. An example of impact assessment for foreign investment, see Rights & Democracy, *Human Right Impact Assessments for Foreign Investment Projects: Learning from Community Experience in the Philippines, Tibet, the Democratic Republic of Congo, Argentina, and Peru* (Montreal: Rights & Democracy, 2007), online: Rights & Democracy <http://www.dd-rd.ca/site/_PDF/publications/globalization/hria/full%20 report_may_2007.pdf> [Rights & Democracy].

18 The EU Commission's 'Impact Assessment Guidelines' indeed mentions that one of the objectives of impact assessments, is to ensure coherence and consistency with the EU's sustainable development strategies. See EC, Commission, *Impact Assessment Guidelines,* online: EU <http://ec.europa.eu/governance/impact/commission_ guidelines/docs/iag_2009_en.pdf> at 6 [EU Impact Assessment Guidelines].

19 EC, *External Trade: Handbook for Sustainability Impact Assessment* (2006), online: EU Commission <http://trade.ec.europa.eu/doclib/docs/2006/march/tradoc_127974. pdf> at 52–6 [EU Handbook for Sustainability Impact Assessment].

Impact assessment mechanisms can be found both at the domestic and international level. At the national level, domestic environmental and planning laws require the impact assessment of major projects. At the international level, some trade and investment negotiations include requirements for assessing the possible impact that negotiated agreements may have on sustainable development. For example, as part of the EU-Canada negotiations of a Comprehensive Economic and Trade Agreement ("CETA"), SIAs were prepared in order to assess the impact of both international trade and investment on economic, social, and environmental issues.[20]

SIAs can promote sustainable development goals in several ways. When applied to foreign investments SIAs allow negotiators to identify aspects of agreements that require mitigation or enhancement measures, in order to derive the most benefits from FDI.[21] By assessing economic, environmental and social impacts of potential measures, decision-makers have a better idea of the advantages and disadvantages of each proposal. SIAs allow decision-makers to fully understand the synergies between the different fields, and how one policy can support another. Alternatively, by addressing more than just environmental or economic aspects, SIAs equip decision-makers with better tools to perform the trade-offs that are necessary in places where the promotion of one policy inherently frustrates the goals of another. Lastly, where the public is effectively invited to take part in this process, SIAs also increase the democratic legitimacy of negotiated agreements.

Substantive dimension: options to improve IIAs

The effects of FDIs, as mentioned before, are complex and multi-faceted. Their impact touches such matters as trade, services, intellectual property, industrial policies, labor issues, movement of personnel and environmental concerns. Furthermore, FDIs can both promote and frustrate sustainable development goals. The challenge faced by treaty negotiators, therefore, is to balance these interests in order to maximize the potential benefits of FDIs. Treaty negotiators, for example, must design tools that will promote sustainable investments by providing them with a secure and stable business environment. On the other hand, they also

---

20 See EC, *A Trade SIA Relating to the Negotiation of a Comprehensive* Economic *and Trade Agreement (CETA) Between the EU and Canada*, online: <http://www.eucanada-sia.org/docs/EU-Canada_SIA_Final_Report.pdf> [EU-Canada SIA]. On investment, see *ibid* at 337.

21 For a detailed review of SIAs, see Gehring, *supra* note 13 at 145.

need to secure ample regulatory flexibility so that states can reform and adapt their policies accordingly.

Although increasing,[22] the explicit presence of sustainable development objectives in investment treaties remains relatively low.[23] The following section discusses some of the examples offered by the substantive rules of IIAs in order to address sustainable development objectives. It should be mentioned that this is not an exhaustive list of possible solutions. In fact, the complex nature of sustainable development requires many different approaches for the numerous issues embedded in this concept. Indeed, what is right for climate change will not necessarily work for smoking prevention, or bio-diversity. However, the following can be used as a starting point from which more complex solutions can be developed.

Preambular language

One solution adopted by states is the inclusion of references to sustainable development objectives in the preambles of IIAs. According to article 31(2) of the Vienna Convention, the context and purpose of a treaty is to be derived *inter alia* from the treaty's preamble.[24] In light of the different interpretations given to legal terms such as "expropriation," "legitimate expectations" and "like-circumstances," as well as the effects these can have on sustainable development objectives,[25] it is clear that preambular language can fulfill a significant role.[26]

Preambular references can be made either directly to the concept of sustainable development as a whole, or to a specific issue such as climate change, labor standards, health, or human rights. There are several ways in which states refer to sustainable development objectives in their

22 Kathryn Gordon and Joachim Pohl, "Environmental Concerns in International Investment Agreements: A Survey" (2011) OECD Working Papers on International Investment, No. 2011/1, online: OECD <http://www.oecd.org/dataoecd/50/12/48083618.pdf> at 8 [Gordon and Pohl].

23 See Kathryn Gordon, "International Investment Agreements: A Survey of Environmental, Labour and Anti-corruption Issues" in OECD, *International Investment Law: Understanding Concepts and Tracking Innovations* (Paris: OECD, 2008), online: OECD <www.oecd.org/dataoecd/3/5/40471550.pdf> at Annex 3.A1 [Gordon].

24 Vienna Convention on the Law of Treaties, May 23, 1969, 1155 UNTS 1980 at art 31(2) [*Vienna Convention*].

25 For a review of these terms and their relations to sustainable development, see Cordonier Segger, Gehring and Newcombe, *supra* note 5.

26 Marie-Claire Cordonier Segger and Andrew Newcombe, "An Integrated Agenda for Sustainable Development in International Investment Law" in Cordonier Segger, Gehring and Newcombe, *supra* note 5 at 126.

preambles. First, states can declare sustainable development to be a specific objective of the treaty. For example, the Canadian Model FIPA states in its preamble that:

> the promotion and the protection of investments of investors of one Party in the territory of the other Party will be conductive to the stimulation of mutually beneficial business activity, to the development of economic cooperation between them and to the promotion of sustainable development.[27]

Similarly in the preamble to NAFTA, the parties express both their determination to promote sustainable development in general, and to address many of the topics that are included under this definition, such as environmental objectives and economic development.[28] Similar examples can be found in the preamble to the Common Market for Eastern and Southern Africa ("COMESA") investment agreement,[29] and several Canadian IIAs.[30] Some agreements also refer to more specific issues, such as the promotion of climate change objectives.[31]

A second type of preambular language, while not referring to sustainable development as a treaty objective *per se*, imposes upon parties to act in accordance with this principle. This type of language can be found in US IIAs. The preamble to the US-Rwanda BIT, for example, defines as treaty objectives *inter alia* the promotion of economic cooperation, the stimulation of private investment, and the creation of a stable business environment. It continues, however, by stating that the parties are: "*Desiring* to achieve these objectives in a manner consistent with the protection of health, safety, and the environment, and the promotion of internationally recognised labor rights."[32]

---

27 Canada model Foreign Investment Promotion and Protection Agreement (2004), online: DFAIT <www.international.gc.ca/trade-agreements-accords-commerciaux/agr-acc/fipa-apie/index.aspx> [Canada Model FIPA].

28 *North American Free Trade Agreement Between the Government of Canada, the Government of Mexico and the Government of the United States*, December 17, 1992, Can TS 1994 No. 2, 32 ILM 289 (entered into force in January 1, 1994) [NAFTA].

29 See *Treaty Establishing the Common Market for Eastern and Southern Africa* (November 5, 1993), 33 ILM 1067 [COMESA], *Investment Agreement for the COMESA Common Investment Area* (May 23, 2007) [COMESA Investment Agreement].

30 See e.g. the Canada-Peru FIPA (2006); Canada-Jordan FIPA (2009).

31 See e.g. *Agreement on Free Trade and Economic Partnership Between Japan and the Swiss Confederation*, February 17, 2009, online: MOFA <http://www.mofa.go.jp/region/europe/switzerland/epa0902/agreement.pdf>.

32 See US Model BIT (2004) see USTR online: <http://ustraderep.gov/assets/Trade_Sectors/Investment/Model_BIT/asset_upload_file847_6897.pdf>; US-Uruguay BIT (2006).

A third example of preambular language can be defined as "non-derogation" language. This language can be found in many of the IIAs signed by states such as Finland, the Netherlands, Japan and the United States.[33] According to these references, the treaty's objectives (often economic in nature) are to be achieved without relaxing regulatory standards in fields such as the environment, health or safety.

Lastly, on very rare occasions, references to sustainable development treaties can be found in the preamble to IIAs. Such references can be found in Model treaties, such as the International Institute for Sustainable Development's Model BIT, in which references to numerous treaties have been made,[34] or the 2007 Norway Model BIT (later abandoned),[35] in which a reference to the United Nations Charter and the Universal Declaration of Human Rights can be found. More relevant examples are found in the preamble to the Singapore-EFTA FTA (which includes investment protection), in which the parties reaffirm "their commitment to the principles set out in the United Nations Charter and the Universal Declaration of Human Rights,"[36] and in the Energy Charter Treaty, in which the parties are "[r]ecalling the United Nations Framework Convention on Climate Change, the Convention on Long-Range Transboundary Air Pollution and its protocols, and other international environmental agreements with energy-related aspects."[37]

Exceptions and reservations

Another way in which states attempt to promote sustainable development objectives is in the use of exceptions and reservations in IIAs. IIAs, like almost any international agreement, impose certain restrictions on a state's regulatory flexibility. Through the use of exceptions, states

---

33 See e.g. Finland-Ethiopia BIT (2006); Finland-Armenia BIT (2004); Netherlands-Suriname BIT (2005); Netherlands-Burundi BIT (2007); US-Mozambique BIT (1998); US-Jordan BIT (2003); US-Bahrain BIT (2001); Japan-Korea BIT (2002); Japan-Vietnam BIT (2003).

34 The IISD Model BIT includes *inter alia* references to the1992 Rio Declaration on Environment and Development; the 2002 World Summit on Sustainable Development and the Millennium Development Goals and the OECD Guidelines for Multinational Enterprises. See Howard Mann et al, "IISD Model International Agreement on Investment for Sustainable Development" (2005), online: ITA <http://italaw.com/documents/investment_model_int_agreement.pdf> [IISD Model BIT].

35 Norway Model BIT (2007), online: ASIL <http://www.asil.org/ilib080421.cfm#t1>.

36 *Agreement between the EFTA States and Singapore*, 26 June 2002, online: EFTA <http://www.efta.int/~/media/Documents/legal-texts/free-trade-relations/singapore/EFTA-Singapore%20Free%20Trade%20Agreement.pdf>.

37 *Energy Charter Treaty*, December 17, 1994, 2080 UNTS 36116, 34 ILM 360 [ECT].

ensure that their ability to regulate certain fields is not restricted by investment treaties.

Exceptions in IIAs appear in several forms. First, some IIAs include provisions that allow for treaty reservations, which are sector-specific carve-outs from treaty obligations. For example, Annex I of the Canada-Peru FIPA includes a list of sectors that are exempted from some of the IIAs' substantive rules.[38] Secondly, a few IIAs adopt general exceptions provisions, modeled on article XX of the GATT.[39] These general exceptions allow IIA parties to adopt or enforce measures relating to the protection of *inter alia* "human, animal, or plant life or health," or to the conservation of exhaustible natural resources. As in article XX of the GATT, these exceptions are subject to non-discriminatory treatment and should not be used as disguised restrictions for investment or trade.[40]

Thirdly, some IIAs include what has been described by some as "non-precluded measures" (or "NPMs").[41] NPMs are intended to exempt certain subject areas (e.g. public health, public security, morality) from the scope of the treaty, or from specific treaty obligations. For example, the protocol to the Germany-Bangladesh BIT states: "Measures that have to be taken for reasons of public security and order, public health or morality shall not be deemed 'treatment less favorable' within the meaning of Article 2."[42]

Exceptions, at least in theory, can promote sustainable development objectives. Their main contribution in this respect is by preventing conflicts between investment rules and sustainable development regulation. The recent Philip Morris claims made against Australia and Uruguay following their anti-smoking regulations (mainly plain-packaging rules) is an excellent example of a case in which general exceptions would have been helpful.[43] However, the authors believe that the use of

---

38 See e.g. Canada-Peru FIPA (2003) at art 9.
39 See *General Agreement on Tariffs and Trade*, October 30, 1947, 58 UNTS 187, Can TS 1947 No. 27 (entered into force January 1, 1948) at art XX.
40 See Andrew Newcombe in ch 15 of this book. See also Andrew Newcombe, "General Exceptions in International Investment Agreements" in Cordonier Segger, Gehring and Newcombe, *supra* note 5 at 358 [Newcombe "General Exceptions"].
41 William Burke-White and Andreas von Staden, "Investment Protection in Extraordinary Times: The Interpretation and Application of Non-Precluded Measures Provisions in Bilateral Investment Treaties" (2008) 48(2) Virginia Journal of International Law 307 [Burke-White and von Staden]; Newcombe "General Exceptions", *supra* note 40 at 358.
42 Germany-Bangladesh BIT (1981). See e.g. general exclusion in U.S.-Panama BIT (1982) at art X.
43 *FTR Holding S.A., Philip Morris Products S.A. and Abal Hermanos S.A. v Oriental Republic of Uruguay*, ICSID Case No. ARB/10/7. Regarding Philip Morris' claim

exceptions should be made with care. First, exceptions should not be overly inclusive. While they may be useful in certain cases of public health, human rights or treatment granted to indigenous people, they may actually frustrate the objectives in fields such as climate change where private investments are badly needed. Alternatively, as stated by Newcombe, in several cases tribunals have acknowledged that measures aimed at the protection of public policy objectives do not breach investment treaty obligations. Providing a closed list of protected areas will therefore simply limit the scope of what can be considered as *bona fide* public policy objectives.[44]

Language clarifications

A third tool available for states in order to promote sustainable development objectives can be described as "language clarification" provisions, or "improved definitions." The field of international investment law relies on several standards of protection, most notably "fair and equitable treatment," non-discriminatory treatment (including "national treatment" and "most-favored nation treatment"), and protection from unlawful expropriation. The definition of each of these standards includes many legal tests, most of which rely on the interpretation of legal terms. For example, the "national treatment" standard relies on arbitrators' interpretation of what may constitute "like-circumstances." Similarly, the "fair and equitable treatment" standard relies on, among other things, the tribunal's interpretation of what investors may "legitimately expect" when making their investment. Other questions that tribunals dispute include the relevance of the purpose of the measure in the expropriation analysis.

All of these questions, and the manner in which tribunals choose to answer them, can affect sustainable development.[45] For example, by deciding that carbon-footprints are irrelevant for what may constitute "like-circumstances," states' attempts to differentiate between low-carbon and carbon-intensive producers (e.g. by imposing carbon taxes)

---

against Australia, see Luke E. Peterson, "Philip Morris puts Australia on notice of treaty claim, but both parties decline to release documents; claim over tobacco regulation would be third treaty-based investor-state claim filed by Philip Morris since 2010", *IA Reporter*, June 30, 2011, online: IAReporter <http://www.iareporter.com/articles/20110630_5>.

44 See Newcombe, ch 15 of this book. See also Newcombe, "General Exceptions", *supra* note 40 at 357–8.

45 For a detailed review of all the potential issues that may arise out of these questions, see Cordonier Segger, Gehring and Newcombe, *supra* note 5.

can be viewed as a violation of the non-discrimination rules. By clarifying the language used in treaties, states can avoid such conflicts.

Indeed, in recent years states have become aware of these potential conflicts and have aimed to clarify legal terms.[46] Most notably, some states have made clarifications with respect to the terms "expropriation" and "indirect expropriation," perhaps due to the wide meaning some tribunals have read into them.[47] In 2004, the United States and Canada included an Annex on expropriation in their Model IIAs.[48] Part of this Annex, as appears for example in the US-Uruguay BIT, states that: "Except in rare circumstances, non-discriminatory regulatory actions by a Party that are designed and applied to protect legitimate public welfare objectives, such as public health, safety, and the environment, do not constitute indirect expropriations."[49]

Similar clarifications can also be found *inter alia* in COMESA investment agreement[50] and the ASEAN-Australia-New Zealand FTA.[51]

Language clarifications can also be found more generally. As mentioned above, commitment to rules of international law implies a certain loss of regulatory flexibility. In some cases, states provide clarifications as

---

46 See e.g. Mahnaz Malik, "Recent Developments in International Investment Agreements: Negotiations and Disputes" (2010) IV Annual Forum for Developing Country Investment Negotiators, Background Papers, online: IISD <http://www.iisd.org/pdf/2011/dci_2010_recent_developments_iias.pdf> at 4–5 [Malik].

47 The Metalclad Tribunal, for example, has stated: "expropriation under NAFTA includes not only open, deliberate and acknowledged takings of property, such as outright seizure or formal or obligatory transfer of title in favour of the host State, but also covert or incidental interference with the use of property which has the effect of depriving the owner, in whole or in significant part, of the use or reasonably-to-be-expected economic benefit of property even if not necessarily to the obvious benefit of the host State". *Metalclad Corpn v Mexico* (2000) ICSID Case No. ARB(AF)97/1 at para 103 [*Metalclad*].

48 Annex B of the US Model BIT (2004); Annex B.13(1) of the Canada Model FIPA (2003).

49 US-Uruguay BIT (2005) at Annex B, art 4(b); *Free Trade Agreement Between the Government of the United States of America and the Government of the Republic of Chile*, June 6, 2003, online: USTR <http://www.ustr.gov/trade-agreements/free-trade-agreements/chile-fta/final-text> at art 4(b); see for a Canadian example *Free Trade Agreement Between Canada and the Republic of Colombia*, November 21, 2008, online: DFAIT <http://www.international.gc.ca/trade-agreements-accords-commerciaux/agr-acc/colombia-colombie/can-colombia-toc-tdm-can-colombie.aspx?view=d> at annex 811.

50 See COMESA, *supra* note 29 at art 20(8).

51 *Agreement Establishing the ASEAN-Australia-New Zealand Free Trade Area*, February 27, 2009, online: ASEAN <http://www.asean.org/22260.pdf> at ch 11 annex, para 4.

to what is included in this "loss" of regulatory flexibility, and what is not. Article 10.12 of the US-Chile FTA ("Investment and Environment") for instance, clarifies that environmental regulation shall not be limited by the investment rules prescribed in this agreement. It is stated:

> Nothing in this Chapter shall be construed to prevent a Party from adopting, maintaining, or enforcing any measure otherwise consistent with this Chapter that it considers appropriate to ensure that investment activity in its territory is undertaken in a manner sensitive to environmental concerns.[52]

Although their impact has been somewhat limited in the past, this type of clause may still prove useful in future disputes, especially as they shed light on the context and the purpose of investment treaties.[53]

Other potential language clarifications can be made in future IIAs as well. For example, it can be emphasized that a specific state commitment is needed in order to establish investors' "legitimate expectations,"[54] and that the mere change in regulation (subject to good-faith and non-discrimination) should not be considered as a breach of such. Furthermore, it can also be clarified that environmental issues, human rights or social considerations, when applied in order to protect such interest, should be considered as part of the "like-circumstances" legal test.

---

52 *Free Trade Agreement Between the Government of the United States of America and the Government of the Republic of Chile*, June 6, 2003, online: USTR <http://www.ustr. gov/trade-agreements/free-trade-agreements/chile-fta/final-text> at art 10.12.

53 For other examples, see Belgium/Luxemburg-Colombia BIT (2009) at art VIII(4); *Canada-Chile Free Trade Agreement*, December 5, 1996, online: DFAIT <http://www. international.gc.ca/trade-agreements-accords-commerciaux/agr-acc/chile-chili/ menu.aspx?lang=en&view=d> art G 14.

54 This is in effect what was done in the ASEAN-Australia-New Zealand FTA where in the Annex on expropriation the parties have included as a factor in the indirect expropriation analysis the following: "whether the government action breaches the government's prior binding written commitment to the investor whether by contract, licence or other legal documents" (rather than a general reference to the "reasonable investment-backed expectations" of the investor. The "specific commitment approach" has been adopted by several investment tribunals. See e.g. *Total S.A. v Argentine Republic* (Decision on Liability, December 27, 2010), ICSID Case No. ARB/04/01 at para 117 [*Total S.A.*]; *Grand River Enterprises Six Nations Ltd, et al v United States of America* (Award, January 12, 2011) UNCITRAL at para 141 [*Grand River*]; *Glamis Gold Ltd v The United States of America* (Award, June 8, 2009) UNCITRAL at paras 766–7 [*Glamis Gold*]; *Joseph Charles Lemire v Ukraine* (Decision on Jurisdiction and Liability, January 14, 2010) ICSID Case No. ARB/06/18 at para 284 [*Lemire*, Decision on Jurisdiction and Liability].

Language clarifications can also be made with respect to the term "investment." The "Salini test," for example, requires "contributions, a certain duration of performance of the contract and participation in the risks of transaction" and "the contribution to the economic development of the host State" in order to establish an "investment."[55] Recently, a prominent scholar cast doubts over whether investment in cigarettes should be considered as "investment."[56] This suggestion was made following the recent Phillip Morris investment claims amid the doubts over whether investment in cigarettes actually promoted states' development. While this proposition is certainly appealing, it is not without fault. Most notably, this proposition leaves investors in doubt as to whether their investment is, or is not, covered by the investment treaty, until such a time as an investment tribunal makes the determination. The term "contribution" is wide and vague, and by itself does not allow investors to know in advance whether their investment is to be considered as "contributing" (and thus covered by the IIA), or not. While agreeing with the general idea, according to which only investments that promote sustainable development should be covered by investment agreements, the authors believe that, ideally, such a determination should be made *ex ante*, before the investment is made, and not *ex post facto*, only after a dispute has arisen. This is required for reasons of predictability and transparency. Furthermore, decisions as to the investment's contribution should be made by professional bodies, and not by arbitrators, who are not suited to making such determinations. It is argued, therefore, that decisions as to the contributing nature of an investment should be made by impact assessment mechanisms, or any other pre-investment examination.

It is true that most states do not, and cannot, approve all incoming investments on an individual basis, and therefore such *ex ante* reviews may not always be available. However, an increased use of SIAs, both at the domestic and international levels, and especially in sensitive areas and for large-scale projects, will provide states with more comprehensive understanding concerning the investment's "contribution," and consequently will also allow foreign investors to know whether their planned investment will be covered by IIAs or not.

---

55 *Salini Costruttori S.p.A. and Italstrade S.p.A. v Kingdom of Morocco*, (Decision on Jurisdiction, July 23, 2001) ICSID Case No. ARB/00/4 at para 52. For a detailed discussion see Marek Jeżewski, "Development Considerations in Defining Investment" in Cordonier-Segger, Gehring and Newcombe, *supra* note 5 at 215.

56 "The Interaction of International Investment Law with Other Fields of Public International Law" (Remarks delivered at Leiden University, April 8–9, 2011) [unpublished].

In conclusion, a word of caution is required. States should not forget that private investments are crucial for sustainable development, and that a stable legal and business environment is essential for their promotion. States should therefore be wary of turning language clarifications into overly sweeping exclusions. States should identify those legal tests that could potentially affect sustainable development goals, and refine them so as to achieve a delicate balance between the need to provide a stable business environment on the one hand, and the need to allow sufficient regulatory flexibility on the other.

Corporate social responsibility

Another way that IIAs can promote sustainable development objectives is through the use of Corporate Social Responsibility ("CSR"). The modern concept of CSR can be traced back to the 1950s, when CSR was defined as "obligations of businessmen to pursue those policies, to make those decisions, or to follow those lines of action which are desirable in terms of the objectives and values of our society."[57] Although nowadays some debate still takes place on the exact definition of CSR,[58] for the purposes of this chapter the words of Supreme Court of Canada's Judge Gonthier will suffice:

> [CSR] generally embodies the notion that a corporation must act in a responsible manner with regard to the environment, community and the society in which it operates. In its most basic form, CSR emphasizes an approach to corporate governance and operations that integrates and balances the self-interests of the corporation, and those of its investors, with the concerns and interests of the public.[59]

Perhaps the most eminent example of a CSR code is the OECD Guidelines for Multinational Enterprises ("the OECD Guidelines"), updated

---

57 H.R. Bowen, *Social Responsibility and Accountability* (New York: Harper & Row, 1953), as cited in Archie B. Carroll, "Corporate Social Responsibility: Evolution of a Definitional Construct" (1999) 38(3) Business & Society 268 at 270 [Carroll].

58 Peter T. Muchlinski, *Multinational Enterprises and The Law* (New York: Oxford University Press, 2007) at 101 [Muchlinski].

59 Hon Charles Doherty Gonthier, "Foreword" in Michael Kerr, Richard Janda and Chip Pitts (eds), *Corporate Social Responsibility: A Legal Analysis* (Ontario: LexisNexis, 2009), as cited in Jarrod Hepburn and Vuyelwa Kuuya, "Corporate Social Responsibility and Investment Treaties" in Cordonier Segger, Gehring and Newcombe, *supra* note 5 at 585 [Hepburn and Kuuya].

in 2011, which have been described by some as an "emerging consensus on the social obligations of MNEs."[60] The OECD Guidelines represent a comprehensive code of conduct, including voluntary standards for environment, employment, combating bribery, science, competition, taxation and now human rights.[61] Another example, albeit one that focuses exclusively on human rights, is the 2011 "principles for responsible contracts" formulated by John Ruggie, the Special Representative of the Secretary-General on the issue of human rights and transnational corporations and other business enterprises.[62] These principles include *inter alia* the planning and management of potential adverse impacts on human rights, project operating standards, community engagement and grievance mechanisms.

The vast majority of CSR norms are considered "soft law," as they are voluntary and rely on self-governance. This, however, does not make them ineffective. Soft law mechanisms often include other "sticks and carrots" besides the threat of legal action,[63] and at least in some cases CSR "soft law" norms have succeeded in enforcing higher standards of social responsibility.[64]

The activity of foreign investors, as discussed above, can impact social, economic and environmental issues. But while some governments are equipped with the means to regulate and control these effects, others are not. This situation can be aggravated where states are eager to attract foreign investment and thus are willing to ignore the adverse effects on issues like human rights or the environment. Furthermore, the existence of governmental corruption, or the mere inability to enforce high standards of regulation, can result in the exploitative behavior of foreign multinationals. All of these scenarios are the result of inefficient enforcement of high standards of corporate social "behavior" on foreign investors. The role CSR can play in this respect is evident. By adhering to

---

60 Muchlinski, *supra* note 60 at 103.
61 OECD, *OECD Guidelines for Multinational Enterprises*, online: OECD, <http://www.oecd.org/daf/investment/guidelines>.
62 UN Human Rights Council, *Report of the Special Representative of the Secretary-General on the issue of human rights and transnational corporations and other business enterprises*, UN GAOR, 17th Session, Agenda item 3, UN Doc A/HRC/17/31/Add.3 (2011), online: UN <http://www.ohchr.org/Documents/Issues/Business/A.HRC.17.31.Add.3.pdf>.
63 Roya Ghafele and Angus Mercer, "Not Starting in Sixth Gear: An Assessment of the U.N. Global Compact's Use of Soft Law as a Global Governance Structure for Corporate Social Responsibility" (2010) 17 U.C. Davis Journal of International Law & Policy 41.
64 John M. Conley and Cynthia A. Williams, "Global Banks as Global Sustainability Regulators?: The Equator Principles" (2011) 33(4) Law & Pol'y 542.

external norms, on top of, or in place of, the norms imposed by host states, higher standards of behavior can be achieved. Furthermore, following CSR principles will assist foreign investors to plan and avoid potential conflicts and enhance their acceptance by the local community.

CSR norms can be incorporated into IIAs in several ways. First, several of the provisions already discussed in this chapter are designed to enforce (as "hard law") higher standards of social activity.[65] And it is certainly conceivable that an arbitral tribunal, where an IIA makes reference to CSR, will interpret compliance with these norms as also influencing its interpretation of value-open norms such as discrimination, fair and equitable treatment or expropriation. As such, in the future it may be the case that where an investor blatantly violates its own CSR commitment, his failure to comply with these norms could be invoked by the host state and set up against his claims of being treated for example unfairly. It would then have to be considered by investment tribunals.

With respect to self-governed "soft law" norms, these can be mentioned in the preambles to IIAs and serve as a source for treaty interpretation. The preamble to the Canada-Peru FTA, for example, "encourages" enterprises to respect CSR norms.[66] A more comprehensive example can be found in the preamble to the IISD Model BIT, where one of its aims is described as:

> Affirming the progressive development of international law and policy on the relationships between multinational enterprises and host governments as seen in such international instruments as the ILO Tripartite Declaration on Multinational Enterprises and Social Policy; the OECD Guidelines for Multinational Enterprises; and the United Nations' Norms and Responsibilities of Transnational Corporations and Other Business Enterprises with Regard to Human Rights.[67]

Furthermore, IIAs can also include more specific treaty provisions with respect to CSR. The IISD Model BIT, for example, includes a CSR provision according to which foreign investors must adhere to a list of CSR codes and guidelines. Another possibility is an *ex ante* review of the investors' CSR policies and their suitability for designated projects. The implementation of such a review may be prescribed as a precondition for

---

65 See Hepburn and Kuuya, *supra* note 61 at 599.
66 Canada-Peru FTA (2009).
67 IISD Model BIT, *supra* note 34.

certain types of investments, especially for those that were identified as sensitive by SIAs. Alternatively, as implied by article 13.6(2) of the EU-Korea FTA (which specifically refers also to FDI), states can also grant preferential treatment to investors that comply with CSR obligations.[68] If such a strategy is to be adopted, states should adjust other treaty provisions, such as the non-discrimination provisions, in order to ensure that CSR-based preferential treatment is not considered as a treaty violation.

Interesting developments in this respect can be found in the evolving EU policy on international investment law. Pursuant to the entry into force of the Treaty of Lisbon, FDI has been integrated into the EU common commercial policy. While the formulation of the EU's future investment policy is still ongoing,[69] it may be predicted that the inclusion of CSR in this policy is highly likely. First, the EU's latest FTAs with Korea and with Colombia and Peru mention CSR standards as a means to promote sustainable development goals.[70] Secondly, in two recent resolutions, the European Parliament expressed its will to see CSR provisions incorporated into future investment and trade agreements.[71] Most notably, in its resolution on the future European international investment policy, it was stated that the Parliament is calling "for a corporate social responsibility clause and effective social and environmental clauses to be included in every FTA the EU signs."[72] Similar recognition was also made by the European Council, in its "conclusion on a comprehensive European international investment policy" from 2010.[73]

---

68 Hepburn and Kuuya, *supra* note 61 at 609.

69 See Armand de Mestral at ch 3 of this book.

70 In both cases FDI is specifically mentioned. See *Free Trade Agreement Between the European Union and its Member States, of the one part, and the Republic of South Kora on the other*, October 15, 2009, online: EU <http://eur-lex.europa.eu/LexUriServ/Lex UriServ.do?uri=OJ:L:2011:127:0006:1343:EN:PDF> at art 13.6; *Trade Agreement Between the European Union and Colombia and Peru* (April 2011) at art 271, online: European Commission Trade <http://ec.europa.eu/trade/creating-opportunities/ bilateral-relations/regions/andean>.

71 European Parliament, *European Parliament resolution of 25 November on corporate social responsibility in international trade agreements* [2010] online: EU <http://www. europarl.europa.eu/sides/getDoc.do?type=TA&language=EN&reference=P7-TA-2010-0446>; European Parliament, *European Parliament resolution of 6 April 2011 on the future European international investment policy* [2011] online: EU <http:// www.europarl.europa.eu/sides/getDoc.do?type=TA&reference=P7-TA-2011-0141& language=EN>.

72 *Ibid.*

73 Council of the European Union, *Conclusion on a comprehensive European international investment policy*, 3041st Foreign Affairs Council Meeting, Luxemburg, October 25,

Interaction with sustainable development treaties

Another aspect that should be addressed in future IIAs is the interaction between IIAs and Multilateral Environmental Agreements. Although IIAs have not yet posed fundamental challenges to other regimes, there have been disputes, both at the WTO and in the investment law regime, directly related to environmental issues. For example, in *Vattenfall v Germany*,[74] the Swedish state-owned company Vattenfall challenged regulations imposed on its coal-fired power plant located near Hamburg which imposed more onerous measures on the plant compared to those originally guaranteed. These measures were enacted after the 2008 elections, when the Green Party had entered power in a coalition in the Hamburg municipal government, and were partly justified by the fact that coal-fired plants affected climate change. Vattenfall claimed a violation of the Energy Charter Treaty[75] (which mandates that investments be accorded fair and equitable treatment), and sought €1.4 billion in damages.

Following Vattenfall's legal actions, the German federal government agreed to a settlement according to which the required permits for Vattenfall's operation would be granted. Furthermore, Vattenfall was released from earlier commitments to reduce environmental damage.[76] This case represents an example of climate-related disputes that could become popular in the future, and it may demonstrate the possibility for IIA provisions to frustrate the objectives of climate change treaties. In the treaty-making process this could be addressed in several ways. For example, article 104 of the NAFTA instructs that in the event of legal conflicts between the NAFTA and a list of environmental treaties, the latter shall prevail.[77] More commonly, as stated above, exceptions and reservations provide the same solution, as they exclude certain fields from the scope of IIAs and *de facto* prioritize these subject-matters over the need to protect foreign investments.

Conclusion

Modern IIAs offer greater possibilities to balance different public policy objectives. This is mainly due to the growing concern of the parties

2010, online: EU <http://www.consilium.europa.eu/uedocs/cms_data/docs/pressdata/EN/foraff/117328.pdf> at para 16.

74 *Vattenfall AB, Vattenfall Europe AG, Vattenfall Europe Generation AG v The Federal Republic of Germany*, Award, ICSID Case No. ARB/09/6 (March 11, 2011) [*Vattenfall*].

75 ECT, *supra* note 37.

76 *Vattenfall, supra* note 77.

77 See NAFTA, *supra* note 28 at art 104.

involved in the negotiation of the agreements regarding the widespread impact that these instruments can have, not only on the environment but also on trade, labor conditions, health issues, etc. This chapter reviewed some of the tools that states may find useful when attempting to incorporate sustainable development objectives into their IIAs. It was explained that the challenge faced by treaty-drafters is multilayered, as states must strike a balance between the need to secure ample regulatory flexibility on the one hand, and to create a stable, transparent and inviting business environment, on the other. These tools, it was emphasized, should be developed and refined in order to maximize the potential embedded in FDI for supporting sustainable development.

In order to conclude this chapter, two parting remarks should be made. First, the essence of the term "sustainable development" lies in the desired balance between economic, social and environmental concerns. All three pillars are important, and all should be taken into consideration. This is what distinguishes "sustainable development" from pure environmental or economic approaches. Following this view, it is argued that states should apply some of the measures discussed with caution, and only after a careful review of their *full* implications. For example, it may be that the easiest way to prevent future conflicts actually frustrates potential synergies. The use of exceptions, for example, may hinder foreign investments and thus frustrate technology transfer or the creation of new jobs.

Secondly, the concept "sustainable development" includes numerous interests, with almost all requiring different balances and different treatment. IIAs should therefore avoid using "one size fits all" solutions for sustainable development as a whole. For example, it would be wrong to address the interaction between economic development and climate change mitigation with the same legal tools used for the interaction between human rights and economic development. More detailed IIAs should therefore be promoted and provisions governing the interaction with other international regimes be encouraged.

17 Direct taxation, tax treaties and IIAs: mixed objectives, mixed results

Martha O'Brien and *Kim Brooks***

Introduction

This chapter explores the relationship between international taxation and FDI, and the ways double taxation conventions ("tax treaties") and IIAs address the rights and obligations of states, investors and taxpayers. We use the Canadian network of tax treaties and IIAs to illustrate the potential for interaction between the two types of agreements, as Canada has an interesting perspective as a jurisdiction that is both capital-importing and capital-exporting, and as a founding member of the OECD. Further, Canada has formulated a model FIPA[1] and has a demonstrable policy of concluding tax treaties with its IIA partners.[2]

Tax treaties and IIAs have much in common. They share the same purpose of facilitating FDI, and they provide similar legal protections, such as prohibitions of discriminatory treatment of non-nationals and access to binding dispute resolution. Among other objectives, they are intended to reduce risk and create security and predictability, allowing investors to plan and carry out commercially viable activities under the protection of an international legal regime. In this sense, they both contribute to ensuring the sustainability of FDI and the legal regimes

---

* Professor, University of Victoria, Faculty of Law.
** Dean, Dalhousie University, Schulich School of Law.
1 See Department of Foreign Affairs and International Trade Canada (DFAIT), *Canada's FIPA Model*, online: DFAIT <http://www.international.gc.ca/trade-agreements-accords-commerciaux/assets/pdfs/2004-FIPA-model-en.pdf> [Canada's FIPA Model].
2 For the list of Canada's tax treaties, see Department of Finance Canada (DFC), online: DFC <http://www.fin.gc.ca/treaties-conventions/in_force--eng.asp> [Canada's tax treaties]. For the list of Canada's FIPAs and FTAs containing investment chapters, see online: DFAIT <http://www.international.gc.ca/trade-agreements-accords-commerciaux/agr-acc/index.aspx> [Canada's FIPAs].

that support it. There are other similarities as well. Tax treaties and IIAs have proliferated in tandem during the recent period of intensified globalization. Indeed, they are often negotiated with the same country in close temporal proximity. The same international organizations, the OECD and the UN, have been instrumental in setting standards and drafting models.

Despite their commonalities, international direct taxation and FDI policy as embodied in IIAs seem to inhabit separate spheres of international law and policy. Scholars who are specialists in both taxation and international trade and investment law are rare, although scholarship on taxation and trade and investment has increased in the last 15 years.[3] This is undoubtedly in response to the WTO Agreements of 1994, especially the General Agreement on Trade in Services (GATS), the Agreement on Trade-Related Investment Measures (TRIMS), the Agreement on Subsidies and Countervailing Measures, as well as the exponential growth in the number of RTAs and IIAs, and the advance of globalization generally. In addition, with the reduction or elimination of tariff and non-tariff barriers to trade and investment, and with efforts to minimize investment risk through IIAs, the tax implications of cross-border investment have become more visible and more significant in the decision-making process of investors. In particular, the implications of the GATS for taxation of foreign investors in the services sector,[4] the

3 To cite only a few examples of the literature, all of which cite numerous other works: H.D. Rosenbloom, "What's Trade Got to Do With It?" (1993/94) 49 Tax L Rev 593; Brian J. Arnold and Neil H. Harris, "NAFTA and the Taxation of Corporate Investment: A View From Within NAFTA" (1993/94) 49 Tax L Rev 530 [Arnold and Harris]; L. Friedlander, "The Role of Non-Discrimination Clauses in Bilateral Income Tax Treaties After GATT 1994" (2002) Brit Tax Rev 71 [Friedlander]; Arthur J. Cockfield, *NAFTA Tax Law and Policy—Resolving the Clash between Economic and Sovereignty Interests* (Toronto: Toronto University Press, 2005) [*Cockfield*]; Michael Daly, "Some Taxing Issues for the World Trade Organization" (2000) 48(4) Can Tax J 1053; John W. Boscariol, "The Impact of International Trade and Investment Agreements on Governments' Taxation Powers" 43 *Report of Proceedings of Fifty-Fifth Tax Conference, 2003 Tax Conference* (Toronto: Canadian Tax Foundation, 2004) at 1; Brenda C. Swick and Helen Gray, "Significant Developments in International Trade and Customs Law" 31 *Report of Proceedings of Fifty-Sixth Tax Conference, 2004 Tax Conference* (Toronto: Canadian Tax Foundation, 2005) ch 1 at 42–6 [Swick and Gray]; Michael Lang, Judith Herdina and Ines Hofbauer (eds), *WTO and Direct Taxation* (The Hague: Kluwer Law International, 2005).
4 Catherine Brown, "Tax Discrimination and Trade in Services: Should the Non-discrimination Article in the OECD Model Treaty Provide the Missing Link between Tax and Trade Agreements?" in Arthur Cockfield (ed), *Globalization and its Discontents: Tax Policy and International Investments* (Toronto: University of Toronto Press, 2010) at ch 13.

interaction of direct taxation with the non-discrimination rules in the NAFTA and EU Treaties[5] and the Agreement on Subsidies and Counter-vailing Measures[6] have been examined at length. The unsuccessful negotiations of a MAI in the late 1990s[7] and the proliferation of IIAs in recent years have also sparked interest in the interaction of direct taxa-tion and direct investment.

This chapter cannot cover all the significant tax impediments and incentives to FDI; it is intended merely to illuminate the linkages between international taxation and investment for non-tax specialists. Specifically, this chapter seeks to bring into focus the tax treaty provi-sions most relevant to FDI and their potential interaction with IIAs. Part I provides a general description of tax treaties, Canada's tax treaty network, and the relationship between tax treaty claims and investor-state claims under IIAs. Part II examines some important provisions of tax treaties (and Canadian domestic law) that promote or impede the flow of FDI between Canada and its tax treaty partners to ensure tax compliance and to prevent differential treatment of investors.

Tax and treaties and IIAs

After a brief introduction to tax treaties in general, Canada's practice is described, followed by an analysis of the interactions between taxation and IIAs.

Introduction to tax treaties

Tax treaties apply only to direct taxation in the form of income, corpor-ate profits and capital taxes. They do not apply to indirect taxes, except in limited or exceptional ways.[8] Value added taxes, excise taxes and customs duties are a central concern in international agreements for the liberalization of trade in goods and services, and also give rise to investor-state disputes under IIAs. In contrast, as this chapter will

---

5 Catherine Brown and Martha O'Brien, "Tax Discrimination and the Cross-Border Provision of Services—Canada/UK Perspectives" in Christopher P.M. Waters (ed), *British and Canadian Perspectives in International Law* (Leiden: Martinus Nijhoff, 2006) at ch 16.

6 Friedlander, *supra* note 3 at 98.

7 Michael Daly, "Some Taxing Questions for the Multinational Agreement on Invest-ment (MAI)" (1997) 20(6) The World Economy 787.

8 It is quite common to extend the non-discrimination article to all taxes imposed by a contracting state. See the discussion of non-discrimination provisions in tax treaties below in Part II.

discuss, direct taxation is generally expressly excluded from the scope of such agreements.

The OECD and the UN have both contributed to the development of model tax treaties. Since 1961, the OECD Committee on Fiscal Affairs has been more influential. The OECD Model[9] was drafted and has evolved from the perspective of its members, all relatively wealthy industrialized democracies, and is generally viewed as favoring the interests of capital exporting countries. The UN Model reflects more closely the interests of capital importing countries. The first UN Model Convention was published in 1980, and a revised UN Model was published in 2001.[10]

The Committee on Fiscal Affairs of the OECD is composed of senior officials of the tax authorities of the member countries, and now includes a number of non-member countries participating as observers and offering their views on proposed revisions. The Model was originally intended as a template for tax treaty negotiations between OECD members, although it is widely used in negotiations by non-member countries as well. OECD members are not bound by the Model or commentaries, and may reserve their position, and enter recorded observations, in respect of particular articles or commentaries.[11]

The current OECD and UN Models are broadly similar in their scope, organization and content. While the OECD Model assumes that the contracting states will be more or less equal in economic and industrial development, bargaining power and the two-way exchange of services, capital and investment, the UN Model is designed to balance the disparate interests of developed and developing countries. Accordingly, the UN Model tends to favor taxation on the basis of source over residence, so that a capital importing country's tax base is not unduly eroded by concessions to investors from capital exporting nations.[12]

Today there are approximately 3,000 bilateral tax treaties based on the OECD Model[13] in force globally. Tax treaties traditionally state their

---

9 *OECD Model Tax Convention on Income and on Capital*, loose-leaf (Paris: OECD) (Published in loose-leaf since 1992) [OECD Model Tax Convention].

10 A much more comprehensive history of the development of the model tax conventions is found in United Nations, Dept of Economic and Social Affairs, *United Nations Model Double Taxation Convention between Developed and Developing Countries* (New York: United Nations, 2001) at vi–xxii (introduction) [UN Model DTC].

11 See OECD Model Tax Convention, *supra* note 9 at paras 30–2.

12 See UN Model DTC, *supra* note 10, Introduction at vii–viii, paras 4–5.

13 This estimate appears in OECD Centre for Tax Policy and Administration, *The Granting of Treaty Benefits with Respect to the Income of Collective Investment Vehicles* (Paris: OECD, 2009) at 7 para 22.

primary purposes in the title: "for the avoidance of double taxation and the prevention of fiscal evasion with respect to taxes on income."[14] But beyond these stated goals, they undoubtedly also provide predictability and certainty to international investors, and access to legally binding dispute resolution between taxpayers and the contracting states (as well as a state-to-state dispute resolution by a mutual agreement procedure). Although tax treaties are concluded between states, they are normally made part of the binding tax law of the contracting states, often with priority over domestic law to the extent of any inconsistency.[15]

Most countries tax their residents on their worldwide income and non-residents on income derived from sources within their territory, raising the obvious potential for juridical double taxation, or the taxation of the same taxpayer on the same income by two states. Tax treaties apply to residents of one or both contracting states, and apportion taxing jurisdiction on income that flows between the state of source and the state of residence. Tax treaties are said to be relieving, that is, they cannot increase, but may reduce a taxpayer's liability as determined under a contracting state's domestic law. In a tax treaty, the contracting states reciprocally renounce the full measure of tax sovereignty they may otherwise assert (and do assert) in their domestic law. Thus one effect of tax treaties is to reduce or eliminate juridical double taxation.

In resolving disputes concerning tax treaties, the very extensive commentaries to the UN and OECD Models, as well as the treaty interpretation principles of the Vienna Convention[16] are consulted and generally applied by the national courts of the contracting states with jurisdiction in tax matters. National courts also frequently consider the interpretations given in rulings of other jurisdictions so that a fairly consistent international jurisprudence of tax treaty interpretation and application has developed.[17] However, as there is no international tax court and no world tax organization, it should not be assumed that the

---

14 See e.g. titles of Canada's tax treaties, *supra* note 2.
15 The status of tax treaties in the legal hierarchy of a contracting state obviously varies considerably, and a discussion of the various ways they are enforced in national legal systems is beyond the scope of this chapter. Canada brings its tax treaties into force by Act of Parliament. Each such Act provides that the scheduled tax treaty takes priority over any inconsistent law. See e.g. *Tax Conventions Implementation Act*, SC 2010, c.15, ss 3–5.
16 *Vienna Convention on the Law of Treaties*, May 23, 1969, 1155 UNTS 331, 8 ILM 679.
17 See e.g. *Saipem UK Ltd v R*, 2011 TCC 25 and *American Income Life Insurance Co v R*, 2008 TCC 306 for two recent cases where the Tax Court of Canada refers to judgments of other jurisdictions' tax courts.

interaction of tax treaties with domestic and foreign tax laws is the same, or predictable in each jurisdiction.

In addition to its remedies against either host or home country in the courts, an investor that alleges it has not been granted the treatment to which it is entitled under a tax treaty can request the competent authority of its state of residence to review and resolve the problem, if necessary through mutual agreement with the other contracting state's competent authority. Provisions for the resolution of disputes regarding the application of tax treaties by arbitration binding on both contracting states are still quite rare, but are becoming more common in tax treaties, although they are subject to the consent of both contracting states and sometimes also the taxpayer.[18]

Overview of Canada's tax treaties

Canada has concluded 92 tax treaties, 88 of which are in force as of March 2011.[19] Canada's network includes treaties with its NAFTA partners, all OECD member countries,[20] all the EU Member States, the so-called BRIC emerging economies and South Africa, and numerous developing countries.[21] Canada's treaties are based on the OECD Model,

---

18 Article 23 of Canada's tax treaty with Mexico is an example of the mutual agreement procedure. The Canada-Mexico and Canada-United States tax treaties also provide for binding arbitration where the mutual agreement procedure is unsuccessful. Paragraph 1 is typical of tax treaties based on the OECD Model:
1. Where a person considers that the actions of one or both of the Contracting States result or will result for that person in taxation not in accordance with the provisions of this Convention, that person may, irrespective of the remedies provided by the domestic law of those States, address to the competent authority of the Contracting State of which that person is a resident an application in writing stating the grounds for claiming the revision of such taxation. To be admissible, the said application must be submitted within three years from the first notification of the action which gives rise to taxation not in accordance with the Convention.
Convention Between the Government of Canada and the Government of the United Mexican States for the Avoidance of Double Taxation and the Prevention of Fiscal Evasion with Respect to Taxes on Income, online: DFC <http://www.fin.gc.ca/treaties-conventions/mexico_1-eng.asp> at art 23(1) [Canada-Mexico Tax Treaty].

19 See Canada's tax treaties *supra* note 2.

20 The treaty with Turkey is signed, but not yet in force as of March 2011. See *Agreement Between Canada and the Republic of Turkey for the Avoidance of Double Taxation and the Prevention of Fiscal Evasion with Respect to Taxes on Income and on Capital*, online: DFC <http://www.fin.gc.ca/treaties-conventions/turkey_1-eng.asp>.

21 The only G-20 member with which Canada does not have a tax treaty is Saudi Arabia. Brian J. Arnold, *Reforming Canada's International Tax System Toward Coherence and Simplicity* (Toronto: Canadian Tax Foundation, 2009) at ch 12 suggests that Canada's network has become too large and unwieldy.

but adopt provisions of the UN Model in some aspects, reflecting either the preference of the other contracting state, or the fact that Canada is a capital importing state in relation to some countries, and an exporter in relation to others, and that its older treaties may reflect its former status as a net importer of capital.[22] Also, Canada has reserved in relation to a number of OECD Model provisions, in particular with respect to the non-discrimination obligations discussed in more detail in Part II. Canada's reservations are reflected in its tax treaties.

Canada's tax treaties do not apply to provincial, territorial or local taxation, or indirect taxes such as the GST/HST, excise taxes or import duties. In Canada, tax treaties are brought into force by federal statute, and take precedence over inconsistent federal law.[23] Foreign investors in Canada are entitled as taxpayers to the relief provided by Canadian tax treaties in determining their Canadian tax liabilities. If the Canada Revenue Agency ("CRA") denies the benefit of a tax treaty to an investor, the Tax Court of Canada has exclusive original jurisdiction to resolve the dispute following a trial on the merits with full procedural safeguards. Thus there is a transparent, public, judicial process for taxpayer-state dispute resolution.

IIAs and direct taxation

The wall separating international direct tax policy from trade and investment policy in Canada's international affairs is demonstrated by the fact that DFAIT is responsible for negotiating trade and investment agreements, while officials from the Department of Finance are charged with tax treaty negotiations. When a country with which Canada is negotiating a FIPA suggests a change to the taxation provision (Model FIPA article 16),[24] the matter may be referred to the finance department. Otherwise, no one from the first department participates in the negotiations led by the second, or *vice versa*.

Canada's unofficial policy seems to be to have a comprehensive tax treaty in place before, or within a short time after, entering into an IIA with a particular country.[25] The official position of DFAIT is that FIPA

---

22 See the *Final Report of the Advisory Panel on International Taxation* (Ottawa: Department of Finance, 2008) at 5 paras 2, 9.

23 See *supra* note 15.

24 See Canada's FIPA Model, *supra* note 1 at art 16.

25 One might note the early precedent of Canada's conclusion of a tax treaty with Mexico (1991, replaced 2006) coincident with the NAFTA negotiations, and with Chile (1992, replaced 1999) in tandem with the Canada-Chile FTA of 1997. As of

partners are selected according to potential commercial benefit and need for protection of Canadian investors, as well as the likelihood of concluding an agreement, together with "trade policy or other foreign policy interests."[26] The latter may be interpreted as including international tax policy. However, it may no longer be true to say Canada insists on having a tax treaty in place with its FIPA partners, given the new policy of negotiating Tax Information Exchange Agreements (TIEAs) with jurisdictions that have no interest in a comprehensive tax treaty, but may be destinations for significant outbound foreign investment.[27]

So far, there has been only one (unsuccessful) arbitral tribunal ruling in a case where a direct tax measure was alleged to contravene an IIA.[28] This is undoubtedly because IIAs, and RTAs which include investment protection, generally "carve out" tax measures from their application by stating that nothing in the agreement applies to tax measures (or "tax matters"), and that any dispute is to be resolved as provided by an applicable tax treaty.[29] There are normally limited exceptions to the

July 2010, Canada has signed FIPAs (or RTAs with investment chapters) with only three countries with which it has no tax treaty or Tax Information Exchange Agreement, and with which it has no negotiations underway: Panama, El Salvador and Uruguay. Most notably, Canada has not announced negotiations for a tax treaty or TIEA with Panama, despite having signed a free trade agreement with that country on May 14, 2010, which includes provisions on trade in services, investment protection corresponding to the Model FIPA, and government procurement guarantees. In contrast, Canada's very significant two-way trade and investment with Hong Kong and Taiwan has not yet resulted in tax treaties with these jurisdictions. See Canada's tax treaties and Canada's FIPAs *supra* note 2.

26 DFAIT, "Canada's FIPA Program: Its Purpose, Objective and Content", online: DFAIT <http://www.international.gc.ca/trade-agreements-accords-commerciaux/ agr-acc/fipa-apie/fipa-purpose.aspx?lang=en&menu_id=43&menu=R>.

27 See The Budget Plan 2007, online: DFC <http://www.budget.gc.ca/2007/pdf/ bp2007e.pdf> Ann 5 at 422–3.

28 See *Plama Consortium Ltd v Bulgaria*, Award, ICSID Case No. ARB/03/24 (ECT) (August 27, 2008) [*Plama*]. Another possible case is *Antoine Goetz and Others v Republic of Burundi*, Award, ICSID Case No. ARB/95/3 (February 10, 1999). In that case, Belgian investors claimed that the withdrawal by Burundi of a free zone certificate entitling their company, AFFIMET, established under Burundian law, to benefit from general exemptions for both tax and customs duties was an expropriation of their investment prohibited by the BIT between the Belgian-Luxembourg Economic Union and Burundi. It is not clear whether the free zone certificate exempted AFFIMET from direct taxes as well as indirect taxes, but it is reasonable to assume this was the case. The claim was settled without a formal award, but the tribunal did find that Burundi's actions were tantamount to an expropriation. *See* the discussion in *Swick & Gray*, *supra* note 3 at 43–4.

29 Canada's Model FIPA, *supra* note 1 at art 16 para 1, is not atypical:
    Except as set out in this Article, nothing in this Agreement shall apply to taxation

general exclusion of tax measures from the protection of the IIA, and the exceptions vary widely from one agreement to another. Many IIAs do not exclude tax measures from their protections where the tax measures violate obligations assumed under an investment agreement between the host state and the investor, or amount to an expropriation of the investment.[30]

The NAFTA also generally excludes taxation measures from the state parties' obligations.[31] NAFTA article 2103(1) provides that "Except as set out in this Article, nothing in this Agreement shall apply to taxation measures."[32] Article 2103(2) provides that the rights and obligations of a Party under a tax convention shall be unaffected, and the tax convention shall apply to the extent of any inconsistency. The national treatment and MFN obligations of NAFTA Chapter 11 (Investment) are specifically excluded in respect of direct taxes (article 2103(4)(b)).

In the sole arbitral award to date on the compatibility of a direct tax measure with the ECT's investment protection guarantees, *Plama*, the tribunal found no discriminatory treatment, expropriation or breach of the obligation of fair and equitable treatment.[33] The investor, a Cyprus corporation, purchased shares of a Bulgarian corporation in a series of transactions, which had disastrous tax consequences for it under Bulgarian tax law. Although the investor was later able to obtain a remission of the tax

measures. For further certainty, nothing in this Agreement shall affect the rights and obligations of the parties under any tax convention. In the event of any inconsistency between the provisions of this Agreement and any such convention, the provisions of that convention shall apply to the extent of the inconsistency.

30 See e.g. the Canada-Latvia FIPA (2009), *supra* note 2 at art XII(3), (4).

31 See Catherine Brown and Martha O'Brien, "Tax Discrimination and the Cross-Border Provision of Services—Canada/UK Perspectives" in Christopher P.M. Waters (ed), *British and Canadian Perspectives in International Law* (Leiden: Martinus Nijhoff, 2006) at 324–7 (where these provisions of the NAFTA are described and analyzed in more detail). See also the discussion of the relationship between tax and trade arbitration in William W. Park, "Arbitration and the Fisc: NAFTA's 'Tax Veto'" (2001) 2 Chicago J Int'l L 231; Canada-Mexico Tax Treaty, *supra* note 18 at art 23 para 6 acknowledges the potential application of the GATS, but requires the agreement of both treaty partners that a measure is not within the scope of the tax treaty for a dispute to be brought under the GATS. The *Convention Between Canada and the United States of America With Respect to Taxes on Income And on Capital*, June 14, 1983, online: DFC <http://www.fin.gc.ca/treaties-conventions/USA_-eng.asp> at art XXIX(6) treaty creates a different hierarchy between the GATS and the tax treaty.

32 See *North American Free Trade Agreement Between the Government of Canada, the Government of Mexico and the Government of the United States*, December 17, 1992, Can Ts 1994 No 2, 32 ILM 289 at art 2103(2) [NAFTA].

33 See *Plama, supra* note 28.

liability, during the interim period it had to pay the tax, which it claimed made it impossible to obtain the necessary financing to operate the acquired investment. The tribunal noted that article 21 of the ECT specifically excluded taxation measures of a contracting state from the ECT's investment protection. Where a tax measure is alleged to be discriminatory or an expropriation, the issue must be referred to the host state's tax authority, which was not done. The tribunal went on to find "no action by [Bulgaria] which comes anywhere near to being unfair or inequitable treatment or amounting to expropriation."[34]

Despite the dearth of arbitral tribunal rulings on IIAs and direct taxation, there have been some notable decisions concerning indirect taxes (not covered by tax treaties) that could be relevant when such a case arises. As a threshold test, it has been held that to constitute a tax, a levy must be "imposed by law" and must "[impose] a liability on classes of persons to pay money to the State for public purposes."[35] The general exclusion of tax matters from the guarantees provided by an IIA applies to both direct and indirect taxes.[36]

Differential taxation by a host (or source) country can undoubtedly constitute a breach of the national treatment commitments made in an IIA (unless taxation is expressly excluded from such guarantees).[37] The

---

34 *Ibid* at para 267.
35 *EnCana Corpn v Republic of Ecuador*, Award, UNCITRAL (February 3, 2006) at para 142(4) [*Encana*]. We thank Andrew Newcombe and Céline Lévesque for their assistance in our research of investment arbitration awards related to taxation. Any errors or misstatements in this respect are, however, our own.
36 It was argued in *Occidental Exploration and Production Co v The Republic of Ecuador*, Final award, London Court of International Arbitration Administered Case No. UN3467 (July 1, 2004) [*Occidental*] that only direct tax measures, and not the value added tax that was at issue in that case, were excluded under the IIA provision, since tax conventions only apply to direct taxes. The arbitration tribunal chose to avoid ruling on this point at para 69. In *EnCana, supra* note 35, at para 142(2), the arbitral tribunal held that the term "taxation" was not limited to direct taxation; the tribunal in *Duke Energy Electroquil Partners & Electroquil S.A. v Republic of Ecuador*, Award, ICSID Case No. ARB/04/19 (August 18, 2008) followed the *EnCana* tribunal on this point.
37 Discriminatory application of (indirect) tax measures has been held to violate the national treatment obligation of the investment chapter of the NAFTA in *Feldman v Mexico*, Award on Merits, ICSID Case No. ARB(AF)/99/1 (December 16, 2002) [*Feldman*] and in the trio of sweeteners cases against Mexico, including *Archer Daniels Midland Company and Tate & Lyle Ingredients Americas, Inc. v Mexico*, ICSID Case No. ARB(AF)/04/05 (November 21, 2007) [*ADM*]; *Corn Products International, Inc. v Mexico*, Decision on Responsibility, ICSID Case No. ARB(AF)/04/01 (January 15, 2008) [*CPI*] and *Cargill Incorporated v Mexico*, Award, ICSID Case No. ARB(AF)/05/2 (September 18, 2009) [*Cargill*].

MFN obligation could also clearly conflict with specific maximum tax rates and other provisions of tax treaties with third countries if tax is not carved out from this commitment. It has been established in arbitral awards concerning IIAs that tax measures can constitute indirect or creeping expropriation prohibited by an IIA,[38] and can also constitute a breach of the general obligation of fair and equitable treatment.[39] It should be noted, however, that Canada's FIPAs carve out this obligation in relation to taxation in the absence of an expropriation in ways that other countries' IIAs do not. This explains the divergent results in *Occidental* and *EnCana*.[40]

Canada's Model FIPA article 16 is particularly strict in excluding taxation from the obligations of the agreement.[41] The technique that is used allows a Party to refer the issue of whether a measure is a tax measure to the tax authorities of the Parties. Their determination, if made within six months of the reference, is binding on the investor-state or state-to-state arbitral tribunal. If the tax authorities of both states jointly determine that a measure is a taxation measure, then the dispute would be excluded from the jurisdiction of the arbitral tribunal or panel unless the investor claims that the tax measure is in breach of an investment agreement (article 16(3)) or constitutes an expropriation (article 16(4)).[42]

The issue of whether a tax measure is a breach of an investment agreement between the investor and the host state, or constitutes an expropriation, is also initially to be determined by the tax authorities of the Parties.[43] The investor may only submit the claim to arbitration where, six months after the reference of the issue, the tax authorities have not jointly determined that the tax measure is not a breach of an investment agreement or does not constitute an expropriation. While one might think that the tax authorities would have an incentive to agree, in order

38 See *Feldman, supra* note 37; *Occidental, supra* note 36 at para 187. No expropriation was found to have occurred in the circumstances of these cases.

39 *Occidental, supra* note 36, and *Pan American Energy LLC and BP Argentina Exploration Co v Argentine Republic*, Decision on Preliminary Objections, ICSID Case No. ARB/03/13 (July 27, 2006); *El Paso Energy International Co v Argentine Republic*, Decision on Jurisdiction, ICSID Case No. ARB/03/15 (April 27, 2006).

40 See William W. Park, "Tax Arbitration and Investor Protection" in Catherine A. Rogers and Roger P. Alford (eds), *The Future of Investment Arbitration* (Oxford: Oxford University Press, 2009) ch12 at 239–44 (where the author discusses the two cases and compares the IIAs in issue).

41 See Canada's FIPA Model *supra* note 1 at art 16.

42 See *ibid* at art 16(3)–(6).

43 *Ibid* at art 16(5).

to preclude the claim, some cases show otherwise. For example, in the three sweetener cases against Mexico, the tax authorities of the United States and Mexico could not agree that the (indirect) tax at issue did not constitute an expropriation in violation of NAFTA article 1110 (expropriation) and as a result the tribunals ruled on this issue.[44]

In conclusion, Canada's FIPAs, and many other IIAs, carve out most tax matters comprehensively. There are sound policy reasons to keep the non-discrimination obligations of tax treaties and IIAs separate.[45] In Canada's case, there was already a significant network of tax treaties in place when it entered into its first IIA in 1989. Excluding tax measures from the IIA reduces uncertainty as to which agreement was intended to apply in any particular case, the possibility of multiple fora for resolution of the dispute, and the potential for inconsistent rulings from courts and tribunals. It also recognizes the critical link between taxation and state sovereignty and capacity, the need for a country to be able to adjust its tax system to meet economic challenges and the expectations of its citizens, and the political importance of these aspects of taxation.

On the other hand, there is value in identifying the disparities in tax treatment that can inhibit FDI. The literature on international tax competition[46] supports the proposition that tax incentives to FDI have a discernible effect on location decisions, even if they are not very efficient (i.e. the granting of the incentive costs more than the value of the investment attracted). If that is true, then imposing a heavier tax burden on foreign investors in comparison with resident investors logically should inhibit investment. Some of the disparities in treatment that can be viewed as discriminatory and their relationship to tax treaty provisions are outlined in the following section.

The consequences of tax treaties for foreign direct investment

Tax laws can dramatically affect the rates of return on invested capital and consequently have long been regarded as an important determinant of investment decisions. Tax laws are particularly important as determinants of FDI since the returns on such investments might be

---

44 See *Cargill, supra* note 37 at paras 16–17; *ADM, supra* note 37 at para 15.
45 See Cockfield, *supra* note 3, and Arnold and Harris, *supra* note 3.
46 See Alec Easson, "Tax Competition and Investment Incentives" (1996/97) 2(2) EC Tax J 63 at 70–1 [Easson]; Jacques Morisset and Nede Pirnia, "How Tax Policy and Incentives Affect Foreign Direct Investment: A Review" (2005) Research Working Paper No. 2509, online: SSRN <http://papers.ssrn.com/so13/papers.cfm?abstract_id=632579>.

subject to tax in both the originating and the host country. As noted above, many countries levy income tax on corporate profits both on a residency basis (on the worldwide profits of corporations resident in the jurisdiction) and a source basis (on corporate profits with a source in the jurisdiction). Moreover, fundamental tax concepts and detailed rules often differ substantially between countries. Hence, it is easy to see that without coordination between countries, FDI could be discouraged, or at least influenced in unintended ways, through the interaction of domestic tax systems. In both the economic and legal literature there has been an extended debate over whether bilateral tax treaties have in fact facilitated FDI.[47]

Tax treaties serve three primary functions in relation to FDI: reducing administrative barriers, reducing tax costs to cross-border activity, and ensuring a level playing field for non-nationals. Tax treaties also reduce opportunities for tax avoidance and assist administrators to combat tax evasion.

Reducing the administrative barriers to cross-border activity

One potential barrier to FDI is the administrative cost of complying with a country's tax rules when the level of investment in the jurisdiction is modest. Many countries impose their income tax on any foreign corporation "carrying on business" in the jurisdiction.[48] Consequently, a foreign corporation that opens an office in a country to engage in preparatory and auxiliary activities prior to deciding whether to expand its operations in the country, or otherwise undertakes business activities for only a limited purpose or period of time, might well be found to be carrying on business in the country and be liable to tax and required to

---

47 Interestingly, the evidence is inconclusive as to whether tax treaties or investment agreements actually increase FDI. See Andrew Newcombe and Lluís Paradell, *Law and Practice of Investment Treaties* (The Netherlands: Kluwer Law International, 2009) at 62; Fabian Barthel, Mathias Busse and Eric Neumayer, "The Impact of Double Taxation Treaties on Foreign Direct Investment: Evidence from Large Dyadic Panel Data" (July 2010) 28(3) Contemporary Economic Policy 366; W. Steven Clark, "Tax Incentives for Foreign Direct Investment: Empirical Evidence on Effects and Alternative Policy Options" (2000) 48(4) CanTax J 1139; Bruce Blonigen and Ronald Davies, "Do Bilateral Tax Treaties Promote Foreign Direct Investment?" (June 1, 2001) University of Oregon Economics Working Paper No. 2001–12; Tsilly Dagan, "The Tax Treaties Myth" (2000) 32 NYUJ Int'l L& Pol 939 [Dagan].

48 "Carrying on business" may be very broadly defined, as in the Canadian *Income Tax Act*, *infra* note 50 at s 253 where merely offering something for sale or soliciting orders in Canada, without any physical presence, may constitute carrying on business in Canada.

file tax returns. This added administrative cost might discourage corporations from undertaking preliminary steps or modest business activities in another country.

Tax treaties contain a number of articles that reduce the compliance costs for exploratory, auxiliary, or small-scale activities by exempting them from tax in the source country. The most significant of these articles is the business profits article. In all treaties, this article provides that an enterprise resident in one treaty partner will be taxed in the other treaty partner only if it has a permanent establishment in that jurisdiction. The precise definition of a permanent establishment varies from treaty to treaty but generally it requires that the enterprise have a fixed place of business through which the business of the enterprise is wholly or partly carried on. A fixed place of business is defined to include a place of management, branch, office, factory, etc.[49]

Reducing the tax imposed in the source country

All countries seek to alleviate double taxation unilaterally. Most commonly, this is done by providing a tax credit (or exemption) for any foreign taxes paid by residents of that country on income that has a source in another country. Hence, it might appear that the tax imposed in a source country would not affect cross-border investment since that tax would always be credited against the taxes paid in the resident country. However, among other concerns, not all taxes paid in source countries would be fully credited in the resident country. For example, most countries impose a relatively high flat withholding tax on the gross amount of most forms of income from capital and other periodic payments. Canada imposes a 25 per cent withholding tax on interest, dividends, rents and royalty payments made to non-residents.[50] In the residence country, only the net amount of this payment (that is, after deducting the expenses of earning the income) would be subject to tax, and thus in many cases the tax in the source country on the gross payment would exceed the amount that could be credited against the tax liability in the resident country. Consequently, tax treaties invariably

49 For more on the permanent establishment threshold see e.g. Brian Arnold, "Threshold Requirements for Taxing Business Profits under Tax Treaties" (2003) Bulletin for International Fiscal Documentation 476; International Fiscal Association, "Is There a Permanent Establishment?" 94a Cahiers de droit fiscal international (The Hague: SduUitgevers, 2009) at 169; Dale Pinto, "The Need to Reconceptualize the Permanent Establishment Threshold" (July 2006) IBFD-Bulletin at 266.

50 See *Income Tax Act*, RS C 1985, c 1 (5th supp), s 212 [*Income Tax Act*].

reduce the rate of withholding tax that applies to cross-border investment returns. Over the past couple of decades many treaties have reduced these withholding tax rates to 10 or 5 per cent and often have abolished them altogether.[51] In its treaties, normally in article 12, Canada frequently exempts royalties related to computer software, patents, know-how and copyrights from withholding tax.[52]

As another illustration of how tax treaties might reduce the tax cost of foreign investment, the business profits article prescribes the scope of taxation once a business has a permanent establishment in the jurisdiction. So, for example, pursuant to article 7 in most tax treaties, the enterprise is only taxable on profit that the permanent establishment might be expected to make if it were a distinct and separate enterprise engaged in the same or similar activities.[53] In other words, it clarifies and restricts the amount of income that might be thought to be taxable in the source jurisdiction.

Ensuring a level playing field for non-nationals

Tax treaties usually contain a non-discrimination clause that provides that one signatory country will not discriminate against nationals of the other signatory country. These provisions are not nearly as strong or as effective as similar provisions in trade and investment agreements. The OECD Model provides in article 24(1) that "[n]ationals of [Country A] shall not be subjected in [Country B] to any taxation or any requirement connected therewith, which is other or more burdensome than the taxation and connected requirements to which nationals of [Country B] in the same circumstances, in particular with respect to residence, are or may be subjected."[54] This provision has been interpreted strictly, both

---

51 For a discussion of the taxation of dividends, interest and royalties see e.g. Stef vanWeeghel, "Dividends (Article 10 OECD Model Convention)" in Michael Lang (ed), *Source Versus Residence: Problems Arising From the Allocation of Taxing Rights In Tax Treaty Law And Possible Alternatives* (Austin [Tex]: Wolters Kluwer Law and Business, 2008); Niv Tadmore, "Royalties (Article 13 OECD Model Convention)" in Michael Lang (ed), *Source Versus Residence: Problems Arising From the Allocation of Taxing Rights in Tax Treaty Law and Possible Alternatives* (Austin [Tex]: Wolters Kluwer Law & Business, 2008).

52 See Canada's tax treaties, *supra* note 2.

53 *Ibid.*

54 Articles of the Model Convention with Respect to Taxes on Income and on Capital, January 28, 2003, online: OECD <http://www.oecd.org/dataoecd/52/34/1914467. pdf> at art 24(1). For more on the non-discrimination article see e.g. American Law Institute, "Part Four: Non-Discrimination—I. Basic Concept" in Federal Income Tax Project: International Aspects of United States Income Taxation II: Proposals on

in Canada and abroad, so as to allow discrimination on the basis of residence, even where the non-resident is in substantially the same tax circumstances as a resident would be.[55] Further, Canada has a reservation on the non-discrimination article of the OECD model treaty and generally offers a more restricted non-discrimination article to its treaty partners. Notably, Canada preserves its ability to impose a branch tax on non-resident nationals who carry on business in Canada, restrict the deduction of interest payments where a company is thinly capitalized, and provide Canadian-controlled private corporations with generous tax incentives that are not available to foreign corporations, or Canadian corporations controlled by non-residents.

Occasionally, tax treaties include MFN clauses. These clauses guarantee that if treaty partner A offers a more favorable arrangement (e.g. a lower withholding tax rate) to treaty partner C, that treatment will be extended to the treaty partner B, the partner to the tax treaty that includes the MFN clause.[56] Canada sometimes includes an MFN clause in its non-discrimination article, with respect to Canadian enterprises controlled by residents of the other contracting states. The NAFTA Parties extend the non-discrimination article in their three tax treaties to all taxes, not just the usual corporate profits and income taxes to which the treaties generally apply. However, this probably does not add anything to the guarantees in the NAFTA regarding indirect tax measures, and Canada still retains its reservation allowing it to impose differential taxation on residents of the other NAFTA parties and on Canadian corporations controlled by their residents.

United States Income Tax Treaties (San Francisco, May 13, 1991); John F. Avery Jones, "The Non-discrimination Article in Tax Treaties Part 2" (1991) 11/12 Brit Tax Rev 421; Richard M. Hammer, "Nondiscrimination in the International Tax Context: A Look at OECD Model Article 24" (2005) 12 Tax Management International Journal 700; Ruth Mason, "A Theory of Tax Discrimination" (2008) NYU Jean Monnet Working Paper 09/06; Ruth Mason and Herman Bouma, "Nondiscrimination at the Crossroads of International Taxation" (2008) 93b Cahiers de Droit Fiscal International.

55 See the discussion in Friedlander, *supra* note 3 at 77–86. Canada's restrictive approach to its non-discrimination obligations in tax treaties has been affirmed (in the first Canadian case on the issue) in *Saipem UK Ltd v The Queen* 2011 TCC 25 (appeal pending).

56 For more on MFN provisions see e.g. Albert J. Rädler, "Chapter 1: Most-Favoured-Nation Concept in Tax Treaties" in Michael Lang et al (eds), *Multilateral Tax Treaties: New Developments in International Tax Law* (London and Boston: Kluwer Law International, 1998).

Reducing tax avoidance and evasion

The other primary objective of tax treaties is to prevent or reduce the opportunities for international tax avoidance and evasion. "Double non-taxation" through the use of hybrid entities and "treaty shopping" (to be discussed below) may be prevented through specific types of tax treaty provisions limiting access to the benefits of treaties where artificial or conduit structures are used. Prevention of avoidance and evasion are enhanced by provisions allowing the tax authorities of the treaty partners to exchange tax information regarding any person, not just residents of their respective jurisdictions, and extending to all forms of taxes. While these objectives are not aimed at promoting FDI, they are significant in shaping the decision-making of investors as to where to invest, and the form that investment takes.

Reducing opportunities for tax avoidance

The domestic tax laws of two countries often treat private legal constructs differently. Over the past few decades, international tax planners have become increasingly resourceful in exploiting these differences. A typical international tax arbitrage arrangement might involve the use of a legal entity that is classified as a taxpayer in one country (Country A) but a flow-through entity in another country (Country B). Often these are referred to as hybrid entities, and across countries there are a large variety of such legal entities. If a corporation in Country A sets up a hybrid entity in Country B to receive royalties that originate in Country B the result might be that the royalties will escape tax completely. They will not be taxed in County B, where they originate, since Country B will look through the hybrid entity in its country and regard the royalties as having been received by the corporation in Country A. They will not be taxed in Country A either, since that country will view them as having been received by the hybrid entity in Country B, which it regards as a legal taxpayer. In the past, tax treaties have not reduced these kinds of opportunities for tax arbitrage but countries are increasingly using their treaties to attempt to prevent the non-taxation of international capital flows.

Tax treaties present an opportunity for tax avoidance by allowing for what is known as treaty shopping. For example, a multinational that is a resident in Country A and receiving royalties from Country B may have some tax withheld on the payment pursuant to the tax treaty between Countries A and B. However, Country B might have a tax treaty with Country C under which the withholding tax on royalties is less or even completely removed. Therefore, the multinational might establish a presence in Country C for the sole purpose of receiving royalties from Country B free of withholding tax. There is some dispute in the literature as to whether this type of tax planning is appropriate[57] and not all countries are concerned about it. However, tax treaties increasingly provide some form of anti-treaty-shopping mechanism, often referred to as a limitation-of-benefit provision.[58] These provisions restrict the ability of taxpayers to access the beneficial provisions of tax treaties where the taxpayer lacks a real connection to the jurisdiction that is a signatory to the treaty.[59] Specific articles of tax treaties also often contain anti-abuse clauses. For example, some treaties preclude access to reduced withholding tax rates on investment returns where the recipient in the treaty jurisdiction is not the beneficial owner of the shares or debt.[60]

To combat conduit practices, tax treaties may contain provisions that restrict the ability of companies to claim they are residents of a treaty partner where the company is essentially serving as a conduit. For example, Canada's treaty with Mongolia provides that the convention shall not apply where a company is beneficially owned or controlled, directly or indirectly, by non-residents if the amount of tax imposed is substantially lower than the amount that would be imposed by that state if the entity was owned primarily by residents.[61] Similarly, some

---

57 See e.g. Andrian Candu, "Abuse of Tax Treaties" in Michael Schilcher and Patrick Weninger (eds), *Fundamental Issues and Practical Problems in Tax Treaty Interpretation* (Vienna: Linde, 2008); David G. Duff, "Responses to Treaty Shopping: A Canadian Perspective" (Paper Prepared for the Conference on Tax Treaties from a Legal and Economic Perspective, Vienna, Austria, March 18–20, 2010); Raffaele Russo, "Chapter 3: Guiding Concepts for International Tax Planning" in *Fundamentals of International Tax Planning* (Amsterdam: IBFD, 2007).

58 There are additional provisions in Canada's domestic tax legislation that assist in reducing international tax avoidance. See e.g. *Income Tax Act, supra* note 50 at s 245, the general anti-avoidance rule, which applies to deny benefits where there has been a misuse of the provisions of a tax treaty.

59 The 2007 protocol to the Canada–United States treaty includes a limitation on benefits provision that is applicable to both Canada and the United States.

60 For a discussion of these kinds of provisions, see e.g. C. Brown, "Beneficial Ownership and the Income Tax Act" (2003) 51 Can Tax J 402; J.D.B. Oliver et al, "Beneficial Ownership and the OECD Model" (2001) Brit Tax Rev 27; Vern Krishna, "Treaty Shopping and the Concept of Beneficial Ownership in Double Tax Treaties" (August 2009) 19 Can Current Tax 129 at 138.

61 *Convention Between the Government of Canada and the Government of Mongolia for the Avoidance of Double Taxation and the Prevention of Fiscal Evasion with Respect to Taxes on Income and on Capital*, online: DFC <http://www.fin.gc.ca/treaties-conventions/mongolia_-eng.asp> at art 28(3).

countries, most notably the United States, have included limitation on benefits provisions in their tax treaties.

Combating tax evasion

It is relatively easy for a tax department to obtain information about a resident taxpayer in order to combat tax evasion if the information is within the jurisdiction of the department. However, if the information is outside the jurisdiction then it is usually very difficult, if not impossible, to obtain it. For that reason, most capital exporting countries that tax the worldwide income of their residents have insisted that their tax treaties contain an exchange-of-information provision.[62] Indeed, in recent years even jurisdictions that are not parties to a double taxation agreement have been entering into stand-alone Tax Information Exchange Agreements.[63] Many commentators have questioned the effectiveness of these provisions since in order to obtain information from another country pursuant to them the requesting tax administration generally has to have reasonable grounds for suspecting that a specified person has evaded taxes. Further, the requesting tax administration must identify the person under investigation, the information sought, the tax purpose for which it is sought, and the grounds for believing that the information requested is held by the jurisdiction of which the request is made.[64] The OECD is engaged in an on-going project of increasing both the scope and adoption of exchange of information agreements.[65] In addition to cooperating by exchanging information, in some limited cases, tax treaties may enable one jurisdiction to enforce the tax judgments of another jurisdiction and to assist in tax collection.

This brief listing of the functions of tax treaties is sufficient to illustrate why there is a contentious debate about their role in encouraging and directing FDI. Some commentators argue that on balance they are likely to have no, or only a trivial, effect on FDI flows.[66] But whatever their effect, the fact that they are bilateral agreements between countries

---

62 See e.g. Vito Tanzi and Howell Zee, "Taxation in a Borderless World: The Role of Information Exchange" in *International Studies in Taxation: Law and Economics* (London: Kluwer Law International, 1999).

63 See Tax Information Exchange Agreements, online: DFC< http://www.fin.gc.ca/treaties-conventions/tieaaerf-eng.asp>.

64 See e.g. Michael McIntyre, "How to End the Charade of Information Exchange" (October 26, 2009) Tax Notes Intl 255.

65 See OECD, *Tax Co-operation: Towards a Level Playing Field—2008 Assessment by the Global Forum on Taxation* (Paris: OECD, 2008).

66 See e.g. Dagan, *supra* note 47.

limits their scope. It is easy to see why this mechanism for reconciling the effects of different domestic tax systems emerged near the beginning of the last century when only a relatively small number of countries were involved in international trade and investment and domestic tax systems were quite different. However, in the modern era of globalization many have argued that it is time to move to multilateral double tax treaties along the lines of multilateral trade and investment agreements.[67]

Conclusion

A comparison of tax treaties and IIAs reveals some interesting commonalities. Simply to illustrate, both tax treaties and IIAs need to address the pre-establishment period of investment to reduce barriers to entry; tax treaty and IIA negotiators have had to grapple with the appropriate limits on non-discrimination clauses; limitation of benefits clauses have been employed as a means of restricting abuses; tax treaties and IIAs both have to address the resolution of complex disputes; and information sharing concerns have been significant in both contexts. Nevertheless, even in the absence of any obvious and recorded reluctance to merge tax and investment treaty negotiations, the two have remained on parallel but distinct tracks. Ultimately, this chapter highlights that lack of connection. In some respects, tax treaties serve as effective vehicles for bilaterally coordinating domestic tax regimes and for facilitating investment. In other ways, though, they fall short.

Various proposals have been introduced for the better harmonization of international tax arrangements. In fact, as noted above, tax scholars have been taken by the WTO as a model for harmonization of international tax treaties (and tax practices more generally). It seems there is much that tax, trade and investment policy makers could learn from working more closely together.

---

67 See, e.g. Reuven Avi-Yonah, "Treating Tax Issues Through Trade Regimes" (2000–01) XXVI Brook J Intl L 1683; Arthur Cockfield, "The Rise of the OECD as Informal 'World Tax Organization' Through National Responses to E-Commerce Tax Challenges" (2006) 9 Yale Journal of Law and Technology 59; Frances Horner, "Do We Need an International Tax Organization?" (2001) 24 Tax Notes International 179; Dale Pinto, "A Proposal to Create a World Tax Organisation" (2003) 9 New Zealand Journal of Taxation Law and Policy 145; Vito Tanzi, "Is there a Need for World Tax Organization?" in Assaf Rzin and Efraim Sadka (eds), *The Economics of Globalization* (New York: Cambridge University Press, 1999) at 173; Adrian Sawyer, *Developing a World Tax Organisation: The Way Forward* (UK: Fiscal Publications, 2008); Richard Vann, "A Model Tax Treaty for the Asian-Pacific Region? (Part II)" (April 1991) International Bureau of Fiscal Documentation 151 at 160–1.

18 The impact of international law on IIA interpretation

*August Reinisch**

Introduction

The task of improving IIAs cannot be undertaken without a good understanding of the relationship between IIAs and general international law. At a basic level, IIAs as treaties have to be applied and interpreted according to the principles of treaty interpretation codified in the Vienna Convention.[1] But the interaction goes deeper as general international law plays an important gap-filling function for matters either not defined in IIAs (e.g. the definition of "expropriation") or not covered by IIAs (e.g. rules on attribution of state conduct). And there will be cases of overlap between IIAs and general international law that pose particular issues to investment tribunals. The present chapter explores this relationship in order to draw insights for the improvement of IIAs, especially with a view to ensuring the sustainability of the investment law regime.[2]

As to the application of articles 31 and 32 of the Vienna Convention by investment tribunals, it is in no way special or different from what would occur under any other treaty. However, what is special is the hybrid nature of investment arbitration as a form of enforcement of international treaty obligations, on the one hand, and as direct dispute

* Professor of International and European Law, University of Vienna, Austria. The author wishes to thank Christina Knahr and Sahib Singh for their research assistance and comments.
1 *Vienna Convention on the Law of Treaties*, May 23, 1969, 1155 UNTS 331, 8 ILM 679 (entered into force January 27, 1980) [Vienna Convention]. See also G.G. Fitzmaurice, "The Law and Procedure of the International Court of Justice: Treaty Interpretation and Certain Other Treaty Points" (1951) 28 Brit YB Int'l L 1; Sir Ian Sinclair, *The Vienna Convention on the Law of Treaties*, 2nd edn (Manchester: Manchester University Press, 1984); Richard K. Gardiner, *Treaty Interpretation* (Oxford: Oxford University Press, 2008) [Gardiner].
2 See Introduction to this book.

324 Improving international investment agreements

settlement between private parties and states, on the other hand.[3] This latter aspect clearly points to commercial arbitration paradigms where different rules of interpretation are applied. Although the legal reasoning of some investment treaty tribunals display a commercial arbitration pedigree when it comes to interpretation techniques, it is clear that, at least officially, tribunals tend to adhere to an international treaty interpretation approach. The hybrid nature raises the problem that commercial arbitrators unfamiliar with public international law may only pay lip-service to the Vienna Convention rules.

The question of the gap-filling function of general international law, for its part, can be situated in the broader debate concerning "self-contained" regimes and the fragmentation of international law.[4] This question came to the fore notably in the context of the multiple investor claims against Argentina where the defence of necessity both under BITs and customary international law was raised. The tribunals' incoherent approaches to necessity raise many issues. As such, it has been used as an example underscoring the relevance of customary international law in addressing issues not governed by IIAs, while similarly highlighting the dangers of incorporating too much into an IIA governed regime.

The First part of this chapter outlines the reliance of investment tribunals on the rules of treaty interpretation contained in articles 31 and 32 of the Vienna Convention. The Second part of focuses on the specific impact of international law on the interpretation of IIAs which results from the fact that many IIA provisions are closely linked to customary international law concepts, using the concept of necessity as an example.

The interpretation of IIAs

There is general agreement among scholars and arbitral tribunals that IIA provisions have to be interpreted according to the rules of interpretation laid down in articles 31 and 32 of the Vienna Convention.[5] Article 31 of the Vienna Convention provides:

---

3 See Zachary Douglas, "The Hybrid Foundations of Investment Treaty Arbitration" (2003) 74 Brit YB Int'l L 151.
4 *Fragmentation of International Law: Difficulties Arising from the Diversification and Expansion of International Law*, Report of the Study Group of the International Law Commission, finalized by Martti Koskenniemi (in *Report of the International Law Commission*, UNGAOR, 58th Sess, Supp No. 10, UN Doc A/61/10, (2006) at para 414 [ILC Report].
5 See e.g. *Methanex v United States of America*, Final Award, UNCITRAL (August 3, 2005), Part IV, Ch B, para 29 [*Methanex*]; see also generally Ole Kristian Fauchald, "The Legal Reasoning of ICSID Tribunals: An Empirical Analysis" (2008) 19(2) EJIL

1. A treaty shall be interpreted in good faith in accordance with the ordinary meaning to be given to the terms of the treaty in their context and in the light of its object and purpose.

2. The context for the purpose of the interpretation of a treaty shall comprise, in addition to the text, including its preamble and annexes:

    (a) any agreement relating to the treaty which was made between all the parties in connection with the conclusion of the treaty;

    (b) any instrument which was made by one or more parties in connection with the conclusion of the treaty and accepted by the other parties as an instrument related to the treaty.

3. There shall be taken into account, together with the context:

    (a) any subsequent agreement between the parties regarding the interpretation of the treaty or the application of its provisions;

    (b) any subsequent practice in the application of the treaty which establishes the agreement of the parties regarding its interpretation;

    (c) any relevant rules of international law applicable in the relations between the parties.

4. A special meaning shall be given to a term if it is established that the parties so intended.[6]

Article 32 of the Vienna Convention provides:

Recourse may be had to supplementary means of interpretation, including the preparatory work of the treaty and the circumstances of its conclusion, in order to confirm the meaning resulting from

---

301; Thomas W. Wälde, "Interpreting Investment Treaties: Experiences and Examples" [Wälde] in Christina Binder et al (eds), *International Investment Law for the 21st Century, Liber Amicorum Christoph Schreuer* (Oxford: Oxford University Press, 2009) at 724 [Binder et al]; Christoph Schreuer, "Diversity and Harmonization of Treaty Interpretation in Investment Arbitration" (2006) 3(2) Transnational Dispute Management, in Malgosia Fitzmaurice, Olufemi A. Elias and Panos Merkouris (eds), *Treaty Interpretation and the Vienna Convention on the Law of Treaties: 30 Years On* (The Netherlands: Martinus Nijhoff Publishers, 2010) at 129 [Schreuer]; Anthea Roberts, "Power and Persuasion in Investment Treaty Interpretation: the Dual Role of States" (2010) 104(2) AJIL 179; Virtus Chitoo Igbokwe, "Determination, Interpretation and Application of Substantive Law in Foreign Investment Treaty Arbitrations" (2006) 23(4) J Int'l Arb 267.

6 Vienna Convention, *supra* note 1 at art 31.

the application of article 31, or to determine the meaning when the interpretation according to article 31:

(a)   leaves the meaning ambiguous or obscure; or

(b)   leads to a result which is manifestly absurd or unreasonable.[7]

In the case law of international courts and tribunals, both provisions are regarded as codifying customary international law.[8] This jurisprudence has also confirmed that the starting point for any treaty interpretation is the plain wording of the individual provisions of an agreement,[9] aided by a contextual understanding of the entire agreement[10] and supported by teleological considerations about the aims of an agreement.[11] Nevertheless, it is generally accepted that a textual

---

7 *Ibid* at art 32.

8 See e.g. *Libya v Chad* [1994] ICJ Rep 4 at 19, para 41 [*Libya v Chad*]; *Salini Costruttori S.p.A. and Italstrade S.p.A. v Jordan*, Decision on Jurisdiction, ICSID Case No. ARB/02/13 (November 9, 2004) at para 75 [*Salini*]; *Tokios Tokelés v Ukraine*, Decision on Jurisdiction, ICSID Case No. ARB/02/18 (April 29, 2004) at para 27 [*Tokios Tokelés*]; *Mondev International Ltd v United States of America*, Award, ICSID Case No. ARB(AF)/99/2 (October 11, 2002) at para 43 [*Mondev*]; *Noble Ventures, Inc. v Romania*, *Award*, ICSID Case No. ARB/01/11 (October 12, 2005) at para 50 [*Noble*].

9 *Libya v Chad*, *supra* note 8 at 20, para 41 ("[i]nterpretation must be based above all upon the text of the treaty"); *Competence of the General Assembly for the Admission of a State to the United Nations*, Advisory Opinion, ICJ Rep 4, 1950 ("[t]he first duty of a tribunal which is called upon to interpret and apply the provisions of a treaty, is to endeavor to give effect to them in their natural and ordinary meaning [. . .]" at 8); *Sempra Energy International v Argentine Republic*, Decision on Annulment, ICSID Case No. ARB/02/16 (Annulment proceeding) (June 29, 2010) at para 188. [*Sempra*, Annulment]; See also the commentary of the International Law Commission to art 27 (now art 31) in "Draft Articles on the Law of Treaties with commentaries" (UN Doc A/6309/Rev.1) in *Yearbook of the International Law Commission* 1966, vol II (New York: UN, 1967) (UNDOC.A/CN.4/SER.A/1966/Add.1) ("[t]he article as already indicated is based on the view that the text must be presumed to be the authentic expression of the intentions of the parties; and that, in consequence, the starting point of interpretation is the elucidation of the meaning of the text, not an investigation *ab initio* into the intentions of the parties" at 220).

10 See e.g. *Fraport AG Frankfurt Airport Services Worldwide v Philippines*, Award, ICSID Case No. ARB/03/25 (August 16, 2007) at para 339; *Industria Nacional de Alimentos, S.A. and Indalsa Perú, S.A. v The Republic of Peru*, Decision on Annulment, ICSID Case No. ARB/03/4 (Annulment proceeding) (September 5, 2007) at para 80 (Request for annulment of the award in *Empresas Lucchetti, S.A. and Lucchetti Perú, S.A. v Republic of Peru*, Award, ICSID Case No. ARB/03/4 (February 7, 2005).

11 *SGS Société Générale de Surveillance SA v Philippines*, Decision on Objections to Jurisdiction and Separate Declaration, ICSID Case No. ARB/02/6 (January 29, 2004) at para 116; *Occidental Exploration and Production Company v Ecuador*, Final Award, LCIA Case No. UN 3467 (July 1, 2004) at para 183; *Siemens AG v Argentina*, Decision on Jurisdiction, ICSID Case No. ARB/02/8 (August 3, 2004) at para 81

interpretation does not enjoy primacy over the other elements contained in article 31 of the Vienna Convention. Rather, all aspects enjoy equal relevance. Investment tribunals have captured this approach as a "process of progressive encirclement."[12]

It has become a truism for many investment tribunals to state that the wording of IIAs matters and that they will pay specific attention to the actual language of the provisions applicable in various cases.[13] Equally, the object and purpose of a treaty provision are of primary relevance for the interpretation of IIAs.[14] In spite of this general agreement on the use of the rules of treaty interpretation contained in the Vienna Convention, the actual results appear to differ sharply. In fact, the proper meaning of IIA provisions raises interesting interpretation questions; they demonstrate that tribunals may come to diverging results, although the actual difference in the specific wording of the clauses they have to apply will often be limited.

The ordinary meaning

The pre-eminence of the ordinary wording is often stressed by investment tribunals. For instance, the NAFTA tribunal in *ADF v United*

[*Siemens AG*]; *MTD Equity Sdn. Bhd & MTD Chile S.A. v Chile*, Award, ICSID Case No. ARB/01/7 (May 25, 2004) at para 113 [*MTD*, Award]; *Enron Corpn and Ponderosa Assets, L.P. v Argentine Republic*, Award, ICSID Case No. ARB/01/3 (May 22, 2007) at para 259 [*Enron*].

12 *Aguas del Tunari v Bolivia*, Decision on Respondent's Objections to Jurisdiction, ICSID Case No. ARB/02/3 (October 21, 2005) [*Aguas del Tunari,* Jurisdiction] ("[I]nterpretation under Article 31 of the Vienna Convention is a process of progressive encirclement where the interpreter starts under the general rule with (1) the ordinary meaning of the terms of the treaty, (2) in their context and (3) in light of the treaty's object and purpose, and by cycling through this three step inquiry iteratively closes in upon the proper interpretation. [. . .] It is critical to observe [. . .] [that] the Vienna Convention does not privilege any one of these three aspects of the interpretation method" at para 91).

13 See e.g. *M.C.I. Power Group L.C. and New Turbine, Inc. v Ecuador*, Award, ICSID Case No. ARB/03/6 (July 31, 2007) at para 127; *Saluka Investments BV (The Netherlands) v The Czech Republic*, Partial Award, UNCITRAL (March 17, 2006) at para 297 [*Saluka*].

14 See e.g. *Bayindir Insaat Turizm Ticaret Ve Sanayi A.S. v Islamic Republic of Pakistan*, Decision on Jurisdiction, ICSID Case No. ARB/03/29 (November 14, 2005) at para 96; *Lauder v Czech Republic*, Final Award, UNCITRAL (September 3, 2001) at para 292; *MTD*, Award, *supra* note 11 at paras 104, 105; *Siemens AG*, *supra* note 11 at para 81; *Noble*, *supra* note 8 at para 52; *Aguas del Tunari*, Jurisdiction, *supra* note 12 at paras 153, 240–1; *Continental Casualty Co v The Argentine Republic*, Decision on Jurisdiction, ICSID Case No. ARB/03/9 (February 22, 2006) at para 80.

States held that "[w]e understand the rules of interpretation found in customary international law to enjoin us to focus first on the actual language of the provision being construed."[15]

The "ordinary meaning" is regularly invoked in cases where tribunals are called upon to decide on the scope of IIA clauses. For instance, in *Maffezini v Spain*, the tribunal emphasized the wording of the applicable MFN clause which referred to treatment "in all matters subject to this Agreement" in order to conclude that these also covered dispute settlement.[16] This interpretation was reaffirmed in the *Suez v Argentina* case where the tribunal held that dispute settlement was certainly a "matter" governed by the Argentina-Spain BIT and that the "ordinary meaning" of the term "treatment" included the rights and privileges granted by a contracting state to investors covered by the treaty.[17]

Also, the NAFTA tribunal in *Methanex* stressed the importance of the literal interpretation of treaty provisions in the context of giving meaning to NAFTA's national treatment clause.[18] On this basis, the *Methanex* tribunal emphasized the ordinary meaning approach over any other interpretation technique.[19] Sometimes tribunals emphasize the literal interpretation without even invoking the Vienna Convention.[20]

Object and purpose

Article 31 of the Vienna Convention explicitly makes the "object and purpose" of a treaty a relevant interpretation criterion. It is thus not surprising that investment tribunals regularly refer to the "object and purpose" of IIAs—which they often find expressed in their preambles.[21]

---

15 *ADF Group Inc. v United States of America*, Award, ICSID Case No. ARB(AF)/00/1 (January 9, 2003) at para 147 [*ADF*].
16 *Emilio Agustín Maffezini v Kingdom of Spain*, Award on Jurisdiction, ICSID Case No. ARB/97/7 (January 25, 2000) at para 38 [*Maffezini*].
17 *Suez, Sociedad General de Aguas de Barcelona S.A., and Vivendi Universal S.A. v The Argentine Republic*, ICSID Case No. ARB/03/19 and *AWG Group Ltd v The Argentine Republic* (UNCITRAL), Decision on Jurisdiction (August 3, 2006) at para 55 [*Suez and Vivendi*].
18 *Methanex, supra* note 5 at Part IV, ch B, para 29.
19 *Ibid* at para 37.
20 See e.g. *International Thunderbird Gaming Corpn v Mexico*, Arbitral Award, UNCITRAL (January 26, 2006) at para 175.
21 *Compañía de Aguas del Aconquija S.A. and Vivendi Universal v Argentine Republic*, Award, ICSID Case No. ARB/97/3 (August 20, 2007) at para 7.4.4 [*Compañía de Aguas*]; *MTD*, Award, *supra* note 11 at para 113; *LG&E Energy Corpn v Argentine Republic*, Decision on Liability, ICSID Case No. ARB/02/1 (October 3, 2006) at para 124 [*LG&E, Liability*]; *Saluka supra* note 13 at para 299.

A particularly articulate expression of this approach can be found in the *Siemens* decision.[22] In this case, the tribunal relied on the title and preamble of the BIT in ruling that the parties' intention was to create favorable conditions for investments and to stimulate private initiative.[23]

Object and purpose was also particularly relevant in cases where tribunals had to interpret the scope of the dispute settlement often in the context of the reach of MFN clauses. In a number of cases, arbitral tribunals have stressed that effective investor-state dispute settlement is a crucial aspect of investment protection.[24] This has led to calls for an extensive interpretation of MFN clauses to include dispute settlement as well.[25]

Intent of the parties—negotiating history

The intention of the parties is not an express guideline for treaty interpretation pursuant to articles 31 and 32 of the Vienna Convention. In fact the only reference to intent can be found in article 31(4) clarifying that "[a] special meaning shall be given to a term if it is established that the parties so intended." However, it is widely accepted that the intention of the treaty parties is a relevant aspect of interpretation. Thus, it is not surprising that international courts and tribunals often inquire into the intention of the parties in order to ascertain the content of specific treaty provisions.[26] This is also true for investment tribunals.[27]

22 *Siemens AG*, *supra* note 11 at para 81.

23 *Ibid.*

24 See e.g. *National Grid plc v The Argentine Republic*, Decision on Jurisdiction, UNCITRAL (June 20, 2006) at para 76 [*National Grid*, Jurisdiction]; *Eastern Sugar BV v Czech Republic*, Partial Award, SCC Case No. 088/2004, UNCITRAL (March 27, 2007) at para 165; *Suez and Argentina*, *supra* note 17 at para 57.

25 See e.g. *Telefónica SA v Argentine Republic*, Decision of the Tribunal on Objections to Jurisdiction, ICSID Case No. ARB/03/20 (May 25, 2006) at para 98. See also Stephan Schill, *The Multilateralization of International Investment Law* (New York: Cambridge University Press, 2009) at 180.

26 *Case Concerning the Dispute Regarding Navigational and Related Rights (Costa Rica v Nicaragua)*, ICJ Reports (2009) 213, at paras 63, 64.

27 See e.g. *Amco Asia Corpn and others v Republic of Indonesia*, Decision on Jurisdiction, ICSID Case No. ARB/81/1 (September 25, 1983) ("[a] convention to arbitrate is not to be construed *restrictively*, nor, as a matter of fact, *broadly* or *liberally*. It is to be construed in a way which leads to find out and to respect the common will of the parties" at para 14); *Berschader v Russia*, Award, SCC Case No. 080/2004 (April 21, 2006) ("[f]irstly, the tribunal must express its firm view that the fundamental issue in determining whether or not an MFN clause encompasses the dispute resolution provisions of other treaties must always be an assessment of the intention of the contracting parties" at para 175) [*Berschader*]; *Compañía de Aguas*, *supra* note 21 at

Ideally, the wording of a treaty is seen as the best expression of what the parties really intended. This is clearly alluded to in *Methanex* when the tribunal stated: "[. . .] the approach of the Vienna Convention is that the text of the treaty is deemed to be the authentic expression of the intentions of the parties."[28] Whether this is always true may be open to doubt, although the idea as such has been affirmed in investment arbitration practice.

Tribunals often attempt to uncover the intention of treaty parties by having recourse to the *travaux préparatoires* of a treaty. Though mentioned in article 32 of the Vienna Convention only as supplementary means of interpretation,[29] establishing the (re-)constructed will of the parties is frequently the avowed task of arbitration tribunals.[30] Since states often do not specifically negotiate individual treaty provisions, and instead rely on templates taken from national Model BITs, such emphasis on their presumed intention to be unearthed by studying the *travaux* may be overly optimistic.[31]

Many awards fail to explain the legal basis of the tribunal's underlying presumptions and, in particular, why a presumption should work in one direction and not in the opposite. Possibly this is a result of the interpretation principle *in dubio mitius* according to which, in case of doubt, states must be presumed to incur fewer rather than more far-reaching obligations.[32] However,

para 7.4.4; *Parkerings-Compagniet AS v Lithuania*, Award, ICSID Case No. ARB/05/8 (September 11, 2007) ("[t]he Claimant did not show any evidence which could demonstrate that, when signing the BIT, the Republic of Lithuania and the Kingdom of Norway intended to give a different protection to their investors than the protection granted by the *fair and equitable* standard" at para 277).

28 *Methanex supra* note 5 at Part II, ch B, para 22; see also *Berschader*, *supra* note 27 (Separate Opinion by Todd Weiler at para 4).

29 Vienna Convention, *supra* note 1 at art 32.

30 *Plama Consortium Ltd v Bulgaria*, Decision on Jurisdiction, ICSID Case No. ARB/03/24 (February 8, 2005) at paras 189–95; *Pope & Talbot Inc. v Canada*, Award on the Merits of Phase 2, UNCITRAL (April 10, 2001) at paras 39–41; *Mondev*, *supra* note 8 at para 111.

31 See Wälde, *supra* note 5 ("[w]hat these features do is to place a question mark over the use of *travaux* under Article 32 of the Vienna Convention, but also over too much reliance on established interpretation maxims such as '*e contrario*' or the principle of effectiveness of each element of the text. These assume a degree of perfection and information with the drafters that did not exist" at 750).

32 See The *Loewen Group, Inc. and Raymond L Loewen v United States of America*, Award, ICSID Case No. ARB (AF)/98/3 (June 26, 2003) [*Loewen*]; *SGS Société Générale de Surveillance S.A. v Islamic Republic of Pakistan*, Decision on Jurisdiction, ICSID Case No. ARB/01/13 (August 6, 2003) ("[t]he appropriate interpretive approach is the prudential one summed up in the literature as *in dubio pars mitior est sequenda*, or

the validity of such a principle as a guideline for interpretation is controversial.[33]

Contextual interpretation

A contextual interpretation of treaty provisions is clearly mandated by article 31 of the Vienna Convention calling for an interpretation of the "terms in their context."[34] The immediate context of a treaty expression is determined by the grammar and syntax of a sentence.[35] The Vienna Convention makes clear, however, that context specifically relates to the entire text as well as the preamble and annexes of a treaty.[36]

Context within IIAs

Investment tribunals often determine the meaning of provisions by reference to their location within a specific BIT.[37] For the purpose of interpreting MFN clauses, tribunals have frequently looked at the context of such clauses and the relationship to other clauses in an IIA which might shed light on their proper interpretation. One recurrent line of argument, particularly of those tribunals which were willing to allow the extension of MFN clauses to procedural or even jurisdictional provisions in third country IIAs, relates to the implications of certain exceptions to MFN treatment as they are often expressly foreseen in IIAs. At a minimum, many IIAs provide that MFN treatment does not cover benefits granted as a result of preferential trade agreements like customs unions and free trade agreements. *E contrario* or on the basis of the principle of *expressio unius est exclusio alterius*, tribunals have argued that other exceptions should not be read into the text.[38] Thus, where an MFN clause is wide enough to cover procedural or jurisdictional issues, the lack of any express exception in these fields should be interpreted as a clear indication that they are included. This reasoning was adopted by the tribunal in *National Grid v Argentina*[39] and emphasized in *RosInvest v Russia* where

more tersely, *in dubio mitius*" at para 171). See also Gus van Harten, *Investment Treaty Arbitration and Public Law* (Oxford: Oxford University Press, 2007) at 132.

33 See Wälde, *supra* note 5 at 741. See also *Mondev, supra* note 8 at para 43.

34 See Vienna Convention, *supra* note 1 at art 31.

35 Gardiner, *supra* note 1 at 178.

36 Vienna Convention, *supra* note 1 at art 31(1).

37 See e.g. *Saluka, supra* note 13 at para 298.

38 See, for instance, the tribunal in *Tokios Tokelės, supra* note 8 at para 30, on the issue of the correct interpretation of the definition of investor.

39 *National Grid*, Jurisdiction, *supra* note 24 at para 82.

the tribunal specifically noted that the UK-USSR BIT exempted preferential trade and tax agreements from the application of its MFN clause[40] and concluded that:

> [i]t can certainly not be presumed that the Parties "forgot" arbitration when drafting and agreeing on Article 7. Had the Parties intended that the MFN clauses should also not apply to arbitration, it would indeed have been easy to add a sub-section (c) to that effect in Article 7. The fact that this was not done, in the view of the Tribunal, is further confirmation that the MFN-clauses in Article 3 are also applicable to submissions to arbitration in other Treaties.[41]

It thus followed the argument proposed by claimant who had urged the tribunal to apply "the principle of *expressio unius est exclusio alterius.*"[42]

The contextual relevance of other IIAs

When ascertaining the proper meaning of IIA clauses via contextual consideration, tribunals often take a comparative approach by looking at the wording of other IIAs concluded by one of the parties with third states or between third states. To what extent reliance on such "external" context is justified raises complex legal issues.[43] As a matter of empirical fact, investment tribunals like international courts and tribunals in general quite often take into account the formulation of third country treaties in order to confirm or to contrast the interpretation of the treaty rules they have to apply.

The area of interpreting the content of key substantive investment standards, such as fair and equitable treatment or full protection and security,[44] is a particularly clear example of tribunals heavily relying on

---

40 UK-USSR BIT (1989) at art 7.
41 *RosInvestCo UK Ltd v The Russian Federation*, Award on Jurisdiction, SCC Case No. Arb. V079/2005 (October 2007) at para 135.
42 *Ibid* at para 99.
43 See Mārtiņš Paparinskis, "Sources of Law and Arbitral Interpretations of Pari Materia Investment Protection Rules" in Ole Kristian Fauchald and André Nollkaemper (eds), *The Practice of International and National Courts and the (De-) Fragmentation of International Law* (Oxford: Hart Publishing, 2011), online: SSRN <http://papers.ssrn.com/sol3/papers.cfm?abstract_id=1697835>.
44 See Campbell McLachlan, Laurence Shore and Matthew Weiniger, *International Investment Arbitration: Substantive Principles* (Oxford: Oxford University Press, 2007); August Reinisch (ed), *Standards of Investment Protection* (Oxford: Oxford University Press, 2008).

the interpretation of similar clauses contained in third party treaties in the gradual elaboration of a *jurisprudence constante* or *de facto* case law.[45] Strictly speaking, the third country BITs and their interpretation in investment awards is beyond the direct context of interpretation. However, like general (customary) international law on point, it is often relied upon for argumentative purposes.

Such a comparative approach is often used in the field of interpreting the scope of MFN clauses. For instance in the *Salini* case, the tribunal distinguished the MFN clause it had to apply from the one applicable in *Maffezini* to explain why it rejected the idea that it would encompass dispute settlement. It found that "Article 3 of the BIT between Italy and Jordan does not include any provision extending its scope of application to dispute settlement. It does not envisage 'all rights or all matters covered by the agreement'."[46] Thus, it held that its jurisdiction could not be based on another BIT via the applicable MFN clause.

General international law as relevant context

According to article 31(3)(c) of the Vienna Convention, "[t]here shall be taken into account, together with the context any relevant rules of international law applicable in the relations between the parties."[47] This provision which has been termed the "most ambivalent" one of the interpretation rules of the Vienna Convention[48] has received much attention in WTO law.[49] But also in investment law recent developments have led to

---

45 See Gabrielle Kaufmann-Kohler, "Arbitral Precedent: Dream, Necessity or Excuse?" (2007) 23 Arbitration International 357; Andrea K. Bjorklund, "Investment Treaty Arbitral Decisions as *Jurisprudence Constante*" in Colin Picker, Isabella Bunn and Douglas W. Arner (eds), *International Economic Law: State and Future of the Discipline* (Oxford: Hart Publishing, 2008) at 265; August Reinisch, "The Role of Precedent in ICSID Arbitration" in Austrian Arbitration Yearbook (2008) at 495; Andrés Rigo Sureda, "Precedent in Investment Treaty Arbitration," in Binder et al, *supra* note 5 at 830.

46 *Salini, supra* note 8 at para 118.

47 Vienna Convention, *supra* note 1 at art 31(3)(1).

48 Wälde, *supra* note 5 at 769.

49 Isabelle Van Damme, *Treaty Interpretation by the WTO Appellate Body* (Oxford: Oxford University Press, 2009) at ch 9; José E. Alvarez, "The Factors Driving and Constraining the Incorporation of International Law in WTO Adjudication" in Merit E. Janow, Victoria Donaldson and Alan Yanovich (eds), *The WTO: Governance, Dispute Settlement and Developing Countries* (New York: Juris Publishing Inc, 2008) at 622; Mārtiņš Paparinskis, "Equivalent Primary Rules and Differential Secondary Rules: Countermeasures in WTO and Investment Protection Law" in Tomer Broude and Yuval Shany (eds), *Multi-Sourced Equivalent Norms in International Law* (Oxford: Hart Publishing, 2010) at 259.

a more intense debate of this interpretative guideline.[50] The potential of integrating general international law, mainly in the form of custom, as a means to mitigate the dangers of fragmentation stemming from a proliferation of treaty regimes was recognized by the ILC Study Group on Fragmentation.[51] According to the Study Group's conclusions, customary international law and general principles of law are of particular relevance to the interpretation of a treaty under article 31(3)(c) of the Vienna Convention, where the treaty rule is unclear or open-textured,[52] the treaty terms have a recognised meaning in customary law,[53] and where the parties presumptively intended to refer to customary law for questions that were not resolved in the treaty in express terms.[54]

Examples of international law influences on IIA interpretation

Because IIAs are largely building on the existing customary international law protection of foreign investment, as expressed in the principles governing expropriations of foreign property or the respect for treatment in accordance with the international minimum standard, these general international principles often influence the actual interpretation of specific IIA standards in concrete cases.

One of the best known problems concerns the relationship between the treaty standard of fair and equitable treatment, regularly included in IIAs, and the international minimum standard under customary law. Whether and to what extent general international law should, and indeed does, influence the interpretation of the fair and equitable treatment standard has given rise not only to divergent responses by arbitral tribunals[55] and

---

50 Campbell McLachlan, "Investment Treaties and General International Law" (2008) 57 ICLQ 361; Campbell McLachlan, "The Principle of Systemic Integration and Article 31(3)(c) of the Vienna Convention" (2005) 54 ICLQ 279; Mārtiņš Paparinskis, "Investment Protection Law and Systemic Integration of Treaty and Custom" (2010) SIEL Online Proceedings Working Paper 2010/21, online: SSRN <http://ssrn.com/abstract=1632559>; Christoph Schreuer, "Diversity and Harmonization of Treaty Interpretation in Investment Arbitration", *supra* note 5.
51 ILC Report on Fragmentation, *supra* note 4.
52 *Ibid* at para 20(a).
53 *Ibid* at para 20(b).
54 *Ibid* at para 20(c).
55 *Mondev*, *supra* note 8 at para 125; *ADF supra* note 15 at para 179; see also *CMS Gas Transmission Company v The Argentine Republic*, Award, ICSID Case No. ARB/01/8 (May 12, 2005) at para 284 [*CMS Gas*]; *Siemens v Argentina*, Award, ICSID Case No. ARB/02/8 (February 6, 2007) at para 291; *MCI Power Group and New Turbine v Ecuador*, Award, ICSID Case No. ARB/03/6 (July 31, 2007) at para 369. Compare

to academic controversy;[56] it has equally led treaty-makers to clarify the intended meaning of clauses that proved controversial.[57] However, other fields of international law, such as the rules on diplomatic protection, and here in particular on the nationality of claims, are often invoked in investment arbitration in order to provide interpretative guidelines for tribunals. Whether and to what extent investment arbitration rules are meant to replace the traditional rules of diplomatic protection or whether they are intended to be supplemented by them has proven to become highly controversial as well.[58]

Because of the limited space available here, these issues will not be addressed in detail. Rather, one example is highlighted which demonstrates the often unexplored potential of general international law for the interpretation of IIAs. It is the case of the role of treaty provisions permitting derogations from protection standards in emergency situations and their relationship to the general international law of state of necessity.

The relevance of state responsibility rules for IIA interpretation— the example of state of necessity and emergency clauses in IIAs

A particularly rich field of international law influences on IIA interpretation can be observed with regard to state responsibility rules which regularly play an important role in investment cases. To be precise, they are usually particularly relevant for issues not regulated by IIAs. Exam-

with *CME Czech Republic B V v The Czech Republic*, Partial Award, UNCITRAL (September 13, 2001) at para 156; *Técnicas Medioambientales Tecmed S.A. v Mexico*, Award, ICSID Case No. ARB (AF)/00/2 (May 29, 2003) at para 155.

56 Kenneth J. Vandevelde, "A Unified Theory of Fair and Equitable Treatment" (2010) 43 NYU J Int'l L and Pol 43; Campbell McLachlan, "Investment Treaties and General International Law" (2008) 57 ICLQ 361 at 374; J. Roman Picherack, "The Expanding Scope of the Fair and Equitable Treatment Standard: Have Recent Tribunals Gone Too Far?" (2008) 9 Journal of World Investment and Trade 255; Rudolf Dolzer "Fair and Equitable Treatment: A Key Standard in Investment Treaties" (2005) 39 The International Lawyer 87; Christoph Schreuer, "Fair and Equitable Treatment in Arbitral Practice" (2005) 6 Journal of World Investment and Trade 357.

57 See e.g. US Model BIT 2004, online: US Department of State <http://www.state.gov/documents/organization/117601.pdf> at art 5(2).

58 *Loewen supra* note 40 at para 233; *Case concerning Ahmadou Sadio Diallo (Guinea v Congo)*, Preliminary Objections, ICJ Reports (2007) at para 88; see the general discussion in Zachary Douglas, *The International Law of Investment Claims* (Cambridge: Cambridge University Press, 2009) at 10–38; see also Sir Frank Berman QC, "The Relevance of the Law on Diplomatic Protection in Investment Arbitration" in Federico Ortino et al (eds), *Investment Treaty Law: Current Issues II* (London: BIICL, 2007) at 69; Mārtiņš Paparinskis, "Barcelona Traction: A Friend of Investment Protection Law" (2008) 8 *Baltic Yearbook of International Law* 105.

ples are questions of attribution of conduct[59] or rules on the exclusion of wrongfulness, in particular in the context of the invocation of state of necessity.[60] For such questions, BITs usually do not contain any special rules. Thus, customary international law rules in the form of—what is generally regarded as their codification—the ILC Articles on State Responsibility are often resorted to by investment tribunals.

In these situations, the state responsibility rules normally operate as gap-fillers. They are applied because IIAs do not address these issues; thus they are not directly relevant for the interpretation of IIA provisions. However, in some instances interesting overlaps may occur. The relationship between general international law on state of necessity and emergency clauses in IIAs is one such example. A number of investment cases brought against Argentina have addressed this problem.

One of the most hotly debated issues in investment law has been the question whether Argentina's economic emergency measures adopted in the wake of its financial crisis in 2001–02 excluded its responsibility for breaches of BIT obligations. Many cases were in fact brought by US investors on the basis of the Argentina-US BIT[61] which contained a special emergency or non-precluded measures (NPM) clause. Its article XI provided:

> [t]his treaty shall not preclude the application by either Party of measures necessary for the maintenance of public order, the fulfillment of its obligations with respect to the maintenance or restoration of international peace or security, or the protection of its own essential security interests.[62]

In all these cases Argentina invoked both article XI and the customary international law defense of necessity as codified in article 25 of the International Law Commission's Articles on State Responsibility.[63]

59 See e.g. Georgios Petrochilos, "Attribution" in Katia Yannaca-Small (ed), *Arbitration Under International Investment Agreements: A Guide to Key Issues* (Oxford: Oxford University Press, 2010) at 287; Kaj Hobér, "State Responsibility and Attribution", in Peter Muchlinski, Federico Ortino and Christoph Schreuer (eds), *The Oxford Handbook of International Investment Law* (Oxford: Oxford University Press, 2008) at 549.
60 For discussions on necessity, see *infra* note 70.
61 *CMS Gas*, *supra* note 55; *Enron*, *supra* note 11; *Sempra Energy International v Argentine Republic*, Award, ICSID Case No. ARB/02/16 (September 28, 2007) [*Sempra*]; *LG&E, Liability*, *supra* note 21; *Continental Casualty Co v Argentine Republic*, Award, ICSID Case No. ARB/03/9 (September 5, 2008) [*Continental Casualty, Award*].
62 US-Argentina BIT (1991) at art XI.
63 See "Draft articles on Responsibility of States for Internationally Wrongful Acts, with commentaries 2001" (UN Doc A/56/10) in Yearbook of the International Law

Tribunals differed not only with regard to the question whether the level for either the treaty standard or the severity required by article 25 had been met; they also had different views regarding the relationship between the treaty clause and the customary international law defense.[64] The *CMS*,[65] *Enron*[66] and *Sempra*[67] tribunals concluded that article XI reflected the customary international law standard of necessity, while the *LG&E*[68] tribunal treated article XI as a distinct defense.[69]

In the *CMS* award, the relationship between the two legal regimes was not directly addressed. Rather, the tribunal analyzed the availability of the customary international law defense of state of necessity. It relied on article XI of the Argentina-US BIT only in passing so as to confirm its findings on customary law.[70]

The integrative approach was made even more explicit in *Enron* and *Sempra* where the tribunals found that the emergency clause of the Argentina-US BIT could not be regarded as a self-judging clause and held that this "[t]reaty provision is inseparable from the customary law standard insofar as the definition of necessity and the conditions for its

Commission 2001, vol. II, Part Two (New York: UN, 2008) art 25 (UN Doc A/CN.4/SER.A/2001/Add.1) [ILC Articles on State Responsibility].
64 See e.g. Christina Binder, "Changed Circumstances in Investment Law: Interfaces Between the Law of Treaties and the Law of State Responsibility with a Special Focus on the Argentine Crisis" in Binder et al, *supra* note 5 at 608; Andrea K. Bjorklund, "Emergency Exceptions: State of Necessity and *Force Majeure*" in Peter Muchlinski, Federico Ortino and Christoph Schreuer, *The Oxford Handbook of International Investment Law, supra* note 59 at 495; William Burke-White and Andreas von Staden, "Investment Protection in Extraordinary Times: The Interpretation and Application of Non-Precluded Measures Provisions in Bilateral Investment Treaties" (2007) 48 Virginia Journal of International Law 307; Tarcisio Gazzini, "Necessity in International Investment Law: Some Critical Remarks on *CMS v Argentina*" (2008) 26 Journal of Energy and Natural Resources Law 450; Jürgen Kurtz, "ICSID Annulment Committee Rules on the Relationship between Customary and Treaty Exceptions on Necessity in Situations of Financial Crisis" (December 20, 2007) 11(30) ASIL Insight.
65 *CMS Gas, supra* note 55.
66 *Enron, supra* note 11.
67 *Sempra, supra* note 61.
68 *LG&E, Liability, supra* note 21.
69 On these conflicting awards, see in particular, Charles Leben, "L'Etat de nécessité dans le droit international de l'investissement" (2005) 349 Gazette du Palais 19; August Reinisch, "Necessity in International Investment Arbitration—An Unnecessary Split of Opinions in Recent ICSID Cases?" (2007) 8(2) Journal of World Investment and Trade 191; Stephan W. Schill, "International Investment Law and the Host State's Power to Handle Economic Crises" (2007) 24(3) Journal of International Arbitration 265; Michael Waibel, "Two Worlds of Necessity in ICSID Arbitration: CMS and LG&E" (2007) 20 Leiden Journal of International Law 637.
70 *CMS Gas, supra* note 55 at para 374.

operation are concerned, given that it is under customary law that such elements have been defined."[71]

By effectively conflating the IIA standard and the customary international law standard of necessity, the ICSID tribunals also heavily relied upon state responsibility law in their interpretation of article XI of the Argentina-US BIT. In fact, the *Sempra* tribunal expressly considered that it should rely on general international law where the IIA does not provide a sufficiently precise answer. This approach could take place in the context of article 31(3)(c) of the Vienna Convention, whereby a tribunal would rely on the customary international law standard of necessity in order to interpret the relatively undetermined wording of the IIA's NPM clause. However, the *Sempra* tribunal appeared to have gone further by applying customary international law requirements for the invocation of necessity which it found missing in the applicable IIA. It found that because the IIA did not deal with the legal elements necessary for the legitimate invocation of a state of necessity such rule had thus to be found under customary law.[72]

This approach was, however, severely criticized. At first, the *CMS* annulment committee,[73] though upholding the original *CMS* award, found that the tribunal had made grave errors and should have considered article XI as a distinct treaty defense.[74] Pursuant to the *CMS* annulment committee "[o]nly if [a tribunal] concluded that there was conduct not in conformity with the Treaty would it have had to consider whether Argentina's responsibility could be precluded in whole or in part under customary international law."[75]

This reasoning was reinforced by the *Sempra* annulment committee.[76] It concluded that the original tribunal's reliance on article 25 of the ILC Articles on State Responsibility, instead of article XI of the Argentina-US BIT meant that it "has failed to conduct its review on the basis that the applicable legal norm is to be found in article XI of the BIT, and that this failure constitutes an excess of powers within the meaning of the ICSID Convention."[77]

In arriving at this conclusion the committee took an extremely restrictive approach as to the relevance of customary international law

---

71 *Sempra, supra* note 61 at para 376. Similarly, *Enron, supra* note 11 at para 334.
72 *Sempra, supra* note 61 at para 378.
73 *CMS Gas v Argentina*, Decision on Annulment, ICSID Case No. ARB/01/8 (Annulment proceeding) (September 25, 2007).
74 See *ibid* at para 129.
75 *Ibid* at para 134.
76 *Sempra*, Annulment, *supra* note 9.
77 *Ibid* at para 209.

for the interpretation of IIAs. While not denying that such role may be appropriate in certain situations,[78] it held that "from [a] comparison [of the texts of Article 25 ILC Articles and Article XI BIT] [it was apparent] that Article 25 does not offer a guide to interpretation of the terms used in Article XI."[79] While it may be correct to prioritize the application of the primary rule of the IIA (article XI of the Argentina-US BIT) over the secondary rule of state responsibility (article 25 of the ILC Articles on State Responsibility), the total neglect of the latter as rules having a potential "relevance" for the interpretation of the former appears overly strict.

A very different approach made general international law crucial for the annulment of the *Enron* award.[80] The annulment committee in this case found that the way the original tribunal applied the "only way" criterion, the issue of the impairment of essential interests of other states as well as Argentina's contribution to the situation of necessity in the sense of article 25 of the ILC Articles on State Responsibility[81] was "tainted by annullable error."[82] Whether the committee overstepped the distinction between annulling because the proper law was not applied and reforming the award because it was incorrectly applied is a question that goes to the heart of the function of annulment under the ICSID Convention.[83] The committee obviously emphasized its role as that of a detector of the tribunal's failure to apply the applicable law.[84]

As opposed to the *Sempra* annulment committee, the committee in *Enron* did not take issue with the application of customary international law on state of necessity in principle; rather it criticized its wrong application. Instead of less influence of general international law (on necessity) as suggested by the *Sempra* annulment committee, it found that the proper application of the requirements to invoke a state of necessity under customary international law would have required a

78 *Ibid* ("[i]t may be appropriate to look to customary law as a guide to the interpretation of terms used in the BIT" para 197).

79 *Ibid* at para 199.

80 *Enron v Argentina*, Decision on Annulment, ICSID Case No. ARB/01/3 (Annulment proceeding) (July 30, 2010) [*Enron*, Annulment].

81 See art 25 ILC Articles on State Responsibility, *supra* note 67.

82 *Enron*, Annulment, *supra* note 80 at para 395.

83 See on the function of art 52 ICSID Convention, among others, Irmgard Marboe, "ICSID Annulment Decisions: Three Generations Revisited", in Binder et al, *supra* note 5 at 200; Christoph Schreuer, "Three Generations of ICSID Annulment Proceedings" in Emmanuel Gaillard and Yas Banifatemi (eds), *Annulment of ICSID Awards* (Huntington, NY: Juris Pub, 2004) at 17.

84 See with regard to the "only way" criterion, *Enron*, Annulment, *supra* note 89 at para 377.

much more thorough discussion of article 25 of the ILC Articles on State Responsibility and its corresponding customary international law by the tribunal. For instance, with regard to the "only way" criterion, the *Enron* annulment committee was of the view that the tribunal should have gone beyond a literal "interpretation" and inquired whether there would have been available other reasonable means of a proportionate response to the Argentinean financial crisis[85] instead of relying on the expert opinion of an economist stating "that Argentina had other options for dealing with the economic crisis."[86] According to this view, the proper role of general international law should have been much more prominent in determining the outcome of the proceedings.

An alternative can be found in the reasoning of the *Continental Casualty* tribunal.[87] In line with the two annulment committees in *CMS* and *Sempra*, it also regarded article XI as a distinct defense and it stressed the different conditions for the invocation of the treaty defense and the state of necessity defense.[88] It then proceeded to interpret this provision not so much in light of the "customary concept of necessity" which it still considered relevant.[89] Rather, it particularly relied on the GATT and GATT/WTO jurisprudence relating to the GATT article XX exceptions which had "extensively dealt with the concept and requirements of necessity in the context of economic measures derogating to the obligations contained in GATT."[90] On this basis, the ICSID tribunal found that "Argentina's conduct in the face of the economic and social crisis conformed, by and large, with the conditions required for derogating from its obligations under Art. XI of the BIT [. . .]"[91]

This approach represents a middle ground in keeping general international law relevant for the interpretation of an IIA provision, and in the case at hand, of the NPM clause of article XI of the Argentina-US BIT. While reserving a role to customary international law for the interpretation of an IIA as a matter of principle, the *Continental Casualty* tribunal mainly resorted to the meaning given to a related concept in another treaty, the GATT, in order to interpret the provision in question.

85 *Enron*, Annulment, *supra* note 80 at paras 369–73.
86 *Ibid* at para 374.
87 *Continental Casualty*, Award, *supra* note 61.
88 *Ibid* at para 167.
89 *Ibid* at para 168.
90 *Ibid* at para 192.
91 *Ibid* at para 233.

Conclusion

The overview of IIA interpretation and the specific example from investment arbitration practice have demonstrated that general international law plays a highly relevant role in the interpretation of IIAs. As with other special fields of international law, there appears to be a clear tendency to regard investment law and its basis in the form of IIAs, to be a sub-field of international law which cannot be seen in "clinical isolation" from the rest.[92]

The view already expressed in one of the first treaty arbitration cases, *AAPL v Sri Lanka*,[93] that BITs are not "self-contained closed legal systems"[94] has ever since been adhered to in investment arbitration practice to the extent that general international law has played an important gap-filling role, assisting in particular the interpretation of often vague and general IIA provisions.

While this integrative approach has its own dangers, as can be seen from recent ICSID annulment decisions—chastising tribunals for their reliance on general international law instead of strict adherence to IIA provisions—it seems that the trend of firmly embedding IIAs in general international law will make an important contribution to emphasizing the coherence of international law in a time of threatening fragmentation.

It could be argued that reducing the influence of general international law in investment treaty arbitration would be helpful in order to make IIAs more predictable. Indeed, in some circumstances, the relevance of general international law for the interpretation of IIAs may lead to uncertainty in the interpretative process. But that need not necessarily be the case. Where vague IIA provisions are applied "in isolation" from general international law, the outcome of this interpretation exercise need not be more predictable. International law may contribute to a clarification of IIA provisions. This requires, of course, a thorough knowledge of general international law. Only with such knowledge will IIAs, as instruments of public international law, be properly interpreted and applied by tribunals. This will contribute to the sustainability of the IIA system because a more coherent and predictable system will enhance the confidence of its users and thus reinforce reliance on it.

---

92 See *United States—Standards for Reformulated and Conventional Gasoline* (complaint by Venezuela) (April 29, 1996) WTO Doc WT/DS2/AB/R at 17 (Appellate Body Report), online: WTO <http://docsonline.wto.org>; *MTD v Chile*, Decision on Annulment, ICSID Case No. ARB/01/7 (March 21, 2007) at para 61.

93 *Asian Agricultural Products Ltd ("AAPL") v Republic of Sri Lanka*, Award and Dissenting Opinion, ICSID Case No. ARB/87/3 (June 27, 1990).

94 *Ibid* at para 21.

19 The contribution of international investment law to public international law

*Armand de Mestral**

Introduction

The previous chapter sets out the significant contributions that general rules of public international law continue to make in building a body of international law governing foreign investment. Is the reverse also true? Is international investment law capable of contributing to the development of public international law in the same way that international trade law, pursuant to the WTO Agreements[1] and a host of RTAs,[2] has served to enrich international law?[3] This chapter asserts that international investment law is indeed making a significant contribution both to international dispute settlement procedures (Part I) and to the substance of public international law (Part II). In doing so, this chapter argues that, far from contributing to the "fragmentation" of international law, international investment law should be seen as a source of enrichment for public international law.

Contribution to international dispute settlement procedures[4]

International investment law enriches public international law through the increasing adoption of procedures and processes frequently applied

* Emeritus Professor, Jean Monnet Professor of Law, McGill University.
1 See World Trade Organization, *The Legal Texts: The Results of the Uruguay Round of Multilateral Trade Negotiations* (Cambridge: Cambridge University Press, 1999) [WTO Agreements].
2 See World Trade Organization, "Regional Trade Agreements Information System," online: WTO <http://rtais.wto.org/ui/PublicAllRTAList.aspx>.
3 David A. Gantz, *Regional Trade Agreements: Law, Policy and Practice* (Durham, NC: Carolina Academic Press, 2009).
4 Investor-state arbitration is also contributing to the development of legal practice in general. For example, the increased complexity of litigation involved has opened up a new and highly lucrative field of practice, which has led to the expansion of litigation

in national judicial systems. Unlike domestic courts, international dispute resolution processes have traditionally relied on state-centered, closed or secret decision-making processes with limited public participation. Investor-state arbitration, in addition to involving a private party as claimant, is increasingly opening up international litigation to public scrutiny and participation as well as adopting complex judicial procedures and processes characteristic of domestic courts.[5]

Private parties as claimants in international dispute settlement proceedings

As described earlier in Chapter 1, a key development in modern international investment law has been the introduction of investor-state dispute settlement in the late 1960s.[6] While it took a few decades before investors made regular use of this recourse, they now do in large numbers.[7] Private parties are increasingly using investor-state arbitration not only to further their own interests by seeking damages, but also, on occasion, to force the hand of governments or to express dissatisfaction with the results of intergovernmental procedures that may have been instituted.

Two examples of this phenomenon are the *Sweeteners*[8] and the *Softwood Lumber*[9] cases, instituted by several companies under NAFTA

and arbitration departments within major law firms and in government legal departments. A comprehensive discussion of the impact of investor-state arbitration on legal practice is, however, beyond the scope of this chapter. See, for a discussion on one aspect of this question, Arman Sarvarian, "Ethical Standards for Representatives before ICSID Tribunals" (2011) 10 Law and Practice of International Courts and Tribunals 67.

5 On the consolidation of investor-state arbitration proceedings, see C. Lévesque and A. Newcombe at ch 2 of this book.

6 See A. Newcombe at ch 1 of this book. Some investment claims commissions allowed claims based on individual losses, but were generally set up by agreement between the host and home states: see Andrew Newcombe and Lluis Paradell, *Law and Practice of Investment Treaties: Standards of Treatment* (The Netherlands: Kluwers Law International, 2009) at 7 [Newcombe and Paradell].

7 *Ibid* at 58.

8 *Corn Products International Inc. v United Mexican States*, Decision on Responsibility, ICSID Case No. ARB(AF)/04/01 (January 15, 2008) [*Corn Products*]; *Archer Daniels Midland Co and Tate & Lyle Ingredients Americas Inc. v The United Mexican States*, Award, ICSID Case No. ARB(AF)04/05 (November 21, 2007) [*Archer Daniels*]; *Cargill, Incorporated v United Mexican States*, Award, ICSID Case No. ARB (AF)/05/2 [*Cargill*].

9 *Canfor Corpon v United States of America and Terminal Forest Products Ltd v United States of America*, Decision on Preliminary Question, UNCITRAL (June 6, 2006) [*Canfor*].

Chapter 11.[10] In both of these instances there had already been interstate litigation before the WTO[11] and lengthy interstate negotiations that had not brought a change of governmental policy in Mexico and the United States, respectively, that satisfied the private companies involved. In the *Sweeteners* cases, various American producers of high-fructose corn syrup (HFCS) who had been subject to retaliatory taxes and antidumping duties in Mexico, and in the *Softwood Lumber* cases, Canadian softwood lumber companies who had been subject to antidumping and countervailing duties, as well as a special law[12] in the United States, decided to sue for damages. In both instances, the companies were successful either in seeking damages or in provoking further negotiations for the losses they had suffered in violation of the standards of treatment guaranteed under NAFTA Chapter 11. It should be noted that these Chapter 11 arbitrations were also complemented by cases taken before the Mexican courts, using the *amparo* remedy,[13] and before American trade courts.[14]

10 *North American Free Trade Agreement Between the Government of Canada, the Government of Mexico and the Government of the United States*, December 17, 1992, Can TS 1994 No. 2 (entered into force January 1, 1994) [NAFTA].

11 In the HFCS dispute, see *Mexico—Anti-Dumping Investigation of High Fructose Corn Syrup (HFCS) from the United States, Recourse to Article 21.5 of the DSU by the United States* (2001), WTO Doc WT/DS132/AB/RW (Appellate Body Report). In the Softwood Lumber dispute, see *United States—Final Dumping Determination on Softwood Lumber from Canada* (2004 and 2006), WTO Docs WT/DS264/AB/R and WT/DS264/AB/RW (Appellate Body Report); *United States—Investigation of the International Trade Commission in Softwood Lumber from Canada* (2004 and 2006), WTO Docs WT/DS277/R (Panel Report) and WT/DS277/AB/RW (Appellate Body Report). Note that the *Softwood Lumber Agreement Between the Government of Canada and the Government of the United States of America*, September 12, 2006, Can TS 2006/23 (entered into force October 12, 2006), online: DFAIT <http://www.international.gc.ca/controls-controles/softwood-bois_oeuvre/other-autres/agreement-accord.aspx> [SLA] was negotiated and submitted as a Mutually Agreed Solution encompassing the following disputes: WT/DS236, WT/DS247, WT/DS257, WT/DS264, WT/DS277 and WT/DS311.

12 *The Continued Dumping and Subsidy Offset Act*, 19 USC §1002 (August 22, 2005) [*Byrd Amendment*].

13 *Cargill, supra* note 8 at para 112. The *amparo* remedy in Mexico is a determination by the courts that a provision of law or a judicial decision is in violation of the constitution: see Carlos Sánchez Mejorado, "The Writ of Amparo: Mexican Procedure to Protect Human Rights" (1946) 243 Annals of the American Academy of Political and Social Science 107.

14 In the Softwood Lumber Dispute, see e.g. *Tembec, Inc. v United States*, Case No. 06-152 (2006), online: USCIT <http://www.cit.uscourts.gov/slip_op/Slip_op06/06-152.pdf>; *Tembec, Inc. v United States*, Case No 06-109 (2006), online: USCIT <http://www.cit.uscourts.gov/slip_op/Slip_op06/06-109.pdf>; *Abitibi-Consol., Inc. {and Canfor Corpn} v United States*, Case No. 06-83 (2006), online: USCIT <http://www.cit.uscourts.gov/slip_op/Slip_op06/06-83.pdf>.

Recourse to a private suit to force the hand of governments can be illustrated by other cases[15] that have been instituted in the face of ongoing interstate procedures and tensions between governments. Investor-state proceedings are frequently preceded by interstate negotiations on behalf of the investor, as happened in the recent cases against Argentina,[16] where a number of governments protested the treatment of their corporate nationals. Complex negotiations between governments also occurred in earlier arbitrations, such as *Asian Agricultural Products v Sri Lanka*[17] or *Wena Hotels v Egypt*.[18] At some point in the process, private investors decide to rely on the arbitral remedy, especially when they have effectively written off their investment and are seeking to mitigate their losses; but in other cases they use investor-state arbitration as one of several means of pursuing their interests.

This increased participation of private parties in investor-state arbitration calls into question the current status of corporations in international law. Are corporations in the process of becoming subjects, rather than objects, of international law as a result of the substantive and procedural protections that they increasingly enjoy, in particular, under international investment law? This is a complex and delicate question, which is noted here and is treated by Patrick Dumberry in this book.[19]

Participation of non-parties in international dispute settlement

Many domestic legal systems provide for the possibility of intervention in legal proceedings by persons or institutions that have not been directly instrumental in initiating the proceedings. International litigation has traditionally been reserved to states and participation has been further reserved to states that are party to the particular case. This has left very little space for the intervention of would-be "friends of the court" who

---

15 *Canadian Cattlemen for Fair Trade v United States of America*, Award on Jurisdiction, UNCITRAL (28 January 2008) [*Canadian Cattlemen*].

16 *CMS Gas Transmission Co v Argentine Republic*, Award, ICSID Case No. ARB/01/8 (May 12, 2005) [*CMS Gas*]; *Enron Creditors Recovery Corpn & Ponderosa Assets, L.P. v Argentine Republic*, Decision on Annulment, ICSID Case No. ARB/97/3 (Annulment Proceeding) (July 30, 2010) [*Enron*]; *Sempra Energy International v Argentine Republic*, Decision on Annulment, ICSID Case No. ARB/02/16 (Annulment Proceeding) (June 29, 2010) [*Sempra*].

17 *Asian Agricultural Products Ltd v Democratic Socialist Republic of Sri Lanka*, Final Order, ICSID Case No. ARB/87/3 (June 27, 1990).

18 *Wena Hotels Ltd v Arab Republic of Egypt*, Award, ICSID Case No. ARB/98/4 (December 8, 2000).

19 See P. Dumberry at ch 10 in this book.

might have additional insights and information to contribute to the litigation. A number of international procedures, such as those of the ICJ[20] and the WTO,[21] allow for the intervention of interested states. According to many public interest groups, the issues being addressed in international litigation are of great significance to many citizens as well as to the governments directly involved.[22] Furthermore, these groups argue that legal proceedings conducted in the open and subject to public scrutiny are far more likely to lead to a fair and just conclusion and thereby lead to greater public confidence.[23] But change has been slow to come, as most states have been reluctant to open up international litigation to public participation and publicity.

Some of the most significant changes in this regard have begun to occur in investor-state arbitration. Many observers of the NAFTA Chapter 11 investor-state process were critical of the fact that no provision was made in the treaty for *amicus curiae* intervention and many efforts have been made to seek the right to intervene.[24] These efforts came to a head in the NAFTA Chapter 11 *Methanex* arbitration. In this case, a number of environmental NGOs sought to intervene in support of the US position that California had been pursuing legitimate environmental objectives when it banned the sale and use of the gasoline additive MTBE. They were successful in that the tribunal, then including former US Secretary of State Warren Christopher, held that the interventions should be allowed on the grounds that the issues before it were both private and public in nature and that the interventions would bring additional evidence and insights into the public dimensions of the case.[25] The NAFTA parties subsequently demonstrated their approval of this by formally providing for the possibility of *amicus curiae*

---

20 *Rules of the International Court of Justice* [1978] ICJ Acts & Docs 6 at arts 81–6, online: ICJ <http://www.icj-cij.org/documents/index.php?p1=4&p2=3&p3=0> [*ICJ Rules*].

21 See WTO Agreements, *supra* note 1, *Understanding on Rules and Procedures Governing the Settlement of Disputes* [DSU], art 10.

22 See International Institute for Sustainable Development, Communities for a Better Environment, the Bluewater Network of Earth Island Institute, the Center for International Environmental Law's submissions, as summarized in *Methanex Corpn v United States of America*, Decision on Amici Curiae, UNCITRAL (January 15, 2001) at paras 5–8 [*Methanex, Amici*]; see also H. Mann and D. McRae, "Amicus Curiae submissions to the NAFTA Chapter 11 Tribunal: *Methanex Corp. v the United States of America*", UNCITRAL (March 9, 2004), online: IISD <http://www.iisd.org/pdf/2004/trade_methanex_submissions.pdf>.

23 *Ibid.*

24 *Ibid.*

25 *Methanex, Amici*, *supra* note 22 at para 49.

interventions.[26] This right has been used on a number of occasions with varying success.[27]

NAFTA Chapter 11 may have been the first international procedure to move towards acceptance of *amicus* briefs in international arbitral litigation, but it has not been alone.[28] The ICSID Rules[29] have been subsequently amended to allow *amicus* briefs at the discretion of the tribunal, and such briefs have been accepted in a number of cases.[30] Interestingly, ICSID tribunals have also used their general discretion to control their proceedings by seeking information and opinions on matters of EU law from the Commission of the European Union, as was done in the *Eureko v Slovak Republic* arbitration.[31] Increased willingness to receive *amicus* briefs has not been restricted to investor-state arbitral proceedings. The Appellate Body of the WTO issued a statement in 2000 in the *Asbestos* case[32] that it would be prepared to receive such briefs and has, on a number of occasions, accepted them.[33] This generated

26 NAFTA Free Trade Commission, *Statement of the Free Trade Commission on Non-Disputing Party Participation*, in "Celebrating NAFTA at Ten"—NAFTA Commission Meeting, October 7, 2003, online: DFAIT <http://www.international.gc.ca/trade-agreements-accords-commerciaux/assets/pdfs/Nondisputing-en.pdf>.

27 See e.g. *United Postal Service of America Inc v Government of Canada*, Decision on Amici Curiae, UNCITRAL (October 17, 2001) (request for standing as *amicus curiae* granted).

28 The most notable is the CJEU which is both open to the public and allows *amici* briefs. However, the CJEU has always considered itself to be *sui generis* and very different from normal intergovernmental tribunals. See *Consolidated Version of the Rules of Procedure of the European Court of Justice* [2010] OJ, C 177/24 at art 93.

29 See "Rules of Procedure for Arbitration Proceedings," in *ICSID Convention, Regulations and Rules* (effective April 10, 2006), online: ICSID <http://icsid.worldbank.org/ICSID/StaticFiles/basicdoc/basic-en.htm> at Rule 37(2) [ICSID Arbitration Rules].

30 *Suez Sociedad General de Aguas de Barcelona, S.A., and Vivendi Universal S.A. v The Argentine Republic*, Order in Response to Amicus Petition, ICSID Case No. ARB/03/19 (February 12, 2007); *Biwater Gauff (Tanzania) Ltd v United Republic of Tanzania*, Procedural Order No. 5 on Amicus Curiae, ICSID Case No. ARB/05/22 (February 2, 2007).

31 *Eureko B.V. v Slovak Republic*, Award on Jurisdiction, Arbitrability and Suspension, ICSID Case No. 2008–13 (October 26, 2010); *AES Summit Generation Ltd and AES-Tisza Erömü Kft v The Republic of Hungary*, Award, ICSID Case No. ARB/07/22 (September 23, 2010).

32 The Additional Procedures set out by the Appellate Body in *European Communities—Measures Affecting Asbestos and Asbestos-Containing Products* (2001), WTO Doc WT/DS135/AB/R at paras 50–7 (Appellate Body Report) [*EC—Asbestos*] were heavily criticized by the WTO General Council: See WTO, General Council, *Minutes of Meeting* (held on November 22, 2000), WTO Doc WT/GC/M/60, online: WTO <http://docsonline.wto.org> [*WTO Meeting Minutes*].

33 *United States—Lead and Bismuth II* (2000), WTO Doc WT/DS138/AB/R at paras 36–42 (Appellate Body Report); *EC—Asbestos, supra* note 32 at paras 50–7; *European*

some controversy, with some WTO members suggesting that the Appellate Body had acted beyond its powers.[34]

The reception of *amici* interventions has been a slow process but it appears to be gaining momentum. It now is a fact in several different international economic dispute settlement fora and is serving to allow for the introduction of public voices to what once were absolutely closed procedures. Were it not for the reluctance of certain institutions to welcome *amicus* briefs and the uncertainty as to whether they are always well received, this process would have proceeded even faster.

Open proceedings

In most democratic societies, there has been considerable public pressure upon states to open the doors and let the public observe the conduct of international proceedings, as generally happens in national judicial proceedings. This, however, continues to be resisted by the majority of states.[35] While certain international tribunals like the ICJ provide for an open public gallery, many proceedings between governments are conducted behind closed doors.

The confidentiality of NAFTA Chapter 11 investor-state proceedings and the perception of secrecy quickly attracted negative criticism[36] from both the public in general and public interest NGOs in particular. The criticism also focused on the fact that arbitration is conducted by persons chosen by the parties and not by domestic judges. In response to the criticism, the three governments issued a declaration in 2001, stating that: "Nothing in the NAFTA imposes a general duty of confidentiality on the disputing parties to a Chapter Eleven arbitration, and, subject to the application of Article 1137(4), nothing in the NAFTA precludes the Parties from providing public access to documents submitted to, or issued by, a Chapter Eleven tribunal."[37] Today, documents,

---

Communities—Trade Description of Sardines (2002), WTO Doc WT/DS231/AB/R at paras 161–70 (Appellate Body Report).

34 See e.g. *WTO Meeting Minutes, supra*, note 32 at para 11 (debate sparked in response to asbestos case).

35 See *WTO Meeting Minutes, supra* note 32.

36 Howard Mann, *International Investment Agreements, Business and Human Rights: Key Issues and Opportunities* (International Institute for Sustainable Development, February 2008), online: IISD <http://www.iisd.org/pdf/2008/iia_business_human_rights.pdf> at 29 ff.

37 *Notes of Interpretation of Certain Chapter 11 Provisions* (NAFTA Free Trade Commission, July 31, 2001), online: DFAIT <http://www.international.gc.ca/trade-agreements-accords-commerciaux/disp-diff/NAFTA-Interpr.aspx?lang=en> [*NAFTA FTC Notes*].

beginning with notices of intent to submit a claim to arbitration, are now regularly published on governmental[38] and private[39] websites. In 2003, Canada and the US (later joined by Mexico), announced that they would consent, and request the investors to consent, to hearings open to the public.[40] Thus far, a handful of hearings have been open to the public through closed-circuit transmission from the offices of the ICSID, where many NAFTA arbitrations are conducted under the ICSID Additional Facility Rules.[41]

The NAFTA's approach to open proceedings appears to have influenced ICSID, as evidenced in the 2006 amendment of the ICSID Arbitration Rules.[42] Arguably, the NAFTA example has been slowly taken up by the WTO, where selected proceedings conducted at the WTO headquarters in Geneva have been opened to the public via closed-circuit transmission facilities in a number of recent high profile cases.[43] Thus the example of open investor-state arbitration has been felt even in institutions dealing with interstate disputes. Where states have wanted to maintain strict secrecy in their proceedings, they have chosen arbitral institutions, such as the London Court of International Arbitration, whose rules guarantee secrecy.[44]

Substantive contributions to public international law

Arguably, international investment law is having a significant impact on the development of contemporary public international law. International investment law, for example, is becoming a source of inter-

---

38 US Department of State, "International Claims and Investment Disputes", online: <http://www.state.gov/s/l/c3433.htm>; DFAIT, "NAFTA—Chapter 11—Investment Portal," online: <http://www.international.gc.ca/trade-agreements-accords-commerciaux/disp-diff/nafta.aspx?lang=en>; Secretaría de Economía México, "Solución de Controversias Inversionista—Estado," online: <http://www.economia.gob.mx/swb/en/economia/p_Solucion_Controversias_InvEdo>.

39 Online: NAFTA Claims <http://www.naftaclaims.com>.

40 See e.g. *Statement of Canada on open Hearings in NAFTA Chapter Eleven Arbitrations*, in "Celebrating NAFTA at Ten" NAFTA Commission Meeting, October 7, 2003), online: DFAIT <http://www.international.gc.ca/trade-agreements-accords-commerciaux/agr-acc/nafta-alena/open-hearing.aspx?lang=eng>.

41 *NAFTA FTC Notes*, *supra* note 37.

42 ICSID Arbitration Rules, *supra* note 29 at Rule 32.

43 *European Communities—Measures Affecting the Approval and Marketing of Biotech Products (Complaint by the United States of America, Canada, Argentina)* (2004), WTO Docs WT/DS291 (US), WT/DS292 (Canada), WT/DS293 (Argentina), (Panel Report).

44 See e.g. SLA, *supra* note 11 at art XIV(6); London Court of International Arbitration, *LCIA Arbitration Rules* (1998) at art 30, online: LCIA <http://www.lcia.org/Dispute_Resolution_Services/LCIA_Arbitration_Rules.aspx#article30>.

national law both in the use of BITs and the growing arbitration jurisprudence. It is also being used to interpret other treaties and to resolve private claims, even applying treaties directly in domestic legal systems. International investment law is thus facilitating a fascinating dialogue with the traditional substance of public international law, and, thereby, making substantive contributions to public international law.

Capacity of BITs and investor-state arbitrations to serve as sources of international law

Chief among the primary sources of international law that can be applied by the ICJ under its Statute are "international conventions, whether general or particular, establishing rules expressly recognized by the contesting states."[45] "Judicial decisions" are listed among the "subsidiary means for the determination of rules of law."[46] Given that there are more than 2,800 BITs [47] and that there has been an ever-expanding body of investor-state arbitral jurisprudence during the last 15 years,[48] one can legitimately ask whether this does appear to constitute an important new branch of public international law.

What significance can be accorded to the fact that over 2,800 BITs exist and that these BITs display considerable similarity in the standards of treatment provided to foreign investors and investments? Some observers have speculated that the number and similarity of BITs may be declaratory of customary international law.[49] This is a tempting but

---

45 *Statute of the International Court of Justice*, June 26, 1945, Can TS 1945/7 at art 38.1(a), online: ICJ <http://www.icj-cij.org/documents/index.php?p1=4&p2=2& p3=0#CHAPTER_II> [ICJ Statute].

46 *Ibid* at art 38.1(d).

47 See *World Investment Report 2011*, UNCTAD/WIR/2011 [*WIR 2011*] at 100. See also United Nations Conference on Trade and Development list of Bilateral Investment Treaties, online: UNCTAD <http://www.unctadxi.org/templates/ DocSearch____779.aspx> (for country-specific lists, see <http://www.unctad.org/ Templates/Page.asp?intItemID=2344&lang=1>); Kluwer Arbitration database, online: Kluwer <http://www.kluwerarbitration.com/BITs-countries.aspx>.

48 The total of known investment treaty arbitration, as tallied cumulatively from 1987, at the end of 2010 was 390 cases, with the majority of those cases heard under the auspices of ICSID, including its Additional Facility Rules. The cumulative total in 1995 was around 10. See *WIR 2011*, *supra* note 47 at 101–2.

49 Ian A. Laird, "A Community of Destiny—The Barcelona Traction Case and the Development of Shareholder Rights to Bring Investment Claims" in Todd Weiler (ed), *International Investment Law and Arbitration: Leading Cases from the ICSID, NAFTA, Bilateral Treaties and Customary International Law* (London: Cameron May, 2005) at 95–6; Stephen M. Schwebel, "Investor-State Disputes and the Development

essentially false conclusion. One reason that there are so many BITs, rather than a single multilateral agreement, is that bilateral relationships differ so much that states desire to tailor solutions to each individual case. The resistance encountered by the effort in the mid-1990s to promote the MAI suggests the same conclusion.[50] With the exception of expropriation, there is no evidence that states consider that in signing a BIT they are simply codifying rules to which they are already bound by customary international law. Quite the contrary, the evidence suggests that each BIT is *sui generis*. At best, what seems to be occurring is that BITs use "standards" of treatment developed in the context of international trade law,[51] other standards developed in the context of the minimum standard of treatment of aliens,[52] and still other standards refined and developed in the practice of international trade and investment law.[53] Any review of the development of international treaty standards by such bodies as the ILC must consider the contribution of BITs to the definition of these standards.[54] In this context, BITs are without question important evidence of treaty practice defining these international standards, but, with the exception of expropriation, there is no convincing evidence that BITs are themselves declaratory of customary international law. If they were, they would be largely redundant.

of International Law: The Influence of Bilateral Investment Treaties on Customary International Law" (2004) 98 American Society of International Law Proceedings 27; F.A. Mann, "British Treaties for the Promotion and Protection of Investments" (1981) 52 Brit YB Int'l L 249; Andreas Lowenfeld, *International Economic Law*, 2nd edn (New York: Oxford University Press, 2002) at 486.

50 *The Multilateral Agreement on Investment—Draft Consolidated Text*, April 22, 1998, OECD Doc DAFFE/MAI(98)7/REV1, online: OECD <http://www1.oecd.org/daf/mai/pdf/ng/ng987r1e.pdf>. See also Katia Tieleman, "The Failure of the Multilateral Agreement on Investment (MAI) and the Absence of a Global Policy Network" in *UN Vision Project on Global Public Policy Networks 1999*, online: Global Public Policy Networks <http://www.gppi.net/fileadmin/gppi/Tieleman_MAI_GPP_Network.pdf>.

51 See George Schwartzenberger, "The Most-Favoured Nation Standard in British State Practice" (1945) 22 Brit YB Int'l L 96.

52 See *L.F.H. Neer and Pauline Neer (U.S.A.) v United Mexican States* (1926), Reports of International Arbitral Awards, Vol IV at 60–6, online: UN <http://untreaty.un.org/cod/riaa/cases/vol_IV/60-66.pdf> [*Neer*].

53 See e.g. the ban on performance requirements in NAFTA, *supra* note 10 at art 1106.

54 See Martti Koskenniemi (ed), *Fragmentation of International Law: Difficulties Arising from the Diversification and Expansion of International Law*, Report of the Study Group of the International Law Commission" (A/CN.4/L.682) in *Yearbook of the International Law Commission 2006*, General Assembly Official Records, Sixty-first session, Supplement No. 10 (A/61/10), online: ILC <http://untreaty.un.org/ilc/texts/instruments/english/draft%20articles/1_9_2006.pdf>.

In the same vein, BITs generally contain recourse to investor-state arbitration. But practice varies considerably between states[55] and varies even between BITs negotiated by the same states or international persons.[56] There is no evidence in state practice or in BITs that recourse to investor-state arbitration is anything but one form of dispute settlement that states are free to include in their treaties. Private parties have no right under international law to complain about the absence of investor-state arbitration in a given BIT.

The legal significance of investor-state arbitral jurisprudence may raise rather different considerations from BITs. Does the fact that one party to investor-state proceedings is a private person or entity remove this form of dispute settlement from the realm of public international law? To suggest that the presence of a private party removes the matter from the arena of international law would also have the same implication in the spheres of international human rights[57] and international humanitarian law (IHL),[58] where the applicant or the accused respectively are private parties; the very purpose of both of these spheres of modern public international law is to protect the human rights of individuals by granting them direct international remedies or to punish IHL violators through international procedures such as those of the International Criminal Court (ICC).[59]

If they must be seen as part of public international law, can investor-state arbitral awards be equated to other international decisions, whether

55 See e.g. *Treaty Between United States of America and the Argentine Republic concerning the Reciprocal Encouragement and Protection of Investment*, November 14, 1991, TIAS, art VII (entered into force October 20, 1994), and *Agreement Between the Government of the Republic of Croatia and the Government of Canada for the Promotion and Protection of Investments*, February 3, 1997, Can TS 2001/4, art XII (entered into force January 30, 2001).

56 The EU has committed itself to investor-state arbitration in only one agreement: see *Energy Charter Treaty*, December 17, 1994, 2080 UNTS 36116, (entered into force April 16, 1998) at art 26. Many of its cooperation agreements have no dispute settlement provisions and others such as the *EU-South Korea Free Trade Agreement*, October 6, 2010, online: EC <http://ec.europa.eu/trade/creating-opportunities/bilateral-relations/countries/korea/> provide for interstate procedures. Chinese practice varies greatly. See Liu Chunbao, ch 4 in this book.

57 Philip Alston (ed), *Non-State Actors and Human Rights* (Oxford: Oxford University Press, 2005).

58 See William Schabas, *The International Criminal Court: A Commentary on the Rome Statute* (Oxford: Oxford University Press, 2010).

59 *Rome Statute of the International Criminal Court*, July 17, 1998, UN Doc A/CONF 183/9, (entered into force on July 1, 2002) online: International Criminal Court <http://www.icc-cpi.int/NR/rdonlyres/0D8024D3-87EA-4E6A-8A27-05B987C38689/0/RomeStatuteEng.pdf>.

judicial or arbitral? In the first place it should be noted that international judicial decisions do not have precedential value and are only binding upon the immediate parties. This rule, enshrined in state practice and in customary law, as well as in the Statute of the ICJ,[60] is applicable *a fortiori* to arbitral proceedings.[61] But does this necessarily reduce their significance as evidence of the law? In the view of this writer they do not, since they are rendered under international law, by tribunals established under a treaty, by persons versed in international law. As such they are valid evidence of the state of international law on such issues as international responsibility (e.g. on attribution or necessity), the extent of the power to expropriate, the extent of the police power of states, treaty interpretation, and the role of general principles of law, which have arisen as central issues in a number of investor-state arbitrations.

BITs and investor-state arbitration as a source on matters of treaty interpretation

BITs are treaties and issues of treaty interpretation have arisen in many investor-state cases.[62] The most common issue of interpretation has focused on articles 30 and 31 of the *Vienna Convention on the Law of Treaties* and involves the use of the plain meaning of words in their context and the principle of effectiveness in contrast to arguments in favor of broader purposive and more subjective interpretations.[63] These decisions have not necessarily added much to the understanding of the *Vienna Convention* but they certainly confirm the primacy of its approach as declaratory of customary international law.

The primacy of the will of the parties to a treaty as a source of authority has been affirmed on a number of occasions, particularly in those awards

---

60 ICJ Statute, *supra* note 45 at art 59.
61 IIAs usually provide that an award made by a tribunal in a given case shall be binding only on the particular parties to the dispute. See e.g. NAFTA, *supra* note 10 at art 1136(1).
62 See *Tecnicas Medioambientales Tecmed S.A. v The United Mexican States*, Award, ICSID Case No. ARB (AF)/00/2 (May 29, 2003); *Methanex Corpn v United States of America*, Final Award, UNCITRAL (August 3, 2005) [*Methanex, Final Award*]; *Rosinvest UK Ltd v The Russian Federation*, Final Award, SCC Arbitration V 079/2005 (September 12, 2010); *CMS Gas*, *supra* note 39; *LG&E Energy Corpn, LG&E Capital Corpn., LG&E International, Inc. v Argentine Republic*, Award, ICSID Case No. ARB/02/1 (July 25, 2007).
63 *Vienna Convention on the Law of Treaties*, May 23, 1969, 1155 UNTS 331 (entered into force January 27, 1980), online: UN <http://untreaty.un.org/cod/avl/ha/vclt/vclt.html>.

which have considered the Declaration of July 2001 of the NAFTA Parties concerning the content of the "fair and equitable treatment" standard.[64] There had been considerable controversy as to whether the reference to "fair and equitable treatment" constituted a new and higher standard than that found in customary international law governing the treatment of aliens.[65] The three states have intervened, using their powers to issue binding interpretations of the treaty under NAFTA article 1131, to declare that NAFTA article 1105 referred only to the customary international law standard.[66] Subsequent NAFTA tribunals have all assumed that they were bound by this interpretative statement: some have concluded that the standard has in fact evolved beyond the classic 1927 statement in the *Neer*[67] arbitration, while others have decided that they were required to remain close to the 1927 definition.[68] These decisions constitute a remarkable example of both treaty interpretation and the capacity of the NAFTA parties to put an end to a potential interpretation that they deemed inimical to their interests and intentions.

The significance of using public international law to resolve private claims

International investment law and investor-state arbitration also bring into sharper focus the suitability of recourse to international law to deal with what are essentially private claims. Certain branches of international law speak to the protection of special categories of protected persons or property. A longstanding example would be the protections and immunities granted to diplomats;[69] a more recent example would be the protection of aircraft, those flying in them, and persons frequenting airports.[70] Decisions by claims tribunals on the minimum

---

64 *NAFTA FTC Notes, supra* note 37.
65 This approach had been endorsed by the tribunal in *Pope & Talbot Inc v The Government of Canada*, Award on the Merits of Phase 2, UNCITRAL (April 10, 2001) at paras 105–18.
66 *NAFTA FTC Notes, supra* note 37.
67 *Neer, supra* note 52. See e.g. *ADF Group Inc v United States of America*, Award, ICSID Additional Facility Rules (January 9, 2003); *Mondev International Ltd v United States of America*, Award, ICSID Additional Facility Rules (October 11, 2002).
68 *Glamis Gold Ltd v United States of America*, Award, UNCITRAL (June 8, 2009); *Cargill, supra* note 8.
69 *Vienna Convention on Diplomatic Relations*, April 18, 1961, 500 UNTS 95 (entered into force April 24, 1964), online: UN <http://untreaty.un.org/ilc/texts/instruments/english/conventions/9_1_1961.pdf>.
70 *Convention on Offences and Certain Other Acts Committed On Board Aircraft*, November 4, 1964, TIAS 6768; *Convention for the Suppression of Unlawful Acts Against the Safety*

standard of treatment of aliens provide another good example.[71] The PCIJ, in the *Danzig* Advisory Opinion,[72] showed long ago that an international treaty could be designed to protect individuals. A BIT constitutes a modern example of a protection of designated categories of individuals and of their property. This form of international protection is considerably enhanced by the right of recourse to arbitration.

A further and equally interesting question arises from the recourse to international law to resolve private claims for economic loss. In these circumstances, international law is used to determine liability, to assess arguments made in mitigation of liability, to assess damages and to regulate the arbitral proceeding. International law must provide answers to claims by states that they should be excused from liability due to circumstances precluding a finding of wrongfulness. To do this, arbitral tribunals have drawn upon the rules of state responsibility[73] and general principles of law, which have been developed primarily to deal with interstate conflicts. The expropriation of the property of aliens has long been a concern of customary international law. Often the terminology adopted by BITs supplements customary international law or adopts very specific solutions that the state parties deem best adapted to their interests.[74] Modern BITs are thus in a fascinating dialogue with international custom, almost always confirming, sometimes going beyond and sometimes deliberately falling short. But it is impossible to ignore BITs as a source of law governing expropriation.

To have recourse to international law to resolve private claims and the correlative state responsibility to satisfy these claims places new demands on international law. The process of analysis requires new answers and a

of Civil Aviation, September 23, 1971, 974 UNTS 178 (entered into force January 16, 1973); *Convention on the Marking of Plastic Explosives for the Purpose of Detection*, March 1, 1991, Can TS 1998/54 (entered into force June 21, 1998); *Protocol for the Suppression of Unlawful Acts of Violence at Airports Serving International Civil Aviation*, February 24, 1988, 974 UNTS 177.

71 See *Neer*, *supra* note 52; *Harry Roberts (U.S.A.) v United Mexican States* (1926), Reports of International Arbitral Awards, vol IV at 77–81, online: UN <http://untreaty.un.org/cod/riaa/cases/vol_IV/77-81.pdf>.

72 *Polish Postal Service in Danzig* (1931), Advisory Opinion, PCIJ (Ser B) No. 11) online: World Courts <http://www.worldcourts.com/pcij/eng/decisions/1925.05.16_danzig.htm>.

73 "Draft articles on Responsibility of States for Internationally Wrongful Acts" (UN Doc A/56/10) in *Yearbook of the International Law Commission 2001*, vol. II, Part Two (New York: UN, 2008) (UN Doc A/CN.4/SER.A/2001/Add.1), online: UN <http://untreaty.un.org/ilc/texts/instruments/english/commentaries/9_6_2001.pdf> [*State Responsibility*].

74 Newcombe and Paradell, *supra* note 6.

vision of the enhanced reach of international law. This process is certainly a source of new complexity and arguably a source of great enrichment for international law.

Strengthening the direct effect of public international law

A few national legal systems treat public international law—both treaties and custom—as constituting an integral part of their legal system. However, the great majority of national legal systems must be qualified as dualist. As a consequence, many rules of treaty law covering major issues are very difficult, if not impossible, for private individuals to invoke as legally binding. One of the most notable exceptions is found in EU law, where certain important provisions of EU treaties are deemed to have "direct effect" and are invoked by individuals and applied to them by national courts.[75] Through investor-state arbitration, BITs are given a form of direct effect. Foreign investors are entitled to invoke the protections of the treaty directly and are dispensed from looking at domestic law. This field of law thus provides a very convincing demonstration that international law can have direct effect in dualist systems.

Conclusion

In the final analysis, it is hard to escape the conclusion that the international law governing the protection of foreign investors and investments is having a significant impact on the development of contemporary public international law. It has accentuated the movement towards the expansion of subsets of law within the broader framework, each governed by a dynamic specific to itself. Furthermore, as it expands into new areas and performs new functions, general international law is not weakened, but enriched.

75 Paul P. Craig and Gráinne De Búrca, *EU Law: Text, Cases, and Materials*, 5th edn (Oxford: Oxford University Press, 2011) at ch 8.

Table of treaties and international instruments

I. BITs

Australia-India (1999) – 152
Austria-FRY Macedonia (2002) – 89
Austria-Lebanon (2001) – 240
Austria-Soviet Union (1990) – 219
Bangladesh-USA (1989) – 219
Belgium/Luxemburg-Colombia (2009) – 295
Canada-Costa Rica (1998) – 87, 89, 201
Canada-Ecuador (1996) – 87
Canada-Jordan (2009) – 290
Canada-Latvia (2009) – 311
Canada-Peru (2006) – 290, 292
Canada-USSR (1989) – 25
Canada-Venezuela (1998) – 219
Chad-Italy (1969) – 17
China-Barbados (1998) – 63
China-Chile (1994) – 62
China-Ecuador (1994) – 62
China-Germany (2003) – 69, 70, 71, 220, 237
China-India (2006) – 73
China-Israel (1995) – 62
China-Japan (1988) – 65
China-Korea (1992) – 69
China-Lithuania (1993) – 62
China-Mexico (2008) – 67, 70, 71
China-Morocco (1995) – 62, 69
China-Netherlands (2001) – 67, 72
China-Russia (2006) – 67
China-Switzerland (2009) – 68

China-Trinidad and Tobago (2002) – **68, 73**
China-Uganda (2004) – **71**
China-UK (1985) – **65, 69**
Croatia-Canada (1997) – **352**
Croatia-Kuwait (1997) – **89**
Czech Republic-Switzerland (1990) – **238**
El-Salvador-Spain (1995) – **200, 201**
El Salvador-USA (1999) – **219**
Finland-Armenia (2004) – **291**
Finland-Ethiopia (2006) – **291**
France-Argentina (1991) – **220**
Germany-Bangladesh (1981) – **292**
Germany-Lebanon (1997) – **87**
Germany-Pakistan (1959) – **15, 16, 17**
Germany-Pakistan (2009) – **56**
Germany-Philippines (1997) – **200**
Germany-Soviet Union (1989) – **219**
Honduras-USA (1995) – **219**
Iran-Sri Lanka (2000) – **89**
Italy-Morocco (1990) – **220**
Japan-Korea (2002) – **291**
Japan-Russia (1998) – **87**
Japan-Vietnam (2003) – **291**
Jordan-Singapore (2004) – **274**
Korea-Austria (1991) – **47**
Lebanon-Belarus (2002) – **89**
Libya-Malta (1973) – **87**
Mexico-Italy (1999) – **237**
Netherlands-Burundi (2007) – **291**
Netherlands-Czech Republic (1991) – **233**
Netherlands-Philippines (1985) – **238**
Netherlands-Romania (1995) – **232**
Netherlands-Soviet Union (1989) – **219**
Netherlands-Suriname (2005) – **291**
Netherlands-Venezuela (1993) – **219**
Pakistan-Switzerland (1995) – **220, 221**
Philippines-Switzerland (1997) – **220**
Slovakia- Switzerland (1990) – **238**
Sweden-India (2000) – **153**
Switzerland-Mexico (1996) – **89**
UK-Albania (1994) – **222**
UK-Bolivia (1988) – **222**

UK-Bulgaria (1995) – 222
UK-El Salvador (1999) – 222
UK-Jamaica (1987) – 222
UK-USSR (1989) – 332
UK-Swaziland (1995) – 87
US-Argentina (1991) – 37, 170, 222, 242, 336–340, 352
US-Bahrain (2001) – 291
US-Egypt (1982) – 25, 170
US-Jordan (2003) – 291
US-Kazakhstan (1994) – 87
US-Morocco (1991) – 222
US-Mozambique (1998) – 291
US-Poland (1990) – 151
US-Turkey (1985) – 151
US-Uruguay (2006) – 78, 294
W. Germany-Singapore (1975) – 87

Model BITs

2004 Canada Model FIPA – 25, 29, 30, 33, 35–40, 51, 151, 222, 240, 274, 277–279, 283, 290, 294, 303, 309, 310, 313
1998 China Model BIT – 60, 66, 69–71
2007 Colombia Model BIT – 68, 167
2006 France Model BIT – 52, 220, 222
2008 German Model BIT – 52, 222
2007 Norway Model BIT (draft, later abandoned) – 188, 191, 291
2004 US Model BIT – 22, 25, 29, 30, 32–40, 52, 72, 117, 151, 153, 188, 208, 219, 221, 222, 240, 242, 278, 283, 290, 294, 335
Asian-African Legal Consultative Organization, *Model Agreement for Promotion and Protection of Investment* (1984) – 20
IISD, *IISD Model International Agreement on Investment for Sustainable Development* (2005) – 20, 192, 279, 291, 299
ICSID, Model Clauses: *Model Clauses Relating to the Convention on the Settlement of Investment Disputes Designed for Use in Bilateral Investment Agreements* (1969) – 17.

II. Other international investment agreements

Agreement among the Government of Brunei Darussalam, the Republic of Indonesia, Malaysia, the Republic of the Philippines, the Republic of Singapore and the Kingdom of Thailand for the Promotion and Protection of Investments, December 15, 1987 – 220, 222.
Agreement between the EFTA States and Singapore, June 26, 2002 – 291

Agreement between the Government of the United States of America and the Government of the Sultanate of Oman, January 1, 2009 – 116

Agreement between the Government of Japan and the Government of Malaysia for an Economic Partnership, December 13, 2005 – 274

Agreement between Japan and Brunei Darussalam for an Economic Partnership, June 18, 2007 – 117

Agreement between Japan and the Republic of Singapore for a New-Age Economic Partnership, January 13, 2002 – 273, 274

Agreement Between the Swiss Federation and the Republic of Columbia on the Promotion and Reciprocal Protection of Investments, May 17, 2006 – 166

Agreement establishing an association between the European Community and its Member States, of the one part, and the Republic of Chile, of the other part, November 18, 2002 – 42

Agreement Establishing the ASEAN-Australia-New Zealand Free Trade Area, February 27, 2009 – 116, 167, 294, 295

Agreement on the European Economic Area—Final Act—Joint Declarations—Declarations by the Governments of the Member States of the Community and the EFTA States—Arrangements—Agreed Minutes—Declarations by one or several of the Contracting Parties of the Agreement on the European Economic Area, May 2, 1992 – 118

Agreement on Free Trade and Economic Partnership between Japan and Swiss Confederation, September 1, 2009 – 116, 167, 168, 290.

Amending Protocol to the Free Trade Agreement Between the Government of the People's Republic of China and the Government of the Islamic Republic of Pakistan, October 16, 2008 – 64

Australia-Chile Free Trade Agreement, July 30, 2008 – 117

Canada-Chile Free Trade Agreement, December 5, 1996 – 295, 309.

Canada-European Union—Trade and Investment Enhancement Agreement, 2004 – 52

Free Trade Agreement Between The Government of The People's Republic of China and The Government of the Islamic Republic of Pakistan, November 24, 2006. – 64

Comprehensive Economic Cooperation Agreement between the Republic of India and the Republic of Singapore, June 29, 2005 – 274

Convention on the Settlement of Investment Disputes between States and Nationals of Other States, March 18, 1965. – 53, 62, 72, 101, 140, 174, 175, 205, 213–215, 218, 221, 226, 234, 247–249, 251, 254, 255, 257, 261–263, 338

EC, *Council Decision 2010/91/EC of 10 November 2009 on the conclusion of an Agreement in the form of a Protocol between the European Community and the Republic of Tunisia establishing a dispute settlement mechanism applicable to disputes under the trade provisions of the Euro-Mediterranean Agreement establishing an Association between the European Communities and their Member States, of the one part, and the Republic of Tunisia, of the other part*, November 10, 2009 – 164, 171

Economic Partnership Agreement between the CARIFORUM States, of the one part, and the European Community and its Member States, of the other part, October 15, 2008 – 54, 128

Energy Charter Treaty, December 17, 1994 – 18, 42, 43, 47, 118, 201, 206, 219, 221, 222, 230, 240–242, 245, 282, 291, 301, 311, 312, 352.

EU-South Korea Free Trade Agreement, October 6, 2010 – 53, 54, 117, 128, 352.

Euro-Mediterranean Agreement establishing an association between the European Communities and their Member States, of the one part, and the Republic of Tunisia, of the other part, July 17, 1995 – 42

Free Trade Agreement between Canada and the Republic of Colombia, November 21, 2008 – 31, 35, 188, 189, 210, 294

Free Trade Agreement between Canada and the Republic of Panama, May 14, 2010 – 116, 127, 132.

Free Trade Agreement between Canada and the Republic of Peru, May 29, 2008 – 31, 189, 210, 299.

Free Trade Agreement Between Canada and the United States of America, January 2, 1988 – 117, 161.

Free Trade Agreement Between the European Union and its Member States, of the one part, and the Republic of South Korea on the other, October 15, 2009 – 300

Free Trade Agreement Between the Government of Canada and the State of Israel, July 31, 1996 – 128

Free Trade Agreement between the Government of New Zealand and the Government of the People's Republic of China, April 7, 2008 – 66–70, 72, 74, 116, 121, 128, 275.

Free Trade Agreement between the Government of the Republic of Korea and the Government of the Republic of Singapore, August 4, 2005 – 275

Free Trade Agreement Between the Government of the United States of America and the Government of the Republic of Chile, June 6, 2003 – 294, 295

Free Trade Agreement between the People's Republic of China and the Government of the Republic of Peru, April 28, 2009 – 116

Free Trade Agreement between the Republic of China and the Republic of Panama, August 1, 2003, – 275

Free Trade Agreement Between The Republic of Peru and the EFTA States June 24, 2010 – 166, 168

India-Korea Comprehensive Economic Partnership Agreement, August 7, 2009 – 116, 127, 130

Investment Agreement for the COMESA Common Investment Area, 2007 – 209, 209, 290.

Malaysia-New Zealand Free Trade Agreement, October 26, 2009 – 275

North American Free Trade Agreement Between the Government of Canada, the Government of Mexico and the Government of the United States, December 17, 1992 – 18, 25, 25, 28, 29, 32, 34.

Partnership and Cooperation Agreement between the European Communities and their Member States, and Ukraine, June 14, 1994 – 42

Peru-Singapore Free Trade Agreement, May 29, 2008 – 117, 127, 130.

Thailand-Australia Free Trade Agreement, July 5, 2004 – 276

Trade Agreement Between the European Union and Colombia and Peru, April 2011 – 300

Treaty of Asuncion, March 26, 1991 – 117

Treaty Establishing the Caribbean Community, July 4, 1973 – 118

Treaty Establishing the Common Market for Eastern and Southern Africa, November 5, 1993 – 275, 290, 294

Treaty of Lisbon amending the Treaty on European Union and the Treaty establishing the European Community, December 13, 2007 – 43, 78, 120

Understanding Concerning Certain U.S. Bilateral Investment Treaties, signed by the U.S., the European Commission, and acceding and candidate countries for accession to the European Union, September 22, 2003 – 48

The United States-Peru Trade Promotion Agreement, April 12, 2006 – 165, 166, 171.

United States-Singapore Free Trade Agreement, May 6, 2003 – 210.

III. Other treaties and international instruments

Agreement Between Canada and the Republic of Turkey for the Avoidance of Double Taxation and the Prevention of Fiscal Evasion with Respect to Taxes on Income and on Capital, July 14, 2009 – 308

Agreement on Air Transport between Canada and the European Community and its Member States, December 18, 2009 – 55

Agreement on Trade-Related Investment Measures, April 15, 1994 – 18, 118, 164, 167, 304

Agreement on Trade-Related Aspects of Intellectual Property Rights, April 15, 1994 – 127, 166, 169, 170

Articles of the Model Convention with Respect to Taxes on Income and on Capital, January 28, 2003 – 317

ASEAN Framework Agreement on Services, December 15, 1995 – 245

Consolidated versions of the Treaty on European Union and the Treaty on the Functioning of the European Union, 2008 – 43

Convention Between Canada and the United States of America With Respect to Taxes on Income and on Capital, June 14, 1983 – 311

Convention Between the Government of Canada and the Government of Mongolia for the Avoidance of Double Taxation and the Prevention of Fiscal Evasion with Respect to Taxes on Income and on Capital, May 27, 2002 – 320

Convention Between the Government of Canada and the Government of the United Mexican States for the Avoidance of Double Taxation and the Prevention of Fiscal Evasion with Respect to Taxes on Income, April 8, 1991 – 308

Convention on the Marking of Plastic Explosives for the Purpose of Detection, March 1, 1991 – 355

Convention on Offences and Certain Other Acts Committed On Board Aircraft, November 4, 1964 – 354

Convention for the Suppression of Unlawful Acts Against the Safety of Civil Aviation, September 23, 1971 – 355

Council of the European Union, *Conclusion on a comprehensive European international investment policy*, October 25, 2010 – 50

Declarations of the Government of the Democratic and Popular Republic of Algeria Concerning the Settlement of Claims by the Government of the United States of America and the Government of the Islamic Republic of Iran, January 19, 1981 – **219, 226**

Declaration on the Establishment of a New International Economic Order, 1974 – **17**

Doha Ministerial Declaration, Ministerial Conference, November 14, 2001 – **284**

"Draft Articles on the Law of Treaties with commentaries", 1967 – **326, 338, 339, 340**

"Draft articles on Responsibility of States for Internationally Wrongful Acts", 2001 – **217, 336, 355**

EC, *Commission Regulation (EC) 847/2004 of the European Parliament and of the Council of 29 April 2004, on the negotiation and implementation of air service agreements between Member States and third countries*, April 29, 2004 – **55**

EC, *Council and Commission Decision 98/181/EC, ECSC, Euratom of 23 September 1997 on the conclusion, by the European Communities, of the Energy Charter Treaty and the Energy Charter Protocol on energy effi ciency and related environmental aspects*, September 23, 1997 – **42**

EC, *Commission Decision 2007/339/EC on the signature and provisional application of the Air Transport Agreement between the European Community and its Member States, on the one hand, and the United States of America, on the other hand*, April 25, 2007 – **55**; European Parliament, *European Parliament resolution of 25 November on corporate social responsibility in international trade agreements*, November 25, 2010 – **300**

European Parliament, *European Parliament resolution of 6 April 2011 on the future European international investment policy*, April 6, 2011 – **300**

General Agreement on Tariffs and Trade, April 15, 1994 – **37,73, 130, 160, 164, 165, 268–270, 273, 275–277, 279–282, 292, 340.**

General Agreement on Trade in Services, April 15, 1994 – **18, 74, 120, 127, 160, 164, 165, 168, 170, 270, 273, 275, 276, 277, 304, 311.**

Johannesburg Declaration on Sustainable Development, September 4, 2002 – **284**

The Multilateral Agreement on Investment – Draft Consolidated Text, April 22, 1998 – **351**

OECD *Draft Convention on the Protection of Foreign Property*, 1963 – **19**

OECD *Draft Convention on the Protection of Foreign Property*, October 12, 1967 – **19**

OECD *Model Tax Convention on Income and on Capital*, (Published in loose-leaf since 1992) – **306, 308**

Protocol for the Suppression of Unlawful Acts of Violence at Airports Serving International Civil Aviation, February 24, 1988 – **355**

Protocol No. 11 to the Convention for the Protection of Human Rights and Fundamental Freedoms, November 1, 1998 – **183**

Resolution adopted by the General Assembly: Administration of Justice at the United Nations, December 16, 2009 – **253, 261**

The Rio Declaration on Environment and Development, June 3–14, 1992 – 284
Rome Statute of the International Criminal Court, July 17, 1998 – 248
Softwood Lumber Agreement Between the Government of Canada and the Government of the United States of America, September 12, 2006 – 344
Statute of the Administrative Tribunal of the International Bank for Reconstruction and Development, July 1, 1980 – 258
Statute of the International Court of Justice, June 26, 1945 – 350, 353
Treaty Establishing a Constitution for Europe, December 16, 2004 [Not in Force] – 43
Treaty of Lisbon amending the Treaty on European Union and the Treaty establishing the European Community, July 23, 2007 – 43
Treaty on European Union, February 7, 1992 – 57
Treaty on the Functioning of the European Union, March 30, 2010 – 43, 118, 120
UNCITRAL Model Law on International Commercial Arbitration, December 11, 1985 – 249
Understanding on Rules and Procedures Governing the Settlement of Disputes, World Trade Organization, April 15, 1994 – 248, 346
United Nations, Charter of Economic Rights and Duties of States, December 12, 1974 – 17, 181
United Nations Convention on the Law of the Sea, December 10, 1982 – 248
United Nations Convention on the Recognition and Enforcement of Foreign Arbitral Awards, June 10, 1958 – 225, 249, 262
United Nations Model Double Taxation Convention between Developed and Developing Countries, 2001 – 306
United Nations Sub-Commission on the Promotion and Protection of Human Rights, *Draft Norms on the Responsibility of Transnational Corporations and other Business Enterprises with Respect to Human Rights (Draft Norms)*, August 26, 2003 – 180
Vienna Convention on Diplomatic Relations, April 18, 1961 – 354
Vienna Convention on the Law of Treaties, May 23, 1969 – 171, 289, 307, 323–325, 330, 331, 333, 334, 338, 353

Rules

ECJ, *Consolidated Version of the Rules of Procedure of the European Court of Justice*, July 2, 2010 – 347
ICC, *Rules of Arbitration of the International Chamber of Commerce*, January 1, 1998 – 248
ICJ, *Rules of the International Court of Justice*, April 14, 1978 – 213, 346
ICSID, *Additional Facility Rules*, April 10, 2006 – 33, 140, 145, 154, 213, 247–249, 349, 350
ICSID, *Rules of Procedure for Arbitration Proceedings*, April 10, 2006 – 33, 145, 149, 154, 208, 213, 248, 259, 347, 349

London Court of International Arbitration, *LCIA Arbitration Rules*, January 1, 1998 – 349

PCIJ, *Rules of the Court*, March 24, 1922 – 213

UNCITRAL, *Arbitration Rules of the United Nations Commission on International Trade Law*, April 28, 1976 – 33, 80, 154, 213, 226, 247–249, 258, 259

Table of cases

I. International investment treaty and contract cases

Abaclat and ors v Argentina, Decision on Jurisdiction, ICSID Case No. ARB07/05 (August 4, 2011) – 235

AbitibiBowater Inc v Government of Canada, Consent Award, UNCITRAL (December 15, 2010) – 143

Accord Alpha Projektholding GmbH v Ukraine, Award, ICSID Case No. ARB/07/16 (November 8, 2010) – 202

ADC Affiliate Limited and ADC & ADMC Management Ltd v The Republic of Hungary, Award, ICSID Case No. ARB/03/16 (October 2, 2006) – 232, 233

ADF Group Inc v United States of America, Award, ICSID Case No. ARB(AF)/00/1 (January 9, 2003) – 126, 156, 328, 334, 354

AES Summit Generation Ltd and AES-Tisza Erömü Kft v The Republic of Hungary, Award, ICSID Case No. ARB/07/22 (September 23, 2010) – 347

Aguas del Tunari v Bolivia, Decision on Respondent's Objections to Jurisdiction, ICSID Case No. ARB/02/3 (October 21, 2005) – 327

Alasdair Ross Anderson and others v Republic of Costa Rica, Award, ICSID Case No. ARB(AF)/07/3 (May 19, 2010) – 199, 200, 201

Alex Genin, Eastern Credit Ltd, Inc and A.S. Baltoil v The Republic of Estonia, Award, ICSID Case No. ARB/99/2 (June 25, 2001) – 215

Alps Finance Trade AG v The Slovak Republic, Award, UNCITRAL (March 5, 2011) – 151, 238, 239

Amco Asia Corpn and others v Republic of Indonesia, Decision on Jurisdiction, ICSID Case No. ARB/81/1 (September 25, 1983) – 329

Amco Asia Corpn and others v Republic of Indonesia, Resubmitted Case, Decision on Jurisdiction, ICSID Case No. ARB/81/1 (May 10, 1988) – 227

American Bell International, Inc v The Government of the Islamic Republic of Iran, et al (June 11, 1984), 6 Iran-US CTR, 74 – 227

Antoine Goetz and Others v Republic of Burundi, Award, ICSID Case No. ARB/95/3 (February 10, 1999) – 310

Archer Daniels Midland Coy and Tate & Lyle Ingredients Americas Inc v The United Mexican States, Award, ICSID Case No. ARB(AF)04/05 (November 21, 2007) – 123, 163, 185, 254, 312, 343

Asian Agricultural Products Ltd ("AAPL") v Republic of Sri Lanka, Award and Dissenting Opinion, ICSID Case No. ARB/87/3 (June 27, 1990) – 341

Asian Agricultural Products Lted v Democratic Socialist Republic of Sri Lanka, Final Order, ICSID Case No. ARB/87/3 (June 27, 1990) – 218, 345

Azurix Corpn v Argentine Republic, Decision on Jurisdiction, ICSID Case No. ARB/01/12 (December 8, 2003) – 216

Bayindir Insaat Turizm Ticaret Ve Sanayi A.S. v Islamic Republic of Pakistan, Decision on Jurisdiction, ICSID Case No. ARB/03/29 (November 14, 2005) – 327

Berschader v Russia, Award, SCC Case No. 080/2004 (April 21, 2006) – 329

Biwater Gauff (Tanzania) Ltd v United Republic of Tanzania, Procedural Order No. 5 on Amicus Curiae, ICSID Case No. ARB/05/22 (February 2, 2007) – 347

Brandes Investment Partners LP v Venezuela, Decision on Rule 41(5) Objection, ICSID Case No ARB/08/3 (February 2, 2009) – 146, 147

Canadian Cattlemen for Fair Trade v United States of America, Award on Jurisdiction, UNCITRAL (January 28, 2008) – 123, 126, 345

Canfor Corpn v United States of America and Terminal Forest Products Ltd v United States of America, Decision on Preliminary Question, UNCITRAL (June 6, 2006) – 278, 343

Cargill, Incorporated v United Mexican States, Award, ICSID Case No. ARB(AF)/05/2 (September 18, 2009) – 123, 163, 185, 254, 312, 314, 343, 344

Cementownia "Nowa Huta" S.A. v Turkey, Award, ICSID Case No. ARB(AF)/06/2 (September 17, 2009) – 204, 207

China Heilonjiang International Economic & Technical Cooperative Corpn et al v Mongolia, PCA, 2010 – 75

CME Czech Republic BV v The Czech Republic), Partial Award, UNCITRAL (September 13, 2001) – 335

CMS Gas Transmission Co v Argentine Republic, Award, ICSID Case No ARB/01/8 (May 12, 2005) – 334, 336, 337, 345, 353

CMS Gas v Argentina, Decision on Annulment, ICSID Case No. ARB/01/8 (Annulment proceeding) (September 25, 2007) – 338

Commerce Group Corpn and San Sebastian Gold Mines, Inc v Republic of El Salvador, Award, ICSID Case No. ARB/09/17 (March 14, 2011) – 30

Compania De Aguas Del Aconquija S.A. & Compagnie Générale des Eaux v Argentine Republic, Award, ICSID Case No. ARB/97/3 (November 21, 2000) – 254, 328

Compania De Aguas Del Aconquija S.A. & Compagnie Générale des Eaux v Argentine Republic, Decision on Annulment, ICSID Case No. ARB/97/3 (July 3, 2002) – 225, 254

Compañiá de Aguas del Aconquija S.A. and Vivendi Universal v Argentine Republic, Award, ICSID Case No. ARB/97/3 (August 20, 2007) – 255, 278, 329

Continental Casualty Co v Argentine Republic, Award, ICSID Case No. ARB/03/9 (September 5, 2008) – 275, 382, 336, 340

Continental Casualty Co v The Argentine Republic, Decision on Jurisdiction, ICSID Case No. ARB/03/9 (February 22, 2006) – 327

Corn Products International Inc v United Mexican States, Decision on Responsibility, ICSID Case No. ARB(AF)/04/01 (January 15, 2008) – **123, 185, 254, 312, 343**

Dow AgroSciences LLC v Canada, Settlement Agreement, UNCITRAL (May 25, 2011) – **141**

Duke Energy Electroquil Partners & Electroquil S.A. v Republic of Ecuador, Award, ICSID Case No ARB/04/19 (August 18, 2008) – **312**

Eastern Sugar BV v Czech Republic, Partial Award, SCC Case No. 088/2004, UNCITRAL (March 27, 2007) – **47, 49, 329**

EDF (Services) Ltd v Romania, Award, ICSID Case No. ARB/05/13 (October 8, 2009) – **207, 283**

Ekran Berhad v People's Republic of China, ICSID Case No. ABR/11/15. (suspended as of July 22, 2011) – **75**

El Paso Energy International Coy v Argentine Republic, Decision on Jurisdiction, ICSID Case No. ARB/03/15 (April 27, 2006) – **313**

Emilio Agustin Maffezini v Kingdom of Spain, Decision of the Tribunal on Objections to Jurisdiction, ICSID Case No. ARB/97/7 (January 25, 2000) – **88, 328**

Empresas Lucchetti, S.A. and Lucchetti Perú, S.A. v Republic of Peru, Award, ICSID Case No. ARB/03/4 (February 7, 2005) – **326**

EnCana Corporation v Republic of Ecuador, Award, UNCITRAL (February 3, 2006) – **312**

Enron v Argentina, Decision on Annulment, ICSID Case No. ARB/01/3 (Annulment proceeding) (July 30, 2010) – **339**

Enron Corporation and Ponderosa Assets, L.P. v Argentine Republic, Award, ICSID Case No. ARB/01/3 (May 22, 2007) – **279, 327, 336, 337**

Enron Creditors Recovery Corpn & Ponderosa Assets, L.P. v Argentine Republic, Decision on Annulment, ICSID Case No ARB/97/3 (Annulment Proceeding) (July 30, 2010) – **345**

Ethyl Corpn v Government of Canada, Award on Jurisdiction, UNCITRAL (June 24, 1998) – **32, 141, 142**

Eureko B.V. v Slovak Republic, Award on Jurisdiction, Arbitrability and Suspension, ICSID Case No 2008–13 (October 26, 2010) – **47, 347**

Europe Cement Investment & Trade S.A. v Republic of Turkey, Award, ICSID Case No. ARB(AF)/07/2 (August 13, 2009) – **204**

Feldman v Mexico, Award on Merits, ICSID Case No. ARB(AF)/99/1 (December 16, 2002) – **312, 313**

Fraport AG Frankfurt Airport Services Worldwide v Philippines, Award, ICSID Case No. ARB/03/25 (August 16, 2007) – **199, 200–203, 206, 211, 326**

Fraport AG Frankfurt Airport Services Worldwide v Philippines, Decision on the Application for Annulment, ICSID Case No. ARB/03/25 (Annulment Proceedings) (December 23, 2010) – **200**

FTR Holding S.A., Philip Morris Products S.A. and Abal Hermanos S.A. v Oriental Republic of Uruguay, ICSID Case No. ARB/10/7 (March 26, 2010) – **169, 292**

GAMI Investments, Inc v The Government of the United Mexican States, Final Award, UNCITRAL (November 15, 2004) – **279, 280**

Generation Ukraine v Ukraine, Final Award, ICSID Case No. ARB/00/9 (September 16, 2003) – **243**

Genin et al v Estonia, Award, ICSID Case No. ARB/99/2 (June 25, 2001) – **203**

Glamis Gold, Ltd v United States of America, Award, UNCITRAL (June 8, 2009) – **35, 126, 295, 354**

Global Trading Resource Corpn and Globex International, Inc v Ukraine, Award, ICSID Case No ARB/09/11 (December 1, 2010) – **146, 147**

Grand River Enterprises Six Nations, Ltd, et al v United States of America, Award, UNCITRAL (January 12, 2011) – **168, 171, 295**

Gustav FW Hamester GmbH & Co KG v Republic of Ghana, Award, ICSID Case No. ARB/07/24 (June 18, 2010) – **202, 203, 205, 215**

Holiday Inns S.A. v Morocco, Decision on Jurisdiction, ICSID Case No. ARB/72/1 (May 12, 1974) – **218**

Impregilo S.p.A. v Islamic Republic of Pakistan, Decision on Jurisdiction, ICSID Case No. ARB/03/3 (April 22, 2005) – **216**

Inceysa Vallisoletana, S.L. v El Salvador, Award, ICSID Case No. ARB/03/26 (August 2, 2006) – **199, 200, 201, 203, 206**

Industria Nacional de Alimentos, S.A. and Indalsa Perú, S.A. v The Republic of Peru, Decision on Annulment, ICSID Case No. ARB/03/4 (Annulment proceeding) (September 5, 2007) – **326**

International Thunderbird Gaming Corpn v Mexico, Arbitral Award, UNCITRAL (January 26, 2006) – **328**

Joseph C. Lemire v Ukraine, Decision on Jurisdiction and Liability, ICSID Case No. ARB/06/18 (January 21, 2010) – **203, 283, 295**

Klöckner Industrie-Anlagen GmbH and others v United Republic of Cameroon and Société Camerounaise des Engrais, Award, ICSID Case No. ARB/81/2 (October 21, 1983) – **218, 227**

Lauder v Czech Republic, Final Award, UNCITRAL (September 3, 2001) – **327**

LG&E Energy Corpn v Argentine Republic, Decision on Liability, ICSID Case No. ARB/02/1 (October 3, 2006) – **328, 336, 337**

LG&E Energy Corpn, LG&E Capital Corpn, LG&E International, Inc v Argentine Republic, Award, ICSID Case No ARB/02/1 (July 25, 2007) – **353**

Liman Caspian Oil BV & NCL Dutch Investment BV v The Republic of Kazakhstan, Award, ICSID Case No. ARB/07/14 (June 22, 2010) – **243, 244, 245**

Limited Liability Company Amto v Ukraine, Final Award, SCC Case No. 080/2005 (March 26, 2008) – **215**

Loewen Group, Inc and Raymond L. Loewen v United States of America, Award, ICSID Case No. ARB (AF)/98/3 (June 26, 2003) – **330, 335**

M.C.I. Power Group L.C. and New Turbine, Inc v Ecuador, Award, ICSID Case No. ARB/03/6 (July 31, 2007) – **327, 334**

Merrill & Ring Forestry L.P. v Canada, Award, UNCITRAL (March 31, 2010) – **35**

Metalclad Corpn v The United Mexican States, ICSID, Case No. ARB (AF)/97/1 (August 30, 2000) – **32, 125, 294**

Methanex Corporation v United States of America, Decision on Amici Curiae, UNCITRAL (January 15, 2001) – **32, 39, 346**

Methanex Corpn v United States of America, Final Award of the Tribunal on Jurisdiction and Merits, UNCITRAL (August 3, 2005) – 275, 324, 328, 330, 353

Mobil Corpn and others v Bolivarian Republic of Venezuela, Decision on Jurisdiction, ICSID Case No. ARB/07/27 (June 10, 2010) – 204, 235, 236

Mondev International Ltd v United States of America, Award, ICSID Case No. ARB(AF)/99/2 (October 11, 2002) – 126, 326, 330, 334, 354

Morrison-Knudsen Pacifi c Ltd v The Ministry of Roads and Transportation et al Harris International, Iran-US Trib. (July 3, 1984) – 227

MTD Equity Sdn. Bhd. & MTD Chile S.A. v Chile, Award, ICSID Case No. ARB/01/7 (May 25, 2004) – 207, 327

MTD v Chile, Decision on Annulment, ICSID Case No. ARB/01/7 (March 21, 2007) – 341

National Grid plc v The Argentine Republic, Decision on Jurisdiction, UNCITRAL (June 20, 2006) – 329, 331

Noble Ventures, Inc v Romania, Award, ICSID Case No. ARB/01/11 (October 12, 2005) – 326, 327

Occidental Exploration and Production Co v Ecuador, Final Award, LCIA Case No. UN 3467 (July 1, 2004) – 312, 313, 326

Owens-Corning Fiberglass Corpn v The Government of Iran et al (May 13, 1983), 2 Iran-US CTR, 322 – 227

Pac Rim Cayman LLC v Republic of El Salvador, Decision on the Respondent's Preliminary Objections under CAFTA Articles 10.20.4 and 10.20.5, ICSID Case No. ARB/09/12 (August 2, 2010) – 30

Pan American Energy LLC & BP Argentina Exploration Co v Argentine Republic, ICSID Case No. ARB/03/13 and *BP America Production Co et al v Argentine Republic*, ICSID Case No. ARB/04/8, Decision on Preliminary Objections (July 27, 2006) – 243, 313

Parkerings-Compagniet AS v Lithuania, Award, ICSID Case No. ARB/05/8 (September 11, 2007) – 330

Petrobart Ltd v The Kyrgyz Republic, Award, Arbitration Institute of the Stockholm Chamber of Commerce, ARB. No. 126/2003 (March 29, 2005) – 241, 243

Phoenix Action Ltd v Czech Republic, Award, ICSID Case No. ARB/06/5 (April 15, 2009) – 190, 192, 205, 206, 233, 234, 235

Plama Consortium Ltd v Bulgaria, Award, ICSID Case No. ARB/03/24 (August 27, 2008) – 192, 199, 201, 206, 310, 311

Plama Consortium Ltd v Bulgaria, Decision on Jurisdiction, ICSID Case No. ARB/03/24 (February 8, 2005) – 242, 244, 245, 330

Pope & Talbot Inc v Government of Canada, Award, UNCITRAL (January 26, 2000) – 122

Pope & Talbot Inc v The Government of Canada, Award on the Merits of Phase 2, UNCITRAL (April 10, 2001) – 125, 279, 280, 330, 354

Pope & Talbot Inc v The Government of Canada, Award in Respect of Damages, UNCITRAL (May 31, 2002) – 39

Rompetrol v Romania, Decision on Respondent's Preliminary Objections on Jurisdiction and Admissibility, ICSID Case No. ARB/06/03 (April 18, 2008) – 232, 236

RosInvestCo UK Ltd v The Russian Federation, Award on Jurisdiction, SCC Case No. Arb. V079/2005 (October 2007) – 332

Rosinvest UK Ltd v The Russian Federation, Final Award, SCC Arbitration V 079/2005 (September 12, 2010) – 353

RSM Production Corpn v Grenada, Award, ICSID Case No. ARB/10/6 (December 10, 2010) – 146, 147

Rumeli Telekom A.S. and Telsim Mobil Telekomunikasyon Hizmetleri A.S. v Republic of Kazakhstan, Award, ICSID Case No. ARB/05/16 (July 29, 2008) – 202

Saba Fakes v Turkey, Award, ICSID Case No. ARB/07/20 (July 14, 2010) – 205

Salini Costruttori S.p.A. and Italstrade S.p.A. v Jordan, Decision on Jurisdiction, ICSID Case No. ARB/02/13 (November 9, 2004) – 296

Salini Costruttori S.P.A. and Italstrade S.P.A. v Kingdom of Morroco, Decision on Jurisdiction, ICSID Case No. ARB/00/4 (July 16, 2001) – 151, 234, 326, 333

Saluka Investments B.V. v The Czech Republic, Decision on Jurisdiction over the Czech Republic's Counterclaim, UNCITRAL (May 7, 2004) – 201, 214, 215, 217, 224, 228

Saluka Investments BV (The Netherlands) v The Czech Republic, Partial Award, UNCITRAL (March 17, 2006) – 36, 47, 232, 233, 327, 328, 331

S.D. Myers, Inc v Government of Canada, Partial Award, UNCITRAL (November 13, 2000) – 122, 142, 280

S.D. Myers, Inc v Government of Canada, Second Partial Award, UNCITRAL (October 21, 2002) – 123

S.D. Myers, Inc v Government of Canada, Separate Concurring Opinion, UNCITRAL (13 November 2000) – 280

Sergei Paushok, CJSC Golden East Co, CJSC Vostokneftegaz Co v The Government of Mongolia, Award on Jurisdiction and Liability, UNCITRAL (April 28, 2011) – 215, 225, 228

SGS Société Générale de Surveillance S.A. v Islamic Republic of Pakistan, Decision on Jurisdiction, ICSID Case No. ARB/01/13 (August 6, 2003) – 216, 220, 221, 223, 330

SGS Société Générale de Surveillance SA v Philippines, Decision on Objections to Jurisdiction and Separate Declaration, ICSID Case No ARB/02/6 (January 29, 2004) – 216, 220, 278, 326

Sempra Energy International v Argentine Republic, Award, ICSID Case No. ARB/02/16 (September 28, 2007) – 336, 337, 338

Sempra Energy International v Argentine Republic, Decision on Annulment, ICSID Case No ARB/02/16 (Annulment Proceeding) (June 29, 2010) – 326, 338, 345

Siemens v Argentina, Award, ICSID Case No. ARB/02/8 (February 6, 2007) – 334

Siemens AG v Argentina, Decision on Jurisdiction, ICSID Case No ARB/02/8 (August 3, 2004) – 278, 326, 327, 329

Southern Pacific Properties (Middle East) Ltd v Arab Republic of Egypt, Award on the Merits, ICSID Case No. ARB/84/3 (May 20, 1992) – **216**

Suez, Sociedad General de Aguas de Barcelona S.A., and Vivendi Universal S.A. v The Argentine Republic, ICSID Case No. ARB/03/19 and *AWG Group Ltd v The Argentine Republic* (UNCITRAL), Decision on Jurisdiction (August 3, 2006) – **328, 329**

Suez Sociedad General de Aguas de Barcelona, S.A., and Vivendi Universal S.A. v The Argentine Republic, Order in Response to Amicus Petition, ICSID Case No. ARB/03/19 (February 12, 2007) – **347**

Tecnicas Medioambientales Tecmed S.A. v The United Mexican States, Award, ICSID Case No ARB (AF)/00/2 (May 29, 2003) – **335, 353**

Telecommunications, Inc v Islamic Republic of Iran, Partial Award, Iran-US Trib. (November 2, 1987) – **227**

Telefónica S.A. v Argentine Republic, Decision of the Tribunal on Objections to Jurisdiction, ICSID Case No. ARB/03/20 (May 25, 2006) – **329**

Texaco Overseas Petroleum Co & California Asiatic Oil Co v Libyan Arab Republic, Award (January 19, 1977) – **184**

Tokios Tokelés v Ukraine, Decision on Jurisdiction, ICSID Case No. ARB/02/18 (April 29, 2004) – **202, 232, 326, 331**

Total S.A. v. Argentine Republic, Decision on Liability, ICSID Case No. ARB/04/01(December 27, 2010) – **295**

Trans-Global Petroleum Inc v Jordan, Consent Award, ICSID Case No. ARB/07/25 (April 8, 2009) – **146**

Trans-Global Petroleum Inc v Jordan, Decision on Rule 41(5) Objection, ICSID Case No. ARB/07/25 (May 12, 2008) – **146, 147**

Tza Yap Shum v Republic of Peru, Decision on Jurisdiction and Competence, ICSID Case No. ABR/07/6 (June 19, 2009) – **75**

United Postal Service of America Inc v Government of Canada, Decision on Amici Curiae, UNCITRAL (October 17, 2001) – **347**

Vattenfall AB, Vattenfall Europe AG, Vattenfall Europe Generation AG v Federal Republic of Germany, Award, ICSID Case No. ARB/09/6 (March 11, 2011) – **47, 301**

Waguih Elie George Siag and Clorinda Vecci v the Arab Republic of Egypt, Dissenting Opinion of Professor Francisco Orrego Vicuña, ICSID Case No. ARB/05/15 (June 1, 2009) – **206**

Wena Hotels Ltd v Arab Republic of Egypt, Award, ICSID Case No. ARB/98/4 (December 8, 2000) – **345**

Westinghouse Electric Corpn v The Islamic Republic of Iran et al, Iran-US TRib (February 12, 1987) – **227**

World Duty Free Company Ltd v Kenya, Award, ICSID Case No. ARB/00/7 (October 4, 2006) – **192, 199, 206**

Yukos Universal Limited (Isle of Man) v The Russian Federation, Interim Award on Jurisdiction and Liability, UNCITRAL (November 30, 2009) – **232, 243, 244, 245**

II. PCIJ and ICJ cases

Asylum Case (Columbia v Peru), [1950] ICJ Rep 266 – 213

Case concerning Ahmadou Sadio Diallo (Guinea v Congo), Preliminary Objections, [2007] ICJ Rep – 335

Case Concerning the Dispute Regarding Navigational and Related Rights (Costa Rica v Nicaragua), [2009] ICJ Rep 213 – 329

Competence of the General Assembly for the Admission of a State to the United Nations, Advisory Opinion [1950] ICJ Rep 4 –326

Harry Roberts (U.S.A.) v United Mexican States (1926), Reports of International Arbitral Awards, vol IV at 77–81 – 355

L.F.H. Neer and Pauline Neer (U.S.A.) v United Mexican States (1926), Reports of International Arbitral Awards, vol IV at 60–6 – 351, 354, 355

Libya v Chad [1994] ICJ Rep 4 – 326

Polish Postal Service in Danzig (1931), Advisory Opinion, PCIJ (Ser B) No 11 – 355

Reparations for Injuries Suffered in the Service of the United Nations, Advisory Opinion, [1947] ICJ Rep 174 – 183

GATT and WTO cases

Argentina—Definitive Anti Dumping Duties on Poultry (2003), (Panel Report) – 173

Brazil—Measures Affecting Imports of Retreaded Tyres (2007), (Appellate Body Report) – 271

EC—Measures Affecting Trade in Large Civil Aircraft (2011), (Appellate Body Report) – 173

European Communities—Measures Affecting Asbestos and Asbestos-Containing Products (2001), (Appellate Body Report) – 347

European Communities—Measures Affecting the Approval and Marketing of Biotech Products (Complaint by the United States of America, Canada, Argentina) (2004), (Panel Report) – 349

European Communities—Trade Description of Sardines (2002), (Appellate Body Report) – 348

Korea—Definitive Safeguard Measure on Imports of Certain Dairy Products (1999), (Panel Report) – 271

Korea—Measures Affecting Imports of Fresh, Chilled and Frozen Beef (2001), (Appellate Body Reports) – 162, 344

Mexico—Anti-Dumping Investigation of High Fructose Corn Syrup (HFCS) from the United States, Recourse to Article 21.5 of the DSU by the United States (2001), (Appellate Body Report) – 162, 344

Mexico—Measures on Soft Drinks and Other Beverages (Complaint by the United States) (2005), (Panel Report) – 162, 163

Mexico—Taxes Measures on Soft Drinks and Other Beverages (Complaint by the United States) (2006), (Appellate Body Report) – 162, 173

Turkey—Restrictions on Imports of Textile and Clothing Products (1999), (Appellate Body Report) – 160
United States—Final Dumping Determination on Softwood Lumber from Canada (2004 and 2006), (Appellate Body Report) – 344
United States—Final Anti-Dumping Measures on Stainless Steel from Mexico (Complaint by the United States) (2008), (Appellate Body Report) – 159
United States— Import Prohibition of Certain Shrimp and Shrimp Products (1998), (Appellate Body Report) – 271
United States— Investigation of the International Trade Commission in Softwood Lumber from Canada (2004 and 2006), (Appellate Body Report) – 344
United States—Lead and Bismuth II (2000), (Appellate Body Report) – 347
United States—Measures Affecting the Cross-Border Supply of Gambling and Betting Services (2005), (Appellate Body Report) – 270
United States—Standards for Reformulated and Conventional Gasoline (complaint by Venezuela) (April 29, 1996), (Appellate Body Report) – 341

IV. Other cases and decisions

International

ECHR, *Kin-Stib and Majkíc v Serbia*, No. 12312/05 (20 April 20, 2010) – 168
ECJ, *Commission v Austria*, C-205/06, [2009] ECR I-1301 – 43, 47
ECJ, *Commission v Austria*, C-475/98, [2002] ECR I-9797 – 55
ECJ, *Commission v Belgium*, C-471/98, [2002] ECR I-9681 – 55
ECJ, *Commission v Denmark*, C-467/98), [2002] ECR I-9519 – 55
ECJ, *Commission v Finland*, C-118/07, [2009] ECR I-10889 – 47
ECJ, *Commission v Finland*, C-469/98, [2002] ECR I-9627 – 43, 55
ECJ, *Commission v Germany*, C-476/98, [2002] ECR I-9855 – 55
ECJ, *Commission v Luxemburg*, C-472/98, [2002] ECR I-9855 – 55
ECJ, *Commission v Sweden*, C-249/06, [2009] ECR I-1335 – 43, 47
ECJ, *Commission v Sweden*, C-468/98,[2002]ECR I-9575 – 55
Judicial Decisions: International Military Tribunal (Nuremberg), Judgment and Sentences, (1947) 41(1) AJIL 172 – 187
Opinion 1/94 [1994] ECR I-5267 – 46
Opinion 2/00 [2001] ECR I-09713 – 46
Re Stainless Steel Sheet and Strip in Coils from Mexico (Mexico v United States) (2010), USA-MEX-2007–1904–01 (Ch 19 Panel) – 159
United States of America v Canada, Award, London Court of International Arbitration Case No. 81010 (January 20 and 28, 2011) – 162
United States of America v Canada, Decision, LCIA Case No. 91312 (September 27, 2009) – 162

Domestic

Abitibi-Consol Inc {and Canfor Corpn} v.United States, Case No. 06–83 (2006) – 344

American Income Life Insurance Co v R, 2008 TCC 306 – 307
Mayor of Bradford v Pickles [1895] AC 587 (HL) – 236
Saipem UK Ltd v R, 2011 TCC 25 (appeal pending) – 307, 318
Tembec, Inc v United States, Case No. 06–109 (2006) – 344
Tembec, Inc v United States, Case No. 06–152 (2006) – 344
The United Mexican States v Metalclad Corporation, 2001 BCSC 664 – 125

Bibliography

Books

Alston, Philip (ed), *Non-State Actors and Human Rights* (Oxford: Oxford University Press, 2005).

Alvarez, José Enrique, *The Public International Law Regime Governing International Investment* (The Hague: The Hague Academy of International Law, 2011).

Alvarez, Jose E. and Karl P. Sauvant, *The Evolving International Investment Regime Expectations, Realities, Options* (Oxford: Oxford University Press, 2011).

Amerasinghe, Chittharanjan F., *Jurisdiction of International Tribunals* (The Hague: Kluwer Law International, 2003).

Arnold, Brian J. *Reforming Canada's International Tax System Toward Coherence and Simplicity* (Toronto: Canadian Tax Foundation, 2009).

Binder, Christina et al (eds), *International Investment Law for the 21st Century, Liber Amicorum Christoph Schreuer* (Oxford: Oxford University Press, 2009).

Bowen, H.R., *Social Responsibility and Accountability* (New York: Harper and Row, 1953).

Brown, Chester and Devashish Krishan (eds), *Commentaries on Selected Model Investment Treaties* (Oxford University Press, forthcoming).

Brown, Chester and Kate Miles (eds), *Evolution in Investment Treaty Law and Arbitration* (Cambridge: Cambridge University Press, 2011).

Brundtland, Gro Harlem et al, *Our Common Future: World Commission on Environment and Development* (Oxford: Oxford University Press, 1987).

Chauffour, Jean-Pierre and Jean-Christophe Maur (eds), *Preferential Trade Agreement Policies for Development: A Handbook* (Washington, DC: The World Bank, 2011).

Cheng, Bin, *General Principles of Law as Applied by International Courts and Tribunals* (New York: Cambridge University Press, 2006).

Cockfield, Arthur J, *NAFTA Tax Law and Policy—Resolving the Clash between Economic and Sovereignty Interests* (Toronto: Toronto University Press, 2005).

Cordonier Segger, Marie-Claire and Ashfaq Khalfan, *Sustainable Development Law: Principles, Practices and Prospects* (Oxford: Oxford University Press, 2004).

Cordonier Segger, Marie-Claire, Markus W. Gehring and Andrew Paul Newcombe (eds), *Sustainable Development in World Investment Law* (The Hague: Kluwer Law International, 2011).

Court de Fontmichel, Alexandre. *L'arbitre, le juge et les pratiques illicites du commerce international* (Paris: Editions Panthéon Assas, 2004).

Craig, Paul P. and Gráinne De Búrca, *EU Law: Text, Cases, and Materials*, 5th edn (Oxford: Oxford University Press, 2011).

Dolzer, Rudolf and Christoph Schreuer, *Principles of International Investment Law* (Oxford: Oxford University Press, 2008).

Dolzer, Rudolf and Margrete Stevens, *Bilateral Investment Treaties* (The Hague: Martinus Nijhoff Publishers, 1995).

Dong Wang, *China's Unequal Treaties: Narrating National History* (Maryland: Lexington Books, 2005).

Douglas, Zachary, *The International Law of Investment Claims* (Cambridge: Cambridge University Press, 2009).

Dugan, Christopher F. et al, *Investor-State Arbitration* (New York: Oxford University Press, 2008).

Dupuy, Pierre-Marie et al (eds), *Human Rights in International Investment Law and Arbitration* (Oxford: Oxford University Press, 2009).

Franck, Thomas M., *The Power of Legitimacy Among Nations* (New York: Oxford University Press, 1990).

Gallagher, Norah and Wenhua Shan, *Chinese Investment Treaties: Policies and Practice* (Oxford: Oxford University Press, 2009).

Gantz, David A., *Regional Trade Agreements: Law, Policy and Practice* (Durham, NC: Carolina Academic Press, 2009).

Gardiner, Richard K., *Treaty Interpretation* (Oxford: Oxford University Press, 2008).

Griebel, Jörn, *Internationales Investitionsrecht* (Munich: Beck Verlag, 2008).

Haddad, Mona and Constantinos Stephanos (eds), *Financial Services and Preferential Trade Agreements: Lessons from Latin America* (Washington, DC: The World Bank, 2010).

Henkin, Louis et al, *International Law, Cases and Materials*, 3rd edn (St-Paul: West Publ. Co, 1993).

Hoekman, B. and K. Saggi, "Multilateral Disciplines for Investment-Related Policies" in Paolo Guerrieri and Hans-EckartScharrer (eds), *Global Governance, Regionalism and the International Economy* (Baden-Baden: NomosVerlagsgesellschaft, 2000).

Ijalaye, David Adedayo, *The Extension of Corporate Personality in International Law* (New York: Oceana Publications, 1978).

Jägers, N., *Corporate Human Rights Obligations: In Search of Accountability* (Antwerpen: Intersentia, 2002).

Jennings, R. and A. Watts (eds), *Oppenheim's International Law*, 9th edn, vol. 1 (London: Longman, 1992).

Jessup, Philip C., *A Modern Law of Nations, an Introduction* (New York: Macmillan, 1948).

Karsten, Kristine and Andrew Berkely (eds), *Arbitration—Money Laundering, Corruption and Fraud* (Paris: ICC, 2003).

Kauffmann, Céline and Cristina Tébar Less, *Transition to a Low-carbon Economy: Public Goals and Corporate Practices* (Paris: OECD, 2010).

Kerr, Michael et al, *Corporate Social Responsibility: A Legal Analysis* (Markham, Ont: LexisNexis, 2009).

Kinnear, Meg N. et al, *Investment Disputes under NAFTA: An Annotated Guide to NAFTA Chapter 11* (The Hague: Kluwer Law International, 2006).

Kläger, Roland. *'Fair and Equitable Treatment' in International Investment Law* (Cambridge: Cambridge University Press, 2011).

Koremenos, Barbara et al, *The Rational Design of International Institutions* (Cambridge: Cambridge University Press, 2004).

Lang, Michael, Judith Herdina and Ines Hofbauer (eds), *WTO and Direct Taxation* (The Hague: Kluwer Law International, 2005).

Lardy, Nicholas R., *Integrating China into the Global Economy* (Washington, DC: Brookings Institution Press, 2002).

Lowenfeld, Andreas, *International Economic Law*, 2nd edn (New York: Oxford University Press, 2002).

Markert, Lars, *Streitschlichtungsklauseln in Investitionsschutzabkommen* (Baden-Baden: Nomos, 2010).

Maskus, Keith, *Intellectual Property Rights in the Global Economy* (Washington: Institute for International Economics, 2000).

Matsushita, Mitsuo et al, *The World Trade Organization: Law, Practice and Policy* 2nd edn (Oxford: Oxford University Press, 2006).

McLachlan, Campbell, Laurence Shore and Matthew Weiniger, *International Investment Arbitration: Substantive Principles* (Oxford: Oxford University Press, 2007)

Merciai, Patrizio, *Les entreprises multinationales en droit international* (Brussels: Bruylant, 1993).

Mitchell, Andrew, *Legal Principles in WTO Disputes* (Cambridge: Cambridge University Press, 2008).

Montt, Santiago, *State Liability in Investment Treaty Arbitration* (Oxford: Hart Publishing, 2009).

Muchlinski, Peter T., *Multinational Enterprises and the Law* (New York: Oxford University Press, 2007).

Newcombe, Andrew and Lluís Paradell, *Law and Practice of Investment Treaties: Standards of Treatment* (The Netherlands: Kluwer Law International, 2009).

Nguyen, Quoc Dinh, Patrick Daillier and Alain Pellet, *Droit international public*, 6th edn (Paris: LGDJ, 1999).

Okeke, Chris N., *Controversial Subjects of Contemporary International Law*, 3rd edn (Rotterdam: Rotterdam University Press, 1974).

Qureshi, Asif and Andreas R. Ziegler, *International Economic Law*, 3rd edn (London: Thomson Sweet & Maxwell, 2011).

Reinisch, August (ed), *Standards of Investment Protection* (Oxford: Oxford University Press, 2008).

Richardson, Benjamin. *Socially Responsible Investment: Regulating the Unseen Polluters* (Oxford: Oxford University Press, 2008).

Rogers, Catherine (ed), *The Future of Investment Arbitration* (Oxford: Oxford University Press, 2009).

Ruggie, John. "International Regimes, Transactions, and Change: Embedded Liberalism and the Post-war Economic Order" (1982) 36 *International Organization* 379.

Salacuse, Jeswald. *The Law of Investment Treaties* (Oxford: Oxford University Press, 2010).

Sauvant, Karl P. (ed), *Appeals Mechanism in International Investment Disputes* (New York: Oxford University Press, 2008).

Sauvant, Karl P. and Lisa E. Sachs (eds), *The Effect of Treaties on Foreign Direct Investment Bilateral Investment Treaties, Double Taxation Treaties, and Investment Flows* (Oxford: Oxford University Press, 2009).

Sawyer, Adrian, *Developing a World Tax Organisation: The Way Forward* (UK: Fiscal Publications, 2008).

Sayed, Abdulhay, *Corruption in International Trade and Commercial Arbitration* (The Hague: Kluwer Law International, 2004).

Schill, Stephan W., *International Investment Law and Comparative Public Law* (Oxford: Oxford University Press, 2010).

Schill, Stephan W., *The Multilateralization of International Investment Law* (Cambridge: Cambridge University Press, 2009).

Schabas, William, *The International Criminal Court: A Commentary on the Rome Statute* (Oxford: Oxford University Press, 2010).

Schreuer, Christoph, *The ICSID Convention: A Commentary* (New York: Cambridge University Press, 2009).

Shany, Yuval, *Regulating Jurisdictional Relations between National and International Courts* (New York: Oxford University Press, 2007).

Shelp, Ronald et al, *Service Industries and Economic Development: Case Studies in Technology Transfer* (New York: Praeger Publishing, 1984).

Sinclair, Sir Ian, *The Vienna Convention on the Law of Treaties*, 2nd edn (Manchester: Manchester University Press, 1984).

Sornarajah, M., *The International Law on Foreign Investment*, 2nd edn (New York: Cambridge University Press, 2004).

Tienhaara, Kyla, *The Expropriation of Environmental Governance* (Cambridge: Cambridge University Press, 2009).

Trebilcock, Michael and Robert Howse, *The Regulation of International Trade*, 3rd edn (London: Routledge, 2005).

Tung, William L., *China and the Foreign Powers: The Impact of and Reaction to Unequal Treaties* (New York: Oceana Publications, 1970).

UNCTAD, *International Investment Instruments: A Compendium, Vol III* (New York: UN, 1996).

Van Damme, Isabelle, *Treaty Interpretation by the WTO Appellate Body* (Oxford: Oxford University Press, 2009).

Van den Bossche, Peter, *The Law and Policy of the World Trade Organization*, 2nd edn (Cambridge: Cambridge University Press 2008).

Vandevelde, Kenneth J. *United States International Investment Agreements* (Oxford: Oxford University Press, 2009).

Vandevelde, Kenneth J., *United States Investment Treaties: Policy and Practice* (Boston: Kluwer Law and Taxation, 1992).

Van Harten, Gus, *Investment Treaty Arbitration and Public Law* (Oxford: Oxford University Press, 2007).

Vernon, Raymond, *Sovereignty at Bay: The Multinational Spread of U.S. Enterprises* (New York: Basic Books, 1971).

Waibel, Michael et al., *The Backlash Against Investment Arbitration: Perceptions and Reality* (The Hague: Kluwer Law International, 2010).

World Trade Organization, *The Legal Texts: The Results of the Uruguay Round of Multilateral Trade Negotiations* (Cambridge: Cambridge University Press, 1999).

Ziegler, Andreas R., *Droit international économique de la Suisse—Une introduction* (Berne, Stämpfli: 2010).

Articles and book chapters

Abbott, Frederick, "NAFTA and the Legalization of World Politics: A Case Study" (2000) 54(3) International Organization 519.

Abi Saab, Georges, "The International Law of Multinational Corporations: A Critique of American Legal Doctrines" (1971) 2 Annales d'études internationals 97.

Adlung, Rudolf and Martín Molinuevo, "Bilateralism in Services Trade: Is There Fire Behind the (BIT-) Smoke" (2008) 11(2) J Int'l Econ L 365.

Allee, Todd and Clint Peinhardt, "Contingent Credibility: The Impact of Investment Treaty Violations on Foreign Direct Investment" (2011) 65(3) International Organization 401.

Allee, Todd and Clint Peinhardt, "The Least BIT Rational: An Empirical Test of the 'Rational Design' of Investment Treaties" (Presentation delivered at the Political Economy Organization Conference in Monte Carlo Verità, Switzerland February 3–8, 2008) online: <http://www.cis.ethz.ch/events/past_events/PEIO2008/Allee.Peinhardt_BITs.Rational.Design>.

Alvarez, Jose E., "Critical Theory and the North American Free Trade Agreement's Chapter Eleven" (1997) 28 U Miami Inter-Am L Rev.

Alvarez, José E., "The Factors Driving and Constraining the Incorporation of International Law in WTO Adjudication" in Merit E. Janow, Victoria Donaldson and Alan Yanovich (eds), *The WTO: Governance, Dispute Settlement and Developing Countries* (New York: Juris Publishing, Inc, 2008).

Alvarez, José E., "Implications for the Future of International Investment Law" in Karl P. Sauvant and Michael Chiswick-Patterson (eds), *Appeals Mechanism in International Investment Disputes* (New York: Oxford University Press, 2008) 16.

Alvarez, José E., "The Return of the State" (2011) 20(2) Minnesota Journal of International Law 223.

Alvarez, José Enrique and Tegan Brink, "Revisiting the Necessity Defense" (2011–12) *Yearbook of International Investment Law and Policy* (forthcoming), online <http://www.iilj.org/publications/documents/2010-3.Alvarez-Brink.pdf>.

Andenas, Mads and Stefan Zleptnig, "Proportionality: WTO Law in Comparative Perspective" (2007) 42(3) Tex Int'l LJ 370.

Anzilotti, Dionisio, "La Demande Reconventionnelle en Procédure Internationale" (1930) 57 Journal du Droit International 857.

Arnold, Brian, "Threshold Requirements for Taxing Business Profits under Tax Treaties" (2003) Bulletin for International Fiscal Documentation 476.

Arnold Brian J and Neil H. Harris, "NAFTA and the Taxation of Corporate Investment: A view from within NAFTA" (1993/94) 49 Tax L Rev 530.

Atik, Jeffery, "Legitimacy, Transparency and NGO Participation in the NAFTA Chapter 11 Process" in Todd Weiler (ed), *NAFTA Investment Law and Arbitration: Past Issues, Current Practice, Future Prospects* (New York: Transnational Publishers, 2004) 135.

Avi-Yonah, Reuven, "Treating Tax Issues Through Trade Regimes" (2000–2001) XXVI Brook J Intl L 1683.

Baade, Hans W, "The Legal Effect of Code of Conduct for Multinational Enterprises" in Norbert Horn (ed), *Legal Problems of Codes of Conduct for Multinational Enterprises* (Boston: Kluwer, 1980).

Bachand, Rémie and Stéphanie Rousseau, "International Investment and Human Rights: Political and Legal Issues" (2003) International Centre for Human Rights and Democratic Development 16.

Barberis, Julio A, "Nouvelles questions concernant la personnalité juridique internationale" (1983) I:179 Rec des Cours 157.

Barthel, Fabian, Mathias Busse and Eric Neumayer, "The Impact of Double Taxation Treaties on Foreign Direct Investment: Evidence from Large Dyadic Panel Data" (July 2010) 28:3 Contemporary Economic Policy 366.

Berezowski, C, "Les problèmes de la subjectivité internationale" in V Ibler (ed), *Mélanges offerts à Juraj Andrassy* (The Hague: Martinus Nijhoff Publ., 1968).

Berger, Axel, "The Politics of China's Investment Treaty-Making Program" in Tomer Broude, Marc L. Busch and Amelia Porges (eds), *The Politics of International Economic Law* (Cambridge: Cambridge University Press, 2011).

Berman QC, Sir Frank, "The Relevance of the Law on Diplomatic Protection in Investment Arbitration" in Federico Ortino et al (eds), *Investment Treaty Law: Current Issues II* (London: BIICL, 2007).

Binder, Christina, "Changed Circumstances in Investment Law: Interfaces Between the Law of Treaties and the Law of State Responsibility with a Special Focus on the Argentine Crisis" in Christina Binder et al (eds), *International Investment Law for the 21st Century, Liber Amicorum Christoph Schreuer* (Oxford: Oxford University Press, 2009).

Bishop, Doak, "The Case for an Appellate Panel and its Scope of Review" (2005) 2 *Transnational Dispute Management* 8.

Bjorklund, Andrea K., "Emergency Exceptions: State of Necessity and *Force Majeure*" in Peter Muchlinski, Federico Ortino and Christoph Schreuer, *The Oxford Handbook of International Investment Law* (Oxford: Oxford University Press, 2008).

Bjorklund, Andrea K., "Investment Treaty Arbitral Decisions as *Jurisprudence Constante*" in Colin Picker, Isabella Bunn and Douglas W. Arner (eds),

International Economic Law: State and Future of the Discipline (Oxford: Hart Publishing, 2008).

Bjorklund, Andrea K and Sophie Nappert, "Beyond Fragmentation" (2011) UC Davis Legal Studies Research Paper No. 243, online: SSRN <http://ssrn.com/abstract=1739997>.

Blomeyer, Arwed, "Types of Relief Available (Judicial Remedies)" in Mauro Cappelletti (ed), VXI *International Encyclopedia of Comparative Law* (Tübingen: Mohr, The Hague: Nijhoff, 1982).

Blonigen, Bruce and Ronald Davies, "Do Bilateral Tax Treaties Promote Foreign Direct Investment?" (June 1, 2001) University of Oregon Economics Working Paper No. 2001–12.

Bodansky, Daniel, "The Concept of Legitimacy in International Law" in *Legitimacy of International Law* (Berlin: Springer, 2008).

Boscariol, John W., "The Impact of International Trade and Investment Agreements on Governments' Taxation Powers" 43 *Report of Proceedings of Fifty-Fifth Tax Conference, 2003 Tax Conference* (Toronto: Canadian Tax Foundation, 2004).

Brainard, Lael, "An Empirical Assessment of the Factor Proportions of Multinational Sales" (1993) NBER Working Paper 4580.

Brainard, Lael, "An Empirical Assessment of the Proximity-Concentration Tradeoff between Multinational Sales and Trade" (1997) 87 American Economic Review 520.

Branstetter, Lee et al, "Intellectual Property Rights, Imitation, and Foreign Direct Investment Theory and Evidence" (2007) NBER Working Paper 13033.

Branstetter, Lee G., Raymond Fisman and C Fritz-Foley, "Do Stronger Intellectual Property Rights Increase International Technology Transfer? Empirical Evidence from US Firm-Level Data" (2006) 121(1) Quarterly Journal of Economics 321.

Brower, Charles and Stephan Schill, "Is Arbitration a Threat or a Boon to the Legitimacy of International Investment Law?" (2009) 9 Chi J Int'l L 471.

Brower II, Charles H., "The Functions and Limits of Arbitration and Judicial Settlement under Private and Public International law" (2008) 18 Duke J Comp and Int'l L 259.

Brower II, Charles, "Obstacles and Pathways to Consideration of the Public Interest in Investment Treaty Disputes" in Karl P. Sauvant (ed), *Yearbook of International Investment Law and Policy* (2008–09) 347.

Brown, C., "Beneficial Ownership and the Income Tax Act" (2003) 51 Can Tax J 402.

Brown, Catherine, "Tax Discrimination and Trade in Services: Should the Non-discrimination Article in the OECD Model Treaty Provide the Missing Link between Tax and Trade Agreements?" in Arthur Cockfield (ed), *Globalization and its Discontents: Tax Policy and International Investments* (Toronto: University of Toronto Press, 2010).

Brown, Catherine and Martha O'Brien, "Tax Discrimination and the Cross-Border Provision of Services—Canada/UK Perspectives" in Christopher

P.M. Waters (ed), *British and Canadian Perspectives in International Law* (Leiden: Martinus Nijhoff, 2006).

Brown, Chester, "The Relevance of the Doctrine of Abuse of Process in International Adjudication" (2011) 2 *Transnational Dispute Management*.

Brummer, Chris, "The Ties That Bind? Regionalism, Commercial Treaties, and the Future of Global Economic Integration" (2007) 60(5) V and L Rev 1349.

Burke-White, William W. and Andreas von Standen, "Investment Protection in Extraordinary Times: The Interpretation of Non-precluded Measure Provisions in Bilateral Investment Treaties" (2007) 48(2) Va J Int'l L 307.

Byers, Michael, "Abuse of Rights: An Old Principle, A New Age" (2002) 47:2 McGill LJ 389.

Candu, Andrian, "Abuse of Tax Treaties" in Michael Schilcher and Patrick Weninger, eds, *Fundamental Issues and Practical Problems in Tax Treaty Interpretation* (Vienna : Linde, 2008).

Caplan, Lee and Jeremy Sharpe, "The 2004 U.S. Model Bilateral Investment Treaty" in Chester Brown and Devashish Krishan (eds), *Commentaries on Selected Model International Investment Agreements* (Oxford University Press, forthcoming).

Caron, David D., "Reputation and Reality in the ICSID Annulment Process: Understanding the Distinction between Annulment and Appeal" (1992) 7(1) ICSID Rev 21.

Carr, David L., James R Markusen and Keith E. Maskus, "Estimating the Knowledge Capital Model of the Multinational Enterprise" (2001) 91(3) The American Economic Review 693.

Carroll, Archie B., "Corporate Social Responsibility: Evolution of a Definitional Construct" (1999) 38(3) Business and Society 268.

Carter, Justin, "The Protracted Bargain: Negotiating the Canada-China Foreign Investment Promotion and Protection Agreement" (2009) 47 Can YB Int'l Law 197.

Chalamish, Dr Efraim, "The Future of Bilateral Investment Treaties: A De Facto Multilateral Agreement?" (2009) 34(2) Brook J Int'l L 304.

Chalker, James, "Case Note: Eastern Sugar B.V. v. The Czech Republic" (2009) *Transnational Dispute Management 1*.

Chalker, James, "Making the Energy Charter Treaty Too Investor Friendly: Plama Consortium Limited v. Republic of Bulgaria" (2006) 5 *Transnational Dispute Management*.

Chandler, Aaron M., "BITs, MFN Treatment and the PRC: The Impact of China's Ever-Evolving Bilateral Investment Treaty Practice" (2009) 43 Int'l Lawyer 1301.

Charney, Jonathan I., "Transnational Corporations and Developing Public International Law" (1983) Duke LJ 773.

Chellaraj, Ganaraj, Keith E. Maskus and Aaditya Mattoo, "Labor Skills and Foreign Direct Investment in a Dynamic Economy: Estimating the Knowledge Capital Model for Singapore" (2009) East West Centre Working Paper, Economic Series 100.

Choukroun, Sylvie, *Enron in Maharashtra: Power Sector Development and National Identity in Modern India* (M.A. Thesis, University of Pennsylvania, 2002) online: <http://lauder.wharton.upenn.edu/pages/pdf/SylvieChoukroun_Thesis.pdf>.

Clark, W. Steven, "Tax Incentives for Foreign Direct Investment: Empirical Evidence on Effects and Alternative Policy Options" (2000) 48(4) Can Tax J 1139.

Clodfelter, Mark A., "The Adaptation of States to the Changing World of Investment Protection through Model BITs" (2009) 24(1) ICSID Rev 165.

Cockfield, Arthur, "The Rise of the OECD as Informal 'World Tax Organization' through National Responses to E-Commerce Tax Challenges" (2006) 9 Yale Journal of Law and Technology 59.

Coe, Jack, "Settlement of Investor-State Disputes Through Mediation—Preliminary Remarks on Processes, Problems and Prospects" in R. Doak Bishop, ed, *Enforcement of Arbitral Awards Against Sovereigns* (New York: Huntington, JurisNet LLC, 2009)

Coe Jr, Jack J, "Towards a Complementary Use of Conciliation in Investor-State Disputes—A Preliminary Sketch" (2005) 12:7 UC Davis J Int'l L and Pol'y 7.

Cohen-Jonathan, Gérard, "L'arbitrage Texaco-Calasiatic contre Gouvernement Libyen" (1977) 23 :1 AFDI 452.

Congyan Cai, "China-US BIT Negotiations and the Future of Investment Treaty Regime: A Grand Bilateral Bargain with Multilateral Implications" (2009) 12 J Int'l Econ L 457.

Conley, John M. and Cynthia A. Williams, "Global Banks as Global Sustainability Regulators?: The Equator Principles" (2011) 33(4) Law and Pol'y 542.

Cordonier Segger, Marie-Claire and Andrew Newcombe, "An Integrated Agenda for Sustainable Development in International Investment Law" in Marie-Claire Cordonier Segger, Markus W. Gehring and Andrew Newcombe (eds), *Sustainable Development in World Investment Law* (Netherlands: Kluwer Law International, 2010).

Cosbey, Aaron, "The Road to Hell? Investor Protections in NAFTA's Chapter 11" in Lyuba Zarsky (ed), *International Investment for Sustainable Development: Balancing Rights and Rewards* (London: Sterling, VA: Earthscan, 2005).

Crawford, James, "Is There a Need for an Appellate System?" (2005) 2 *Transnational Dispute Management* 8.

Cremades, Bernardo, "Corruption and Investment Arbitration" in Gerald Aksen et al (eds), *Global Reflections on International Law, Commerce and Dispute Resolution, Liber Amicorum in honour of Robert Briner* (Paris: International Chamber of Commerce, 2005).

Crespo, Mariana Hernandez, "From Paper to People: Building Conflict Resolution Capacity and Frameworks for Sustainable Implementation of IIAs to Increase Investor-State Satisfaction" in UNCTAD, *Investor-State Disputes: Prevention and Alternative to Arbitration II: Proceedings of the Washington and Lee University and UNCTAD Joint Symposium on International Investment and Alternative Dispute Resolution, held on March 29, 2010 in*

Lexington, Virginia, United States of America (New York and Geneva: United Nations, 2011).

Crook, John R., "Four Tribunals Apply ICSID Rule for Early Ouster of Unmeritorious Claims" 15(10) ASIL Insights, 2011 online <http://www.asil.org/insights110426.cfm>.

Dagan, Tsilly, "The Tax Treaties Myth" (2000) 32 NYU J Int'l L and Pol 939.

Daly, Michael, "Some Taxing Issues for the World Trade Organization" (2000) 48(4) Can Tax J 1053.

Daly, Michael, "Some Taxing Questions for the Multinational Agreement on Investment (MAI)" (1997) 20(6) The World Economy 787.

Davey, William J. and André Sapir, "The Soft Drinks Case: The WTO and Regional Agreements" (2009) 8(1) World Trade Review 5.

De Mestral, Armand, "The Lisbon Treaty and the Expansion of EU Competence Over Foreign Direct Investment and the Implications for Investor-State-Arbitration" in Karl P. Sauvant (ed), *Yearbook on International Investment Law and Policy 2009–2010* (New York: Oxford University Press, 2010).

De Mestral, Armand, "NAFTA Dispute Settlement: Creative Experiment or Confusion" in Lorand Bartels and Federico Ortino (eds), *Regional Trade Agreements and the WTO Legal System* (Oxford: Oxford University Press, 2006).

De Paula, Guilherme Morales, "A cláusula de eleição de foro do Protocolo de Olivos e seus efeitos contraproducentes para o Mercosul" (2005) 6(1) Revista *Escuela Direito Pelotas* 167.

Dempsey, Paul Stephen, "Competition in the Air: European Union Regulation of Commercial Aviation" (2001) 66(3) J Air L and Com 979.

Desbordes, Rodolphe and Vincent Vicard, "Foreign Direct Investment and Bilateral Investment Treaties: An International Political Perspective" (2009) 37(3) Journal of Comparative Economics 372.

DiMascio, Nicholas and Joost Pauwelyn, "Nondiscrimination in Trade and Investment Treaties: Worlds Apart or Two Sides of the Same Coin" (2008) 102 AJIL 48.

Dobbin, Frank et al, "The Global Diffusion of Public Policies: Social Construction, Coercion, Competition, or Learning?" (2007) 33(1) Annual Review of Sociology 449.

Dobbins, Robert N., "The Layered Dispute Resolution Clause: From Boilerplate to Business Opportunity" (2005) 1 Hasting Business Law Journal 176.

Dolzer, R., "Fair and Equitable Treatment: A Key Standard in Investment Treaties" (2005) 39 Int'l Lawyer 87.

Dominicé, Christian, "L'émergence de l'individu en droit international public" (1987–8) 16 Annales d'études internationales 8.

Dominicé, Christian, "La personnalité juridique dans le système du droit des gens" in Jerzy Makarczyk (ed), *Theory of International Law at the Threshold of the 21st Century: Essays in Honour of Krzysztof Skubiszewski* (The Hague: Kluwer, 1996).

Douglas, Z., "The Hybrid Foundations of Investment Treaty Arbitration" (2004) 74 Brit YB Int'l L 151.

Drabek, Zdenek, "A Multilateral Agreement on Investment: Convincing the Sceptics" (1998) WTO ERAD Staff Working Paper 98–05.

Duff, David G., "Responses to Treaty Shopping: A Canadian Perspective" (Paper Prepared for the Conference on Tax Treaties from a Legal and Economic Perspective, Vienna, Austria, March 18–20, 2010).

Dumberry, Patrick, "L'entreprise, sujet de droit international? Retour sur la question à la lumière des développements récents du droit international des investissements" (2004) 108(1) RGDIP.

Dumberry, Patrick and Érik Labelle-Eastaugh, "Non-State Actors in International Investment Law: The Legal Personality of Corporations and NGOs in Investor State Arbitration" in Jean d'Aspremont (ed), *Participants in the International Legal System: Multiples Perspectives on Non-State Actors in International Law* (New York: Routledge-Cavendish, 2011).

Easson, Alec, "Tax Competition and Investment Incentives" (1996/97) 2(2) EC Tax J 63.

Egger, Peter and Michelle Pfaffermayr, "The Impact of Bilateral Investment Treaties on Foreign Direct Investment" (2004) 32(4) Journal of Comparative Economics 788.

Ekholm, Karolina, "Factor Endowments and the Pattern of Affiliate Production by Multinational Enterprises" (1997) CREDIT Working Paper 97/19, University of Nottingham.

Ekholm, Karolina, "Headquarter Services and Revealed Factor Abundance" (1998) 6 Review of International Economics 545.

Ekholm, Karolina, "Multinational Production and Trade in Technological Knowledge" PhD dissertation, Lund Economic Studies (1995).

Ekholm, Karolina, "Proximity Advantages, Scale Economies, and the Location of Production" in Pontus Braunerhjeim and Karolina Ekholm (eds), *The Geography of Multinational Firms* (Boston: Kluwer Academic, 1998).

Elkins, Zachary et al, "Competing for Capital: The Diffusion of Bilateral Investment Treaties, 1960–2000" (2006) 60(4) International Organization 811.

Falsafi, Alireza, "Regional Trade and Investment Agreements: Liberalizing Investment in a Preferential Climate" (2008) 36(1) Syracuse J Int'l L and Com 43.

Fauchald, Ole Kristian, "The Legal Reasoning of ICSID Tribunals: An Empirical Analysis" (2008) 19(2) EJIL 301.

Fitzmaurice, G.G., "The Law and Procedure of the International Court of Justice: Treaty Interpretation and Certain Other Treaty Points" (1951) 28 Brit YB Int'l L 1.

Flavell, CJ Michael, QC, Martin G. Masse and Cyndee Todgham Cherniak, "Buy American or What?" (2009) International Trade Brief, online: McMillan <http://www.mcmillan.ca/Buy-American-or-What>.

Franck, Susan, "Integrating Investment Treaty Conflict and Dispute Systems Design" (2007) 92(1) Minn L Rev161.

Franck, Susan D., "The Legitimacy Crisis in International Treaty Arbitration: Privatizing Public International Law Through Inconsistent Decisions" (2005) 73(4) Fordham L Rev 1521.

Friedlander, L., "The Role of Non-Discrimination Clauses in Bilateral Income Tax Treaties After GATT 1994" (2002) Brit Tax Rev 71.

Friedmann, W., "General Course in Public International Law" (1969) II 127 Rec des Cours 121.

Fry, James D, "International Human Rights in Investment Arbitration: Evidence of International Law's Unity" (2007) 18 Duke J Comp and Int'l L 77.

Gaffney, John P., "'Abuse of Process' in Investment Treaty Arbitration" (2010) 11(4) Journal of World Investment and Trade 515.

Gaillard, Emmanuel, "Treaty-Based Jurisdiction: Broad Dispute Resolution Clauses" (2005) 234 NYLJ 68.

Gantz, David A., "An Appellate Mechanism for Review of Arbitral Decisions in Investor-State Dispute: Prospects and Challenges" (2006) 39 V and J Transnat'l L 39.

Gazzini, Tarcisio, "Necessity in International Investment Law: Some Critical Remarks on *CMS v Argentina*" (2008) 26 Journal of Energy and Natural Resources Law 450.

Gehring, Markus W., "Impact Assessments of Investment Treaties" in Marie-Claire Cordonier Segger, Markus W. Gehring and Andrew Newcombe (eds), *Sustainable Development in World Investment Law* (Netherlands: Kluwer Law International, 2010).

Geiger, Rainer, "The Multifaceted Nature of International Investment Law" in Karl P. Sauvant and Michael Chiswick-Patterson (eds), *Appeals Mechanism in International Investment Disputes* (New York: Oxford University Press, 2008).

Ghafele, Roya and Angus Mercer, "Not Starting in Sixth Gear: An Assessment of the U.N. Global Compact's Use of Soft Law as a Global Governance Structure for Corporate Social Responsibility" (2010) 17 U.C. Davis Journal of International Law and Policy 41.

Gibson, Christopher, "A Look at the Compulsory License in Investment Arbitration: The Case of Indirect Expropriation" (2010) 25 Am U Int'l L Rev 357.

Gilardi, Fabrizio, "Who Learns from What in Policy Diffusion Processes?" (2010) 54(3) American Journal of Political Science 650.

Gill, Judith, "Inconsistent Decisions: An Issue to be Addressed or a Fact of Life?" (2005) 2 *Transnational Dispute Management* 12.

Glass, Amy and Kamal Sassi, "Intellectual Property Rights and Foreign Direct Investment" (2002) 56(2) Journal of International Economics 387.

Goldstein, Judith et al, "Introduction: Legalization and World Politics" (2000) 54(3) International Organization 385.

Gonthier, Hon Charles Doherty, "Foreword" in Michael Kerr, Richard Janda and Chip Pitts (eds), *Corporate Social Responsibility: A Legal Analysis* (Ontario: LexisNexis, 2009).

Griebel, Jörn, "Die Einbeziehung von 'contract claims' in internationale Investitionsstreitigkeiten über Streitbeilegungsklauseln in Investitionsschutzabkommen" (2006) German Arbitration Journal 306.

Guiguo Wang, "China's FTAs: Legal Characteristics and Implications" (2011) 105(3) AJIL 493.

Guzman, Andrew T., "Why LDCs Sign Treaties That Hurt Them: Explaining the Popularity of Bilateral Investment Treaties" (1998) 38(4) Va J Int'l L 639.

Haas, Peter M., "Introduction: Epistemic Communities and International Policy Coordination" (1992) 46(1) International Organization 1.

Hallward-Driemeier, Mary, "Do Bilateral Investment Treaties Attract FDI? Only a bit . . . and they could bite" (2003) World Bank Policy Research Working Paper Series No. 3121, online: SSRN <http://papers.ssrn.com/sol3/cf_dev/AbsByAuth.cfm?per_id=327728>.

Hamelmann, Sandy, "Internationale Jurisdiktionskonflikte und Vernetzungen transnationaler Rechtsregime: Die Entscheidungen des Panels und des Appellate Body der WTO in Sachen 'Mexico—Tax Measures on Soft Drinks and Other Beverages'" (2006) 58 *Beiträge zum transnationalen Wirtschaftsrecht* 1.

Hammer, Richard M., "Nondiscrimination in the International Tax Context: A Look at OECD Model Article 24" (2005) 12 Tax Management International Journal 700.

Hansen, Robin F., "The International Legal Personality of Multinational Enterprises: Treaty, Custom and the Governance Gap" (2010) 10(1) Global Jurist.

Hansen, Robin F., "Parallel Proceedings in Investor-State Treaty Arbitration: Responses for Treaty-Drafters, Arbitrators and Parties" (2010) 73(4) Mod L Rev 523.

Hansen, Robin, "The Systemic Challenge of Corporate Investor Nationality in an Era of Multinational Business" (2010) 1(1) Journal of Arbitration and Mediation 81.

Harrison, James and Alessa Goller, "Trade and Human Rights: What Does 'Impact Assessment' Have to Offer?" (2008) 8(4) Human Rights Law Review 587.

Hasbrouk, Brandon and Jason Ratigan, "The Way Forward" in UNCTAD, *Investor-State Disputes: Prevention and Alternative to Arbitration II: Proceedings of the Washington and Lee University and UNCTAD Joint Symposium on International Investment and Alternative Dispute Resolution, held on 29 March 2010 in Lexington, Virginia, United States of America* (New York and Geneva: United Nations, 2011).

Haugeneder, Florian, "Corruption in Investor-State Arbitration" (2009) 10(3) J World Investment and Trade 319.

Henckels, Caroline, "Overcoming Jurisdictional Isolationism at the WTO-FTA Nexus: A Potential Approach for the WTO" (2008) 19(3) EJIL 571.

Henkin, Louis, "International Law: Politics, Values and Functions" (1989) IV: 216 Rec des Cours.

Hepburn, Jarrod and Vuyelwa Kuuya, "Corporate Social Responsibility and Investment Treaties" in Marie-Claire Cordonier Segger, Markus W. Gehring and Andrew Newcombe (eds), *Sustainable Development in World Investment Law* (The Hague: Kluwer Law International, 2011).

Hiber, Dragor and Vladimir Pavić, "Arbitration and Crime" (2008) 25(4) J Int'l Arb 461.

Hillman, Jennifer, "Conflicts Between Dispute Settlement Mechanisms in Regional Trade Agreements and the WTO" (2009) 42(2) Cornell Int'l LJ 193.

Hjälmroth, Carolinn and Stefan Westerberg, "A Common Investment Policy for the EU" in *The Contribution of Trade to a New Growth Strategy*, 2009 online: Kommers <http://www.kommers.se/upload/Analysarkiv/In%20 English/Analyses/LS%20Investments.pdf>.

Hobér, Kaj, "State Responsibility and Attribution" in Peter Muchlinski, Federico Ortino and Christoph Schreuer (eds), *The Oxford Handbook of International Investment Law* (Oxford: Oxford University Press, 2008).

Hoffmann, Anne K., "Counterclaims by Respondent State in Investment Arbitrations" (2006) German Arbitration Journal 317.

Horner, Frances, "Do We Need an International Tax Organization?" (2001) 24 Tax Notes International 179.

Igbokwe, Virtus Chitoo, "Determination, Interpretation and Application of Substantive Law in Foreign Investment Treaty Arbitrations" (2006) 23(4) J Int'l Arb 267.

Institut de droit international, "Les entreprises multinationales" (1978) II: 57, Ann inst dr int.

International Fiscal Association, "Is There a Permanent Establishment?" 94a Cahiers de droit fiscal international (The Hague: SduUitgevers, 2009).

Jacob, Marc, *International Investment Agreements and Human Rights* (2010) INEF Research Paper Series.

Jagusch, Stephen, "Denial of Advantages under Article 17(1)" (Presentation delivered to the Investment Protection and the Energy Charter Treaty Conference Washington DC, May 18, 2007) [unpublished].

Jeżewski, Marek, "Development Considerations in Defining Investment" in Marie-Claire Cordonier Segger, Markus W. Gehring and Andrew Newcombe (eds), *Sustainable Development in World Investment Law* (Netherlands: Kluwer Law International, 2010).

Johns, Fleur, "The Invisibility of the Transnational Corporation: An Analysis of International Law and Legal Theory" (1994) 19 Melbourne UL Rev 893.

Jones, John F. Avery, "The Non-discrimination Article in Tax Treaties Part 2" (1991) 11/12 Brit Tax Rev 421.

Juillard, Patrick, "Bilateral Investment Treaties in the Context of Investment Law" (Paper delivered at the OECD Investment Compact Regional Round-table on Bilateral Investment Treaties for the Protection and Promotion of Foreign Investment in South East Europe, Dubrovnik, Croatia, May 28–29, 2001) online: OECD <http://www.oecd.org/dataoecd/44/41/ 1894794.pdf>.

Juillard, Patrick, "The Law of International Investment: Can the Imbalance be Redressed?" in Karl P. Sauvant (ed), *Yearbook in International Investment Law and Policy 2008–2009* (New York: Oxford University Press, 2009).

Juillard, Patrick, "Variation in the Substantive Provisions and Interpretation of International Investment Agreements" in Karl P. Sauvant and Michael Chiswick-Patterson (eds), *Appeals Mechanism in International Investment Disputes* (New York: Oxford University Press, 2008) 81.

Kalb, Johanna, "Creating an ICSID Appellate Body" (2005) 10 UCLA J Int'l and Foreign Aff 179.

Karl, J., "The Promotion and Protection of German Foreign Investment Abroad" (1996) 11 ICSID Rev 1.

Kaufmann-Kohler, Gabrielle, "Annulment of ICSID Awards in Contract and Treaty Arbitrations: Are There Differences?" in E. Gaillard and Y. Banifatemi (eds), *Annulment of ICSID Awards* (New York: Juris Publishing, 2004) 189.

Kaufmann-Kohler, Gabrielle, "Arbitral Precedent: Dream, Necessity or Excuse?" (2007) 23 Arbitration International 357.

Kaufmann-Kohler, Gabrielle, "In Search of Transparency and Consistency: ICSID Reform Proposal" (2005) 2 *Transnational Dispute Management* 1.

Kelley, Glen, "Multilateral Investment Treaties: A Balanced Approach to Multinational Corporations" (2001) 39(2) Colum J Transnat'l L 483.

Kelsey, Jane, "Embedding the Neoliberal Transformation of Government Services Through Trade in Service Agreements" in Shawkat Alam, Natalie Klein and Juliette Overland (eds), *Globalisation and the Quest for Social and Environmental Justice: The Relevance of International Law in an Evolving World Order* (New York: Routledge, 2011).

Kim, Dohyun, "The Annulment Committee's Role in Multiplying Inconsistency in ICSID Arbitration: The Need to Move Away from an Annulment-based System" (2011) 86 NYU Law Review 242.

Kingsbury, Benedict and Stephen W. Schill, "Investor-State Arbitration as Governance: Fair and Equitable Treatment, Proportionality and the Emerging Global Administrative Law" (September 2, 2009), NYU School of Law, Public Law Research Paper No. 09–46. Available at SSRN: <http://ssrn.com/abstract=1466980>.

Kinley, David and Junko Tadaki, "From Talk to Walk: The Emergence of Human Rights Responsibilities for Corporations at International Law" (2004) Va JL Int'l L 931.

Kinley, David and Rachel Chambers, "The UN Human Rights Norms for Corporations: The Private Implications of Public International Law" (2006) 3 Human Rights Law Review.

Knahr, Christina, "Investments 'in accordance with host state law'" (2007) 4(5) *Transnational Dispute Management.*

Knull III, William H. and Noah D. Rubins, "Betting the Farm on International Arbitration: Is it Time to Offer an Appeal Option?" (2000) 11 Am J Int'l Arb 531.

Kobrin, Stephen J., "The MAI and the Clash of Globalizations" *Foreign Policy* (September 1998) 97.

Koller, Christian, *Aufrechnung und Widerklage im Schiedsverfahren* (Vienna: Manzsche Verlags und Universitätsbuchhandlung, 2009).

Kolo, Abba, "Witness Intimidation, Tampering and Other Related Abuses of Process in Investment Arbitration: Possible Remedies Available to the Arbitral Tribunal" (2010) 26:1 Arb Int'l 43.

Kolo, Abba and Thomas W. Wälde, "Renegotiation and Contract Adaptation in International Investment Projects—Applicable Legal Principles and Industry Practices" (2000) 1(1) The Journal of World Investment and Trade 5.

Koremenos, Barbara, "Contracting Around International Uncertainty" (2005) 99(4) American Political Science Review 549.

Kreindler, Richard H, "Aspects of Illegality in the Formation and Performance of Contracts" in Albert Jan van den Berg (ed), *ICCA Congress Series No. 11* (The Hague: Kluwer Law International, 2003).

Kriebaum, Ursula, "Illegal Investments" in Klausegger et al (eds), *Austrian Yearbook on International Arbitration* (Austria: Manz, 2010).

Krishna, Vern, "Treaty Shopping and the Concept of Beneficial Ownership in Double Tax Treaties" (August 2009) 19 Can Current Tax 129.

Krommendijk, J and Dr John Morij, "'Proportional' by What Measure(s)? Balancing Investor Interests and Human Rights by Way of Applying the Proportionality Principle in Investor-State Arbitration" in Pierre-Marie Dupuy et al (eds), *Human Rights in International Investment Law and Arbitration* (Oxford: Oxford University Press, 2009).

Kryvoi, Yaraslau, "Counterclaims in Investor-State Arbitration" (2011) LSE Society and Economy Working Papers 8/2011.

Kupfer Schneider, Andrea, "Getting Along: the Evolution of Dispute Resolution Regimes in International Trade Organizations" (1999) 20 Mich J Int'l L 697.

Kupfer Schneider, Andrea, "Using Dispute System Design to Add More Process Choices to Investment Treaty Disputes" in UNCTAD, *Investor-State Disputes: Prevention and Alternative to Arbitration II: Proceedings of the Washington and Lee University and UNCTAD Joint Symposium on International Investment and Alternative Dispute Resolution, held on 29 March 2010 in Lexington, Virginia, United States of America* (New York and Geneva: United Nations, 2011).

Kurkela, M.S., "Criminal Laws in International Arbitration—the May, the Must, the Should and the Should Not" (2008) 26(2) ASA Bulletin 280.

Kurtz, Jürgen, "Adjudging the Exceptional at International Investment Law: Security, Public Order and Financial Crisis" (2010) 59 ICLQ 325.

Kurtz, Jürgen, "ICSID Annulment Committee Rules on the Relationship between Customary and Treaty Exceptions on Necessity in Situations of Financial Crisis" (December 20, 2007) 11(30) ASIL Insight.

Kurtz, Jürgen, "National Treatment, Foreign Investment and Regulatory Autonomy: The Search for Protectionism or Something More?" in P. Kahn and T. Wälde (eds), *New Aspects of International Investment Law* (Leiden: Martinus Nijhoff, 2007).

Kurtz, Jürgen, "The Use and Abuse of WTO Law in Investor-State Arbitration: Competition and its Discontents" (2009) 20 EJIL 749.

Laborde, Gustavo, "The Case for Host State Claims in Investment Arbitration" (2010) 1(1) Journal of International Dispute Settlement 97.

Laird, Ian A., "A Community of Destiny—The Barcelona Traction Case and the Development of Shareholder Rights to Bring Investment Claims" in Todd Weiler (ed), *International Investment Law and Arbitration: Leading Cases from the ICSID, NAFTA, Bilateral Treaties and Customary International Law* (London: Cameron May, 2005)

Laird, Ian, "A Distinction without a Difference?" in Todd Weiler (ed), *International Investment Law: Leading Cases from the ICSID, NAFTA, Bilateral Investment Treaties and Customary International Law* (London: Cameron May, 2005) 201.

Lalive, Pierre and Laura Halonen, "On the Availability of Counterclaims in Investment Treaty Arbitration" in Alexander J Bělohlávek and Naděžda Rozehnalová, *Czech Yearbook of International Law*, vol II (New York: Juris Publishing, 2011) 141.

Larschan, Bradley and Guive Mirfendereski, "The Status of Counterclaims in International Law, With Particular Reference to International Arbitration Involving a Private Party and a Foreign State" (1986–87) 15 Denv J Int'l L and Policy 11.

Lauterpacht, Sir Elihu, "Foreword" in Marie-Claire Cordonier Segger, Markus W. Gehring and Andrew Newcombe (eds), *Sustainable Development in World Investment Law* (Netherlands: Kluwer Law International, 2010).

Leben, Charles, "L'Etat de nécessité dans le droit international de l'investissement" (2005) 349 Gazette du Palais 19.

Leben, C., "Quelques réflexions théoriques à propos des contrats d'Etat" in *Souveraineté étatique et marchés internationaux à la fin du 20ᵉ siècle: Mélange en l'honneur de Philippe Kahn* (Paris: Litec, 2000).

Lee, Jeong-Yeon and Edwin Mansfield, "Intellectual Property Protection and US Foreign Direct Investment" (1996) 78(2) Review of Economic and Statistics 181.

Legum, Bart, "The Difficulties of Conciliation in Investment Treaty Cases: A Comment on Professor Jack C. Coe's 'Toward a complementary use of conciliation in investor-state disputes—A preliminary sketch'" (2006) 21(4) Mealey's International Arbitration Report 1.

Legum, Barton, "Options to Establish an Appellate Mechanism for Investment Disputes" in Karl P. Sauvant and Michael Chiswick-Patterson (eds), *Appeals Mechanism in International Investment Disputes* (New York: Oxford University Press, 2008) 231.

Leitner, Kara and Simon Lester, "WTO Dispute Settlement 1995–2010—A Statistical Analysis" (2011) 14(1) J Int'l Econ L 191.

Lévesque, Céline, "Influences on the Canadian FIPA Model and US Model BIT: NAFTA Chapter 11 and Beyond" (2006) 44 Can YB of Int'l Law 249.

Lévesque, Céline, "Preliminary Legal Assessments of Investor Claims as a Tool to 'Fitting the Forum to the Fuss'" in UNCTAD, *Investor-State Disputes: Prevention and Alternative to Arbitration II: Proceedings of the Washington and Lee University and UNCTAD Joint Symposium on International Investment and Alternative Dispute Resolution, held on 29 March 2010 in Lexington, Virginia, United States of America* (New York and Geneva: United Nations, 2011).

Lévesque, Céline and Andrew Newcombe, "Commentary on the Canadian Model Foreign Investment Promotion and Protection Agreement" in Chester Brown and Devashish Krishan (eds), *Commentaries on Selected Model International Investment Agreements* (Oxford University Press, forthcoming).

Liberti, Lahra, "Investissements et droits de l'homme" in Phillipe Kahn and Thomas W. Walde (eds), *New Aspects of International Investment Law* (Hague Academy of International Law, 2007).

Lowe, A.V., "Corporations as International Actors and International Law Makers" in Benetto Conforti et al (eds), *The Italian Yearbook of International Law* (Leiden: Martinus Nijhoff Publishers, 2004) 23.

Ludwig, Claudia, "Negotiation Clauses in BITs—Empty Words?" (May 24, 2011), online: Kluwer Arbitration Blog <http://kluwerarbitrationblog.com/blog/2011/05/24/negotiation-clauses-in-bits-%E2%80%93-empty-words/>.

Malanczuk, Peter, "Multinational Enterprises and Treaty-Making: A Contribution to the Discussion on Non-State Actors and the Subjects of International Law" in V. Gowlland-Debbas (ed), *Multilateral Treaty-Making: The Current Status of Challenges to and Reforms Needed in the International Legislative Process* (The Hague: Martinus Nijhoff Publishers, 2000) 55.

Malik, Mahnaz, "The IISD Model International Agreement on Investment for Sustainable Development" in Marie-Claire Cordonier Segger, Markus Gehring and Andrew Newcombe (eds), *Sustainable Development in World Investment Law* (The Hague: Kluwer Law International, 2011).

Malik, Mahnaz, "Recent Developments in International Investment Agreements: Negotiations and Disputes" (2010) IV Annual Forum for Developing Country Investment Negotiators, Background Papers, online: IISD <http://www.iisd.org/pdf/2011/dci_2010_recent_developments_iias.pdf>.

Mann, F.A., "British Treaties for the Promotion and Protection of Investments" (1981) 52 Brit YB Int'l L 249.

Mansfield, Edwin, Mark Schwartz and Samuel Wagner, "Imitation Costs and Patents: An Empirical Study" (1981) 91(364) The Economic Journal 907.

Marboe, Irmgard, "ICSID Annulment Decisions: Three Generations Revisited" in Christina Binder et al (eds), *International Investment Law for the 21st Century, Liber Amicorum Christoph Schreuer* (Oxford: Oxford University Press, 2009).

Marceau, Gabrielle and Julian Wyatt, "Dispute Settlement Regimes Intermingled: Regional Trade Agreements and the WTO" (2010) 1(1) Journal of International Dispute Settlement 67.

Markert, Lars, "The Crucial Question of Future Investment Treaties: Balancing Investors' Rights and Regulatory Interests of Host States" in Marc Bungenberg, Jörn Griebel and Steffen Hindelang (eds), *European Yearbook of International Economic Law, Special Issue: International Investment Law and EU Law* (Berlin/Heidelberg/New York: Springer, 2011).

Markusen, James R., "Commitment to Rules on Investment: The Developing Countries' Stake" (2001) 9(2) Review of International Economics 287.

Markusen, James R., "Contracts, Intellectual Property Rights, and Multinational Investment in Developing Countries"(2001) 53 Journal of International Economics 189.

Markusen, James R. and Bridget Strand, "Adapting the Knowledge Capital Model of the Multinational Enterprise to Trade and Investment in Business Services" (2009) 32(1) World Economics 6.

Markusen, James R. and Keith E. Maskus, "Discriminating Among Alternative Theories of the Multinational Enterprise" (2002) 10 Review of International Economics 694.

Markusen, James R. and Keith E. Maskus, "Multinational Firms: Reconciling Theory and Evidence" in Magnus Blomstrom and Linda Goldberg (eds), *Topics in Empirical International Economics: A Festschrift in honour of Robert E. Lipsey* (Chicago: University of Chicago Press, 2001).

Mason, Ruth, "A Theory of Tax Discrimination" (2008) NYU Jean Monnet Working Paper 09/06.

Mason, Ruth and Herman Bouma, "Non-discrimination at the Crossroads of International Taxation" (2008) 93b Cahiers de Droit Fiscal International.

McDougal, Myres S., "International Law, Power and Policy: A Contemporary Conception" (1953) Rec des Cours 82.

McIntyre, Michael, "How to End the Charade of Information Exchange" (October 26, 2009) Tax Notes Int'l 255.

McLachlan, Campbell, "Investment Treaties and General International Law" (2008) 57 ICLQ 361.

McLachlan, Campbell, "The Principle of Systemic Integration and Article 31(3)(c) of the Vienna Convention" (2005) 54 ICLQ 279.

McRae, Donald, "The WTO Appellate Body: A Model for an ICSID Appeals Facility?" (2010) 1 Journal of International Dispute Settlement 371.

Mills, Karen, "Corruption and Other Illegality in the Formation and Performance of Contracts and in the Conduct of Arbitration relating Thereto" in Albert Jan van den Berg (ed), *ICCA Congress Series No. 11* (The Hague: Kluwer Law International, 2003).

Mistelis, Loukas A. and Crina Mihaela Baltag, "Denial of Benefits and Article 17 of the Energy Charter Treaty" (2009) 113(4) Penn St L Rev 1301.

Morisset, Jacques and Nede Pirnia, "How Tax Policy and Incentives Affect Foreign Direct Investment: A Review World Bank Policy" (1999) Research Working Paper No. 2509, online: SSRN <http://papers.ssrn.com/so13/papers.cfm?abstract_id=632579>.

Mourre, Alexis, "Arbitration and Criminal Law: Reflections on the Duties of the Arbitrator" (2006) 22(1) Arb Int'l 95.

Muchlinski, Peter, "The COMESA Common Investment Area: Substantive Standards and Procedural Problems in Dispute Settlement" SOAS School of Law Research Paper No. 11/20102, online: SSRN <http://papers.ssrn.com/sol3/papers.cfm?abstract_id=1698209>.

Neumayer, Eric and Laura Spess, "Do Bilateral Investment Treaties Increase Foreign Direct Investment to Developing Countries?" (2005) 33(10) World Development 1567.

Newcombe, Andrew, "A Brief Comment on the 'Public Statement on the International Investment Regime'" (September 3, 2010) online: Kluwer Arbitration Blog <http://kluwerarbitrationblog.com>.

Newcombe, Andrew, "General Exceptions in International Investment Agreements" in Marie-Claire Cordonier Segger, Markus Gehring and Andrew Newcombe (eds), *Sustainable Development in World Investment Law* (The Hague: Kluwer Law International, 2011).

Newcombe, Andrew, "Investor Misconduct: Jurisdiction, Admissibility or Merits" in Chester Brown and Kate Miles (eds), *Evolution in Investment Treaty Law and Arbitration* (Cambridge: Cambridge University Press, 2011).

Novy, Zdenek, "The Illegality of a Contract Contrary to Fundamental Principles of International Law" (2010) online: SSRN <http://ssrn.com/abstract=1685293>.

Nunnenkamp, Peter and Julius Spatz, "Intellectual Property Rights and Foreign Direct Investment: A Disaggregated Analysis" (2004) 140(3) Review of World Economics 393.

Oliver, J.D.B. et al, "Beneficial Ownership and the OECD Model" (2001) Brit Tax Rev 27.

Olson, Stephen and Clyde Prestowitz, "The Evolving Role of China in International Institutions" (Research report prepared for the US-China Economic and Security Review Commission, January 2011), online: US–China Economic and Security Review Commission <http://www.uscc.gov/researchpapers/2011/TheEvolvingRoleofChinainInternationalInstitutions.pdf>.

Paparinskis, Mārtiņš, "Barcelona Traction: A Friend of Investment Protection Law" (2008) 8 *Baltic Yearbook of International Law* 105.

Paparinskis, Mārtiņš, "Equivalent Primary Rules and Differential Secondary Rules: Countermeasures in WTO and Investment Protection Law" in Tomer Broude and Yuval Shany (eds), *Multi-Sourced Equivalent Norms in International Law* (Oxford: Hart Publishing, 2010).

Paparinskis, Mārtiņš, "Investment Protection Law and Systemic Integration of Treaty and Custom" (2010) SIEL Online Proceedings Working Paper 2010/21, online: SSRN <http://ssrn.com/abstract=1632559>.

Paparinskis, Mārtiņš, "Sources of Law and Arbitral Interpretations of Pari Materia Investment Protection Rules" in O.K. Fauchald and A. Nollkaemper (eds), *Unity or Fragmentation of International Law: The Role of International and National Tribunals* (Oxford: Hart Publishing, 2011).

Park, Walter, "Intellectual Property Rights and International Innovation" in Keith Maskus, *Frontiers of Economics and Globalization: Intellectual Property Rights and Globalization* (Amsterdam: Elsevier Science Ltd, 2008).

Park, William W., "Arbitration and the Fisc: NAFTA's 'Tax Veto'" (2001) 2 Chicago J Int'l L 231.

Park, William W., "Tax Arbitration and Investor Protection" in Catherine A. Rogers and Roger P. Alford (eds), *The Future of Investment Arbitration* (Oxford: Oxford University Press, 2009).

Poulsen, Lauge S., "Sacrificing Sovereignty by Chance: Investment Treaties, Developing Countries and Bounded Rationality" (2011) [unpublished, archived at Department of International Relations, London School of Economics].

Paulsson, Jan, "Arbitration Without Privity" (1995) 10(2) ICSID Rev 232.

Paulsson, Jan, "Avoiding Unintended Consequences" in Karl P. Sauvant and Michael Chiswick-Patterson (eds), *Appeals Mechanism in International Investment Disputes* (New York: Oxford University Press, 2008) 241.

Paulsson, Jan, "Jurisdiction and Admissibility" in Gerald Aksen et al, *Global Refections on International Law, Commerce and Dispute Resolution—Liber Amicorum in honor of Rober Briner* (Paris: ICC Publishing, 2005) 601.

Pauwelyn, Joost, "Adding Sweeteners to Softwood Lumber: The WTO–NAFTA 'Spaghetti Bowl' is Cooking" (2006) 9(1) J Int'l Econ L 197.

Pauwelyn, Joost and Luiz Eduardo Salles, "Forum Shopping Before International Tribunals" (2009) 42(1) Cornell Int'l LJ 77.

Perkams, Markus, "Piercing the Coporate Veil in International Investment Agreements—The Issue of Indirect Shareholder Claims Reloaded" in August Reinisch and Christina Knahr (eds), *International Investment Law in Context* (Utrecht: Eleven International Publishing, 2007).

Petersmann, Ernst-Ulrich, "Justice as Conflict Resolution: Proliferation, Fragmentation and Decentralization of Dispute Settlement in International Trade" (2004) EUI Working Paper Law No. 2004/10, online: SSRN <http://ssrn.com/abstract=836324>.

Peterson, Luke E. and Kevin Gray, "International Human Rights in Bilateral Investment Treaties and Investment Treaty Arbitration" (2003) Working Paper for the Swiss Ministry for Foreign Affairs.

Petrochilos, Georgios, "Attribution" in Katia Yannaca-Small (ed), *Arbitration Under International Investment Agreements: A Guide to Key Issues* (Oxford: Oxford University Press, 2010).

Picherack, J. Roman, "The Expanding Scope of the Fair and Equitable Treatment Standard: Have Recent Tribunals Gone Too Far?" (2008) 9 Journal of World Investment and Trade 255

Pinto, Dale, "The Need to Reconceptualize the Permanent Establishment Threshold" (July 2006) IBFD—Bulletin.

Pinto, Dale, "A Proposal to Create a World Tax Organisation" (2003) 9 New Zealand Journal of Taxation Law and Policy 145.

Poirat, F., "L'article 26 du Traité relatif à la Charte de l'énergie : procédures de règlement des différends et statut des personnes privées" (1998) 102 RGDIP.

Price, Daniel M., "US Trade Promotion Legislation" (2005) 2 *Transnational Dispute Management* 47.

Protopsaltis, Panayotis M., "The Challenge of the Barcelona Traction Hypothesis: Barcelona Traction Clauses and Denial of Benefits Clauses in BITs and IIAs" (2010) 11 Journal of World Investment and Trade 561.

Rädler, Albert J., "Chapter 1: Most-Favoured-Nation Concept in Tax Treaties" in Michael Lang et al (eds), *Multilateral Tax Treaties: New Developments in International Tax Law* (London and Boston: Kluwer Law International, 1998).

Radu, Anca, "Foreign Investors in the EU. Which 'Best Treatment'? Interactions Between Bilateral Investment Treaties and EU Law" (2008) 14 Eur LJ 237.

Raeschke-Kesslar, H., "Corrupt Practice in the Foreign Investment Context: Contractual and Procedural Aspects" in Norbert Horn (ed), *Arbitrating Foreign Investment Disputes: Procedural and Substantive Aspects* (The Hague: Kluwer Law International, 2004).

Raeschke-Kesslar, Hilmar, "Corruption" in Peter Muchlinski et al (eds), *The Oxford Handbook of International Investment Law* (Oxford: Oxford University Press, 2008).

Ratner, Steven R., "Corporations and Human Rights: A Theory of Legal Responsibility" (2001) 111 Yale LJ 443.

Reiner, Clara and Christoph Schreuer, "Human Rights and International Investment Arbitration" in Pierre-Marie Dupuy, Francesco Francioni and Ernst-Ulrich Petersmann (eds), *Human Rights in International Investment Law* (Oxford: Oxford University Press, 2009).

Reinisch, August, "Necessity in International Investment Arbitration—An Unnecessary Split of Opinions in Recent ICSID Cases?" (2007) 8(2) Journal of World Investment and Trade 191.

Reinisch, August, "The Role of Precedent in ICSID Arbitration" in *Austrian Arbitration Yearbook* (2008).

Reinisch, August, "Selecting the Appropriate Forum" in UNCTAD (ed), *Dispute Settlement: International Center for the Settlement of Investment Disputes* (New York and Geneva: United Nations, 2003).

Reisman, W. Michael, "The Breakdown of the Control Mechanism in ICSID Arbitration" (1990) 4 Duke LJ 739.

Reisman, W. Michael, "International Investment Arbitration and ADR: Married but Best Living Apart" in UNCTAD, *Investor-State Disputes: Prevention and Alternative to Arbitration II: Proceedings of the Washington and Lee University and UNCTAD Joint Symposium on International Investment and Alternative Dispute Resolution, held on 29 March 2010 in Lexington, Virginia, United States of America* (New York and Geneva: United Nations, 2011).

Rigaux, François, "Transnational Corporations" in M. Bedjaoui (ed), *International Law: Achievement and Prospects* (Paris: Unesco, 1991).

Rigo Sureda, Andrés, "Precedent in Investment Treaty Arbitration" in Christina Binder et al (eds), *International Investment Law for the 21st Century, Liber Amicorum Christoph Schreuer* (Oxford: Oxford University Press, 2009).

Robbins, J., "The Emergence of Positive Obligations in Bilateral Investment Treaties" (2006) 13 U Miami Int'l and Comp L Rev 403.

Roberts, A, "Power and Persuasion in Investment Treaty Interpretation: The Dual Role of States" (2010) 104(2) AJIL 179.

Rose-Ackerman, Susan and Jennifer Tobin, "Foreign Direct Investment and the Business Environment in Developing Countries: The Impact of Bilateral Investment Treaties" (2005) Yale Law and Economics Research Paper No. 293.

Rosenbloom, H.D., "What's Trade Got to Do With It?" (1993/94) 49 Tax L Rev 593.

Rubins, Noah, "Comments to Jack C. Coe Jr's Article on Conciliation" (2006) 21(4) Mealey's International Arbitration Report 1.

398 *Improving international investment agreements*

Russo, Raffaele, "Chapter 3: Guiding Concepts for International Tax Planning" in *Fundamentals of International Tax Planning* (Amsterdam: IBFD, 2007).

Salacuse, Jeswald W., "Is There a Better Way? Alternative Methods of Treaty-Based, Investor-State Dispute Resolution" (2007) 31 Fordham Int'l LJ 138.

Salacuse, Jeswald, "The Treatification of International Investment Law" (2007) 13 Law and Business Review of the Americas 155.

Salacuse, Jeswald W. and Nicholas P. Sullivan, "Do BITs Really Work?: An Evaluation of Bilateral Investment Treaties and Their Grand Bargain" (2005) 46 Harv Int'l LJ 67.

Sánchez Mejorado, Carlos, "The Writ of Amparo: Mexican Procedure to Protect Human Rights" (1946) 243 Annals of the American Academy of Political and Social Science 107.

Sander, Frank E.A. and Stephen B. Goldberg, "Fitting the Forum to the Fuss: A User-Friendly Guide to Selecting and ADR Procedure" (1994) 10(1) Negotiation Journal 49.

Sarvarian, Arman, "Ethical Standards for Representatives before ICSID Tribunals" (2011) 10 Law and Practice of International Courts and Tribunals 67.

Sauvant, K.P. and V. Aranda, "The International Legal Framework for Transnational Corporations" in A.A. Fatouros (ed), *Transnational Corporations—The International Legal Framework* (New York: Routledge, 1994).

Scherer, M., "International Arbitration and Corruption—Synopsis of Selected Arbitral Awards" (2001) 19(4) ASA Bulletin 710.

Schill, Stephan W., "International Investment Law and the Host State's Power to Handle Economic Crises" (2007) 24(3) Journal of International Arbitration 265.

Schill, Stephan, "Tearing Down the Great Wall: The New Generation Investment Treaties of the People's Republic of China" (2007) 15 Cardozo J Int'l and Comp L 73.

Schlemmer, Engela C., "Investment, Investor, Nationality, and Shareholders" in Peter Muchlinski, et al (eds), *The Oxford Handbook of International Investment Law* (Oxford: Oxford University Press, 2008).

Schreuer, C. "*Why Still ICSID?*" (2011) Transnational Dispute Management.

Schreuer, Christoph, "Consent to Arbitration" in Peter T. Muchlinski, Federico Ortino and Christoph Schreuer (eds), *Handbook of International Investment Law* (Oxford/New York: Oxford University Press, 2008).

Schreuer, Christoph, "Diversity and Harmonization of Treaty Interpretation in Investment Arbitration" (2006) 3(2) *Transnational Dispute Management* in M. Fitzmaurice, O.A. Elias and Panos Merkouris (eds), *Treaty Interpretation and the Vienna Convention on the Law of Treaties: 30 Years On* (The Netherlands: Martinus Nijhoff Publishers, 2010).

Schreuer, Christoph, "Fair and Equitable Treatment in Arbitral Practice" (2005) 6 Journal of World Investment and Trade 357.

Schreuer, Christoph, "Investment Treaty Arbitration over Contract Claims— the Vivendi I Case Considered" in Todd Weiler (ed), *International Investment Law and Arbitration* (Huntington: JurisNet, LLC, 2008).

Schreuer, Christoph, "Preliminary Rulings in Investment Arbitration" in Karl P. Sauvant and Michael Chiswick-Patterson (eds), *Appeals Mechanism in International Investment Disputes* (New York: Oxford University Press, 2008) 207.

Schreuer, Christoph, "Three Generations of ICSID Annulment Proceedings" in Emmanuel Gaillard and Yas Banifatemi (eds), *Annulment of ICSID Awards* (Huntington, NY: Juris Pub, 2004).

Schwartzenberger, George, "The Most-Favoured Nation Standard in British State Practice" (1945) 22 Brit YB Int'l L 96.

Schwebel, Stephen M., "Investor-State Disputes and the Development of International Law: The Influence of Bilateral Investment Treaties on Customary International Law" (2004) 98 American Society of International Law Proceedings 27.

Schwebel, Stephen M., "The United States 2004 Model Bilateral Investment Treaty: An Exercise in the Regressive Development of International Law" in Gerald Aksen et al (eds), *Global Reflections on International Law, Commerce and Dispute Resolution: Liber Amicorum in Honour of Robert Briner* (Paris: ICC Publishing, 2005).

Seck, Sara L., "Conceptualizing the Home State Duty to Protect Human Rights" in Karin Buhmann et al (eds), *Corporate Social and Human Rights Responsibilities: Global Legal and Management Perspectives* (New York: Palgrave Macmillan, 2010).

Seck, Sara L., "Unilateral Home State Regulation: Imperialism or Tool for Subaltern Resistance?" (2008) 46(3) Osgoode Hall LJ 565.

Seidl-Hohenveldern, I., "The Theory of Quasi-International and Partly International Agreements" (1975) 11 Rev BDI 570.

Shishi Li, "Bilateral Investment Promotion and Protection Agreements: Practice of the People's Republic of China" in Paul de Waart, Paul Peters and Erik Denters (eds), *International law and Development* (Netherlands: Martinus Nijhoff Publishers, 1988).

Shore, Laurence, "The Jurisdiction Problem in Energy Charter Treaty Claims" (2007) 10 Int'l Arb L Rev 58.

Simons, Penelope, "Corporate Voluntarism and Human Rights: The Adequacy and Effectiveness of Voluntary Self-Regulation Regimes" (2004) 59(1) Industrial Relations 101.

Sinclair, Anthony C, "The Substance of Nationality Requirements in Investment Treaty Arbitration" (2005) 20 ICSID Rev-FILJ 357.

Smith, Stephanie and Janet Martinez, "An Analytical Framework for Dispute Systems Design" (2009) 14 Harvard Negot L Rev.

Snyder, Francis, "China, Regional Trade Agreements and WTO Law" (2009) 43 Journal of World Trade 1.

Soloway, Julie A., "Environmental Trade Barriers Under NAFTA: the MMT Fuel Additives Controversy" (1999) 8(1) Minn J Global Trade.

Soloway, Julie A., "NAFTA's Chapter 11—The Challenge of Private Party Participation" (1999) 16(2) Journal of International Arbitration 1.

Stevens, Margrete and Ben Love, "Investor-State Mediation: Observations on the Role of Institutions" in Arthur W. Rovine (ed), *Contemporary Issues in International Arbitration and Mediation: Fordham Papers 2009* (The Netherlands: Martinus Nijhoff, 2009).

Stiglitz, Joseph E., "Regulating Multinational Corporations: Towards Principles of Cross-border Legal Frameworks in a Globalized World" (2008) 23 Am U Int'l L Rev.

Stone Sweet, Alec and Jud Mathews, "Balancing and Global Constitutionalism" (2008) 47 Colum J Transnat'l L 68.

Stout, Taylor G., "NAFTA Dispute Settlement Procedures" (2011) International Judicial Monitor, online: International Judicial Monitor <http://www.judicialmonitor.org/archive_winter2011/spotlight.html>.

Sungjoon Cho, "Linkage of Free Trade and Social Regulation: Moving Beyond the Entropic Dilemma" (2005) 5 Chicago J Int'l L 625.

Supnik, Kate M., "Making Amends: Amending the ICSID Convention to Reconcile Competing Interests in International Investment Law" (2009–10) 59 Duke LJ 343.

Swenson, Deborah L., "Why Do Developing Countries Sign BITs?" (2005) 12(1) UC Davis J Int'l L and Pol'y 131.

Swick, Brenda C. and Helen Gray, "Significant Developments in International Trade and Customs Law" 31 *Report of Proceedings of Fifty-Sixth Tax Conference, 2004 Tax Conference* (Toronto: Canadian Tax Foundation, 2005) ch 1.

Tadmore, Niv, "Royalties (Article 13 OECD Model Convention)" in Michael Lang (ed), *Source Versus Residence: Problems Arising From the Allocation of Taxing Rights In Tax Treaty Law And Possible Alternatives* (Austin [Tex]: Wolters Kluwer Law and Business, 2008).

Taillant, Jorge Daniel and Jonathan Bonnitcha, "International Investment Law and Human Rights" in Marie-Claire Cordonier Segger, Markus W. Gehring, and Andrew Newcombe (eds), *Sustainable Development in World Investment Law* (Netherlands: Kluwer Law International, 2011).

Tams, Christian J., "Is There a Need for an ICSID Appellate Structure?" in R. Hoffman and Christian J. Tams (eds), *The International Convention for the Settlement of Investment Disputes: Taking Stock After 40 Years* (Nomos: Baden Baden, 2007) 223.

Tanzi, Vito, "Is there a Need for World Tax Organization?" in Assaf Rzin and Efraim Sadka (eds), *The Economics of Globalization* (New York: Cambridge University Press, 1999).

Tanzi, Vito and Howell Zee, "Taxation in a Borderless World: The Role of Information Exchange" in *International Studies in Taxation: Law and Economics* (London: Kluwer Law International, 1999).

Thirlway, Hugh, "Counterclaims Before the International Court of Justice: The *Genocide Convention* and the *Oil Platforms* Decisions" (1999) 12 Leiden J Int'l Law 197.

Tieleman, Katia, "The Failure of the Multilateral Agreement on Investment (MAI) and the Absence of a Global Policy Network" in *UN Vision Project on*

Global Public Policy Networks 1999, online: Global Public Policy Networks <http://www.gppi.net/fileadmin/gppi/Tieleman_MAI_GPP_Network.pdf>.

Toral, Mehmet and Thomas Schultz, "The State, a Perpetual Respondent in Investment Arbitration?" in Michael Waibel et al (eds), *The Backlash against Investment Arbitration: Perceptions and Reality* (The Hague: Wolters Kluwer, 2010) 577.

Tsatsos, Aristidis, "ICSID Jurisprudence: Between Homogeneity and Heterogeneity. A Call for Appeal?" (2009) 6 *Transnational Dispute Management* 1.

Turrin, Alessandro and Dieter M. Urban, "A Theoretical Perspective on Multilateral Agreements on Investment" (2008) 16(5) Rev Int Econ 1023.

Van Aaken, A., "Fragmentation of International Law: The Case of International Investment Protection" (2008) 17 Finnish Yearbook of International Law 93.

Vandevelde, K.J., "A Unified Theory of Fair and Equitable Treatment" (2010) 43 NYU J Int'l L and Pol 43.

Vandevelde, Kenneth, "A Comparison of the 2004 and 1994 US Model BITs: Rebalancing Investor and Host Country Interests" (2008–09) *Yearbook of International Investment Law and Policy* 283.

Vann, Richard, "A Model Tax Treaty for the Asian-Pacific Region? (Part II)" (April 1991) International Bureau of Fiscal Documentation 151.

VanWeeghel, Stef, "Dividends (Article 10 OECD Model Convention)" in Michael Lang (ed), *Source Versus Residence: Problems Arising From the Allocation of Taxing Rights In Tax Treaty Law And Possible Alternatives* (Austin [Tex]: Wolters Kluwer Law and Business, 2008).

Veenstra-Kjos, Hege Elisabeth, "Counterclaims by Host States in Investment Treaty Arbitration" (2007) 4(4) *Transnational Dispute Management* 1.

Verhoosell, Gaetan, "The Use of Investor-State Arbitration under Bilateral Investment Treaties to Seek Relief for Breaches of WTO Law" (2003) 6(2) J Int'l Econ L 493.

Verrill Jr, Charles Owen, "Are WTO Violations Also Contrary to the Fair and Equitable Treatment Obligations in Investor Protection Agreements" (2005) 11(2) ILSA Journal of International and Comparative Law 287.

Vincentelli, Ignacio A., "The Uncertain Future of ICSID in Latin America" (2010) 16 Law and Business Review of the Americas 409.

Voon, Tania, "NAFTA Chapter 19 Panel Follows WTO Appellate Body in Striking Down Zeroing" (2010) 14(29) American Society of International Law, 14(2)9 ASIL Insights, online: ASIL <http://www.asil.org/files/insight 100923pdf.pdf>.

Waibel, Michael, "Two Worlds of Necessity in ICSID Arbitration: CMS and LG&E" (2007) 20 Leiden Journal of International Law 637.

Wälde, Thomas, "Alternatives for Obtaining Greater Consistency in Investment Arbitration: An Appellate Institution after the WTO, Authoritative Treaty Arbitration or Mandatory Consolidation?" (2005) 2 *Transnational Dispute Management* 71.

Wälde, Thomas W., "Interpreting Investment Treaties: Experiences and Examples" in Christina Binder et al (eds), *International Investment Law for the*

21st Century, Liber Amicorum Christoph Schreuer (Oxford: Oxford University Press, 2009).

Wälde, Thomas W. and Borzu Sabahi, "Compensation, Damages and Valuation" in Peter T. Muchlinski, Federico Ortino and Christoph Schreuer (eds), *Handbook of International Investment Law* (Oxford/New York: Oxford University Press, 2008) 1049.

Walker Jr, Herman, "Provisions on Companies in United States Commercial Treaties" (1956) 50 Am J Int'l L 373.

Webb Yackee, Jason, "Bilateral Investment Treaties, Credible Commitment, and the Rule of (International) Law: Do BITs Promote Foreign Direct Investment?" (2008) 42(4) Law and Soc'y Rev 805.

Wei Shen, "The Good, the Bad or the Ugly? A Critique of the Decision on Jurisdiction and Competence in *Tza Yap Shum v. The Republic of Peru*" (2011) 10 Chinese Journal of International Law 55.

Weil, Prosper, "Le droit international en quête de son identité" (1992) VI: 237 Rec des Cours.

Weiler, Todd, "Balancing Human Rights and Investor Protection: A New Approach for a Different Legal Order" (2004) 27 BC Int'l and Comp L Rev ICLR.

Welsh, Nancy A., "Mandatory Mediation and its Variations" in UNCTAD, *Investor-State Disputes: Prevention and Alternative to Arbitration II: Proceedings of the Washington and Lee University and UNCTAD Joint Symposium on International Investment and Alternative Dispute Resolution, held on 29 March 2010 in Lexington, Virginia, United States of America* (New York and Geneva: United Nations, 2011).

Welsh, Nancy A. and Andrea K. Schneider, "The Application of Dispute Settlement Design Principles and Procedural Justice Theories to the Potential Use of Mediation and Other Consensual Processes in the Investor-State Context" [manuscript—on file with author].

Williamson, Oliver E., "Credible Commitments: Using Hostages to Support Exchange" (1983) 73(4) The American Economic Review 519.

Wölker, Ulrich, "The EU as a Player in the BIT arena: Current and Future Legal Challenges" (Paper delivered at the 50 Years of Bilateral Investment Treaties Conference, Frankfurt) reproduced in (2009) 24(2) ICSID Rev 43.

Wolski Bobette, "Recent Developments in International Commercial Dispute Resolution: Expanding the Options" (2001) 13(2) Bond Law Review, online <http://epublications.bond.edu.au/blr/vol13/iss2/2>.

Yackee, Jason Webb, "Bilateral Investment Treaties, Credible Commitment, and the Rule of (International) Law: Do BITs Promote Foreign Direct Investment?" (2008) 42(4) Law and Soc'y Rev 805.

Yingyi Qian, "The Process of China's Market Transition (1978–98): The Evolutionary, Historical, and Comparative Perspectives" (2000) 156 Journal of Institutional and Theoretical Economics 151.

Ziegler, Andreas R., "Multilateraler Investitionsschutz im Wirtschaftsrecht" in Dirk Ehlers and Hans-Michael Wolffgang (eds), *Rechtsfragen internationaler Investitionen* (Frankfurt: Verlag Recht und Wirtschaft 2009).

Ziegler, Andreas R., "The Nascent International Law on Most-Favoured-Nation (MFN) Clauses in Bilateral Investment Treaties (BITs)" in Christoph Herrmann and Jörg Philipp Terhechte (eds), *European Yearbook of International Economic Law* (Heidelberg, Germany: Springer, 2010).

Ziegler, Andreas R. and Bertram Boie, "The Relationship between International Trade Law and International Human Rights Law" in Erika de Wet and Yure Vidmar (eds), *Hierarchy in International Law* (Oxford: Oxford University Press, forthcoming).

Reports and official documents

American Law Institute, "Part Four: Non-Discrimination—I. Basic Concept" in Federal Income Tax Project: International Aspects of United States Income Taxation II: Proposals on United States Income Tax Treaties (San Francisco, May 13, 1991).

Australian Government, Department of Foreign Affairs and Trade, "Gillard Government Trade Policy Statement: Trading our way to more jobs and prosperity", April 2011, online: Australian Government <http://www.dfat.gov.au/publications/trade/trading-our-way-to-more-jobs-and-prosperity.html>.

Centre for Effective Dispute Resolution, CEDR Commission on Settlement in International Arbitration, Final Report, November 2009, online: CEDR <http://www.cedr.com/about_us/arbitration_commission/Arbitration_Commission_Doc_Final.pdf>.

Chinese Ministry of Commerce (MOFCOM), "Signed BITs with 130 countries" *Xinhua* (November 1, 2010), online: Xinhua <http://news.xinhuanet.com/fortune/2010-11/01/c_12724364.htm>.

Commentary to the MAI Negotiating Text, April 1998, online: OECD <www1.oecd.org/daf/mai/pdf/ng/ng988r1e.pdf>.

Committee on International Trade, Draft Report for a regulation of the European Parliament and of the Council establishing transitional arrangements for bilateral investment agreements between Member States and third countries, November 18, 2010.

Council of the European Union, 2007 EFC Report to the Commission and the Council on the Movement of Capital and Freedom of Payments, Doc. Nr. 5123/08, No. 15.

Council of the European Union, Conclusions on a comprehensive European international investment policy, 3041st Foreign Affairs Council Meeting, October 25, 2010.

Council of the EU, *Minimum Platform for Investment for the EU FTAs,* Brussels March 6, 2009, 7242/09 (first issued as *Minimum platform on investment for EU FTAs—Provision on establishment in template for a Title on "Establishment, trade in services and e-commerce,"* Note to the 133 Committee, European Commission DG Trade, Brussels, 28 July, 2006, D (2006) 9219).

EC, *A Trade SIA Relating to the Negotiation of a Comprehensive Economic and Trade Agreement (CETA) Between the EU and Canada* (2011), online: <http://www.eucanada-sia.org/docs/EU-Canada_SIA_Final_Report.pdf>.

EC, *External Trade: Handbook for Sustainability Impact Assessment* (2006), online: EU Commission <http://trade.ec.europa.eu/doclib/docs/2006/march/tradoc_127974.pdf>.

EC, Commission, *Impact Assessment Guidelines*, online: EU <http://ec.europa.eu/governance/impact/commission_guidelines/docs/iag_2009_en.pdf>.

EU Commission, Communication from the Commission to the Council, the European Parliament, the European Economic and Social Committee and the Committee of the Regions. Towards a comprehensive European international investment policy, July 7, 2010, COM (2010) 343 final.

EU Commission, Proposal for a Regulation of the European Parliament and the Council establishing transitional arrangements for bilateral investment agreements between Member States and third countries, July 7, 2010, COM (2010) 344 final.

European Commission, A European Strategy for Sustainable, Competitive and Secure Energy, March 8, 2006, COM (2006) 105 final.

European Commission, Communication from the Commission on relations between the Community and third countries in the field of air transport. Proposal for a European Parliament and Council Regulation on the negotiation and implementation of air service agreements between Member States and third countries, February 26, 2003, COM (2003) 94 final.

European Commission, Towards a Dynamic European Economy. Green Paper on the Development of the Common Market for Telecommunications Services and Equipment. Appendices, June 30, 1987, COM (87) 290 final/appendices.

Final Report of the Advisory Panel on International Taxation (Ottawa: Department of Finance, 2008).

Koskenniemi, Martti (ed), *Fragmentation of International Law: Difficulties Arising from the Diversification and Expansion of International Law*, Report of the Study Group of the International Law Commission (in *Report of the International Law Commission*, UNGAOR, 58th Sess, Supp No. 10, UN Doc A/61/10, 2006). Also, in *Yearbook of International Law Commission 2006*, General Assembly Official Records, Sixty-first session, Supplement No. 10 (A/61/10), online: ILC <http://untreaty.un.org/ilc/texts/instruments/english/draft%20articles/1_9_2006.pdf>.

Gordon, Kathryn, "International Investment Agreements: A Survey of Environmental, Labour and Anti-corruption Issues" in OECD, *International Investment Law: Understanding Concepts and Tracking Innovations* (Paris: OECD, 2008).

Gordon, Kathyrn and Joachim Pohl, "Environmental Concerns in International Investment Agreements: A Survey" (2011) *OECD Working Papers on International Investment, No. 2011/1*, OECD Investment Division, online: <http://www.oecd.org/daf/investment>.

ICSID, "The ICSID Caseload—Statistics", online: ICSID <http://icsid.worldbank.org/ICSID/FrontServlet?requestType=ICSIDDocRH&actionVal=ShowDocument&CaseLoadStatistics=True&language=English21>.

ICSID, Notifications Concerning Classes of Disputes Considered Suitable or Unsuitable for Submission to the Centre, online: ICSID <http://icsid. worldbank.org/ICSID/FrontServlet?requestType=ICSIDDocRH&actionVal =ShowDocument&Measures=True&language=English> ICSID/8-D.

ICSID Convention, Regulations and Rules, *Report of the Executive Directors on the ICSID Convention*, online: ICSID <http://icsid.worldbank.org/ICSID/Static Files/basicdoc/partB.htm>.

ICSID Secretariat, "Possible Improvements of the Framework for ICSID Arbitration" October 22, 2004, Discussion Paper.

ILA, *Final Report of the International Law on Foreign Investment Committee* (2008).

IMF, World Economic Outlook April 2011, online: IMF <http://www.imf.org/ external/pubs/ft/weo/2011/01/pdf/text.pdf>.

International Law Association, *New Delhi Declaration of Principles of International Law Relating to Sustainable Development,* (2002) 49(2) Netherlands International Law Review 299.

Mann, Howard. *International Investment Agreements, Business and Human Rights: Key Issues and Opportunities* (International Institute for Sustainable Development, February 2008), online: IISD <http://www.iisd.org/pdf/2008/iia_ business_human_rights.pdf>.

Mann, H. and D. McRae, "Amicus Curiae submissions to the NAFTA Chapter 11 Tribunal: *Methanex Corp. v the United States of America*", UNCITRAL (March 9, 2004), online: IISD <http://www.iisd.org/pdf/2004/trade_ methanex_submissions.pdf>.

NAFTA Free Trade Commission, *Statement of the Free Trade Commission on Non-Disputing Party Participation*, in "Celebrating NAFTA at Ten"—NAFTA Commission Meeting, October 7, 2003, online: DFAIT <http://www. international.gc.ca/trade-agreements-accords-commerciaux/assets/pdfs/ Nondisputing-en.pdf>.

NAFTA Free Trade Commission, *Notes of Interpretation of Certain Chapter 11 Provisions* July 31, 2001), online: DFAIT <http://www.international.gc.ca/ trade-agreements-accords-commerciaux/disp-diff/NAFTA-Interpr. aspx?lang=en>.WTO, General Council, *Minutes of Meeting* (held on November 22, 2000), WTO Doc WT/GC/M/60, online: WTO <http:// docsonline.wto.org>.

OECD, Committee on International Investment and Multinational Enterprises, *Foreign Direct Investment for Development: Maximising benefits, minimising costs* (Paris: OECD, 2002).

OECD, Drafting Group No. 2 on Selected Topics Concerning Treatment of Investors and Investment (Pre/Post Establishment), Note by the Chairman, *Mechanisms for Standstill, Rollback and Listing of Country Specific Reservations*, February 15, 1996, DAFFE/MAI/DG2(95)3/REV1.

OECD, "International Investment Agreements: A Survey of Environmental, Labour and Anti-corruption Issues" in *International Investment Law: Understanding Concepts and Tracking Innovations* (Paris: OECD, 2008).

OECD, *International Investment Law: Understanding Concepts and Tracking Innovations* (Paris: OECD, 2008).

OECD, *OECD Guidelines for Multinational Enterprises*, online: OECD <http://www.oecd.org/daf/investment/guidelines>.

OECD, *Tax Co-operation: Towards A Level Playing Field—2008 Assessment by the Global Forum on Taxation* (Paris: OECD, 2008).

OECD, Working Papers on International Investment, Number 2006–3, *Interpretation of the Umbrella Clause in Investment Agreements* (October 2006), online: OECD <http://www.oecd.org/dataoecd/3/20/37579220.pdf>.

OECD Centre for Tax Policy and Administration, *The Granting of Treaty Benefits with Respect to the Income of Collective Investment Vehicles* (Paris: OECD, 2009).

"Public Statement on the International Investment Regime" (August 31, 2010), online: Osgoode Hall Law School <http://www.osgoode.yorku.ca/public_statement>.

Rao, Someshwar, Malick Souare and Weimin Wang, "Canadian Inward and Outward Direct Investment: Assessing the Impacts", Foreign Affairs and International Trade, Trade Policy Research 2010: Exporter dynamics and productivity 315.

Report of the Advisory Committee on International Economic Policy Regarding the Model Bilateral Investment Treaty, presented to The Department of State, 30 September 2009, online: Department of State, Press Release <http://www.state.gov/r/pa/prs/ps/2009/sept/130097.htm>.

Report of the Special Representative of the Secretary-General of the United Nations on the issue of human rights and transnational corporations and other business enterprises, HRC, UNGAOR, 4th Sess, UN Doc A/HRC/4/74 (2007).

Rights and Democracy, *Human Right Impact Assessments for Foreign Investment Projects: Learning from Community Experience in the Philippines, Tibet, the Democratic Republic of Congo, Argentina, and Peru* (Montreal: Rights and Democracy, 2007).

Secretary-General of the OECD, *OECD Benchmark Definition of Foreign Direct Investment*, 4th ed (Paris: OECD, 2008), online: OECD<http://www.oecd.org/dataoecd/26/50/40193734.pdf>.

Statement of Canada on Open Hearings in NAFTA Chapter Eleven Arbitrations, October 2003, online: DFAIT <http://www.international.gc.ca/trade-agreements-accords-commerciaux/agr-acc/nafta-alena/open-hearing.aspx?lang=eng>.

Statement of Canada on open Hearings in NAFTA Chapter Eleven Arbitrations, in "Celebrating NAFTA at Ten" NAFTA Commission Meeting, October 7, 2003), online: DFAIT <http://www.international.gc.ca/trade-agreements-accords-commerciaux/agr-acc/nafta-alena/open-hearing.aspx?lang=eng>.

Stern, Nicholas, "The Stern Review on the Economics of Climate Change", online: National Archive <http://webarchive.nationalarchives.gov.uk/+/http://www.hm-treasury.gov.uk/stern_review_report.htm>.

"The Benefits of Services Trade Liberalization," International Chamber of Commerce Policy Statement, September 7, 1999, ICC Doc 103/210.

UNCTAD, *The Development Dimension of International Investment Agreements*, TD/B/C.II/MEM.3/2, December 2, 2008.

UNCTAD, "Development Implications of International Investment Agreements" (2007) 2 IIA Monitor 6.

UNCTAD, *International Investment Arrangements: Trends and Emerging Issues* UNCTAD/ITE/IIT/2005/11.

United Nations Conference on Trade and Development (UNCTAD), *Investor-State Disputes: Prevention and Alternatives to Arbitration* (New York and Geneva: United Nations, 2010).

UNCTAD, *Investor-State Disputes: Prevention and Alternative to Arbitration II: Proceedings of the Washington and Lee University and UNCTAD Joint Symposium on International Investment and Alternative Dispute Resolution, held on 29 March 2010 in Lexington, Virginia, United States of America* (New York and Geneva: United Nations, 2011).

UNCTAD, "Latest Developments in Investor-State Dispute Settlement" (2010) IIA ISSUES NOTE No. 1 International Investment Agreements, online: UNCTAD <http://www.unctad.org/en/docs/webdiaeia20103_en.pdf>.

UNCTAD, "Latest Developments in Investor-State Dispute Settlement" (2011) IIA Issues Note 1, online: UNCTAD <http://www.unctad.org/en/docs/webdiaeia20113_en.pdf>.

UNCTAD, "Recent Developments in International Investment Agree-ments" (2007–June 2008), IIA Monitor No. 3 (2009) (New York, Geneva, 2009).

UNCTAD, "Recent Developments in International Investment Agreements" (2008–June 2009) 3 IIA Monitor 1, (New York and Geneva).

UNCTAD, "The Role of International Investment Agreements in Attracting Foreign Direct Investment to Developing Countries," *UNCTAD Series on International Investment Policies for Development*, (New York and Geneva: UN, 2009).

UNCTAD, "Selected Recent Developments in IIA Arbitration and Human Rights" (2009) 2 IIA Monitor 8.

UNCTAD, *Scope and Definition*, Series on Issues in International Investment Agreements II (New York and Geneva: United Nations, 2011).

UNCTAD, *Trade and Development Report* (2007) UNCTAD/TDR/2007.

UNCTAD, *World Investment Report 2008: Transnational Corporations, and the Infrastructure Challenge* (New York and Geneva: UNCTAD, 2008).

UNCTAD, *World Investment Report 2011: Non-equity Modes of International Production and Development*, UNCTAD/WIR/2011 (New York and Geneva: UNCTAD, 2011).

UNFCCC, *Investment and Financial Flows to Address Climate Change* (2007), online: UNFCCC <http://unfccc.int/cooperation_and_support/financial_mechanism/items/4053.php>.

UN Human Rights Council, *Report of the Special Representative of the Secretary-General on the issue of human rights and transnational corporations and other business enterprises*, UN GAOR, 17th Session, Agenda item 3, UN Doc A/HRC/17/31/Add.3 (2011). World Trade Organization, Appellate Body, *Annual Report for 2010*, WT/AB/15, June 2011.

WTO General Council, *Minutes of Meeting* (held on December 14, 2010) WTO Doc WT/COMTD/71.

WTO General Council, *Minutes of Meeting* (held on December 14, 2010) WTO Doc WT/L/806.

News reports

"China, EU could begin investment pact negotiations next month: official" September 22, 2011, online: *China Post* <http://www.chinapost.com.tw/business/asia-china/2011/09/22/317383/China-EU.htm>.

DFAIT, "Background on the Canada-'EU6' Foreign Investment Promotion and Protection Agreement (FIPA) Negotiations", online: DFAIT <http://www.international.gc.ca/trade-agreements-accords-commerciaux/agr-acc/fipa-apie/eu6-ue6.aspx?menu_id=30&menu=R>.

"EU investment policy needs to balance investor protection and public regulation, says International Trade Committee", Press release, online: European Parliament <http://www.europarl.europa.eu/en/pressroom/content/20110314IPR15476/html/EU-investment-policy-needs-to-balance-investor-protection-and-public-regulation>.

"EU and Vietnam to Launch Free Trade Negotiations" March 2, 2010, online: Europa <http://trade.ec.europa.eu/doclib/press/index.cfm?id=518&serie=319&langId=en>.

"EU to start bilateral trade negotiations with Singapore" March 3, 2010, online: Europa <http://trade.ec.europa.eu/doclib/press/index.cfm?id=519&serie=320&langId=en>.

European Commission, "EU and Canada take stock of historic Free Trade Agreement negotiations", online: Europa <http://trade.ec.europa.eu/doclib/press/index.cfm?id=664&serie=389&langId=en>.

"European Commission proposes relaunch of trade negotiations with Mercosur countries" May 4, 2010, online: Europa <http://trade.ec.europa.eu/doclib/press/index.cfm?id=566&serie=339&langId=en>.

"Legal Proceedings" (December 3, 2009), online: Siemens AG <http://w1.siemens.com/press/pool/de/events/corporate/2009-q4/2009-q4-legal-proceedings-e.pdf>.

Marotte, Bertrand and John Ibbitson, "Provinces on hook in future trade disputes: Harper" *The Globe and Mail* (August 26, 2010).

McCarthy, Shawn, "Failed ban becomes selling point for MMT. Not enough scientific evidence to prove additive a risk, minister says, promising to give manufacturers $19-million" *The Globe and Mail* (July 21, 1998) A3.

"Middle East Free Trade Area Initiative," online: Office of the United States Trade Representative <http://www.ustr.gov/trade-agreements/other-initiatives/middle-east-free-trade-area-initiative-mefta>.

Moyers, Bill, "Trading Democracy" Public Broadcasting System, online: PBS <http://www.pbs.org/now/transcript/transcript_tdfull.html>.

"News in Brief: Uruguay prepares defense against Philip Morris" *Investment Treaty News* (December 16, 2010), online: IISD <http://www.iisd.org/itn/2010/12/16/news-in-brief-2/>.

Ostry, Sylvia and Julie Soloway, "The MMT case ended too soon. Taking it to arbitration would have helped settle some crucial questions" *The Globe and Mail* (July 24, 1998) A15.

Peterson, Luke Eric, "Analysis: Tribunal in Grand River v. U.S.A. arbitration declines to import non-investment law obligations into NAFTA; role of other 'relevant' legal obligations in treaty interpretation under Vienna Convention is not discussed" *IA Reporter*, March 6, 2011, online: IA Reporter <http://www.iareporter.com/articles/20110306_3>.

Peterson, Luke Eric, "Canada releases new BITs with several EU member-states reflect EU requirements and Canadian reform agenda" (2009) 2(8) *IA Reporter* 7.

Peterson, Luke Eric, "Italy, Slovenia and Malta concur with Czech Republic on lack of necessity for intra-EU BITs; Italy-Czech treaty has been terminated" (2009) 2(13) *IA Reporter*.

Peterson, Luke E., "Philip Morris puts Australia on notice of treaty claim, but both parties decline to release documents; claim over tobacco regulation would be third treaty-based investor-state claim filed by Philip Morris since 2010" (2011) *IA Reporter*, June 30, 2011, online: IA Reporter <http://www.iareporter.com/articles/20110630_5>.

Peterson Luke E. and Ana C. Simões e Silva, "Brazilian Government Mandated to Pursue Limited Range of Investment Protection Standards; Prospects for Ratification of 1990s-era BITs With Various Developed Countries Remain Highly Unlikely" (2008) 1(9) *IA Reporter* 7.

Sosnow, Cliff, "Canada-China Investment Protection Agreement—A Significant Stepping Stone to Deeper Economic Co-Operation", (2005), online: Blakes <http://www.blakes.com/english/view_disc.asp?ID=43>

The Council of Canadians, "Blame NAFTA, not Williams, for costly AbitibiBowater settlement," online <http://www.canadians.org/media/trade/2010/27-Aug-10.html>.

"Towards a comprehensive European international investment policy: An interview with Tomas Baert, European Commission, Directorate General for Trade, Services and Investment" in *Investment Treaty News* (September 23, 2010), online: IISD <http://www.iisd.org/itn/2010/09/23/towards-a-comprehensive-european-international-investment-policy-an-interview-with-tomas-baert-european-commission-directorate-general-for-trade-services-and-investment/>.

"Trade By Any Other Name" *The Economist*, November 3, 1998.

"U.S.-Bulgaria Investment Treaty Additional Protocol Sent to Senate," January 22, 2004, online: America <http://www.america.gov/st/washfile-english/2004/January/200401221522291CJsamohT0.7042353.html>.

Vis-Dunbar, Damon, "Norway Shelves its Draft Model Bilateral Investment Treaty," June 8, 2009, online: Investment Treaty News <http://www.iisd.org/itn/2009/06/08/norway-shelves-its-proposed-model-bilateral-investment-treaty/>.

WTO, "Members debate cigarette plain-packaging's impact on trademark rights" June 7, 2011, online: WTO <http://www.wto.org/english/news_e/news11_e/trip_07jun11_e.htm>.

Index

abuse of corporate nationality: clauses requiring additional links with home state 237–239; 'denial of benefits' clauses 32, 240–245; IIA provisions generally 237; incorporation test *see* incorporation test; national practice 71–72

appellate mechanism: appointment to 259–260; arguments for and against 249–250; confidence-enhancing role of 255–256; consistency of awards 250–252; costs and delays 254–255; issues generally 247–249, 263–264; management of proceedings 262–263; model proposal for 257–258; practicality of implementation 257; problem of multiplicity of IIA rule sets 252–254; standard of review 260–262; standing appeals body proposal 258–259; structure of 259–260

arbitration *see also* appellate mechanism; dispute settlement; jurisdiction: as aid to treaty interpretation 353–354; appeals *see* appellate mechanism; 'connexity' between claim and counterclaim 226–228; consent clauses 15, 17; consent to 218–219; and corporate nationality *see* abuse of corporate nationality; corporate nationality; delegation of treaty interpretation to 79, 89–90, 90*fig*; growth in number of claims 1; ICSID *see* International Centre for Settlement of Investment Disputes (ICSID); merits spectrum for claims *see* dispute settlement; model clauses 17, 20, 29–30, 33, 53, 139; publication of awards 72; as source of international law 350–353; statistics 140, 255; UNCITRAL Rules 33, 80, 226, 247, 248, 249, 258, 259; WTO *see* World Trade Organization (WTO)

bilateral investment treaties (BITs): as aid to treaty interpretation 353–354; attraction of FDI by 81, 90, 94; coalescing of trade and investment law 127; dispute settlement 127–128; as distinct entity 116; efficiency in treaty practice 130–133; growth in use of ('treatification') 16–19, 23–24; mandate to negotiate 121; model BITs 19–22, 23–24, 51–55, 117; overlap in trade and investment standards 127; possible decline of 115, 116–117, 122, 129; regulatory provision in 119; renegotiation of 22–23; scope of investment protection 124–126;

as source of international law
350–353

Canada: balancing of investor and
state rights 34; clarification of
substantive provisions 34–37;
criticisms of IIA regime 30–31;
dispute settlement 28–30, 32–34,
38–39; efficiency in IIA practice
26; exceptions provisions 37; IIA
coverage and scope 27–28, 31–32;
IIA practice generally 25–26,
39–41; legitimacy in IIA
practice 30–31; sustainability
in IIA practice 34; sustainable
development provisions 38;
taxation *see* tax treaties; taxation
China: abuse of corporate nationality
71–72; accession to ICSID 62;
development of IIA programme
60; dispute settlement 69–70;
efficiency in IIA practice 65;
exceptions provisions 73–74;
expropriation provisions 74; FDI
to 59, 61, 63, 64; first-generation
IIAs 60–61; FTAs with BIT-
like investment chapters 65; IIA
practice generally 59–60, 75;
investor misconduct provisions
70–71; legitimacy in IIA practice
70; MFN provisions 67–68;
model BIT 60, 61, 63–64, 66–74;
national treatment provisions
65–67; regulatory powers
provisions 74; second-generation
IIAs 62; sustainability in IIA
practice 72; sustainability
provisions in treaty preambles
72–73; third-generation IIAs
63–64; transfer rights provisions
68–69; transparency provisions 72
Committee on Regional Trade
Agreements (CRTA): creation
of 130
corporate investors *see entries at*
investor

corporate nationality *see also* abuse
of corporate nationality: and
arbitration generally 230–231,
245–246; incorporation test
see incorporation test
corporate social responsibility (CSR):
IIAs and sustainable development
297–300
costs of exports: analysis of IIA
benefits for developing countries
107
counterclaims: balancing of investor
and state rights 216–217;
'connexity' between claim and
counterclaim 226–228; consent
to arbitration 218–219; exclusive
jurisdiction of national courts
224–226; investor's acceptance of
arbitration 223–224; jurisdiction
over 217–218; scope of IIA
provisions 219–221; standing of
host state 221–222; use generally
212–216, 228–229
coverage and scope of IIAs: efficiency
in IIA practice 27–28; legitimacy
in IIA practice 31–32; national
practice 27–28, 31–32
criminal law: ICC proceedings 352

delegation of treaty interpretation to
neutral third parties: as research
metric 79, 89–90, 90*fig*
'denial of benefits' clauses: use of 32,
240–245
developed countries: as promotors of
IIAs 82–83
developing countries: avoidance of
'holdup' problem 95–96; balance
of IIA benefits and costs 110;
benefits of IIAs generally 95; cost
of exporting to 107; defection
of local agents to competitors
108–109; direct export to
104–107; disadvantages of IIAs
generally 99; and IIAs generally
93–95; knowledge capital model

of MNE investment 97–99; and MAI 101; negative results from IIA enforcement 101–104, 111–112*appendix*; negotiating power as to profit distribution 100; non-discrimination issue 101; penalty mechanisms 109; power to optimize trade policy 107–108; reputational benefits of IIAs 96–97; self-enforcing contracts 104–107

direct taxation *see* tax treaties; taxation

dispute settlement *see also* appellate mechanism; arbitration; jurisdiction: appeals *see* appellate mechanism; claims of uncertain merit 148–150; co-existence of regimes 160–161; complexity of treaty network 163–165; convergence of trade and investment issues 127–129; counterclaims *see* counterclaims; current IIA practice 150–154; efficiency in IIA practice 28–30, 69–70; improvements in future IIAs 150; incorporation test *see* incorporation test; legitimacy in IIA practice 32–34; management of proceedings 262–263, 347, 349; meritorious claims 138–144; merits spectrum generally 135–138, 156–157; national practice 28–30, 32–34, 38–39, 69–70; open proceedings 348–349; options for improvement of provisions 154–156; overlap in procedures generally 158–160, 174–176; overlap situations 161–163; participation of non-parties 345–348; private parties as claimants 343–345; procedural overlap of provisions 171–173; scope of IIA provisions 219–221; substantive overlap of provisions 165–171; sustainability in IIA

practice 38–39; unmeritorious claims 144–148

double taxation conventions *see* tax treaties

efficiency in IIA practice: dispute settlement *see* dispute settlement; IIA coverage and scope 27–28, 65–69; national practice 26, 65; RTAs 130–133

emergency clauses: and interpretation of IIAs 335–340

enforcement of IIAs: consequences for developing countries 101–104; penalty mechanisms 109; self-enforcing contracts 104–107

environment: FDI effect on 276

EU competence: foreign direct investment (FDI) 120–121, 128

European Union: Commission's approach 47–50; competence over FDI 23, 42, 43, 44–47, 48, 50, 120–121, 128; development of IIA treaty making role 44; IIA practice generally 42–44; influence on BIT system 55–58; Member States' approach 47–50; model BIT proposal 43, 51–55, 58

exceptions *see also* general exceptions: national provision for 37, 73–74; sustainability in IIA practice 37, 73–74

export costs: analysis of IIA benefits for developing countries 107

expropriation: national practice 74

foreign direct investment (FDI): amount worldwide compared to level of arbitration 137; attraction by IIAs 27, 77, 80, 85, 93, 95, 110, 130–131; benefits generally 286, 288–289; BITs as means to attract 81, 90, 94; to China 59, 61, 63, 64; environmental impact 276; knowledge capital model 97–99; liberalization by MAI 97;

OECD definition 285; protection
by IIAs 1; public international
law applied to 85; SIAs and 288;
specific treaty references to 300;
and sustainable development
generally 285, 302; and taxation
see tax treaties; taxation
free trade agreements (FTAs):
BIT-like investment chapters in
65; effect on FDI 28, 65

General Agreement on Tariffs and
Trade (GATT) *see also* World Trade
Organization (WTO): Article XX
general exceptions 9, 37, 73–74,
160, 268, 269–272, 279–281,
292, 340; and RTAs 160, 165–173
general exceptions: effects of 276–
282; GATT Article XX 9, 37, 73–
74, 160, 268, 269–276, 279–281,
292, 340; in IIA treaties 272–276;
use in general 267–269, 282–283

'holdup' problem: avoidance by use
of IIA 95–96
human rights: accountability under
IIAs 184–187; current IIA practice
188–190; lack of investors'
treaty obligations generally
179–180, 193–194; options for
strengthening IIA provisions
190–193

impact assessments: IIA provisions
286–288
'improved definitions': IIAs and
sustainable development 293–297
incorporation test: 'abuse of rights'
theory interpretation 233–237;
formalistic interpretation 231–
233; interpretation by tribunals
generally 231
International Centre for Settlement
of Investment Disputes (ICSID):
access to 221; annulment process
174, 175, 339; and appellate

mechanism 247–249, 251, 254–
255, 257, 258–263; arbitration by
57, 70, 80, 128, 205; arbitration
statistics 140, 255; China's
accession to 62; denunciations of
215; early-dismissal procedure
154; expedited review process
145–148; jurisdiction 218, 226,
234; management of proceedings
347, 349; model arbitration
clauses 17, 20, 29–30, 33, 53,
139; proposals for rule changes
191; publication of awards 72;
reference to case law 175; referral
to 29–30, 242; standing before
221; strike-out provisions 208;
and treaty interpretation 338–340
International Criminal Court (ICC):
proceedings 352
International Investment
Agreements (IIAs) *see also* bilateral
investment treaties (BITs);
regional trade agreements (RTAs);
trade and investment agreement
(TIAs): attraction of FDI by
27, 77, 80, 85, 93, 95, 110,
130–131; Canadian practice *see*
Canada; Chinese practice *see* China;
coverage and scope of *see* coverage
and scope of IIAs; criticisms of 2,
30–31; developed countries and
see developed countries; developing
countries and *see* developing
countries; EU practice *see* European
Union; exceptions *see* exceptions;
general exceptions; greater
complexity of 15, 18–19; growth
in use of 1, 15; and human rights
see human rights; interpretation of
see interpretation of IIAs; literature
on 2; making of *see* treaty-making;
'modelization' 19–22, 23–24;
multiplicity of rule sets 252–254;
political economy approach to
see political economy analysis of
IIAs; renegotiation of 22–23;

scope and structure of book 3–11; and sustainable development *see* sustainable development provisions; and taxation *see* tax treaties; taxation; 'treatification' 16–19, 23–24; US practice *see* USA

international investment law: arbitration *see* arbitration; and public international law generally 342–343, 356; resolution of private claims 354–356; strengthening of direct effect of public international law 356; substantive contributions to public international law 349–350

international law: arbitration as source of 350–353; BITs as source of 350–353; and interpretation of IIAs *see* interpretation of IIAs; public international law and international investment law *see* international investment law

interpretation of IIAs: arbitration as aid to 353–354; BITs as aid to 353–354; context of general international law 333–334; context within IIAs 331–332; contextual interpretation generally 331; contextual relevance of other IIAs 332–333; emergency clauses and 335–340; examples 334–335; intent of parties 329–331; and international law generally 323–324, 341; object and purpose of treaty 328–329; ordinary meaning 327–328; state of necessity clauses and 335–340; state responsibility rules and 335–340; Vienna Convention rules 324–327

investment: in developing countries *see* developing countries; provisions in RTAs *see* regional trade agreements (RTAs); scope of treaty protection 124–126; trade activities qualifying as 122–124

investor misconduct: legitimacy in IIA practice generally 195–197; mapping 198–199; mapping by arbitration phase 205–207; mapping by investment phase 199–205; national practice 70–71; need for changes to treaty practice 207–211

investor rights: acceptance of arbitration 223–224; balancing with state rights 34, 216–217

investors' legal personality: corporations in international law 180–183; human rights accountability *see* human rights; lack of obligations generally 179–180, 193–194

jurisdiction: exclusive jurisdiction of national courts 224–226; ICSID 218, 226, 234; over counterclaims 217–218

knowledge capital model of MNE investment: analysis of IIA benefits for developing countries 97–99

language clarification provisions: IIAs and sustainable development 291–293

language of treaties: preambular language *see* preambles to treaties; precision as research metric 78, 87–88, 88*fig*; sustainable development *see* sustainable development provisions

legitimacy in IIA practice: corporate nationality *see* abuse of corporate nationality; corporate nationality; dispute settlement *see* appellate mechanism; counterclaims; dispute settlement; general exceptions *see* general exceptions; human rights *see* human rights; IIA coverage and scope 31–32, 70–72; investor misconduct *see* investor misconduct; investors' legal personality *see* investors' legal personality; national practice 30–31, 70

local agents: defection to competitors 108–109; direct export without use of 104–107

merits spectrum for claims *see* dispute settlement

model BITs: CSR provision 299; 'denial of benefits' clauses 32, 240; EU proposal 43, 51–55, 58; features of 29–30; references to sustainable development 291; specific provisions in 66–74, 151, 153, 188, 221–222; and treaty interpretation 330; use of 18–22, 23–24, 25–26, 39–40, 60, 61, 63–64, 117, 208; variations within 22

most-favoured nation (MFN) treatment: national practice 67–68

Multilateral Agreement on Investment (MAI): general exceptions 282; objections to 101, 351; proposal for 97, 142, 190, 305

multinational enterprizes (MNEs): costs of exports 107; defection of local agents to competitors 108–109; direct export by 104–107; investment in developing countries *see* developing countries; knowledge capital model of investment 97–99

national treatment: national practice 65–67

non-discrimination: developing countries and 101; tax treaties 317–318

non-parties: participation in arbitration 345–348

obligation under IIAs: as research metric 78, 88–89, 89*fig*

operationalization: application to IIA research 85–87

Organisation for Economic Co-operation and Development (OECD): definition of FDI 285; MAI *see* Multilateral Agreement on Investment (MAI)

parties to agreement: negotiating history as aid to interpretation 329–331

political economy analysis of IIAs: approach generally 76–79; conclusions 91–92; delegation of treaty interpretation to neutral third parties 79, 89–90, 90*fig*; developed countries and IIAs 82–83; extent of obligation under IIAs 78, 88–89, 89*fig*; literature 79–82; operationalization and measurement 85–87; precision of treaty language 78, 87–88, 88*fig*; research frameworks 83–85; trends in IIAs 87–91

preambles to treaties: sustainable development provisions in 72–73, 289–291

precision of treaty language: as research metric 78

private parties: as claimants 343–345

public international law: application to FDI 85; and international investment law *see* international investment law

regional trade agreements (RTAs): coalescing of trade and investment law 127; collocation of trade and investment obligations 118–121; content of chapter 115; and continuance of BITs 129; continuing trend of investment provision inclusion 133–134; convenience of inclusion of investment chapters 129; CRTA 130; dispute settlement 127–129;

efficiency in treaty practice
130–133; impact of investment
chapters 121–122; inclusion of
investment chapters 116–118;
interpretation of investment
chapters 122; overlap in trade
and investment standards 127;
scope of investment protection
124–126; trade and investment
agreement (TIAs) *see* trade and
investment agreement (TIAs);
trade qualifying as investment
122–124; use of 116; WTO
review of investment provisions
129–130
regulatory powers: national
practice 74
reservations *see* exceptions

self-enforcing contracts:
consequences for developing
countries 104–107
state of necessity clauses: and
interpretation of IIAs 335–340
state responsibility rules: and
interpretation of IIAs 335–340
state rights: balancing with investor
rights 34, 216–217; standing as to
claims 221–222
subsidiaries *see also* local agents:
direct export without use of
104–107
Sustainability Impact Assessments
(SIAs): effect on FDI 288
sustainability in IIA practice:
balancing of investor and
state rights 34; clarification
of substantive provisions
34–37; exceptions provisions *see*
exceptions; general exceptions;
international investment law
see international investment
law; interpretation of IIAs *see*
interpretation of IIAs; national
practice 34, 72; sustainable
development *see* sustainable

development provisions; taxation
see tax treaties; taxation
sustainable development provisions:
corporate social responsibility
297–300; exceptions and
reservations 291–293; and FDI
generally 285, 302; IIA provisions
generally 284–286, 301–302;
impact assessments (SIAs)
286–288; 'improved definitions'
293–297; interaction of IIAs
with sustainable development
treaties 301; language clarification
provisions 291–293; national
practice 38, 72–73; options for
substantive improvements in IIAs
288–289; preambular language
289–291; sustainability in IIA
practice 38, 72–73; in treaty
preambles 72–73
sustainable development treaties:
interaction with IIAs 301

tax treaties: anti-avoidance generally
319; Canadian practice generally
308–309; effects on FDI generally
314–315; and IIAs generally
303–305, 322; non-discrimination
317–318; overview of 305–308;
reduction of administrative
barriers to FDI 315–316;
reduction of source country
taxation 316–317; reduction of
tax avoidance 319–321; tax
evasion measures 321–322
taxation: IIAs and direct taxation
309–314
trade and investment agreement
(TIAs): coalescing of trade
and investment law 127; and
continuance of BITs 129; dispute
settlement 127–129; efficiency in
treaty practice 130–133; impact
of investment chapters 121–122;
interpretation of investment
chapters 122; overlap in trade

and investment standards 127; scope of investment protection 124–126; use of 116–117; WTO review of investment provisions 129–130

trade policy: developing countries' power to optimize 107–108

transfer rights: national practice 68–69

transparency provisions: national practice 72

'treatification': process of 16–19, 23–24

treaty interpretation: delegation of as research metric 79, 89–90, 90*fig*

United Nations Commission on International Trade Law (UNCITRAL): Arbitration Rules 33, 80, 226, 247, 248, 249, 258, 259

USA: balancing of investor and state rights 34; clarification of substantive provisions 34–37; criticisms of IIA regime 30–31; dispute settlement 28–30, 32–34, 38–39; efficiency in IIA practice 26; exceptions provisions 37; IIA coverage and scope 27–28, 31–32; IIA practice generally 25–26, 39–41; legitimacy in IIA practice 30–31; sustainability in IIA practice 34; sustainable development provisions 38

Vienna Convention on the Law of Treaties: interpretation of IIAs 324–327

World Trade Organization (WTO) *see also* General Agreement on Tariffs and Trade (GATT): affirmation of existing rights and obligations under 165–173; appeals 263; Appellate Body 255, 256, 270, 347–348; arbitration by 128, 301; China's accession to 22, 63, 64; Committee on Regional Trade Agreements (CRTA) 130; creation of 163; dispute settlement provisions 6, 50, 158; efficiency of 164–165; entry into force 171; and general exceptions 271, 275; integration of trade and investment provisions 18, 122, 127, 133–134, 163–164; investment and 119–120; legitimacy of 164–165; non-party involvement in arbitration 346; notification of RTAs to 116; open proceedings 349; overlap of dispute settlement provisions with other regimes 160–163; and public international law 342, 344; reference to case law 175; referral to 159, 275; review of RTA investment provisions 129–130; and RTAs 164–165; taxation and 304, 322; and treaty interpretation 333, 340

For Product Safety Concerns and Information please contact our
EU representative GPSR@taylorandfrancis.com Taylor & Francis
Verlag GmbH, Kaufingerstraße 24, 80331 München, Germany